HANDBOOK ON HYBRID ORGANISATIONS

Handbook on Hybrid Organisations

Edited by

David Billis

Emeritus Reader, London School of Economics, UK

Colin Rochester

Honorary Research Fellow, University of Kent, UK

EE Edward **Elgar**
PUBLISHING

Cheltenham, UK • Northampton, MA, USA

Published by
Edward Elgar Publishing Limited
The Lypiatts
15 Lansdown Road
Cheltenham
Glos GL50 2JA
UK

Edward Elgar Publishing, Inc.
William Pratt House
9 Dewey Court
Northampton
Massachusetts 01060
USA

A catalogue record for this book
is available from the British Library

Library of Congress Control Number: 2019952342

This book is available electronically in the **Elgar**online
Social and Political Science subject collection
DOI 10.4337/9781785366116

ISBN 978 1 78536 610 9 (cased)
ISBN 978 1 78536 611 6 (eBook)

Typeset by Servis Filmsetting Ltd, Stockport, Cheshire
Printed and bound in Great Britain by TJ International Ltd, Padstow

Contents

About the editors

David Billis is Emeritus Reader at the London School of Economics (LSE) where he did his first degree and, after ten years as a member of a kibbutz, a PhD. His academic career spans all three sectors in which he has extensive research and consultancy experience. He began at Brunel University researching social services. There he also founded in 1978 the first university-based programme working with voluntary organisations (PORTVAC). In 1987 he returned to the LSE to became founding director of the LSE Centre for Voluntary Organisation which extended the work of PORTVAC. Recent posts include Visiting Professor at Imperial College London. He co-founded the journal *Nonprofit Management and Leadership* and was the first non-American to receive the distinguished lifetime achievement award from ARNOVA, the leading international third sector research association. As an organisational theorist he developed the work-levels approach which was implemented globally in Unilever, Tesco and BG Group. Currently his main interest is the continuous development of his theory of hybrid organisations. He has published widely in academic journals, and his books include *Welfare Bureaucracies*, *Organisational Design* (with Ralph Rowbottom), *Organising Public and Voluntary Agencies* and most recently, (as editor) *Hybrid Organisations and the Third Sector*.

Colin Rochester has worked with volunteers and in voluntary organisations for 50 years, initially as a practitioner and manager and more recently as a consultant, researcher and writer. He has been the National Development Officer of the Workers Educational Association and Head of Cambridge House Settlement and, after becoming one of the first cohort of postgraduate students studying the voluntary sector at Brunel University, has held academic posts at the London School of Economics and Roehampton University. He is currently an Honorary Research Fellow in the Centre for Philanthropy at the University of Kent. The most recent of his publications is *Rethinking Voluntary Action: The Beat of a Different Drum* (2013) and he has co-authored *Volunteering and Society in the 21st Century* (with Angela Ellis Paine and Steven Howlett, 2010) and co-edited *An Introduction to the Voluntary Sector* (with Justin Davis Smith and Rodney Hedley, 1995), *Voluntary Organisations and Social Policy: Perspectives on Change and Choice* (with Margaret Harris, 2001) and *The Roots of Voluntary Action* (with George Gosling, Alison Penn and Meta Zimmeck, 2011).

Contributors

Erynn Beaton, Ohio State University, USA.

Anita Blessing, University of Birmingham, UK.

Anthony E. Boardman, University of British Columbia, Canada.

Börje Boers, University of Skövde Sweden and Universität Witten/Herdecke, Germany.

Richard Bolden, University of the West of England, UK.

Curtis Child, Brigham Young University, USA.

Chris Cornforth, Open University, UK.

Jo Crotty, Edge Hill University, UK.

Jean-Louis Denis, Montreal University, Canada.

Bob Doherty, University of York, UK.

Elena Dowin Kennedy, Elon University, USA.

Angela Ellis Paine, University of Birmingham, UK.

Adalbert Evers, Ruprecht-Karls-Universität Heidelberg, Germany and Ersta Sköndal Bräcke University College, Sweden.

Ewan Ferlie, King's College London, UK.

Lars Fuglsang, Roskilde University, Denmark.

Johan Gärde, Ersta Sköndal Bräcke University College, Sweden.

Magnus Gulbrandsen, University of Oslo, Norway.

Nardia Haigh, University of Massachusetts-Boston, USA.

Kelly Hall, University of Birmingham, UK.

Helen Haugh, University of Cambridge, UK.

Matt Hill, Youth Impact, UK.

Diane Holt, University of Leeds, UK.

Kath Hulse, Swinburne University of Technology, Melbourne, Australia.

Benjamin Huybrechts, Emlyon Business School, France.

Claus Jacobs, Bern University of Applied Sciences, Switzerland.

Philip Marcel Karré, Erasmus University Rotterdam, Netherlands.

Karin Kreutzer, EBS Universität für Wirtschaft und Recht, Germany.

Hana Lipovská, Masaryk University, Czech Republic.

David Littlewood, University of Sheffield, UK.

Sergej Ljubownikow, University of Sheffield, UK.

Fergus Lyon, Middlesex University, UK.

Ross Millar, University of Birmingham, UK.

Robin Miller, University of Birmingham, UK.

Vivienne Milligan, University of New South Wales, Sydney, Australia.

Jørn Kjølseth Møller, Roskilde University, Denmark.

Mark A. Moore, Simon Fraser University, Vancouver, Canada.

David Mullins, University of Birmingham, UK.

Mattias Nordqvist, Jönköping University, Sweden.

Victor Pestoff, Ersta Sköndal Bräcke University College, Sweden.

Julie Rijpens, University of Liège, Belgium.

Aurélie Soetens, University of Liège, Belgium.

Jana Soukopová, Masaryk University, Czech Republic.

Anna Thomasson, Lund University, Sweden.

Taran Thune, University of Oslo, Norway.

Gabriela Vacecová, Masaryk University, Czech Republic.

Nicolette van Gestel, Tilburg University, Netherlands.

Arlette Cindy van Lint, ORMIT Nederland, Netherlands.

Patrick A.M. Vermeulen, Radboud University Nijmegen, Netherlands.

Aidan R. Vining, Simon Fraser University, Canada.

David L. Weimer, University of Wisconsin-Madison, USA.

Richard Winter, Australian National University, Australia.

Acknowledgements

Putting together the major volume that is this *Handbook* is the work of many hands and we owe a great debt of gratitude to the authors who have contributed to its contents and are listed in the Contributors section. Our thanks to them is all the greater because of the delays and disruptions to the work brought about by the serious health issues experienced by both editors and now happily overcome. We want to thank our contributors for the patience and support they have shown us during these difficult times. We are also grateful to Rachel Downie of Edward Elgar Publishing for her support and her faith in us during the long gestation period of the *Handbook*.

Above all we owe a great deal to two people who have provided us with consistent support and helped to keep us relatively sane. Jacquie Billis, David's wife, who, despite the pressures of his illness and the demands of the *Handbook*, was always there to support him with love and wisdom. He is a very lucky man, but then he has known that for a very long time. And Meta Zimmeck, Colin's partner, has more or less graciously accepted that too much of his time has been spent with the *Handbook* rather than with their joint activities and has remained supportive of the project. He is extremely grateful to her for this and much else.

Grateful acknowledgements are made to the following for permission to use previously published material in this book.

The Leadership Foundation for Higher Education for 'Leadership roles and approaches in UK HEI' (Figure 10.1), previously published in Bolden, R., Petrov, G. and Gosling, J. (2008), *Developing Collective Leadership in Higher Education: Final Report*, London: Leadership Foundation for Higher Education.

Taylor & Francis for the use of 'The third sector and the welfare triangle' (Figure 18.1), previously published in Pestoff, V. (2008), *A Democratic Architecture for the Welfare State*, London, UK and New York, USA: Routledge.

SAGE for the use of material in Chapter 19 previously published in Ljubownikow, S. and Crotty, J. (2017), 'Managing boundaries: the role of non-profit organizations in Russia's managed democracy', in *Sociology*, 51 (5), http://doi.org/10.1177/0038038515608111.

SAGE for the use of material in Chapter 19 previously published in Crotty, J. and Hall, S.M. (2013), 'Environmental responsibility in a transition context', *Environment and Planning C: Government and Policy*, 31 (4), pp. 667–681.

SpringerNature for the use of 'Three sectors and their hybrid zones' (Figure 25.1), previously published in Billis, D. (2010), *Hybrid Organisations and the Third Sector*, Basingstoke: Palgrave Macmillan.

Selected abbreviations

ANT	Actor Network Theory
APOPO	Anti-Personnel Landmines Detection Product Development
AWO	Arbeiterwohlfahrt / Workers Welfare
BEN	Bicycling Empowerment Network
BC	British Columbia
BoP	base of the pyramid
BTR	below the radar
CBT	Columbia Basin Trust
CEE	Central and Eastern Europe
CEO	chief executive officer
CIC	community interest company
CPC	Columbia Power Corporation
CSO	civil society organisation
CSR	corporate social responsibility
DBFOM	design, build, finance, operate and maintain
DH	Department of Health
DIV	deprived, isolated or vulnerable people
DSE	Dialogue Social Enterprise
ESOP	employee stock ownership programme
EU	European Union
FBO	faith-based organisation
FHFA	Federal Housing Finance Agency
FPO	family personal-organisation
FPR	fractionalised property rights
GFC	global financial crisis
GS	Google Scholar
GSE	government-sponsored enterprise
HEI	higher education institution
HO	hybrid organisation
HTSO	housing third sector organisation
HTPP	hybridity tensions positioning protocol
INPC	International Nut Producers Cooperative
KCC	Khayelitsha Cookie Company
L3C	low-profit limited liability company
LA	local authority
LLC	limited liability company
LSE	London School of Economics
LtE	learn to earn
MCA	Mumwa Crafts Association
ME	mixed enterprise

MENA	Middle East and North Africa
MNC	multinational corporation
NESTA	National Endowment for Science and Technology
NGO	non-governmental organisation
NHS	National Health Service
NOR	New Organisational Reality
NPG	New Public Governance
NPM	New Public Management
NRAS	National Rental Affordability Scheme
OECD	Organisation for Economic Co-operation and Development
PORTVAC	Programme of Research and Training into Voluntary Action
PNH	public–nonprofit hybrids
PO	personal-organisation
PPP	public–private partnership
RD	regional director
RE	renewable energy
RNLI	Royal National Lifeboat Institution
RtR	Right to Request
SANCO	South African National Civic Organisation
S-D	service-dominant
SDGs	Sustainable Development Goals
SOE	state-owned enterprise
TESSEA	Thematic Network for Social Economy
TPA	traditional public administration
TSO	third sector organisation
UNICEF	United Nations Children's Fund
V4	Vysegrád Four
VOC	Verenigde Oost-Indische Compagnie
WELP	Waneta Expansion Limited Partnership

1. Introduction to the *Handbook on Hybrid Organisations*
David Billis and Colin Rochester

1.1 BEYOND THE COMFORT ZONE

The title of this section of our Introduction is intended to reflect our contention that we are writing in a fascinating period for organisational studies during which the rise of hybrid organisations (HOs) is causing us to reconsider the way we understand the world of organisations. The 'new kids on the block' are turning out to be not so young, nor so few in numbers, nor so inconsequential as is sometimes assumed. The growing excitement and fascination of these times is sometimes tempered by a sense of discomfort and uncertainty. Are HOs making a positive contribution to our society? Or are their problems causing too many difficulties? Should we keep well away from them?

Before responding to these questions, we first provide the background for and scope of the book, and in so doing note some of the new theories that will most likely provide both excitement and constructive discomfort. We then begin to introduce two crucial issues: the contribution of HOs and their potential problems. Section 1.2 provides a systematic summary of all the chapters, and section 1.3 briefly speculates on the past, present and future of the study of HOs.

1.1.1 The Background and Scope of the Book

The academic background to this book is a period in which the study of hybrid organisations and their number, scope and importance have begun to be fully appreciated. It is becoming increasingly evident that they are distinctive organisations that play a unique role in their responses to human problems. The impressive number and wide variety of HOs, their potential longevity and their global coverage are increasingly recognised. What is now also under way is both the identification of historic HOs and the creation of new ones. After centuries of invisibility we can now say with confidence that the HO genies have slipped out of many of their bottles. As far as we can judge, this is a process which appears to have begun more systematically in the last quarter of the 20th century when academics began to explore these seemingly new organisational phenomena.

So what are these hybrid organisations? For the moment, we describe them as formal organisations that utilise the distinctly different principles of more than one of the three sectors (private, public and third). Although not yet a complete working definition it immediately points to what has become the main challenge in the study of HOs: the clash of organisational principles which, while it provides them with the flexibility that is the basis of their unique contribution, can also be the cause of their unique problems.

There are multiple objectives of this *Handbook*. The broad ambition is to advance our understanding of these comparatively new players in the study of organisations.

1

Importantly, and in contrast to other studies of HOs, we have approached the study of hybrid organisations as a global multi-sector phenomenon of formal organisations. However, our intention is even more ambitious. It is to increase the range and broaden the boundaries of the study of hybrid organisations themselves by beginning to drill downward into the history of HOs; by bringing the role of volunteers out of the cold and into the study of hybridity; and by analysing and including non-formal organisations and family businesses into the study of formal organisations. The end result is a new map of the range of hybrid organisations, and the need to rethink existing organisational approaches.

The increasing range of HOs is demonstrated in the following 28 chapters by 53 contributors from 13 countries, which break new ground in the diversity of their content and perspectives. Different kinds of hybrid organisations are arranged by sector and discuss specific types such as government-sponsored enterprises, social enterprises, public–private partnerships, and many more. A variety of fields in which HOs operate are covered; examples include health, housing, religion and higher education. Numerous organisational issues are addressed, including governance, strategic planning, social impact and mission. We have also been successful in the geographical coverage of the *Handbook*, which discusses issues faced by HOs in countries from different areas: Western Europe, Eastern Europe, North America, Africa and Australia. The range of academic disciplines and fields is no less extensive, including public administration, social policy, organisational theory, management studies, history, law and economics.

More radical organisational territory is also explored in Chapter 27 which highlights the importance of volunteers and voluntarism, not only in their primary role in the third sector but also in their contributions to the work of government organisations. The final part of the *Handbook* also contains a new theory that brings the non-formal or 'personal-organisation' (not to be confused with informal organisations) into the family of organisations. Indeed, the concluding chapter (Chapter 29) contends that HOs play a pivotal role in a groundbreaking new approach: the New Organisational Reality.

When planning the organisation of the book, we considered a number of possibilities but finally concluded that the best choice was to base it on sectors. This decision emerged from the contention that the three sectors (public, private and third) play a key role in the development of HO research. This is demonstrated by the many contributors to our *Handbook* who either clearly utilise the terminology of sectors or utilise language that is similar to the sectoral division. We have in mind, as one example, the chapters that discuss 'social enterprise', which is in essence a hybrid between the third sector (or one of its alternative names) and the private sector. Other contributors have also been drawn to the utility of the sector concept, or some close alternative name, as a powerful boundary concept. There is another important reason for our choice. This use of sectors makes sense in the arenas of practice and public policy where the broad notion of sectors remains influential. The choice of the sector in the analysis of HOs thus seemed a sensible organising principle.

Below, we discuss the two questions that reverberate throughout the chapters: what is the essential contribution of HOs? Then we explore the other side of the coin, the problems of HOs. If the discussions are to be useful, a working definition is required and we have followed the sector-driven organisation of the book by utilising the approach that covers all three sectors (Chapter 24). Briefly, based on the criticality of formal organisations in responding to human problems, it recognises their historic adherence to the distinctive principles of one sector, but argues that this ideal sector model is unrealistic. It is therefore replaced by the authentic sector model which includes HOs and reflects organisational reality. The continued strength of the principles of the three sectors led to the definition of HOs as organisations that retain their prime adherence to the principles of one of the three sectors, but have absorbed some of the principles of one or both of the other sectors.

In conclusion, despite their problems, we have personally long taken an optimistic approach to the importance of HOs. It is an approach based on the contention that HOs are a distinct form of organisation that is inexorably being recognised as such. With recognition comes the realisation that our understanding of the world of organisations is changing. We are moving beyond the organisational comfort zone.

1.1.2 The Distinctive Contribution of Hybrid Organisations

The organisational comfort zone is so well known that it is not usually recognised as such. Dominated by formal organisations, it is a taken-for-granted essential part of everyday life in most developed countries. The situation differs from country to country and in different periods, but there is widespread awareness that, put crudely, for some things we can turn for support to government agencies, for other needs we have choices and pay for ourselves; for yet other issues we can become members of third sector organisations that we support with contributions, fees and voluntary work.

The reality is that the taken-for-granted assumptions about formal organisations have, as we shall shortly demonstrate, been incomplete for centuries. The strength of the three sectors of formal organisations will continue, possibly for more centuries. They are not going anywhere soon. Nonetheless, the steady unveiling of hybrid organisations and the greater complexity of the organisational world present a major challenge for organisational studies. The complexities of this new organisational reality are an intrinsic part of the *Handbook*.

The main objective of the remainder of this part of the chapter is to provide an introduction to the two key aspects of hybrid organisation: the distinctive character of their contribution, and the distinctive problems that they face. Section 1.2 will provide summaries of key aspects of all the chapters. In contrast, we draw on the contributions of contributors and external sources more specifically in order to illustrate these two key aspects.

Despite the increased recognition in the academic world of the existence of hybrid organisations there is some way to go before we fully understand the real range of their positive contributions. We begin therefore by noting their general intrinsic contribution: it is their potential to solve problems that cannot be resolved solely by traditional non-hybrid organisations. Their ability to utilise the principles of several sectors can enable them to obtain additional resources in order for them to maintain, change and survive in their objective of responding to human problems.

In this section we draw attention to the value of HOs by noting, perforce only fleetingly, the work of several contributors and other commentators. We begin by drawing attention to two case studies that remind us of the longevity and success of HOs, their historic and continuing contribution and, not least, the importance of organisational roots. This last point is especially relevant for the stability of HOs in which roots – the reasons for their existence and their organisational DNA – can be confused.

The value of roots

The importance of roots is demonstrated by two chapters that present historic case studies of hybrids. The first of these is Thomasson's study of the Swedish corporate model (Chapter 8) that can be traced back to the late 19th century. In the 1960s and 1970s the model was more widely utilised with the expansion of the public sector and the development of the social welfare state, and it experienced a further boost in the middle of the 1980s resulting from the influence of the New Public Management ((NPM). A strong message is reserved for the end of the chapter, where Thomasson declares that without understanding its history it would be easy, but erroneous, to assume that the Swedish corporate model was a result of the strong impact of NPM on the development of public services and their hybrid character. On the contrary, what we see today results from the influence that the public as well as the private sector logics have had on the model during that period: '[it] teaches us not to forget our history'. This provides a salutary warning for HO researchers in an exciting and rapidly increasing field (see section 1.3 of the chapter).

Roots and interdependence

There are older hybrid organisations that have been identified as existing many hundreds of years ago. This is illustrated in the pioneering case study of the rise of the Dutch East India Company founded in 1602 (Vermeulen and van Lint, Chapter 11). It is a detailed and fascinating study which examines the enduring conflicting demands, and mutual dependence between the company and the state. The authors utilise the work of Gelderblom et al. (2010, p. 16) whose work highlights the character of the company 'as a private commercial company with superimposed public responsibilities'. While the state officially kept the final authority to itself, the company received the public power to make decisions in the name of the States General. The authors suggest that this was the first hybrid organisation combining state and commercial logics. The company lasted until 1799 without a master plan in mind. Instead its hybrid strategy unfolded by actions and responses along the way. It was certainly an impressive achievement and the particular lessons to be learned are the enduring importance of its enacted hybrid roots and the key role of mutual dependence. It is a success story which is only slightly modified by its eventual failure.

Both these cases may help us to understand and learn from this additional historical dimension of hybrid organisations. Other hybrid centenarians and some even older are also to be found as societal pillars in many countries; these include universities, cathedrals, mosques, museums, theatres, learned societies, leisure and sports organisations, and political parties. Indeed, Chapter 26 by Johan Gärde, whose objective is to better understand the hybrid arrangements that have arisen from the interaction between church and faith-based organisations in the three sectors, is introduced by an account of a conference in the Vatican with its 2000-year history.

Hybrid research institutes: innovation and interdependence

Another important lesson is provided by an example in which the private sector stakeholders' principles of the market are interwoven with public sector research principles in the search for innovation. The possibility of developing new innovative approaches to problems is an attractive prospect for stakeholders. In Chapter 7, for example, Gulbrandsen and Thune analyse research institutes as organisations that have research and development as a main activity, whose funding is most often predominantly public, and which are not part of the higher education system. They suggest that an important driver of these structures is the assumption that the creativity and radical solutions, associated with public research organisations, can be implemented in private firms. Overall, effective hybrid arrangements tend to be realised only through repeated collaborative and integrative efforts over a long period of time. In this collaboration, it seems that both sides can, but do not always, achieve the objective of melding the competing principles of public research with those of private sector implementation.

1.1.3 The Contribution of Hybrid Organisation Research to Society

As demonstrated in this *Handbook* the development of interest in HOs and its associated theories has resulted in the development of new research insights and the deeper understanding of organisations in all three sectors. Inevitably, new insights bring with them new problems. Although we discuss some of these in the following section, one of these is so important that we raise it now. The perspective which clearly differentiates non-hybrids from hybrids necessitates reappraising how we determine organisational failure and success. To what extent does hybridity contribute to either of these situations? The potential implications of successfully using a theory of hybridity are at this stage seemingly limitless. Even at the current stage of research it is possible to ask searching questions before any proposed creation of a hybrid organisation. The tools and methodology are in place to clarify accountability for decision-making ownership, governance and operational priorities.

The value of a theory of hybrid organisations may be particularly helpful in the case of HOs such as social enterprises, family businesses and housing organisations that have attracted their own body of dedicated researchers and associated journals and research events. They all have in common the need to understand organisations that have been steadily recognised as HOs (see Cornforth, Chapter 13; Blessing and Mullins, Chapter 16; Milligan and Hulse, Chapter 21). Together, these three areas of hybrid organisations make a critical contribution in their different ways to the economy and to the response to social problems. They also share the problem, in varying degrees of intensity, of uncertainty about their boundaries.

Social enterprises are an interesting example of chronic boundary confusion. In an upcoming international conference devoted to social enterprises (EMES, 2019) one of the major themes contains the call for contributors to respond to the questions: What do we think social enterprise is, and what could it be? The conference organisers point out that for the last 20 years different scholars have sought to define the approaches to social enterprise (SE). What are the boundaries? In an authoritative article in *Public Policy and Administration*, Simon Teasdale answered similar questions by arguing that the definition of SE was deliberately kept loose by policy-makers, 'to allow for the inclusion of almost any organisation claiming to be a social enterprise. This allowed them to amalgamate the positive characteristics of the different organisational forms, and so claim to be addressing a wide range of social problems using social enterprise as a policy tool' (Teasdale, 2011, p. 99).

The recognition that SEs are hybrid organisations is an important first step in deconstructing the hodgepodge of organisations that benefit from the warm glow that is emitted from the SE brand. At some point in the history of SEs it is likely that they will be required to clear up the confusion and clarify the boundary. Failure will lead to an uncertain long-term future for SEs, which are likely to remain susceptible to the malign influence of others, beyond government, that accidentally or deliberately improperly utilise the SE 'brand'.

HO research and government

Whether, or to what degree, this analysis is applicable at an international level it nonetheless appears plausible in the United Kingdom (UK) situation. It may be out of fashion, but it also raises issues about the morality of governments that claim credit when none is due. The issue of morality is inescapably attached to the consequences of its failure. This of course is hardly a new phenomenon. Nonetheless, confusion over conceptual boundaries provides a golden opportunity, an almost irresistible temptation, for governments to exploit the territory. In the case of SEs the practical consequences might be comparatively modest but the unintentional implementation of public policy, even with the best of intentions, but based on confused concepts, is highly likely to be inefficient and expensive; and the deliberate implementation of such concepts may be both costly and morally questionable. Confused public policy is often critically analysed by a number of disciplines. However, scholarly analysis may now need to take into consideration the possibility that the target of the analysis might be a hybrid organisation with its own distinctive organisational characteristics.

The contribution of research for government policy

We have previously fleetingly noted the relevance of hybridity theory for government, with its huge expenditures. We now delve a little deeper into an area in which HO research and the better understanding of hybridity can make a major contribution.

The path to hybrid organisations is attractive for governments. Often this is a result of the pressure to meet political manifestoes and public commitments, combined with the constant need to avoid additional taxes. UK governments have been prone to create structures which involve eye-watering expenditure (seemingly without appreciating the uniqueness of hybrids). A popular but controversial approach is the practice in which private companies provide public services and infrastructure. This public–private partnership model that involves private firms taking on the risk of delivering projects in exchange for payments from the state has been developed over several decades. It has created what has been called in Chapter 24, an 'entrenched hybrid'. The model has recently come under severe criticism from the UK Treasury as being 'inflexible and overly complex' (Davies, 2018). A few months earlier, a governmental enquiry was informed by the most senior official from the Cabinet Office that, 'the entire PFI [private finance initiative] structure is to keep the debt off the public balance sheet. That is where we start.' The enquiry committee declared this to be a 'shocking' admission from the government (Wearden, 2018). To paraphrase Laurel and Hardy, 'here's another nice mess you've gotten us into, Minister'. It is not essential to be an optimist in order to believe that a valuable contribution could be made to the public purse by better understanding the nature of hybrid organisations.

1.1.4 Problems of Hybrid Organisations: Emerging from the Comfort Zone

All organisations face problems, and to claim otherwise is to be 'economical with the truth'. Although we have so far focused on the potential positive contribution of HOs, we are acutely aware of the problems arising from the conflict of principles present in all hybrid organisations. In this section we have attempted to explore some of the major problems that are distinctive for HOs. Foremost amongst them are those caused by lack of clarity about ownership, combined with the concomitant confusion of accountability. These twin characteristics reflect the essence of the DNA of hybrid organisations. Many, perhaps most, cases of significant organisational problems in HOs are likely to be traceable back to confusion surrounding the roles of these twins. They are also the driving forces behind disturbances in the comfort zone.

As reflected in section 1.1, the study of HOs is approached from many different vantage points and levels of problem. We have consequently focused on the principle of ownership and, sometimes by implication, its related problem of accountability.

Ownership and accountability

The previous section concentrated on the advantages of HOs for stakeholders, but it also concluded with a salutary reminder of their possible disasters. The most compelling example was the spectacular collapse of the outsourcer Carillion in early January 2018, which cost the taxpayers £150 million and had a devastating impact on 43 000 employees. In the immediate aftermath of the disaster the overwhelming reaction of the majority of serious observers was to blame poor management and technical failures. One exception was the contribution by Chris Blackhurst (2018) who argued, in summary, that the real problem was the mismatch between private and public when a private company was asked to perform a public service, as is the case with the private–public partnership This was nowhere near a meeting of equals; there was no match of like minds and values, not in terms of how a company is charged and assessed, nor how it is run, nor in operations. One side is for growing profits and producing dividends for shareholders; the other is about getting something for as little as possible (ibid.). A blunt assessment, but one that gets to the heart of the nature of hybridity, the problems of different principles, and the consequence of the absence of shared and transparent knowledge by both sides of their competing principles.

Similar issues are discussed by Boardman and Moore in Chapter 4 where they analyse three forms of local government mixed enterprises. It is the public–private partnership (PPP) form in which government uses the private sector to carry out public purposes that is most relevant. The authors point out that, as a result of the structure in which managers directed by the private sector owners are without direction from public sector officials, there are two sets of owners and severe conflict can arise between them. Their analysis identifies what is seen as a key problem: 'that despite being described as "partnerships", the private sector and public sector owners generally have fundamentally different goals'. This analysis has much in common with the three-sector theory of Billis in Chapter 24 which suggests that HOs have severe difficulties in functioning with decision-making owners from two different sectors. Vining and Weimer in Chapter 6 explore similar territory using a property rights approach that reaches similar conclusions. They remind us that the first and most fundamental dimension of property rights is the degree of ownership fragmentation, and that with a single owner there is no potential for conflict among owners. They conclude by offering advice to organisational designers: be wary of hybrid designs that fractionalise property rights across the public and private sectors. This insight corresponds to the general direction of Chapters 4 and 24.

At first glance, the connection between Chapter 10 by Winter and Bolden and the discussion in the previous paragraph may seem rather distant. For example, their approach is based on a social constructionist perspective (Berger and Luckmann, 1967 [1971]) in which different individuals and occupational groups interpret the central work of the organisation at a particular time and in a given cultural context. Ownership and accountability do not appear to be central to their analysis. But closer examination reveals, despite its different theoretical approach and area of concern, a contribution that is considering the same problems of owners with fundamentally different goals and the presence of ownership fragmentation. Their contribution is powerful and may be (painfully) familiar to most academics. The authors are discussing hybridity in higher education institutions, and the heavy weight of their evidence provides a powerful confirmation of the internal conflicts and contradictions in these hybrid organisations. Their focus is on problems such as divided loyalties, contradictory expectations, values and assumptions, cultures and beliefs. But all these are set within the overarching problem of the clashes of principles and approaches of: (1) the academic collegiate mission and its emphasis on intellectual rigour and scholarship; with (2) the market and hierarchical structures; and (3) the vagaries of government policy.

Chapter 14 by Doherty, Haugh and Lyon explores the strategic management tensions encountered when seeking to balance the commercial, social and environmental objectives of SE. Given that they define the aim of strategic management as the creation of a shared plan of action for the organisation, it is to be expected that such a high-level decision will inevitably rise to the top of all pyramids and be the concern of the decision-makers in all organisations. However, the authors persuasively lay out the case that the distinctive features of hybrid organisation warrant further research into the nature of their appropriate strategic management. We surmise that without such research the accountable owners and many more staff will be destined to share their space with the permanent presence of the infamous 'elephant in the room'. Other important contributions are made by authors who also consider potential problems that can reach the highest level of decision-making. Thus Huybrechts, Rijpens, Soetens and Haugh (Chapter 23) reflect on their research into the ways in which newly established social enterprise hybrids have, with modest success, endeavoured to build legitimacy. Kreutzer and Jacobs in Chapter 22 tackle the difficult problem of mission drift and present the development of a framework that responds to these problems.

Earlier, we briefly referred to the 'unfashionable' consideration of the possible lack of morality in the actions of governments with respect to the SE approach. In a thoughtful and extensive contribution that also discusses social enterprise, Curtis Child (Chapter 12) has produced a diplomatic but nonetheless powerful critique about the morality of social enterprises. His concern about their morality is 'that the pursuit of social value could be limited by the tools of the market upon which, by definition, social enterprises rely'. He suggests that it is easy to think that using them towards moral ends can only turn out well. 'But it is possible – some say likely – that efforts to address social problems are not best governed by the tools of capitalism, and that efforts to make them do moral things might have an adverse effect.' He concludes that it would be 'appropriate for social enterprise scholars to think more deeply about the moral consequences of social enterprise', suggesting that 'it is constructive to reflect critically on whether encouraging social enterprise is ultimately a worthy pursuit'. We might say that he has (constructively) put the 'cat amongst the pigeons'; a British idiom with several alternative unsavoury origins but whose general meaning is fairly obvious. A more delicate approach is to suggest that it might take many of us out of our comfort zones, which returns us to the main theme of this section and our own conclusions.

1.1.5 Summary of Section 1.1

The chapter began by laying out in the opening subsection 1.1.1 the background and scope of the book, the rationale behind the choice of presentation of the chapters, and a definition of hybrid organisations. We decided that the following subsections should provide a limited introduction to the most crucial questions confronting the existence and continued development of HOs: what are their distinctive potential advantages? And what are their inherent problems? In response to these questions section 1.1.2 discusses the advantages of hybrid organisations and section 1.1.3 contains some reflections on the contribution of HO research.

Section 1.1.2 begins by explaining what we mean by the organisational 'comfort zone': the taken-for-granted assumptions about formal organisations. Following this, it moves rapidly into the main discussion about the distinctive contribution of HOs. It lists many of the areas in which their ability to utilise the principle of sectors and solve problems that cannot be resolved solely by traditional non-hybrid organisations has proved valuable. From this point onwards a number of examples are provided and begin by discussing the value of organisational roots and the proven longevity of HOs which can survive, at least, for several centuries (Chapters 8, 11 and 26). They also point to the importance of interdependence, an advantage which is also noted by Gulbrandsen and Thune in the context of research institutes in Chapter 7.

Section 1.1.3 moves beyond the contribution of HOs and considers the contribution of HO research to society, firstly with respect to groups of HOs, using the example of social enterprise; and secondly, discussing the contribution for government policy. But since HO research is primarily undertaken in universities which are themselves hybrid organisations (see Chapter 10) that are dependent, for example, on fees, donations, legacies and, most importantly, the collegium of academics, the end products of the university are themselves making significant contributions to society. In addition to work with individual organisations, an important contribution to groups of HOs such as SEs is to utilise hybridity theory to help clarify the potentially existential problem of their confused boundary. The second more specific, but still potential, contribution is to clarify the presence and nature of hybrid organisations before governments establish them without understanding their complexity.

Section 1.1.4 illustrates the other side of the coin: the distinctive problems of hybridity. It concentrates on the two most serious issues: those of unclear accountability and ownership. It illustrates the major disaster of a national private–public partnership, Carillion, and the conflicts resulting from mixed private and public sector ownership of local government mixed enterprises (a form of PPP). We return to two forms of organisation whose advantages have already been noted: universities and social enterprises. The study of universities confirms that they are indeed HOs, with severe internal conflicts over issues such as divided loyalties, values and cultures, but these are all played out within the overarching problem of competition between the academic collegiate mission, the market and government policy.

There are two very different studies of SEs that remind us of broader considerations. The study of strategic management tensions, although it begins by discussing the problems, is firmly balanced by the later presentation of responses and solutions. The broader point is that the division into advantages and disadvantages of HOs is rather artificial and, as will be evident from this section, and the chapters themselves, many chapters address both problems and solutions. That said, the second broader consideration, also about SEs, adopts one of the most valuable academic approaches by raising difficult questions, in this instance about their morality. With this contribution we have returned to the theme of moving beyond our comfort zone.

1.2   CONTENTS OF THE HANDBOOK

In the 28 chapters that follow this Introduction we have assembled a rich variety of insights into the nature of hybrid organisations and the challenges they pose. The material is divided into four parts. The first nine chapters focus on public sector hybrids. Part II consists of six chapters which look at hybrid organisations rooted in the private sector. In Part III we turn our attention to the seven chapters that examine third sector hybrids. And the six remaining chapters that make up the Part IV of the *Handbook* provide insights into all three of the sectors and their boundaries.

1.2.1   Part I: Public Sector Hybrids

The first two chapters after this Introduction provide some theoretical guidance to the complexities and tensions involved in public–private sector hybrids. In Chapter 2, Philip Marcel Karré sets out a conceptual model which maps hybridity across ten dimensions where the private and the public mix and can be used to identify an organisation's hybrid thumbprint. He defines the ten dimensions as: (1) legal form; (2) ownership; (3) activities; (4) funding; (5) market environment; (6) value orientation; (7) strategic orientation; (8) relationship with public principal; (9) managerial autonomy; and (10) executive autonomy. He suggests that the organisational thumbprint derived from their analysis can be used to highlight areas of tension; to facilitate discussion about the organisation's strategic course; and to identify the dimensions on which these organisations can be beneficial or hazardous.

Chapter 3, by Nicolette van Gestel, Jean-Louis Denis and Ewan Ferlie, discusses four theoretical frameworks that, according to the authors, make sense of hybrid organisations, drawing on recent empirical works to help understand how public service organisations deal with hybridity in strategy and practice. The four frameworks are: governance theory and the emergence of mixed forms; institutional logics where the focus is on organisational change; Actor Network Theory focusing on the process of organising; and the identity framework which explores how individuals and organisations experience hybridity in public organisations. The authors conclude that: 'All four of the frameworks we explored were found to capture some, but not all, facets of the answer.' The chapter provided 'a rich variety of alternative theoretical perspectives which can be used to inform further empirical studies of hybridisation in the public services'.

Chapter 4 focuses on some of the legal issues involved in public–private organisations and the implications of them for their performance. Anthony E. Boardman and Mark A. Moore distinguish between different kinds of local government mixed enterprises: the classic form where a local government directly or indirectly owns some of the common shares in an organisation and private investors also owns some of them; the public–private partnership, a long-term contract between the private sector and a government agency which goes beyond the contracting-out of a government service; and the complex form, involving a variety of public arrangements and contractual solutions for engaging the private sector. The authors identify different ways in which these MEs perform. Some of them provide 'the best of both worlds' and maximise the provision of social welfare; others are hamstrung by conflicts between public and private values; while a third offers 'the worst of both worlds' where public and private owners maximise profit at the expense of consumers.

In Chapter 5, Ross Millar, Kelly Hall and Robin Miller present a case study of social enterprises established under the 'Right to Request' programme that formed new organisations into which public services could be 'spun out' from the National Health Service (NHS) in England. Drawing on elements of the four 'theoretical prisms' set out by van Gestel and her colleagues in Chapter 3 of this *Handbook*, Miller et al. identify some approaches that have offered ways of resolving some of the contradictions and multiple logics of social enterprises within the context of public sector delivery. In particular, insights gleaned from Actor Network Theory has clarified the need for greater financial support from the government while identify theory helped to create a better understanding of the need to adapt to different audiences. These findings provide useful insights into the sustainability of hybrid organisations.

Aidan R. Vining and David L. Weimer, in Chapter 6, use six dimensions of property rights to explore the differences between different kinds of public–private hybrid organisations and some aspects of their performance. The different dimensions are: (1) the degree of fragmentation of ownership; (2) 'the extent to which various dimensions of property rights are comprehensively and unambiguously assigned and specified among owners and other claimants'; (3) 'the ease with which current property rights can be reallocated': (4) security from trespass or 'the extent to which either duty-bearers or third parties respect property rights claims': (5) 'the expectation that the current allocation of rights will exist over time': and (6) the extent to which owners and managers have autonomy within the system. The authors apply these dimensions to empirical evidence about the performance of different public–private organisational forms and conclude that, while all of them risked some goal conflict, the challenge was likely to be greatest for public–private partnerships and government-sponsored enterprises and less severe in mixed enterprises.

Chapter 7, by Magnus Gulbrandsen and Taran Thune, addresses an accelerating trend to hybridisation in universities and research institutes through the development of new organisational arrangements that combine research with innovation and/or commercialisation. These not only bring together aspects of the public and private sectors but also combine the goals of furthering scientific understanding with the commercial exploitation of this knowledge. The chapter reviews three different types of organisational set-up for achieving integration between private and public goals before concluding that hybridity in research is particularly complex, entailing not just the combination of public and private sector forms but also two different perspectives on science. Research-based hybrids may not resemble hybrids in other fields and require significant and patient investment.

In Chapter 8, Anna Thomasson reviews the experience of the Swedish corporate model, the hybrid organisational form of the corporations owned by Swedish municipalities and developed long before the introduction of New Public Management. She suggests that the growth in the numbers of these corporations has been fuelled by their perceived advantages: greater clarity about the relationship between performance and income through the separation of the corporation's budget and increased managerial autonomy leading to greater efficiency and effectiveness. On the other hand, managerial autonomy has increasingly been seen to risk eroding accountability to the municipality, and there was a danger of mission drift as public sector values were overshadowed by the values of the market. Historically the model has been seen to work because of the honesty of politicians and faith in the democratic system but the impact of NPM and some recent corruption scandals have brought the boards and managers of the corporations – and the model itself – under scrutiny.

The main purpose of Chapter 9 by Lars Fuglsang and Jørn Kjølseth Møller is to develop a framework for understanding how hybridity can lead to innovation. The first part of this approach is through adopting the logic of servitisation, which introduces a market-like approach to public services where citizens are treated more as if they were individual customers. The second part uses the ideas of boundary concepts, skills and hybrid regions to explain how actors can develop 'a new idea that gives meaning to and pulls together diverse supporters around a shared meaning' for innovation; how they can use the skills and identify the materials needed to develop new ideas; and how they can work within a 'hybrid region' that provides the autonomy to connect and integrate the elements of experimental practice through overlapping principles.

In Chapter 10, Richard Winter and Richard Bolden look at the ways in which higher education institutes are made up of competing professional and managerial beliefs and value systems. The professional or normative value system emphasises public service, professional autonomy, collegial practice and tradition, while the managerial or utilitarian alternative is characterised by profit-making, corporate management, customer service and change. The chapter discusses different approaches to synthesising, bridging and reconciling differences in logic and values. These include considering universities as 'dual identity' organisations and regarding academic leaders as managers with an alternate professional identify. The key challenge remained how to devise governance structures and leadership processes for orienting academic work around change and enterprise ideals whilst simultaneously enabling academics and professional staff to retain their professional identities.

1.2.2   Part II: Private Sector Hybrids

Chapter 11 focuses on one of the oldest hybrids of them all: the Dutch East India Company, founded in 1602 as a national trading company with a state monopoly of trade with the East and using investments from shareholders. Patrick A.M. Vermeulen and Arlette Cindy van Lint review the history of the company and its attempts to secure the support it needed from different internal and external parties: the directors of the company, the shareholders and the States General. The conceptual basis of the chapter is the competition between two central logics – the commercial and the state – and the ways in which organisations respond to conflicting institutional pressures. It examines three key stages of the development of the company: an attempt to combine both logics; a second phase eventually resolved by the application of commercial logic; and a third phase that led to the bankruptcy when the hybrid character that had made the company so powerful also caused its downfall.

In Chapter 12, Curtis Child introduces the discussion of social enterprises by identifying three 'classes of concerns' that they need to address as hybrid organisations. He suggests that the first of these – issues of consonance involved in trying to reconcile the very different logics of the market and social welfare – can be addressed by appropriate structures for accountability and governance. The second concern is trustworthiness – to what extent can external actors trust the organisation's claims? – to which the response can take the form of new legal forms of organisation and certification. For the third set of moral concerns, which deals with the ethical consequences of merging commercial and social goal and values, Child offers no simple responses but suggests that scholars need 'to think more deeply' about these issues.

Chris Cornforth focuses on governance structures in Chapter 13. He identifies two main approaches for social enterprises in managing the pressure to maintain their social goals in the face of commercial pressures in the form of strategies that either integrate or compartmentalise competing institutional logics. He lists four kinds of integrative strategies: developing legal structures such as the new community interest company; adopting external accreditation of standards; defining the membership of the organisation and the composition of its board; and developing control mechanisms that manage both social and financial performance. Strategies for compartmentalisation are of two kinds: either segregation – separating social and commercial activities into legally distinct but connected organisations; or segmentation – separating parts of the organisation with different logics within the same organisation.

In Chapter 14, Bob Doherty, Helen Haugh and Fergus Lyon explore the strategic management tensions involved in balancing commercial, social and environmental objectives in social enterprises, and discuss how they can be managed. They highlight three ways in which organisations can respond to the tensions involved: by prioritising one of the conflicting demands at the expense of the others; by separating the customers and the beneficiaries of social enterprises into different stakeholder groups; or by striving to develop an integrated model in which all business functions support the achievement of the dual mission of 'pursuing viable commercial markets at the same time as generating social and environmental value'. They bring these elements together into a conceptual framework that provides a guide to the alternative strategic options available to social enterprise hybrids.

Chapter 15 by Elena Dowin Kennedy, Erynn Beaton and Nardia Haigh looks at how the corporate governance practices of both traditional firms and social enterprises might use them to increase their social impact. It assesses them against the six corporate governance principles developed by the Organisation for Economic Co-operation and Development (OECD): ensuring the basis for an effective corporate governance framework; protecting the rights and equitable treatment of shareholders; addressing the responsibilities of institutional investors; understanding the role of stakeholders in corporate governance; ensuring the need for disclosure and transparency; and addressing the responsibilities of the board. The authors conclude that traditional firms were likely to increase their social impact if they were to adopt the governance practices of social enterprises, and that both traditional firms and social enterprises would increase their social impact if they adhered more strictly to OECD corporate governance principles.

Finally in this section, we turn to Chapter 16 in which Anita Blessing and David Mullins, drawing on the experience of the United States (US) and using the lens of organisational hybridity, look at ways in which profit-oriented investors respond to state and civic governance mechanisms for encouraging societally beneficial investments in affordable rental housing. They discuss a pair of mechanisms that can be seen as working in tandem to develop an affordable rental housing industry. The 'carrot' of Low Income Housing Tax Credit which provided tax exemptions for organisations with tax liabilities was combined with the 'stick' of the Community Reinvestment Act of 1977 which obliged banks to meet the credit needs of the communities in which they operate. These measures have been implemented by hybrid organisations through community development corporations and community development financial institutions. The authors conclude that these measures have had an impact on the provision of local affordable housing and also provided a significant effect on the development of inter-organisational hybridity.

1.2.3   Part III: Third Sector Hybrids

In Chapter 17, Adalbert Evers argues that third sector organisations experience two very different kinds of hybridity that point in very different directions for research and practice. The first of these – inter-sectoral hybridity – involves the 'intertwining of usually separated institutional logics and organisational fields'. The second – multipurpose hybridity – refers to 'organisational forms that combine distinct purposes, such as service provision and advocacy, value change and mutual help'. Evers feels that the inter-sectoral approach needs to be complemented by multi-purpose hybridity so that 'a richer variety of organisations comes into focus and service provision will not be the most important feature'. He calls for research based on this dual approach that addresses 'issues that concern the vitality of civil society, the third sector and the rich variety of its organisations'.

Chapter 18 from Victor Pestoff provides us with an important context for research and action on third sector organisations. He suggests that the elements that comprise different kinds of public administration regimes (PARs) have clear implications for hybridity, co-production and the third sector, and argues that changes in public administration regimes will determine the focus of the leaders of third sector organisations. The four PARs he identifies are traditional public administration based on the provision of public goods delivered by public servants guided by bureaucratic norms; New Public Management where the market replaces the state as the main mechanism for governing citizens' preferences; New Public Governance where citizens play a more active role as co-producers; and communitarianism which involves radical budget cuts for public services and the expectation that families, communities and the third sector will fill the vacuum.

In Chapter 19, Sergej Ljubownikow and Jo Crotty look at the impact of the system of 'managed democracy' on non-profit organisations (NPOs) in the Russian Federation.

Their case studies focus on NPOs engaged in health and education on the one hand, and those involved in environmental issues on the other. In both cases, they argue, NPOs have become hybrids – agents of the state as well as agents of the non-profit sector – but for different reasons. Those engaged in health and education have encountered state-led committees or roundtables which have provided a means of developing an overlap between the roles and responsibilities of individuals active in the NPOs and those working within the agencies of the state. This has blurred the line between the responsibilities of the state and the work of NPOs. In the case of environmental NPOs, dependency on state funding has meant that their concerns have been restricted to activities that were acceptable to the state.

Chapter 20 looks at the growing pains of civil society organisations and, in particular, social enterprises in the transitional economy of the Czech Republic. Gabriela Vaceková, Hana Lipovská and Jana Soukopová argue that, despite the deep transformation of the Czech economy as it moves from a state-controlled economic system to one that is driven by the market, the development of social enterprises has been hindered by the legacy of communism. Czechs have found it difficult to adjust to the loss of state monopoly of public services and are suspicious of the association of businesses with a social dimension with socialism. Legal structures and the security of property rights are underdeveloped. In the absence of legislation and a more secure funding base, social enterprises remain vulnerable and make a only a limited contribution to the economy.

The case study presented in Chapter 21 by Vivienne Milligan and Kath Hulse reviews the recent development of housing third sector organisations (HTSOs) in Australia. The majority of the 40 or so larger organisations that dominate the sector are enacted hybrids rooted in government initiatives in specialist housing provision, with a limited pool of members and increasingly financed by major financial organisations. They are increasingly market-driven due to 'capricious government behaviour' and 'bureaucratic inertia'; the influence of powerful land developers and banks; and the weakness of their connections with the third sector. In the process HTSOs have moved from their original status of state–third sector hybridity to one which involves the state, the third sector and the market.

In Chapter 22, Karin Kreutzer and Claus Jacobs also use a case study of the United Nations Children's Fund (UNICEF) Germany as a worked example of a tool they have developed to address the key issue of mission drift in hybrid organisations. Their framework, the hybridity tensions positioning protocol (HTPP), can be used to identify, surface and specify four generic organisational tensions as a means of reaching decisions about how to develop the organisation's mission. The HTPP charts social and commercial logics across the four kinds of organisational tension to provide a map of the organisation's current positioning. This enables it to discuss and agree how to address its future needs and any necessary revisions to its mission statement. As well as contributing to a transformation of potential conflict into productive tensions, Kreutzer and Jacobs claim that the protocol can also provide an organisation with aspects of a strategic capability.

Another case study is presented by Benjamin Huybrechts, Julie Rijpens, Aurelie Soetens and Helen Haugh in Chapter 23. Their focus is on a federation of community-owned renewable energy co-operatives which explored ways of building legitimacy in these social enterprise hybrids which suffered from the liability of newness. The REScoop.eu federation adopted four kinds of discourse in order to build legitimacy in its member organisations: developing a critique of the dominant logic of policy-makers and corporations; promoting a new model in the form of a social enterprise; engaging in advocacy of the new kind of organisation; and using a wide range of activities to spread knowledge about the new hybrid model. The authors conclude that these activities have had some success, but have not yet fully engaged the support of stakeholders.

1.2.4 Part IV: The Three Sectors and Their Boundaries

The driving force of Chapter 24 by David Billis is his concern about a lack of understanding about the contribution made by hybrid formal organisations to responding to human problems, and his primary objective is to identify a greater clarity of accountable ownership. The chapter outlines the author's theoretical approach before presenting two models. The first of these analyses the three sectors in which each of them consists of individual formal organisations with common principles of organisation. The second model builds on this to present an 'authentic sector model' which contains both ideal-typical organisations and their hybrids. This section of the chapter also uses a suite of concepts to identify different kinds of hybridity. The chapter goes on to present three case studies – of global disaster, national uncertainty and local disturbance – that demonstrate the ways in which the new concepts help to clarify the problems of confused ownership. It ends by looking ahead to the continued development of this theory of the New Organisational Reality and discussing the need to rethink the changing role of organisational theory.

The objectives of Chapter 25 by David Littlewood and Diane Holt are: to examine the state of research on hybrid organisations in sub-Saharan Africa; to explore the types of hybrid organisation found there; and to identify challenges facing them. The authors point out the complexities associated with sub-Saharan African contexts. The private sector is distinguished by the prevalence of the informal and subsistence economy and the importance of multinational enterprises. The public sector is 'characterised by limited resources and capacity, regulatory voids, and also challenges of corruption, excessive bureaucracy and a lack of accountability'. And the third sector 'has been heavily influenced by international dynamics and actors', its organisations tend to be informal and they are also less able to hold governments to account. The chapter identifies some key challenges and strategies for third sector, public sector and private sector hybrids in sub-Saharan Africa and outlines some insights for research, theory and practice.

The purpose of Chapter 26 by Johan Gärde is to better understand the hybrid arrangements that have arisen from the interaction between churches, faith-based organisations and other sectors. This is approached by exploring drivers for and against the development of hybridity and by developing a rough draft of some of the new hybrid relationships between churches and faith-based organisations and the other sectors. Faith-based organisations face diminishing congregations and have responded by interactions with public, private and other civil society organisations, some of which have led to hybrid types. The author also suggests that faith communities and their organisations are striving to resolve not only the problem of declining membership but also the challenge of wider humanitarian tragedy.

Colin Rochester, Angela Ellis Paine and Matt Hill set out in Chapter 27 to assess the extent to which the involvement of volunteers can be seen as a way of defining the hybrid character of organisations across all three sectors. The chapter begins by mapping the geography of hybrid organisations developed by Billis in Chapter 24 in order to identify the organisational settings where volunteers might be found. The chapter then takes a close look at the ideal type of third sector organisation – the association – which is used as a kind of template for volunteer involvement in other organisations. It discusses the role of volunteers in third sector hybrids, before looking at the status and roles of volunteers in the other two: public and private. Finally, it seeks to identify the part played by volunteers in each sector and the extent to which they can be seen as contributing to the hybrid nature of organisations.

In Chapter 28, Börje Boers and Mattias Nordqvist explore the nature of family businesses as hybrid organisations by examining two case studies of companies that were family-owned and had been listed on the stock exchange. Both organisations exhibited high levels of potential conflict due to the centrality of their competing logics, but there were clear differences between them. In one of them the logic of family ownership remained paramount. In the other, tensions between family members – the majority – and other members of the board led to the development of 'a hybrid professional family firm' with a non-family chief executive officer (CEO) and chair; the family, while remaining active and interested owners, no longer controlled the organisation.

Finally, Chapter 29 by David Billis builds on the analysis of the three sectors – public, private and third – presented in Chapter 24 and argues that the exclusive focus of that chapter on formal organisations failed to take into account the 'personal world' of individuals, families, friends and neighbours. Chapter 29 therefore sets out to explore the overlapping territory between formal organisations and the personal world. The chapter discusses some key items of relevant literature; presents a case study of 15 book clubs; uses the case study to introduce and presents a model of a new form called the 'personal-organisation' (PO) which differentiates its principles from those of formal organisations; distinguishes between different kinds of PO including the distinctive type of the 'family personal-organisation'; and speculates on the different ways in which hybrid organisations could arise from the personal world, and how principles of the personal world can be adopted by formal organisations.

1.3 REFLECTIONS AND SPECULATIONS ON THE PAST, PRESENT AND FUTURE OF THE STUDY OF HYBRID ORGANISATIONS

1.3.1 Introduction: The Purpose and the Journey

Our purpose

The first section of this chapter presented the background and scope of the *Handbook* and argued that the advances in the study of hybrid organisations are leading us to move beyond our organisational comfort zone. Section 1.2 deepened the understanding of the contents of the book by providing a systematic summary of all the chapters and their contribution to the advances of our understanding of HOs. This section is rather different. It does not focus on the book itself but explores the academic journey of the study of HOs. Where did the journey begin? Where has it arrived? And where is the next likely destination?

This approach came up against a number of limitations: data identification and collection, and limited resources, being at the top of the list. In the preparation of this final section it also became evident that answering the three questions would require a mixture of different approaches. In response to the first, historical question, we decided to utilise Google Scholar (GS) to track the growth of HO publications over a period of 58 years in order to get a sense of the broad development of the academic engagement with HOs. Several academic reviews were consulted about its suitability before using GS (see Harzing, 2018). This proved to be a useful exercise indicating that GS would be appropriate for the task of mapping the development of interest in hybrid organisations.

In our response to the first question (which we set out in section 1.3.2 below, on the pioneering period) the number of publications identified by GS was manageable enough to permit extracts from those that were considered to make important contributions. The second question (which we discuss in section 1.3.3, on the interregnum) addressed, as its name implies, a period that signalled the approach of a new period of HO research. Here again, in this period, it was possible to continue using the publications approach. In section 1.3.4, however, both the current position and the possible future for the study of HOs have been included in the same section as a result of the pace of development revealed in the publications exercise. An exhilarating period of research had arrived in which traditional organisational approaches were being challenged. The interregnum was left behind, and the book is written in the third period: that of recognition. During this period our reflections and speculations are confronted by an accelerating body of publications that is now increasing at more than 1000 a month. The publications exercise served its main purpose for this book and provided us with enough material which, together with our own personal experiences, could be blended into this final section.

Our journey
Before responding to the three questions, our starting point is to consider the growth of publications about HOs; an exercise which we hope will provide an indication of the general direction. The following time-boundaries and data should therefore be treated as broad indicators of the growth of research interest.

Utilising Google Scholar we decided that, although there were occasional earlier mentions of the early use of hybrid organisations, it would make sense to begin our search in 1960, when there were ten publications. The number then meandered along until 1990 by which time scholars had 170 publications at their disposal. It seemed a snail-like pace and yet it represented steady progress each decade. These three decades might be considered as the pioneering period during which researchers became increasingly concerned about the blurred and confusing overlap between the sectors.

The following period – from 1990 to 2000 – can be thought of as the interregnum, since by the end of the decade the total number of publications had grown to 677. It was a period in which research interest began to solidify and lay the foundations for the leap into what we might now call the period of recognition from 2000 onwards. We decided on this title since the increase of publications in the following period is so considerable and consistent that it is difficult to escape the conclusion that a wide range of academics had begun to recognise the existence and importance of hybrid organisations. The chapter now moves on to discuss these three periods.

1.3.2 Where Were We? The Pioneering Period: Blurring (1960–1990)

Our reflections draw on a deep involvement with third sector research and their hybrid organisations, which began in 1978 with the establishment at Brunel University of the first centre for the systematic postgraduate teaching and study of the third sector, which later transferred to the London School of Economics (LSE) in 1987. One of the chronic problems facing both the third and the public sector, as Lan and Rainey (1992, p. 7) pointed out, was that social scientists have been exploring blurring on the boundaries between public and private organisations 'for decades'. Both sectors were worried about their boundaries. However, if the concern of the public sector was mainly about elements of the boundary between the public and the private sector, the third sector had more substantial problems. It was preoccupied with its overall boundary, and the lack of recognition of its true societal contribution. This anxiety about boundaries led many third sector scholars, amongst numerous others, to describe them as 'messy' and 'blurred' (e.g., Lohmann, 1992; Van Til, 1988). In 1987 the *Journal of Voluntary Action Research* published a two-volume special edition devoted to the blurring of the sectors in which one of the guest editors, Susan Ostrander, declared: 'the papers in this collection take this principle of blurred boundaries as a premise' (Ostrander, 1987, p. 7). They were not alone since, as noted by Lan and Rainey, blurring was the default response to the problem of sector boundaries. In time, it became clearer that utilising words such as 'blurring' and 'messy' was inadequate to describe the boundaries between the sectors. It stood in the way of developing anything that might resemble an explanatory theory.

The use of 'blurring' as a description of the boundary problems between sectors slowly decreased, but is still used; for example, there is an interesting defence of the continuing utility of 'blurring' to be found in Bromley and Meyer (2017). In our own research it had become increasingly clear that without a theoretical explanation it would be impossible to understand the boundary phenomenon. In the late 1980s, David Billis encountered the work of the distinguished anthropologist Edmund Leach, and his short book *Culture and Communication* (Leach, 1976). His work on boundaries and his use of a Venn diagram to depict what he called the 'ambiguity' of the overlap between them (ibid., pp. 34–35) was to prove invaluable. His concept of ambiguity and the Venn diagram were rapidly transported to the different field of formal organisations and were employed for lectures and publications about the third sector. Within two years, 'blurring' was replaced by 'ambiguity', and this, in turn, was replaced by the beginnings of a theory of hybrid organisations that has been continually tested and developed until its latest presentation in this *Handbook*.

These reflections are not intended to be a comprehensive history of HOs. Nonetheless, it is possible to get a strong sense that, by the end of the pioneering period, the notion of hybrid arrangements and organisations was beginning to take grip. Admirers of the advantages of the private sector found support in the influential book by Savas (1987), *Privatization: The Key to Better Government*, whose title did not do justice to the contents of a book that, whilst it made a strong case for the virtues of the private sector, went well beyond crude boosterism. Considerable space was also given to the thoughtful analysis of 'alternative arrangements for providing goods and services' (ibid., pp. 58–115). Amongst these was the suggestion that 'hybrid arrangements' might be one of the ways of overcoming the problems of human services contracting (ibid., p. 83). Although they are only briefly mentioned and not fully defined, his book is packed with detailed examples of numerous organisations that would now be regarded as hybrid organisations.

In an intriguing contrast, public administration writers were already making a very different case some years earlier. Musolf and Seidman (1980), for example, were concerned about the increasing 'vesting of responsibility for the performance of important government activities in "quasi-government" or "quasi-private" [agencies] . . . The burgeoning use of these and other hybrid organisations . . . raises serious questions of appropriateness' (ibid., p. 124). Musolf and Seidman do not refer to hybrid organisations again, but the essence of their argument is that these hybrids have led to the blurred boundaries of public administration and unclear lines of accountability which are undesirable in a constitutional democracy. To support their case they provide 23 high-profile examples (ibid., pp. 129–130).

This work was drawn upon by Bozeman who, also writing from a public administration approach, produced a seminal book in 1987: *All Organizations Are Public: Bridging Public and Private Organizational Theories* (Bozeman, 1987). Bozeman is wrestling with problems similar to those raised by Musolf and Seidman, and other authors in the pioneering period – and well beyond – to come to grips with the vexed issues of boundaries, blurring and accountability. Also utilising numerous examples, he considers that these problems are the result of 'government and business organisations becoming more and more similar in respect to their functions, management approaches, and public visibility' (ibid., p. 5). But he goes well beyond Musolf and Seidman in that he defines and utilises the concept of hybrid organisations in all three sectors throughout the book. And he suggests (as an almost incidental definition) that they add an additional element of complexity which comes from 'this growth of "hybrid" (partly government, partly private) organizations and "third-sector" nonprofit organisations' (ibid.).

We chose these three examples because they are all concerned with the enduring issues but approach them from the different perspectives of private and public sector research. Furthermore, they indicate how the idea of hybrid organisations had begun to appear. Undoubtedly there were other scholars on a similar path, and still others for whom blurring remained and still remains an acceptable explanation. Our own experience, bolstered by the scan through the literature, is that it was also a period of development in the study of HOs in which the issues of boundaries, blurring and nascent ideas of hybridity were mainly limited to a discourse between scholars from the same sectoral interests and disciplinary approaches. It was also a period during which researchers had begun to understand the unique nature and problems of hybrid organisations. By the end of the pioneering period in 1990 there had been 170 publications.

1.3.3   Interregnum (1990–2000)

So far, we have been primarily interested in gaining a broad sense of the increase of scholarly interest in HOs by noting how the number of publications had grown. In the period of the interregnum – from 1990 to 2000 – the number of reported publications reached 677.

Before moving on to review the interregnum period, however, it might be helpful to briefly digress and explore a little deeper to see whether the idea of the three different periods of development might also be reflected in differences in the importance that authors gave to hybrid organisations. If this could be achieved it would provide another useful indicator for the present and future health of the study of HOs.

We again reviewed the publications, but this time the objective was to find how many of the publication had the words 'hybrid organisation' or 'hybridisation' in their title. The title of a paper by authors is not chosen lightly; it usually reflects the main area of interest and purpose of their contribution. Google helpfully lists publications in order of relevance, beginning with those that have 'hybrid organisation', or something close to that, in the title. We found that in the 30 years of the pioneering period there were six such publications, whereas eight titles were produced in just the ten years of the interregnum. Many of these publications appeared towards the end of the period; one sign that the interregnum was coming to an end. More importantly, in the decade of the interregnum the number of publications rose from 170 to 677 publications.

What stands out from the comparison between the pioneering and interregnum periods is not only that there were more publications and titled publications in the shorter period of time; there were also hints of things to come. In brief, scholars from different backgrounds were now writing papers titled with 'hybrid organisation' or similar. The public sector provided three of the titles, but the rest were spread amongst business, management, third sector, economics and organisational journals. It seems that a wider range of disciplines were entering the discussions. And academics who had been working in the pioneering period were continuing to focus on HOs while new ideas were beginning to flourish.

An interregnum scholar: some reflections

In order to illustrate several of the characteristics of this period described above we briefly discuss an important work of the distinguished scholar Claude Ménard. We are not qualified to discuss his detailed economic analysis, and this is not the reason why we are offering a profile of a few of his publications. More important for our purposes are the insights that he provides into the internal conflicts amongst economists regarding different approaches to hybrid organisations. He is very much an interregnum scholar whose work on HOs spans all three of the periods and, as an organisational economist, adds a valuable approach to the study of HOs.

His first publication that acknowledges the presence of HOs appears in 1996: 'On Clusters, Hybrids and Other Strange Forms' (Ménard, 1996). But a draft of his most relevant and influential paper, 'The Economics of Hybrid Organizations' was delivered as his Presidential Address for the International Society for New Institutional Economics in 2002. He begins by criticising one of his colleagues for raising questions about the need for considering HOs in economics, and counters this by predicting that it is highly likely that their considerable role 'will generate a growing flow of theoretical models and empirical studies. And I expect new institutional economists to take a significant share of these researches' (Ménard, 2002, pp. 1–2). His address is helpful in appreciating the opposition that could be faced by HO scholars, not only from within the society of economists. More generally it alerts us to the conflicts that can arise from new theoretical theories that question entrenched approaches. In a later passage, he reinforces his views by contrasting the negative approach of his colleagues to HOs, and what he implies is the more enlightened approach of other disciplines. He declares that: 'to my knowledge, there is no extensive survey of the literature on hybrid organisations in economics. But at least two relatively extensive surveys on papers published in sociology or management journals are available' (ibid., p. 6).

By the time we have reached the end of the paper it becomes increasingly evident that Ménard is deeply concerned that there are significant groups of economists who do not regard HOs as an important area of study. In his conclusions he is careful to present a list of issues and problems to explore, and also acknowledges the contribution of managerial sciences, marketing and sociology to their identification. However, it seems that these issues are also presented in order to ask the rhetorical question: is the study of HOs worth the effort? His answer again emphasises that the argument that hybrid organisations have characteristics of their own, and that they deserve extensive study, has been challenged. His parting words are crystal clear:

> In short, discrete hybrid organisations exist. We must explain why and what makes them viable substitutes to alternative modes of governance. I agree with Coase that hybrids are not 'strange forms'. Rather, they are a major if not predominant mode of organising transactions and, therefore, economic activities. But these forms are highly complex, which makes their study challenging. Challenging, and stimulating. (ibid., p. 25)

This contribution reflects what appeared to be a fundamental debate surrounding the approach to hybrid organisations in an earlier era. Whilst this contributes to an understanding of intellectual debates in the interregnum, it also has implications for the current situation. Another interpretation of the two sides of what Ménard refers to as 'the fence' is that it was a clash between theories based in a hybrid-free world and those who recognised the critical, perhaps even predominant, role of hybrids. The dilemma for the former, traditional view was therefore what to do about the pesky hybrid newcomers. In other words, can they just be integrated into the existing dominant approach? No disrespect is intended towards our colleagues, but we shall call this the 'economists' dilemma' despite its widespread presence in many disciplines. Almost two decades later we shall suggest that, in a more modern form, this question and the dilemma still require answers. For us, as with Ménard, this is also a rhetorical question, albeit a rather different one.

The 1990s was the decade in which the study of HOs became of increased interest and segued into the wider recognition of HOs that we know today. In the next subsection we will go on to discuss the current period but, at this stage, we would suggest that our tripartite division may be a reasonable reflection of the stages in the development of HOs.

1.3.4   Where Are We Now? And What Is the Future? Recognition (2000 and Beyond)

The introduction to this section of the chapter proposed that the history of research into hybrid organisations might be usefully divided into three periods. Having now completed part of the publications exercise it seems that it will provides a useful contribution to the understanding of HO history. One thing is evident: notwithstanding the growth of publications since 2000, the foundations for today's developments began around 1960, and by the beginning of the period of recognition in 2000 publication numbers had reached 677. From then on the history of the study of hybrid organisations changes dramatically. By 2010 the number of publications had grown to 3850, and in the period until 2018 it had increased to 12 800.

We do not wish to drown the narrative in statistics and we conclude by noting that in every year in the period 2000–2018 the percentage of publications has steadily increased. In the year 2010/11 there were 620 additional publications and in the year 2017/18 the number had leapt to 1600. The number of publications is far more than we had envisaged and it was equally surprising to observe the scale and consistency of the increase year by year.

The first speculation: drivers of growth
Moving briefly outside the bubble of the academic study of HOs and what is sometimes negatively described as the 'ivory tower', the world at large can be seen as chaotic and unpredictable; it would be presumptuous to venture any speculations about future economic, political and environmental conditions that might drive or slow down the future of HO research. The good news is that, even in a period of often uncomfortable changes in higher education (see Chapter 10 by Winter and Bolden in this *Handbook*), academics – as is evident throughout this *Handbook* – are increasingly seeking new and innovative ways of understanding the HO phenomenon. Yet, academic inquisitiveness and enthusiasm, whilst essential, are only part of the story of the path to publication.

Underpinning the growth of HO publications is a web of forces. A few processes that come to mind are interacting influences such as a higher public profile for HOs, or a group of them, as a result of severe problems – such as the recent crisis in non-governmental organisations (NGOs), particularly in Oxfam concerning claims of sexual misconduct by aid workers – that may attract academic and/or government interest. There are many other less complex drivers. For example, funding for research at all levels from individual academics to research centres may continue to be provided by government, foundations and wealthy individuals seeking new ways to respond to societal problems.

A powerful driver in the development of research has been the increasing recognition of entire categories of organisations as HOs. A prominent example of this is the widely acknowledged understanding of social enterprises as HOs, which has led to the rapid development of a body of literature. Other HO categories are housing associations (Chapters 16 and 21 in this *Handbook*), state-owned enterprises (Bruton et al., 2015) and societally important categories of hybrid organisations such as faith-based organisations (Chapter 26 in this *Handbook*) and the newest and very important group, family businesses (Chapter 28 in this *Handbook*).

In addition to the recognition of specific organisational categories as hybrids, growth has been driven by the knowledge that many of the areas of growth that were noted in the initial stages of HO development are still in their infancy. The geographical coverage of HOs has steadily increased but global coverage is patchy, as is the range of organisational types that were considered in the early days of the study of hybrids and which is still the case today. The study of the history of HOs, with a few ground-breaking exceptions, remains an unexplored area. And the territory of (non-formal) personal-organisations is also hardly explored.

More traditional ways of increasing interest for particular academic approaches and problems, and publications, are the development of initiatives such as presentations at broader-based conferences, entire conferences dedicated to HO studies, and special editions of journals. Looking at the present situation, several of these have already occurred and played their part in driving the development of publications about HOs. These types of initiatives will naturally increase as the scope of HOs and their full impact and contributions are more fully appreciated. To summarise, then, our first speculation based on the discussion in this subsection of some of the numerous current drivers of growth, and potentially many more, is that it is highly likely that the future of HO studies will continue to grow and advance.

The second speculation: the academic condition
Although publications have served as a useful indicator of growth and change in the study of HOs, there are additional considerations to be taken into account when reflecting on the future. An important element is to attempt to understand the present state of HO research: the academic condition.

First, we return to the description of the current period as one of recognition, a word that requires some explanation. The intention was to indicate this that this is a period in which, although hybrids are increasingly recognised as distinctive types of organisational forms, there are different approaches towards understanding them. The wide range of different approaches to the study of HOs is illustrated in the various chapters in this *Handbook*. For example, approaches may include different theories or suite of theories, specialisation in a specific field of interest such as health, different geographic territories and organisational levels. And all these and other approaches can be combined together for more precise descriptions of an area of study. A bewildering number of combinations can emerge. Given the complexity of approaches, comments have been restricted to just two of the broad developments that we speculate will be significant players in the future scenario of HOs. The first speculation, in the previous subsection, discussed the drivers for the growth of HO research that will continue to grow. The second speculation concerns the present and future state of the academic condition.

The second speculation flows from the first. It involves a consideration of the consequences for academic approaches of the continued growth of a New Organisational Reality (NOR) resulting from the inexorable uncovering of the essential role of hybrid organisations. The NOR is already in progress, with the consequence that traditional approaches – defined as those based on the 'pure' ideal model of formal organisations that belong to one of the three sectors – are being revisited. Academic approaches are increasingly compelled to adjust to the fact that their bedrock is changing and now increasingly contains hybrid organisations. This is the developing academic condition, the state of cautious engagement with HOs.

This engagement is manifested in a number of different responses. In the beginning these were of lack of interest, or of dismissal. This was understandable in light of the low profile of HOs, and the continuing power of the traditional approach based on the importance of the historic and current roles of pure formal organisations. It is an approach with strong roots in academia, where it underpins many disciplines, departments and courses, with numerous journals that are similarly divided.

But the situation has now become a challenge for traditional approaches that is likely to intensify if the developments of personal-organisations and their role in hybridity, presented in Chapter 29 of this *Handbook*, gain acceptance. The rethinking that is required to include these types of HOs in organisational studies has already begun. An example is the studies of family businesses, that are increasingly being analysed as hybrid organisations positioned between the private sector and POs.[1] The realisation of the increasing complexity of the organisational world has led to more constructive responses than the original attitude of 'dismissal'. Valuable research has been undertaken, utilising and expanding a variety of traditional approaches to respond to and analyse real problems and contribute to the body of knowledge.

But it might be prudent to be cautious when the theory in question is defined so broadly that it has no boundaries and just about any conflict of principles at any level can be included, and squeezed into the theoretical sphere of influence. We have in mind the institutional logics perspective, which is defined as 'the socially constructed, historical patterns of cultural symbols and material practices, assumptions, values, and beliefs by which individuals produce and reproduce their material subsistence, organise time and space, and provide meaning to their daily activity' (Thornton and Ocasio, 1999, p. 804). Not surprisingly, therefore, this perspective, which can be defined at different levels of analysis including world systems, societies and organisations (ibid.), is regarded as important. But what does the study of HOs most require at its current stage of development?

We shall reflect on this question in the following subsection. For the moment, however, summarising both sets of speculations, our conclusion is that the drivers of growth bode well for the health of HO research. Existing drivers are likely to maintain their relevance and, in the light of the expansion of the field itself and the prospect of new responses to problems, they may well increase. Overwhelmingly, the state of the academic condition of the study of HOs is therefore healthy.

1.3.5   Theory and the Challenge of a New Organisational Reality

This section of the Introduction has focused on the academic journey of the study of hybrid organisations. It has provided a sense of a history that is substantially more long-standing, rich and fast-developing than might have previously been envisaged, even by the pioneers in this field. In the journey since 1960 we have argued that the study of HOs has reached the period of recognition. These concluding reflections discuss the relationship between the study of hybrid organisations and their presence in a New Organisational Reality (NOR).

The balance: is there a gap between theory and reality?
After previously laying out in some detail the substantial progress that has been made so rapidly, it sounds churlish even to ask the question. The existing abundance of available research on HOs seems an answer in itself. Nonetheless, we suggest that there is in fact a gap that is made wider by the reality of the New Organisational Reality. The relationship between theory and reality will be regarded as two interacting processes in motion: on the one hand their study, and on the other, their reality.

It is dubious whether this has ever been a balanced interaction, and this may well be the case with most similar types of interaction. Hybrid organisations have been around for centuries but it is only comparatively recently that they have begun to be recognised and understood. It is not surprising therefore that most of the research and literature of organisations is hybrid-free. Whilst it has had its full measure of debate and fierce disagreement, research has mainly operated within an organisational comfort zone that has not significantly challenged the theoretical dominance of the pure formal organisation.

In the meantime, when faced with the reality of societal problems, stakeholders have been busy – both accidentally and deliberately – establishing new HOs. Governments around the world have been particularly involved in this activity, sometimes on a monumental scale, as is the case of state-owned enterprises (Bruton et al., 2015). And John Kay, the distinguished British economist and a newcomer to HO research, has laid bare an impressive list of new governmental hybrids. Intriguingly, his title is 'Hybrid Organisations: The Ambiguous Boundary between Public and Private Activity' (Kay, 2018), the subtitle of which takes us back to earlier periods of the study of HOs. This is by no means a criticism of a fascinating article which has much to offer. The contributions from Bruton and his colleagues and Kay remind us that many additional HOs may await analysis and, in the case of the latter, how HO research would benefit from additional and more structured ways of the dissemination and discussion of ideas amongst the relevant academic communities. The growth of the reality of hybrid organisations on a global scale will require such new initiatives if the gap between theory and reality is not to grow wider. This more general theme of responding to the challenge of the NOR will be elaborated next.

The challenge of the New Organisational Reality
Realistically, it is now possible to say with confidence that HOs exist on a global scale and comprise a complex collection of different types and combinations of activities, geography and scale. In response to the challenge of this complexity, HO research can offer a large body of ideas. Despite this, there are two areas of possible concern. The first is whether these theoretical responses are capable of reducing the gap between the theory and the reality of today's global coverage. It is probable that the current focus on individual HOs and groups of them will continue to illuminate the field, possibly for decades. But are some approaches constrained by the hybrid-free foundations of their theoretical approach, and possibly also from an absence of interest in the structural reality of organisations? Arguably, such constraints might weaken the analysis of HOs and limit their utility in the study of hybrid organisations.

The second area of concern, which may also include the first, is whether existing theoretical approaches will meet the additional complexity presented by the NOR. This new reality brings with it the inclusion of hybrid organisations that will transform the nature of organisational studies. It will do this by expanding the definition of an organisation, a transformation of organisational reality that has already begun by recognising family businesses as hybrids. These are not HOs that utilise the principles of more than one formal organisation; but despite this they are hybrids, because they draw on the principles not only of formal organisations but also of personal-organisations such as family businesses and many others (see Chapters 28 and 29 in this *Handbook*). All in all, it is a daunting challenge for HO theory.

Helpfully, we encountered a chapter by Haveman and Gualtierig, who while surveying institutional logics (IL) proposed, unduly modestly, 'three gentle corrections . . . to guide future research' (Haveman and Gualtierig, 2017, p. 1). More relevantly for these reflections, they provide examples of some of the problems facing IL that might assist HO theory in responding to the challenge of the New Organisational Reality. Severely summarising part of their detailed argument, Havemen and Gualtierig declare that logics are not material constructs such as organisational structures. On the contrary, institutional logics are 'fundamentally, cultural phenomena' that most previous research has inappropriately taken to be 'purely rational constructs' (ibid., p. 22). In essence they argue that putting the two interpretations together is a mess; they should be kept separate. More elegantly: putting them together results in an 'ontologically heterogeneous, concept' (ibid.).

They continue by complaining that the proliferation of research about IL 'on ever-more-specialised topics has not made any appreciable accumulation of knowledge, either within topic or overall', even though this is the main purpose of social scientists (ibid., p. 23). This is the beginning of a devastating critique of the current IL situation which begins by declaring that: 'We cannot make progress by simply adding more studies to the pile . . . we are in danger of making IL nothing more than an empty buzzword'. On the following page they make the damning criticism that the current state of research makes it difficult to develop theory (ibid., p. 24). This will be expanded in the following subsection and is an important relevant observation.

Obviously, the main message is for those utilising IL, for whom the final pages of Havemen and Gualtierig's argument will not make easy reading. Nevertheless, as students of hybrid organisations, it would be sensible to look carefully at some of their criticisms of the current state of IL. The 'standout' problems of IL, the most worrying ones, are those that have arisen from a confused and contradictory definition that result in scattered propositions, some of which are contradictory and others loosely connected, and together make it extremely difficult to develop a theory of IL (ibid., pp. 24–25). We do not suggest that HO research shares the worrying situation that they are describing; but we propose an initial 'health check' that will be increasingly essential as we enter the period of the global complex reality of the New Organisational Reality.

1.3.6 A Healthy HO Theory: A Constructive Challenge for Organisational Theory

We conclude these personal reflections with the contention that the totality of contributions in this *Handbook* present a body of research that does justice to the exciting development of organisational reality. It is healthy because it demonstrates constructive criticism, the development of new theories, the advance into new territories both geographical and sectoral, and the continuation and development of theoretical approaches by our contributors who include some of the notable pioneers in the field such as Adelbert Evers and Victor Pestoff.

Most importantly, our personal evaluation is that the pivotal problem of avoiding confused definitions and their consequences have been well addressed in Chapters 24 and 29. To say otherwise would be inappropriately coy and contradict the lessons of the 40 years of continuous testing of the numerous stages of painstaking development. This, together with the more recent work on volunteering in hybrid organisations in Chapter 27, present a suite of concepts and an overarching theory that present a constructive challenge of the existing organisational theory. This was achieved by reconceptualising the nature and role of formal organisations in a number of stages, involving:

1. Developing a theory of their roots and strengths arising from three competing and distinct distinctive and unambiguously organisational principles of responding to human problems.

2.   Developing a bottom-up theory of the 'pure' three sectors based on the accumulation of individual organisations with their three different principles.
3.   Developing a theory of HOs as major forms of formal organisations that retain their main prime accountability to one of the three distinctive sectors, but absorb to different degrees one or both of the other sector principle.
4.   Developing a map illustrating the overlapping of the three sectors and the existence of nine different combinations of HOs.
5.   Demonstrating the interacting and interdependent nature of the three sectors.
6.   Developing a range of concepts that enable the analysis of HOs at individual, group and societal levels.
7.   Reconceptualising the nature of organisations by researching, analysing and defining personal-organisations and demonstrating that they are extensive and serious contributors in the response to social problems; have their own organisational language and distinctive principles; and consist of seven new types of hybridity with formal organisations.
8.   Developing an embryonic theory of family organisations as hybrid organisations.
9.   Analysing the role of volunteers and their role in hybrid organisations.

The New Organisational Reality
Together, these glimpses of the theoretical contributions of Chapters 24 and 29 reflect a research-based overarching theory which not only expands the boundaries of hybrid organisations but also challenges the very foundations of organisational theory. It achieves this by identifying a more realistic world consisting of an interdependent body of organisations comprising: traditional formal organisations and those that are hybrids; and personal-organisations and their hybrids with formal organisations, and vice versa. It is not only personal-organisations that should be seen as part of the realistic world; as Chapter 27 demonstrates, the role of volunteers is also an intrinsic part of the New Organisational Reality.

The NOR is far more than just another stage in the development of approaches to hybrid organisations since, as has been noted above, it presents an alternative basis for organisational theory itself. We believe, as we have tried to demonstrate, that an overarching theory of hybrid organisations is critical. It provides the precondition for understanding the reality of the radical New Organisational Reality that we are entering.

NOTE

1.   See Chapter 29 in this *Handbook* for further discussion.

REFERENCES

Berger, Peter L. and Thomas Luckmann (1967 [1971]), *The Social Construction of Reality*, London: Allen Lane, Penguin Press; reprinted 1971, Penguin University Books.
Blackhurst, Chris (2018), 'Carillion Collapse: A Flawed System is to Blame', *Independent*, 22 January.
Bozeman, Barry (1987), *All Organizations Are Public: Bridging Public and Private Organizational Theories*, San Francisco, CA: Jossey Bass Publishers.

Bromley, Patricia and John W. Meyer (2017), 'They Are All Organizations: The Cultural Roots of Blurring Between the Nonprofit, Business, and Government Sectors', *Administration and Society*, 49(7), pp. 939–966.

Bruton, Garry D., Mike W. Peng, David Ahlstrom, Stan Ciprian and Xu Kehan (2015), 'State-Owned Enterprises Around the World as Hybrid Organizations', *Academy of Management Perspectives*, 29(1), pp. 92–114.

Davies, Rob (2018), 'Hammond Abolishes PFI Contracts for New Infrastructure Projects', *Guardian*, 29 October.

EMES (2019), 'Conference Call for 7th EMES International Research Conference on Social Enterprise', International Research Network (EMES).

Gelderblom, O., A. de Jong and J. Jonker (2010), 'An Admiralty for Asia: Isaac le Maire and Conflicting Conceptions about the Corporate Governance of the VOC'. ERIM: ERS-2010-026-FandA.

Harzing, Anne-Wil (2018), 'The Good, the Bad, and the Better', Google Scholar Citation Profiles, 24 November.

Haveman, Heather A. and Gillian Gualtieri (2017), 'Institutional Logics', in Ray Aldag (ed.), *Oxford Research Encyclopaedia of Business and Management*. DOI: https://dx.doi.org/10.1093/acrefore/9780190224851.013.137.

Kay, John (2018), 'Hybrid Organisations: The Ambiguous Boundary between Public and Private Activity', *Welsh Economic Review*, 26, pp. 46–56. DOI: http://doi.org/10.18573/wer.232.

Lan, Z. and H.G. Rainey (1992), 'Goals, Roles, and Effectiveness in Public, Private, and Hybrid Organizations: More Evidence on Frequent Assertions about Differences', *Journal of Public Administration Research and Theory*, 2(1), pp. 5–28.

Leach, Edmund (1976), *Culture and Communication*, Cambridge: Cambridge University Press.

Lohmann, Roger A. (1992), *The Commons: New Perspective on Nonprofit Organisations and Voluntary Action*, San Francisco, CA: Jossey-Bass.

Ménard, Claude (1996), 'On Clusters, Hybrids and Other Strange Forms: The Case of the French Poultry Industry', *Journal of Institutional and Theoretical Economics*, 152(1), pp. 154–183.

Ménard, Claude (2002), 'The Economics of Hybrid Organizations', Presidential Address for the International Society for New Institutional Economics.

Musolf, Lloyd D. and Harold Seidman (1980), 'The Blurred Boundaries of Public Administration', *Public Administration Review*, 40(2), pp. 124–130.

Ostrander, Susan (1987), 'Towards Implications for Research, Theory and Policy on Nonprofits and Voluntarism', *Journal of Voluntary Action Research*, 16(1/2), pp. 126–133.

Savas, E.S. (1987), *Privatization: The Key to Better Government*, Jackson, NJ: Chatham House Publishers.

Teasdale, Simon (2011), 'What's in a Name? Making Sense of Social Enterprise Discourses', *Public Policy and Administration*, 27(2), pp. 99–119.

Thornton, Patricia and William Ocasio (1999), 'Institutional Logics and the Historical Contingency of Power in Organisations: Executive Succession in the Higher Education Publishing Industry, 1958–1990', *American Journal of Sociology*, 105(3), pp. 801–843.

Van Til, J. (1988), *Mapping the Third Sector: Volunteerism in a Changing Social Economy*, New York: Foundation Centre.

Wearden, Graeme (2018), 'Carellian Collapse Exposed Government Outsourcing Flaws – Report', *Guardian*, 9 July.

PART I

PUBLIC SECTOR HYBRIDS

2. Hybrid organisations: between state and market
Philip Marcel Karré

INTRODUCTION

Hybrid organisations are defined by the mixing of different and inherently contradictory characteristics. Their hybridity makes them contested phenomena. While their proponents claim that they can combine the best of different worlds – in the words of the United Kingdom (UK) periodical *The Economist*, 'the security of the public sector and the derring-do of the private sector' – their adversaries claim that they only combine the worst. Hybridity, the more critical voices warn, leads to 'inherently confused organisations, buffeted by all sorts of contradictory pressures. This means that their internal operations can be hard to understand and their behaviour may be hard to predict' (*The Economist*, 2009).

This contradiction and contention is perhaps most severe where state and market meet each other and organisations have to combine the characteristics of the public and the private sector in the provision of public goods and services. It is those public–private hybrids that are looked at in this chapter. In the model developed by Billis (2010b, p. 57) they inhabit 'zone three', where the public and the private sector overlap.

Examples of such public–private hybrid organisations are state-owned enterprises, agencies and other forms of quasi non-governmental organisations (or quangos) that not only operate at arm's length from their political masters but also undertake commercial activities on behalf of government, mixing them with their activities related to public interests (Bruton et al., 2015; Pollitt et al., 2001, 2004; Pollitt and Talbot, 2004; van Thiel, 2000; Verhoest, 2011). Such hybrid organisations can be found in many countries (Billis, 2010a; Grohs, 2014; Grossi and Thomasson, 2015; Karré, 2011; Koppell, 2003; Kosar, 2008; Rhodes and Donnelly-Cox, 2014; Seidman, 1988) and are not a new phenomenon. There are many experiences of public–private hybrid organisations in history. The Netherlands and Britain for example amassed huge amounts of wealth by virtue of hybrid trading companies such as the British and the Dutch East India companies (for the latter, see Vermeulen and van Lint, Chapter 11 in this *Handbook*). And in many countries it was not the state that started many of what we now see as critical public functions and services such as education, health and public infrastructures, but societal groups such as churches, citizens concerned with social issues and businessmen who saw commercial opportunities in building railways or providing water supplies for sprawling cities.

After the Second World War the public sector grew, as the state began to play a more prominent role in the provision of public goods and services in Western countries (Jackson, 2003). But now hybridity and hybrid organisations are once more on the rise. Over the last few years, many countries have moved from the 'welfare state' to a 'welfare mix' (Defourny, 2014, p. 20; Seibel, 2015). Government agencies are no longer the sole provider of public services. Governments make use of commercial companies for the provision of public services and public sector service providers are now also expected to embrace private sector management techniques, to become more outgoing and responsive and to engage in the market place. They now: '(1) involve a variety of stakeholders, (2) pursue multiple and often conflicting goals and (3) engage in divergent or inconsistent activities' (Mair et al., 2015, p. 714). By doing so, they have become hybrid organisations, 'heterogeneous arrangements, characterized by mixtures of pure and incongruous origins, (ideal) types, "cultures", "coordination mechanisms", "rationalities", or "action logics"' (Brandsen et al., 2005, p. 750). These hybrid organisations include a mixture of the characteristics of societal sectors, different modes of governance and different institutional logics.

This change from the 'welfare state' to the 'welfare mix', and the rise of hybrid organisations that accompanied it, is often explained by the rise of two broad movements or trends (some would call them fashions) of the last 30-odd years: New Public Management (NPM) (Christensen and Lægreid, 2011a, 2011b; McLaughlin et al., 2002; Pollitt et al., 2007) and New Public Governance (NPG) (Durose and Richardson, 2015a, 2015b; Fotaki, 2011; Osborne, 2010b; Pierre and Peters, 2000). New Public Management's underlying logic is to run government like a business through the introduction of private sector management techniques with a focus on economy, efficiency and outputs. NPM also advocates a purchaser–provider split, in which public goods and services are provided via contractual relationships by a collection of independent agencies that are in competition with one another. By contrast, New Public Governance 'posits both a *plural state*, where multiple interdependent actors contribute to the delivery of public services, and a *pluralist state*, where multiple processes inform the policy-making system' (Osborne, 2010a, p. 9). Here the focus is on the ways in which public service organisations interact with their environment and the governance of these interactions and their effectiveness and outcomes.

NPM and NPG followed each other in time, but did not substitute one another. On the contrary, different reform strategies were combined while the core values of traditional public administration remained intact, leading to some sort of a layering or sedimentation process (Olsen, 2009; Osborne, 2010a; Streeck and Thelen, 2005). Because of this, public service provision and public administration as a whole have become more complex and more hybrid, 'resulting in multiple-layer structural and cultural features' (Christensen and Lægreid, 2010, p. 407). Emery and Giauque (2014) make the same point in an article describing the hybrid universe of public administration in the 21st century.

As the whole system of government and public administration has become more mixed, the set, predictable blueprint for governmental organisations – if such a thing ever existed – has become less prevalent. More and more organisations operate in the fuzzy world between the public and the private realm. These hybrid organisations come in all sorts of different shapes and sizes. Therefore, the first step in understanding these organisations, and of standing a chance of minimising the perceived risks and maximising possible beneficial effects, is to explore just what makes them hybrid.

This chapter sets out do so by providing a conceptual model of public–private hybrid organisations. It is based on insights from the fields of public administration and political science, and summarises several characteristics of hybrid organisations that exist between state and market on an array of different dimensions. This model also makes it possible to distinguish between different forms of hybrids and can therefore be used as a taxonomy of hybrid organisations.

The chapter focuses on the following two questions:

1. On what dimensions can an organisation be hybrid?
2. What are the possible positive and negative effects of an organisation's hybridity?

The first question is examined in the next section of this chapter by taking a closer look at the labels 'public' and 'private' and what they mean when it comes to organisations. I will look at how ideal-typical public and private sector organisations differ from one another with regard to (among other issues) their funding, autonomy and core values. I will argue that a dichotomous view of public versus private bears little resemblance to reality where there is a fuzzy border between public and private. By contrast, I will develop the model of a multidimensional continuum in which ideal-typical public and private sector organisations are the extremes between which many different hybrid organisational forms can exist. I will describe several dimensions of such a continuum and show how the model can be used to chart hybrid organisations.

I will focus on the second question concerning hybridity's effects in the following section. I will do so by examining the literature on hybridity's benefits and risks and assessing the financial, cultural and political benefits and risks every hybrid organisation faces potentially. I will also discuss which effects (positive and negative) are most likely for what kind of hybrid organisation based on the multidimensional continuum developed in the preceding section. The chapter ends with some general conclusions on hybridity in organisations and a discussion of what that means for research and practice.

THE CONTINUUM BETWEEN PUBLIC AND PRIVATE

Public Versus Private as a Grand Dichotomy

The distinction between public and private – between the realm of the state and that of the market place – is often seen as a dichotomy. In this view, state and market are not only fundamentally dissimilar but are also mutually exclusive domains. The state safeguards public interests through coercion and by providing essential public services through public organisations. And the market, driven by individual self-interest and the quest for making a profit, provides commercial goods and services through private organisations.

Dahl and Lindblom (1953) distinguish between agencies as ideal-typical governmental organisations on the one hand and enterprises, or ideal-typical business firms, on the other (cf. Rainey, 1997, pp. 61–63; Rainey and Chun, 2007, pp. 75–76). A comparable distinction is made by Simon (1989), who speaks of task and market organisations (see Joldersma and Winter, 2002 for an English translation). Since then, many authors have refined Dahl and Lindblom's distinction; see Rainey and Chun (2007) for an overview.

Agencies produce public goods and services, which means that their outputs are not readily transferable to economic markets at a market price. Instead they rely on governmental appropriations for their financial resources. Because of this their autonomy is limited. They function under governmental authority and oversight, which leads to more red tape and more elaborate bureaucratic structures. Agencies often have a monopoly and do not have to fight off competitors.

Enterprises thrive in economic markets where they constantly have to prove to the customer that their goods and services are more desirable than those of their competitors. They are financed through sales and fees. Enterprises, of course, also have to adhere to public laws and regulations, but in general they have a considerable degree of autonomy concerning their transactions and relations.

Another way to differentiate between ideal-typical public and private organisations is to look at the values that guide their organisational and managerial behaviour. The discussion about similarities and differences of organisational values in the public and the private sector is extensive and not less contested than that about hybrid organisations themselves (for an overview of the debate, see van der Wal et al., 2008; van der Wal and van Hout, 2009). For the purposes of comparing ideal-typical public and private organisations I focus on two approaches which have played a role in the discussion on hybrid organisations in the field of public administration: Jane-Erik Lane's distinction between guiding principles in public administration and public management, and Jane Jacobs's distinction between two moral syndromes.

In a seminal article, Lane (1994) set out to describe the differences between an approach to public service provision dominated by the traditional public sector values commonly referred to as classic public administration and one dominated by New Public Management, a management style in which private sector values were introduced into the public sector. In the value system of public administration, which is prevalent in ideal-typical public organisations, guiding principles such as rules, openness and legality are important, and employees enter the organisation because they see it as their vocation to serve the public interest. Contrary to these values, Lane's public management approach is guided by principles also at play in ideal-typical private sector organisations. Here objectives, secrecy and effectiveness are important and the whole organisation is aimed at making a profit.

A second way of distinguishing between ideal-typical public and private sector organisations based on their value orientations is featured in Jacobs's (1992) book on 'moral syndromes'. Here this urban theorist, who is better known for her other works on cities and urban planning, explores the morals and values that underpin working life. She distinguishes between two moral systems (which she calls syndromes): the Guardian Moral Syndrome, which is at play in governments, armies, religion and some big, bureaucratic private organisations; and the Commercial Moral Syndrome, which is at play with regard to all human activities concerning trade and the production of goods. The syndromes are each driven by 15 precepts.

The two main values in the Guardian Moral Syndrome are taking and force. Trading and other commercial activities are shunned. This is a culture that thrives on tradition, obedience, discipline, hierarchy and loyalty, and in which expert knowledge gives power. Vengeance and deception are permitted, as long as they are for the sake of the task at hand or, to put it differently, in the public interest. Other values, which are not necessarily virtues but are core to the guardian syndrome, are the rich use of leisure (or laziness, if one wants to be cruel), ostentation, exclusivity and fatalism. Honour, largesse and fortitude are also important.

By comparison, trading (in the sense of commercial activity) is the main value of the Commercial Moral Syndrome. This culture is all about cooperation, honesty and abiding by contracts, as well as about competition, initiative and enterprise, innovation and efficiency.

Jacobs's two syndromes are arguably a black and white (some might even call it caricature-like) depiction of the differences between the guiding principles of state and market. For the purpose of constructing a sharp distinction between public and private sector organisations, however, her ideal types – as well as those of Lane – fulfil an important task. They are not meant to be taken as literally true, but, in the tradition of Weber, are to be understood as a way of carving out as clearly and sharply as possible how two phenomena can be distinguished by using abstract, hypothetical constructs.

In theory there are thus a number of ways of distinguishing between public and private organisations, but in practice these clear distinctions are often hard to make. The reality in which organisations engaged in public service provision operate is messy and fuzzy and they do not necessarily always stick to the ideal-typical roles outlined before. There has always been a fuzzy border between public and private: '[s]ince human societies formed, there have always been complex relations and interplay between purportedly private economic activity and governmental entities' (Dahl and Lindblom, 1953; as cited in Rainey and Chun, 2007, pp. 73–74).

Treating the categories of public and private as a dichotomy involves drawing a picture of a stable society in which both state and market place have their own and specific roles, activities, responsibilities and realms of influence. In such a world there are no hybrids; except perhaps as some sort of deviance or as a halfway house for the short period when an organisation leaves one sector and enters another, such as through the processes of nationalisation and privatisation. Society, however, has become more complex, as described in the introduction to this chapter. This complexity breeds hybridity as hybrid organisational forms find their place in a world in which institutional logics are not static but mingle and mix freely. From such a perspective it seems more helpful to see public and private not as a dichotomy but rather as a continuum consisting of several dimensions based on the various characteristics of different organisations.

Public and Private as Poles of a Multidimensional Continuum

In this chapter, I argue that here is no clear-cut dichotomy between public and private and, what is more, there is no trichotomy between homogenous public, private and hybrid organisations either. Public organisations behave differently from private organisations, and hybrid organisations behave differently still. Furthermore, one hybrid organisation will behave very differently from another. Within the hybrid area between public and private, all kinds of different styles and shapes of hybrid entities operate. The term 'hybrid' alone says very little about an organisation; one might even argue (to paraphrase the title of Bozeman's, 1987 classic book) that all organisations are hybrid to some extent and hybridity is therefore a poor predictor of the possible dangers or benefits attributed to this status.

This chapter therefore looks at the various characteristics that define an organisation as hybrid. If there is a continuum between public and private, which criteria do you use to determine where on that continuum a specific organisation fits? We may look at the legal form of an organisation and get a very clear answer on whether it is public or private. Yet few other characteristics give such a black and white picture. An ideal-typical public organisation would be 100 per cent funded by public (taxpayer) money, and the public, or its representatives, would have a 100 per cent say over its activities. However, few organisations are that pure. To name but some examples, many public sector schools and cultural organisations are happy to accept donations (whether in money, materials or time); and why would the public library not let out its function rooms after closing time to earn some extra cash? This argument also runs the other way: some organisations seem at first sight to belong to the private realm, but dig a little deeper and one might find out that, for example, the local municipal government owns a substantial stake in that otherwise private commercial Local Airport Ltd.

We can devise several possible axes between ideal-typical public organisations on the one extreme and ideal-typical private organisations on the other. In the remainder of this chapter, I will refer to these axes as dimensions of hybridity. There are already several models for doing so, of which some are one-dimensional (Dahl and Lindblom, 1953; Fottler, 1981) and others multidimensional (Billis, 2010b; Bozeman, 1987; Denis et al., 2015; Evers et al., 2002; Perry and Rainey, 1988; van Thiel, 2000; Wamsley and Zald, 1973). Summarising all these individual models, ten dimensions of hybridity can be distinguished (Karré, 2011):

- Legal form: does the organisation fall under commercial law or is it an entity under public law?
- Ownership: the continuum between public ownership (by the government) and private ownership (either by a single business owner or a group of shareholders).
- Activities: the continuum between statutory activities (at the behest of government) and purely commercial activities.
- Funding: the continuum between government appropriation and private funding.
- Market environment: the continuum between a monopoly and full competition.
- Value orientation: the continuum between a public and a private sector value orientation. The first is defined here by the guiding principles of Lane's public administration approach and Jacobs's Guardian Moral Syndrome. The second is defined here by the guiding principles of Lane's public management approach and Jacobs's Commercial Moral Syndrome.
- Strategic orientation: the continuum between a strategy mainly aimed at government and public sector goals, and one aimed more at the market and its own commercial interests.
- Relationship with public principal: this is the continuum between a hierarchical relationship between the organisation and government in dealings between the two, and a vertical relationship of equals based on a contract under private law.
- Levels of autonomy: the last two dimensions of the model presented here concern the amount of autonomy the senior executives of an organisation possess in their day-to-day activities. I make a distinction here between autonomy on issues concerning the internal processes of the organisation (managerial autonomy), and autonomy on issues concerning how it executes its tasks, in other words how it delivers the public services it has been tasked to fulfil (executive autonomy):
    - managerial autonomy is the continuum between no and full autonomy for the organisation's senior executives to engage in strategic management, which means to specify the organisation's objectives, translate them into policies and plans and to allocate resources to implement them;

– executive autonomy is the continuum between no and full autonomy for senior executives on how to design and organise the organisation's operational processes, that is, how to execute the production of public goods and services.

Charting Hybrid Organisations

An organisation can be defined as 'hybrid' if it mixes public and private sector characteristics or one or more of the above-mentioned dimensions. However, given the many interrelations between the public and the private sector, the number of organisations that are hybrid on one or a small number of dimensions is quite substantial. It is therefore necessary not only to take into account whether an organisation mixes public and private, but also the intensity of this mix, which is defined here as an organisation's 'hybridness'. This hybrid thumbprint of an organisation can be illustrated by scoring it on a radar chart, for example by using the following scores: completely public (0), mostly public (2), somewhat public (4), halfway between public and private (5), somewhat private (6), mostly private (8), and completely private (10).

So how do these charts work? A hypothetical organisation, represented as only a dot at the centre of the chart, would be 100 per cent public on all of the dimensions featured before: the ideal-typical agency. As the surface area grows, the organisation becomes more private to the maximum of covering the full chart, which represents an organisation that scores 100 per cent private on all dimensions, the ideal-typical enterprise. A prototypical hybrid organisation would be half agency, half enterprise and could be visualized as portrayed in Figure 2.1.

However, reality is far messier and such perfect hybrids are only rarely to be found. Most hybrid organisations do not score evenly on all dimensions but rather show heterogeneous scores. Figures 2.2 and 2.3 show examples of such heterogeneous hybrids. These examples are fictitious but were inspired by real-life cases. For a study in which this model has been used to chart three hybrid organisations in the Dutch waste management sector, see Karré (2011).

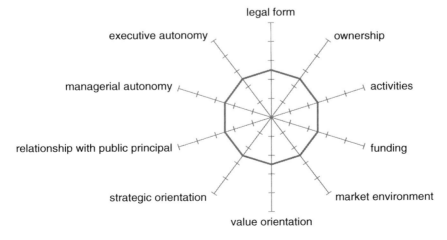

Figure 2.1   Ideal-typical hybrid organisation

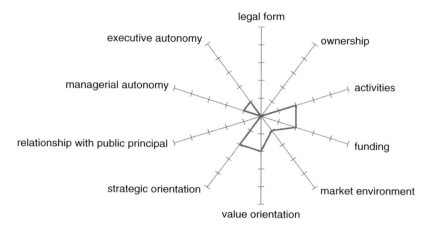

Figure 2.2   A hybrid municipal service

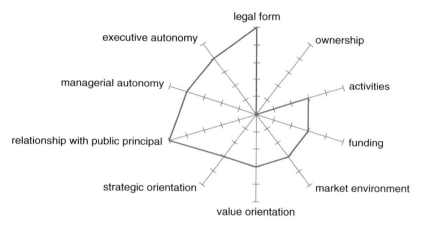

Figure 2.3   A hybrid quango

Figure 2.2 visualizes a hybrid organisation that is a municipal service. It conducts some activities for commercial customers but is still mostly funded by a municipality. Its culture still is more bureaucratic than entrepreneurial, and the organisation's strategy is mostly aimed at the public sector. The organisation's director only has limited autonomy concerning how they run the organisation and how it conducts its services.

Figure 2.3 visualizes a quite different organisation. This hybrid organisation has been located at arm's length as a quango. A governmental department is still its principal but it already conducts most of its activities for private partners and hence generates a substantial amount of its income from commercial activities. This organisation operates in a competitive market environment and embraces commercial values and strategy. The organisation's chief executive officer (CEO) has a considerable amount of managerial as well as executive autonomy.

Obviously scoring an organisation on these ten dimensions is no exact science, and the *raison d'être* of such charts is not to pretend that it is possible to come to an absolute measure of an organisation's degree of hybridity. They can, however, be used to compare different organisations – or one organisation at different points in time – and as an indicative-diagnostic tool to highlight those dimensions on which an organisation's hybrid status can be expected to cause tensions. The radar charts presented here can also be used as a tool to help an organisation's stakeholders visualise how they see the organisation at the moment and how they would like to see it in the future. As such, they are meant to start a further discussion (especially within the organisation in question) about its hybridity.

For example, I used this model to facilitate discussions in a Dutch public agency about the further strategic course of the organisation. I asked respondents, all employees of the organisation, to score the organisation as they saw it now and as they would like it to be in the future. This exercise made it clear that views differed widely not only on the organisation's future, but also on how the organisation functioned currently. The model established these differences and provided the agency's team members with a starting point for their conversation and with the language needed to discuss their differences.

Besides being understood descriptively, these spider charts can also be used as an indicative-diagnostic tool to highlight those dimensions on which an organisation's new hybrid status can be expected to be either beneficial or hazardous. Both the organisations visualized in Figures 2.2 and 2.3 are hybrid organisations. However, they differ from one another in regard to the degree of their hybridness, which is more intense for the latter than the former. The organisation visualized in Figure 2.2 for example is hybrid on the dimensions concerning its activities, funding, market environment, value and strategic orientation as well as those concerning its managerial and executive autonomy. Based on these observations, we might expect that the positive and negative effects of its hybridity will also occur on these dimensions. I will develop this point further, by looking at the possible positive and negative effects of hybridity in the next section.

THE EFFECTS OF HYBRIDITY

The chapter now turns to possible positive and negative effects of hybridity. I summarize the arguments brought forward about benefits and risks in the literature and also link them to the conceptual model developed in the preceding section by discussing which effects (positive and negative) seem to be most likely for what kind of hybrid organisation.

Risks

The literature on hybrid organisations tends to focus mostly on the possible risks of hybridity rather than on its potential benefits. Brandsen and Karré (2011) speak of three kinds of risk – financial, cultural and political – which tend to focus on the danger of corruption.

Financial risks concern the possible loss of public funds due to an organisation's hybridity. This could occur either directly through investment in risky ventures or indirectly through exposure to unfair competition. One form of unfair competition by hybrid organisations concerns the use of cross-subsidies, in which the organisation uses government funds to compete in commercial markets by keeping its cost price low thanks to the use of publicly funded overheads (accommodation, administrative staff). This is problematic on two accounts: firstly, it can lead to a loss of public money when the commercial activities of the organisation turn out to be less successful than planned and public funds are needed to compensate for private losses. The second and less obvious – though arguably more common – effect of this use of cross-subsidies is that it creates implicit overcapacity at the taxpayer's expense.

Other forms of unfair competition are the use of confidential government data for commercial means (granting the organisation a competitive edge over its competitors), the forming of public monopolies and the combination of conflicting roles, such as an agency that also starts to produce goods and services in a sector which it regulates.

Cultural risks are due to a decline in public service ethos and the impact of moral degeneration as the result of clashing values. As early as 1992, Jacobs had warned that introducing a profit orientation in public service provision would lead to corruption. Koppell (2003) makes that point in his study of mortgage lenders Freddie Mac and Fanny Mae; while Denis et al. (2015) elaborate on this kind of risk. Based on institutional theory (for example, as developed by Thornton et al., 2012), they write that combining several organisational archetypes and institutional logics will lead to unstable organisations. Using Actor Network Theory (based on work by, among others, Latour, 2003, 1987; Law, 1991) they argue that the various values, norms and instruments of different regulatory regimes may not be readily combined. And from an identity perspective (which Noordegraaf, 2015, for example, also uses to discuss hybrid professionalism) they make the point that a mixing of multiple identities can lead to challenges and dilemmas for individual practitioners when, for example, an organisation attracts new, more business-minded employees for its commercial activities who do not fit in with its more veteran staff.

Political risks deal with the danger that governments will no longer be able to control organisations effectively once they have become hybrids. Putting an organisation at arm's length and allowing it to enter the market place, it is feared, will lead to its developing its own identity and opportunistic behaviour. As hybrid organisations focus mostly on their own interests and have to please a wider array of stakeholders, they become less dependable partners for their political principals in the provision of public services, and this could lead to an accountability gap (Grossi and Thomasson, 2015). This is also a point made by Mair et al. (2015, p. 715) who warn that hybridity leads to 'ambiguity about incentives and value dispositions in performance measures' as it 'involves accountability to a diverse array of stakeholders'. Similarly, Ebrahim et al. (2014) point to mission drift and accountability challenges in hybrid organisations.

Linking these ideas about hybridity's risks with the conceptual model developed in the previous section, we can assume that negative financial effects will mainly be an issue for organisations that are hybrid on the dimensions labelled structure and activities. These deal with the ways in which an organisation is funded and under how much commercial pressure it has to operate (referred to here as the market environment). Hybridity's negative cultural effects will mainly be an issue for organisations that are hybrid on the dimensions labelled culture and strategy, as these deal with the clashes that can occur due to the mixing of various values, norms and instruments of different regulatory regimes and of contradictory identities. Finally, we can assume that negative political effects will mainly be an issue for organisations that are hybrid on the dimensions labelled governance and politics. An organisation that is hybrid on these dimensions, and its political principals, needs to be aware of mission drift and accountability issues.

Benefits

Besides the risks of hybridity, the literature also describes several possible positive effects. The main benefit of hybridity appears to be synergy, as hybrid organisations can combine the best of different worlds (Brandsen, 2010, p. 841). Here the fact that hybrid organisations have to combine organisational archetypes, values, norms, instruments and identities is not seen as a weakness but as a strength. In addition, the whole notion that organisations fall apart without a single dominant cultural syndrome is questioned (van der Wal and van Hout, 2009). Mair et al. (2015, p. 715) mention several possible positive effects identified by scholars who:

> suggest that operating in institutional interstices and combining multiple logics (i.e. considering and adhering to multiple prescriptions) might open up opportunities, as organizations can access broader sets of resources and expand their practices and which allows them to be innovative, to create new products and services and to pioneer new ways or organizing.

The synergetic effects that hybridity produces can be seen on the same broad fields on which hybridity's negative effects show themselves: financial, cultural and political. One example of a financial benefit would be the access to new markets and new resources gained by an organisation that enables government to reduce its contributions. This was originally one of the main reasons why public organisations were put at arm's length, based on the ideas behind New Public Management. A cultural benefit of synergy is the idea – already mentioned – that hybrid organisations can combine the best of both worlds. This could take the form of an agency that learns how to be more customer-oriented, efficient and innovative while at the same time upholding its public service ethos. And a political benefit of synergy through hybridity could be that the organisation does indeed embrace all of its shareholders, which in many public organisations include citizens and clients as well as government. This would help the organisation to retain its legitimacy in the new world of New Public Governance.

The potential positive effects of hybridity can be linked to the conceptual model developed in the preceding section. We can assume that positive financial effects will mainly be an issue for organisations that are hybrid on the dimensions labelled structure and activities. By engaging in new activities, organisations can expand their practices and access new financial and other resources. Hybridity's positive cultural effects will mainly occur in organisations that are hybrid on the dimensions labelled culture and strategy. It is by combining the best of both worlds in terms of values, norms and practices that these positive effects can occur. Finally, we can assume that positive political effects will mainly be an issue for organisations that are hybrid on the dimensions labelled governance and politics. By granting the organisation more autonomy, it also has the freedom to engage with other societal actors as well as those involved in politics.

Table 2.1   Risks and benefits of hybridity

	Risks	Benefits
Financial	Loss of public funds	Access to new funding and other resources
Cultural	Decline in public service ethos and moral degeneration	Innovation
Political	Loss of control by politics	More legitimacy through broader group of stakeholders

Discussion of Risks and Benefits

Table 2.1 summarises hybridity's risks and benefits. It is interesting to note that these benefits and risks are not mutually exclusive: in practice they are often two sides of the same coin. Whether an effect is seen as a positive or as negative is often in the eye of the beholder and thus depends on who is making the assessment. Based on discussions undertaken in various research projects aimed at the effects of hybridity in Dutch hybrid organisations between state and market (Algemene Rekenkamer, 2005, 2006; Brandsen et al., 2006; Brandsen and Karré, 2011; Karré, 2011) this point can be elaborated on.

For example, CEOs of hybrid organisations often cite increased turnover and higher profits due to their additional commercial activities as positive effects of hybridity; their organisations can benefit economically from a more entrepreneurial course of action. Whether an organisation's improved financial position is also positive for the government that owns it or for the citizen who depends on the services it provides, however, is debatable. After all, if the hybrid organisation turns a profit, even though this is public money, it is not part of the public purse and not at the disposal of public budgeters. So an organisational financial benefit due to hybridity does not necessarily have to be beneficial for government or the public as a whole.

Whether the competitive advantages a hybrid organisation might have are interpreted as positive or negative, moreover, seems to be a matter of interpretation. It is not uncommon for an organisation's private competitors, guarding their own business interests, to claim that hybrid organisations have unfair advantages on the market place because of their links with government. But from a political standpoint, or that of the citizen, unfair competition may be desirable and may be not perceived to be a problem because it has beneficial effects for the public; there are often other motivations for choosing the public option than cost alone (such as creating local jobs or working to a higher environmental standard than a commercial competitor could provide).

Hybridity's cultural effects are also in fact two sides of the same coin. Managing an organisation in a more business-like manner can increase its effectiveness and efficiency and thus save money. But some commentators point out that efficiency should not be the only goal in public service provision. For example, more business-like home care has been criticised for providing a stripped-down service, focused on providing only those tasks mandated by contract, in as little time as possible, and thereby ignoring the real needs of patients. Another flipside of a more business-like approach is that a hybrid organisation might be tempted to put more energy into providing commercially more advantageous services to its private customers and thereby neglecting its public customers. Behaviour appropriate in the market place, such as always choosing the cheapest or most profitable option, is not necessarily beneficial in a public setting. Furthermore, not all employees of an organisation might be capable of working in an entrepreneurial fashion and might be triggered to leave. This can also, of course, be seen as a positive effect, as it cuts the organisation's dead wood.

Finally, the political effects of hybridity can be seen in terms of different sides of the same coin. On the one hand its new hybrid status often leads to an organisation opening up and engaging in conversations and accountability dialogues with a variety of stake-holders. On the other hand, however, this can also be interpreted in a negative way, as government has less say on how the organisation provides its services and how it spends what is, in essence, public money.

Both benefits and risks have a flipside, which makes it impossible to state from the outset whether hybridity will be a salvation or an abomination. All depends, it would seem, on how hybridity is dealt with or managed. The model described earlier in this chapter can help to start a discussion about the best way to do this (see Karré, 2011 for an illustration of how this can be done).

CONCLUSIONS AND DISCUSSION

This chapter has looked at hybrid organisations from a public administration and management perspective. Hybridity has been seen as a public–private mix where public is understood to indicate the state, and private the market. I suggested that the distinction between public and private is often seen as a dichotomy. However, in reality the border between state and market has always been rather blurred and has tended to shift, and there always have been hybrid organisations that straddle that border between the sectors.

Recently their number has grown, as the rise of New Public Management and New Public Governance has made public administration in general, and public service provision especially, not only more complex but also more hybrid. Organisations engaged in the production of public goods and services now have to combine different and contradicting governance regimes and institutional logics as they mix the characteristics of public and private sector organisations. This can lead to innovation but also to confusion. Therefore I concluded that in order to understand hybridity in organisations and to start a discussion about its risks and benefits it was necessary to learn more about what makes a hybrid organisation really hybrid.

A first step to do so is to establish how ideal-typical public and private sector organisations ('agency' and 'enterprise' in the distinction introduced by Dahl and Lindblom) differ from one another. For this I looked at work undertaken by Rainey and Chun and others who distinguished them with regard to the environments they functioned in, their interaction with their environment and their organisational roles, structures and processes.

A second step in establishing how an organisation can be described as a public–private hybrid was to discuss how hybrid organisations can be positioned with regard to agency and enterprise. For this it proved difficult to approach public and private as a dichotomy as this either/or view seemed to exclude the existence of hybrid organisations from the outset. It also did not seem to fit with the prevalent view in research on public administration and management across the world that they were inherently complex and hybrid. To overcome this limitation I sketched a multidimensional continuum between the ideal-typical public and private sector organisations. Between these poles organisations could (summarizing conclusions drawn in a variety of studies) be located on ten axes or dimensions on which they can mix public and private. Those dimensions were: (1) legal form; (2) ownership; (3) activities; (4) funding; (5) market environment; (6) value orientation; (7) strategic orientation; (8) relationship with public principal; (9) managerial autonomy; and (10) executive autonomy. These ten dimensions can be used for the purposes of discussion and as a starting point for further enquiry as a means of charting organisations. This can help to develop a first understanding of the nature of their 'hybridness' or their hybrid thumbprint.

I not only concluded that there is a variety of hybrid organisational forms in the continuum between public and private but also that there are a number of theories concerning the effects of their hybridity as possible benefits and risks. Both can be seen as financial, cultural and political. Financial risks concerned a loss of public funds and financial benefits access to new funding and other resources. Cultural risks concerned a decline in ethics and cultural benefits innovation through new combinations of values. Political risks concerned the loss of control by politicians and political benefits a strengthening of legitimacy as organisations enlarge their circle of stakeholders.

A closer inspection of the benefits and risks of hybridity as discussed in the literature showed that they were essentially two sides of the same coin, indicating that it is not clear from the outset whether hybridity will lead to positive effects, negative effects or perhaps both. Charting an organisation using the ten dimensions presented in this chapter can help to draw attention to possible effects (both positive and negative) making it possible to devise plans on how to minimise the perceived risks and maximise the possible beneficial effects.

A last question, taking these conclusions into account, is where to go from here both in theory and practice. I propose that there are at least three challenges that need to be overcome in order to further advance our understanding of hybrid organisations.

First, we need to improve our understanding of the essence of hybridity in organisations. In other words we have to find out more about what makes a hybrid organisation hybrid. This should not remain a purely theoretical or abstract activity but should be undertaken by conducting research in a variety of fields. The model presented in this chapter can be a helpful tool in this process, as it is a first step to getting to grips with the variety and diversity of hybrid organisational forms. But it is by no means the last thing that should be said on the matter. On the contrary, the model presented here and the thinking behind it could be used as an instrument to start discussions in both academia and the world of practice with the goal not only to test and develop it further but to also to enhance our understanding about the practical manifestations of hybridity in organisations.

Second, we also need to understand hybridity's benefits and risks; the circumstances under which they occur; with what intensity they are found; and what practitioners can do in order to get the most out of its positive effects while effectively controlling its negative effects. And this should not remain a purely academic activity, but should be undertaken together with practitioners, for example in the form of action research. Managers of hybrid organisations will often have already found ways to deal with hybridity's effects and will also have a better understanding of how, when and why they manifest themselves.

Third, there seems to be more academic interest in hybridity and hybrid organisations. Recent examples are found not only in this *Handbook* but also in special issues of scientific journals, such as *Public Administration* (see Denis et al., 2015) and *International Studies of Management and Organisation* (see Anheier and Krlev, 2015, for an introduction). In these times of inherent complexity and hybridity in public administration this interest is laudable, but research on hybrid organisations is often fragmented and there is too little contact and exchange between various groups, each of which seems to approach the subject from another angle and with another background. Much could be won should we succeed in working closer together while still employing a broad perspective, approaching hybrid organisations from various disciplines and angles. By doing so we not only stand a better chance of grasping the variety and diversity of hybrid organisations but can also hope to develop a better understanding of the complex and hybrid world of public administration in the 21st century.

REFERENCES

Algemene Rekenkamer (2005) *Publiek ondernemerschap: toezicht en verantwoording bij publiek-private arrangementen.* Sdu Uitgevers,'s-Gravenhage.

Algemene Rekenkamer (2006) *Goed bestuur tussen publiek en privaat: Ontwikkelingen in bestuur, beleid en regelgeving.* Algemene Rekenkamer, Den Haag.

Anheier, H.K. and G. Krlev (2015) Guest Editors' Introduction. *International Studies of Management and Organisation*, 45, pp. 193–206. doi:10.1080/00208825.2015.1006026.

Billis, D. (2010a) *Hybrid Organisations and the Third Sector: Challenges for Practice, Theory and Policy.* Palgrave Macmillan, Basingstoke, UK and New York, USA.

Billis, D. (2010b) Towards a Theory of Hybrid Organisations. In D. Billis, *Hybrid Organisations and the Third Sector: Challenges for Practice, Theory and Policy.* Palgrave Macmillan, Basingstoke, UK and New York, USA, pp. 46–69.

Bozeman, B. (1987) *All Organisations Are Public: Bridging Public and Private Organisational Theories*, 1st edn. Jossey-Bass, San Francisco, CA, USA.

Brandsen, T. (2010) Hybridity/Hybridization. In H.K. Anheier and S. Toepler (eds), *International Encyclopedia of Civil Society.* Springer, New York, USA, pp. 839–842.

Brandsen, T. and P.M. Karré (2011) Hybrid Organisations: No Cause for Concern? *International Journal of Public Administration*, 34, pp. 827–836. doi:10.1080/01900692.2011.605090.

Brandsen, T., W. van de Donk and P. Kenis (2006) *Meervoudig bestuur: publieke dienstverlening door hybride organisaties.* Lemma, Den Haag.

Brandsen, T., W. van de Donk and K. Putters (2005) Griffins or Chameleons? Hybridity as a Permanent and Inevitable Characteristic of the Third Sector. *International Journal of Public Administration*, 28, pp. 749–765. doi:10.1081/PAD-200067320.

Bruton, G.D., M.W. Peng, D. Ahlstrom, C. Stan and Xu Kehan (2015) State-Owned Enterprises Around the World as Hybrid Organisations. *Academy of Management Perspectives*, 29, pp. 92–114. doi:10.5465/amp.2013.0069.

Christensen, T. and P. Lægreid (2010) Complexity and Hybrid Public Administration – Theoretical and Empirical Challenges. *Public Organization Review*, 11, pp. 407–423. doi:10.1007/s11115-010-0141-4.

Christensen, T. and P. Lægreid (2011a) *The Ashgate Research Companion to New Public Management.* Ashgate, Farnham, UK.

Christensen, T. and P. Lægreid (2011b) *Transcending New Public Management: The Transformation of Public Sector Reforms.* Ashgate, Farnham, UK.

Dahl, R., and C.E. Lindblom (1953) *Politics, Economics and Welfare Planning and Politico-Economic Systems Resolved into Basic Social Processes.* Harper & Row, New York, USA.

Defourny, J. (2014) From Third Sector to Social Enterprise: A European Research Trajectory. In Jacques Defourny, Lars Hulgård, Victor Pestoff (eds), *Social Enterprise and the Third Sector: Changing European Landscapes in a Comparative Perspective.* Routledge, Abingdon, UK, pp. 17–41.

Denis, J.-L., E. Ferlie and N. van Gestel (2015) Understanding Hybridity in Public Organisations. *Public Administration*, 93, pp. 273–289. doi:10.1111/padm.12175.

Durose, C., and L. Richardson (2015a) *Designing Public Policy for Co-production.* Policy Press, Bristol, UK.

Durose, C. and L. Richardson (2015b) *Rethinking Public Policy-making Why Co-production Matters*. Policy Press, Bristol, UK.

Ebrahim, A., J. Battilana and J. Mair (2014) The Governance of Social Enterprises: Mission Drift and Accountability Challenges in Hybrid Organisations. *Research in Organizational Behavior*, 34, pp. 81–100.

The Economist (2009) The Rise of the Hybrid Company, 3 December. http://www.economist.com/node/15011 307.

Emery, Y. and D. Giauque (2014) The Hybrid Universe of Public Administration in the 21st Century. *International Review of Administrative Sciences*, 80, pp. 23–32. doi:10.1177/0020852313513378.

Evers, A., U. Rauch and U. Stitz (2002) *Von öffentlichen Einrichtungen zu sozialen Unternehmen: hybride Organisationsformen im Bereich sozialer Dienstleistungen*. Edition Sigma, Berlin.

Fotaki, M. (2011) Towards Developing New Partnerships in Public Services: Users as Consumers, Citizens and/or Co-Producers in Health and Social Care in England and Sweden. *Public Administration*, 89, pp. 933–955. doi:10.1111/j.1467-9299.2010.01879.x.

Fottler, M.D. (1981) Is Management Really Generic? *Academy of Management Review*, 6, pp. 1–12.

Grohs, S. (2014) Hybrid Organisations in Social Service Delivery in Quasimarkets: The Case of Germany. *American Behavioral Scientist*. doi:10.1177/0002764214534671.

Grossi, G. and A. Thomasson (2015) Bridging the Accountability Gap in Hybrid Organisations: The Case of Copenhagen Malmo Port. *International Review of Administrative Sciences*, 81, pp. 604–620. doi:10.1177/002085 2314548151.

Jackson, P.M. (2003) The Size and Scope of the Public Sector: An International Comparison. In A. Bovaird and E. Loffler (eds), *Public Management and Governance*. Routledge, London, UK and New York, USA, pp. 24–40.

Jacobs, J. (1992) *Systems of Survival: A Dialogue on the Moral Foundations of Commerce and Politics*, 1st edn. Random House, New York, USA.

Joldersma, C. and V. Winter (2002) Strategic Management in Hybrid Organisations. *Public Management Review*, 4, pp. 83–99.

Karré, P.M. (2011) *Heads and Tails: Both Sides of the Coin: An Analysis of Hybrid Organisations in the Dutch Waste Management Sector*. Eleven International Publishing, The Hague.

Koppell, J.G. (2003) *The Politics of Quasi-Government: Hybrid Organisations and the Dynamics of Bureaucratic Control*. Cambridge University Press, Cambridge, UK.

Kosar, K.R. (2008) *The Quasi Government: Hybrid Organisations with both Government and Private Sector Legal Characteristics* (RL30533). Washington, DC: Congressional Research Service.

Lane, J.-E. (1994) Will Public Management Drive Out Public Administration? *Asian Journal of Public Administration*, 16, pp. 139–151. doi:10.1080/02598272.1994.1080029.

Latour, B. (1987) *Science in Action: How to Follow Scientists and Engineers Through Society*. Harvard University Press, Cambridge, MA, USA.

Latour, B. (2003) *We Have Never Been Modern*. Harvester Wheatsheaf, New York, USA.

Law, J. (1991) *A Sociology of Monsters: Essays on Power, Technology, and Domination*. Routledge, London, UK and New York, USA.

Mair, J., J. Mayer and E. Lutz (2015) Navigating Institutional Plurality: Organisational Governance in Hybrid Organisations. *Organization Studies*, 36, pp. 713–739.

McLaughlin, K., S.P. Osborne and E. Ferlie (2002) *New Public Management: Current Trends and Future Prospects*. Routledge, London, UK and New York, USA.

Noordegraaf, M. (2015) Hybrid Professionalism and Beyond: (New) Forms of Public Professionalism in Changing Organisational and Societal Contexts. *Journal of Professions and Organization*, jov002. doi:10.1093/jpo/jov002.

Olsen, J.P. (2009) Change and Continuity: An Institutional Approach to Institutions of Democratic Government. *European Political Science Review*, 1, pp. 3–32. doi:10.1017/S1755773909000022.

Osborne, S.P. (2010a) Introduction. The (New) Public Governance: A Suitable Case for Treatment? In S.P. Osborne, *The New Public Governance? Emerging Perspectives on the Theory and Practice of Public Governance*. Routledge, Abingdon, UK, pp. 1–16.

Osborne, S.P. (2010b) *The New Public Governance? Emerging Perspectives on the Theory and Practice of Public Governance*. Routledge, Abingdon, UK.

Perry, J. and R.G. Rainey (1988) The Public–Private Distinction in Organisation Theory: A Critique and Research Strategy. *Academy of Management Review*, 13 (2), pp. 182–201.

Pierre, J. and B.G. Peters (2000) *Governance, Politics and the State*. Palgrave Macmillan, Basingstoke, UK.

Pollitt, C. and C. Talbot (2004) *Unbundled Government: A Critical Analysis of the Global Trend to Agencies, Quangos and Contractualisation*. Routledge, London, UK.

Pollitt, C., K. Bathgate, J. Caulfield, A. Smullen and C. Talbot (2001) Agency Fever? Analysis of an International Policy Fashion. *Journal of Comparative Policy Analysis*, 3, pp. 271–290. doi:10.1023/A:1012301400791.

Pollitt, C., C. Talbot, J. Caulfield and A. Smullen (2004) *Agencies: How Governments Do Things Through Semi-Autonomous Organisations*. Palgrave Macmillan, New York, USA.

Pollitt, C., S. Thiel and V. van Homburg (2007) *New Public Management in Europe: Adaptation and Alternatives*. Palgrave Macmillan, Basingstoke, UK.

Rainey, H.G. (1997) *Understanding and Managing Public Organisations*, 2nd edn. Jossey-Bass, San Francisco, CA, USA.

Rainey, H.G. and Y.H. Chun (2007) Public and Private Management Compared. In E. Ferlie, L.E. Lynn and C. Pollitt (eds), *The Oxford Handbook of Public Management*. Oxford University Press, Oxford, UK, pp. 72–102.

Rhodes, M.L. and G. Donnelly-Cox (2014) Hybridity and Social Entrepreneurship in Social Housing in Ireland. *Voluntas. International Journal of Voluntary and Nonprofit Organizations*, 25, pp. 1630–1647.

Seibel, W. (2015) Welfare Mixes and Hybridity: Analytical and Managerial Implications: 'Welfare Mix' and Hybridity: Divergent but Compatible Concepts. *Voluntas. International Journal of Voluntary and Nonprofit Organizations*, 26, pp. 1759–1768.

Seidman, H. (1988) The Quasi World of the Federal Government. *Brookings Review*, 6, pp. 23–27. doi:10.2307/20080040.

Simon, M. (1989) *De Strategische Functie Typologie: Functioneel Denkraam voor Management*. Kluwer Bedrijfswetenschappen, Deventer.

Streeck, W. and K. Thelen (2005) Introduction: Institutional Change in Advanced Political Economies. In W. Streeck and K. Thelen (eds), *Beyond Continuity*. Oxford University Press, Oxford, UK, pp. 1–39.

Thornton, P.H., W. Ocasio and M. Lounsbury (2012) *The Institutional Logics Perspective: A New Approach to Culture, Structure, and Process*. Oxford University Press, Oxford, UK.

van der Wal, Z. and E.T.J. van Hout (2009) Is Public Value Pluralism Paramount? The Intrinsic Multiplicity and Hybridity of Public Values. *International Journal of Public Administration*, 32, pp. 220–231. doi:10.1080/01900690902732681.

van der Wal, Z., G. De Graaf and K. Lasthuizen (2008) What's Valued Most? Similarities and Differences Between the Organisational Values of the Public and Private Sector. *Public Administration*, 86, pp. 465–482. doi:10.1111/j.1467-9299.2008.00719.x.

van Thiel, S. (2000) *Quangocratization: Trends, Causes and Consequences*. Interuniversity Center for Social Science Theory and Methodology, Amsterdam.

Verhoest, K. (2011) *Government Agencies: Practices and Lessons from 30 Countries*. Palgrave Macmillan, Basingstoke, UK.

Wamsley, G. and M.N. Zald (1973) *The Political Economy of Public Organisations: A Critique and Approach to the Study of Public Administration*. Lexington Books, Lexington, MA, USA.

3. Hybridity in public organisations
Nicolette van Gestel, Jean-Louis Denis and Ewan Ferlie

INTRODUCTION

Recent special editions of the *International Review of Administrative Sciences* (Emery and Giauque, 2014) and *Public Administration* (Van Gestel et al., 2015) have drawn attention to the important issue in contemporary public management and the non-profit sector of dealing with the growth of hybridity (see also Denis et al., 2015; Skelcher and Smith, 2015). Although hybrid public organisations are not entirely novel, pure or ideal-typical public sector forms have been in retreat since the 1980s as the boundaries between the many actors, organisations and sectors now involved in the delivery of public services become increasingly porous (Christiansen and Laegreid, 2011).

How, first of all, do we define such hybrid forms? In our view what characterises these hybrid public organisations is a mix of different origins and elements that 'do not come from one single logic or one single genre' (Emery and Giauque, 2014, p. 23). Instead, these organisations have to deal with various institutional pressures, often derived from both public and private regimes (Seibel, 2015). Such pressures directing and circumscribing organisational behaviour can be broadly understood as 'the rules of the game' (Kraatz and Block, 2008, p. 243). We define (public) organisations as hybrid when they have to play 'in two or more games at the same time' (Kraatz and Block, 2008, p. 243), for example balancing different market and hierarchical-based logics of action.

Among the critical forces driving change toward hybridity are public management reforms taking place in various jurisdictions (Ferlie and Ongaro, 2015). Most obviously, New Public Management (NPM) reforms have created or expanded public–private partnerships in many countries and invented new business-like organisational forms inside the public sector, in particular in Anglo-Saxon countries such as the United Kingdom (UK), Australia and the United States of America (USA) (Kickert, 2008; Pollitt and Bouckaert, 2011). But NPM is not the whole story and private firms are not the only ones expanding their role in delivering public services. In areas such as continental Europe, where NPM has had less impact (Christiansen and Laegreid, 2011; Meyer et al., 2013), some governments use novel steering mechanisms which include greater cooperation with non-governmental organisations (NGOs), the third sector and civil society, again producing a blurring across traditional sectoral boundaries (Billis, 2010; Pollitt and Bouckaert, 2011).

As a result, public organisations have to deal simultaneously with diverse governance mechanisms such as central performance indicators (hierarchy); market mechanisms such as tenders and competition (market); and citizens' and stakeholder's expectations of client-oriented behaviour and horizontal collaboration (networks). While the mixed or hybrid nature of public organisations is the result of a series of pressures for reform (Christensen and Laegreid, 2011; Meyer et al., 2013), it is the management and professionals in public organisations who are challenged to meet these multiple expectations when dealing with their strategies and practices (Reay and Hinings, 2009).

In this chapter, we aim to encourage a cross-disciplinary conversation on the topic of hybrid public organisations across the fields of public administration and organisational studies (as has been previously advocated, for example, by Rhodes, 2007; Arellano-Gault et al., 2013; Bozeman, 2013; and in our special edition in *Public Administration*, Van Gestel et al., 2015). Public services, after all, are delivered by organisations and increasingly through strategic alliances or inter-organisational networks as well as by the traditional single vertically integrated public organisation. Our meso or organisational level focus is a middle-range unit of analysis, distinct both from the micro-level focus on service delivery and the macro-level focus on public policy making. Our central question is: how can we understand hybridity in public services organisations, in particular regarding the roles and identities of management and professionals? We will use different theoretical perspectives on hybridity and illustrate these by using empirical studies.

The chapter is structured as follows. We discuss four theoretical frameworks – governance theory, institutional theory, Actor Network Theory and identity approaches – that we have introduced in our earlier work to make sense of hybrid organisations (Denis et al., 2015). From each theoretical angle we discuss some applications, drawing on recent empirical works to understand how public service organisations deal with hybridity in strategy and practice. We use examples of hybrid organising and the impact of them on public management and professionals across various nations and policy areas. Finally, we discuss the extent to which the four theoretical frameworks help us to understand how public organisations deal with hybridity in practice, and we suggest some avenues for further research.

GOVERNANCE THEORY: UNDERSTANDING HYBRID MODES

In the governance literature, a classic distinction is drawn between hierarchies, markets and networks or clans as three 'pure' alternative modes of governance (Kooiman, 2003; Powell, 1990). During the heyday of traditional public administration (TPA), hierarchy was perceived as the dominant principle. In later years, with increasing demands for integral and client oriented public services, public sector hierarchies were considered rigid and inflexible (Bryson et al., 2014). Hierarchical governance with its far-reaching specialisation according to Weberian principles had led to a fragmentation of services provision which turned out to be less adequate in solving complex, 'wicked' problems (Agranoff, 1991; Weber and Khademian, 2008).

The two most widely discussed alternatives to traditional governance in the public sector are New Public Management with its emphasis on market-based mechanisms to improve efficiency, and the network approach where government agencies are expected to collaborate in 'horizontal' coalitions with various stakeholders (Ferlie and Ongaro, 2015; Klijn and Koppenjan, 2012; O'Toole, 2015). As Hill and Lynn (2005, p. 173) have argued, this latter approach 'reflects a widespread (though not universal) belief that the focus of administrative practice is shifting from hierarchical government towards greater reliance on horizontal, hybridised, and associated forms of governance', in line with other changes associated with networked governance (Moore and Hartley, 2008; Newman, 2001), such as managed networks, multi-agency working and inter-sectoral partnerships. A third option is provided by the model of the neo-Weberian state, a template that combines the 'old public administration' with a call for improving the expert knowledge of professionals and a focus on responsiveness to citizens (Pollitt and Bouckaert, 2011).

So far, alternative modes of governance have turned out to be less ideal in practice than suggested by their advocates. For example, the applications of NPM ideas tend to focus on the internal efficiency of the public administration system while neglecting the importance of involving external stakeholders and other public values such as equity, due process and legitimacy of agency decision-making (Pollitt and Bouckaert, 2011). The network approach in the public sector stresses collaboration between public organisations and private and non-profit actors, aiming for integral services, but does not provide a clear connection to improved performance (Ferlie et al., 2003). As O'Toole (2015, p. 361) has argued in his overview of network studies in the public sector over two decades: 'More needs to be known about the ways in which networks and networking behavior can shape performance and affect the most salient values in our governance systems.'

It has often been suggested in the literature that over time one dominant ideal type is replaced by another: we may witness a change, for example, from hierarchy to market or from hierarchy to networks (Blatter, 2003; Kooiman, 2003). Other authors, however, have expressed their doubts 'that there is an inevitable and irreversible paradigmatic shift towards market- or network-organisation' (Olsen, 2006, p. 1). During the past two decades, in particular, the idea has grown that alternative modes of governance do not (fully) replace each other but may coexist and simultaneously influence contemporary management. This can be perceived as a major driver of hybridity in public domains (Bryson et al., 2014; Emery and Giauque, 2014; Meyer et al., 2013). The resulting multiple modes of governance, based on various principles, lead to a lack of adequate alignment and coordination between them, and this in turn promotes tensions and conflicts in implementing public policies (Denis et al., 2015; Emery and Giauque, 2014).

Overall, hybrid forms have thus been developed between the three 'pure' modes. They include relational markets (which mix markets and networks), managed markets (which mix markets and management), managed networks (which mix management and networks), and even 'relational bureaucracies' (another mix of hierarchy and network). Such examples of mixed governance can be easily extended (Seibel, 2015). These pervasive intermediate forms require more intensive analysis in both public services and third sector settings. Whether these different governance principles can be successfully held in balance, and if so, how, are ultimately empirical questions (Seibel, 2015). What is unlikely is that any kind of 'one size fits all' concept will meet the case given that national and sector characteristics are relevant in specific contexts (Denis et al., 2015; Meyer et al., 2013).

Some Applications to the Study of Hybrids in Public Services Settings

We now turn to some empirical studies to examine how the current diversity of governance mechanisms, based on hierarchy, market and networks, is balanced in hybrid public organisations. We include case studies of various nations, and sector and policy domains, to understand how mixed modes of governance may impact on public organisations and in particular on local managers and professionals.

In one survey of public organisations in continental Europe, Meyer et al. (2013) studied 271 public sector executives in the city of Vienna who were experiencing reform initiatives across a range of different policy fields (involving cultural, infrastructural, social and regulatory activities). The authors found that, despite recent waves of managerial and market reform initiatives, public sector executives still felt strongly linked to the Weberian ideal in traditional public administration, but they were open at the same time to the use of managerial concepts and instruments (ibid., p. 17). These findings confirmed that earlier (traditional) modes of governance had not disappeared and that different modes of governance could coexist. Interestingly, and contrary to the study's expectations, Meyer et al. (2013) also found that public sector executives who adhered more strongly to a managerial focus in public administration displayed a higher overall public service motivation and felt more attracted to policy-making than colleagues who primarily linked themselves to a legalistic-bureaucratic framework.

A study in Switzerland (Emery et al., 2008) showed that frontline workers within local public organisations had a different orientation from that found in the executives in Meyer et al.'s study. The differences may suggest that the social position of public servants is important to understanding their ability to deal with hybrid governance. The study is based on 36 interviews with frontline workers across many policy domains. Emery et al. (2008) studied the perceptions of the performance of street-level public servants without management responsibilities who were operating in a context of NPM-type changes. The authors concluded that these frontline workers had a rather pragmatic view on hybrid governance; they strove for a highly capable public sector and pointed to an implementation gap where the objectives of reforms did not necessarily lead to the effects that they were intended to achieve (Emery et al., 2008, p. 318). The frontline workers felt a strong attachment to the efficiency and the traditional ethos of the state's role promoted by the 'Weberian' model of public administration, and did not support the commercial values introduced by Swiss NPM policies (ibid., p. 317). They seemed to aim for a synthesis which 'modernised' traditional public administration approaches but did not disturb them radically in line with the template of a neo-Weberian state (Pollitt and Bouckaert, 2011) which seeks to keep but also update the basic form of the Weberian public agency (in Germany, for example).

In a study of local government organisations in Germany, France and Italy, Kuhlmann (2010) assessed the impact of managerial and NPM ideas on traditional public administration. The study's focus on local public organisations was justified by its claim that they were 'acknowledged to be more advanced in reform implementation than are upper levels of government' (ibid., p. 1116). The study showed, however, that here NPM had a low impact on traditional public administration: 'There can be no doubt that the NPM doctrine has clearly left its mark in the Continental European administrative landscape . . . Yet, there was no shift to a managerial administration and the NPM has lost most of its initial attraction' (ibid., p. 1128). Hybridity at the local government level in the three countries thus implies the coexistence of TPA and NPM, which may (or may not) culminate over time in a neo-Weberian state. As Kuhlmann (2010, p. 1128) argued:

> Since there is little interest on the part of political as well as administrative actors to be restricted to an exclusively strategic or managerial role, it is not surprising, particularly in Germany and Italy where this approach was debated, that most of the political reform elements have barely functioned or have more or less been quietly abolished. The final outcome of a 'Neo-Weberian' amalgamation of legalist and managerial elements still remains to be seen.

In a Scandinavian context, Fossestol et al. (2015) found that NPM and post-NPM (network) templates for reform had created a hybrid governance environment for executive organisations in Norwegian welfare and employment services. The study demonstrated that there was growing hybridity even in highly institutionalised (mature) fields of the public sector, and that hybridisation had endured over the past decade. In a comparison of organisational responses from ten executive organisations, the study found that in most cases managers and professionals tended to separate out different kinds of governance demands in order to avoid the indecisiveness and ambiguous responses that were seen as the result of hybridity. In only a few cases, with a post-NPM (network) form of organising, were the local actors able to synthesise multiple institutional demands, and these seemed to be largely associated with lower work pressures and small and medium-sized organisations.

Hybrid Governance: Conclusion

The studies cited above confirmed that various modes of governance were simultaneously at play, and this had created a hybrid environment for public sector executives and professionals who had used their room for discretion to influence their preferred style of governance. Top executives had more freedom in navigating between different modes of governance than public servants with a lower status, largely due to fragmentation of agency roles and a process of de-professionalising at the front line which combined to reduce their freedom of action. Interestingly, and contrary to expectations from studies with a macro-analytical perspective, executives in a context of traditional public administration (such as Vienna) expressed a higher public service motivation when they were associated with managerial and market modes of governance. This counterintuitive finding is one reason to recommend further examination of the consequences of hybrid governance for public organisations. We also recognised in the empirical studies problems with preserving the quality of public services in a context of hybrid governance incentives. The relationship between hybrid governance and the quality of public services thus seems another relevant avenue for future research.

INSTITUTIONAL THEORY: MULTIPLE LOGICS

Institutional theory and its focus on resilient social structures to explain non-rational behaviour (Scott, 2014) provides our second prism. Institutionalism is a major and expanding stream within organisational studies that may be highly applicable to the study of public services organisations that are inherently built on more than one particular logic. Traditionally this has focused on the state and the professions, but more recently it has embraced the management and market. Despite its early founders and followers (Selznick, 1949; Zilber, 2002) the main focus of institutional theory has long been on the level of the organisational field rather than on understanding single organisations. As Greenwood et al. (2014, p. 1206) argue: 'We have become overly concerned with explaining institutions and institutional processes, notably at the level of the organisation field, rather than with using them to explain and understand organisations.'

For a long time, too, the explanatory focus of institutional theory was on stability and continuity rather than on change (Pierson, 2000; Mahoney, 2000). Institutions were considered powerful forces that could explain the non-rational behaviour of organisations and in particular their path-dependency. The early assumptions of institutional theory that organisations would move to a single coherent archetype (where structures, processes and underlying values were in alignment) were not confirmed by empirical studies which instead suggested 'sedimented' formations (Cooper et al., 1996) and the presence of multiple logics which somehow managed to coexist (Reay and Hinings, 2009). The normative dimension of values – and long-term value shifts – rather than a pure focus on formal structure was thus a major concern. As Meyer and Höllerer (2014) have argued, a focus on formal organisations might lead attention away from the study of alternative modes of organising and the underlying dynamics that have created complex public organisations.

More recently, and in line with the early institutionalists (Selznick, 1949), growing attention has been devoted to understanding change, and institutions have been considered both potential constraints and enablers for change (Clemens and Cook, 1999; Dacin et al., 2002). Responding to earlier criticisms that institutional theory lacked an adequate account of agency, more recent literature has also developed concepts of institutional entrepreneurship, or skillful and embedded action by well-placed actors within organisations (Dorado, 2005; Edwards and Jones, 2008). These harked back to earlier studies that have emphasised the entrepreneurial role of 'organised actors with sufficient resources' (DiMaggio, 1988, p. 14). Building on DiMaggio (1988) and Oliver (1991), Lawrence and Suddaby (2006) developed the concept of institutional work to understand the 'purposive actions of individuals and organisations aimed at creating, maintaining and disrupting institutions' (Lawrence and Suddaby, 2006, p. 2015; see also Garud et al., 2007; Levy and Scully, 2007). The attention to agency and to processes of change has enhanced the sensitivity in institutional theory to the role of hybridity in organisations and fields.

One of the most influential perspectives on hybridity within recent institutional theory is the institutional logics stream. Institutional logic has become a buzzword (Thornton and Ocasio, 2008) which has been used to highlight the leading principles that may guide organisations' and other actors' behaviour. Recently, the existence of multiple competing logics has been termed 'institutional complexity' (Greenwood et al., 2011) and there has been a marked increase in the attention given to the responses and actions of actors (Pache and Santos, 2010, 2013). There is some overlap between the institutional logics perspective and the governance literature, as both refer to the interaction between hierarchy or state and market on the one hand, and civil society and networks on the other. The logics literature, however, includes a much broader range of leading principles including logics based on family, religion and professions (Friedland and Alford, 1991; Thornton et al., 2012), as well as logics related to specific fields or topics (logics of welfare attitudes, Larsen, 2008; and logics of performance appraisal, Townley, 1997). This wide application of the logics perspective has led some institutional scholars argue that institutional theory is losing its focus (Meyer and Höllerer, 2014).

Some Applications to the Study of Hybrids in Public Services Settings

We turn now to some empirical studies derived from institutional theory, in particular on institutional logics, and focusing on hybridity in public organisations. In a study of blended logics in two hospitals in the English National Health Service (NHS), Currie and Spyridonidis (2016) found that nurse consultants were able to blend professional and policy-driven logics for positional gain. This ability was attributed to the ambiguous status of the nurse consultants compared to those of doctors: their external status was seen as low, but within the nursing profession it was high. The relationship between the two logics was more problematic in one of the two hospitals than in the other. In the more problematic case the hospital's financial and performance problems led to greater pressure on the staff and a stronger impact on the (managerial) policy-driven logic that, in turn, created greater competition and conflict with the interests of more powerful professionals (doctors). The combined impact of the financial problems, the managerial logic and the resistance of the doctors meant that there was less room for manoeuvre for the less powerful nurse consultants. The study demonstrates that the extent to which logics can be blurred and blended depends on the ways in which different professionals are affected by the specific logics of their profession and the ways in which they impact on them.

Johansen et al. (2015) looked at three organisations in Norway, one private (a savings bank) and two public organisations (a municipality and a hospital), and highlighted the perception of their managers about the hybrid situations they experienced and the ways in which they responded to them as individuals. They found that the managers felt that multiple logics competed for priority in all organisations, but that it was less clear who were the 'winners' in public organisations where commercial aims did not automatically prevail. They also found that the way in which managers dealt with hybridity and its multiple, competing logics was not dependent on their social position and related power and influence (as in the study of Currie and Spyridonodis and others discussed above), but on their identity ('Who am I?'). The same study by Johansen et al. also found that a strategy of compartmentalisation to deal with competing logics was more applicable in the municipality than in the hospital. Currie and Spyridonidis (2016) also noted that actors in hospitals needed to blend different logics, rather than keeping them apart in different jurisdictions, because the demands of patient care required a high level of interdependency in healthcare.

Cloutier et al. (2016) studied the processes in Quebec's publicly funded healthcare system in Canada of the adoption by its managers of top-down reform initiatives and their integration into existing institutionalised forms and practices. They found that the managers responsible for four newly formed healthcare organisations were responsible both for defining and carrying forward their individual missions and, at the same time, implementing the government's mandate for reform. The study thus focused on managers who operate at the interface between those responsible for developing policy and those who carry out operational activities. In particular, the relational part of their work is considered crucial for matching the strategic and conceptual elements with the operational focus. Relational skills and activities (such as the ability to build coalitions, networks, trust and support) seem here even more essential in bridging top-down reform and bottom-up missions than for less senior managers. So how individual actors involved in change efforts in public services construct their role seems to matter (see also Currie and Spyridonisis, 2016, for empirically observed variety in such role construction by potential change agents in the English healthcare sector).

Institutional Logics: Conclusion

Despite a growing number of studies on public organisations dealing with the complexity of multiple institutional logics, the conditions for successful logic blending are still hard to detect. This may be due to the fact that institutional research 'currently suffers from too much heterogeneity, especially with regard to the definition and identification of institutional logics' (Meyer and Höllerer, 2014, p. 1227). The illustrative empirical studies discussed in this section suggest that variables such as the social position and self-image of managers and professionals; their feeling of urgency to find a workable mix given their clients' dependency on public services; and the relational work necessary to bridge macro designs with operational activities, play an important role in understanding whether – and how – logics are combined to provide a hybrid synthesis in daily practice. Refining theory-building about hybridity based on the institutional logics perspective should be informed by a more systematic account of these variables and their effects in different public contexts.

ACTOR NETWORK THEORY: LOOSE NETWORKS OF DIVERSE ACTORS AND ACTANTS

Another literature stream reflects ideas drawn from Actor Network Theory (ANT), which was originally developed in science and technology studies where it was interested in the process of how science was practised and how scientific inventions became widely accepted in their fields (Latour, 1987) and turned into accepted 'black boxes'. It has now become an influential approach to various social sciences.

ANT represents a move away from the adoption of taken-for-granted centres of control (Lee and Stenner, 1999). Taking a post-structuralist position which has some affinity with Foucauldian analysis (see also Callon, 1990; Law, 1991) it sees collective social action as embedded in a complex network of human and non-human elements (known as actants). Computer hardware or software may, for instance, be important actants in many contemporary organisations. ANT assumes that social actors are not just puppets of broader forces but have some autonomy, and that each actor in a network exercises some autonomy as a mediator rather than a mere intermediary. It does not see social actions as determined by macro-societal contexts but rather as shifting constellations of different forces that may be (provisionally) assembled. These clusters are brought together in loose networks over what is often an extensive domain, which is investigated by following a complex chain formed by the actors and actants themselves, which may proliferate as there are no a priori limits to a network's extent.

Latour (2005) offers a useful overview of basic ANT concepts. ANT no longer sees social aggregates as given, but sees them rather as evident in 'a trail of associations between heterogeneous elements' (ibid., p. 5). The task of research becomes to trace these associations, understand how they can be seen as a design, and identify whether any assemblages endure in the long term. Thus ANT studies do not aim solely at deconstruction but also explore how the social can be reassembled: 'it is much more important to check what are the institutions, procedures and concepts able to collect and to reconnect the social' (ibid., p. 11). Latour argues that such a perspective is especially usefully in non-determined situations where innovations proliferate, where group boundaries are uncertain and where the range of entities can shift: 'at this point, the last thing to do would be to limit in advance the shape, stage, heterogeneity and combination of associations' (ibid.). The emphasis is on the fluidity of associations and the skill needed to bring a complex chain together in what may be a temporary assembly.

Latour's (1993, 2005) emphasis on associations, intermediaries and fluidity is consistent with our ideas about hybridity, and regards this as a core issue (Latour, 2005). ANT views social phenomena as an assemblage of different elements in which there is open communication between them. This makes it possible for mediators to emerge and bring together different domains either taking on conditions of hybridity or acting as catalysts for wider processes of hybridisation. This is part of what Lee and Stenner (1999, p. 95) refer to as 'the monstrous rumble of hybrid activity' in modern society.

Some Applications to the Study of Hybrids in Public Services Settings

We now give two examples of how an ANT prism has been used concretely to study public services hybrids. Firstly, some sociologically orientated accounting researchers used ANT to study hybrid elements in public services settings that, in their view, went beyond the narrow emphasis within organisational studies on exploring hybrid organisational forms. They also viewed hybrid practices, processes, bodies of expertise and objects as possible foci for analysis.

Miller et al. (2008) drew on ANT ideas to explore a growing hybridity between accounting practices and a rising discourse of risk management in UK and US corporate governance policy. While risk management practices are often developed within vertically integrated organisations, they also needed to consider the increasingly important role of inter-organisational relations, networks and more fluid boundaries. Their interpretation of ANT texts cited (ibid., p. 944) suggests conditions of pervasive impurity and ready hybridisation: 'the world is populated by hybrids or intermediaries that constantly mix up and link up apparently disparate and heterogeneous things'; and they recognise that hybrids may struggle to achieve stability. The focus of their study is on the changing nature of accounting knowledge and practices as they increasingly cross traditional organisational boundaries (Hopwood, 1996).

Miller et al. (2008) provide an example of the hybridisation of medical and financial knowledge in New Public Management (NPM) style healthcare settings, although they acknowledged that this hybridity is unstable over both space and time (ibid., p. 955). They found that the hybridisation of clinical and accounting expertise (see also Kurunmäki, 2004) was more highly developed in the Finnish healthcare system than in the UK equivalent as the result of the greater willingness of doctors there to acquire accounting-based expertise. This perspective highlights the possible development of new hybrid roles by individuals; in this case the emergence of a clinical managerial hybrid role. McGivern et al. (2015) explored how doctors in the English NHS who moved into part-time managerial posts enacted these hybrid roles, and how the changes in their roles varied from the more incidental to the strategic. These developments were linked to a focus on identity shifts, which we discuss below.

A second brief example comes from the law courts. Lee and Stenner (1999) exemplify their general argument by exploring how the position of a child witness has been changing in law. The traditional position that children should not testify in court is being eroded by the development of new interviewing techniques and video recording (an actant). They suggest that: 'an absolute exclusion, a firm division, instituted at some moment in legal history is approached by the gradual and creeping boundary dissolution of an actor network' (ibid., p. 101).

ANT: Conclusion

We suggest that ANT provides a useful additional theoretical perspective for analysing hybrids in public services settings along the same lines as its application to other settings, such as laboratories. The interest here is in charting hybrid practices, processes, knowledges and roles that moves beyond the study of hybrid organisational forms. In disciplinary terms, ANT has had a strong influence in sociological accounting research, in critical information systems research (Doolin and Lowe, 2002), and in science and technology studies which include the study of publicly funded science laboratories. Areas of application within the public services include the possible combination of professional and financial knowledges and roles, along with the study of attempts (not always effective) to enrol a diverse set of heterogeneous actors around new information systems (Doolin, 1999).

AN IDENTITY PERSPECTIVE: EFFECTS OF HYBRIDITY ON PEOPLE

Work on hybridity has moved far beyond its initial focus on the emergence of new structural arrangements. We have observed a push toward a practice turn (Schatzki et al., 2001) in the study of hybridity, with a growing focus on how individuals deal in their day-to-day practices with – and contribute to shaping – the pressures of hybridisation in contemporary organisations. Individual roles and identities are a locus through which broader institutional pressures for hybridisation take forms which are accommodated or reformulated. Researchers on hybridity have thus recently responded to the call made by neo-institutionalists for a focus on the micro-practices of actors and on their agentic capacity (Suddaby, 2010). Hybridisation is not a fully predetermined phenomenon in which organisations and actors are passive recipients of external pressures and changes. An identity perspective not only analyses the impact of hybridity on individual work experience and sense of belonging, but also takes into account the nature of the responses of actors involved in the hybridisation process where sense-making, resistance and agentic capacity are at play.

Organisational identity and identities within organisations have been the object of numerous scholarly works (Pratt and Foreman, 2000; Pratt et al., 2006; Dutton et al., 2010). Social identity theories have identified three dimensions, which can be characterised as individual, group and organisational identity (Albert and Whetten, 1985). Firstly, identity refers to the definition of self: the 'Who am I?' or 'Who are we?' questions. Secondly, identity refers to a set of elements that make one person or a group of individuals distinct from others ('What makes me or what make us distinct from others?'). And thirdly, it refers to something that is relatively enduring. The combination of these three dimensions means that identity-related phenomena play an important role in organisations (Pratt et al., 2006; Fiol et al., 2009).

Despite the sense of stability and continuity conveyed by the term, organisational scholars have paid more and more attention to the unstable and changing properties of identity in organisations. Studies have looked, for example, at intractable identity conflicts and at identity violations and explored the strategies used by actors to deal with these perceived threats (Pratt et al., 2006; Fiol et al., 2009). In their 1985 paper, Albert and Whetten discuss hybrid identity as being composed of multiple identities that would not normally be found together. Organisational identity is not set in stone and does not take a permanent form, nor is it shared by all organisational members (Pratt and Rafaeli, 1997). Studies of different approaches that people can take to 'identity work' in organisations (Sveningsson and Alvesson, 2003; Alvesson, 2010), and more process-based approaches to identity struggles or transitions over time (Langley et al., 2012), make it clear that the academic domain of identity studies is a lively and contested terrain.

Change and pressures within one's environment will often challenge one's own sense of belonging (Creed et al., 2010). In many organisations such as in the cultural industries, higher education and the healthcare sector, the confrontation of multiple and distinct logics and identities (such as between artists and managers, or between managers and professionals) challenge current identity patterns (Skelcher and Smith, 2015). Identity is developed over time through interaction with others and through complex processes of social identification (Pratt and Rafaeli, 1997), or attachment to particular and culturally distinct social groups. Identity has a significant impact on the development of the individual's own organisational and work roles (Spyridonidis et al., 2015). Recent studies on organisational hybrids and on the process of hybridisation have been increasingly concerned by a more critical and dynamic approach to identity phenomena (Denis et al., 2015; McGivern et al., 2015). We will now review some key studies on the broad theme of identity and hybridity in the public sector.

Some Applications to the Study of Hybrids in Public Services Settings

Exploring the dynamic between hybridity and identity development at a personal level is one landmark of contemporary public administration scholarship. Meyer et al. (2013), for example, found a high proportion of hybrid identities among public servants in the form of a mix of a commitment to Weberian-style bureaucracy and an orientation to reform through the use of managerial and market tools.

The evolution of identities is influenced by the contexts in which people work, and evolving identities shape roles and practices. Blomgren and Waks (2015) studied the introduction of a requirement for a national system of benchmarking reports to compare levels of quality in the Swedish healthcare system. Using case studies of county and regional councils, the authors looked at the ways in which reports based on comparisons of healthcare quality were used and at the roles played in this process by various actors (such as medical specialists and medical experts groups). The use of these reports involved the confluence of a variety of institutional logics (democratic, managerial, market and professional). The authors observed that to 'manage' this institutional complexity actors needed to embody this kind of hybridity, and that hybrid professionals were considered a precondition and a mechanism for dealing with institutional complexity.

In another study, Buffat (2014) looked at the development and use of identities in a public insurance company in Switzerland that had been exposed both to public values and to managerial practices analogous to the private sector. They observed that public officials were deeply aware of and sensitive to changes in their environment as it came increasingly under the influence of hybridity. Their identities had evolved in response to these changes that included the creation of multiple identities among the actors. The author suggested that the organisational hybridisation involved actors in a process of diversifying their markers of belonging, or the visible signs of their social identification. The hybrid identity thus provided actors with a strategic resource which they can use to deal with challenges to legitimacy and environmental pressures.

In a study of the life trajectory of gay, lesbian, bisexual and transgender ministers in the Protestant church, Creed et al. (2010) observed that individuals relied on a set of cultural resources, biblical narratives and Protestant traditions to reconcile the contradiction between their self-identity and the affirmed or authoritarian rules of the church. The authors identified a form of identity work, which they labelled as 'reconciliation work', that identified the levers through which individual experience and emotions were reconciled with the aspirations of being ministers of the Protestant church. This study highlighted the active roles of individuals in reconciling institutional contradictions and, at the same time, challenging long-standing institutional prescriptions. In this case, certain individuals were the active catalyst of social change in their reconciliation work – which in our terms can be seen as a process of hybridisation – set within a broader context of institutional inertia.

Kodeih and Greenwood (2014) carried out a longitudinal study of the strategies used by business schools in France, a highly institutionalised form based on the system of Grandes Écoles. The business schools had come under pressure from the influence of international norms, and especially from the emphasis placed on the need to promote productivity in terms of research activities and publications. Their study focuses on how the identity of a business school influenced how it responded to situations of institutional complexity. The authors concluded that responses to hybridisation pressures depended less on the current identity and status of the school and more on the schools' aspirations for a future identity. The study highlighted the nature of identity phenomena at a more aggregate level and suggested that the influence of hybrid pressures was mediated by the organisation's identity aspirations.

Recent works (McGivern et al., 2015; Spyridonidis et al., 2015) have looked at the place of identity work among groups of NHS hybrid professionals, namely physicians in managerial roles or in leading roles in various types of clinical networks. The individuals are pushed by the healthcare context toward a new kind of relationship between professionals and organisations. McGivern et al. (2015) identified empirically two types of hybrid roles: the incidental hybrids and the willing hybrids. While the incidental hybrids accommodated pressures for hybridisation in a more or less sporadic way, the willing hybrids got engaged in a transformational process of their identity where professionalism was reformulated around the ethos of addressing the best care for patients collectively (as opposed to a micro-level clinical focus). Such changes in identity in turn had implications for the relationship between the willing hybrids and their peers. Willing hybrids also adopted the role early in their career, while the practice of the new managerial roles enabled them to align their existing identity in the organisation.

Conclusion: Identity Perspectives

Overall, as these different empirical studies indicated, hybridity pressures influenced the development of individual and organisational identities. This, however, is not a one-way relationship. Individuals are aware of the pressures and they reframe the nature of hybrid organisations through the processes of sense-making and, more broadly, through identity work (Bévort and Suddaby, 2016). One common finding that came across from those studies is that the agency of individuals is at the core of the strategies developed to deal with institutional complexity. The contradictions and tensions at various levels gave rise to the need for reconciliation through identity work at the level of the individual. The hybrid identities as a result of these processes were not fixed entities but took shape and operated through a constant tension between external pressures, contingencies and individual agency.

DISCUSSION AND IMPLICATIONS

Based on our previous review of the academic literature that explored the phenomenon of hybridity in public organisations, we discuss here what we have learned from the four theoretical perspectives we identified and some of their empirical applications. Finally, we suggest some further avenues for research.

Comparing Theoretical Frameworks on Hybrid Public Organisations

In this chapter we asked: how can we understand hybridity in public services organisations, in particular regarding the roles and identities of management and professionals? All four of the frameworks we explored were found to capture some, but not all, facets of the answer.

Governance theory has so far focused on the macro level of public sector reform and has broadly suggested a shift away from the traditional Weberian model and the development of alternative mechanisms for coordination provided either by markets or by networks. The empirical studies that we reviewed here, however, found evidence of the survival of traditional principles for public administration together with the development of hybridity in the form of multiple mechanisms for coordination that existed simultaneously and were often difficult to reconcile. Our empirical illustrations showed that managers and professionals felt concerned about negative effects of shifts in governance and their impact on the continuation of public services and the maintenance of high-quality services. The studies also concluded that in non-Anglo-Saxon countries the practice of NPM-type reforms was flawed, especially in parts of Europe where the state traditionally had a central position in society and where there was a strong tradition of the importance of legal safeguards for civic rights (Pollitt and Bouckaert, 2011). We also identified variations at the local level of implementation that could not easily be captured by a governance perspective; for example, the variations in attitudes of executives and frontline workers towards NPM-type tools and instruments. The governance framework thus may benefit from complementary theoretical input, in particular at the meso- and micro-organisational level.

Similarly, the growing literature on institutional logics has shown that hybridity in public organisations can be understood from the simultaneous play of a multiplicity of organising principles. Where governance theory presents three basic modes of governance (hierarchy, market, network), the institutional logics literature distinguishes six societal logics, based on the seminal article of Friedland and Alford (1991), which are complemented by specific logics applied to particular issues. Some authors have perceived the heterogeneity of institutional logics found in empirical studies to be an important barrier for further theory development (Meyer and Höllerer, 2014). Another problem for institutional theory might be its tendency to switch from an overemphasis on an institutional focus to a narrow focus on the strategies and responses of actors. The empirical studies discussed here from the institutional perspective found some interesting variables that deserve further attention in explaining variation in the role of managers and professionals in hybrid public organisations. These included their social position and self-image; the degree of clients' dependency on public services, and the type and quality of 'relational work' (Cloutier et al., 2016) that could bridge macro designs and operational activities.

Actor Network Theory differs from the previous two perspectives in concentrating on the more micro or meso level of service settings, networks or even loose arenas. These arenas may be populated by a considerable range of disparate actors and actants. In contrast to most studies on public organisations, ANT focuses on the process of organising rather than on the organisations themselves. Empirical studies based on ANT demonstrate that hybridity is often fragile and unstable in, for example, combining knowledges from different fields or in hybrid roles of actors (such as professional and manager). Empirical studies of ANT have also illustrated how new technologies (actants) may cause changes in definitions of human rights, leading to a lower protection by legal rules in local practices. ANT does not, however, focus on individual framing and identity.

The identity framework may complement the other perspectives with its interest in how individuals and organisations experience hybridity in public organisations. As the empirical studies have illustrated, the ability of managers and professionals to incorporate multiple identities can become a resource through which individuals can frame and deliver public services according to the different expectations of stakeholders. But we also observed important variations where some individuals resisted the development of hybrid roles while others felt attracted to them as a means to improving public services and/or the social position of the individual. The range of different impacts (positive as well as problematic) of hybridity on public sector workers means that research on hybrid roles and identity is in need of more systematic and longitudinal comparison in order to discover ways in which hybridity and its (non-)appreciation by individuals is changing over time.

A review of the value of all four of our theoretical frameworks and their applications reveals that there remain gaps in the understanding of hybridity in public organisations. We therefore put forward some ideas for further development of the theoretical streams informing the study of hybrid public organisations.

Some Avenues for Further Development of the Theoretical Streams

The four theoretical approaches may offer different degrees of purchase at different levels of analysis which may lead to further questions, as follows:

- Governance theory: since it operates mainly at the level of the inter-organisational field and at the top of individual public services organisations (the board level), future research questions could include the following. What are the consequences of more mixed forms of governance for the strategic management of such organisations?

How is the balance between hierarchical, market-based and network-orientated modes shifting, and is the networks-based element really increasing as has been suggested in the literature (Klijn and Koppenjan, 2012; O'Toole, 2015)? Can these different governance logics be blended, or are there enduring tensions between them?

- Institutional theory: its primary focus on the evolution of organisational fields is close to governance theory. It too has the concept of 'sedimented' logics which may blend together to complement paradigmatic modes of change. It is perhaps more interested than governance theory in the dynamics of organisational change (and also resistance to it). This leads to research questions such as the following. Do organisations and fields move to hybrid positions and stay there rather than experience a pure paradigm or archetype transition? If so, why? And what is the role of skilled institutional entrepreneurs who may sponsor novel hybrid conditions in public organisations?

- Actor Network Theory: ANT literature focuses on the construction of (perhaps shifting) networks, with a special interest in the construction of hybrid practices and knowledge bases which might, for example, bring together professional and managerial knowledges. These foci could both be useful to future research. ANT work is also concerned to explore the role of non-human actants (such as software or information systems) which may help to align human actors. It brings with it important ideas from the field of science and technology studies (with an interest in the study of such settings as scientific labs, which may of course be funded through public science) and also sociologically orientated accounting and information studies literatures, which broaden the field considerably.

- Identity: this stream of literature operates at the most micro level and studies the individual in public services organisations who is often challenged to move from a single professional focus to a more mixed role, and possibly even to a change in personal identity. This perspective addresses a more social and psychologically orientated literature on identity at work, identity strains and identity transitions. A central question for future research is: how do individuals shape, adapt, or indeed resist pressures towards the enactment of more hybrid roles and identity? The literature currently examines identity issues in the case of professional–managerial hybrids, but it is possible that other hybrid roles may also trigger identity transitions.

The major contribution of this chapter has been a detailed discussion of how hybridity in public organisations can be understood from the point of view of four theoretical frames. It brought together a substantial body of conceptual literature with empirical illustrations, on the understanding that advances in our knowledge of hybridity were more likely to take place when theoretical frameworks were applied to the experience of real public organisations. Although limited in number and scope, the empirical studies discussed here have demonstrated the ability of the frameworks to interpret the phenomenon of hybridity from a range of different angles. This, we suggest, provides a rich variety of alternative theoretical perspectives which can be used to inform further empirical studies of hybridisation in the public services.

REFERENCES

Agranoff, R. (1991), 'Human services integration: past and present challenges in public administration', *Public Administration Review*, 51 (6), pp. 533–542.

Albert, S. and Whetten, D.A. (1985), 'Organisational identity', *Research in Organisational Behavior*, 7, pp. 263–295.

Alvesson, M. (2010), 'Self-doubters, strugglers, storytellers, surfers and others: Images of self-identities in organisations', *Human Relations*, 63 (2), pp. 193–217.

Arellano-Gault, D., Demortain, D., Rouillard, C. and Thoenig, J.-L. (2013), 'Bringing public organisation and organising back in', *Organisation Studies*, 34 (2), pp. 145–167.

Bévort, F. and Suddaby, R. (2016), 'Scripting professional identities: how individuals make sense of contradictory institutional logics', *Journal of Professions and Organization*, 3, pp. 17–38.

Billis, D. (2010), 'Towards a theory of hybrid organisation', in D. Billis (ed.), *Hybrid Organisations and the Third Sector*, Basingstoke: Palgrave Macmillan, pp. 46–69.

Blatter, J. (2003), 'Beyond hierarchies and networks: institutional logics and change in transboundary spaces', *Governance: An International Journal of Policy, Administration, and Institutions*, 16 (4), pp. 503–526.

Blomgren, M. and Waks, C. (2015), 'Coping with contradictions: hybrid professionals managing institutional complexity', *Journal of Professions and Organisation*, 2 (1), pp. 78–102.

Bozeman, B. (2013), 'What organisation theorists and public policy researchers can learn from one another: publicness theory as a case-in-point', *Organisation Studies*, 34 (2), pp. 169–188.

Bryson, J.M., Crosby, B.C. and Bloomberg, L. (2014), 'Public value governance: moving beyond traditional public administration and the New Public Management', *Public Administration Review*, 74 (4), pp. 445–456.

Buffat, A. (2014), '"Public on the outside, private on the inside": the organisational hybridisation, sense of belonging and identity strategies of the employees of a public unemployment insurance fund in Switzerland', *International Review of Administrative Sciences*, 80 (1), pp. 70–88.

Callon, M. (1990), 'Techno-economic networks and irreversibility', *Sociological Review*, 38 (S1), pp. 132–161.

Christensen, T. and Laegreid, P. (2011), 'Complexity and hybrid public administration: theoretical and empirical challenges', *Public Organisation Review*, 11 (4), pp. 407–423.

Clemens, E.S. and Cook, J.M. (1999), 'Politics and institutionalism: explaining durability and change', *Annual Review of Sociology*, 25, pp. 441–466.

Cloutier, C., Denis, J.-L., Langley, A. and Lamothe, L. (2016), 'Agency at the managerial interface: public sector reform as institutional work', *muv009 Journal of Public Administration Research and Theory*, 26 (2), pp. 259–276.

Cooper, D.J., Hinings, B., Greenwood, R. and Brown, J.L. (1996), 'Sedimentation and transformation in organisational change: the case of Canadian law firms', *Organisation Studies*, 17, pp. 623–647.

Creed, W. D., DeJordy, R. and Lok, J. (2010), 'Being the change: resolving institutional contradiction through identity work', *Academy of Management Journal*, 53 (6), pp. 1336–1364.

Currie, G. and Spyridonidis, D. (2016), 'Interpretation of multiple institutional logics on the ground: actors' position, their agency and situational constraints in professionalized contexts', *Organisation Studies*, 37 (1), pp. 77–97.

Dacin, M.T., Goodstein, J. and Scott, W.R. (2002), 'Institutional theory and institutional change: introduction to the Special Research Forum', *Academy of Management Journal*, 45 (1), pp. 45–56.

Denis, J.L., Ferlie, E. and Van Gestel, N. (2015), 'Understanding hybridity in public organisations', *Public Administration*, 93 (2), pp. 273–289.

DiMaggio, P.J. (1988), 'Interest and agency in institutional theory', in L.G. Zucker (ed.), *Institutional Patterns and Organisations: Culture and Environment*, Cambridge, MA: Ballinger, pp. 3–22.

Doolin, B. (1999), 'Sociotechnical networks and information management in health care', *Accounting, Management and Information Technologies*, 9 (2), pp. 95–114.

Doolin, B. and Lowe, A. (2002), 'To reveal is to critique: actor-network theory and critical information systems research', *Journal of Information Technology*, 17 (2), pp. 69–78.

Dorado, S. (2005), 'Institutional entrepreneurship, partaking, and convening', *Organisation Studies*, 26 (3), pp. 385–414.

Dutton, J.E., Roberts, L.M. and Bednar, J. (2010), 'Pathways for positive identity construction at work: four types of positive identity and the building of social resources', *Academy of Management Review*, 35 (2), pp. 265–293.

Edwards, T. and Jones, O. (2008), 'Failed institution building: understanding the interplay between agency, social skill and context', *Scandinavian Journal of Management*, 24 (1), pp. 44–54.

Emery, Y. and Giauque, D. (2014), 'The hybrid universe of public administration in the 21st century', *International Review of Administrative Sciences*, 80 (1), pp. 23–32.

Emery, Y., Wyser, C., Martin, N. and Sanchez, J. (2008), 'Swiss public servants' perceptions of performance in a fast-changing environment', *International Review of Administrative Sciences*, 74 (2), pp. 307–323.

Ferlie, E. and Ongaro, E. (2015), *Strategic Management in Public Services Organisations: Concepts, Schools and Contemporary Issues*, London, UK and New York, USA: Routledge.

Ferlie, E., Hartley, J. and Martin, S. (2003), 'Changing public service organisations: current perspectives and future prospects', *British Journal of Management*, 14, pp. 1–14.

Fiol, C.M., Pratt, M.G. and O'Connor, E.J. (2009), 'Managing intractable identity conflicts', *Academy of Management Review*, 34 (1), pp. 32–55.

Fossestol, K., Breit, E., Andreassen, T.A. and Klemsdal, L. (2015), 'Managing institutional complexity in public sector reform: hybridisation in front-line service organisations', *Public Administration*, 93 (2), pp. 290–306.

Friedland, R. and Alford, R.R. (1991), 'Bringing society back in: symbols, practices, and institutional contradictions', in W.W. Powell and P.J. DiMaggio (eds), *The New Institutionalism in Organisational Analysis*, Chicago, IL: University of Chicago Press, pp. 232–263.

Garud, R., Hardy, C. and Maguire, S. (2007), 'Institutional entrepreneurship as embedded agency: an introduction to the Special Issue', *Organization Studies*, 28 (7), pp. 957–969.

Greenwood, R., Hinings, C.R. and Whetten, D. (2014), 'Rethinking institutions and organisations', *Journal of Management Studies*, 51 (7), pp. 1206–1220.

Greenwood, R., Raynard, M., Kodeih, F., Micelotta, E.R. and Lounsbury, M. (2011), 'Institutional complexity and organisational responses', *Academy of Management Annals*, 5, pp. 317–371.

Hill, C. and Lynn, L. (2005), 'Is hierarchical governance in decline? Evidence from empirical research', *Journal of Public Administration Research and Theory*, 15 (2), pp. 173–195.

Hopwood, A.G. (1996), 'Looking across rather than up and down: on the need to explore the lateral processing of information', *Accounting, Organisations and Society*, 21 (6), pp. 589–590.

Johansen, S.T., Olsen, TH., Solstad, E. and Torsteinsen, H. (2015), 'An insider view of the hybrid organisation: how managers respond to challenges of efficiency, legitimacy and meaning', *Journal of Management and Organisation*, 21 (6), pp. 725–740.

Kickert, W. (ed.) (2008), *The Study of Public Management in Europe and the US: A Comparative Analysis of National Distinctiveness*, London: Routledge.

Klijn, E.-H. and Koppenjan, J. (2012), 'Governance network theory: past, present and future', *Policy and Politics*, 40 (4), pp. 587–606.

Kodeih, F. and Greenwood, R. (2014), 'Responding to institutional complexity: the role of identity', *Organisation Studies*, 35 (1), pp. 7–39.

Kooiman, J. (2003), *Governing as Governance*, London: SAGE.

Kraatz, M.S. and Block, E.M. (2008), 'Organisational implications of institutional pluralism', in R. Greenwood, C. Oliver, K. Sahlin and R. Suddaby (eds), *The SAGE Handbook of Organisational Institutionalism*, London: SAGE, pp. 243–275.

Kuhlmann, S. (2010), 'New public management for the classical continental European administration: modernization at the local level in Germany, France and Italy', *Public Administration*, 88 (4), pp. 1116–1130.

Kurunmäki, L. (2004), 'A hybrid profession – the acquisition of management accounting expertise by medical professionals', *Accounting, Organisations and Society*, 29 (3), pp. 327–347.

Langley, A., Golden-Biddle, K., Reay, T., Denis, J.L., Hébert, Y., et al. (2012), 'Identity struggles in merging organisations renegotiating the sameness–difference dialectic', *Journal of Applied Behavioral Science*, 48 (2), pp. 135–167.

Larsen, C.A. (2008), 'The institutional logic of welfare attitudes: how welfare regimes influence public support', *Comparative Political Studies*, 41, pp. 145–168.

Latour, B. (1987), *Science in Action*, Cambridge, MA: Harvard University Press.

Latour, B. (1993), *We Have Never Been Modern*, Hemel Hempstead: Harvester Wheatsheaf.

Latour, B. (2005), *Reassembling the Social: An Introduction to Actor Network Theory*, Oxford: Oxford University Press.

Law, J. (ed.) (1991), *A Sociology of Monsters: Essays on Power, Technology and Domination*, London, UK and New York, USA: Routledge.

Lawrence, T.B. and Suddaby, R. (2006), 'Institutions and institutional work', in S.R. Clegg, C. Hardy, T.B. Lawrence and W.R. Nord (eds), *Handbook of Organisation Studies*, 2nd edition, London: SAGE, pp. 215–254.

Lee, N. and Stenner, P. (1999), 'Who pays? Can we pay them back?', in J. Law and J. Hassard (eds), *Actor Network Theory and After*, Oxford: Blackwell, pp. 90–112.

Levy, D. and Scully, M. (2007), 'The institutional entrepreneur as modern prince: the strategic face of power in contested fields', *Organisation Studies*, 28 (7), pp. 971–991.

Mahoney, J. (2000), 'Path-dependency in historical sociology', *Theory and Society*, 29, pp. 507–548.

McGivern, G., Currie, G., Ferlie, E., FitzGerald, L. and Waring, J. (2015), 'Hybrid manager-professionals' identity work: the maintenance and hybridisation of medical professionalism in managerial contexts', *Public Administration,* 93 (2), pp. 412–432.

Meyer, R.E. and Höllerer, M. (2014), 'Does institutional theory need redirecting?', *Journal of Management Studies*, 51 (7), pp. 1221–1233.

Meyer, R.E., Egger-Peitler, I., Höllerer, M.A. and Hammerschmid, G. (2013), 'Of bureaucrats and passionate public managers: institutional logics, executive identities, and public service motivation', *Public Administration*, 92 (4), pp. 861–885.

Miller, P., Kurunmäki, L. and O'Leary, T. (2008), 'Accounting, hybrids and the management of risk', *Accounting, Organisations and Society*, 33 (7), pp. 942–967.

Moore, M. and Hartley, J. (2008), 'Innovations in governance', *Public Management Review*, 10 (1), pp. 3–20.

Newman, J. (2001), *Modernising Governance: New Labour, Policy and Society*, London: SAGE.

Oliver, C. (1991), 'Strategic responses to institutional processes', *Academy of Management Review*, 16 (1), pp. 145–179.

Olsen, J.-P. (2006), 'Maybe it is time to rediscover bureaucracy', *Journal of Public Administration Research and Theory*, 16 (1), pp. 1–24.

O'Toole, L.J. (2015), 'Networks and networking: the public administrative agendas', *Public Administration Review*, 75, pp. 361–371.

Pache, A.-C. and Santos, F. (2010), 'When worlds collide: the internal dynamics of organisational responses to conflicting institutional demands', *Academy of Management Review*, 35, pp. 455–476.

Pache, A.-C. and Santos, F. (2013), 'Inside the hybrid organisation: selective coupling as a response to competing institutional logics', *Academy of Management Journal*, 56, pp. 972–1001.

Pierson, P. (2000), 'Increasing returns, path dependence, and the study of politics', *American Political Science Review*, 94, pp. 251–267.

Pollitt, C. and Bouckaert, G. (2011), *Public Management Reform: A Comparative Analysis – New Public Management, Governance, and the Neo-Weberian State*, 3rd edition, Oxford: Oxford University Press.

Powell, W.W. (1990), 'Neither market nor hierarchy: network forms of organisation', *Research in Organisational Behavior*, 12, pp. 295–336.

Pratt, M.G. and Foreman, P.O. (2000), 'The beauty of and barriers to organisational theories of identity', *Academy of Management Review*, 25 (1), pp. 141–143.

Pratt, M.G. and Rafaeli, A. (1997), 'Organisational dress as a symbol of multilayered social identities', *Academy of Management Journal*, 40 (4), pp. 862–898.

Pratt, M.G., Rockmann, K.W. and Kaufmann, J.B. (2006), 'Constructing professional identity: the role of work and identity learning cycles in the customization of identity among medical residents', *Academy of Management Journal*, 49 (2), pp. 235–262.

Reay, T. and Hinings, C.R. (2009), 'Managing the rivalry of competing institutional logics', *Organisation Studies*, 30 (6), 629–652.

Rhodes, R.A. (2007), 'Understanding governance: ten years on', *Organisation Studies*, 28 (8), pp. 1243–1264.

Schatzki, T.R., Knorr-Certina, K. and Von Savigny, E. (eds) (2001), *The Practice Turn in Contemporary Theory*, London, UK and New York, USA: Routledge.

Scott, W.R. (2014), *Institutions and Organisations: Ideas, Interests and Identities*, 4th edition, Los Angeles, CA: SAGE Publications.

Seibel, W. (2015), 'Studying hybrids: sectors and mechanisms', *Organisation Studies*, 36 (6), pp. 697–712.

Selznick, P. (1949), *TVA and the Grass Roots: A Study in the Sociology of Formal Organisation*, Berkeley, CA: University of California Press.

Skelcher, C. and Smith, S.R. (2015), 'Theorizing hybridity: institutional logics, complex organisations, and actor identities: the case of nonprofits', *Public Administration*, 93 (2), pp. 433–448.

Spyridonidis, D., Hendy, J. and Barlow, J. (2015), 'Understanding hybrid roles: the role of identity processes amongst physicians', *Public Administration*, 93 (2), pp. 395–411.

Suddaby, R. (2010), 'Challenges for Institutional Theory', *Journal of Management Inquiry*, 19, pp. 14–20.

Sveningsson, S. and Alvesson, M. (2003), 'Managing managerial identities: organisational fragmentation, discourse and identity struggle', *Human Relations*, 56, pp. 1163–1193.

Thornton, P.H. and Ocasio, W. (2008), 'Institutional logics', in R. Greenwood, C. Oliver, K. Sahlin and R. Suddaby (eds), *The SAGE Handbook of Organisational Institutionalism*, London: SAGE, pp. 99–129.

Thornton, P.H., Ocasio, W. and Lounsbury, M. (2012), *The Institutional Logics Perspective: A New Approach to Culture, Structure and Process*, New York: Oxford University Press.

Townley, B. (1997), 'The institutional logic of performance appraisal', *Organisation Studies*, 18, pp. 261–285.

Van Gestel, N., Denis, J.-L. and Ferlie, E. (eds) (2015), 'Understanding public hybrids', *Public Administration*, Special Edition, 93 (2), pp. 273–556.

Weber, E.P. and Khademian, A.M. (2008), 'Wicked problems, knowledge challenges, and collaborative capacity builders in network settings', *Public Administration Review*, 68, pp. 334–349.

Zilber, T.B. (2002), 'Institutionalization as an interplay between actions, meanings, and actors: the case of a rape crisis center in Israel', *Academy of Management Journal*, 45 (1), pp. 234–254.

4. Local government mixed enterprises
Anthony E. Boardman and Mark A. Moore*

INTRODUCTION

Local governments typically provide a variety of services including roads, primary and secondary education, bus and other public transportation services, fire prevention, garbage collection, parks, policing, social assistance, and water and wastewater treatment. Many of these services require physical facilities in order to operate. Much public infrastructure is old and needs to be replaced. In many regions, the capacity of the infrastructure needs to be expanded. The cost of providing new or refurbished infrastructure continues to increase and, at the same time, many voters oppose tax increases.

In attempts to do more for less, local governments have explored alternative forms of service delivery. Many services have been contracted out to the private sector, most notably for garbage collection but also in other areas. More recently, local governments have formed hybrid organisations to provide local services. This chapter focuses on hybrid organisations in which a local government and the private sector are partners in the sense that each sector has property rights pertaining to the organisation. We refer to these organisations as local government mixed enterprises (local MEs).

There are many different forms of local MEs. Given the proliferation of institutional forms and the inherent difficulty of modelling complex organisational forms, it is not surprising that there are significant theoretical and empirical gaps in the literature concerning the behaviour and performance of local MEs. The main purposes of this chapter are to address some of the gaps in both classification and theory, and to present some tentative predictions concerning the expected behaviour and performance of this type of hybrid organisation.

It is somewhat difficult to specify theoretically clear and appropriate boundaries between local MEs and other hybrid entities with local government interest, and between different forms of local MEs. Nonetheless, the next section of this chapter presents a definition of a local ME, classifies local MEs into three distinct forms and discusses each form: the classic form, the public–private partnership form and the complex form. This classification and discussion are important precursors to theory development. Our theory examines the extent to which a particular organisational form affects social welfare, that is, in terms of the net benefit that accrues to society as a whole. There are three major sets of actors in a local ME: government owners, private sector owners and the managers of the organisation. Although the goals of government owners and private sector owners will generally differ, a local ME with both sets of owners may achieve the 'best of both worlds', that is, provide more social welfare than either a pure private organisation or a pure public organisation. However, in another local ME, goal conflicts between owners, or between owners and managers, may reduce organisational efficiency. This organisation may be the 'worst of both worlds', that is, have lower social welfare than either a pure private organisation or a pure public organisation. In the third situation, public and private owners collude and maximise profit at the expense of consumers. We first provide the intuition behind these different models and then offer graphical explanations. The graphical explanations consider a local ME that is a monopolist provider of a local good or service, such as a school or a wastewater treatment plant.

CLASSIFICATION OF LOCAL GOVERNMENT MIXED ENTERPRISES

Traditionally, a ME was defined on the basis of the presence of both private sector and public sector (that is, government) common share ownership (Boardman et al., 1986). While MEs existed in the 19th century, they grew in numbers and importance during the Great Depression and even more so during the 1960s and 1970s. At that time, they were both widespread and economically important in many developed countries, such as Canada, France, Germany, Italy, Japan and the United Kingdom (UK). Examples of this classic form of ME include British Petroleum, IRI, SNCF and Statoil. The privatisation wave, which began in the mid-1980s in the UK and then became a global phenomenon, resulted in many MEs becoming completely private sector firms, although some governments did retain a golden share in some strategically important privatised firms such as Rolls-Royce. At the same time many state-owned enterprises (SOEs) were partially privatised, thereby creating more MEs in developed and developing countries. Most of these MEs were partially owned by federal governments, although some were owned by subnational-level governments, such as provinces in Canada. In developed countries, few involved local (or regional) governments until recently.

The traditional definition of a ME does not encompass more recent forms of ME-like organisations. In our view, it is now more appropriate to define MEs in terms of the property rights that are held by both private sector and public sector actors. Specifically, we define a ME as an organisation where both the private sector and the public sector can legitimately and meaningfully exercise authority and influence over the organisation's behaviour at some time because each has formalised and significant property rights. Thus, both the public and private sector actors can potentially influence and benefit from the ME, although not necessarily at the same time. By requiring property rights we exclude private firms that are only influenced by government through regulatory authority, or by informal threat of legislative or executive action.

A local government ME is a ME in which local government is one of the public sector property rights holders. Local government may be the only government property right holder or it may be one of a number of different governments. While the term 'local government' usually refers to a single municipality, we use the term to include regional governments (or regional districts) that provide municipal services to areas covered by more than one local government (municipalities) and usually operate under the direction of those municipalities. For example, the regional district of Metro Vancouver operates under the direction of 23 local municipalities, including the City of Vancouver. Local government does not refer to larger political jurisdictions such as states (in the United States of America), provinces (in Canada) or counties (in the UK). This remainder of this section identifies and discusses three forms of local MEs.

The Classic Form of Local Government ME

In the classic form of local ME, a local government directly or indirectly owns some, but not all, of the common shares in an organisation, and private investors own some, but not all, of the common shares. Dexia (2004) reports rapid increases in the number of this type of ME in most European countries, except Belgium. Marra (2007) finds that there has been a significant shift in the ownership of local utilities in the European Union, with many previously local public enterprises replaced by privatised enterprises or MEs. Examples of the classic form of local ME for the provision of water services can be found in Italy (Bognetti and Robotti, 2007; Romano and Guerrini, 2011; Da Cruz and Marques, 2012; Massarutto and Ermano, 2013), Portugal (Da Cruz and Marques, 2012), Spain (García-Valiñas et al., 2013), France (Lobina and Hall, 2007) and Germany (Bauby, 2012). However, in many countries, water supply (including sewage disposal) is operated, for the most part, by public enterprises (Bauby, 2012).

The local government may hold shares in local MEs for a variety of reasons. It might be due to imperfect capital markets, to assist where the private sector does not have enough cash or because the local government itself does not have enough cash. It might be to create jobs, or it might be a way to ensure that the local community benefits from some project that has negative externalities. Such goals are referred to as socio-political goals. Given these non-profit-maximising goals, some authors have questioned why private shareholders would own shares in such a ME. Presumably, investors' expectations about the risks of government interference capitalise into the share price. Sometimes governments interfere in ways that reduce profits and sometimes they do not; either way, private investors have a probability distribution around this interference risk *ex ante* and expect to earn at least a normal return. Pargendler et al. (2013) have developed a theory of how legal and extra-legal constraints can explain private investment in MEs.

The Public–Private Partnership Form of Local Government ME

The term 'Public–Private Partnership' (PPP) has been used in many different ways. This chapter concerns the provision of local government services. In this context, an archetypical PPP is a long-term contract between a consortium of private sector firms and a local government agency according to which the private sector engages in the DBFOM (design, build, finance, operate and maintain) or DBFM (design, build, finance and maintain) of some new infrastructure.[1] It is now generally accepted that the private sector does not have to perform 100 per cent of the DBFM activities for a contract to qualify as a PPP. In our view, in a PPP the private sector must provide significant project financing and engage in most of the other activities. Thus, a contract where the private sector provides design, construction and some project finance qualifies as a PPP, even though the contract may not have a long term. But a fixed-price design–build contract is not a PPP according to our definition. Provision of significant private sector capital during the construction phase of the project is a necessary condition to qualify as a PPP. This requirement ensures that the private sector has some 'skin in the game'. The term of these contracts is typically 20–30 years. In exchange for providing the set of services, the consortium receives a stream of payments over the contract period. Sometimes, the payments are linked to usage levels (that is, output), but usually not. At the end of the contract term, ownership and control of the asset transfers to the public sector.

Given our definition of PPP, there is a clear distinction between a PPP contract and contracting out of government services. A PPP results in a new facility in which the private sector engages in a number of activities, while contracting out may pertain to only one activity and require no new facility. There is also a clear distinction between a PPP contract and the sale or long-term lease of an existing facility. Some governments have transferred operations and maintenance for a specific existing highway to the private sector through a so-called asset monetisation concession (Boardman and Vining, 2011b; Geddes, 2011). In effect, government sells the long-term operating rights to the asset (and maintenance obligations) in exchange for an upfront payment. Typically, the private sector receives revenue from the highway tolls it collects. Examples include the Chicago Skyway and the Indiana Toll Road in the United States of America (USA). In our view, such long-term asset leases are more usefully thought of and classified as privatisation rather than as a form of PPP. They differ from PPPs because the infrastructure (for example, a highway) already exists and so there is little, if any, design element or new construction (build): in short, they are 'brownfield' projects rather than 'greenfield' projects.

PPPs are not classic MEs in the sense of shared or joint share ownership by both parties at the same time. However, this form of infrastructure provision fits within our definition of a local ME because both local government and the private sector have authority and influence that emanate from their contracted property rights. In a PPP, the private sector controls and owns (that is, it claims the residual profits from) the project for a specified concessionary period. At the end of this period, formal ownership reverts to government. The government partner influences the project in a number of ways throughout its life. It draws up the initial specifications for the project, and provides input and exerts influence during the pre-contract negotiating period. During construction or subsequently, there will be some negotiating between the government and the private sector participants. After all, they are supposed to be partners. Furthermore, government is the ultimate property owner at the end of the contract period. At a minimum, the difference between a PPP and a classic ME is that while a classic ME entails simultaneous jointly shared property rights, a PPP essentially involves sequential property rights, or at least sequentially dominant property rights.

There are many reasons why governments form PPPs; see Boardman et al. (2015) for a comprehensive discussion of these reasons. In brief, PPPs may be more efficient due to better incentives or economies of scope. Also, government may obtain political benefits, such as risk transfer, a higher chance that the project comes in on time and on budget, and the ability to provide services now but pay for them later. However, many of these political motives may increase the cost of PPPs, often significantly. One additional reason that pertains to local governments is that they may obtain assistance from a higher level of government. Consider, for example, PPP Canada, which is a Crown corporation, 100 per cent owned by the federal government. Its mandate is to provide 'expertise and advice in assessing and executing PPP opportunities at the federal level as well as leveraging greater value for money from Government of Canada investments in provincial, territorial, municipal and First Nations infrastructure through the PPP Canada Fund' (PPP Canada, 2015). Thus, the federal government is an important potential source of funds for municipalities that want to use PPPs. Critically, in Canada the federal government will only provide funding to municipalities for new infrastructure if it is procured via a PPP.

Some PPPs have an important characteristic that make them more attractive to the private sector than the classic form of local ME. In an availability-based PPP (the most common form of PPP) the private sector's revenues are contractually guaranteed, subject only to the extent that the specified assets and services are made available to the government or service users. Thus, the private sector bears no revenue risk.

Many authors have examined the behaviour and performance of PPPs, generally with little regard to the level(s) of government; see, for example, Hodge and Greve (2007). PPPs with local government partners have been used to build schools, roads, water and wastewater treatment plants in many countries. For an overview of studies that examine these PPPs, see Da Cruz and Marques (2012).

The Complex Form of Local Government ME

In addition to the two forms of local government ME discussed above, there are a variety of emerging complex organisational forms. Antonioli and Massarutto (2012) provide an overview and assessment of urban waste management over almost all of Europe. They conclude:

> increasing integration . . . is occurring between both segments, once almost fully separated, and now characterised by intense transactions and flows in both directions (ibid., p. 508).

> there are many different public arrangements (direct labour, public-law enterprise, private-law limited companies owned totally or partially by municipalities, public–private partnerships) as well as many different contractual solutions for involving the private sector (ibid., pp. 620–622).

Grossi and Reichard (2008) reach a similar conclusion. Interestingly, there are also new complex hybrid arrangements in the USA; see, for example, Kosar (2008)'s review of 'quasi-government' entities in the USA.

In many cases these arrangements are not only complex, they are essentially unique. One example, which is located near Trail, British Columbia (BC), Canada, is the Waneta Expansion Limited Partnership (WELP).[2] WELP can generate up to 335 megawatts of electricity from a powerhouse on the Pend d'Oreille River. Initially, Fortis Inc., a publicly traded private corporation, owned 51 per cent of WELP, and the Columbia Power Corporation (CPC), which is a provincial SOE, owned 32.5 per cent. The Columbia Basin Trust (CBT), also a provincial SOE, owned the remaining 16.5 per cent. CBT is governed by a board consisting of independent local directors and an equal number of directors appointed by the provincial government. CBT, in partnership with CPC, has invested in a number of hydroelectric power plants. Its profits are distributed via grants to regional programmes and initiatives to support local activities, including youth development programmes and environmental projects. In addition to building community capacity, the CBT grants have helped to garner local support for WELP and other local infrastructure projects, some of which have negative local impacts.

WELP exhibits complex contractual relationships. BC Hydro, which owns the water rights, has contracted to buy the electrical energy from WELP under a long-term contract and has also committed sufficient annual water supply to permit WELP to generate the energy it has committed to supply to BC Hydro. WELP's other major customer is Fortis BC, a regulated utility in BC, and a subsidiary of Fortis Inc. Thus, a private company is both an equity holder and a customer, and a SOE is both a supplier (of water) and a customer. SNC Lavalin constructed the powerhouse under a performance-based design–build contract with a fixed price and completion schedule. Construction of the powerhouse was completed in 2015 under budget and ahead of schedule. Another Fortis subsidiary operates the powerhouse under a traditional cost-plus services contract with WELP.

THREE THEORIES RELATING TO THE BEHAVIOUR AND PERFORMANCE OF LOCAL MEs

The behaviour and performance of a local ME are likely to depend on its particular characteristics. This section develops three general theories of local MEs. One is that local MEs are the 'best of both worlds', while a second is that they are the 'worst of both worlds'. These polar theories are simple, but point to testable hypotheses in terms of organisational behaviour and outcomes. One pole is that local MEs perform better than the alternative delivery mechanisms, that is, relative to both a pure private organisation and to a pure public organisation. The opposite pole is that they perform worse than the alternatives. In a third model, both sets of owners seek to maximise local ME profit at the expense of consumers: the 'profit collusion world'.

Local MEs as the 'Best of Both Worlds'

To begin, we suppose that a local government has decided to provide a local good or service. Given that provision of such goods or services should be for society's benefit, it is most appropriate to evaluate different forms of provision in terms of their impact on social welfare, that is, in terms of the net benefits that accrue to society as a whole (Boardman and Vining, 2011a). Economists often assume that society consists of four groups: consumers, employees, firms and government. Social welfare equals the sum of the net benefits flowing to these four groups. For simplicity, we will assume in most of what follows that employees are paid their marginal product and, consequently, the net benefit to them is zero. Since the private sector, the public sector or both sectors have property rights in any particular organisational form, we combine the net benefits that accrue to these two groups into a single measure and refer to it as profits. (Economic) profits may be positive or negative.[3] Naturally, the way profits are distributed between the private sector and public sector owners depends on the contractual arrangements (that is, on the ownership structure). Social output reflects the net benefits accruing to consumers. Thus, social welfare equals social output plus profits.

We also suppose that the provider would be a monopoly, that is, there would only be one organisation providing this local good or service. When analysts or decision-makers evaluate any mode of government service delivery *ex ante* or *ex post*, it is necessary to consider the options. One alternative to a local ME would be an unregulated private firm (PF). However, the more likely alternative to a local ME is some form of government provision, either by a line department of government or by a quasi-governmental organisation owned by government, including a state-owned enterprise. Simplifying somewhat, we refer to all of these government mechanisms as public provision (SOE). We now examine the level of social welfare if the good or service were provided by a private sector firm, if it were provided by a state-owned firm and if it were provided by a ME.

Suppose the good or service is provided by an unregulated, profit-maximising firm (denoted PF). If it is operated efficiently and in the interests of its owners, it will maximise profits (these accrue to the private sector owners). It will choose a relatively high price and a relatively low rate of output per period. These decisions will achieve the highest possible amount of profit, but a relatively low level of social output. Alternatively, the government could form a SOE with the goal of maximising social output. This organisation would choose a relatively low price and a relatively high level of output. Social output would be maximised, but profits would be very small (probably negative), as the SOE incurs production costs but earns little or no revenue. In support of this argument see, for example, García-Valiñas et al. (2013), who find that in-house state provision of water services across 386 municipalities in Spain leads to the lowest residential water prices of any institutional ownership form.

Under either pure private sector ownership (PF) or pure public sector ownership (SOE), social welfare (the sum of profits and social output) may be good but not great. Now consider mixed ownership. As the ownership mix changes from purely private towards purely public, the change in property rights alters the organisation's goals: the ME places a greater weight on social output and a lower weight on profit maximisation. Price is lowered, and output is increased. As a result, profits decrease but social output increases. At least initially the increase in social output is larger than the decrease in profits and, therefore, social welfare increases. Similarly, we can consider the effects as the ownership mix changes from purely public towards purely private. Price would increase and output would decrease, resulting in an increase in profits that is larger than the decrease in social output. Social welfare would increase, at least initially. Thus, mixed or hybrid ownership provides more social welfare than either pure private or pure public ownership; in this sense it is the 'best of both worlds'.

Local MEs as the 'Worst of Both Worlds'

An important potential problem with a hybrid organisation is that of goal conflict between the owners. The public sector and private sector owners have different goals, and each property right holder will try to exert authority and influence over the ME's managers to increase the probability of attaining its own preferred goal(s). In a local ME, private sector owners will normally want to maximise profits all of the time, while the public sector owner will only pursue this goal in some circumstances. Generally, public sector owners will want to maximise something else rather than profit. The previous section assumed that government seeks to maximise social output. Sometimes, government seeks to maximise votes or political benefits (Downs, 1957). Clearly, there are many potential ways that the government might choose to act in order to maximise its chances of re-election. These goals are all different types of socio-political goals; all are different from pure profit-maximisation. This goal divergence is likely to lead to conflict among the owners (Mazzolini, 1979; Viallet, 1983; Brooks, 1987; Boardman and Vining, 2012).

In addition to potential conflict between the public and private owners, there will almost certainly be conflict between one or both sets of owners (the principals) and the managers of the firms (their agents) (Jensen and Meckling, 1976; Holmstrom, 1979;

Grossman and Hart, 1983; Dixit, 2002). In reality, managers are self-interested and may not always strive their utmost to achieve the owners' goal(s).

Boardman and Vining (1991) characterize the classic form of a local ME as a situation in which there are two principals (the public and the private owners) and one agent (the managers). They argue that because the goals of the principals diverge, conflict between them is inevitable (see also Mazzolini, 1979; Brooks, 1987). Furthermore, managers will be subject to divergent pressures from the owners. As a result, they are likely to experience a form of cognitive dissonance as they attempt to reconcile the goal divergence. Some ME managers may engage in self-interested behaviour; for example, they may strategically exploit the conflict between the owners to play one off against the other and thereby maximise their own well-being by inflating their own salaries, reducing their efforts or otherwise pursuing their own interests at the expense of the owners. Effectively, the organisation's costs as well as its goals are affected by the ownership mix. The result will be less efficiency (higher costs), lower profits and lower social welfare in a local ME than with only private sector ownership or government ownership – leading to the 'worst of both worlds'. In general, as the ownership becomes more mixed, profits, social output and social welfare all decrease.

In the PPP form of local ME, governmental uses the private sector to carry out some public purpose. The private sector typically owns and manages the delivery organisation for the concessionary period. During this period, managers are directed by the private sector owners and will not receive direction from public sector officials. Therefore, principal–agent problems are likely to be minimal. However, conflict may arise between the two sets of owners. Thus, the situation can be described as a principal–principal problem. Unfortunately, this problem is potentially severe and thus PPPs may be particularly prone to exhibit the worst of both worlds. A key problem is that, despite being described as 'partnerships', the private sector and public sector owners generally have fundamentally different goals: often one gains at the other's expense. Furthermore, PPP contracts are individually negotiated, long-term and relatively inflexible. Either partner may behave opportunistically and try to take advantage of the other partner. These and other characteristics imply that PPPs will likely have high transaction costs relative to a SOE, the most likely alternative to a PPP (Vining and Boardman, 2008). Lobina and Hall (2007), for example, provide a detailed case study of endemic profit extraction attempts by the private sector participants leading to re-municipalization. Another problem is that the cost of financing for a PPP is higher than for a SOE. High transaction costs and high financing costs imply that a PPP may result in significantly lower social welfare than a SOE (Moore et al., 2017).

Local MEs as a 'Profit Collusion World'

Both our 'best of both worlds' and 'worst of both worlds' models assume that government organisations want to maximise social output or some other socio-political goal. Now suppose that government is primarily interested in earning as much profit as possible from the local ME. In this situation, government will have the same goal as private investors. There is, in effect, 'profit collusion'.

Governments will be most tempted to engage in this behaviour if voters do not perceive the high prices they pay to the local ME as being equivalent to the taxes that they pay directly to the government – that is, if voters are subject to 'fiscal illusion' (Puviani, 1903 [1967]); Downs, 1957; Buchanan, 1967; Joulfaian and Marlow, 1991; Dollery and Worthington, 1996; Ura and Socker, 2011). Fiscal illusion can more easily arise when voters perceive the ME as an entity separate from government; most importantly, if it is not seen as part of the tax machinery.[4]

Government can take advantage of voter/taxpayer fiscal illusion in two ways. First, it can use a ME as a revenue source and either reduce direct taxes or increase provision of government services. Of course this logic applies to some degree to fully state-owned enterprises as well, and this is one reason why state-owned oil companies have become so large (Wolf and Pollitt, 2009; Tordo et al., 2011). However, SOEs have the disadvantage that they are more obviously part of the governmental state apparatus and therefore it is harder to maintain the illusion. Second, a ME allows government to leverage private capital more than in a SOE. Most importantly, private capital reduces current government investment in a ME. Thus, the government can provide services (benefits) to voters now while minimizing current taxes and on-balance-sheet debt (Boardman and Vining, 2012).[5]

When local government is primarily interested in the profit that it can extract from a local ME there might be only minimal conflict with the private sector owners: both want to maximise profits. For an illustration, see the discussion of Berlin Wasserbetriebe in Da Cruz and Marques (2011). If, in addition, the ME were efficient, then the profit-colluding ME would choose the same price and output as the PF does in our 'best of both worlds' model.

However, this outcome is unlikely to be stable indefinitely. Sometimes exogenous factors or random events cause socio-political goals to become paramount and trump the government's desire for profit. In effect, a political shock will cause government to shift away from profit maximisation and focus, at least for a while, on other goals, such as increasing social output. For example, voters might create an outcry over high prices prior to an election. After taking a majority position in the Royal Bank of Scotland (RBS) the UK government left it to get on with maximising profits. But once the UK media raised concerns over bankers' bonuses, the government told RBS management to reduce its diversification and focus more on services in the UK, a form of social output. However, as we discussed in the previous model, if the organisation puts more emphasis on social output and less on pure profit maximisation, then it might end up in the 'worst of both worlds' situation.

GRAPHICAL PORTRAYALS OF THE MAIN ARGUMENTS

We now present graphically our argument that a local ME can be the 'best of both worlds'. To begin, consider Figure 4.1 which presents the standard market diagram for a local monopoly, assuming both managerial efficiency (the lowest possible costs for any rate of output) and, for simplicity, constant average costs (AC) equal to marginal costs (MC).[6] Price (and cost) per unit is on the vertical axis and output (units per period) is on the horizontal axis. Given the cost curve (MC = AC) and the demand curve (D), an unregulated private sector firm would maximise its profit by setting marginal revenue (MR) equal to marginal cost (MC), which occurs at output rate Q_π. It would charge a price of P_π and earn profits per period represented by area B. Social output would equal

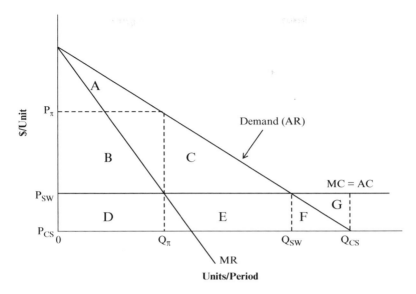

Figure 4.1   A local monopoly

area A, the difference (for all the units that are sold) between the maximum amount that consumers would be willing to pay for the good and the amount that they do pay, here, P_π.

Figure 4.2 shows the performance of an organisation with profits on the vertical axis and social output on the horizontal axis. Points in the north-eastern quadrant have higher levels of social welfare (profits plus social output). As shown in Figure 4.1, a profit-maximising monopoly would earn profits equal to area B, social output would equal area A, and social welfare would equal A + B. This outcome corresponds to point PF* in Figure 4.2.

In contrast, a SOE that maximised social output would operate at output rate Q_{CS} in Figure 4.1 where price, which is denoted P_{CS}, would be zero. Social output would equal area A + B + C + D + E + F, but profits would be negative, represented by the area – (D + E + F + G). Social welfare, the sum of profits and social output, would equal A + B + C – G, which corresponds to point SOE* in Figure 4.2.[7] This level of social welfare may be higher or lower than at PF*, depending on whether C is larger than G or not (that is, it depends upon the elasticity of the demand curve).

The curve denoted EPF* in Figure 4.2 is the efficient enterprise possibility frontier – that is, it shows the best possible combinations of profits and social output that are attainable by cost-minimizing managers. The slope of EPF* shows how much profit must be sacrificed to achieve a given increase in social output (or vice versa). The line denoted SIC* is a social indifference curve: it shows the combinations of profit and social output that provide constant levels of social welfare. Higher SIC curves (as one moves in a north-east direction) indicate higher levels of welfare. Social welfare is attainable and maximised when there is a tangency between SIC* and EPF*, which occurs at SW*. In Figure 4.1, this point occurs where AR equals AC, that is, where the price equals P_{SW} and

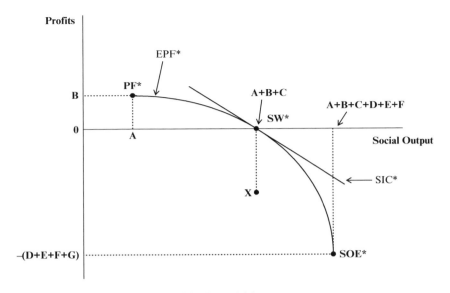

Figure 4.2   Local ME as the 'best of both worlds'

the output equals Q_{SW}. At this point profit equals zero and social output, which equals social welfare, equals A + B + C.[8]

Any position on EPF* between PF* and SOE* will have higher social welfare than at PF* or SOE*. Therefore, any local ME will achieve higher welfare than a completely privately owned or a completely government-owned local ME. As the output rate and price level of the local ME move closer to Q_{SW} and P_{SW}, respectively, social welfare increases and is higher than at either PF* or SOE*. Thus, a local ME can be the 'best of both worlds' for a range of output and prices. The exact position of the local ME on EPF* will depend on the weights it attaches to profit maximisation and social output, which will likely depend on the distribution of the property rights between the public and private owners.

A variety of alternative situations can be described using Figure 4.2. For example, a SOE might try to maximise social welfare, but it may be managerially inefficient. That is, it attempts to operate at Q_{SW} and P_{SW} in Figure 4.1, but its costs are higher than P_{SW}. Consequently, it would have lower profits and would operate at a point such as X in Figure 4.2. In contrast, if a local ME were adopted rather than a SOE, then private sector owners could pressure the managers of the ME to reduce costs and improve profits, moving the outcome closer to SW* (Eckel and Vining, 1985). Therefore, a local ME might be better from the perspective of society as a whole than a SOE that tried to maximise social welfare but was inefficient.

Another potential alternative organisational form is a regulated private sector firm, which has often been adopted in the US and UK. However, for reasons explained in Vining et al. (2014), regulation is unlikely to be a panacea and often results in managerial inefficiency. Furthermore, informational problems mean that regulators often do a poor job of achieving the optimal output level. Regulators require information on demand and costs to determine either price caps or rate-of-return regulation prices. The firm has an incentive to overstate its costs, so that prices may end up above the social welfare-maximising or zero profit level (and output below these levels). Given these problems, a local ME may be a welfare-improving organisational form. Some government ownership may also reduce underinvestment by a regulated private monopoly, which would otherwise fear that regulators might not allow it a reasonable return on its investments. It might also promote better information on costs, which would allow regulated price or output levels to be set closer to the welfare-maximising levels.

We now present diagrammatically the argument that a local ME may result in the 'worst of both worlds'. Recall that the EPF* represents an ideal set of possibilities, achievable only if the managers act in the owners' interests and are efficient (that is, they achieve the lowest possible costs). Even in a purely privately owned firm, ownership and control are typically separate and we would not expect managers to act completely in the shareholders' interests. If this principal–agent problem occurs, then the average cost curve in Figure 4.1 would rise, to MC' = AC' (not shown). A profit-maximising private firm would produce where MC' = MR, resulting in lower output, a higher price, reduced profits and lower social output. Thus, the highest level of profit attainable by a private firm would be at a point to the southwest of PF*, such as PF' in Figure 4.3.[9] Similarly, SOE managers will also act in their own self-interest when possible. This would result in higher costs and so the maximum attainable social output by a SOE would result in greater losses than at SOE*, at a point such as SOE'.[10]

According to Boardman and Vining (1991), a classic ME can expect to experience two types of problems. First, there will be principal–agent problems (between the owners and managers) and, as a result, the effective enterprise possibility frontier, EPF', is everywhere inside EPF*. But, in addition, the presence of two sets of principals and their attempts to achieve a mix of profit and social goals worsens the principal–agent problem. Suppose ownership is initially all private and the organisation is at PF' in Figure 4.3. As government ownership increases, there will be more emphasis on social output as a goal. Conflict

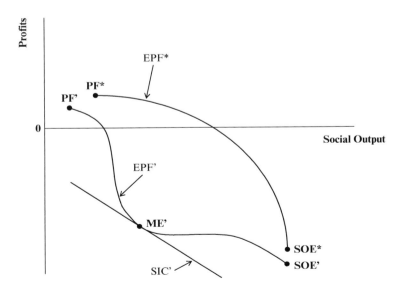

Figure 4.3   Local ME as the 'worst of both worlds'

between the owners and between the owners and the mangers will increase and managerial inefficiency will worsen, that is, the AC' = MC' curve will rise even higher. As a result, any increase in social output results in increasingly larger sacrifices of profits. Similarly, as the ownership changes from purely public to mixed, with increasing emphasis on profitability as a goal, any given increase in profit results in increasingly larger sacrifices of social output. With greater inefficiency than occurs with a purely private or a purely public firm, the EPF' becomes bowed in. Conceivably, the ME might operate at a point such as ME', where social welfare is given by SIC'. There are clearly higher levels of social welfare attainable, including points PF' or SOE'. In this sense, the ME would result in the 'worst of both worlds'.

CONCLUSION

A local government mixed enterprise is a special form of hybrid organisation in which both the private sector and government have formal property rights. It is a relatively new organisational form but its use is increasing in many countries for the provision of local goods and services. Local governments are attracted to these organisations due to the need or desire to provide new infrastructure, and because local MEs bring expertise and funding from the private sector. However, partially because it is a new organisational form, both theory and evidence on the behaviour and outcomes of these organisations are undeveloped. In particular, policy analysts do not know whether this organisational form is superior to purely privately owned firms, SOEs or regulated private sector firms. This chapter attempts to fill part of this gap by developing some theories about the behaviour and performance of local MEs.

To begin, this chapter develops a taxonomy which is a necessary precursor to theory development. It identifies three forms of ME: the classic form of local ME, the PPP form of local ME, and the complex form of local ME. All three forms involve much more complex contractual arrangements than do purely private organisations or SOEs. Generally, the private sector partners want to maximise profits while the government partner has some socio-political goal(s).

The main purpose of this chapter is the development of three potential theories of local ME behaviour and performance. We focus on the provision of a local good or service, such as a school or a wastewater treatment plant, and compare a local ME to purely private provision and to SOE provision. We argue that in some circumstances a local ME might result in the 'best of both worlds' in the sense that it provides more social welfare (profits plus consumer net benefits) than either of the two alternatives. However, a local ME has (at least) two principals (a public and a private owner) and an agent (the managers). Thus, there is the potential for principal–principal conflict as well as for principal–agent conflict. These conflicts might lead to more goal conflict with managers and result in higher costs than in either a purely private firm or a SOE, hence the local ME may be the 'worst of both worlds'. In our third model, government colludes with the private sector to maximise profits. However, this outcome is unstable because it is based on fiscal illusion that can be quickly destroyed by an exogenous shock. While there is some limited evidence that MEs may achieve better cost-efficiency than SOEs, the effects on social welfare are usually not clear (Vining et al., 2014).

It is possible that local MEs are 'the best of both worlds'. But our theory and the evidence suggest that this is often not the case. Institutional designers considering a local ME may face a trade-off between obtaining managerial cost-efficiency and achieving the social welfare-maximising amount of output. Where government owners have some socio-political goals, there may be conflicts between owners or between owners and managers that lead to higher managerial costs and relatively poor social welfare in a local ME. However, despite this potential outcome, local MEs may be the only viable alternative. Indeed, it is hard to imagine why the complex form of local ME actually exists except for this reason. Importantly, this chapter suggests that caution should be applied in this situation and for PPP local MEs. If the government owners wish to maximise profit (that is, to use the ME as a cash cow), then social welfare will not be maximised. Furthermore, an exogenous shock may result in this form producing a 'worst of both worlds' outcome. Pure private sector provision combined with an appropriate tax on the excess profits might be a better way of improving welfare, requiring less public sector investment.

NOTES

*   The authors wish to thank Aidan Vining, who co-authored an earlier article that we draw on extensively (Vining et al., 2014). We also wish to thank Don Fairbairn who explained the structure of the Waneta Expansion Limited Partnership.

1.   Operations are usually performed by the public sector. But this is not always the case. The private sector may, for example, provide hospital, educational or correctional services in addition to DBFM activities.

2.   Don Fairbairn kindly provided this description of the WELP.

3.   Formally we are referring to economic profits, which is any profit (revenues minus accounting costs) remaining after subtracting the 'normal' (that is, risk-adjusted) profits for this type of investment. In simple terms, a firm has to do better than average in order to have positive economic profits. Obviously, therefore, economic profits are often negative (even if accounting profits are positive).

4.   See Dollery and Worthington (1996, pp. 5–30) for a description of all forms of fiscal illusion. For applications at the local government level of revenue-complexity fiscal illusion, see, for example, Pommerehne and Schneider (1978) and Baker (1983).

5.   While this can be conceived as the 'debt illusion' version of fiscal illusion, it could also be formulated as rational collusion between a current government and current voters/taxpayers at the expense of future generational cohorts of voters/taxpayers.

6.   If our analysis concerns a local natural monopoly, then we should show economies of scale and so decreasing average costs. However, this would complicate Figure 4.1 and its interpretation considerably without affecting the analysis. Natural monopolies typically occur in the presence of large, upfront costs due to investment in inputs such as infrastructure to distribute water, electricity, gas, and so on. Once these costs have been incurred, we can treat them as non-recoverable and ignore them because they should not affect future decisions or returns.

7.   We assume, for simplicity, that if there is an accounting loss then it can be funded by lump sum taxes that do not affect social welfare.

8.   At this point, the marginal social benefit (given by the demand curve) equals the marginal social cost (given by the MC curve). Therefore, net social benefits are maximised.

9.   To the extent that the higher costs represented greater employee net benefits (workers or managers paid more than the minimum that they require), then it is possible that social output (employee plus consumer net benefits in this case) does not fall and might even increase, but any increase would be smaller than the loss of profits, so PF' would still be inside EPF*.

10. Because consumer net benefits are still maximised when price is set to zero at output rate Q_{CS} in Figure 4.1, the only consequence of managerial inefficiency is greater losses; social output is unchanged between SOE* and SOE'. If these greater losses are due to (increased) employee net benefits, social output might actually increase relative to SOE*, but the overall level of social welfare would still decline.

REFERENCES

Antonioli, B. and A. Massarutto (2012), 'The municipal waste management sector in Europe: Shifting boundaries between public service and the market', *Annals of Public and Cooperative Economics*, **83** (4), 505–532.

Baker, S. (1983), 'The determinants of median voter tax liability: An empirical test of the fiscal illusion hypothesis', *Public Finance Quarterly*, **11** (1), 95–108.

Bauby, P. (2012), 'Local services of general economic interest in Europe. Water services: What are the challenges?' *Annals of Public and Cooperative Economics*, **83** (4), 561–583.

Boardman, A. and A. Vining (1991), 'The behavior of mixed enterprises', *Research in Law and Economics*, **14**, 223–250.

Boardman, A. and A. Vining (2011a), 'Assessing the economic worth of public–private partnerships', in G. Hodge, C. Greve and A. Boardman, (eds), *International Handbook on Public–Private Partnerships*, Cheltenham, UK and Northampton, MA, USA: Edward Elgar Publishing, pp. 159–186.

Boardman, A. and A. Vining (2011b), 'P3s in North America: Renting the money (in Canada), selling the roads (in the US)', in G. Hodge, C. Greve and A. Boardman (eds), *International Handbook on Public–Private Partnerships*, Cheltenham, UK and Northampton, MA, USA: Edward Elgar Publishing, pp. 354–398.

Boardman, A. and A. Vining (2012), 'The political economy of public–private partnerships and analysis of their social value', *Annals of Public and Cooperative Economics*, **83** (2), 117–141.

Boardman, A., C. Eckel and A. Vining (1986), 'The advantages and disadvantages of mixed enterprises', in A. Negandhi, H. Thomas and K. Rao (eds), *Multinational Corporations and State-Owned Enterprises: A New Challenge*, Vol. 1 of *Research in International Business and International Relations*, Greenwich, CT: JAI Press, pp. 221–244.

Boardman, A., M. Siemiatycki and A. Vining (2015), 'The theory and evidence concerning public–private partnerships in Canada and elsewhere', paper presented at the 2015 Urban Policy Program Symposium, The School of Public Policy, University of Calgary, 2–3 June.

Bognetti, G. and L. Robotti (2007), 'The provision of local public services through mixed enterprises: The Italian case', *Annals of Public and Cooperative Economics*, **78** (3), 415–437.

Brooks, S. (1987), 'The mixed ownership corporation as an instrument of public policy', *Comparative Politics*, **19** (2), 173–191.

Buchanan, J. (ed.) (1967), *Public Finance in Democratic Process: Fiscal Institutions and Individual Choice*, Chapel Hill, NC: University of North Carolina Press.

Da Cruz, N. and R. Marques (2011), 'Accountability and governance in local public services: The particular case of mixed companies', *Innovar: Revista de Ciencias Administrativas y Sociales*, **21** (42), 41–54.

Da Cruz, N. and R. Marques (2012), 'Mixed companies and local governance: No man can serve two masters', *Public Administration*, **90** (1), 737–758.

Dexia (2004), *Local Public Companies in the 25 Countries of the European Union*, Paris: Dexia Editions.

Dixit, A. (2002), 'Incentives and organisations in the public sector: An interpretative review', *Journal of Human Resources*, **37** (4), 696–727.

Dollery, B. and A. Worthington (1996), 'The empirical analysis of fiscal illusion', *Journal of Economic Surveys*, **10** (3), 261–297.

Downs, A. (1957), *An Economic Theory of Democracy*, New York: Harper.

Eckel, C. and A. Vining (1985), 'Elements of a theory of mixed enterprise', *Scottish Journal of Political Economy*, **32** (1), 82–94.

García-Valiñas, M., F. González-Gómez and A. Picazo-Tadeo (2013), 'Is the price of water for residential use related to provider ownership? Empirical evidence from Spain', *Utilities Policy*, **24**, 59–69.

Geddes, R. (2011), *The Road to Renewal: Private Investment in the US Transportation Infrastructure*, Lanham, MD: Rowman & Littlefield Publishing.

Grossi, G. and C. Reichard (2008), 'Municipal corporatization in Germany and Italy', *Public Management Review*, **10** (5), 597–617.

Grossman, S. and O. Hart (1983), 'An analysis of the principal–agent problem', *Economica*, **51** (1), 7–45.

Hodge, G. and C. Greve (2007), 'Public–private partnerships: An international performance review', *Public Administration Review*, **67** (3), 545–558.

Holmstrom, B. (1979), "Moral hazard and observability', *Bell Journal of Economics*, **10** (1), 74–91.

Jensen, M. and W. Meckling (1976), 'Theory of the firm: Managerial behavior, agency costs and ownership structure', *Journal of Financial Economics*, **3** (4), 305–360.

Joulfaian, D. and M. Marlow (1991), 'The relationship between on-budget and off-budget government', *Economic Letters*, **35** (3), 307–310.

Kosar, K. (2008), *The Quasi Government: Hybrid Organizations with Both Government and Private Sector Legal Characteristics*, Washington, DC: Congressional Research Service.

Lobina, E. and D. Hall (2007), 'Experience with private sector participation in Grenoble, France, and lessons on strengthening public water operations', *Utilities Policy* **15**, 93–109.

Marra, A. (2007), 'Internal regulation by mixed enterprise: The case of the Italian water sector', *Annals of Public and Cooperative Economics*, **78** (2), 245–275.

Massarutto, A. and P. Ermano (2013), 'Drowned in an inch of water: How poor regulation has weakened the Italian water reform', *Utilities Policy*, **24**, 20–31.

Mazzolini, R. (1979), *Government Controlled Enterprises*, Winchester: Wiley-Interscience.

Moore, M., A. Boardman and A. Vining (2017), 'Analyzing risk in PPP provision of utility services: A social welfare perspective', *Utilities Policy*, **48**, 210–218.

Pargendler, M., A. Musacchio and S. Lazzarini (2013), 'In strange company: The puzzle of private investment in state-controlled firms', *Cornell International Law Journal*, **46** (3), 569–610.

Pommerehne, W. and F. Schneider (1978), 'Fiscal illusions, political institutions, and local public spending', *Kyklos*, **31** (3), 381–408.

PPP Canada (2015), 'About us', accessed 30 June 2015 at http://www.p3canada.ca/en/about-us/.

Puviani, A. (1903 [1967]), *Teoria Della Illusione Finanziaria*, Milan: Remo Sandon, partially translated and edited by Buchanan, J. (1967) as 'The fiscal illusion', in *Public Finance in Democratic Process: Fiscal Institutions and Individual Choice*, Chapel Hill, NC: University of North Carolina Press.

Romano, G. and A. Guerrini (2011), 'Measuring and comparing the efficiency of water utility companies: A data envelopment analysis approach', *Utilities Policy*, **19**, 202–209.

Tordo, S., B. Tracy and N. Arfaa (2011), *National Oil Companies and Value Creation*, Washington. DC: World Bank Working Paper, No. 218.

Ura, J. and E. Socker (2011), 'The behavioural political economy of budget deficits: How starve the beast policies feed the machine', *Forum*, **9** (2). doi:10.2202/1540-8884.1430.

Viallet, C. (1983), 'Resolution of conflicts of interest in the ownership of the firm: The case of mixed firms', *Annals of Public and Cooperative Economics*, **54** (3), 255–270.

Vining, A. and A. Boardman (2008), 'Public–private partnerships in Canada: Theory and evidence', *Canadian Public Administration*, **51** (1), 9–44.

Vining, A., A. Boardman and M. Moore (2014), 'The theory and evidence pertaining to local government mixed enterprises', *Annals of Public and Cooperative Economics*, **85** (1), 53–86.

Wolf, C. and M. Pollitt (2009), 'The welfare implications of oil privatization: A cost–benefit analysis of Norway's Statoil', Energy Policy Research Group Working Paper, No. 0907; Cambridge Working Paper in Economics No. 0907.

5. Hybrid organisations in English health and social care
Ross Millar, Kelly Hall and Robin Miller

INTRODUCTION

Against a backdrop of the New Public Management (NPM) drive for quasi markets, provider diversity and business processes on the one hand, and the promotion of New Public Governance and co-production with citizens on the other (Osborne, 2006), much is being made of public service organisations becoming less distinctive. Established polarities between public and private sectors are being brought into question (Powell and Miller, 2013) with an increasing sense of 'inter-sectoral blurring' becoming apparent (Denis et al., 2015, p. 273). This situation is leading to range of discussions and debates about public service delivery needing to be reframed to capture the diversity of these organisational forms (Hall et al., 2016; Anderson, 2013).

The concept of hybridity is one approach that has been tabled to make sense of such growing differentiation (Denis et al., 2015). Within the context of public sector reform, healthcare has come to represent a notable case in point with contributions that have looked to capture processes of hybridisation (Waring, 2015; Allen et al., 2011). The purpose of this chapter is to build on growing interest in the study of organisational hybridity in health and social care with a particular focus on social enterprise. Drawing on a case study of 'Right to Request' social enterprises in England, we aim to further understand the nature and impact of hybridity through the use of a multi-perspective approach (Denis et al., 2015).

The chapter begins with an overview of recent hybrid developments in English health and social care. It then presents details about the case study in question – 'Right to Request' social enterprises in England – before presenting an overview of the multi-perspective approach being taken. The chapter then presents a frame analysis looking at the extent to which social enterprise reflects different perspectives of hybridity put forward by Denis et al. (2015). The chapter concludes by arguing that a multi-perspective approach provides a useful means for analysts to re-imagine the hybrid nature of social enterprise by drawing on different analytical perspectives.

HYBRID DEVELOPMENTS IN ENGLISH HEALTH AND SOCIAL CARE

Successive healthcare reform agendas in England have promoted greater competition and choice of provider as a way to encourage greater responsiveness, innovation and efficiency in the delivery of care (Allen et al., 2011; Millar et al., 2012).

The implication of these various developments have led to suggestions that health and social care services are increasingly associated with hybrid modes of governance, organisation and delivery (Billis, 2010; Waring, 2015). A prime example of the promotion of hybridity in healthcare policy is that of National Health Service (NHS) Hospital Foundation Trusts (FTs). These were introduced by the United Kingdom's (UK) New Labour government under the Health and Social Care (Community Health and Standards) Act in 2003, and continued under the subsequent Coalition and Conservative governments. FT status is intended to enable greater financial freedoms, encourage organisational autonomy from central government, and provide additional oversight given by a council of governors that would include employees, patients, and carers (Ham and Hunt, 2008). The approach taken by FTs was said to be modelled on co-operative and mutual traditions of ownership and accountability to staff, patients and members of the public (Allen et al., 2012). However, these are not truly mutuals as members cannot decide to dissolve the entity and use the proceeds, and they do not have full discretion on how to use any income surplus (Birchall, 2008).

An alternative example of new hybrid organisational forms in the health and care sector is that of micro enterprises. Defined as very small local enterprises with five or fewer workers that are independent of any larger organisation (Community Catalysts, 2011), micro enterprises have supported the UK government's 'personalisation' agenda encouraging 'a diverse market that provides real choice to people' (Department of Health and NAAPS, 2009, p. 2). They vary widely, with some having characteristics and structures aligned with both the third sector and the private sector (Needham et al. 2016). They have been regarded as sectorless, in not belonging to the public, private or third sector; a state which is further compounded by their very small size and often informal management structures (Donahue, 2011; Fox, 2013).

BACKGROUND TO THE CASE STUDY

A third organisational form that challenges the polarity perspective between public and private – and which is the main focus of this chapter – is that of social enterprise. Successive UK governments have actively encouraged social enterprises to deliver public services on the grounds of their potential to achieve more innovative, cost-efficient and responsive public services (Millar and Hall, 2013; Buckingham, 2012; Dickinson et al., 2012). Defined as businesses with primarily social objectives whose surpluses are reinvested to address a social or environmental need (Department for Trade and Industry, 2002; Department of Health, 2008b), social enterprises have been encouraged in healthcare as a means of combining the best of the public, private and third sector organisations. Policy initiatives in England have included a Social Enterprise Investment Fund, a pathfinder programme and various guidance reports recommending the merits of social enterprise to NHS purchasers (Hall et al., 2012a, 2012b; Tribal Newchurch, 2009; Department of Health, 2006).

In 2008, the Transforming Community Services initiative gave English NHS community healthcare services a 'Right to Request' (RtR) to apply to their commissioners to form new organisations into which public services could be transferred (sometimes referred to as 'spin-outs') (Department of Health, 2009; Miller et al., 2012a, 2012b). The Coalition government extended this option within health and social care under the

'Right to Provide' (Department of Health, 2011), and to other parts of the public sector workforce under the Mutuals in Health Pathfinder Programme (Cabinet Office, 2011). RtR and these other policy initiatives included assumptions that these spin-out organisations were able to combine various elements from the public, private and third sectors. For example, the Right to Request guidance to staff described social enterprises as having similarities to the public sector in their 'common set of values and principles including a commitment to deliver high quality services, a desire to empower their staff and place the communities and people they serve at their core' (Department of Health, 2009, p. 5). They also differed from the public sector in that their 'business' focus would enable them to 'adopt flexible management structures, unique governance arrangements, and put into practice more innovative service models' (Department of Health, 2009, p. 5).

A variety of research has documented the arrival of these social enterprises as they grow and develop (Miller et al., 2012a, 2012b; Hall et al., 2012b; Millar et al., 2013). Some attempt has also been made to theorise these developments, drawing attention to isomorphism (Millar, 2012), strategic change (Millar et al., 2013) and 'publicness' (Hall et al., 2016) regarding social enterprise sectoral identities, characteristics and behaviours. What has yet to be fully explored is the nature and impact of RtR social enterprises in terms of their hybridity. Often defined as 'hybrid' organisations (Battilana and Lee, 2014; Billis, 2010), social enterprises provide obvious candidates as organisations that are seen as blurring the boundaries among the private, public and third sectors (Dart, 2004). As Doherty et al. (2014) note, by pursuing financial and social aims, hybridity provides an appropriate and useful lens through which to critically analyse social enterprise and the challenges associated with managing conflicting institutional logics.

A MULTI-PERSPECTIVE APPROACH

Our entry point into understanding social enterprise hybridity builds on the work of Denis et al. (2015) in their presentation of a multi-perspective approach to understanding hybridity in public service organisations. Drawing attention to the limits of broad definitions of hybridity as a 'mixed origin or composition of elements' (Gittell and Douglas, 2012, cited in Denis et al., 2015, p. 275), Denis et al. (2015) support the view of others that analysing the hybrid nature of public service organisations requires more precise definitions (Skelcher, 2012; Skelcher and Smith, 2015). Furthermore, these authors call for approaches to analysing hybridity that go beyond understandings of hybrids as predominantly focused on governance structures, calling for an integrated and inclusive approach that draws on wider literatures emanating from public administration and organisational studies (Denis et al., 2015, pp. 274–275).

In looking to understand the multiple manifestations of hybridity in public services and their consequences for individuals, organisations and the (in)stability of reforms, Denis et al. (2015) map the literature of hybridity across the fields of public administration and organisation studies. In doing so, they identify four perspectives or 'alternative theoretical prisms' to help understand various aspects of hybridity in public services organisations (Denis et al., 2015, p. 275). These perspectives focus on:

1. governance forms: theories that seek to understand how shifts in structures and governance (hierarchy, network, market) affect organisational hybridity;
2. the institutional dynamics of hybridity: theoretical perspectives on institutional dynamics of hybrids (using organisational archetype theory and institutional logics);
3. the social interactions of hybridity: theoretical perspectives for understanding hybrid agency and practices; and
4. the identities of hybridity: theoretical perspectives exploring the individual consequences of hybridity for roles, work practices and identities.

Building on the dimensions of structure, agency, institutional context and identities, Denis and his colleagues argue that these various theoretical perspectives can be used to grasp different dimensions of hybridity in public services. They argue that taking such a perspective has a number of benefits in enabling analysts to explore relationships across a variety of different levels, as well as pay attention to the tensions and possible contradictions between different analytic levels. Exploring the concept of hybridity at multiple levels can also encourage a greater dialogue between the neighbouring disciplines of public administration and organisational studies.

The following sections will operationalise this approach by applying the four theoretical prisms as frames through which to make sense of social enterprise in English health and social care. Our frame analysis builds on the perspective of Rein and Schön's (1993) concepts of 'frames' and 'framing'. Jones and Exworthy (2015, p. 197) neatly summarise how the concept of interpretive frames stems from the work of Goffman (1974), who defined them as organising principles that govern the meaning we assign to social events (Goffman, 1974, p. 10). Evidently different frames can lead to things being seen in different ways that can support different courses of action concerning 'what is to be done, by whom, and how to do it' (Rein and Schön, 1993, p. 147). The following sections analyse how far such a multi-perspective approach can illuminate different aspects of social enterprise hybridity.

GOVERNANCE THEORY

Denis et al. (2015) summarise how governance theory can provide a useful prism through which to understand hybridity in public services. Building on the classic distinctions of hierarchies, markets and networks/clans (Ouchi, 1979) as three 'pure' alternative modes of governance, the literature in this area points to how hybrid modes can develop between these arrangements. Denis et al. (2015) cite the work of Billis (2010) as a hybrid governance perspective which documents how organisations might have their basic roots in one sector but will incorporate aspects of others. In this chapter we present the example of NHS Foundation Trusts as a mainly public sector organisation but with some third sector principles in its model of governance.

The assumptions underpinning hybrid governance theory can be identified in the arrival of social enterprise on to the health and social care policy agenda. Characterised within a hybrid space of a Third Way between the free market and state control, social enterprise was synonymous with the New Labour government's (1997–2010) approach to developing a mixed economy of healthcare provision. The *Our Health, Our Care, Our Say* policy white paper (Department of Health, 2006) encouraged social enterprise through a range of initiatives that included setting up the Department of Health's Social Enterprise Unit, the Social Enterprise Investment Fund and Social Enterprise Pathfinder Programme. In the primary and community health sector, social enterprises were one of the organisational forms that could be considered under the Transforming Community Services programme (Department of Health, 2009). This policy commitment was highly significant in that NHS employees were to be given a 'Right to Request' (RtR) to 'spin out' and set up social enterprise organisations to deliver community health services (Department of Health, 2008a).

Department of Health (DH) guidance which was produced to promote and explain the process explained the benefits of RtR for staff within these hybrid arrangements. Working in a social enterprise created conditions where staff could 'innovate and lead rather than being told what to do' (Department of Health, 2008b), have 'the independence, flexibility and responsiveness to innovate and improve services and outcomes', as well as achieve organisational efficiency 'through less-bureaucratic processes and a more engaged staff-group' (Department of Health, 2009, p. 8). The main opportunities set out in policy documents (referred to as 'hooks' by Hall et al., 2012b) for NHS services to become social enterprises are detailed in Box 5.1. They demonstrate that the goal of social enterprise as one of working between markets and hierarchies as a distinct form of hybrid governance.

Research into the introduction of social enterprises appears to support the value of these hybrid governance arrangements. Early research documenting the experience of the initial 38 Right to Request social enterprises (Miller et al., 2012b) reported notable benefits of becoming a social enterprise that centred on improving outcomes for patients, communities and frontline staff to have more influence over services (Hall et al., 2012b). Opportunities to develop greater innovation, increased autonomy, the provision of a wider range of services, and efficiency savings were also reported within this hybrid governance space (Miller and Millar, 2011; National Audit Office, 2011; Hall et al., 2012b; Miller et al., 2012b).

Research into these Right to Request social enterprises also identified structural challenges associated with the entry of social enterprises into established healthcare

---

BOX 5.1   CENTRAL GOVERNMENT 'HOOKS' TO ENCOURAGE NHS STAFF TO SET UP SOCIAL ENTERPRISES

- Improving services through innovation, flexibility and new partnerships
- Putting patients and communities at the centre of services
- Engaging staff with organisations (and vice versa)
- Addressing health inequalities and/or unmet needs
- Escaping a cumbersome and bureaucratic system
- Retaining public sector values and brand
- Delivering wider social and environmental value

Source: Hall et al. (2012b).

governance arrangements. Hybrid governance arrangements meant that these organisations found it difficult to fit into established public sector commissioning (purchasing) frameworks. Commissioners have been highlighted as particularly problematic, as they may equate social enterprises with being 'not business-like enough' (Baines et al., 2010, p. 54). As social enterprises remained dependent on the NHS providing them with public sector contracts, they expressed concerns that they would struggle to compete with other public, private and third sector providers to secure contracts (Hall et al., 2012a).

These experiences suggest that the arrival of social enterprise was by no means representative of a linear progression away from established governance modes of delivery (Denis et al., 2015, p. 276). Social enterprise therefore warrants further analysis regarding the dimensions and dynamics of these organisational forms within health and social care contexts.

INSTITUTIONAL THEORY

Denis et al. (2015, p. 277) set out a second approach to understanding hybridity. This has its roots in new institutionalism, with a theoretical focus on organisational archetypes and institutional logics. Drawing on studies of organisational change (Denis et al., 2001), Denis et al. (2015, p. 278) suggest that an institutional perspective explores how tensions among governance structures, managers and professionals can encourage hybrid organisational forms. Examples might include an 'uneasy truce' between two institutional logics where the logic of professional dominance has been 'subdued but not eliminated' by managerial groups (Reay and Hinings, 2005, p. 364). The perspective is interested in exploring institutional instability, with a focus on 'becoming' rather than taking institutions as stable 'beings' (Bjerregaard and Jonasson, 2014). Such a perspective is also aligned with a stronger emphasis on the everyday practice of managing high institutional complexity (Jarzabkowski et al., 2007).

Elements of the hybrid institutional perspective can be found in a variety of studies exploring the experience of working in health and social care social enterprises. An example of this uneasy truce within the social enterprise hybrid arrangements can be found in qualitative research by Hall et al. (2012b). This examines the motivations of NHS staff who went through the Right to Request programme to become a social enterprise, and identifies key tensions between policy and practice. While policy articulated the benefits of becoming a social enterprise linked to bottom-up staff empowerment and enhanced outcomes for patients and communities, in reality the experience of becoming a social enterprise was often linked to top-down government restructuring programmes designed to increase competition and cut costs (Addicott, 2011). Faced with the threat of closure, merger or being put out to tender, staff reported being pushed out of the NHS and into social enterprises. Interestingly, what followed from this push, and the multiple tensions that it involved, was the expression of opportunity, as staff believed social enterprise represented more organisational autonomy and innovation (Addicott, 2011; Hall et al., 2012a), as well as personal empowerment and fulfilment (Hall et al., 2012b). The tensions brought about by becoming a social enterprise led to the organisational form being framed as a collective opportunity to improve existing services, to lead and manage improvements to service delivery, with employees empowered to shape decision making.

Connected to the hybrid institutional arrangements of becoming a new organisation within unstable institutions, qualitative research by Millar et al. (2013) also explored the transition involved in becoming a social enterprise. This research employed a strategic change perspective to focus on how those leading the RtR articulated the change through sense-making (see, e.g., Gioia and Thomas, 1996). The experience of strategic change created a number of tensions in the balance between existing professional requirements and workloads on the one hand, and the incorporation of managerial business-like responsibilities on the other. 'Entrepreneurial readiness' was clearly an issue (Miller and Millar, 2011), as the business practices associated with planning and finance required for a social enterprise were difficult to incorporate and balance within the context of fulfilling the public service duties of meeting patient and public needs (Hazenberg and Hall, 2014; Hall et al., 2012a).

The strategic change associated with becoming a social enterprise also highlighted the 'sense-giving' practices leaders required as they communicated the idea of social enterprise to others in order to gain their support (Gioia and Chittipeddi, 1991). The research found evidence of internal success in communicating the financial and social advantages of the change, engaging the organisation in collective decision-making, and enabling staff to exercise the freedom to express ideas. However, the research also identified evidence of failure to effectively communicate the idea of social enterprise to external audiences, namely existing public sector managers and public sector commissioning organisations. In these contexts, resistance to social enterprise stemmed from it being seen as a new and untested organisational form. As a result, social enterprise practices struggled to form part of the fields or systems defining current activity, as the RtR lacked both senior management buy-in and supportive commissioning environments (Miller and Millar, 2011; Hazenberg and Hall, 2014). In support of hybrid institutional theory, Millar et al. (2013) suggest that becoming a social enterprise in health and social care involves both a reordering of priorities and the disruption of established relationships. It depends not only on the ability of the social enterprise organisation to implement new structures and processes, but also on its ability to convey the new mission and priorities to the health and social care system.

The implication of the institutional perspective illustrates how the experience of being a social enterprise can be associated with multiple institutional logics. Becoming a social enterprise appears something akin to walking a tightrope between meeting the top-down accountabilities of public sector policy-makers and commissioners to meet appropriate standards; working with and communicating organisational changes to the workforce; needing to develop new business processes; and nurturing a responsive service to meet the needs of patients and communities.

ACTOR NETWORK THEORY

A third perspective from the literature provides a focus on agency and practices. This is based on a view of organisations and systems that comprise a complex actor network that is fragile, diverse and shifting, and where hybrids can emerge in some instances but not necessarily in others (Denis et al., 2015, p. 279). A promising avenue within this perspective is the analysis of boundaries and how they are transgressed in social and organisational settings, particularly 'the conditions under which boundaries generate differentiation or dissolve to produce hybridity or new forms of categorization' (Lamont and Molnàr, 2002, p. 187). Denis et al. remark how ANT-style heterogeneous networks may reflect boundary-shifting and redefinition in social and organisational settings. The perspective underlies the multi-level nature of hybridity as a mixture of individuals, groups, organisations and macro-societal processes.

Social enterprise hybrids in health and social care can be analysed in terms of the ideas derived from actor networks. It has been documented elsewhere how network organisations such as the Social Enterprise Coalition (SEC) represent paradigm-building actors that have been influential in establishing discourses, narratives and ideal types that characterise the early-stage development of social entrepreneurship (Nicholls, 2010). In healthcare, the Social Enterprise Investment Fund (SEIF) represents a key example of such an organisation. Introduced in 2007, the SEIF provided financial and developmental investment to both new and existing social enterprises to enable them to set up or become sustainable within the English health and social care market. The fund provided grants and loans to the value of £100 million over a four-year period from 2007 to 2011, but was then extended by a further year with an additional £19 million (Hall et al., 2012a). An evaluation of the SEIF (Alcock et al., 2012; Hall et al., 2012a) found that the funding was instrumental in enabling the Right to Request social enterprises to secure financial and business support (also see National Audit Office, 2011). In particular the SEIF was used to fund consultancy start-up costs or legal expenses, or to employ business support managers. For most, this was the only source of funding available to support these developmental processes and was seen as central to their successful establishment.

Yet the nature and implementation of this funding highlighted the delicate situation in which these social enterprises found themselves. Frustrations with the length of time needed to apply for and then actually receive SEIF funding created delays and difficulties in launching them (Alcock et al., 2012). Investment in the SEIF, moreover, was predominantly in the form of grants, and this brought into question the long-term sustainability of social enterprises. The fragile nature of such funding also raised questions about the extent to which social enterprises had the capacity and the skills to adapt to the political and financial environments in which health and social care operated (Dees and Anderson, 2003; Macmillan, 2007; Hall et al., 2012a). The implication of this perspective shows how the networks and systems within which social enterprises are located are fragile and may either help or hinder their emergence and survival. Networks that facilitate access to funding are particularly crucial and the most important of them tend to involve grant funding through government sources, with the SEIF being one key example.

IDENTITY THEORY

Denis et al. propose an identity perspective which focuses on the individual level, in particular how hybrid work identities might form within the context of growing boundary permeability and the ways in which the individual's perceptions may influence the adaption or resistance to hybrid roles and demands. They summarise literature that draws attention to how the mixing of multiple identities or the construction of a new identity can present challenges and dilemmas for public service practitioners (Denis et al., 2015, pp. 279–280). The identity perspective also identifies tensions and dilemmas as well as possible resistance from individuals facing hybridisation. Denis et al. draw attention to post-colonial theories of management (e.g., Frenkel and Shenav, 2006; Frenkel, 2008) which suggest that hybridity can be considered as a form of accommodation to coercive pressures (a colonisation by new systems, norms and codes of conduct) without becoming totally absorbed by such pressures.

The challenges and dilemmas of mixing multiple identities or constructing a new identity for those working in social enterprises are readily apparent. Workforce concerns regarding job security, the potential loss of public sector branding and the future of pension schemes have been documented as important challenges to the resulting change in identity (Sankelo and Akerblad, 2008; Addicot, 2011). Sectoral change has also brought uncertainty in terms of their alignment with the public, private or third sectors. Hall et al. (2016) explored the 'publicness' of social enterprise spin-outs in relation to the extent to which they embraced the constructions of new identities. This research and that of others (Allen et al., 2011; Billis, 2010; Battilana and Lee, 2014) has indicated that, rather than aligning with a particular sector, social enterprise organisations have embraced elements of each sector: public, private and third.

Hall et al. (2016) have drawn attention to how this sectoral ambiguity has created both advantages and challenges for those working in social enterprises. A social enterprise can enjoy the best of both worlds: having public (and third) sector values in terms of community engagement and staff empowerment; but at the same time, having a private sector business focus to enable it to adopt flexible management structures and develop more innovative service models. This flexible identity means that social enterprises can adopt the approach that works best for the organisation rather than the sector, and this can also enable them to make the most of any potential partnerships and opportunities (as also outlined by Hazenberg and Hall, 2014). A fluid identity can bring with it a range of skills in managing impressions, as social enterprises can adapt their sectoral affiliation in response to the audience; for example, being more 'public' to public sector commissioners and more 'third' to non-profit funders (Hall et al., 2016). However, such sector ambiguity can also put social enterprises at a disadvantage. Being caught in 'no man's land' without a clearly defined place can lead to low levels of trust and uncertainty among commissioners, service users and potential partners about what sort of organisation they are, thereby making them reluctant to engage with them. Furthermore, it remains to be seen how far RtR social enterprises can ever be outside of the 'public' identity, given their reliance on the public sector for contracts and their need to fulfil the regulatory requirements of the Care Quality Commission (Hall et al., 2016; Allen et al., 2011).

The implication of the identity perspective draws attention to the performative roles and demands involved in being a social enterprise. Evidently, a social enterprise is associated with multiple identities. Such a hybrid position brings not only opportunities to further establish and accumulate access to resources through successful impression management, but also challenges in relation to their associated ambiguity which can lead to perceptions of risk and low trust by external audiences.

DISCUSSION AND CONCLUSION: SOCIAL ENTERPRISE AS A HYBRID ORGANISATIONAL FORM

We have selected a multi-perspective approach on the grounds that, like Denis and his colleagues, we are interested in how different theoretical perspectives can highlight distinctive manifestations of hybridity at different levels of analysis. By drawing on and combining governance theory, institutional theory, Actor Network Theory and identity theory in relation to social enterprise, we are able to open up new analytical perspectives and insights into hybridity. Table 5.1 summarises our assumptions and our analysis of each theoretical perspective in relation to social enterprise hybridity.

Our analysis of RtR social enterprises in England based on the theoretical perspectives set out by Denis and his colleagues suggests that these organisational forms demonstrate

Table 5.1   A multi-perspective approach to understanding social enterprise hybridity

Theoretical perspective	Key assumptions	Elements identified in social enterprise hybridity
Governance theory	Hybrid modes develop between classic market, hierarchy, network alternatives Organisations have roots in one sector but incorporate aspects of others	Social enterprise framed in policy documents as best of both worlds between market and state Structural benefits reported by organisations
Institutional theory	Multiple institutional logics produce inconsistencies and tensions which provoke change Tensions between competing logics become apparent A focus on 'becoming' and the study of everyday practice	An uneasy truce between top-down enforced organisational change and bottom-up opportunities for entrepreneurial action Tensions between professional requirements and business responsibilities Tensions in communicating with internal (organisational) and external (institutional environment) audiences
Actor Network Theory	Organisations and systems occupy fragile and diverse states where hybrids can emerge Attention to boundary-shifting and boundary dynamics	Start and growth funding from government is key to developing social enterprises Boundaries are fragile, with a reliance on grant funding Limited capacity and skills to acquire more sustainable funding
Identity theory	The development of hybrid individual identities The process of constructing new identities to support being a hybrid Resistance to hybridisation leads to forms of accommodation without being totally absorbed	Workforce concerns around leaving their public sector identity Social enterprise sector ambiguity creates advantages in relationship building honing messages to different audiences Social enterprise sector ambiguity creates disadvantages with distrust and uncertainty about role and remit

distinctive manifestations of hybridity at different levels of analysis. Considered from the four theoretical perspectives, social enterprise hybrids are characterised by: mixed governance structures; mixed institutional logics; combinations of knowledge, values and processes; and hybrid identities between individuals and groups. In this section we summarise our findings and make suggestions for further research to explore these perspectives further.

Our analysis of the shifts in structures and governance associated with RtR social enterprises suggest that the drivers for this change have been government-led. Successive policy, particularly between 2008 and 2011, has looked to promote social enterprise in the delivery of primary and community care services. Research in relation to this shift in governance gives some support to the government drive based on the benefits of social enterprise in relation to innovation, responsiveness and independence. Yet this transition in governance is by no means straightforward, with challenges raised regarding internal support, external investment and understanding, and uncertainty regarding the sustainability of these arrangements.

As a result, our analysis gives support to institutional theories in exploring the extent to which RtR organisations can resolve the contradictions and multiple logics of social enterprises within an institutional context of public sector delivery. An uneasy truce is surfaced in how those within RtR organisations make sense of this new organisational form; whether they jumped towards RtR or were pushed by the need to survive in the face of service closure. What appears crucial to resolving these tensions is the ability to give sense to these new arrangements: the ability of those leading change to communicate or frame any new arrangements internally to staff and externally to commissioners and funders.

What also appears to be central to the case of RtR is the additional support from government. Drawing on insights gleaned from Actor Network Theory, the role of the Social Enterprise Investment Fund was seen to be central to the start-up and growth of these new arrangements. The presence of such network-building actors looks to be important in this regard. When we turn to identity perspectives, the findings suggest a continued ambiguity surrounding RtR organisations. Such chameleon-like qualities can provide a source of advantage in terms of adapting messages to different audiences. However, these qualities also created uncertainty and possible mistrust about relatively unknown phenomena in the eyes of external audiences.

Our analysis points to key issues and dynamics within RtR organisations and has prompted us to take up the call by Denis et al. (2015) to seek to combine these levels of analysis in order to open up new analytical perspectives and insights on hybridity. A multi-perspective approach has clear benefits in this regard. However, limitations to such an approach are apparent. Denis and his colleagues appear to provide a selective account of organisational studies and public administration fields on which they base their propositions. The multi-perspective approach may omit key contributions to understanding and analysing hybridity with a long history of scholarship in this area, including those scholars contributing to this *Handbook*. Care also needs to be taken with an approach which looks to categorise contrasting perspectives where such demarcation of assumptions and theories might constrain rather than further our understanding of hybridity.

Despite these limitations, through our study of social enterprise and using these perspectives we have been able to assess both the relative coherence and the fragility of these organisational forms. We also contribute to wider debates regarding the nature of social enterprise hybridity, the role of institutional contexts in shaping organisational developments, and the experience of those working within such organisational contexts (Doherty et al., 2014). Based on this evidence, we suggest that further research is required with a view to updating the field regarding the sustainability of social enterprises. Where much of the research studying social enterprise in healthcare has captured these emergent forms as they interact with existing institutional fields, we propose that future research analyses the extent to which these different forms of hybridity become embedded and sustained within such contexts. Questions regarding the institutional dynamics of social enterprise hybridity remain unresolved, particularly the extent to which these hybrid forms can either be stabilised or collapse through internal contradictions. The most recent work exploring the identity of RtR organisations (Hall et al., 2016) appears to suggest that this is not the case, and indeed might well be not a preferable option as organisations need to keep fleet of foot within ever-challenging public sector environments. Yet, the 'normalisation' (May and Finch, 2009) of social enterprise in health and social care remains a key issue requiring further investigation.

In conclusion, this chapter has analysed a case study of social enterprise in order to understand hybrid organisations in English health and social care. In doing so, it has drawn on recent thinking that introduces different theories of hybridity for public service contexts. Our findings suggest that the drivers of social enterprise have resulted from government initiatives to open up health and social care services to new providers in order to encourage a change in the nature of service provision based on greater innovation, responsiveness, autonomy and well-being. The evidence suggests that, while these characteristics and processes have been evident, competing organisational and institutional logics have also led to instability and tensions. Central to overcoming these tensions appears to the ability to communicate or give sense to this new organisational form. In addition, the presence and support of network-building actors appears crucial to the facilitation of their efforts. Based on these findings, our chapter suggests that further research is needed that goes beyond current conversations about social enterprise as an emergent form into studies of the embeddedness and normalisation of these organisations within existing institutional contexts.

REFERENCES

Addicott, R. (2011) *Social Enterprise in Health Care: Promoting Organisational Autonomy and Staff Engagement*, London: Kings Fund.

Alcock, P., R. Millar, K. Hall, F. Lyon, A. Nicholls and M. Gabriel (2012) Start up and growth: national evaluation of the Social Enterprise Investment Fund (SEIF). Department of Health Policy Research Programme (PRP).

Allen, P., W. Bartlett, V. Pérotin, G. Matchaya, S. Turner and B. Zamora (2011) Healthcare providers in the English National Health Service: public, private or hybrids? *International Journal of Public and Private Healthcare Management and Economics*, 1 (3): pp. 1–18.

Allen, P., J. Townsend, P. Dempster, J. Wright, A. Hutchings and J. Keen (2012) Organizational form as a mechanism to involve staff, public and users in public services: a study of the governance of NHS Foundation Trusts. *Social Policy and Administration*, 46 (3): pp. 239–257.

Anderson, S. (2013) Publicness, organisational characteristics and performance: an investigation of public and private hospitals in England. *International Journal of Public and Private Healthcare Management and Economics*, 3 (1): pp. 33–50.

Baines, S., M. Bull and R. Woolrych (2010) A more entrepreneurial mindset? Engaging third sector suppliers to the NHS. *Social Enterprise Journal*, 6 (1): pp. 49–58.

Battilana, J. and S. Dorado (2010) Building sustainable hybrid organizations: the case of commercial microfinance organizations. *Academy of Management Journal*, 53 (6): pp. 1419–1440.

Battilana, J. and M. Lee (2014) Advancing research on hybrid organizing. *Academy of Management Annals*, 8 (1): pp. 397–441.

Billis, D. (2010) Towards a theory of hybrid organization. In D. Billis (ed.), *Hybrid Organizations and the Third Sector*, Basingstoke: Palgrave Macmillan, pp. 46–69.

Birchall, J. (2008) The 'mutualisation' of public services in Britain: a critical commentary. *Journal of Co-operative Studies*, 41 (2): pp. 5–16.

Bjerregaard, T. and C. Jonasson (2014) Managing unstable institutional contradictions: the work of becoming. *Organization Studies*, 35 (10), pp. 1507–1536.

Buckingham, H. (2012) Capturing diversity: a typology of third sector organisations' responses to contracting based on empirical evidence from homelessness services. *Journal of Social Policy*, 41 (3): pp. 569–589.

Cabinet Office (2011) *Mutual Pathfinder Progress Report*, London: Cabinet Office.

Community Catalysts (2011) *Enterprise for all: Care or Community Support Services Run by People Who Have Experienced Them: A Practical Guide for Enterprising People*, Harrogate: Community Catalysts.

Dart, R. (2004) The legitimacy of social enterprise. *Nonprofit Management and Leadership*, 14 (4): pp. 411–424.

Dees, J.G. and B.B. Anderson (2003) Sector bending: blurring lines between non-profit and for-profit. *Society*, 40 (4): pp. 16–27.

Denis, J.-L., E. Ferlie and N. Van Gestel (2015) Understanding hybridity in public organizations. *Public Administration*, 93 (2): pp. 273–289.

Denis, J.-L., L. Lamothe and A. Langley (2001) The dynamics of collective leadership and strategic change in pluralistic contexts. *Academy of Management Journal*, 44 (4): pp. 809–837.

Department for Trade and Industry (DTI) (2002) *Social Enterprise: A Strategy for Success*, DTI, London.

Department of Health (2006) *Our Health, Our Care, Our Say*, London: Stationery Office.

Department of Health (2008a) *High Quality Care For All: NHS Next Stage Review*, London: Stationery Office.

Department of Health (2008b) *Social Enterprise, Making a Difference: A Guide to the Right to Request*, London: Stationery Office.

Department of Health (2009) *Transforming Community Services: Enabling New Patterns of Provision*, London: Stationery Office.

Department of Health (2011) *Making Quality Your Business: A Guide to the Right to Provide*, London: Stationery Office.

Department of Health and NAAPS (2009) *Supporting Micromarket Development: A Concise Practical Guide for Local Authorities*, London: Department of Health.

Dickinson, H., K. Allen, P. Alcock, R. Macmillan and J. Glasby (2012) *The Role of the Third Sector in Delivering Social Care*, London: NIHR School for Social Care Research.

Doherty, B., H. Haugh and F. Lyon (2014) Social enterprises as hybrid organizations: a review and research agenda. *International Journal of Management Reviews*, 16: pp. 417–436.

Donahue, K. (2011) Have voluntary sector infrastructure support providers failed micro organisations? *Voluntary Sector Review*, 2 (3): pp. 391–398.

Ferlie, E., L. FitzGerald, G. McGivern, S. Dopson and C. Bennett (2013) *Making Wicked Problems Governable? The Case of Managed Networks in Health Care*, Oxford: Oxford University Press.

Fox, A. (2013) *Putting People into Personalisation: Relational Approaches to Social Care and Housing*, Lincoln: ResPublica.

Frenkel, M. (2008) The multinational corporation as a third space: rethinking international management discourse on knowledge transfer through Homi Bhabha. *Academy of Management Review*, 33 (4): pp. 924–942.

Frenkel, M. and Y. Shenav (2006) From binarism back to hybridity: a postcolonial reading of management and organization studies. *Organization Studies*, 27 (6): pp. 855–876.

Gioia, D.A. and K. Chittipeddi (1991) Sensemaking and sensegiving in strategic change initiation. *Strategic Management Journal*, 12: pp. 433–448.

Gioia, D.A. and J.B. Thomas (1996) Identity, image and issue interpretation: sensemaking during strategic change in academia. *Administrative Science Quarterly*, 41: pp. 370–392.

Gittell, J.H. and A. Douglas (2012) Relational bureaucracy: structuring reciprocal relationships into roles. *Academy of Management Review*, 37 (4): pp. 709–733.

Goffman, E. (1974) *Frame Analysis: An Essay on the Organisation of Experience*, Cambridge, MA: Harvard University Press.

Hall, K., P. Alcock and R. Millar (2012a) Start up and sustainability: marketisation and the Social Enterprise Investment Fund in England. *Journal of Social Policy*, 41 (4): pp. 733–749.

Hall, K., R. Miller and R. Millar (2012b) Jumped or pushed: what motivates NHS staff to set up a social enterprise? *Social Enterprise Journal*, 8 (1): pp. 49–62.

Hall, K., R. Miller and R. Millar (2016) Public, private or neither? Analysing the publicness of healthcare social enterprises. *Public Management Review*, 18 (4): pp. 539–557.

Ham, C. and P. Hunt (2008) Membership governance in NHS Foundation Trusts: a review for the Department of Health. Mimeo.

Hazenberg, R. and K. Hall (2014) Public service mutuals: towards a theoretical understanding of the spin-out process. *Policy and Politics*, 44 (3): pp. 441–463.

Jarzabkowski, P., J. Balogun and D. Seidl (2007) Strategizing: the challenges of a practice perspective. *Human Relations*, 60 (1): pp. 5–27.

Jones, L. and M. Exworthy (2015) Framing in policy processes: a case study from hospital planning in the National Health Service in England. *Social Science and Medicine*, 124: pp. 196–204.

Kurunmäki, L. (2004) A hybrid profession: the acquisition of management accounting knowledge by medical professionals. *Accounting, Organization and Society*, 28: pp. 327–347.

Lamont, M. and V. Molnàr (2002) The study of boundaries in the social sciences. *Annual Review of Sociology*, 28: pp. 167–195.

Macmillan, R. (2007) Understanding the idea of 'grant dependency' in the voluntary and community sector. *People, Place and Policy Online*, 1 (1): pp. 30–38.

May, C. and T. Finch (2009) Implementing, embedding, and integrating practices: an outline of normalization process theory. *Sociology*, 43 (3): pp. 535–554.

Millar, R. (2012) Social enterprise in health organization and management: hybridity or homogeneity? *Journal of Health Organization and Management*, 26 (2): pp. 143–148.

Millar, R. and K. Hall (2013) Social return on investment (SROI) and performance measurement: the opportunities and barriers for social enterprises in health and social care. *Public Management Review*, 15 (6): pp. 923–941.

Millar, R., K. Hall and R. Miller (2013) A story of strategic change: becoming a social enterprise in English health and social care. *Journal of Social Entrepreneurship*, 4 (1): pp. 4–22.

Millar, R., M. Powell and A. Dixon (2012) What was the programme theory of New Labour's Health System Reforms? *Journal of Health Services Research and Policy*, 17 (1): pp. 7–15.

Miller, R. and R. Millar (2011) Social enterprise spin-outs from the English health service: a Right to Request but was anyone listening? Working Paper No. 52, University of Birmingham Third Sector Research Centre, Birmingham, January.

Miller, R., K. Hall and R. Millar (2012a) Right to Request social enterprises: a welcome addition to third sector delivery of English healthcare? *Voluntary Sector Review*, 3 (2): pp. 275–285.

Miller, R., R. Millar and K. Hall (2012b) Spin-outs and social enterprise: the 'Right to Request' programme for health and social care services. *Public Money and Management*, 32 (3): pp. 233–236.

National Audit Office (NAO) (2011) *Establishing Social Enterprises under the Right to Request Programme*, London: Stationary Office.

Needham, C., K. Allen and K. Hall (2016) *Micro-Enterprise and Personalisation: What Size is Good Care?* Bristol: Policy Press.

Nicholls, A. (2010) The legitimacy of social entrepreneurship: reflexive isomorphism in a pre-paradigmatic field. *Entrepreneurship Theory and Practice*, 34 (4): pp. 1042–2587.

Osborne, S.P. (2006) The New Public Governance? *Public Management Review*, 8 (3): pp. 333–348.

Ouchi, W.G. (1979) A conceptual framework for the design of organizational control mechanisms. *Management Science*, 25: pp. 833–848.

Powell, M. and R. Miller (2013) Privatizing the English National Health Service: an irregular verb? *Journal of Health Politics, Policy and Law*, 38 (5): pp. 1051–1059.

Provan, K.G. and P.N. Kenis (2008) Modes of network governance: structure, management, and effectiveness. *Journal of Public Administration Research and Theory*, 18 (2): pp. 229–252.

Reay, T. and C.R. Hinings (2005) The recomposition of an organizational field: health care in Alberta. *Organizational Studies*, 26 (3): pp. 351–383.

Rein, M. and D. Schön (1993) Reframing policy discourse. In F. Fischer and J. Forester (eds), *The Argumentative Turn in Policy Analysis*, London: Duke University Press, p. 147.

Sankelo, M. and L. Akerblad (2008) Nurse entrepreneurs attitudes to management, their adoption of the managers role and managerial assertiveness. *Journal of Nursing Management*, 17 (7): pp. 829–836.

Skelcher, C. (2012) What do we mean when we talk about 'hybrids' and 'hybridity' in public management and governance? Working Paper, Institute of Local Government Studies, University of Birmingham.

Skelcher, C. and S. Smith (2015) Theorising hybridity: institutional logics, complex organisation and actor identities: the case of non profits. *Public Administration*, 93 (2): pp. 433–448.

Tribal Newchurch (2009) *Social Enterprise Pathfinder Programme Evaluation: Final Report*, London: Department of Health.

Waring, J. (2015) Mapping the public sector diaspora: towards a model of inter-sectoral cultural hybridity using evidence from the English healthcare reforms. *Public Administration*, 93 (3): pp. 345–362.

6.   Public–private hybrids: a property rights perspective
Aidan R. Vining and David L. Weimer

THE PUBLIC–PRIVATE HYBRID

Hybrid organisations, which must accommodate the interests of multiple principals if they are to survive, take many forms. Intra-sector hybrids, either with only public sector principals, such as the Port Authority of New York and New Jersey, or with only private sector principals, such as social enterprises that seek to promote both social purpose and profitability, typically face tensions between goals that complicate the tasks of managers, sometimes resulting in the dominance of the goal of one, or one kind of, principal to resolve the tension. The potential for goal tension is more acute in cross-sector hybrid organisations that have both public and private principals (public–private hybrids) especially when the private principal seeks to maximise profit and profit maximisation is not the primary public purpose of the hybrid. Based on the fractionalised property rights (FPR) framework we describe below, we argue that the extent to which the potential for dysfunctional conflict materialises depends on the specific characteristics of the property rights that define the claims and duties of the organisation's principals and managers (Vining and Weimer, 2016). Further, we present a diagnostic FPR framework based on what we consider to be the six most important dimensions of organisational property rights. The unpacking of the FPR framework helps to explain why certain kinds of public–private hybrids are more or less prone to dysfunction, and consequently the framework may assist organisational designers in reducing the chances of dysfunction within a category of hybrids.

If public–private hybrids are particularly vulnerable to goal tensions, why have they become so common? There are several reasons why public–private hybrids are especially attractive to legislative and bureaucratic organisational designers. From a normative perspective, public–private hybrids offer the pleasant prospect of marrying public purposes to private sector efficiency and strategic flexibility (Eckel and Vining, 1985; Pargendler et al., 2013). They also offer political benefits. By employing the private sector, legislative and executive actors can obscure responsibility for performance outcomes, while implying that they are dragging reluctant bureaucrats towards more 'business-like' behaviour. This message is attractive to right-of-centre politicians who are critical of the Leviathan, but who still wish to provide services to voters.

Another political benefit of public–private hybrids is that the private sector can bring capital to the table; Boardman and Vining (2012) explain why this is a political, not an economic, benefit. As many governments reach their debt limits, competition for public funds for capital-intensive projects have become intense. The use of hybrids facilitates off-budget expenditures (Vining and Boardman, 2008a, 2008b; Barlow et al., 2013). Even governments that are able to fund capital projects often prefer to smooth expenditures over time or shift them to future governments and taxpayers. Offered an (expected) risk-adjusted satisfactory rate of return, private sector actors will provide such funds. Indeed, specialist entities will arise to do so. These fiscal rationales can induce even left-of-centre governments to embrace hybrids. Finally, many political and administrative actors are attracted to 'innovative' organisational forms (Weimer, 1980; DiMaggio and Powell, 1983), even when there is little evidence of their effectiveness.

Our analysis proceeds in three steps. First, we set out and describe what we believe to be the most important property rights dimensions for assessing hybrid organisations of all kinds. We do so by contrasting fully public and fully private organisations in terms of each of the six FPR dimensions. Second, we apply the framework to four categories of public–private hybrids: mixed enterprises (MEs), public–private partnerships (PPPs), government-sponsored enterprises (GSEs), and government–nonprofit hybrids (GNHs). In general, based on the fractionalised property rights analysis and consistent with empirical evidence, the most common property rights configurations in PPPs and GSEs tend to be more problematic than those in MEs and GNHs. Third, we offer some advice for hybrid designers. (Or advice for those called in to repair faulty initial designs.) We conclude, most importantly, that the devil is in the property right details.

CRITICAL PROPERTY RIGHT DIMENSIONS

Property rights structure the relationships among people concerning the use of things (Furubotn and Pejovich, 1972). As use has multiple dimensions, property rights themselves are complex bundles of claims and duties (Barzel, 1989). Claims and duties can be formal in the sense that they are legally defined and enforced either by or through institutions of the state, or they are informal, gaining force through shared norms or self-enforcement. (Often both formal and informal enforcement are required.) Ideally, the selected configuration of property rights creates incentives for claimants to maximise the benefits of their rights and for those that bear duties to rights holders to minimise the costs of their compliance. Achieving an efficient balance can be relatively straightforward in the single (unified) ownership of an asset or organisation. In the presence of various forms of fractionalised ownership, however, much greater potential for misalignment of benefits and costs arises.

Drawing on frameworks for analysing property rights systems in general (Riker and Weimer, 1993; Vining and Weimer, 1998), we focus on six dimensions of property rights that are relevant to understanding the behaviour and performance of public–private hybrids. To sharpen the exposition, we compare hybrids to pure public and pure private organisations in terms of these dimensions. We do so because these are the canonical alternative organisational designs. These ideal types abstract from important details, such as the problem of multiple principals for public agencies, complex stock arrangements for private sector firms, and the degree and nature of ownership fragmentation within hybrids, all of which are also relevant to actual organisational performance. Subsequently, we look at several common public–private hybrids in terms of property rights fractionalisation (Vining and Weimer, 2016).

Degree of Fragmentation of Ownership

The first, and most fundamental, dimension of property rights is the degree of ownership fragmentation: the number of parties who have claims to organisational assets or the residuals the assets create. With a single owner, there is no potential for conflict among owners (although there may be conflict between the owner and managers). Fragmentation of ownership begins at 'an *N* of 2' owners. Fragmentation beyond a few owners (but especially among large numbers of owners with equal fractions of ownership) inevitably results in some separation of ownership from control. Managers then exercise de facto decision rights (Berle and Means, 1932; Jensen and Meckling, 1976). Once this occurs, ownership fragmentation creates incentives for an individual owner to free-ride on the monitoring of managers. The free-riding problem tends to worsen (perhaps in an exponential fashion) as the number of owners increases. Indeed, Adam Smith was famously doubtful of the potential survivability of the joint-stock design (Anderson and Tollison, 1982, p. 1241; Vining and Weimer, 2017) because of the potential for free-riding, noting that: 'the greater part of those proprietors seldom pretend to understand anything of the business . . . and when the spirit of faction happens not to prevail among them, give themselves no trouble about it'. As we know, his scepticism was somewhat unjustified, but only as a result of the development of hundreds of years of external institutional regulation (Stigler and Friedland, 1983). It has also been pointed out that the wide dispersion of share ownership is not that common, especially when viewed from a global perspective (La Porta et al., 1999).

Free-riding in the monitoring of managers creates potential inefficiency even when owners share the same goal. However, when owners have different goals, such as with respect to short- versus long-term returns or, most relevant for our purposes, with respect to profit versus public purposes, the need to reconcile goals creates the potential for greater inefficiencies.

Public–private hybrids clearly embody fragmented ownership: there is at least one public owner and one private sector owner. Recognition of conflict between owners in hybrids is not a new insight. For example, as Adams (1996, p. 16) points out regarding the early European colonial trading hybrids: 'Even when [patrimonial principals were] engaged in joint enterprises, they were wont to aim at goals that were contingently incompatible at best (the monarch seeking territorial aggrandizement and members of the estates pursuing mercantile profit, to put one common situation crudely).' This quote echoes Adam Smith's sardonic comment about the dual owners of the British East India Company, namely that 'no two characters seem more inconsistent than those of trader and sovereign' (Smith, 1776, as cited in Hanke, 1987, p. 3).

The literature on conflicting institutional logics also provides some theory and enlightening case studies on the tension of multiple owners, conflicting goals and conflicted identities within organisations. However, only one of the empirical case studies of hybrids in the conflicting logics literature pertains to a public–private hybrid that involves a clear trade-off between an owner with a profit-maximisation goal and an owner with a (non-profit-maximising) social purpose (Saz-Carranza and Longo, 2012). Rather, these studies focus on social entrepreneurship organisations and non-governmental organisations (NGOs) that engage in quasi-commercial activities, such as microfinance (Austin et al., 2006; Jay, 2013; Kraatz and Block, 2008; Lee and Battilana, 2013; Pache and Santos, 2010, 2013). Although these organisations involve some degree of conflicting logics over profit versus public service, they do not involve multiple owners with sharply conflicting goals. One might expect the tension to be relatively muted. However, the evidence suggests that these tensions are still very difficult to manage (Glynn, 2000; Battilana and Dorado, 2010; Fiol et al., 2009).

Most pertinent to an analysis of public–private hybrids, owner conflict or goal opaqueness has also been observed and studied in public–private partnerships (Boardman and Vining, 2012), in mixed enterprises (Vining et al., 2014), and in government-sponsored enterprises (Koppell, 2001). Because some level of ownership fragmentation is a necessary condition for an organisation to qualify as a hybrid organisation, it is tempting to equate ownership fragmentation with fractionalisation of property rights. We seek to persuade readers that, while ownership fragmentation is crucial, it is not the only important dimension of fractionalisation variability.

Clarity of Allocation

Clarity of allocation refers to the extent to which various dimensions of property rights are comprehensively and unambiguously assigned and specified among owners and other claimants. De facto allocations typically supplement de jure rights, which are often incomplete. Even in cases of highly fragmented ownership, such as occur with common property resources, clarity of allocation can be crystallised if the owners can self-organise effectively (Ostrom, 1990). If not, lack of clarity generally increases inefficiency and discourages worthwhile investments (Knack and Keefer, 1995).

In countries with effective legal and political institutions, both public agencies and private sector firms generally exhibit reasonably clear allocations of property rights. Public agencies and their managers are subject to numerous *ex ante* rules that provide clarity of allocation, especially civil service rules prohibiting organisational members from taking financial residuals as income and specifying how revenues can be used (Johnson and Libecap, 1989). Although agency managers may muddy the clarity of allocation by creating organisational common property, the rights framework usually gives them the opportunity to clarify at the level of the individual organisational member (Vining and Weimer, 1999). Property rights over outputs or inputs shared with other public agencies, however, are often not clearly spelled out. For example, a probation bureau may have minimal say over the number or type of inmates discharged to it from prisons. Nonetheless, allocations of property rights to public agencies in jurisdictions with strong commitments to the rule of law are generally clear enough. However, in the absence of a strong rule of law, corruption can produce a substantial lack of clarity.

The allocation of property rights to assets in private sector firms is typically very clear. Indeed, the availability of willing investors depends crucially on clarity of ownership of the residual. Civil law frameworks (contract, property, and tort) provide defaults for many aspects of ownership not explicitly set out in contracts. Nonetheless, clarity can be clouded to some extent by fragmentation of ownership and other property rights inherent in the joint stock company (Berle and Means, 1932; Jensen and Meckling, 1976). Multiple classes of shares, especially in jurisdictions where courts have not fully specified the boundaries of the rights of each class often exacerbate lack of clarity and create tension between different classes of owners. This can result in misalignment of incentives across owners, but also between owners and managers—agency loss, or principal–agent problems—as we discuss below. However, the crucial point is that in the private sector firm owner tension around clarity of allocation, when it occurs, is restricted to conflict about who gets the residual, not about what it consists of or how it should be measured.

The clarity of allocation of property rights in public–private hybrids is dimmed by the very fact of goal incongruence. At the design stage (behind the 'veil of ignorance'), of course, public and private principals can try to mitigate looming tension by detailed contract-writing. However, the complexity of the world makes writing complete contracts difficult for all organisations. In addition to procedural incompleteness, which results from incomplete information about contingencies, asymmetry in bargaining and uncertainty about compliance, contracts may also have 'strategic incompleteness' which may be introduced by a party anticipating an advantage during renegotiation (Cooley and Spruyt, 2009).

Administrative law fills many of the gaps in clarity for public agencies, and civil and criminal laws do so for private firms. These bodies of law essentially function as quasi-constitutions for all organisations. In contrast, in most countries the legal principles that would be necessary for a comprehensive legal framework for hybrids are currently lacking or sparse and provide little background clarity. The mixing of private and public assets without detailed specification of responsibilities for their maintenance over extended time periods is likely to result in especially unclear property right regimes, potentially creating common property problems within the organisation. However, as we discuss further in the conclusion, greater *ex ante* attention to the development of public–private hybrid 'constitutions' would result in reduced property rights ambiguity.

Calculating and specifying ownership of most organisations' financial residual (whether positive or negative) is relatively straightforward. In most cases, however, if the residual is only meant to be fiscal, there is little normative rationale for the use of public–private hybrids (again, with the exception of those cases where the public principal also wishes to maximise profit exclusively). However, specifying and calculating the total residual that is valued by all principals is likely to be difficult. (Needless to say, if this residual is difficult to specify and calculate comprehensively, then it is difficult to maximise in practice.) If some output is either not sold in markets or sold at non-market prices, then total hybrid 'revenue' must be imputed. Further, when output depends on either the use of public assets with opaque user costs (because the assets are not traded in markets) or the use of private assets whose user costs may differ from market rentals (because they are locked into mixed configurations), the calculation of the residual is contentious. These valuation problems blur the allocation of rights to the residual. On this dimension of property rights, we conjecture that the allocation of property rights in public–private hybrids is always somewhat unclear and, therefore, uncertain.

Cost of Alienation

Cost of alienation refers to the ease with which current property rights can be reallocated. A low cost of alienation facilitates the movement of resources to their most productive social uses as circumstances change. De jure allocations usually facilitate low-cost alienation while de facto allocations often make it costly. However, de jure allocation among multiple owners often involves high costs of alienation for an individual fractional owner. The need for agreement by all owners on alienation provides every owner with leverage in preserving commitment to particular goals or strategies. This is valuable for the maintenance of cooperation and stability (Araral, 2009) but detrimental to the efficient use of assets across organisations.

By design, the cost of alienation of the assets of most public agencies is almost always very high. Mechanisms that permit managers to sell unwanted assets or even trade assets with other public agencies are uncommon. Instead, alienation typically requires collective action by elected government principals or oversight agencies. The conflicting interests of multiple stakeholders, some of whom may claim the right to bestow a 'social licence' (which can be thought of as a quasi-property right if unchallenged) make such collective action costly for the principals. Consequently, public agencies tend to face high costs of alienation with respect to both internal assets and the termination of the agencies themselves. The presence of opposing and organised interest groups makes reform of ineffective public agencies more difficult but also increases the credibility of persistence of the agency. The cost of alienation of the assets of private sector firms is relatively low. Clear allocations of rights facilitate the sale of the firm's assets. Although there may be a collective action problem when ownership is fragmented among many stockholders, the firm itself, or parts thereof, can be readily sold, thus facilitating firm termination, takeover or merger.

The cost of alienation of assets for public–private hybrids is typically high, because decisions about the sale of assets or termination can often only be made through direct negotiations between the public and private principals. Depending on the nature of the initial allocation of rights to the assets of the hybrid, the cost of alienation may well be as high as for a public agency. Yet, with respect to the potential termination of a public–private hybrid, the alienation cost is likely to be even higher than for a public agency if the public principal has to negotiate with the private principals over compensation or post-termination liability. A government shareholding in a commercially profitable mixed enterprise can be an exception (see below), unless there is strong political opposition to public disinvestment (which there often is).

Security from Trespass

Security from trespass refers to the extent to which either duty-bearers or third parties respect property right claims. Effective enforcement against trespass through the institutions of effective states can provide high levels of security. However, ineffective enforcement of de jure allocations or weak norms supporting de facto allocations, both typically common in fragile states, results in poor security that deters productive investments, diverts investments to self-protection, or even induces predatory behaviour (Baumol, 1990). The strength of the rule of law largely determines the security of property from trespass in both public agencies and private sector firms. A major purpose of United States (US) civil service reform was to prevent public assets from being diverted either for private gain or for partisan political purposes (Johnson and Libecap, 1989). The managers of private sector firms are usually incentivised to preserve assets for organisational use; larger private sector firms typically strengthen the security of their assets by investing in their own enforcement, especially in terms of preventing the unsanctioned diversion of assets by organisational members.

The security of assets within a public–private hybrid is likely to be less than in either of the pure unitary forms simply because the nature and value of the residual is inevitably less well specified, as discussed above. As a result, managers may face weaker incentives to protect the present value of assets (however it is specified). At the very least, protection will be harder work. The resulting weaker protection may manifest itself in the shifting of costs from private to public assets, or the shifting of risk from private to public owners. In extreme cases, especially in environments with a weak rule of law and limited oversight capacity of public owners, managers may actually degrade or loot public assets. This occurred during the initial de facto privatisation of state enterprises in the formerly socialist countries (Campos and Giovannoni, 2006) and during the collapse of the Saddam Hussein regime in Iraq.

Credibility of Persistence

Credibility of persistence refers to the strength of the expectation that the current allocation of rights will persist over time. Of course, rights holders of all kinds face a risk that governments will alter de jure rights even extending to the exercise of eminent domain or to outright nationalisation. Owners may also face risks related to changes in internal norms that support the emergence of new de facto rights, for example, those that legitimise 'squatting' (Murtazashvili, 2013). High credibility of the persistence of property rights normally facilitates the efficient use of resources over time; the willingness of claimants to defer immediate consumption to allow investments that permit greater consumption in the future depends on it. Credibility of persistence is also undermined if the allocation is temporally uncertain: trespassers may be able to acquire de facto or even de jure property rights, especially in jurisdictions with weak or changing institutions (Besley, 1995).

The credibility of persistence of all organisational property rights, of course, is highly dependent on the broader political and institutional environment (North, 1990; Rodrik et al., 2004). Property rights are intrinsically less credible in North Korea, Venezuela and Argentina than in most other places, for reasons of regime, government, and history, respectively. However, even in more favourable institutional environments, the credibility that property rights of, and within, public agencies will persist depends on the stability of the political and legal environment. For example, in the recent *Tsilqot'in* case, the Supreme Court of Canada considerably expanded and strengthened the property rights of First Nations (aboriginal Canadians) to traditional lands surrounding their reserves, and weakened those of government agencies and those with subsurface resource exploitation property rights. Then, in 2017, the Court more clearly specified the limits of those property rights (*Ktunaxa Nation v. British Columbia*).

In stable institutional environments, civil service systems generally provide credibility to public employees that encourage them to invest in agency-specific human capital that may have low market value outside the agency context. A threat of organisational termination reduces the credibility of this commitment. In democratic political systems, there is always a risk of governmental change that can fundamentally alter attitudes toward organisational designs. The credibility of persistence of property rights in private sector firms generally depends on the strength of the rule of law and the stability of the regime that provides it. Strong rule of law in stable regimes provides credibility; either weak rule of law or an unstable regime undercuts it. To the extent that de facto property rights within an organisation depend on norms, the possibility of the norms changing, say because of changes in corporate culture, will undercut the credibility of persistence.

The credibility of persistence of property rights within a public–private hybrid is always somewhat uncertain because it ultimately depends on the commitment of the political master of the public owner, which may well vary with the ideological preferences of the government or governing party. Because of the ongoing potential for electoral turnover in democratic countries, these preferences are more variable than those of private owners seeking profit. In non-democratic countries, the preferences of governments over time can be even more unstable. In 2015, the Chinese government demonstrated that it was quite willing to manipulate property rights, including those of mixed enterprises on the Shanghai stock exchange, in the interests of (hoped-for) stock price stability. Credibility can also suffer, for example, when the private principals must rely on contract continuation or renewal by the political principals, as is often the case with public–private partnerships. Anticipation of the possibility of cancellation or non-renewal reduces the incentive of private managers to maintain assets as the closing date approaches. Private owners know that the government has the power to declare *force majeure* to void the contract during unfavourable circumstances, such as economic or fiscal crises. More mundanely, credibility may be undercut if the allocation of rights over time is not very clearly specified, or specified without attention to how changes in allocation should respond to changing circumstances.

Because specific kinds of hybrids tend to have specific ideological appeal (although for whom will vary with the type of hybrid), they are intrinsically quite vulnerable on the credibility of persistence dimension. If a right-of-centre government, for example, gains power it can relatively easily and quietly engage in mixed enterprise termination by selling its shares (Vining et al., 2014). If a left-of-centre government gains power, then it can eliminate an existing public–private partnership at low political cost by buying out the private owner at a premium. The credibility of persistence is also lowered (from the perspective of the public principals) if a private owner can exit the hybrid without substantial penalty. Private owners are usually able to abandon assets (liabilities) through bankruptcy if continued participation becomes unprofitable. The knowledge that terminating participation in this way is possible creates a moral hazard: private owners have incentives to encourage managers to make risky decisions with the expectation that they will profit from success but avoid the full costs of unfavourable outcomes. As we document later, such opportunistic behaviour has been common in public–private partnerships, especially where private owners have been allowed to use stand-alone subsidiaries to participate in the public–private partnership (Boardman and Vining, 2012).

Autonomy

The degree of autonomy measures the extent to which pertinent actors retain discretion within a property rights system (Vining and Weimer, 1998). In the context of organisational property rights (as opposed to individuals' property rights), autonomy has two facets: the autonomy of owners (from external actors) and the autonomy of managers (mostly from owners, but sometimes from external actors as well, especially where politics played a role in the selection and retention of managers). An assessment of owner autonomy considers the extent to which owners can actually exercise their property rights (reasonably) free from interference from external actors. Managerial autonomy refers to the opportunity that managers have to restructure property rights within their organisations without the *ex ante* consent of owners. Some level of managerial discretion is essential to organisational efficiency because efficiency requires that resource use be adjusted in response to changing environments. A reasonable level of managerial autonomy facilitates this strategic readjustment.

Within public agencies (at least in developed countries with good institutions), *ex ante* civil service rules and oversight agencies limit the autonomy of public managers over the use and reallocation of property rights. In contrast, managers of private sector firms are less constrained on a day-to-day basis. Nonetheless, a (too) high level of managerial autonomy in private sector firms creates its own problems. 'Hidden information' and 'hidden action' confront organisational designers with the problem of minimising 'the costs of structuring, monitoring, and bonding a set of contracts among agents with conflicting interests, plus the residual loss incurred because the cost of full enforcement of contract exceeds the benefits' (Jensen and Meckling, 1976, p. 305). Nonetheless, competition in firms' product markets (Alchian and Demsetz, 1972) and contestability of ownership of firms (De Alessi, 1983) both help to ensure that agency cost will be minimised, at least over time. The rise of activist investors and aggressive hedge funds demonstrates this reality (Brav et al., 2008). The market, then, tends to rely on *ex post* controls to limit inappropriate managerial discretion in the private sector. However, evidence suggests that firms with dispersed ownership (that is, high levels of ownership fractionalisation) experience greater degrees of agency loss because these *ex post* controls are somewhat less effective.

Is it likely that public–private hybrids occupy an intermediate position with respect to autonomy? An optimistic affirmative answer to this question seems to underlie the view of hybrids as offering the 'best of both worlds' (such as, for example, high profits and some valued social purpose). Although rarely addressed explicitly, holders of this view seem to be assuming that the level of managerial autonomy is about right in the public–private hybrid, or at least in the mixed enterprise version of it. In contrast, we postulate that it is likely that managers in hybrid organisations have greater de facto autonomy than do either their public or private sector counterparts. As argued earlier, a higher level of managerial autonomy arises primarily from the intrinsic lack of clarity of ownership that results from multiple owners with different goals. Only managers on the organisational ground are in a position to resolve goal tensions. Therefore, they have discretion in practice and considerable autonomy. Further, their autonomy is reinforced by the high cost of alienation and the weakened security from trespass associated with many kinds of hybrids. But discretion is likely to create its own problems for hybrid managers. They may well experience cognitive dissonance, also known as the problem of 'conflicting institutional logics' in the management and sociological literatures, as they manage owner expectations (Jay, 2013; Lee and Battilana, 2013; Pache and Santos, 2013). These problems are likely to be more severe in the public–private hybrid because of more severe goal divergence (Saz-Carranza and Longo, 2012).

APPLICATION TO COMMON PUBLIC–PRIVATE HYBRID ORGANISATIONAL FORMS

We apply the FPR framework to four common types of public–private hybrids. We consider these types in the order of systematic knowledge about their performance: mixed enterprises, public–private partnerships, government-sponsored enterprises, and government–nonprofit hybrids. Table 6.1 summarises the assessment.

Table 6.1   Property rights in common hybrid organisational forms

	Mixed enterprises	Public–private partnerships	Government-sponsored enterprises	Government–nonprofit hybrids
Degree of fragmentation of ownership	Depends on nature of government shares Fragmentation less relevant if 'profit collusion'	High fragmentation in terms of timing of effective ownership Goal conflict inherent	Asymmetric fragmentation: stockholders own positive financial residual but government can owns losses Goal conflict over risk	Degree of fragmentation varies depending on specific contract or charter Shared goals may reduce conflict
Clarity of allocation	High clarity if common share ownership; less clarity with special or golden shares	Lack of clarity in measurement of residual Lack of clarity resulting from long-term contract	Clear when profitable Unclear when unprofitable	Less clear the broader the scope of initial contract between principals or charter mandate
Cost of alienation	Low for public owner compared to pure public form; somewhat higher for private owner than pure private form	High for both public and private owners	Low for private owners High for public owners	High for nonprofit with resource dependence Potentially high for government because of lock-in
Security from trespass	Equivalent to private corporate form in same environments	Risk of shifting of costs to public principals	Government role creates moral hazard for private principals and hybrid managers	Generally high for established nonprofits with congruent missions
Credibility of persistence	Depends on government ability to change nature of shares	Risk of private owner bankruptcy Government initiated renegotiation	Risk of mission change Risk of change in government sponsorship	Risk of resource reductions from government partner
Autonomy	High autonomy for managers	Somewhat constrained by rules imposed by public principal	High autonomy for managers	Depends on specificity of charter

Mixed Enterprises

Mixed enterprises (MEs) are hybrids with some combination of public sector and private sector share ownership. MEs have been widespread and economically important in many developed countries, including the United Kingdom (UK), France and Canada (Boardman et al., 1986; Mazzolini, 1981). However, many of these governments engaged in extensive privatisations in the last decades of the 20th century. As a result, their economic importance decreased in these countries for a time. In contrast, many other countries, including rapidly growing ones such as Brazil, India, and China, have increasingly come to rely on MEs for state-related economic purposes, rather than on wholly owned state enterprises. MEs have also re-emerged in importance in developed countries, but often using complex pyramid ownership or involving local or regional governments rather than national governments (Bortolotti and Faccio, 2008).

Vining et al. (2014) identify and comprehensively analyse four distinct categories of ME that have now become common. Here we focus on the classic ME form in which a government owns shares in a domestic firm. Because ownership share in the classic ME is allocated by the percentage of shares owned, this form is relatively transparent compared to other public–private hybrids on most dimensions, including the nature and extent of ownership fragmentation. Ownership rights are clearly allocated when all parties hold common stock. However, government-owned shares with special privileges tend to reduce the clarity of allocation. Government has lower cost for alienating its ownership than it would in disposing of the assets of a state-owned enterprise or an agency. If government shares have no special privileges, then alienation by private owners should be low-cost; any controls on trading implied by special privileges of government shares ('golden shares') would raise the cost of alienation for private owners.

Managers generally enjoy a considerable degree of day-to-day autonomy. Indeed, it is this autonomy that potentially creates the opportunity for efficiency relative to state-owned enterprises or direct government provision, effectively substituting *ex post* monitoring for *ex ante* rules. Provided the stock of an ME is publicly traded, the share price is public, and changes to it over time should transparently capitalise into managerial behaviour with respect to profit. Managerial autonomy may be reduced if one principal, usually the government owner, dominates share ownership. Nonetheless, where managers do have discretion, they may well experience cognitive dissonance as they attempt to reconcile the goal differences of public and private owners (Vining et al., 2014; Vining and Weimer, 2016). In stock markets in developed countries, stock price changes of MEs quickly reveal changes in managerial behaviour, whether toward or away from profit maximisation. This is a major reason why researchers know quite a lot about their behaviour and performance. Thus, the manner in which managers try to resolve the cognitive dissonance or conflicting logics will also be transparent.

Although it is not universally the case, the aggregate evidence does suggest that MEs do exhibit a greater profit orientation, including a greater focus on cost-efficiency, when compared to state-owned enterprises (Vining et al., 2014; Vining and Weimer, 2016; Wolf and Pollitt, 2009). Vining et al. (2014) conclude that this emphasis on cost and profit is best characterised as resulting in a 'profit collusion world' rather than the 'best of both worlds' that their optimistic designers claimed, or the 'worst of both worlds' as some more sceptical commentators have argued.

Why might a profit collusion world outcome that focuses on joint profit maximisation not be equivalent to a 'best of both worlds' world? We have argued that a profit collusion world would likely be a relatively stable and sustainable outcome that satisfies both private and public principals. However, the best normative rationale for public sector principals to participate in a public–private hybrid is when it is the best, or at least the only practical, way to nudge an organisation towards some social purpose (Vining and Moore, 2017), even if only to the extent that the public principal requires some constraint on the extent of profit maximisation. Unless this is the case, public principals can increase revenue by simply taxing and regulating private sector organisations, and then use the tax receipts to achieve their public purposes. Private sector principals inevitably put much greater pressure on hybrid managers to focus on profitability, regardless of whether this involves the exercise of any monopoly pricing power. However, success at monopoly pricing (that is, pricing above social marginal cost) is not the appropriate way to judge the social value of public–private hybrid organisations (Vining, 2011). (Pricing below social marginal cost is also inefficient as it results in the waste of scarce resources; however, private principals can be relied upon to discourage any tendency in that direction.) Nonetheless, many governments participating in public–private hybrids can easily fall prey to a tendency to regard profit increases as 'better performance'. Thus, many governments in practice treat the profit collusion world as being equivalent to an ideal world.

Public–Private Partnerships

The 'public–private partnership' (PPP) label covers many different organisational forms (Hodge and Greve, 2007). The number of PPPs has grown enormously in many countries over the past 30 years (Hodge et al., 2011). The canonical PPP is a long-term infrastructure contract in which a private sector corporation or consortium finances, designs, builds, operates, and maintains some infrastructure ultimately owned by the public sector. The infrastructure might be a highway, bridge, water treatment plant or hospital. Ownership of the infrastructure ultimately reverts to the contracting government, but often only after an extensive concessionary period (for example, 30 years). The financing activity is usually central to a PPP, but the other contracted activities vary enormously. Thus, for example, a PPP might entail only private sector financing or the design and building of some facility as well. In exchange for providing the finance and other services, the private sector consortium receives a stream of payments, sometimes based on tolling, sometimes linked to usage levels (or output), or 'shadow tolling', but sometimes not.

Although the PPP asset reverts to and is ultimately owned by the government, the private partner has either a preliminary formal ownership or a bundle of use rights that effectively create ownership for an extended time period. Thus, fragmentation of ownership is sequential rather simultaneous. During the period that the private partner enjoys use rights, numerous aspects of the allocation of property rights can be unclear (Vega 2013–14). One reason is that the language of many actual PPP contracts still allocates some important property rights to the public owner during the period of private control. Another reason lies in the difficulty of anticipating many contingencies over a decades-long contract period. Further, even in contracts that spell out returns to the partners on financial residuals (profits), there will still often be ambiguity in how the financial residual is to be measured, especially in assigning costs to the use of long-lived assets.

Long-term contracts that restrict the future actions of the partners generally make the cost of alienation high for all partners. The less specific the restrictions, the more opportunity for either party to trespass on the other. This could emerge through actions such as the private partner shifting costs to public assets, or the public partner requiring the private party to provide services not explicitly set out in the original contract. The greatest threat to the credibility of persistence is the opportunity for the private partner to declare bankruptcy if the contract becomes unprofitable.

In spite of the partnership language, goal tension between owners is often stark: the government is, or should be, interested in cost (price) minimisation; while the private participant is interested in profit maximisation. Nonetheless, we postulate that PPPs usually do not result in as much managerial autonomy as is found in MEs. First, in most PPPs managers are closely monitored by private sector principals and may anticipate returning to work for them directly. Second, most PPP contracts clearly bestow managerial authority on agents of the private owners, as the private owners bring both capital and technical expertise. Therefore, managers who perceive themselves as working for the private owners will focus on private owner profits, and are likely to exhibit somewhat lower levels of dissonance. However, along with private owners, PPP managers are likely to be in conflict with public owners.

Considerable evidence has accumulated showing high rates of renegotiation of PPP contract terms, a likely indicator of tensions arising from fractionalised property rights. Drawing on a variety of studies, Estache and Saussier (2014), for example, find renegotiation rates ranging from 40 per cent for highway projects in the United States to 92 per cent for water projects in Latin America and the Caribbean. Of course, governments cannot credibly commit future governments, so renegotiation could also result from governments' opportunistic *ex post* alteration of property right allocations.

A great deal of evidence suggests that tension over goals has led to opportunistic bankruptcies or other behaviour (such as repeatedly raising tolls) that have forced governments to buy out private partners. Studies that document these kinds of tensions include Acerete et al. (2009, 2011), Reeves (2008), Vining and Boardman (2008a), Boardman and Vining (2012), Bloomfield (2006), Hodge (2005), Johnston (2010), Beh (2010), Bharti and Ganesh (2010), Dagdeviran (2011), Hayllar (2010), Jarvis (2010), Turhani (2013), Mouraviev et al. (2012), Jooste and Scott (2012) and Estache (2006). Based, for example, on their assessment of PPP arrangements for infrastructure investment in the water, waste, transportation, and education sectors in Portugal, da Cruz and Marques (2012, p. 737) conclude that: 'the extreme complexity involved in the whole life-cycle management of these companies usually leads to a poor protection of the public interest'. (For further evidence, see Boardman and Vining, 2012.)

We pick one major PPP to illustrate some of the conflict, confusion, and failure created by lack of clarity of property right allocations (although we could pick many others). Metronet was a £15.7 billion PPP signed in 2003 that was championed by the then UK Chancellor of the Exchequer, Gordon Brown, who subsequently became Prime Minister. Metronet was one of the largest rail infrastructure projects in the world until it collapsed into bankruptcy in 2007. It was meant to refurbish and expand a significant part of the London Underground rail system. Its failure illustrates almost all of the dimensions of property rights problems (see Vining and Boardman, 2008b; Juppe, 2009; Ricketts, 2009; Currie and Teague, 2015). Goal conflict emerged almost immediately when the public and private parties disagreed on the fundamental allocation of property rights: the government acted as if it had purchased an output-based fixed-price contract, while the private sector consortium acted as though it had agreed to a series of heterogeneous, cost-plus contracts. The lack of clarity of property rights also included vagueness, and ultimate disagreement, on the extent of risk transfer (who was responsible for negative fiscal residuals). Not only was most risk not transferred to the private owners, but the risk that was transferred quickly ended up in the hands of very widely dispersed debt-holders. This is a quite common outcome in PPPs (Estache et al., 2007). In aggregate, these factors opened up the PPP to endemic opportunism. As a result, private principals probably made money in the end in spite of Metronet's bankruptcy.

At least in the United Kingdom (although as a result of costly experience), the importance of having an *ex ante* agreement on the distribution of risks is now recognised. Since 2007 the Treasury has required that extensive 'risk matrices' that attempt to identify all possible risks (and the responsibilities for bearing them) be appended to PPP contracts (Iossa and Martimort, 2014). Of course, the more complex and the longer the time horizon of the project—factors that typically make the PPP politically more attractive—the less likely it is that all important risks will be anticipated and included in its risk matrix.

Government-Sponsored Enterprises

The government-sponsored enterprise (GSE) is a stockholder-owned organisation created by government to promote a public purpose (Muslof and Seidman, 1980; Perry and Rainey, 1988; Stanton, 2007). The most notable, if not notorious, GSEs in the US are the Federal National Mortgage Association (Fannie Mae) and the Federal Home Loan Mortgage Corporation (Freddie Mac). They originated during the Great Depression as government enterprises created to promote liquidity in housing markets, but were converted to hybrids in 1970 when Congress required the sale of their assets to private investors through the issuing of common stock. With ownership by private shareholders, the boundaries of these public goals became opaque. To foster the public goals, their features included lines of credit with the federal Treasury, an implicit (and actually realised) federal guarantee of their securities, exclusion from many regulations that apply to private firms, and appointment of a minority of members of their boards of directors by the President.

The fractionalisation of ownership in financial GSEs such as Fannie Mae, Freddie Mac, and the Farm Credit System gives ownership of profits to the private owners, and ownership of losses to the government, creating an asymmetric relationship in risk-sharing (Jensen, 2000). During periods of profitability, the corporate form clearly allocates rights to the private owners. However, as government guarantees may not be explicit but rather arise from the GSE being 'too big to fail', the allocation of rights (now duties) during periods of unprofitability are much less clear. Private owners face low costs of alienation, but—again because of the problem of being 'too big to fail'—government owners face high costs of alienation. Government alienation may also be high if private owners engage in political activity to protect their asymmetric ownership rights. Managers have a high degree of autonomy, both because of an arm's-length relationship with government and because the asymmetric ownership rights give private owners little incentive to monitor managers. Both managerial autonomy and asymmetry in ownership incentives create a moral hazard with respect to risk-taking. It also may enable managers to shift the mission of the GSE in response to changing market conditions.

The history of Fannie Mae and Freddie Mac illustrates the consequences of managerial autonomy and asymmetric ownership rights or duties. They initially purchased and held mortgages originated by local banks but later began securitising portfolios of mortgages that were sold to investors internationally. During the 1990s, however, they began to face competition from private firms in the securitising of mortgages. Although managers did maintain standards on mortgage origination to minimise default risk even into the mid-2000s, pressure from stockholders led them to increase the volume of mortgages securitised and to relax loan standards (Boyack, 2011). Managerial remuneration tended to follow loan volume, so managers had little incentive to resist something that was in their interest and which seemed congruent with the fairly vague public purpose of promoting housing market liquidity. The perception of a government guarantee for Fannie Mae and Freddie Mac securities, of course, contributed to their sales even amid growing concerns about the quality of the mortgages included in the securitised portfolios.

The federal guarantee for Fannie Mae and Freddie Mac, credible because they were 'too big to fail', created a moral hazard that encouraged managers to take on risk that was beneficial to them, but not to the government (Verret, 2010). Moreover, government 'owners' were so diffuse and disparate that this form of moral hazard was almost inevitable. The federal government ended up with a property right to a liability. Koppell (2001) argues that the 'too big to fail' syndrome was buttressed by opportunistic managers and directors. These GSEs enjoyed the political advantages of being perceived as both public and private organisations. Indeed, they were more politically influential than if they were either fully private or fully public. On the private side, they had financial resources that they used to fund contributions to important congressional committee members, they pointed to constituent-valued business that they conducted in every congressional district, they used loyal allies in the housing sector, and they had a centrality in the network of organisations involved in housing finance. On the public side, they emphasised their widely valued public mission and (comparable to a federal agency) substantive expertise. The result was a financial failure that required a substantial government bailout.

Government–Nonprofit Hybrids

Governments become entwined with nonprofit organisations in a variety of ways. Most directly, governments sometimes create nonprofit organisations to serve specific public purposes. For example, the US Congress created the National Academy of Sciences during the American Civil War to provide expertise in support of the war effort. More commonly, governments contract with nonprofit organisations for the provision of specific social services that replace or supplement those services provided by public agencies. Also, increasingly, governments can foster and join networks of nonprofit organisations sharing common goals that can be promoted through coordinated efforts. When do these types of relationships cross some threshold, such that a network is more usefully viewed as a hybrid organisation?

No established definition provides a clear basis for determining when a government–nonprofit arrangement crosses the threshold to becoming a hybrid organisation. Especially in light of the ubiquity of government contracting with nonprofits, and the increasingly common formation of networks aimed at coordinating the provision of social services, a restrictive definition seems necessary to make government–nonprofit coordination an analytically meaningful form of public–private hybrid. We propose defining government–nonprofit hybrids as only encompassing those arrangements in which there is joint governance of the use of resources by the various owners.

With respect to nonprofits with government charters, this definition would exclude organisations such as the National Academies in the United States, which interact with the federal government primarily by performing narrowly defined contract work. Marginal cases include charter nonprofits that receive funding from a government but with few strings attached, such as the National Bureau of Economic Research in the United States, or nonprofits that raise significant resources to supplement government operations, or what Smith (2010) calls 'affiliated foundations'. A clearer case is the Organ Procurement and Transplantation Network (OPTN) in the United States, which received a charter from Congress and operates under oversight by the Department of Health and Human Services to develop the content of rules for the allocation of transplant organs (Weimer, 2010). In many countries, government bureaus contract with nonprofit organisations (as well as for-profit firms) for the delivery of social services. These kinds of contractual arrangements effectively become hybrid organisations by our definition when they embed strong 'relational contracts'. Relational contracts are characterised by mutual dependence that creates an expectation of a continuing relationship, typically because the government partner comes to rely on expertise provided by the nonprofit partner that would be difficult to replace quickly, and the nonprofit partner receives a majority of its funding from the government partner that would also be difficult to replace quickly. For example, a bureau may rely on a single nonprofit to deliver services to a minority population that it would otherwise find difficult to reach (Andrews and Entwistle, 2010).

The degree of fragmentation of ownership depends on the specifics of the charter mandate or contractual relationship. Hybrids with charters may have goals that deviate from those of their founding governments. For example, the OPTN as created by the US Congress requires all transplant centres to be members in good standing. However, the members have at times held different preferences for the extent of geographic sharing of donated transplant organs that guaranteed some segment of the membership would be in disagreement with the preferences of the Department of Health and Human Services (Weimer, 2007). In relational contracts, the mission of the nonprofit and the multiple goals of the government partner, that typically include cost containment, may conflict. In general, the broader the scope of the charter or contract, the more likely it is that the allocation of the fractionalised property rights will be unclear.

The cost of alienation is likely to be high for a number of reasons. The nonprofit partner may not have alternative sources of funding and may not dissolve as easily as a for-profit firm through bankruptcy; or, in the case of charter nonprofits, it may not have authority to dissolve. It may also develop specific assets for the hybrid relationship that do not have much value outside the relationship. The cost to government of changing the relationship is also high if an alternative partner with sufficient expertise is not readily available.

Their advantage in expertise and tacit knowledge will generally protect the nonprofit partner from trespass; these same advantages create an opportunity to divert resources toward its own mission. However, the possibility of the government partner reducing resource contributions does reduce the credibility of persistence for the nonprofit partner.

These reductions may occur for a variety of reasons, such as reductions during periods of fiscal stress, change in the leadership of the government partner, or even a perception that the problem motivating the relationship has been solved.

The autonomy of managers depends on the degree of delegation of authority to them in charters of nonprofits, or the degree of feasible oversight by the government partner in contractual hybrids. As heavy reliance on government contracts generally appears to pose a risk to the identity of nonprofits (Smith and Lipsky, 1993), it is reasonable to expect that goal tensions would likely drive managers toward emphasising those organisational goals that align most closely with those of the government sponsor.

CONCLUSION: AVOIDING THE WORST OF BOTH WORLDS

When considering the consequences of organisational property rights, the devil really is in the details. We believe that the FPR framework presents the most important dimensions of property rights for assessing and predicting the performance of public–private hybrids. Most importantly, the nature of the fractionalisation of rights, and the clarity with which the rights of the public and private owners are specified, fundamentally affect organisational performance, especially when the partners have very different goals. The challenge to performance is likely to be greatest for PPPs or GSEs, where pursuit of private profit is most likely to conflict fundamentally with public goals. Goal conflicts tend to be less severe in MEs if the public partner also favours a profit goal, or in government–nonprofit hybrids if the nonprofit broadly shares the public goal. Nonetheless, all four forms of public–private hybrids risk some goal conflict for which managers often provide a de facto resolution by adopting one or the other goal as dominant.

Do we have any advice to offer organisational designers? Yes: be wary of hybrid designs that fractionalise property rights across the public and private sectors. In view of the inherent problems, one would want to have clearly explained reasons for such hybridisation. Where these reasons do exist, recognise that managers will face dissonance and must be given discretion to address and resolve it. Be prepared to specify who has property rights *ex ante* in great detail; inability to do so for either technical or political reasons should raise a red flag about future dangers. The six dimensions of property rights we set out provide a starting point for getting the details right.

REFERENCES

Acerete, B., J. Shaoul and A. Stafford (2009) Taking Its Toll: The Private Financing of Roads in Spain. *Public Money and Management* 29(1), 19–26.
Acerete, B., A. Stafford and P. Stapleton (2011) Spanish Healthcare Public Private Partnerships: The 'Alzira Model'. *Critical Perspectives on Accounting* 22(6), 533–549.
Adams, J. (1996) Principals and Agents, Colonialists and Company Men: The Decay of Colonial Control in the Dutch East Indies. *American Sociological Review* 61(1), 12–28.
Alchian, A. and H. Demsetz (1972) Production, Information Costs, and Economic Organization. *American Economic Review* 62(5), 777–795.
Anderson, G.M. and R.D. Tollison (1982) Adam Smith's Analysis of Joint-Stock Companies. *Journal of Political Economy* 90(6), 1237–1256.
Andrews, R. and T. Entwistle (2010) Does Cross-Sectoral Partnership Deliver? An Empirical Exploration of

Public Service Effectiveness, Efficiency, and Equity. *Journal of Public Administration Research and Theory* 20(3), 679–701.

Araral, E., Jr (2009) What Explains Collective Action in the Commons? Theory and Evidence from the Philippines. *World Development* 37(3), 687–697.

Austin, J., H. Stevenson and J. Wei-Skillern (2006) Social and Commercial Entrepreneurship: Same, Different, or Both? *Entrepreneurship Theory and Practice* 30(1), 1–22.

Barlow, J., J. Roehrich and S. Wright (2013) Europe Sees Mixed Results from Public–Private Partnerships for Building and Managing Health Care Facilities and Services. *Health Affairs* 32(1), 146–154.

Barzel, Y. (1989) *Economic Analysis of Property Rights.* Cambridge: Cambridge University Press.

Battilana, J. and S. Dorado (2010) Building Sustainable Hybrid Organizations: The Case of Commercial Microfinance Organizations. *Academy of Management Journal* 53(6), 1419–1440.

Baumol, W.J. (1990) Entrepreneurship: Productive, Unproductive, and Destructive. *Journal of Political Economy* 89(5 Pt 1), 893–921.

Beh, L.-S. (2010) Development and Distortion of Malaysian Public–Private Partnerships: Patronage, Privatised Profits and Pitfalls. *Australian Journal of Public Administration* 69(s1), S74–S84.

Berle, A.A. and G.G.C. Means (1932) *The Modern Corporation and Private Property.* New York: Transaction Books.

Besley, T. (1995) Property Rights and Investment Incentives: Theory and Evidence from Ghana. *Journal of Political Economy* 103(5), 903–937.

Bharti, N. and G. Ganesh (2010) Public–Private Partnerships in India's Urban Water Public Utilities: A Case of Sonia Vihar Water Project. *Journal of Management and Public Policy* 1(2), 63–73.

Bloomfield, P. (2006) The Challenging Business of Long-Term Public–Private Partnerships: Reflections on Local Experience. *Public Administration Review* 66(3), 400–411.

Boardman, A., C. Eckel and A. Vining (1986) The Advantages and Disadvantages of Mixed Enterprises. In A. Negandhi, H. Thomas and K.L.K. Rao (eds), *Multinational Corporations and State-Owned Enterprises: A New Challenge*, Vol. 1 of *Research in International Business and International Relations*. Greenwich, CT: JAI Press, pp. 221–244.

Boardman, A.E. and A.R. Vining (2012) The Political Economy of Public–Private Partnerships and Analysis of Their Social Value. *Annals of Public and Cooperative Economics* 83(2), 117–141.

Boardman, A.E., A.R. Vining and D.L. Weimer (2016) The Long-Run Effects of Privatization on Productivity: Evidence from Canada. *Journal of Policy Modeling* 38(6), 1001–1017.

Bortolotti, B. and M. Faccio (2008) Government Control of Privatized Firms. *Review of Financial Studies* 22(8), 2907–2939.

Boyack, A.J. (2011) Laudable Goals and Unintended Consequences: The Role and Control of Fannie Mae and Freddie. *American University Law Review* 60(5), 1489–1560.

Brav, A., W. Jiang, F. Partnoy and R. Thomas (2008) Hedge Fund Activism, Corporate Governance, and Firm Performance. *Journal of Finance* 63(4), 1729–1775.

Campos, N.F. and F. Giovannoni (2006) The Determinants of Asset Stripping: Theory and Evidence from the Transition Economies. *Journal of Law and Economics* 49(2), 681–706.

Cooley, A. and H. Spruyt (2009) *Contracting States: Sovereign Transfers in International Relations.* Princeton, NJ: Princeton University Press.

Currie, D. and P. Teague (2015) Conflict Management in Public–Private Partnerships: The Case of the London Underground. *Negotiation Journal* 31(3), 237–266.

da Cruz, N.F. and R.C. Marques (2012) Mixed Companies and Local Governance: No Man Can Serve Two Masters. *Public Administration* 90(3), 737–758.

Dagdeviran, H. (2011) Political Economy of Contractual Disputes in Private Water and Sanitation: Lessons from Argentina. *Annals of Public and Cooperative Economics* 82(1), 25–44.

De Alessi, L. (1983) Property Rights, Transaction Costs, and X-Efficiency. *American Economic Review* 73(1), 64–81.

DiMaggio, P.J. and W.W. Powell (1983) The Iron Cage Revisited: Collective Rationality and Institutional Isomorphism in Organizational Fields. *American Sociological Review* 48(2), 147–160.

Eckel, C. and A.R. Vining (1985) Elements of a Theory of Mixed Enterprise. *Scottish Journal of Political Economy* 32(1), 82–94.

Estache, A. (2006) PPI Partnerships vs. PPI Divorces in LDCs. *Review of Industrial Organization* 29(1/2), 3–26.

Estache, A. and S. Saussier (2014) Public–Private Partnerships and Efficiency: A Short Assessment. *Journal of Institutional Comparisons* 12(3), 8–13.

Estache, A., E. Juan and L. Trujillo (2007) Public–Private Partnerships in Transport. Policy Research Working Paper, 4436, World Bank.

Fiol, C.M., M.G. Pratt and E.J. O'Connor (2009) Managing Intractable Identity Conflicts. *Academy of Management Review* 34(1), 32–55.

Furubotn, E. and D. Pejovich (1972) Property Rights and Economic Theory: A Survey of Recent Literature. *Journal of Economic Literature* 10(4), 1137–1162.

Glynn, M.A. (2000) When Cymbals Become Symbols: Conflict Over Organizational Identity Within a Symphony Orchestra. *Organization Science* 11(3), 285–298.

Hanke, S.H. (1987) Privatization and Nationalization. *Proceedings of the Academy of Political Science* 36(3), 1–3.

Hayllar, M. (2010) Public–Private Partnerships in Hong Kong: Good Governance – The Missing Ingredient? *Australian Journal of Public Administration* 69(s1), S99–S119.

Hodge, G. (2005) Public–Private Partnerships: The Australian Experience with Physical Infrastructure. In G. Hodge and C. Greve (eds), *The Challenge of Public–Private Partnerships: Learning from International Experience*. Cheltenham, UK and Northampton, MA, USA: Edward Elgar Publishing, pp. 305–331.

Hodge, G. and C. Greve (2007) Public Private Partnerships: An International Performance Review *Public Administration Review* 67(3), 545–558.

Hodge, G., C. Greve and A.E. Boardman (eds) (2011) *International Handbook of Public-Private Partnerships*. Cheltenham, UK and Northampton, MA, USA: Edward Elgar Publishing.

Iossa, E. and D. Martimort (2014) Corruption in Public–Private Partnerships, Incentives and Contract Incompleteness. *Journal of Institutional Comparisons* 12(3), 14–16.

Jarvis, D.S.L. (2010) Institutional Processes and Regulatory Risks: A Case Study of the Thai Energy Sector. *Regulation and Governance* 4(2), 175–202.

Jay, J. (2013) Navigating Paradox as a Mechanism of Change and Innovation in Hybrid Organizations. *Academy of Management Journal* 56(1), 137–159.

Jensen, F.E. (2000) The Farm Credit System as a Government-Sponsored Enterprise. *Review of Agricultural Economics* 22(2), 326–338.

Jensen, M. and W. Meckling (1976) Theory of the Firm: Managerial Behavior, Agency Costs and Ownership Structure. *Journal of Financial Economics* 3(4), 305–360.

Johnson, R.N. and G.D. Libecap (1989) Bureaucratic Rules, Supervisor Behavior, and the Effect of Salaries in the Federal Government. *Journal of Law Economics and Organization* 5(1), 53–82.

Johnston, J. (2010) Examining 'Tunnel Vision' in Australian PPPs: Rationales, Rhetoric, Risks and 'Rogues'. *Australian Journal of Public Administration* 69(s1), S61–S73.

Jooste, S.F. and W.R. Scott (2012) The Public–Private Partnership Enabling Field: Evidence From Three Cases. *Administration and Society* 44(2), 149–182.

Juppe, R. (2009) New Labour, Public–Private Partnerships and Rail Transport Policy. *Economic Affairs* 29(1), 20–25.

Knack, S. and P. Keefer (1995) Institutions and Economic Performance: Cross Country Tests Using Alternative Institutional Measures. *Economics and Politics* 7(3), 207–227.

Koppell, J.G.S. (2001) Hybrid Organizations and the Alignment of Interests: The Case of Fannie Mae and Freddie Mac. *Public Administration Review* 61(4), 468–481.

Kraatz, M.S. and E.S. Block (2008) Organizational Implications of Institutional Pluralism. In R. Greenwood, C. Oliver, R. Suddaby and K. Sahlin-Andersson (eds), *Handbook of Organizational Institutionalism*. London: SAGE Publications, pp. 243–275.

La Porta, R., F. Lopez-de-Silanes and A. Shleifer (1999) Corporate Ownership Around the World. *Journal of Finance* 54(2), 471–517.

Lee, M. and J. Battilana (2013) How the Zebra Got Its Stripes: Imprinting of Individuals and Hybrid Social Ventures. Harvard Business School Working Paper, July 9.

Mazzolini, R. (1981) Strategic Decisions in Government-Controlled Enterprises. *Administration and Society* 13(1), 7–31.

Mouraviev, N., N. Kakabadse and I. Robinson (2012) Concessionary Nature of Public–Private Partnerships in Russia and Kazakhstan: A Critical Review. *International Journal of Public Administration* 35(6), 410–420.

Murtazashvili, I. (2013) *The Political Economy of the American Frontier*. New York: Cambridge University Press.

Muslof, L.D. and H. Seidman (1980) The Blurred Boundaries of Public Administration. *Public Administration Review* 40(2), 124–130.

North, D. (1990) *Institutions, Institutional Change, and Economic Performance*. New York: Cambridge University Press.

Ostrom, E. (1990). *Governing the Commons: The Evolution of Institutions for Collective Action*. New York: Cambridge University Press.

Pache A.C. and F. Santos (2010) When Worlds Collide: The Internal Dynamics of Organizational Responses to Conflicting Institutional Demands. *Academy of Management Review* 35, 455–476.

Pache, A.C. and F. Santos (2013) Embedded in Hybrid Contexts: How Individuals in Organizations Respond to Competing Institutional Logics. *Research in the Sociology of Organizations* 39, 3–35.

Pargendler, M., A. Musacchio and S.G. Lazzarini (2013) In Strange Company: The Puzzle of Private Investment in State-Controlled Firms. *Cornell International Law Journal* 46(3), 569–610.

Perry, J.L. and H.G. Rainey (1988) The Public–Private Distinction in Organization Theory: A Critique and Research. *Academy of Management Review* 13(2), 182–201.

Reeves, E. (2008) The Practice of Contracting in Public–Private Partnerships: Transaction Costs and Relational Contracting in the Irish Schools Sector. *Public Administration* 86(4), 969–986.

Ricketts, M. (2009) The Use of Contracts by Governments and Its Agents. *Economic Affairs* 29(1), 7–12.

Riker W.H. and D.L. Weimer (1993) The Economic and Political Liberalization of Socialism: The Fundamental Problem of Property Rights. *Social Philosophy and Policy* 10(2), 79–102.

Rodrik, D., A. Subramanian and F. Trebbi (2004) Institutions Rule: The Primacy of Institutions over Geography and Integration in Economic Development. *Journal of Economic Growth* 9(2), 131–165.

Saz-Carranza, A. and F. Longo (2012) Managing Competing Institutional Logics in Public–Private Joint Ventures. *Public Management Review* 14(3), 331–357.

Smith, S.R. (2010) Hybridization and Nonprofit Organizations: The Governance Challenge. *Policy and Society* 29(3), 219–229.

Smith, S.R. and M. Lipsky (1993) *Nonprofits for Hire: Welfare State in the Age of Contracting*. Cambridge, MA: Harvard University Press.

Stanton, T.H. (2007) The Life Cycle of the Government-Sponsored Enterprise: Lessons for Design and Accountability. *Public Administration Review* 67(5), 837–845.

Stigler, G.J. and C. Friedland (1983) The Literature of Economics: The Case of Berle and Means. *Journal of Law and Economics* 26(2), 237–268.

Turhani, A. (2013) Governance of Public–Private Partnerships: Lessons Learned from an Albanian Case. *Journal for East European Management Studies* 18(3), 371–385.

Vega, A. (2013–14) Eurostat, Soft Law and the Measurement of Public Debt: The Case of Public–Private Partnerships. *European Journal of Legal Studies* 6(2), 96–118.

Verret J.W. (2010) Treasury Inc.: How the Bailout Reshapes Corporate Theory and Practice. *Yale Journal on Regulation* 27(2), 283–350.

Vining, A.R. (2011) Public Agency External Analysis Using a Modified 'Five Forces' Framework. *International Public Management Journal* 14(1), 63–105.

Vining, A.R. and A.E. Boardman (2008a) Public–Private Partnerships: Eight Rules for Government. *Public Works Management and Policy* 13(2), 149–161.

Vining, A.R. and A.E. Boardman (2008b) Public–Private Partnerships in Canada: Theory and Evidence. *Canadian Public Administration* 51(1), 9–44.

Vining, A.R. and M.A. Moore (2017) Potash Ownership and Extraction: Between a Rock and a Hard Place in Saskatchewan. *Resources Policy* 54(December), 71–80.

Vining, A.R. and D.L. Weimer (1998) Informing Institutional Design: Strategies for Comparative Cumulation. *Journal of Comparative Policy Analysis* 1(1), 39–60.

Vining, A.R. and D.L. Weimer (1999) Inefficiency in Public Organizations. *International Public Management Journal* 2(1), 1–24.

Vining, A.R. and D.L. Weimer (2016) The Challenges of Fractionalized Property Rights in Public–Private Hybrid Organizations: The Good, the Bad, and the Ugly. *Regulation and Governance* 10(2), 161–178.

Vining, A.R. and D.L. Weimer (2017) Adam Smith Was Skeptical of Hybrids – Should We Be Less So? *Public Money and Management* 37(6), 387–389.

Vining, A.R., A.E. Boardman and M.A. Moore (2014) The Theory and Evidence Pertaining to Local Government Mixed Enterprises. *Annals of Public and Cooperative Economics* 85(1), 53–86.

Weimer, D.L. (1980) Federal Intervention in the Process of Innovation in Local Public Agencies: A Focus on Organizational Incentives. *Public Policy* 28(1), 83–116.

Weimer, D.L. (2007) Public and Private Regulation of Organ Transplantation: Liver Allocation and the Final Rule. *Journal of Health Politics, Policy and Law* 32(1), 9–49.

Weimer, D.L. (2010) *Medical Governance: Values, Expertise, and Interests in Organ Transplantation*. Washington, DC: Georgetown University Press.

Wolf, C. and M. Pollitt (2009) The Welfare Implications of Oil Privatization: A Cost–Benefit Analysis of Norway's Statoil', EPRG Working Paper #EPRG0905 and Cambridge Working Paper in Economics #0912.

7. Hybridity and research organisations
Magnus Gulbrandsen and Taran Thune

INTRODUCTION

This chapter discusses hybridity and hybrid organisations within research and innovation. Although this might represent a context in which hybrid organisations are prevalent, there have been few investigations and cases from research organisations, scientific work and science policy in the broader literature on hybrid organisations (Rainey and Bozeman, 2000; Gulbrandsen et al., 2015). Hybridity is not, however, a new concept in the literature on research organisations. It has been used to understand complex, contested and often temporary organisational set-ups that have often aimed to bring public research and development (R&D) closer to the needs and demands of industry and society. The emergence of new organisational structures that straddle established boundaries is partly related to internal developments within the scientific enterprise itself, where intellectual and organisational boundaries may be crossed in the pursuit and application of new knowledge (Gieryn, 1983).

We can draw a distinction between two broad kinds of research organisation: universities and research institutes. We use the term 'universities' for higher education institutions – including specialised and regional colleges – that conduct research and teaching. Research institutes are organisations that have research and development as a main activity, whose funding is most often predominantly public, and which are not part of the higher education system. Formally, universities and institutes may be private (mostly non-profit) or public but universities and research institutes have often defined themselves as part of a separate sector – the research and higher education sector, or academia – distinct from industry and also quite different in some respects from the public sector.

Both types of organisation have experienced changed expectations and policies, and they have responded with a range of new organisational arrangements that work to combine research with innovation and commercialisation. In this chapter we argue that this represents a trend to hybridisation that has accelerated and is increasingly fostered by policies aiming for research to solve societal grand challenges and to contribute to economic growth. Rather than looking at hybridisation within the scientific realm in general, we will discuss specific forms of research organisation that mix private and public sector elements or are set up as collaborations between private and public organisations. From this point of view we aim to address several important questions: what happens in organisations that are set up to combine goals of furthering scientific knowledge and at the same time exploit this knowledge commercially? How are such units organised and managed? Do they develop into profoundly hybrid organisations or are these organisations only 'shallow' hybrids (Billis, 2010)?

To answer these questions we examine three kinds of organisations. First, we look at how public science is moved into the private market, and at the technology transfer offices that are established to facilitate this exchange. Second, we address research organisations that are set up as collaborations between public research organisations and private firms: collaborative research centres. Finally, we look at public research organisations that are established to serve a private market, so-called contract research organisations.

In these settings hybridity is an outcome of the combination of public (or non-profit) and private (for-profit) sectors in specific organisational arrangements. It is also the result of the combination of research-based activities with activities connected to the use of research results in order to facilitate innovation or other forms of impact of research. Hybridity in research can be seen as multi-layered and particularly complex. It not only entails a public–private dimension but also highlights a number of other dimensions of hybridity including knowledge, intellectual property rights and ownership, and norms and practices in research and development activities. Before discussing the three different kinds of organisational set-ups for achieving integration between private and public goals, we will define some of the key terms and discuss at a more general level what hybridity in research might involve.

HYBRID ORGANISATIONS AND RESEARCH[1]

Hybridity and Tensions

'Hybridity' is a term used for a variety of organisational arrangements that are typically found at the intersection of very different organisations or societal spheres such as public and private sectors, and for-profit and not-for-profit domains (Borys and Jemison, 1989; Williamson, 1991; Ménard, 2004). Most hybrid organisations strive to combine or balance different sectoral or institutional logics in a way that may solve complex societal problems and realise new ideals of governance and public administration (de Boer et al., 2007; Battilana and Dorado, 2010; Capano, 2011). Often the idea is to infuse public sector-related organisations with aspects of the private sector that are seen as important for effectiveness and efficiency. This is an important feature in university–industry relations and other research-related hybrids but is not the only rationale for hybridity. It is also driven by an assumption that the creativity and radical solutions associated with public research organisations can be implemented in private firms.

Hybridity has become a key term in discussions of forms of governance and organisation that deviate from the perceived traditional divisions of labour between the private and public sectors, not least within the so-called 'third sector' of non-government organisations (Billis, 2010). Influential authors have looked at how 'hybrid organisations' share some attributes with market organisations and other attributes with government hierarchical organisations (Williamson, 1991), and discussed varieties of 'hybrid organisational arrangements' that combined the characteristics of private and public spheres (Ménard, 2004). Some hybrids can be the result of formal public policy initiatives while others appear as types of alliances between firms or other actors in order to realise common goals (Borys and Jemison, 1989) or to overcome barriers to growth (Shane, 1996). Studies of public services have tended to focus on the education and health sectors, where they have highlighted new formal organisations and forms of governance while important insights have been gained into different types of hybridity and the influence of contextual factors (see, e.g., Brown and Barnett, 2004; Noordegraaf and de Wit, 2012).

Scholars have also outlined different types or modes of hybridity based on whether the nature and dynamics of hybridity in the organisation were shallow or entrenched, and whether they had developed organically or been 'enacted' from outside (Billis, 2010). These distinctions can be tied to different aspects of an organisation such as its origins, governance mechanisms, relationship between different types of staff and accountability, and whether hybridity concerns one organisation or a cross-sector or inter-organisational partnership (Nguyen et al., 2012).

Hybrid organisational forms are in most cases tied to situations of mutual dependency between various actors and exhibit high degrees of uncertainty (Ménard, 2004). They are often unstable, with many forces pushing towards change (Ménard, 2004; Keast et al., 2007; Battilana and Dorado, 2010), and they may encounter resistance, unease and distrust (Battilana and Dorado, 2010; Billis, 2010; Gulbrandsen, 2011; Denis et al., 2015). Prior research has focused on different degrees of integration ranging from boundary-crossing practices (individuals/tasks remain in one sphere but collaborate); to boundary organisations (that explicitly straddle two or more spheres); and to 'true' or 'organic' hybrids that represent a novel combination that cannot be taken apart and be reduced to its originating parts (e.g., Billis, 2010). The distinctive characteristics and practices of the different spheres lead to tensions which can be addressed by their translation into concepts and routines through which the hybrids develop their own unique characteristics, although this may not be the general rule in hybrid research organisations (Gulbrandsen et al., 2015).

Hybridity and Non-Hybridity in Research

The nature of the new and unique organisational practices and configurations that are found in hybrid organisations and the tensions between different elements within them can be clarified by distinguishing them from 'non-hybrid' forms (Billis, 2010). In the field of research this involves analysing the distinction between the ideal type of 'public science' versus the ideal type of 'private science' (Dasgupta and David, 1994). Billis (2010) identifies five elements that are relevant for the study of the public–private distinction: ownership, governance, operational principles, human resources and other resources. We will briefly touch upon such issues to define the 'non-hybrid' states of research.

Probably the most influential framework for understanding public science is the normative approach of Merton (1942 [1973]) who argued that public science was strongly influenced by an 'ethos' or a set of powerful institutional imperatives that were reflected in many different aspects of research organisations. Merton proposed four norms, in the form of communism (research results are everyone's property and are exchanged for individual credibility and esteem; see also Latour and Woolgar, 1979); universalism (research should strive for benefits regardless of benefactor and should be freely available); disinterestedness (researchers should not have a self-interest in particular results and should not be motivated by personal gain); and organised scepticism (results should be scrutinised by the wider research community). These norms are institutionalised in processes and systems such as the hiring procedures of universities and the publication and peer review system. A particular aspect of public science is that the individuals engaged in it typically have 'dual memberships': they are both employees at a research organisation such as a university, and members of a professional research field or specialty (Allen, 1977). The priorities and incentives of the latter often take precedence and, as a result, public research organisations (especially universities) give a high degree of autonomy to members of their scientific staff. The scientific enterprise has been compared to a republic, where employees of different organisations collaborate as members of a self-governing and closely knit network (Polanyi, 1962). This represents a traditional perspective on public research. Although Merton and others have emphasised the ideal-typical nature of such frameworks and the heterogeneity of research organisations, in practice these features are also seen as fundamental elements of what has made universities and other research organisations unique and able to survive for hundreds of years in radically shifting societies. By contrast, private research or private science displays fundamentally different characteristics along these dimensions (Dasgupta and David, 1994). Questions and results are typically oriented at a specific firm's interests; they are to a much greater extent kept secret or protected through intellectual property rights mechanisms (patents in particular); and the employees enjoy a much lesser degree of freedom.

One type of research is not necessarily 'better' than the other, but it has been argued that there are two ideal types that represent a division of labour between universities and firms that have long historical roots (Rosenberg and Nelson, 1994; Mowery et al., 2004). Although notable industrial innovations have emerged in various forms of partnerships between academic science and private firms, the partnerships have typically been based on a clear perception of the boundary and distinction between the actors involved (Rosenberg, 1983, 1994; Rosenberg and Nelson, 1994). New forms of hybridity, however, have challenged this traditional division of labour.

Hybridity is not a new concept in the context of universities and science policy. It has partly emerged as a critique of the traditional dichotomous view of public and private research and has also been used to understand complex, contested and often temporary organisational set-ups that have often aimed to bring public R&D closer to industrial and societal needs and demands. 'Boundary work' is a term coined by Gieryn (1983) to understand the ways in which scientists make a distinction between the activities they are engaged in and other activities, which are then viewed as either partly or entirely 'non-science'. Scientists do this in order to gain material and symbolic resources and a certain degree of autonomy, but the growing distinction between science and non-science may also be seen as a starting point for policies aimed at increasing interaction and hybridity. Gieryn argues that there is 'an unyielding tension between basic and applied research, and between the empirical and theoretical aspects of inquiry' (ibid., p. 787), but despite obvious differences the boundary between science and non-science is blurred and needs to be actively constructed. Similarly, 'boundary organisations' (Guston, 2001) are often found closely related to universities, in the form of technology transfer offices and science parks, which are frequently founded by and sometimes (partly or fully) owned by the universities themselves. Here a space is created for participants from research and from the other side of the boundary where professionals work in a mediating but also quite independent role: 'The boundary organization thus gives both the producers and the consumers of research an opportunity to construct the boundary between their enterprises in a way favourable to their own perspectives' (ibid., p. 405).

Empirical investigations have described how 'hybrid organisations' or intermediary organisations can play a key role in the commercialization of new technologies (cf. Lynn et al., 1996). Fransman (2001) discusses the role of 'hybrid institutions' in economic, technological and scientific development, and focuses on the specific case of the cloned sheep Dolly and the role of the Roslin Institute in Edinburgh together with PPL Therapeutics and Edinburgh University. The term 'hybrid institution' refers here to a combination of organisations which has a government research institute at its core, together with its spin-off companies and neighbouring university. Tuunainen (2005) uses the term 'hybrid organisation' to describe an academic spin-off company and its slow and tension-filled development from a university-internal project to a separate entity with clear boundaries with the university environment.

In several cases, scholars of science policy have proposed new concepts to describe hybrid work practices and/or organisational arrangements. 'Mode 2' (Gibbons et al., 1994; Nowotny et al., 2001) refers to the ways in which traditional disciplinary academic science is gradually being replaced by a form of knowledge production with much higher emphasis on transdisciplinarity and the application of science. The 'triple helix' perspective (Etzkowitz and Leydesdorff, 2000) portrays a transformation in which new forms of close and direct collaboration between universities, industry and governments are becoming ever more central to innovation processes and thus to economic and social change. This is accompanied by changes in the norms of science, with commercial and traditional scientific goals being increasingly combined to some extent in new configurations (Etzkowitz, 1998). Stokes (1997) argues that many of the leading academics across all periods of history have been carrying out activities that combined a quest for fundamental understanding with considerations of practical use. These claims have been heavily debated but they have lent legitimacy to new policies to promote hybridity in science and to systematic attempts at creating more cross-sector collaboration.

Although the boundary perspectives discussed here seem to argue that hybridity and its blurred boundaries represent the 'natural state' for research, policy-makers all over the world have nevertheless attempted to bring research organisations and users in society, especially industry, closer together. There may also be a distinction between hybridity that emerges organically (Billis, 2010) and hybridity which is more the outcome of changes in public policy. This is an issue we will explore further in the next sections of the chapter.

Our brief discussion of large and, to some extent, contested issues has served to show that a traditional distinction between public and private research has increasingly come into question as 'hybridity' has become a central concept. For our purpose it is relevant to talk about different elements of hybridity in research. One is related to the goals: a hybrid organisation often aims to combine public sector and commercial goals. Another is related to ownership and legal status: is the hybrid organisation owned by both public and private actors, and how is ownership exercised in practice? A third is related to funding: is funding split evenly between partners, how are revenues distributed and so on. And a fourth aspect is related to the cognitive dimension, when people with different backgrounds and expertise work together to try to create new work practices or new areas of knowledge. These aspects will be discussed below with reference to three examples of hybrid organisations related to contract research, university–industry relations and commercialisation of public research.

THREE EXAMPLES OF HYBRID ORGANISATIONS AT THE SCIENCE–INDUSTRY INTERFACE

Organisations Involved in the Commercialisation of Research

Intermediary hybrid organisations are found at the intersection between universities and their external environment, most often with an explicit mandate to work with commercialisation and other forms of knowledge transfer. Examples of them include technology transfer offices (TTOs; sometimes called technology licensing offices), science parks and industrial liaison units. With their position at the boundary between universities and the commercial world of firms and investors, they need to combine and mediate between very different cultures and motives (Siegel et al., 2003).

A growing awareness emerged in the late 1970s that new high-technology firms tended to cluster around leading research universities such as MIT and Stanford in the United States (US) and Cambridge in the United Kingdom (UK). Silicon Valley became a global catchphrase and phenomenon, studied by researchers and policy-makers alike, and was a starting point for numerous attempts at emulation and learning. The strong growth in electronics and computing technologies and the emergence of biotech became associated with hybrid settings and seemed to require new forms of support (Mowery et al., 2004). The leading US and some other universities had pioneered the setting up of a support structure for commercialisation in the shape of science parks, innovation centres and incubators with offices and services for newly established firms, technology transfer and licensing offices that would help scientists structure deals with industry and patent research results, and industrial liaison offices that would negotiate collaboration agreements with firms and help to set up joint programmes and centres (Rasmussen et al., 2006).

Early literature provided case studies and focused on preconditions for hybridity in the universities. Central topics were the ways in which the interface to the external environment was organised and the kinds of rules that were needed to guide researchers who wanted to adopt a commercial approach and engage with industry (dubbed academic entrepreneurs) (e.g., Stankiewicz, 1986; McMullan and Melnyk, 1988). Some observers (e.g., Fairweather, 1988) noted the importance of scientific excellence within specific fields and subfields in engineering, medicine and natural science, and the inherent warning that not all universities were likely to succeed by involving themselves in hybrid arrangements. Some research organisations have a broader research base that may limit their capacity to engage in hybrid arrangements.

Researchers in the field of innovation studies have been critical about the value of commercialisation-oriented organisations and have argued that their possible effects on the goals, finances and cognitive aspects of public science in the long run may be negative. The importance of long-term research and education activities for industrial innovation has been highlighted, and Rosenberg and Nelson (1994) and many later scholars (e.g., Dasgupta and David, 1994; Mowery and Sampat, 2005) have warned against the danger of placing too strong an emphasis on commercialisation and the hybrid organisations that this seemed to lead to. Innovation scholars have tried to measure empirically whether the commercial engagement of scientists might negatively affect traditional university activities, but the effects seemed to be positive or curvilinear rather than negative (Larsen,

2011). At least at the level of the individual researcher, hybridity appears to be a viable and frequently successful approach, although researchers still point to the bottom-up nature of these activities and the limited role played by formal hybrid organisations in supporting and facilitating them.

Some science policy scholars have been more optimistic about the impact of hybrid forms and the popular 'triple helix' perspective has gained a lot of attention. This characterises innovation as something that increasingly happens in a collaborative effort between universities, industry and government (Etzkowitz and Leydesdorff, 1997; Etzkowitz, 1998). Much of the triple helix-inspired literature has focused on incubators, technology transfer offices and the role of institutional frameworks. A common example of the latter is the so-called Bayh–Dole Act in the US (1980) which gave the universities ownership of federally funded research and a clear responsibility for commercialisation. This led to a significant growth in the number of hybrid organisations, first in the US, and then in the host of countries which have implemented their own versions of this legislation (Mowery et al., 2004; Grimaldi et al., 2011).

Researchers seem to agree that the growth of intermediary hybrid organisations can be strongly related to legislative changes and new policy instruments such as public seed and venture capital. But they remain divided about the likely effects and importance of these new organisations. Some have argued forcefully that the effects may be negative and that many of these new organisations do not seem to reach their often ambitious goals (Mowery et al., 2004; Mowery and Sampat, 2005). Others state that the establishment of the hybrid organisations is an important result in itself, and that these new organisations may need several decades in order to prove that they can operate successfully at the intersection of science and the commercial world (e.g., Grimaldi et al., 2011). The literature points to high failure rates and many controversies about the effects and usefulness of these intermediary organisations.

The empirical results are fairly clear: few TTOs are able to make a profit, and in many cases science parks seem to have weak influences on innovation (Siegel et al., 2003; Phan et al., 2005), although there are indications of an increase in the number of commercialisations helped by TTOs (Siegel et al., 2007). The optimism about some of these hybrid arrangements is still maintained in policy circles and among some academics, but newer case studies are more likely to highlight tensions and challenges, not least due to the radical and sometimes disruptive nature of the activities taking place (e.g., Rasmussen and Gulbrandsen, 2011). It has been found that age is the most important variable explaining TTO success, and this may highlight the view that hybridity takes a very long time to achieve. Typically the universities that are seen as global success cases in creating new firms and profitable licensing deals are also the ones that pioneered hybrid intermediary organisations (Fairweather, 1988).

The hybrid nature of these intermediary organisations is based on the way in which they combine commercial and public goals in their fundamental mission (Guston, 2001). Some of them are also seen as hybrid in a legal or financial sense by receiving funding from both private and public sources and by including owners representing different sectors (Rasmussen et al., 2006). A third possibility is that they may be hybrid in a cognitive or practical sense (Gulbrandsen, 2009). Many intermediary organisations hire specialised staff and become affiliated to interest organisations such as the American Association of University Technology Transfer Managers. As such the organisations do not mix or combine different spheres but may represent a new form of organisation that seeks to promote hybridity elsewhere, particularly in academia. It is clear, for example, that the tasks and goals of the technology transfer offices, which deal directly and explicitly with scientists, firms and investors, are very complex to fulfil and require high degrees of cross-disciplinary and cross-domain expertise (Siegel et al., 2003). The professionalisation of the technology transfer function can be seen both as an attempt to deal with the contested and often temporary nature of hybrid organisations but also as an institutionalisation of the intermediary type of organisation.

Cooperative Research Centres as Hybrid Organisations

In contrast with TTOs, cooperative research centres (CRCs) do not aim at bringing research to the market, but rather serve as platforms where firms and researchers work jointly on research topics of relevance to both science and industry. New research and innovation centres have been created in many countries in addition to traditional university departments or other established structures for research. Such centres often target specific societal or economic needs that can be addressed by cooperation between several scientific specialisations and areas of competence situated both inside and outside the scientific domain. There are many explanations for this growth in the number of CRCs, including the growing complexity of the social and economic problems that science has to tackle, the increased specialisation of scientific insights, and dependence on expensive and complex technologies to achieve scientific objectives. Moreover, the development of knowledge-based economic sectors where scientific insights are important for the development of new products and processes and, as a result, the growing use of open and collaborative R&D and innovation models in firms (Chesbrough, 2006; Enkel et al., 2009), are important drivers behind increasing use of public–private research cooperation.

Some of these initiatives are intended to facilitate cooperation between academics from different scientific disciplines within multidisciplinary research areas such as life sciences, material sciences and neuroscience, while others aim to bring scientists together with non-scientific participants and stakeholders. The ambitions for the second kind of collaboration are more far-reaching than producing new knowledge: they also include putting knowledge to use. This is the most common way in which the term 'cooperative research centre' is used, expressed for example in the following definition of a CRC: 'A cooperative research center is an organization or unit within a larger organization that performs research and also has an explicit mission (and related activities) to promote, directly or indirectly, cross-sector collaboration, knowledge and technology transfer, and ultimately innovation' (Boardman and Gray, 2010, p.450).

CRCs thus have a hybrid function: they aim to promote scientific or public goals by developing new knowledge, and commercial or private goals by utilising knowledge for commercial ends – by transferring knowledge to firms or others or by supporting commercialisation of knowledge through licensing or the establishment of new firms (Gulbrandsen et al., 2015). To achieve these different goals, centres involve different participants and partners in their work and establish organisational structures to facilitate cooperation between them (Boardman and Gray, 2010). These structures include industry boards, partnership forums, joint facilities or labs, secondment arrangements, mobility stipends, and more. The centres are nonetheless hosted by one organisation, usually a university. Centre leaders and the majority of the staff are academic staff and the contribution from industry is more often in the role of a stakeholder or as a recipient of knowledge that plays an active part in a late phase of the research and development process (Boardman et al., 2012). Centres, however, are expected to produce both scientific results (measured for instance by publications and graduates) and commercial outputs (measured by patents, licences, use of knowledge in innovation, formation of firms and more).

The centres are hybrids in the particular sense that they are basically academic organisations that have been infused with a commercial rationale rather than boundary organisations like the technology transfer offices discussed above (Gulbrandsen et al., 2015). CRCs are also characterised as hybrids from a cognitive perspective since they bring together participants who are specialists in very different knowledge bases and areas of expertise. They might, for example, bring together individuals with medical expertise and those with technology expertise to work jointly towards the development of new medical technologies, or share the very different skills of information and communication technology (ICT) experts and geologists to cooperate in developing new visualisation methods for oil exploration activities. Hybridisation is therefore a central means through which new fields of scientific discovery can be developed.

The CRC model is not, of course, new in itself; cooperative research has been important to the development of science and technology not least in large multinational centres such as CERN (the European Organisation for Nuclear Research). It has played an increasingly central role in science policy, and the growing attention and funding it has received has accelerated the institutionalisation of cooperative research in a wider range of national and regional cooperative efforts. Boardman and Gray (2010) refer to this change as a policy shift towards a 'cooperative paradigm for research policy'. Likewise, arrangements for supporting cooperative research were initially used in technology and engineering in particular, for instance through the establishment of the Industry/University Cooperative Research Centres Program in the US in the 1970s, but they can now be found in many different fields of science.

As the number of such centres has increased and they have become more visible in policy terms they have captured the interest of analysts and researchers who work on sociological and organisational studies of science. A number of studies have addressed cooperative research centres and the antecedents, internal organisation and processes, outcomes and effects of such arrangements (e.g., Boardman et al., 2012; Boardman and Gray, 2010; Corley et al., 2006; Boardman and Corley, 2008; Youtie et al., 2006; Turpin et al., 2011; Thune and Gulbrandsen, 2011; Gulbrandsen et al., 2015). One important question which they have addressed has been the extent to which centres that have been explicitly set up to foster cooperation between science and industry have actually increased scientists' cooperative behaviour (Boardman and Corley, 2008). There is a general assumption in this literature that, while cooperative research centres have established hybrid organisational arrangements (including decision-making bodies and arenas for cooperation), the development of hybrid practices takes time and might not always be successful.

In a recent study of the Nordic context, Gulbrandsen et al. (2015) investigated several examples of cooperative research centres in Norway and Sweden, and found that centres developed practices that served to integrate different communities to varying degrees and that this also had an impact on their ability to reach their goals. Centres in relatively mature fields of science and those based on a set of well-defined and common problems were more successful in achieving their goals than those working in more novel scientific fields or in centres that are set up to handle broad societal challenges. The message here was that hybrid goals (promoting scientific discovery and utilising the discoveries for commercial ends) were possible and that they might be achieved through hybrid organisational arrangements, but for this to happen the knowledge base needed to be shared more widely among participants in industry and in science. To some extent all CRCs are enacted (Billis, 2010), in the sense that they receive funding and support from a specific public policy instrument; Gulbrandsen et al. (2015) and other studies seem to indicate that hybrid goals are best realised when the centre builds upon a more organic and informal cross-sector collaboration. This is not necessarily something that can be achieved by design, but might also be an outcome after years of experience with the CRC.

A final point to be made is that this is not a one-way process. Most of the literature assumes that hybridisation is about academics becoming more commercially oriented. Studies of cooperative research and innovation in highly knowledge-intensive fields, however, show that shared knowledge and shared understanding of the demands and opportunities emerge across organisational boundaries in such a way that participants are able to understand and take full note of the perspective of other contributors (Powell and Sandholz, 2012). We see a similar tendency in the Nordic cases. Industry representatives' understanding and appreciation of scientific norms and methods and scientists' understanding of industry's demands for concrete deliverables, resource scarcity and limited ability to take risk can, over time, lead to a mutual understanding of when and how both commercial results and scientific goals can be pursued. This does not mean that tensions and challenges do not arise, but rather that organisational arrangements are mobilised to solve such problems. In centres that do not yet have such a mutual understanding and a pool of shared knowledge, their organisational arrangements may not be sufficient to stabilise the partnership if problems arise.

Applied Research Institutes as Hybrid Organisations[2]

Research institutes are organisations that are engaged in research and development activities but, for the most part, not formally involved in teaching, although they may include doctoral students among their staff and have close relations to universities in their vicinity. Ownership, orientation and financial structure vary between types of institutes and between countries but here we focus on organisations that are defined and perceived neither as higher education institutions nor as private for-profit companies. There are many names for these entities – such as 'public institutes', 'government laboratories' and 'research and technology organisations' – which indicates the obvious heterogeneity among them. There are numerous investigations of the role universities play in economic, political and social development, but comparatively few of the role played by research institutes (notable exceptions include Crow and Bozeman, 1998; Larédo and Mustar, 2001; Doern and Kinder, 2002; Beise and Stahl, 1999). One reason for this could be that the hybrid nature of these organisations challenges simple dichotomies between pure and applied science; between public and private sector organisations; and between knowledge as 'public' (non-appropriable, results from basic research, and so on) and 'private' (appropriable, stemming from industrial R&D), as outlined earlier in the chapter. The dearth of empirical and theoretical investigations may thus reflect a wider neglect of forms of hybrid organisations (Miller, 2001).

Some applied research institutes are very old (especially if, for example, we count astronomical observatories in this category) and we can distinguish between three kinds of historical origins (Gulbrandsen, 2008). First, many research institutes are related to specific public missions. These include: the exploration of the planet and space (geography, geology, and so on); tasks related to nature and natural resources (weather forecasting, agriculture and fishing, environmental mapping, and more); and particular national interests (defence, energy, and so on). Some of them were created as part of a policy that has long been abandoned, such as the European 'national champions' policy of supporting domestic firms in areas such as telecommunications and nuclear technology with national R&D institutes. Even when the mission has gone, the institutes have often lived on with a broader customer base and public support for specific applied research areas (Larédo and Mustar, 2001, 2004; Larédo, 2003) and with higher emphasis on industrial contract research (Beise and Stahl, 1999; Larédo and Mustar, 2001).

Second, some research institutes have been started with explicit goals of industrial and economic growth, with a view to offering R&D services to industry and to bridging a perceived gap between companies and universities, often in attempts to transfer results from universities into practical use. This model of creating industry-close and industry-specific public R&D organizations originated in Germany in the late 19th century and has been copied by many other countries (Whitley, 2002; Beise and Stahl,1999). This kind of hybrid can thus be very long established. Some of them are very large, employing thousands of scientists and engineers. Examples include the Netherlands Organisation for Applied Scientific Research (TNO), Fraunhofer (Germany), Austrian Competitive Research Centers, the VTT Technical Research Centre (Finland) and the Foundation for Industrial and Technical Research (SINTEF) (Norway).

And third, some institutes have been started within research funding agencies to carry out specific research tasks, quite often fundamental research but within a narrowly defined area. This is a rather unusual model; in most countries funding for research and the actual practice of research are found in different organisations. But in some countries such as Italy, Canada and to some extent Spain and France, large funding organisations also have operated their own research institutes. Still, the challenges of liberalisation, marketisation, New Public Management and other political developments have been felt by many organisations of this kind and these have led to a string of reorganisations, mergers, privatisations and separations of institutes from their original founder (Larédo and Mustar, 2001). Some institutes, moreover, had their roots in specific historical contexts such as the Cold War, the arms race, and a belief in the now-refuted linear model of innovation which assumed that all innovations begin with basic research. They are now faced with different political environments in which they receive significantly less support.

As a response to these challenges and to the changing landscape of research and innovation policies as outlined above, a degree of convergence between the three types of institutes discussed here may be observed. Those that were mission-oriented have incorporated the goals of industrial development; industry-oriented institutes have assumed broader responsibilities for fundamental R&D within certain technologies; and agency institutes have become increasingly autonomous (Beise and Stahl, 1999; Larédo and Mustar, 2001; Nerdrum and Gulbrandsen, 2009). This convergence of goals has strengthened the hybrid nature of the institutes, while those found in many countries have remained strong despite the changes that have occurred in some of their fundamental goals (Larédo and Mustar, 2004).

Research institutes nevertheless remain in the middle of very different cultures within science policy, and it is this which makes them well suited for a broader discussion about hybridity. Elzinga and Jamison (1995) claim that science policy is a staging ground for four competing cultures: the academic culture, the industrial culture, the bureaucratic culture and the civil-political culture. Each is based on sets of norms and values that often differ markedly from the others, and the institutions, organisations and development processes of science policy are continually influenced by the struggle between these four cultures. The academic culture emphasises autonomy and academic freedom and upholds an image of 'pure', 'unrestricted', and 'curiosity-driven' research as an ideal which often serves as the foundation for all types of R&D. The industrial culture emphasises values such as competitive advantage and innovation. R&D is typically seen as a tool through which to promote these values and it should consequently be based on the articulation of demands among users who are striving to become innovative and competitive. Bureaucratic culture is founded on values related to orderly rules, rationality and planning. This implies that R&D is largely viewed in an instrumental light, both as a tool to create achievable goals and efficient rules, and as a source of authority for planners and regulators. Civil society culture is more difficult to characterise, but its influence is often most explicitly seen in various protest movements against the values of some (or all) of the other three cultures (Kallerud, 2002). This culture emphasises democratic deliberation, disagreement and possibly also consensus-building among a large number of stakeholders.

Applied research institutes have to balance norms and values stemming from the different extremes of these four cultures (Elzinga and Jamison, 1995). They can therefore be considered as hybrids along two dimensions (Gulbrandsen, 2011). First, they occupy a middle point between science and non-science or society; and second, they most often have characteristics both of private firms and government bureaucracies, unlike the CRCs discussed above which are mostly hosted by universities and organised accordingly.

The two dimensions of hybridity in research institutes provide a starting point for a discussion of the tensions that exist between them. On the science–non-science dimension, tensions can be related to a lack of 'balance', which has been called both the 'Stockholm Syndrome' and the 'Lima Syndrome' (Gulbrandsen, 2011). The first of these refers to the challenge that research institutes may be – or may be perceived to be – 'in the pockets' of their users, which means they are unable to offer R&D services that correspond to academic ideals of objectivity, criticism, balance and independence. Like the hostages in the original Stockholm Syndrome, the institutes develop sympathies with the 'hostage-takers' and their perspectives. The Lima Syndrome describes the opposite tendency, which is related to the challenge of actual or perceived academic drift. This leads to the belief that central actors feel that the research institutes risk becoming less useful and/or that the more practically oriented R&D activities are viewed as low status.

The most important tensions on the public–private dimension are those related to 'unfair competition'. Research institutes will face this dilemma if they compete in the same market as private firms while at the same time enjoying the benefits of the hybrid position such as public basic R&D funding, access to certain funding arenas closed to for-profit organisations, and reduced taxes. This kind of tension could be exacerbated by the development of an increasing number of sophisticated R&D-based companies such as academic spin-offs. Another tension is found in research institutes with an identity which is closer to the public sector which can also be met with fairly traditional accusations of excessive 'red tape' including excessive conformity to rules and regulations and inefficient operations.

The large Norwegian research institute, SINTEF, may serve as an example of the tensions and dilemmas found in this kind of hybrid. Originally set up in 1950 by the technical university in Trondheim as a means of providing a bridge between the university and industry, it outgrew the initial service and bridging role and over time has become an autonomous institute. It now has the expertise and authority to set up departments and units sometimes related to the needs of existing or future industry and sometimes with the interests of the university in mind. One particularly noteworthy aspect is the high level of mobility among its personnel; each year a large share of its staff (compared to a university setting) will find a job elsewhere. It has moved from being fully owned by the university to become an independent foundation, and the subsequent relationship with the university has been close but uneasy. SINTEF is counted as a public organisation in the national R&D statistics, but as a private firm in the Organisation for Economic Co-operation and Development (OECD) statistics; it is defined as a non-profit foundation, yet was recently forced to pay taxes like a firm; and it has been criticised both for 'academic drift' with too strong an emphasis on publishing, and for competing too directly with consultancy firms. Some of the institute's main partners are also competitors when it comes to R&D funding. Overall this example shows how all the dilemmas and tensions discussed above are experienced in practice by one organisation.

Because research institutes as a type of organisation are older than both technology transfer offices and collaborative research centres, they may provide a useful insight into how a hybrid position can be maintained in the long run in the research context despite the tensions and challenges involved. One important aspect is for them to participate in open scientific publication and to adopt other practices such as university-like career structures and promotion criteria. This provides a counterbalance to the applied and user-oriented nature of many of their activities. Another is to find a formal organisational structure that signals an intermediary position such as a stock company with public shareholders and no annual dividends or a private non-profit foundation.

Unlike the collaborative research centres and many other intermediary organisations, applied research institutes are not always hybrid when it comes to goals and ownership. They may have long-standing and well-defined goals and, like SINTEF, they can be independent foundations with a clear sense of identity as something distinct in its own right rather than a combination of different spheres of engagement. On the other hand, research institutes are often hybrid when it comes to funding, with a clearer mix of contract research and competitive public funding than is found in universities. They are also hybrid in a cognitive sense and in terms of their knowledge base, often combining very practical work at the edge of the 'D' in R&D with state-of-the-art research. Collaborative research centres and intermediary organisations such as technology transfer offices are easily recognised as hybrids that provide an immediate perception of their challenges and position. Research institutes, on the other hand, are more easily identified as hybrids as the result of the activities in which they are engaged, or because of the controversies they sometimes spark in science policy.

DISCUSSION AND CONCLUSIONS

In this chapter we have looked at hybrid organisations in a research setting. Research is increasingly called for as a solution to society's grand challenges such as health issues, environmental problems and economic stagnation. The mechanisms being promoted are often hybrid and involve increased interaction between public research, private firms and non-profit organisations, as the problems are seen as too complex to be solved by a single kind of organisation. But while hybrid organisations in the research setting have been growing in importance, hybridisation and hybrid organisations are neither new nor unusual in research. We have shown that the concept of hybridity has been used in analyses of science policy and the research system for a long time, but with few linkages to the broader literature on hybrid organisations. We have used the concept to discuss the development of forms of research organisations at the intersection between science and society. We have looked at three examples of hybrid organisations that are prevalent in the research setting: intermediary organisations such as technology transfer offices set up to move research results from the universities to commercial applications; research centres built on collaboration between universities and firms; and applied research institutes.

Hybridity in research is particularly complex. It not only entails a combination of public and private spheres – or of government hierarchies with market-based organisational forms – but also involves another and equally fundamental combination. Broadly speaking this involves two very different perspectives on research. In the first place it is carried out in universities and similar organisations in way that involves long time perspectives and often has no specific use or user in mind. It is communicated openly and is added to the repository of (more or less) freely available knowledge. By contrast, research in firms and many non-profit organisations is frequently tied to existing products, services and issues; it is often oriented towards incremental improvements and defending the status quo; and it is a strategic resource which can be kept secret or proprietary. Combining these two very different approaches to research, as can be expected, is often tension-filled and unsuccessful.

Intermediary organisations have hybrid goals. Technology transfer offices work to move research results into industry and to structure different forms of deals between the two sectors; while science parks aim to create attractive and synergistic meeting places for academic research and actors that require such research to be competitive or entrepreneurial. These intermediary organisations are not always themselves hybrid, however; they are likely to be either administrative units based at a university or limited companies wholly or partly owned by a university. Although their activities may be termed hybrid, a main goal for them is often to create hybrid practices elsewhere, such as increased patenting and entrepreneurial behaviour among academics. These organisations may therefore best be viewed not as hybrids in themselves but as a category of organisations with its own logic, promoted by large interest organisations in North America, Europe and Asia. They have a strong self-image of as hybrids, however. In the science and innovation literature, intermediary organisations are viewed as controversial. Many of them seem to fail to reach their goals (make a profit, create synergies) and, in general, the ones that seem to be successful seem to be those that have been established over the longer term and have had many years of experience.

Collaborative research centres (CRCs) are hybrids in the sense that they are set up as formal consortia or organisations with members from different sectors, both public and private, with a rationale of creating new combinations of activities and outputs. Empirical studies show that many of them are not really hybrid in practice: the partners do not interact, one partner may dominate, and partner exits are common. They find it difficult to overcome tensions related to developing combined research agendas, exploring new forms of interaction and decision-making, and dealing with the ownership of results, unless the partners have long experience of working together and they work in a comparatively mature field of research. They experience difficulty in finding the right people from different sectors who are able to work together on research that also aims for high scientific originality.

Intermediary organisations and CRCs exemplify many of the challenges and aspects of hybrid organisations in the broader literature that we discussed earlier. They are unstable, (often) temporary, and there is a high degree of uncertainty involved in them; not only because of the complexity of their organisational set-up but also because, by definition, research involves questions to which the answers are not known. In those organisations where hybridity has become institutionalised there are considerable variations in their practices and in their results, and much depends on the institutional and disciplinary context of their work. Many of these organisations do not emerge out of situations of mutual dependency. Instead, many of them are top-down constructions built upon ideas of commercialisation and research-based innovation, but where the partners initially do not need to work with one another directly. Overall effective hybrid arrangements tend to be realised only through repeated collaborative and integrative efforts over a long period of time. This means that research-based hybrid organisations require significant and patient investment; a difficult condition to meet.

Unlike the first two organisational forms we reviewed, applied research institutes are often not formally hybrid; they represent collections of more or less autonomous organisations working within an applied framework to solve specific problems or to serve a specific set of users. In practice, however, they have hybrid characteristics: they mix activities from different spheres, they have a comparatively high degree of mobility among their personnel, and they work with funding from many different sources simultaneously. They may be seen as representing the longest-standing form of hybrid organisation in research, dating back much further than intermediaries and CRCs. However, even those institutes that have achieved a high degree of institutionalisation are still questioned continuously about their relevance, legitimacy, research quality and other fundamental aspects. Many countries have privatised institutes or merged them with universities; even after decades of experience, hybrid organisations may represent less stable organisational forms.

In Table 7.1 we compare the different types of research-oriented hybrid organisations along some central dimensions. As the table shows, the three types are significantly different from one another, although they may all be termed hybrid due to their goals and (intended) practices. Our discussion of hybrid organisations in research suggests that they can be of very different types and have different origins (see, e.g., Billis, 2010). Furthermore, they seemingly combine hybrid and non-hybrid elements. For example, collaborative centres may have formal goals that combine excellent research and industrial innovation, but their work practices may reflect a 'side-by-side' type of hybridity that first and foremost respects and maintains a fairly traditional division of labour between academia and the private sector. Hybrid organisations in a research setting seem to have this double nature. On the one hand they are hybrids which aim (and sometimes succeed)

Table 7.1   Comparison of three types of hybrid organisations in research

	Knowledge transfer organisations	Collaborative research centres (CRCs)	Applied research institutes
Goal	Make public science discoveries available for commercial exploitation	Perform research of relevance to both public and private partners	Perform research activities as responses to societal demand/by contract
Sectors and hybridity	Intra- and inter-organisational hybridity	Inter-organisational hybridity	Intra-organisational hybridity
Origin/emergence	Enacted: decision by university and possibly others	Enacted but sometimes based on organic partnerships	Enacted: decision typically by ministries, possibly other users
Ownership	Mixed, usually owned by universities	Joint ownership, often hosted by universities	Independent companies/foundations
Funding	Mainly public, and income from licensing/exits	Public and private, normally mostly public	Public and private, sometimes more private
Staff	Staff from industry, academics as clients	Staff in universities and industry	Academic staff, clients from industry
Practices across public–private sector dimension	Facilitate deals, make academics more entrepreneurial	Develop common research agendas for further collaboration	Solve problems for continued contractual relationships
Institutionalisation of hybridity	Varied and frequently entrenched	Varied	High

in transferring knowledge between researchers and users, and translating fundamental research results into something that can be exploited in practice (Etzkowitz, 1998; Fransman, 2001; Gulbrandsen et al., 2015). On the other hand they are also boundary organisations which through their goals and activities, however hybrid and combinatory in nature, serve to define and demarcate the blurry borderline between basic and applied research and between research and use of research (Guston, 2001).

It is not clear whether hybrids in other fields than science display similar characteristics. The research context is unique in some respects and this may make it difficult to draw general conclusions from it. First and foremost, research is an unpredictable activity and there is a significant degree of uncertainty about whether hybrid goals and expectations will actually be met; not because the hybrid organisations fail but because the hypotheses and research propositions may not turn out as expected. Research is also highly specialised with a dedicated expert language, which means that there is a high probability of hybrids remaining shallow, at least in the short and medium term, and especially in research fields that are not very mature. Finally, research represents powerful values and norms and there may be a risk that hybrid organisations, not least those enacted and initiated to meet external demands, will in practice be valued primarily for their contributions to academic knowledge production. This might entail that the increasing number of hybrid organisations in science might represent hybridity at a shallow level. We nonetheless argue that the context of scientific research is interesting for studies of hybrid organisations, and particularly for understanding how hybrid practices, routines, identities, knowledge and norms develop and struggle to become institutionalised within hybrid organisations.

NOTES

1. Some paragraphs in this section are based directly on Gulbrandsen (2011) and Gulbrandsen et al. (2015).
2. This section builds upon Gulbrandsen (2011).

REFERENCES

Allen, T.J. (1977), *Managing the Flow of Technology*. Boston, MA: MIT Press.
Battilana, J. and S. Dorado (2010), Building sustainable hybrid organizations: the case of commercial microfinance organizations. *Academy of Management Journal*, 53(6): 1419–1440.
Beise, M. and H. Stahl (1999), Public research and industrial innovations in Germany. *Research Policy*, 28(4): 397–422.
Billis, D. (2010), *Hybrid Organizations and the Third Sector*. Basingstoke: Palgrave Macmillan
Boardman, C. and D. Gray (2010), The new science and engineering management: cooperative research centers as government policies, industry strategies, and organizations. *Journal of Technology Transfer*, 35(5): 445–459.
Boardman, C., D.O. Gray and D. Rivers (eds) (2012), *Cooperative Research Centers and Technical Innovation: Government Policies, Industry Strategies, and Organizational Dynamics*. New York: Springer Science & Business Media.
Boardman, P.C. and E.A. Corley (2008), University research centers and the composition of research collaborations. *Research Policy*, 37(5): 900–913.
Borys, Bryan and David B. Jemison (1989), Hybrid arrangements as strategic alliances: theoretical issues in organizational combinations. *Academy of Management Review*, 14: 234–249.
Brown, Laurie and J. Ross Barnett (2004), Is the corporate transformation of hospitals creating a new hybrid health care space? *Social Science and Medicine*, 58: 427–444.
Capano, Giliberto (2011), Government continues to do its job: a comparative study of governance shifts in the higher education sector. *Public Administration*, 89: 1622–1642.
Chesbrough, H.W. (2006), The era of open innovation. *Managing Innovation and Change*, 127(3): 34–41.
Corley, E.A., P.C. Boardman and B. Bozeman (2006), Design and the management of multi-institutional research collaborations: theoretical implications from two case studies. *Research Policy*, 35(7): 975–993.
de Boer, H.F., J. Enders and L. Leisyte (2007), Public sector reform in Dutch higher education: the organizational transformation of the university. *Public Administration*, 85: 27–46.
Crow, M. and B. Bozeman (1988), *Limited by Design: R&D Laboratories in the US National Innovation System*. New York: Columbia University Press.
Dasgupta, Partha and Paul A. David (1994), Toward a new economics of science. *Research Policy*, 23(5): 487–521.
Denis, Jean-Louis, Ewan Ferlie and Nicolette van Gestel (2015), Understanding hybridity in public organizations. *Public Administration*, 93(2): 273–289.
Doern, B.G. and J.S. Kinder (2002), One size does not fit all: Canadian government laboratories as diverse and complex institutions. *Journal of Canadian Studies*, 37(3): 33–55.
Elzinga, Aant and Andrew Jamison (1995), Changing policy agendas in science and technology. In Sheila Jasanoff, Gerald E. Markle, James C. Petersen and Trevor Pinch (eds), *Handbook of Science and Technology Studies*. Thousand Oaks, CA: SAGE Publications, pp. 572–597.
Enkel, E., O. Gassmann and H. Chesbrough (2009), Open R&D and open innovation: exploring the phenomenon. *R&D Management*, 39(4): 311–316.
Etzkowitz, H. (1998), The norms of entrepreneurial science: cognitive effects of the new university–industry linkages. *Research Policy*, 27(8): 823–833.
Etzkowitz, H. and L. Leydesdorff (1997), *Universities and the Global Knowledge Economy: A Triple Helix of University–Industry–Government Relations*. Andover: Thomson Learning.
Etzkowitz, Henry and Loet Leydesdorff (2000), The dynamics of innovation: from national systems and 'Mode 2' to a Triple Helix of university–industry–government relations. *Research Policy*, 29: 109–123.
Fairweather, J.S. (1988), *Entrepreneurship and Higher Education: Lessons for Colleges, Universities, and Industry*.

ASHE-ERIC Higher Education Report no. 6. Washington, DC: Association for the Study of Higher Education.

Fransman, Martin (2001), Designing Dolly: interactions between economics, technology and science and the evolution of hybrid institutions. *Research Policy*, 30: 263–273.

Gibbons, M., C. Limoges, H. Nowotny, S. Schwartzman, P. Scott and M. Trow (1994), *The New Production of Knowledge: The Dynamics of Science and Research in Contemporary Societies*. London: SAGE.

Gieryn, Thomas F. (1983), Boundary work and the demarcation of science from non-science: strains and interests in professional ideologies of scientists. *American Sociological Review*, 48: 781–795.

Grimaldi, R., M. Kenney, D.S. Siegel and M. Wright (2011), 30 years after Bayh–Dole: reassessing academic entrepreneurship. *Research Policy*, 40(8): 1045–1057.

Gulbrandsen, Magnus (2008), The co-evolution of research institutes with universities and user needs: a historical perspective. In Eli Moen (ed.), *Science and Society Relationships in the Age of Globalization: Past Reforms and Future Challenges*. Oslo: Research Council of Norway, pp. 188–213.

Gulbrandsen, M. (2009), The relationship between a university and its technology transfer office: the case of NTNU in Norway. *International Journal of Technology Transfer and Commercialisation*, 9(1/2): 25–39.

Gulbrandsen, M. (2011), Research institutes as hybrid organisations: central challenges to their legitimacy. *Policy Sciences*, 44: 215–230.

Gulbrandsen, M., T. Thune, S.B. Borlaug and J. Hanson (2015), Emerging hybrid practices in public–private research centres. *Public Administration*, 93(2): 363–379.

Guston, David H. (1999), Stabilizing the boundary between US politics and science: the role of the office of technology transfer as a boundary organization, *Social Studies of Science*, 29: 87–111.

Guston, David H. (2001), Boundary organizations in environmental policy and science: an introduction, *Science, Technology and Human Values*, 26: 399–408.

Kallerud, Egil (2002), Vitenskap, teknologi og makt – fire perspektiver på evaluering. In Bjørn Stensaker (ed.), *Kunnskaps- og teknologivurdering. Perspektiver, metoder og refleksjoner*. Oslo: Cappelen akademisk forlag, pp. 31–54.

Keast, Robyn, Kerry Brown and Myrna Mandell (2007), Getting the right mix: unpacking integration meanings and strategies. *International Public Management Journal*, 10(1): 9–33.

Larédo, Philippe (2003), Six major challenges facing public intervention in higher education, science, technology and innovation. *Science and Public Policy*, 30(1): 4–12.

Larédo, Philippe and Philippe Mustar (eds) (2001), *Research and Innovation Policies in the New Global Economy. An International Comparative Analysis*. Cheltenham, UK and Northampton, MA, USA: Edward Elgar Publishing.

Larédo, Philippe and Philippe Mustar (2004), Public-sector research: a growing role in innovation systems. *Minerva*, 42: 11–27.

Larsen, T.M. (2011), The implications of academic enterprise for public science: an overview of the empirical evidence. *Research Policy*, 40(1): 6–19.

Latour, B. and S. Woolgar (1979), *Laboratory Life: The Construction of Scientific Facts*. Princeton, NJ: Princeton University Press.

Lynn, Leonard H., N. Mohan Reddy and John D. Aram (1996), Linking technology and institutions: the innovation community framework. *Research Policy*, 25: 91–106.

McMullan, W.E. and K. Melnyk (1988), University innovation centres and academic venture formation. *R&D Management*, 18: 5–12.

Ménard, Claude (2004), The economics of hybrid organizations, *Journal of Institutional and Theoretical Economics*, 160: 345–376.

Merton, Robert K. (1942 [1973]), The normative structure of science. Reprinted in *The Sociology of Science: Theoretical and Empirical Investigations*. Chicago, IL, USA and London, UK: University of Chicago Press, pp. 286–324.

Miller, Clark (2001), Hybrid management: boundary organizations, science policy, and environmental governance in the climate regime. *Science, Technology and Human Values*, 26: 478–500.

Mowery, D.C. and B.N. Sampat (2005), Universities in national innovation systems. In J. Fagerberg, D.C. Mowery and R.R. Nelson (eds), *The Oxford Handbook of Innovation*. Oxford: Oxford University Press, pp. 209–239.

Mowery, D.C., R.R. Nelson, B.N. Sampat and A.A. Ziedonis (2004), *Ivory Tower and Industrial Innovation. University–Industry Technology Transfer Before and After the Bayh–Dole Act in the United States*. Stanford, CA: Stanford University Press.

Nerdrum, Lars and Magnus Gulbrandsen (2009), The technical-industrial research institutes in the Norwegian innovation system. In Jan Fagerberg, David C. Mowery and Bart Verspagen (eds), *Innovation, Path-Dependency, and Policy: The Norwegian Case*. Oxford: Oxford University Press, pp. 327–348.

Nguyen, Mai Thi, William M. Rohe and Spencer Morris Cowan (2012), Entrenched hybridity in public housing agencies in the USA. *Housing Studies*, 27(4): 457–475.

Noordegraaf, Mirko and Bas de Wit (2012), Responses to managerialism: how management pressures affect managerial relations and loyalties in education. *Public Administration*, 90: 957–973.

Nowotny, H., P.B. Scott and M.T. Gibbons (2001), *Re-thinking Science: Knowledge and the Public in an Age of Uncertainty*. London: Polity Press.

Phan, P.H., D.S. Siegel and M. Wright (2005), Science parks and incubators: observations, synthesis and future research. *Journal of Business Venturing*, 20: 165–182.

Polanyi, M. (1962), The republic of science: its political and economic theory. *Minerva*, 1(1): 54–73.

Powell, W.W. and K.W. Sandholtz (2012), Amphibious entrepreneurs and the emergence of organizational forms. *Strategic Entrepreneurship Journal*, 6(2): 94–115.

Rainey, Hal G. and Barry Bozeman (2000), Comparing public and private organizations: empirical research and the power of the a priori. *Journal of Public Administration Research and Theory*, 10: 447–469.

Rasmussen, E. and M. Gulbrandsen (2011), Government support programmes to promote academic entrepreneurship: a principal–agent perspective. *European Planning Studies*, 20(4): 527–546.

Rasmussen, E., Ø. Moen and M. Gulbrandsen (2006), Initiatives to promote commercialization of university knowledge. *Technovation*, 26(4): 518–533.

Rosenberg, Nathan (1983), *Inside the Black Box: Technology and Economics*. Cambridge: Cambridge University Press.

Rosenberg, Nathan (1994), *Exploring the Black Box: Technology, Economics, and History*. Cambridge: Cambridge University Press.

Rosenberg, N. and R.R. Nelson (1994), American universities and technical advance in industry. *Research Policy*, 23: 323–348.

Shane, Scott A. (1996), Hybrid organizational arrangements and their implications for firm growth and survival: a study of new franchisors. *Academy of Management Journal*, 39: 216–234.

Siegel, Donald S., Reinhilde Veugelers and Mike Wright (2007), Technology transfer offices and commercialization of university intellectual property: performance and policy implications. *Oxford Review of Economic Policy*, 23(4): 640–660.

Siegel, D.S., D. Waldman and A. Link (2003), Assessing the impact of organizational practices on the relative productivity of university technology transfer offices: an exploratory study. *Research Policy*, 32: 27–48.

Stankiewicz, R. (1986), *Academics and Entrepreneurs: Developing University–Industry Relations*. London: Frances Pinter.

Stokes, D.E. (1997), *Pasteur's Quadrant: Basic Science and Technological Innovation*. Washington, DC: Brookings Institution Press.

Thune, T. and M. Gulbrandsen (2011), Institutionalization of university–industry interaction: an empirical study of the impact of formal structures on collaboration patterns. *Science and Public Policy*, 38(2): 99–107.

Turpin, T., R. Woolley and S. Garrett-Jones (2011), Cross-sector research collaboration in Australia: the Cooperative Research Centres Program at the crossroads. *Science and Public Policy*, 38(2): 87–97.

Tuunainen, Juha (2005), Hybrid practices? Contributions to the debate on the mutation of science and university. *Higher Education*, 50: 275–298.

Whitley, R. (2002), Developing innovative competences: the role of institutional frameworks. *Industrial and Corporate Change*, 11: 497–528.

Williamson, Oliver E. (1991), Comparative economic organization: the analysis of discrete structural alternatives. *Administrative Science Quarterly*, 36: 269–229.

Youtie, J., D. Libaers and B. Bozeman (2006), Institutionalization of university research centers: the case of the National Cooperative Program in Infertility Research. *Technovation*, 26(9): 1055–1063.

8.   The Swedish corporate model
Anna Thomasson

INTRODUCTION

In common with other countries with a developed economy Sweden has, over recent years, experienced a major shift towards the marketisation of its public services. Influenced by the ideas informing New Public Management (NPM) this has involved radical changes to the way in which public services are organised and delivered. The aim of these reforms is to increase the efficiency and accountability of the public sector by replacing governance based on bureaucratic ideas and values with management approaches and accounting tools inspired by private sector practice (Osborne and Gaebler, 1992; Hood, 1995; Pollitt and Bouckaert, 2011). The influence of NPM in public sectors around the world has resulted in what can be referred to as a blending of sectors (Antonsen and Jörgensen, 1997) followed by the hybridisation of public services (André, 2010; Koppell, 2003).

At first sight, the idea that Sweden has been an eager adopter (Pollitt and Bouckaert, 2011) and an energetic implementer (Wockelberg and Ahlback Öberg, 2016) of NPM reforms is surprising. Sweden has a long tradition of investment in its public sector and the idea of the social welfare state is deeply rooted in the minds of Swedish people. During the last century this commitment has grown, spread and highly influenced the development of the Swedish public sector (Child, 1936; Marklund, 2009). Sweden is also a country where the proverb 'Moderation in all things', or as the Swedes say, *lagom*, is a motto by which many live and one that guides all types of decisions, from how much sugar to put in your coffee to the making of public policy. This notion of *lagom* has led Sweden to take the middle road on many occasions. Perhaps the most notable of these was the decision not to follow the example of either of the superpowers by subscribing to the planned economy of the Soviet Union on the one hand, or the market economy of the United States of America (USA) on the other. Instead the road chosen was that of a strong social welfare state, high taxes and a market economy influenced by a large public sector and government regulation; the so-called 'Middle Way' (Child, 1936; Cox, 2004; Marklund, 2009).

And the reforms have not been uncontroversial. Recent debates in the media and among researchers show how defenders of the Swedish welfare system based on a large public sector can challenge and question NPM values and reforms (Bringselius, 2015; Hall, 2017; Strandhäll and Shekarabi, 2017). This debate, moreover, extends beyond the role and performance of the hybrid organisational forms that have been created as a result of the adoption of NPM approaches to focus on the role of a much older hybrid, the corporations owned by Swedish municipalities that are collectively referred to as the 'Swedish corporate model'. The use of publicly owned corporations to provide public services has a long history which predates NPM by many years with its origins in the Swedish Middle Way and a long tradition of blending the public and private sectors in Sweden rather than the marketisation of public services.

This chapter will focus on the history of the Swedish corporate model and the issues of accountability raised by this kind of hybrid organisation. Its purpose is twofold: first to present the Swedish corporate model and analyse the nature of its hybrid character; and second, to identify the issues this hybrid model raises in regard to governance and accountability, and the ways in which these problems have been addressed. The aims of such an analysis are to develop our understanding of the governance of hybrid organisations and to explore to what extent existing models of understanding hybridity can be applied to a specific empirical example.

The material presented in this chapter is based on the results of ten years of empirical research on the corporate model in Sweden. The empirical material mainly consists of interviews and archival studies. The latter consists of corporate mission statements, political policy documents and agreements. Interviews were carried out with chief executive officers (CEOs), managers and board members of corporations owned or co-owned by Swedish local governments and politically appointed auditors. All this empirical material has been collected by the author herself.

The rest of the chapter is organised in the following way. The next section provides an introduction to the Swedish corporate model and the perceived advantages and disadvantages of the hybrid form; this is followed by an account of the characteristics of the model and an attempt to define the nature of its hybridity; the chapter then looks at the issues of accountability, governance and control, before concluding by discussing the way forward and presenting the implications of the study.

THE SWEDISH CORPORATE MODEL

The first examples of the use of the corporation in a public sector context in Sweden can be traced back to as early as the late 19th century (Meyer et al., 2013). It was in the 1960s and 1970s, however, that the use of the corporate model became more widely spread among Swedish municipalities with the expansion of the public sector and the development of the social welfare state (Hansson and Collin, 1991; Meyer et al., 2013). The model experienced a further boost in the middle of the 1980s as the influence from NPM grew stronger in Sweden (Erlingsson et al., 2014).

It is difficult to say why the corporate form emerged in the first place, especially considering how early it emerged in the Swedish public sector. And few studies have been conducted over the years investigating the purpose and use of the corporate model in Sweden. One likely explanation, however, is the long tradition of close collaboration between the public and private sectors in Sweden (Child, 1936; Marklund, 2009). Another possible explanation is that several of the services that today are considered a public sector responsibility in Sweden actually had their origin in private sector initiatives such as, for example, the provision of water and sewage services (Hansson et al., 1993; Malmer, 2003).

Since the 1960s the use of the corporate model in Sweden has gradually become more and more popular and the number of corporations owned by Swedish local government is currently estimated to be around 1700 (SCB, 2011). The corporate model is predominately used by municipalities to organise technical services as well as infrastructure, energy, public housing, waste management, and water and sewage services (SCB, 2011). It is in these areas that the corporate model had its roots. There are, however, more recent examples of the model being used for organising the provision of social welfare such as care of the elderly and social services, but that is less common (SCB, 2011). The most recent figures show that the municipal corporations in Sweden currently have a combined turnover of approximately 350 billion Swedish crowns (SCB, 2011)

Recent studies, especially those conducted in the light of NPM, suggest that the perceived benefits from using the corporate form as a mean of organising and providing public services include the ability to separate the management of a service from the other services provided by the same municipality (Hallgren and Helleryd, 2007). A separate budget is considered especially advantageous for those services that are financed by fees where there is a clear relationship between performance and income as, for example, in the case of public housing, waste management, and water and sewage.

The corporate model is regarded as a means of improving governance and facilitating decision-making: it clarifies the chain of command and makes the service less exposed to, or influenced by, politics and political decision making and in this way is able to increase autonomy and flexibility (Hallgren and Helleryd, 2007; Ringkjøb et al., 2008). It is also believed that it will strengthen the role of the manager, and facilitate the use of management tools and economic incentives which will improve efficiency as well as effectiveness. The similarities between the perceived benefits of the corporate model and the overall objectives of NPM reforms are thus striking.

The corporate model has not only advantages, but also disadvantages. The risk of erosion of accountability increases if the corporations are given a higher degree of autonomy (Thynne, 1994; Ryan and Ng, 2000; Luke, 2010; Erlingsson et al., 2014; Thomasson and Grossi, 2013; Grossi and Thomasson, 2015). How to govern and manage corporations owned by public government is thus a key issue (Clatworthy et al., 2000; Christensen and Laegreid, 2003; Bozec and Breton, 2003; Bozec et al., 2004; Grossi and Reichard, 2008; Thomasson, 2009; Luke, 2010; Erlingsson et al., 2014). Another – related – issue is the risk of mission drift, that is, the risk of public sector values being overshadowed by such market-oriented values as efficiency and effectiveness (Sands, 2006; André, 2010; Shaoul et al., 2012).

HYBRIDITY AND THE SWEDISH MODEL

The increased attention given to hybrid organisations in the 21st century by scholars researching the management and governance of public sector organisations (see, e.g., Kickert, 2001; Koppell, 2003; Kurunmäki and Miller, 2006; Miller et al., 2008; Skelcher, 2009; André, 2010; Billis, 2010; Pache and Santos, 2013; Denis et al., 2015; Nyland and Pettersen, 2015) can give the misleading impression that they are a new phenomenon. But the idea of hybrid organisations that combined public or private sector characteristics or dimensions predated the move towards NPM by many years. The term 'hybrid' was used in study of the Swedish Middle Way as long ago as 1936 (Child, 1936). In 1953, Dahl and Lindblom published a study that discussed the combination of public and private characteristics in organisations on a continuum ranging from 'core public' at one end of the spectrum to 'core private' at the other. This approach was later pursued by Bozeman (1987), who argued that all organisations had some kind of public dimension and thus many of them could be seen as hybrid forms.

A more common approach, however, is to start from a conception of ideal forms of organisation (Lan and Rainey, 1992; Nutt and Backoff, 1993; Bozeman and Bretschneider, 1994; Kickert, 2001; Billis, 2010). This approach involves detailing the key characteristics of each ideal form of organisation and defining hybrids as organisations that have adopted characteristics from more than one ideal form (Kickert, 2001; Koppell, 2003; Lan and Rainey, 1992; André, 2010; Billis, 2010).

Billis (2010) argues that in all three sectors – public, private and third – there are five core generic elements: ownership, governance, operational priorities, distinctive human resources and distinctive other resources. However, each sector has its own set of distinctive principles that embody these five core elements. Thus, the distinctive ownership in the private sector is by shareholders, in the public sector it is by citizens, and in the third sector by members. Organisations become hybrids when significant distinctive features of one sector are adopted in one or both of the other sectors. Nevertheless, Billis argues that hybrid organisations have a primary adherence to the principles of one sector based on the inherent contradictory conflicting principles of each of them (ibid., p. 56). The 'prime sector' of each organisation can be identified by uncovering the principal owners: those who can close the organisation down, or change its fundamental boundary and mission (ibid., p. 50). Table 8.1 summarises the core elements and principles of the three sectors, and the next section draws on this framework developed by Billis (2010, p. 55) to analyse the hybrid nature of the Swedish corporate model.

Table 8.1   *The mix of private and public sector principles in the Swedish corporate model*

Core elements	Private sector principles	Public sector principles	Swedish corporate model
1. Ownership	Shareholders	Citizens	Shareholders are municipalities, indirectly citizens
2. Governance	Share ownership size	Public elections	Municipality responsible for governance through Municipal Assembly and council
3. Operational priorities	Market forces and individual choices	Public services and collective choice	Market forces and competition combined with public monopoly
4. Distinctive human resources	Paid employees in managerially controlled firm	Paid public servants in legally backed bureau	Paid employees, but sometimes overlap with the role of public servants
5. Distinctive other resources	Sales, fees	Taxes	Mainly fees

Source: Based on the model in Billis (2010, p. 55).

OWNERSHIP AND GOVERNANCE

Municipal corporations in Sweden are fully owned by the municipalities. They hold all the shares in the corporations which are thus indirectly owned by the citizens who ultimately have the authority to govern them through the electoral process. To that extent they exhibit the key characteristics of the public sector as defined by Billis. At the same time all limited corporations, regardless of ownership and whether they are listed on a stock exchange or not, fall under the same legislation (*Aktiebolagslagen*) (Stattin, 2007). As a result, Swedish municipal companies have an ownership structure as well as a governance and accountability system that is similar to that for limited corporations in the private sector. Ownership of municipal limited corporations is thus regulated by the use of shares and, in effect, the owners of those shares are the municipality and not the citizens. According to the legislation, responsibility for governing the corporation is vested in the Municipal Assembly. This means that there is an overlap between the legislation concerning limited corporations (*Aktiebolagslagen*) and that which regulates municipalities (*Kommunallagen*) (Stattin, 2007).

Public services that are corporatised are thus not only subject to the same requirements as other corporations, but also have the same obligations as do public services in general. In accordance to these obligations the Municipal Assembly elects representatives to the Annual General Meeting and these representatives in turn elect board members and auditors. In Sweden, municipal corporations have two types of auditors: those that are formally qualified on the one hand, and laymen non-auditors on the other who are selected from members of political parties based on the result of general elections. Hence politicians not only occupy seats on the board but also take part in auditing the organisation. The Swedish municipal corporation can thus be seen to combine two sets of sector characteristics in terms of its ownership and governance, and can be considered to be a public–private hybrid.

OPERATIONAL PRIORITIES

The third core element found in the Billis model is operational priorities, where private sector principles are based on market forces and individual choice while public sector principles are based on public service and collective choice. The extent to which Swedish municipal corporations adhere to either of these principles varies according to the type of service provided by the corporation. The majority of them operate in the area of technical services such as housing, energy, electricity, waste management, and water and sewage services. These services are all financed by fees and several of them are subject to competition and operate partly in a deregulated market.

Waste management (with the exemption of household waste), for example, was deregulated in the 1990s and early 2000s. Several of the municipal corporations providing waste management services were established before the market was deregulated and have therefore gradually been subjected to competition, and a similar development has taken place in the electricity and energy sectors. The housing market is regulated but subject to competition. Public housing companies compete with privately owned (and often listed) companies in providing rental apartments. Similarly, housing for children and treatment homes for families and individuals in crisis or need of care are provided by municipal as well as private corporations. The supply of housing for these groups is thus purchased by municipalities in a market that is subject to competition. The only exception to the rule is the provision of water and sewage services, which are financed by fees but are public monopolies. There is also a group of municipal corporations that provide services within the area of tourism and culture. These are slightly different from the other municipal corporations in Sweden, since they may be financed by taxes but still provide services in competition with private sector or third sector organisations. The majority of the Swedish municipal corporations operate under a mix of market forces and public service logics.

DISTINCTIVE HUMAN RESOURCES AND DISTINCTIVE OTHER RESOURCES

The final core elements – distinctive human resources and distinctive other resources – also provide evidence for considering the Swedish corporate model a hybrid form. According to Billis, human resources in the private sector consist of employed people working in a corporation, while other resources are provided by sales and fees. In the public sector, on the other hand, human resources consist of public servants working in a bureau, while other resources come in the form of taxes. As already mentioned above, the majority of municipal corporations in Sweden are financed by fees from monopoly services or by a combination of these and fees for services provided in a deregulated market. Only a few are financed by tax money (for example, municipal corporations providing services for tourists and cultural activities). While municipal corporations in Sweden vary in the extent to which their resources come from private sector forms, the majority of them are financed by fees and revenues from a deregulated market.

Like the other core elements, human resources constitute a complex blend of public and private sector principles. People employed by municipal corporations work for a corporation and not a bureau. The intrinsic nature of hybridity in the Swedish municipal corporation causes problems for its governing bodies and those who serve on them (see later section). But these contradictions between public and private principles can also trickle down throughout the organisation and cause tensions for the management of human relations where the principles of the firm conflict with those involved in the bureau. Once again we can see how the Swedish municipal corporation exhibits of a blend of public and private principles.

SUMMARY

On the basis of the core elements developed in the model developed by Billis we can conclude that Swedish municipal corporations are hybrid organisations, since they combine 'built-in' or what Billis calls 'enacted' principles from the private and public sector within each element. This blend of public and private principles makes it difficult to identify the boundary between what is public and what is private in these corporations.

These findings are especially interesting since they challenge the whole idea that there is a continuum of hybrid forms, and tend to support those such as Billis (2010) and Karré

(2011) who offer a different approach. Billis (2010, p. 57), for example, has developed the concept of hybrid zones where principles from different sectors overlap to define different kinds of hybrid organisations. These hybrid forms emerge as their owners, managers or policy-makers (the principal owners) take more or less deliberate decisions to cross sector boundaries. The history of the Swedish corporate model provides two initiatives that illustrate this kind of development. In the first place, hybrids were created due to the 'politicisation' of the economy and the creation of the so-called 'Middle Way' and the social welfare state in the 1930s and onwards (Child, 1936; Marklund, 2009). Secondly, we can see how the influence of NPM has created a new wave of hybridisation as the delivery of public services came to involve the private sector approach and the boundaries between the sectors became blurred (Antonsen and Jörgensen, 1997).

According to Billis (2010) it is a governance responsibility to address the issues of hybridity and make decisions about what logic is to prevail when an organisation crosses the boundary of a sector and moves into a hybrid zone. This enables the organisation to manage the ambiguity associated with goal conflicts in hybrid organisations and the issues about how they can deal with questions of accountability. There are, however, reasons to question whether this approach holds true in the case of the Swedish corporate model.

Swedish municipal corporations lack boundaries. The intrinsic combination of public and private sector principles found in them makes it difficult – or perhaps even impossible – to determine where the boundaries are at whatever level in the organisation we attempt to define them. The nature of the legislative framework under which the municipal corporations have been established, the principles underpinning their system of governance, and the nature of their management and operational principles, including access to and the use of resources, all demonstrate the ways in which public and private principles are intertwined in Swedish municipal corporations. This blend of different principles can be seen to be intrinsic and thus difficult to untangle. As a result the identity of the municipal corporation is fundamentally ambiguous.

ISSUES OF GOVERNANCE, ACCOUNTABILITY AND CONTROL

In a number of studies, hybrid organisations have been described as ambiguous, exposed to goal conflicts and lacking in accountability (see, e.g., Kickert, 2001; Koppell, 2003; Cooney, 2006; Thomasson, 2009; André, 2010; Luke, 2010; Shaoul et al., 2012; Pache and Santos, 2013; Skelcher and Smith, 2015). The weakening of accountability in particular has been attributed to a change in the roles of and relationships between citizens and politicians when the delivery of public services occurs at arm's-length from political governance (André, 2010; Billis, 2010; Shaoul et al., 2012; Grossi and Thomasson, 2015).

Historically, the corporation as an entity was created as a means of managing risk in profit-oriented activities. When a corporation is created a separation occurs between its ownership and the control of its assets. The separation of ownership and control has given rise to what is referred to as an agency problem (Aguilera, 2005): that is, the difficulty of securing the interest of the owners as the responsibility for their assets and investments are handed over to an external actor (in the case of corporations, that is the board and the CEO). This creates a need for the owners to secure their interests and to establish a relationship and a chain of command between them and the actors involved in the governance of corporations (Aguilera, 2005; Huse, 2007). This is a well-known problem that has been analysed and debated by a number of scholars within the field of corporate governance (Fama, 1980; Donaldson, 1990; Walsh and Seward, 1990; Shleifer and Vishny, 1997; Gedajlovic and Shapiro, 1998). The use of the corporate form for the production and delivery of public services exacerbates the problem of agency by altering the relationship between politicians and the voters, and complicating their roles and the interaction between them (Deleon, 1998; Hodge and Coghill, 2007; Hodges, 2012).

In the private sector the interests of the owners can be secured through the implementation of various instruments to measure financial performance (Huse, 2007; Thomsen, 2011). These instruments, and the assumptions on which they are based, are of limited value in a public sector context where other values prevail and financial resources are merely a means to an end. In the circumstances, a question arises about the extent to which hybrid organisations need a governance system that is tailor-made to meet their needs to secure accountability (André, 2010; Shaoul et al., 2012; Grossi and Thomasson, 2015). This question of accountability is closely related to the issue of mission drift: the tendency in hybrid organisations for social ends to be neglected in favour of financial goals that are easier to measure (Shaoul et al., 2012; Grossi and Thomasson, 2015).

The processes used for governance and control creates a conflict between logics and interests that is inherent to the hybrid solution and reflected in different stakeholder expectations (Koppell, 2003; Miller et al., 2008; Thomasson, 2009; Denis et al., 2015; Nyland and Pettersen, 2015; Skelcher and Smith, 2015). Mixing private sector practices with the expectations related to public sector values creates tensions within and around hybrid organisations that can lead to an accountability gap which can threaten their legitimacy. This accountability gap and the tendency to mission drift experienced by hybrid organisations can probably be explained by the fact that the system used for governance and control tends to be a replica of the one used in the private sector (Grossi and Thomasson, 2015; Battilana and Dorado, 2010).

The corporate model used by local governments in Sweden was developed long before Sweden jumped onto the NPM bandwagon and thus also long before the discussion of accountability in hybrid organisations emerged onto the research agenda. When the Swedish corporate model was developed, the template was not the private sector corporation but the idea of a democratic government. Values other than those of the private sector shaped the development of the Swedish corporate model and its content. It may be possible that the Swedish corporate model contains processes that are better aligned with democratic values than those found in the hybrid organisations that have developed in the wake of NPM.

SYSTEMS FOR GOVERNANCE AND CONTROL IN THE SWEDISH CORPORATE MODEL

In Sweden the same legislation applies to all limited companies regardless of ownership. Consequently, municipal corporations are subject to the same system of governance as private corporations. The difference is that the relationship between the municipality and the corporation also falls under the legislation concerning municipalities where the control of ownership control is emphasised. This governance system provides the owner with the following main control mechanisms.

The principal owners of municipal corporations have the right to vote at the Annual General Meeting (and as the municipality holds all the shares it also commands all the votes), they can appoint the members of the board, appoint auditors, issue instructions and define the purpose of the corporation. It is these mechanisms that municipalities can use to govern their corporations and secure their accountability. These formal mechanisms are similar to a large extent to what is also found in corporations in other countries (Thomsen, 2011).

More interesting is how the mechanisms are implemented in a given situation and how the owner, in this case the municipality, secures accountability through the governance process. Sweden, with its long tradition of municipal corporations, differs from other countries. In Sweden it is the practice for local governments to appoint politicians to the board of the corporations they own. By doing so they believe that the decision-making process of the board will be made more transparent and that the interest of the public will be secured. The owners – that is, the municipality – send a signal that public sector principles and democratic values ought to have precedence in this hybrid context (Billis, 2010).

The problem is that when theory meets reality the outcome can be different, and other issues emerge of which the most prominent are discussed here. When an elected representative assumes the role of board member the same person occupies two formal roles within the same system. As a board member they represent the corporation and are obliged to protect the corporation's interests according to the legislation; they are thus legally obliged not to make a decision or act in any way that can damage the corporation. As an elected politician, however, a person has a responsibility to the voters (as well as to the political party to which they belong) and is expected to protect their interests. As an elected politician a board member may feel the need to inform the general public about an issue related to the corporation, but be constrained from doing so since it might damage the corporation.

One example of such a situation is that of an elected politician and board member of a local waste management corporation who felt the need to let the general public know that the corporation was in financial difficulties, but was threatened by the other members of the board with legal action based on the claim that by making this information public he had damaged the corporation. To put elected politicians on the board thus transfers the ambiguity of the hybrid context and organisation to the individual, and it is the individual who in any given situation has to manage that ambiguity. Rather than increasing transparency, the arrangement provides a breeding ground for conflicts between legal systems and moral obligations.

Another aspect to consider is the occupation by elected politicians of other positions in local government alongside their membership of the board of a corporation. The legislation concerning local government in Sweden stipulates that the local government's board has a legal responsibility to oversee the corporations it owns. If an elected politician occupies a seat on the local government board (the executive organ in the local government with representatives from the largest parties with seats in the council) as well as on the board of a corporation, that person is actually overseeing him or herself, and from an accountability perspective this is highly problematic. A similar situation emerges if the elected politician is a corporation board member at the same time as they occupy a seat on the local government council (the parliament of the local government with elected representatives from all political parties) which has oversight of the corporation on the basis of an audit report and annual statement. Once again this is a potential conflict of interest, and an example of how the ambiguity of the hybrid organisation is transferred to the individual in a way that raises issues of accountability and lack of transparency. It happens quite frequently that elected politicians in Swedish local governments have seats on the council and/or the local government board at the same time as they are members of a municipal corporation. There is no formal regulation that prohibits an elected politician from occupying several seats within the local government even though this might give rise to a conflict of interest.

Another effort to reduce the accountability gap in the Swedish corporate model involves the appointment of politically appointed auditors alongside the more conventional professional financial auditors. These are politicians selected by local government to scrutinise the activities of the corporation and assess to what extent they comply with the purpose of the corporation as defined by its owners. Like the appointment of board members this is intended to reduce the accountability gap and increase transparency about the services that have been corporatised by local governments. Unlike the appointment of elected politicians to the board of a corporation the non-professional auditors are not allowed to occupy any other seat in the local government. This part of the Swedish corporate model thus does not give rise to the same kind of ambiguity as does the practice of appointing elected politicians as board members. The system, however, does require that the person appointed as non-professional auditor is able to distinguish between their role as politician and the role as auditor. This is far from uncomplicated since the non-professional auditor's assignment is to audit their political peers.

SUMMARY

Before a public service becomes corporatised it is a part of the local government and therefore also a part of the democratic system and subject to the mechanisms of accountability that this system involves. When the service is corporatised it is expected to move away from the democratic system into the governance system designed for profit-oriented corporations. When the public sector owners use their legal powers to appoint board members and auditors from among elected politicians, the two previously separated systems for governance and accountability become intertwined and the governance system becomes politicised.

The merging of systems adds to the hybrid character of the corporate model, as hybridity is transferred from the contextual and organisational level to the individual. Elected politicians are legally required as board members to look after corporate interests, but morally obliged and expected by their voters to act as politicians and promote the public good. In this situation it becomes more difficult for stakeholders to discern who is responsible for what, and how accountability is secured. The effort made in the spirit of the *lagom* culture and the Middle Way to 'neutralise' the market element and increase transparency can thus actually be argued to be counterproductive. These findings tend to support the suggestions made by previous studies of hybrid organisations of a need to focus more on individuals in organisations and how they, on an individual level, manage the different logics that hybrid organisations comprise (Pache and Santos, 2013).

CURRENT ISSUES

A prerequisite for a system which depends on elected politicians to enhance transparency is the ability of politicians to honour their commitments. Thus in many ways the Swedish corporate model is symbolic of the strong faith Swedes traditionally had in politicians and the democratic system as well as in the social welfare state that was the breeding ground for the Swedish corporate model. As Child describes it in his book on the Swedish Middle Way from 1936: 'the Swedes have an inherent honesty' (Child, 1936, p. 112) and 'the state, the consumer and the producer have intervened to make capitalism work in a reasonable way for the greatest good of the whole nation' (ibid., p. 143).

A great deal has happened since Child wrote his book, and the situation in Sweden is very different today. During recent decades it, like many other countries, has been influenced by NPM and the marketisation of public services that followed. This increasing market orientation has come to challenge the Swedish Middle Way in a number of ways. While the recent reforms that have opened up public services to market forces have been subject to questioning and debate, at the same time the Swedish corporate model, in spite of its long tradition in Sweden, has been questioned, scrutinised and heavily criticised. One reason for the public criticism of the Swedish model and its publicly owned corporations has been a series of recent scandals that have, in turn, raised questions about how to secure transparency and accountability in municipally owned corporations (Amnå et al., 2013; Andersson et al., 2010; Hyltner and Velasco, 2009). On several occasions corporations owned by municipalities have been accused of corruption and failure to live up to the requirements of current legislation. In particular the boards and managers of the corporations have come under scrutiny. Probably the largest scandal involving several of the corporations and their boards took place in Gothenburg in 2010, when a large corruption scheme was discovered that involved several of the corporations and their boards (Amnå et al., 2013).

Corruption and unfair competition combined with a failure to disclose information are the issues that have recently been raised in relation to the use of the Swedish corporate model. They have challenged the strong faith Swedes previously had in their politicians and the government, as well as the Swedish tradition of the Middle Way. In the wake of NPM and recent corporate scandals in local governments, the context as well as the mindset of people seems to have changed. Recent events have shown how the presence of politicians on the board as well the use of politicians as non-professional auditors have secured neither transparency nor accountability. As a result, faith in the system as well as support for the welfare state, and with that the Swedish corporate model, has gradually been eroded. This has led to calls to revisit the existing systems of governance and accountability in the Swedish corporate model, and this is the focus of the next section of this chapter and its conclusion.

THE WAY FORWARD

The negative attention attracted by the corporate model over the last couple of years has implications for its governance system. There is an inherent tension in the corporate model between the control exercised by the owner and the autonomy enjoyed by the agent (the 'agency problem' is a feature of the literature; see, for example, Fama, 1980; Aguilera, 2005). The governance systems of the Swedish model were intended to take account of this tension by bridging the gap between the local government authorities that owned municipal corporation on the one hand, and their agents on the other, and securing trust between them. Current events in Sweden have shown that existing systems of governance and accountability have failed to fill that gap or, perhaps, have not stood the test of time. As market-oriented ideas became rooted in Sweden and converged with the existing social welfare system the context of the corporate model has changed, but the governance of the model has not been adapted to the new circumstances in which it is operating. Private sector principles became dominant in the Swedish corporate model as the result of the deregulation of public services which opened them up to competition. This is not to argue that the new set of principles replaced the original public sector values, but that the two approaches came to overlap over time to create the intrinsic web of public and private sector principles that the Swedish corporate model has developed into (Hyndman and Liguori, 2016).

One response to current events has been action to strengthen the role of the owner and to ensure that local government lives up to the responsibility involved in owning municipal corporations. The legislation governing relationships between municipalities and the corporations they own has been adapted to emphasise the responsibility of local governments to monitor their corporations and the need for them to make clear the public and social value of the corporation. More reforms and further changes to the legal framework are expected as the result of the current revision of the legislation. This focuses not only on the roles and responsibilities of the owners but also on the rest of the governance system, including the role of the auditors.

The measures taken in the last couple of years can be considered as a step back to the principles upon which the public sector has traditionally rested. To reintroduce or re-emphasise public sector values might be what is needed. Both Hoggett (2005) and du Gay (2005) distinguish between the ways in which bureaucracies are organised and the nature of bureaucratic values. It can be argued that recent attempts to avoid the perceived inefficiencies of bureaucracies have led to the erasure of bureaucratic values, and that the way to secure greater accountability in public–private sector hybrid organisations might involve not the creation of bureaucracy, but the reinstatement of bureaucratic values (Hoggett, 2005).

CONCLUSIONS AND IMPLICATIONS

What can we learn from the Swedish corporate model? It enables us to look at the context in which a specific type of organisation emerged and its subsequent history. Without an understanding of its history we might assume that the Swedish corporate model was a result of the strong impact that NPM has had on how public sector services has developed in Sweden during recent decades. And we might draw the conclusion that its hybrid character is the result of the introduction of NPM's private sector logics into the delivery of public services. But the reality is more complex. The history of the Swedish corporate model is almost a century old and what we see today is the result of the influence that public as well as private sector logics has had on the model during that period.

In the wake of NPM there is a tendency to see everything that occurs in the public sector as a result of the recent marketisation of the sector. The example of the Swedish corporate model teaches us not to forget history. And the relevance of the historical context is not restricted to analysis of the Swedish model. A recently published study of the development of the public sector in the United Kingdom shows that trends such as NPM do not come and go or replace each other; instead, systems tend to blend and coexist as reforms are added to already existing solutions (Hyndman and Liguori, 2016). To take history into account is thus not only relevant for understanding a specific type of hybrid organisation that has emerged in Sweden, but also relevant for our understanding of all public sector reforms including the development of hybrid organisations. One lesson (or at least a friendly reminder) to be learned from the Swedish example is thus to include context and history in the analysis of change.

A second issue that is raised by this analysis of the Swedish corporate model is the extent to which existing models and definitions of hybrid organisations are applicable. This analysis drew on the Billis (2010) model and took as its starting point two key aspects of this approach: the idea of hybrid zones based on the overlap between clearly defined sectors, and the definition of the core elements of each of the sectors. By applying this model to the analysis of the Swedish corporate model we were able to describe and define the nature and source of its hybrid character. This study thus supports the conclusions of previous studies on hybrid organisations that are based on the idea that hybridity can be traced back to organisational characteristics or elements (Lan and Rainey, 1992; Nutt and Backoff, 1993; Bozeman and Bretschneider, 1994; Kickert, 2001; Billis, 2010).

The model also enabled us to identify the lack of clarity between fundamental public and private sector principles in the organisation, and the consequent intrinsic web of conflicting logics. This created ambiguity, complicated governance and raised issues of accountability. The study did not provide a means of solving these issues any more than previous research on hybrid organisations had been able to. One possible solution, however, was identified: to let the two systems coexist better by reintroducing bureaucratic values alongside market-oriented solutions (Hoggett, 2005; du Gay, 2005; Hyndman and Liguori, 2016).

This study also sheds some light on how organisational hybridity at the governance level can be experienced as severe problems for individual members of governing bodies. These findings support previous studies of hybrid organisations which suggested a need to highlight the role of individuals in organisations and how they manage the different logics that hybrid organisations comprise (Pache and Santos, 2013).

A fourth issue that is raised by the analysis of the Swedish corporate model is to what extent models and systems of governance and accountability stand the test of time. Looking at the ways in which the Swedish corporate model is being challenged currently, it is apparent that hybrid organisations need to adapt to new challenges. This is of course true for any organisation, but it may be especially important in a hybrid organisation that is exposed to dual logics and systems and is thus more likely to experience changing conditions.

Finally, this analysis of the Swedish corporate model demonstrates the need for further research on specific kinds of hybrid organisations. This chapter has been able to raise some of the key issues they face, but only some of them. Recent studies have identified other issues, and Denis et al. (2015) have provided us with an extensive (though perhaps not exhaustive) list of areas related to hybrid issues in need of research. This chapter has provided an example of how focusing on one form of hybrid organisation can contribute to our greater understanding of hybridity in action.

REFERENCES

Aguilera, Ruth V. (2005), 'Corporate Governance and Director Accountability: An Institutional Comparative Perspective', *British Journal of Management*, 16, 39–53.

Amnå, Erik, Czarniawska, Barbara and Marcusson, Lena (2013), 'Tillitens gränser: Granskningskommissionens slutbetänkande', Göteborg: Granskningskommissionen i Göteborgs stad.

Andersson, Staffan, Bergh, Anderas and Erlingsson, Gissur (2010), *Korruption, maktmissbruk och legitimitet*, Stockholm: Nordstedts.

André, Rae (2010), 'Assessing the Accountability of Government-sponsored Enterprises and Quangos', *Journal of Business Ethics*, 97(2), 271–289.

Antonsen, Marianne and Jörgensen, Torben Beck (1997), 'The Publicness of Public Organisations', *Public Administration*, 75(2), 337–357.

Battilana, Julie and Dorado, Silvia (2010), 'Building Sustainable Hybrid Organisations: The Case of Commercial Microfinance Organisations', *Academy of Management Journal*, 53(6), 1419–1440.

Billis, David (2010), *Hybrid Organisations and the Third Sector: Challenges for Practice, Theory and Policy*, New York: Palgrave Macmillan.

Bozec, Richard and Breton, Gaétan (2003), 'The Impact of the Corporatization Process on the Financial Performance of Canadian State-Owned Enterprises', *International Journal of Public Sector Management*, 16, 27–47.

Bozec, Richard, Zéghal, Daniel and Boujenoui, Ameur (2004), 'The Effect of the Reform of Canadian State-Owned Enterprises on Major Corporate Governance Mechanisms', *Australian Journal of Public Administration*, 63, 79–94.

Bozeman, Barry (1987), *All Organisations are Public: Bridging Public and Private Organisational Theories*, San Francisco, CA: Jossey-Bass.

Bozeman, Barry and Bretschneider, Stuart (1994), 'The Publicness Puzzle in Organisational Theory: A Test of Alternative Explanations of Differences between Public and Private Organisations', *Journal of Public Administration Research and Theory*, 4(2), 197–224.

Bringselius, Louise (2015), 'Sverige behöver en mer nyanserad debatt om NPM', *Dagens Nyheter*, 20 June.

Child, Marquis W. (1936), *Sweden The Middle Way: The Story of the Constructive Compromise Between Socialism and Capitalism*, New York: Penguin Books.

Christensen, Tom and Laegreid, Peter (2003), 'Coping with Complex Leadership Roles: The Problematic Redefinition of Government Owned Enterprises', *Public Administration*, 81, 803–831.

Clatworthy, Mark A., Mellet, Howard J. and Peel, J. Michael (2000), 'Corporate Governance under New Public Management: An Exemplification', *Corporate Governance: An International Review*, 8, 166–176.

Cooney, K. (2006), 'The Institutional and Technical Structuring of Nonprofit Ventures: Case Study of US Hybrid Organisation Caught between Two Fields', *Voluntas*, 17, 143–161.

Cox, Robert (2004), 'The Path-dependency of an Idea: Why Scandinavian Welfare States Remain Distinct', *Social Policy and Administration*, 38(2), 204–219.

Dahl, Robert. A and Lindblom, Charles Edward (1953), *Politics, Economics and Welfare*, New York: Harper & Brothers.

Deleon, Linda (1998), 'Accountability in a "Reinvented" Government', *Public Administration*, 76(3), 539–558.

Denis, Jean-Louis, Ferlie, Ewan and Van Gestel, Nicolette (2015), 'Understanding Hybridity in Public Organisations', *Public Administration*, 93(2), 1–17.

Donaldson, Lex (1990), 'The Ethereal Hand: Organisational Economics and Management Theory', *Academy of Management Review*, 15(3), 369–381.

du Gay, Paul (ed.) (2005), *The Values of Bureaucracy*, Oxford: Oxford University Press.

Erlingsson, Gissur, Fogelgren, Mattias, Olsson, Fredrik, Thomasson, Anna and Öhrvall, Rickard (2014), 'Hur styrs och granskas kommunala bolag? Erfarenheter och lärdomar från Norrköpings kommun', Linköping, Sweden: Centrum för Kommunstrategiska studier, Linköpings universitet.

Fama, Eugene F. (1980), 'Agency Problems and the Theory of the Firm', *Journal of Political Economy*, 88(2), 288–307.

Gedajlovic, Eric R. and Shapiro, Daniel M. (1998), 'Management and Ownership Effects: Evidence From Five Countries', *Strategic Management Journal*, 19, 533–553.

Grossi, Giuseppe and Reichard, Christoph (2008), 'Municipal Corporatization in Germany and Italy', *Public Management Review*, 10(5), 597–617.

Grossi, Giuseppe and Thomasson, Anna (2015), 'Bridging the Accountability Gap in Hybrid Organisations: The Case of Malmö-Copenhagen Port', *International Review of Administrative Science*, 81(3), 604–620.

Hall, Patrik (2017), 'Allt fler styr och kontrollerar – allt färre gör', *Dagens Nyheter*, 28 September.

Hallgren, Tohmas and Helleryd, Erik (2007), 'Affärsmässiga, samhällsnyttiga och kommunägda', Stockholm: Procredo AB.

Hansson, Lennart and Collin, Sven-Olof (1991), *Kommunalt bolag? En studie av för- och nackdelar med bolagisering av kommunalteknisk verksamhet*, Stockholm: Svenska Kommunförbundet.

Hansson, Lennart, Bryntse, Karin, Isaksson, Ulf and Mattisson, Ola (1993), *Teknisk Service Europa*, Stockholm: Svenska Kommunförbundet.

Hodge, Greame, A. and Coghill, Ken (2007), 'Accountability in the Privatized State', *Governance: An International Journal of Policy, Administration and Institutions*, 20(4), 26–51.

Hodges, Ron (2012), 'Joined-up Government and the Challenges to Accounting and Accountability Researchers', *Financial Accountability and Management*, 28(1), 26–51.

Hoggett, Paul (2005), 'A Service to the Public: The Containment of Ethical and Moral Conflicts by Public Bureaucracies', in du Gay, Paul (ed.), *The Values of Bureaucracy*, Oxford: Oxford University Press, pp. 165–190.

Hood, Christopher (1995), 'The "New Public Management" in the 1980s: Variations on a Theme', *Accounting Organisation and Society*, 20(2), 93–109.

Huse, Morten (2007), *Boards, Governance and Value Creation*, Cambridge: Cambridge University Press.

Hyltner, Mårten and Velasco, Micha (2009),'Kommunala bolag: laglöst land?', Stockholm, Sverige: Den nya välfärden.

Hyndman, Noel and Liguori, Mariannunziata (2016), 'Public Sector Reforms: Changing Contours on an NPM Landscape', *Financial Accountability and Management*, 32(1), 388–408.

Karré, Philip Marcel (2011), *Heads and Tails: Both Sides of the Coin: An Analysis of Hybrid Organisations in the Dutch Waste Management Sector*, Den Haag: Eleven International Publishing.

Kickert, Walter. J.M. (2001), 'Public Management of Hybrid Organisations: Governance of Quasi-Autonomous Executive Agencies', *International Public Management Journal*, 4, 135–150.

Koppell, Jonathan G.S. (2003), *The Politics of Quasi-Government: Hybrid Organisations and the Dynamics of Bureaucratic Control*, Cambridge: Cambridge University Press.

Kurunmäki, Lisa and Miller, Peter (2006), 'Modernising Government: The Calculating Self, Hybridisation and Performance Measurement', *Financial Accountability and Management*, 22(1), 87–106.

Lan, Zhiyong and Rainey, Hal G. (1992), 'Goals, Rules and Effectiveness in Public, Private and Hybrid Organisations: More Evidence on Frequent Assertions about Differences', *Journal of Public Administration Research and Theory*, 2(1), 5–28.

Luke, Belinda (2010), 'Examining Accountability Dimensions in State-Owned Enterprises', *Financial Accountability and Management*, 26(2), 134–162.

Malmer, Stellan (2003), *Ett pris blir till: Om förklaringar till kommunala avgifter och taxor*, Köpenhamn: Santérus förlag.

Marklund, Carl (2009), 'The Social Laboratory, the Middle Way and the Swedish Model', *Scandinavian Journal of History*, 34(3), 264–258.

Meyer, Lars, Mårtensson, Pär and Nilsson, Ola (2013), *Kommunala bolag; ägarstyrning och styrelsefunktion*, Lund: Studentlitteratur.

Miller, Peter, Kurunmäki, Liisa and O'Leary, Ted (2008), 'Accounting, Hybrids and the Management of Risk', *Accounting Organisation and Society*, 33, 942–967.

Nutt, Paul C. and Backoff, Robert W. (1993), 'Organisational Publicness and its Implications for Strategic Management', *Journal of Public Administration Research and Theory*, 3(2), 209–231.

Nyland, Karin and Pettersen, Johanne (2015), 'Hybrid Controls and Accountabilities in Public Sector Management', *International Journal of Public Sector Management*, 28(2), 90–104.

Osborne, David and Gaebler, Ted (1992), *Reinventing Government: How the Entrepreneurial Spirit is Transforming the Public Sector*, Reading, Mass: Addison-Wesley.

Pache, Anne-Claire and Santos, Fillipe (2013), 'Inside the Hybrid Organisation: Selective Coupling as a Response to Competing Institutional Logics', *Academy of Management Journal*, 56(4), 972–1001.

Pollitt, Christopher and Boukaert, Geert (2011), *Public Management Reform – A Comparative Analysis: New Public Management, Governance, and the Neo-Weberian State*, Oxford: Oxford University Press.

Ringkjøb, Hans-Erik, Aars, Jacob and Vabo, Signy (2008), 'Lokalt folkestyre AS: Eierskap og styringsroller i kommunale selskap', Bergen.

Ryan, Christine and Ng, Chew (2000), 'Public Sector Corporate Governance Disclosures: An Examination of Annual Reporting Practices in Queensland', *Australian Journal of Public Administration*, 59, s.11–23.

Sands, Valarie (2006), 'The Right to Know and Obligation to Provide: Public–Private Partnerships, Public Knowledge, Public Accountability, Public Disenfranchisement and Prison Cases', *UNSW Law Journal*, 29(3), 334–341.

SCB, Statistics Sweden (2011),'Offentligt ägda företag 2010', Statistiska Centralbyrån, Statistiska meddelanden, OE 27 SM1101, Stockholm: Statistics Sweden.

Shaoul, Jean, Stafford, Anne and Stapleton, Pamela (2012), 'Accountability and Corporate Governance of Public–Private Partnerships', *Critical Perspectives on Accounting*, 23(3), 213–229.

Shleifer, Andrei and Vishny, Robert W. (1997), 'A Survey of Corporate Governance', *Journal of Finance*, 52(2), 737–783.

Skelcher, Chris (2009), 'Public–Private Partnerships and Hybridity', in Ferlie, Ewan, Lynn Jr, Laurence E. and Pollitt, Christopher (eds), *The Oxford Handbook of Public Management*, Oxford: Oxford Handbooks online, pp. 347–370. https://doi.org/10.1093/jopart/mup040.

Skelcher, Chris and Smith, Rathgeb (2015), 'Theorizing Hybridity: Institutional Logics, Complex Organisations, and Actor Identities: The Case of Nonprofits', *Public Administration*, 93(2), 433–448.

Stattin, Daniel (2007), *Kommunal Aktiebolagsrätt: Bolagsrätt och bolagsstyrning för kommun- och landstingsägda bolag*, Stockholm: Nordstedts Juridik.

Strandhäll, Annika and Shekarabi, Ardalan (2017), 'Välfärdens proffs måste ges större friheter i arbetet', *Svenska Dagbladet*, 17 August.

Thomasson, Anna (2009), 'Exploring the Ambiguity of Hybrid Organisations: A Stakeholder Approach', *Financial Accountability and Management*, 25(3), 385–398.

Thomasson, Anna and Grossi, Giuseppe (2013), 'Governance and Accountability of Joint Ventures: A Swedish Case Study', in Valkama, Pekka, Bailey, Steven and Anttiroiko, Ari-Veikko (eds), *Organisational Innovation in Public Services: Forms and Governance*, Basingstoke: Palgrave Macmillan, pp. 221–237.

Thomsen, Steen (2011), *An Introduction to Corporate Governance: Mechanisms and Systems*, Copenhagen: DJÖF Publishing Copenhagen.

Thynne, Ian (1994), 'The Incorporated Company as an Instrument of Government: A Quest for a Comparative Understanding', *Governance: An International Journal of Public Administration*, 7(1), 59–82.

Walsh, James P. and Seward, James K. (1990), 'On the Efficiency of Internal and External Corporate Control Mechanisms', *Academy of Management Review*, 15(3), 421–458.

Wockelberg, Helena and Ahlback Öberg, Shirin (2016), 'Reinventing the Old Reform Agenda: Public Administrative Reform and Performance According to Swedish Top Managers', in Hammerschmid, Gerhard, Van de Walle, Steven, Andrews, Rhys and Bezes, Philippe (eds), *Public Administration Reforms in Europe: A View from the Top*, Cheltenham, UK and Northampton, MA, USA: Edward Elgar Publishing, pp. 162–172.

9. Bridging public and private innovation patterns
Lars Fuglsang and Jørn Kjølseth Møller

INTRODUCTION

In this chapter we develop a framework for analysing the challenge of dealing with innovation in hybrid public services. The main objective of the chapter is to analyse how hybridity can lead to innovation. Hybrid organisations are defined by the literature as organisations that combine multiple organisational identities and forms (Battilana and Lee, 2014), multiple institutional logics (Jay, 2013; Battilana and Lee, 2014) or sector principles (Billis, 2010).

For the purpose of this chapter we define hybrid organisations as organisations that combine two or more institutional logics. An institutional logic is a socially constructed pattern of cultural symbols and material practices by which individuals and organisations provide meaning to their daily activity (Thornton et al., 2012, p. 2). For organisations, logics may translate into organisational 'principles' (Billis, 2010) or rules of the game. In this chapter we use logics and principles as almost interchangeable concepts but for us the overarching phenomenon is logics. The example of hybridity we analyse in this chapter is the growing 'servitisation' of public services. Servitisation we understand as a new institutional logic that leads public services to emphasise user-centric innovation approaches. Servitisation and the user-centric logic represent a move towards market sector principles and therefore an increase in sector hybridity.

We follow Billis (2010) in viewing hybrid organisations as having their roots in the logics or 'principles' of one sector. He argues that all organisations have generic structural features or elements, yet the logics or principles by which these are organised are different in each sector. Sector principles are the rules of the game or organisational ideal models for organisations within a sector. Billis finds that while the principles or ideal types seldom exist in a pure form in real life, organisations nevertheless 'derive their strength and legitimacy' from the principles belonging to their ideal type (ibid., p. 48). Based on previous research and studies, he: (1) distinguishes five core elements of public and private sector organisations (ownership, governance, operational priorities, human resources and other resources); and (2) clarifies how these are organised according to different ideal principles in public, private and third sector organisations. Also drawing on previous research, he finds that organisations always have their primary adherence to one of the three sets of sector principles. However, sectors have what Billis calls 'hybrid zones' where sector principles overlap. Organisations may want to move across deliberately or unconsciously slide into these zones.

Building on Billis's research, we have created a framework that can be used to analyse how organisations, rooted in one sector's ideal principles, enact hybrid logics. To explain this, we use the notion of 'hybrid regions' as a complement to Billis's 'hybrid zones'. By this we mean regions of activity, such as experimental projects, inter-sectorial collaborative efforts, and more, where overlapping sector principles (the hybrid zones) are enacted.

In such regions of activity, employees and others have more autonomy to experiment with solutions, and to enact hybrid principles or logics in order to solve problems. Thus, we suggest a more agency-oriented approach to hybridity in organisations, stressing the way employees and others enact and make sense of the hybrid zones; this is developed in the next section.

The chapter explores how this framework can guide research on the hybridisation of innovation. Hybridisation of innovation is the process of combining different logics in the innovation process in order to solve problems, meaning that the innovation patterns become hybridised by enacting several logics or principles. This is not a straightforward process, we argue, but it requires certain techniques to facilitate the intertwining of logics. In our model, we draw inspiration from the literature on boundary objects (Star and Griesemer, 1989; Carlile, 2004; Barrett and Oborn, 2010) and practice-based theory to understand how 'boundary concepts' can facilitate the enactment of hybrid principles in the innovation process. Boundary concepts are similar to boundary objects in that they are defined as constructs that have interpretative flexibility and may unite diverse groups around a common broad framework (see Barrett and Oborn, 2010, p. 1200). While a boundary object is a composite material object that has interpretative flexibility, a boundary concept is an image and concept with interpretative flexibility.

We argue that many public organisations are undergoing changes that lead them to adopt a logic of 'servitisation' (Vandermerwe and Rada, 1989). Servitisation is an institutional logic that potentially has an impact on a wide range of organisations in different sectors. In the public sector, servitisation would imply a change of operational priorities away from public service and collective choice (see Billis, 2010) and towards a market-like approach where citizens are treated more as if they were individual customers. Thus, we see servitisation as being grounded mainly in a private sector logic. However, the notion of servitisation may contribute to a nuancing of both the public and the private sector logics. For private sector firms as well as public sector organisations, servitisation is a user-centric logic that coexists with a producer-centric logic. In this way servitisation makes the distinctions between public, private and third sector logics more complex, because it is an alternative, market-inspired and user-centric logic to all of them. In contrast to this, the traditional public service sector approach to innovation is more concerned with public service, collective choice, large-scale universal innovation (Hartley, 2005), improving organisational forms, efficient production of service, and internal controls, such as New Public Management (NPM).

From empirical materials we have developed a model where local interaction and deliberation around broad boundary concepts help employees to enact the hybrid logics of market-inspired servitisation and traditional public administration in the innovation process. In three case vignettes of elderly care and postal services, we identify a number of boundary concepts that actors relate to, enact and link to concrete skills and resources, thereby combining and enacting the different logics in the innovation process. We find that servitisation triggers a sense-making process around specific concepts of servitisation and their integration with available skills and equipment.

In the following section we discuss the literature of servitisation, and how servitisation may emerge in public services. Next we introduce the model of the boundary concept. Then we use this framework to analyse three case vignettes. Finally we discuss cross-case insights and further research perspectives.

SERVITISATION AS AN EMERGING LOGIC FOR PUBLIC SERVICES ORGANISATIONS

In this section, we examine servitisation as an emerging new logic of innovation in public services. We further discuss some of the drivers of, and barriers to, servitisation. Finally we discuss how the logic of servitisation is being adopted as a model of change and innovation in public innovation literature.

Innovation patterns can be defined as principles or processes of innovation that are typical of certain collections of firms and organisations that constitute a sector or subsector. For example, high-tech firms can be characterised by a high level of research and development (R&D)-based innovation. The literature has mostly analysed the specificity of innovation patterns rather than their hybridisation. A seminal study of innovation patterns is that of Pavitt (1984), who distinguished between 'sectorial patterns of technical change', arguing that: 'Most technological knowledge turns out not to be "information" that is generally applicable and easily reproducible, but specific to firms and applications, cumulative in development and varied amongst sectors in source and direction' (ibid., p. 343). Pavitt separated private firms into four main subsectors characterised by different innovation patterns: supplier-dominated firms, scale-intensive firms, specialised suppliers and science-based firms.

The innovation literature has mainly continued to separate innovation patterns and discuss their specificity in order to understand the contextual conditions of innovation. Yet a change of perspective has been introduced by Jensen et al. (2007). They argued that research should look for combined innovation patterns as a more relevant research strategy. More specifically, their paper suggested that two modes of innovation were often combined in innovative firms: the 'science, technology and innovation' mode and the 'doing, using and interacting' mode.

The literature on public innovation also suggests that different patterns or logics of innovation can be distinguished. Most notably, Hartley (2005) argues that innovation takes different forms within different conceptions of public administration. In traditional public administration, innovation is large-scale and universal. In NPM, innovation is concerned with organisational form rather than content. In new forms of networked governance, innovation takes place at the central and local level and is aimed at both large transformations and continuous improvements in frontline services (Hartley, 2005).

Research on public innovation also suggests that new forms of service development and innovation may be evolving. Public innovation comes to rely more on the negotiation of values, meanings and relationships (Osborne, 2010), pays more attention to co-creation with citizens, and aims to increase the usability of services and meeting citizens' needs for everyday creativity.

These are useful distinctions that help us to conceptualise how innovation normally takes place in the public sector. However, studying the public sector by separating innovation patterns downplays their hybridity and simultaneous presence in public organisations.

In the service management and marketing literature, which is concerned mainly with the private sector, a stream of literature on servitisation has evolved that also tends to distinguish dominant patterns of innovation that are being institutionalised. Initially, Vandermerwe and Rada (1989) described a process of change that they argued was happening in almost all industries, which they named 'servitisation'. Manufacturing as well as service enterprises were starting to offer '"bundles" of customer-focused combinations of goods, services, support, self-service, and knowledge' where services tended to dominate (ibid., p. 314). They defined services as 'performed rather than produced and [they] are essentially intangible' (ibid., p. 315). The interaction with customers played a key role. Further, they claimed that the evolution towards servitisation was essentially customer-driven, given that, due to technological and other changes, customers had achieved a better base for negotiation.

Other concepts have been used to describe changes that point increasingly in the direction of combined or hybrid frameworks. Gebauer et al. (2012) use the notion of service strategy to describe how manufacturing companies become more involved with services. Service strategy implies an expansion of the value chain where manufacturers increasingly become involved in service offerings to satisfy increasing customer demand, maintain a competitive advantage and achieve financial growth. Kowalkowski et al. (2012) use the concept of service infusion which, they argue, referring to Lindblom (1979), happens through incremental changes at the organisational level rather than as a radical change of business model. Following this, research has emerged that studies service transformation at the organisational level as a sense-making process in relation to broader institutional changes (see DiMaggio and Powell, 1983). For example, Siltaloppi's (2015) PhD thesis is concerned with the servitisation of the Finnish residential sector – as well as the internal resistance to it in the sector – as a new institutional logic.

In the service marketing literature, Vargo and Lusch have achieved enormous impact with their notion of service-dominant (S-D) logic (Vargo and Lusch, 2004, 2008), which is also described as an institutional logic (see Skålén and Edvardsson, 2016). The S-D logic is inspired by other service marketing theories paying attention to the relationship and interaction with customers, such as Grönroos (1994). But Vargo and Lusch tell a more general story of institutional changes from a goods-dominant to a service-dominant logic. More recently, Vargo has attempted to develop the approach into a much wider ecosystem approach drawing inspiration from layered models in institutional theory (Akaka et al., 2013). In its most recent version, Vargo and Lusch (2016) argue that S-D logic rests on five axioms: (1) service is the fundamental basis of exchange; (2) value is co-created by multiple actors, always including the beneficiary; (3) all social and economic actors are resource integrators; (4) value is always uniquely and phenomenologically defined by the beneficiary; and (5) value co-creation is coordinated through actor-generated institutions and institutional arrangements.

In the public administration literature, Osborne and his colleagues (Osborne et al., 2013, 2015) have picked up this service logic as a framework for public sector services and service innovation, naming it the public-service-dominant approach. It is seen as an alternative approach to New Public Management (NPM). Adopting an S-D logic in public service may, according to Osborne et al. (2013), add value to citizens and users of services, create a robust framework for trust in public service delivery, place the experiences of the service user at the heart of effective public service design and delivery, and will create effective public services rather than merely efficient services. Osborne et al. (2015) have also attempted to specify a new service-oriented framework for public services based on seven foundational principles.

Generally, most of the literature on servitisation tends to describe the change from a product-centric to a user-centric approach in terms of a macro-change or a change of ideology (Siltaloppi, 2015) or a change of institutional logic (Skålén and Edvardsson, 2016). There has been less investigation of how this change is adopted at the organisational level. However, the literature does describe varied drivers, barriers and reactions to servitisation. In a review of the servitisation literature, Baines et al. (2009) identify three types of drivers: financial (gaining a higher profit margin), strategic (gaining competitive advantage) and marketing (using services for selling more products). These drivers reflect changes in the customers' role from passive to more active. Baines et al. also describe other barriers or challenges to servitisation that they find in the literature, such as the problems involved in setting up a service culture in companies.

For public organisations there may be several drivers of and barriers to servitisation that make it attractive to move more in this direction, but also problematic in establishing the dominance of this logic. In some cases, like elderly care or public transportation for example, there is the potential to create more user-friendly services, which has not previously been exploited. On the other hand, if public transportation is not user-friendly, people will use private transportation; and if elderly care is not carried out in a responsible and user-friendly way, it may encourage the elderly and their families to choose informal care, and this may make an indirect impact on the position of women in the labour market. Other factors that drive servitisation include: the need for certain public services, such as libraries and postal services, to change their business model in order to survive; the increasing citizen demand for high-quality services; the need to deal with complex service problems that require attention to the users' situation (for example, crime or refugees); and technological changes and fiscal pressures which push service providers into handing over more responsibility to service receivers and civil society.

Servitisation is not unproblematic and it may cause resistance for a number of reasons. A user-centered, market-like logic that increases hybridity could make it more difficult for citizens to be treated in a fair, just and equal way. Political governance of the public sector is crucial for democratic reasons (Rhodes and Wanna, 2007). Yet political governance becomes more confusing when public service (frontline) employees negotiate, co-produce and co-create value with receivers of services. Finally, some public services have control functions in relation to citizens, for example in education, prison, taxation or the police. This also comes into conflict with servitisation. These important conflicts of institutional logics, rooted in the need for both public service and servitisation, create dilemmas both at the level of public policy and public management and for frontline employees.

Based on the work of Thacher and Rein (2004) and Stewart (2006), Oldenhof et al. (2014) have pointed out different ways in which public organisations can respond to the conflicting institutional frameworks which they call value conflicts. The literature often highlights the ways in which actors are constrained by institutional logics, but researchers also call for studies that examine the active role of organisational agents in constructing legitimate compromises (Oldenhof et al., 2014, p. 52). The same authors quote Boltanski and Thévenot's (2006, p. 18) description of modern organisations as 'composite assemblages that include arrangements deriving from different worlds'. Overall, organisations may respond to conflicts between institutional logics in at least four ways: they can reject or ignore certain logics; they can create units that take care of each logic individually; they can deal with tensions incrementally; or they can seek to achieve compromises between logics. This largely corresponds to Battilana and Lee's (2014) typology of hybridisation approaches, based in turn on the work of Pratt and Foreman (2000) and Kraatz and Block (2008). Battilana and Lee's (2014) idea of hybrid organising also contributes to a more agency-oriented research agenda. Hybrid organising sumarises the ways in which organisational agents actively combine and make sense of elements of multiple organisational forms (ibid., p. 403).

There may be strong arguments in public organisations for both a pure public service logic (such as universalism) and a servitisation logic (such as care for the individual citizen). The two logics could contradict each other in ways that might block change and innovation. On the other hand, research has shown that paradoxes in logics may trigger sense-making and lead to innovations (Jay, 2013). In this chapter, rather than focusing on paradoxes, we take a slightly different approach by extending Billis's (2010) argument that, while organisations are rooted in the logic of one sector (and its ideal typical principles), they may move towards hybrid zones where the primary logic overlaps with other logics. We further argue that organisations can have 'hybrid regions', that is, regions of activity or projects where they deliberately adhere to several logics or principles at the same time. We argue that employees and other actors can make use of boundary concepts in order to facilitate and enact hybrid logics in such hybrid regions. More specifically, in our model a boundary concept also makes it possible to create linkages between public service logics and a servitisation logic.

In summary, servitisation and traditional public administration can be seen as overlapping institutional logics. Research calls for more concrete examples of hybrid situations that can explain how elements from overlapping logics could be combined in practice. We explain, in the following section, how focusing the enactment of hybrid logics through boundary concepts can guide research.

BOUNDARY CONCEPTS, SKILLS AND HYBRID REGIONS

In this section we develop a practice-based, situated approach that enables us to analyse how different institutional logics are combined and enacted in innovation processes. The section draws especially the literature on boundary objects and practice-based theory.

Practice-based theories (Giddens, 1984) are concerned with actions through which social structures come to life. Practices are organised nexuses of action (Schatzki, 2002, p. 77) or routinised behaviours (Reckwitz, 2002, p. 249) through which social structures manifest themselves. The idea of the duality of structure is a valuable notion which suggests that practices can both constrain and enable action. Practices have also been described as associations of actions that connect 'heterogeneous elements into a coherent set' (Gherardi, 2006, p. 34). Practice-based approaches are thus concerned with how social and institutional structures are enacted by connecting actions into coherent frameworks; in other words, practices.

Central to this approach is the notion of the heterogeneity of actions. This means that actions grow out of many different contexts and need to be continuously connected to form workable practices. The development of 'boundary objects' has become a key means through which heterogeneous groups and actions can be pulled together into coherent frameworks. A boundary object is an artefact that has interpretative flexibility and which creates a shared context for groups and actions that belong to different 'worlds' or logics

(Mailhot et al., 2016, p. 60). Star and Griesemer (1989) mention, among others, libraries, museums, diagrams, atlases and standardised forms, as well as geographical areas and countries, as examples of boundary objects. They have different meanings to different actors but they also have a structure which is recognisable to all actors. Some authors distinguish boundary objects from objects that belong to a particular logic. Boundary objects are intentionally fuzzy to enable collaboration across boundaries, whereas objects or 'things' that belong to a particular logic provide information about the particular context (Annisette and Richardson, 2011).

While boundary objects are material objects or artefacts, 'boundary concepts' are mental and symbolic labels. They are used to point out broad ideas across diverse groups that can relate to them. A boundary concept, for example, is different from a scientific concept in that it is more complex (Miettinen, 2012) and it is interpretatively flexible. It is not defined in a very precise way like a scientific concept, but works more like a sketch or a model. For example, the concept of innovation in its everyday (not scientific) use can be a boundary concept with a complex meaning that can be interpreted in different ways dependent on context. Boundary concepts serve the purpose of allowing people from different social or professional worlds to agree about some main directions while being broad and flexible enough to preserve space for local interpretations and practices. A boundary concept enables shared directions of interest and common moral commitments to be articulated, and it facilitates interaction, communication and coordination across boundaries (Miettinen, 2012, pp. 19–20). The vagueness and fuzziness of boundary concepts is seen as an advantage because it can attract different supporters. But it is also a weakness because it may blur and fail to reconcile contradictory expectations and interests across social groups (ibid., p. 20).

Boundary concepts may provide a shared context for innovation. The literature refers to a 'bandwagon effect'. This is when actors label an emerging new idea which is broad enough to give meaning to, and pull together, a number of diverse supporters (Corradi et al., 2010; Fuglsang and Eide, 2013; Fujimura, 1992). This can provide a shared framework for innovation (Fuglsang and Eide, 2013), but the label will need to be integrated with narrower, less abstract, less ambiguous and more concrete elements in order for innovation to take place and be realised in practice. Similarly, Pantzar and Shove (2010) argue that a practice (see Reckwitz, 2002; Schatzki, 2002) can be broken down into three components: image, skill and material. Image is mental activity in the shape of symbolic meaning, corresponding to concept or label (see Figure 9.1). Skill is bodily knowledge and competence. And 'material' refers to the specific objects and things (equipment) that constitute a practice. Pantzar and Shove further define innovation in practice as the integration of image, skill and material.

In summary, boundary concepts can be important for innovation by labelling a new idea that gives meaning to and pulls together diverse supporters around a shared meaning, and they may also facilitate a common moral commitment to innovation. Yet innovation – that is, the formation of new practices that challenge existing practices – is dependent on connecting and integrating these concepts with skills and materials.

We suggest that these insights can be used to explain how actors combine institutional logics in the innovation process and form new practices that challenge previous ones. Actors do so by connecting and integrating mental symbolic activity – that is, symbolic meaning – with skills and material equipment. An emerging hybrid practice thus consists

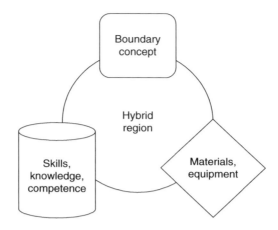

Source: Adapted from Pantzar and Shove (2010).

Figure 9.1   Formation of hybrid practice

of three constitutive elements and the connecting of these elements: (1) bold boundary concepts that give direction to and combine or unite different logics of action around a particular idea and a problem to be solved; (2) the skills, including knowledge and competences, that are required to perform an emerging new practice; (3) and materials and equipment which are drawn upon in the emerging new practice.

In addition to this, we argue that organisations may also have hybrid regions. This means that actors in such regions are given more autonomy to experiment with different solutions and to integrate concepts, skills and materials in new ways. Billis (2010) argues, as mentioned, that sectors have hybrid zones, but we add that organisations have hybrid regions. A hybrid region is a context of actions in which organisational principles, such as principles concerning operational priorities, are relaxed. Actors have more autonomy to connect and integrate the constituent elements of practice in an experimental way according to the varied overlapping sector principles.

Understood in this way, servitisation and traditional public administration are competing logics, and the hybridisation of these logics is the attempt to combine them in the innovation process. Central to this process is the development of boundary concepts and the mobilisation of skills and equipment from diverse practices that can be used to shape new practices of public administration servitisation. The hybrid region is an organisational context where sectorial principles are relaxed, hence providing autonomy for employees to experiment with solutions. Hybrid regions include collaborative projects and experimentations where the organisational principles and the operational priorities of the public sector are open to new practices.

This approach extends previous attempts to understand innovation as partly driven by mental processes and concepts. In the public innovation literature, the notions of conceptual innovation and rhetoric innovation have been introduced to describe the societal development of general conceptual frameworks for innovation. These are distinguished from other types of innovation, such as service innovation, service delivery innovation, process innovation, and administrative and governance innovation. Windrum (2008) has defined conceptual innovation as the development of new worldviews, including new missions, objectives, strategies and rationales. He argues that such conceptual innovations may establish a link between the social economic objectives of a public organisation and its operational rationale. Hartley (2005) defines rhetorical innovations as new language and new concepts. However, in these literatures, conceptual innovation refers to new concepts and language such as 'minimalist state' or New Public Management (Windrum, 2008) or user-orientation rather than to hybrids between logics. Further, conceptual innovation refers to broad discourses in society rather than to the sense-making work that has to be carried out on a day-to-day basis in order to form new practices and innovations. We suggest instead that boundary concepts is an analytical concept for understanding how institutional logics are combined and made sense of in the innovation process at the organisational and practical level.

CASE VIGNETTES

In this section we aim to illustrate how the above practice-based model of the boundary concept, hybrid region and skills and equipment can be an instrument for analysing hybrid innovation. We rely on Billis's (2010) classification of hybrid organisations as having their roots in the principles of one sector, even though organisations may move towards hybrid zones with overlapping logics. Further, we argue that organisations may have hybrid regions where the primary sector principles are relaxed. The case organisations we investigated all adhere to public sector logics, they have created hybrid regions where they experiment with servitisation, and they use boundary concepts as a basis for enacting hybridised logics and principles of the public sector and servitisation.

Method

The three cases have been selected because they illustrate the tendency to servitisation and user-centric approaches in public services where citizens are treated more like customers and sector hybridity is increased. Elderly care and postal services are both expected to perform according not only to a public administration logic (universal and large-scale innovation) but also a servitisation (user-centric) logic. Both work systematically with innovation.

The case studies are based on interviews with key persons. Interviewees were asked to describe the innovation processes, including what, how and where innovation takes place. Interviews were taped and partly transcribed. In addition, several meetings with management were carried out in all three cases. In two of the cases the researchers observed workshops. In all three cases respondents were asked to talk openly about innovation and change processes as they are enacted inside the organisation and made sense of by employees. The case of Post Denmark has previously been published (Fuglsang and Møller, 2014), but this is a new reading and interpretation of the data. The two other case vignettes are part of a longitudinal case study in the municipality of Copenhagen, reported respectively in Fuglsang (2018 and 2019) for other research purposes. The three cases are presented in a condensed version for the purpose of illustrating the method for analysing hybrid innovation.

Case Descriptions

Case 1: Life quality in nursing homes

Five nursing homes for the elderly in the municipality of Copenhagen were selected to participate in a municipal project called 'Life Quality in Nursing Homes' (2015–17) (Fuglsang, 2015). The purpose was to develop new methods through which the nursing homes can help elderly residents to master everyday life and put forward their individual voices and wishes. Residents are to be enabled to continue their previous life as citizens as much as possible. The five subprojects were organised under the umbrella of the municipality's elderly policy, which is called 'Live Strong – The Whole Life' (Københavns Kommune, 2015) concerned with the elderly's 'freedom to live life': 'As you get older in Copenhagen, you must continue to live the life you want to and do the things that matter – even if you need help. Life as elderly should be perceived as a continuation of one's life' (ibid., p. 7). One of the nine reform tracks in the policy states that the municipality must be 'service-minded' (ibid., p. 15):

> Good service occurs when employees and managers are competent and proud of their profession, and good cooperation with citizens gives employees energy and job satisfaction . . . And it reassures that one is met fundamentally with respect and at eye level. It's about highlighting and strengthening interpersonal skills even more, and the responsibility rests both on the employees, managers and citizens.

Funding for the projects was provided through special funds from the Danish government. The project was initiated by policy managers in the municipality's health administration. Yet each nursing home was to develop the new methods bottom-up and discuss their ideas internally and with other nursing homes.

Boundary concepts   The nursing homes came up with certain labels that direct changes, such as 'the good life', 'my life my day', 'residential democracy', 'listen to residents' and 'homeliness'. These labels are boundary concepts in the sense that they provide a bridge between a public administration approach and a more user-centric approach. 'The good life', or 'my day my life', indicate that the elderly should continue their previous life as citizens. This, however, requires a more user-centric approach to care. According to interviews and meetings with managers and employees, the emerging new image of care is seen as representing a change of elderly care from a routinised and standardised approach towards one that listens more to the elderly citizens. Elderly citizens are seen as active fellow citizens rather than as passive beneficiaries of services. Finally, the labels are not defined in a narrow way; they are broad labels that many groups of employees and elderly can relate to from different angles and in a flexible way.

Skills and equipment   The labels are bold concepts that energise existing skills and resources. For example, in one nursing home, an employee turned out to be very good at listening to and talking with elderly residents. She was then allowed to move around freely in the nursing home to inspire others. She also organised debate meetings with the elderly and involved other employees in this. In another nursing home, employees involved the skills of those residents who had been at the home for some time in welcoming new residents. Employees also discussed how they could ask the right questions to new residents to be able to better understand their needs, rather than blindly pursuing professional opin-ions and ethics. Elderly residents are encouraged to arrange weekend trips, write diaries and take pictures in order to improve their everyday life quality. In a third nursing home, a 'troubadour' is hired, who plays music for the elderly based on their own choice. He was hired because the residents wanted someone who could do something with music. In this nursing home, residents are encouraged to generate ideas and are partakers in democratic decision-making processes. People from neighbouring institutions are called upon, such as schoolchildren from a local school to organise activities together with the elderly, citizen-to-citizen, for example a Christmas party. In some nursing homes the personnel exercise their skills of being a good host at dinner tables. In others they experiment with food and music to bring memory and personal voice to the fore.

Hybrid region   The hybrid framework of innovation was protected by a project area where the usual organisational hierarchy is somewhat relaxed. Employees, citizens and public managers mutually negotiated everyday innovation in a pragmatic way. The increased co-creation with citizens required that managers and employees help to mobilise actors, facili-tate meetings and organise events. Ideas and 'practice stories' were exchanged across the five nursing homes at common learning workshops. The purpose of the learning workshops was to share knowledge across the five subprojects, support lasting change and integration in the organisation as a whole, and contribute to the overall evaluation of the project.

Case 2: Life quality in residential areas with many elderly
Case 2, like case 1, is concerned with elderly care but in residential areas with many elderly in Copenhagen. Public managers have organised three subprojects in three residential areas. These subprojects are brought together in common workshops to share knowledge, support lasting change and evaluate the projects. Each subproject is assigned a project manager whose role it is to mobilise resources in local areas across sectors (public, private, third sector).

Boundary concept   In one of the subprojects (focused on here), loneliness is the main boundary concept. Loneliness can probably be defined and examined in a relatively precise manner. Yet loneliness has many faces and can be interpreted in many different ways. Loneliness is addressed as a problem that can call upon both a public service per-spective and a user-centric perspective. From a public service perspective loneliness can be seen as an unintended and unfortunate consequence of the welfare society. However, it may require a user-centred approach to deal with individual problems of loneliness in the short run. The project therefore aims to develop user-friendly methods that can bring people out of unwanted loneliness. Participants in the project include the health administration in the municipality, a private housing company, a civil organisation which runs a local house that offers activities for local citizens, a public activity day centre, a public home-care organisation, a local residents' association, and employees of the housing company, including a janitor. Employees and managers from these different settings are invited to discuss the concept of loneliness. They explore what they can do to detect and minimise unwanted loneliness. A consultant has been invited to explain the concept of loneliness, and how its solutions can be broken down into various small steps. The consultant facilitates a sense-making process. This happens in a reflective learning workshop. Theories and cases of loneliness are discussed in the project group, which consists of several layers of management and frontline employees. Many concrete ideas emerge from this session related to experience and practice for dealing with loneliness.

Skills and equipment   By combining existing skills, experiences and resources in new ways, the personnel create activities for the elderly that counteract loneliness. This includes activities such as common meals, parties with music, singing and dancing, 'krolf' (a combination of croquet and golf), bingo, excursions, cycling (using rickshaws), carpentry, knitting, playing cards, special activities for men only, and special activities for women only. For example, one employee working at the housing association is a trained cook. He serves interesting meals for a small group of elderly. He prepares the meal together with them in a local kitchen in the residential area. The residents' organisation organises various trips by bus. They also refurbished a basement room where the elderly can gather to knit or play cards. Another room has been refurbished as a repair shop and has been equipped with various carpentry tools. The janitor has extensive experience in detecting unwanted loneliness and he is very adept at listening to and talking with lonely elderly.

Hybrid region   These activities take place through interactions between people in a network across sectors. The project context creates a space for mobilising local actors, makes them cooperate in horizontal structures and creates small innovations based on experiences that can help lonely people. Top managers in home-help learn directly from a janitor or a home-helper, and innovation grows out of this protected context of network interaction, which decreases the distance between people geographically, institutionally and hierarchically.

Case 3: Post Denmark
Letter Denmark is a large commercial division in Post Denmark (Fuglsang and Møller, 2014), a publicly held company with a long history and tradition of public service. The business model of postal services is changing. Customer needs and demand for postal services, together with the widespread deregulation of the postal market, are important factors behind these changes. Postal customers increasingly prefer customised services which take into account their specific needs. Letter Denmark has therefore changed its business model and approach to innovation. Letters are still delivered universally in accordance with general postal regulations. But letters must increasingly also be tailored to specific customer needs. Post Denmark has experimented with different types of development units throughout its history. First, a product development department was set up. The task of this unit was to develop innovations decided by top management. Later, a business development department was created. Its role was to foster service innovations proactively. Later again, an innovation team was formed. Its role was to work with external input and inspirations. Innovation has therefore been reorganised from being universal, top-down and large-scale innovation, towards becoming interactive, network-based processes of innovation, or combinations of the two.

Boundary concepts   First of all, the letter has become an important boundary concept in itself. Management holds that the physical letter can still be very useful for customers, despite the growing impact of electronic communication. Yet the meaning of the letter has become more open. On the one hand, it is still delivered in the normal way. On the other hand, it can take new meanings and forms dependent on customer needs. For example, key customers, such as DaneAge (a not-for profit organisation working for a society in which the person is more important than their age), can use letters to collect membership fees, integrating this with other items such as newsletters. To demonstrate the value of the physical letter, new ways of working with the letter and customer value were introduced. So-called documentation studies (quantitative and qualitative studies of the market for letters) were used as boundary frameworks between different relevant groups, including logistic people, salespersons and customers. An idea of sharing documentation studies evolved. Customers together with salespersons could explore new ideas as well as use competencies and experiences of Letter Denmark in their search for new solutions.

Skills and equipment   Letter Denmark was dependent on existing resources and skills. Many employees have worked their entire working lives in Letter Denmark. Logistics and engineering approaches have always been dominant capabilities in postal services. These capabilities are still very important, useful, and essential for conducting documentation studies. Letter Denmark had for a long time also tried to build new 'dynamic capabilities' by either recruiting new personnel or developing new skills among existing personnel. Key account managers had come to play a more prominent role. The innovative potential of the group of key account managers in the encounter with the customers became more emphasised. There was a change in the role of key account managers from a salesperson to a more proactive consultant helping the customer to customise services. Joint documentation studies with customers were conducted, exploring and documenting new ideas for service innovation in the customer's own organisation, helping Letter Denmark to define more general needs for innovation. A stronger innovation culture was developed in the organisation by the reorganisation of the boundary around the developmental organisation (a kind of 'boundary organisation'), for example, reorganising the function of development and innovation by either integrating or separating the development and innovation unit from the main organisation. They all focused on changes in structures, routines and practices entrenched in the organisation of Post Denmark, with a focus on the customisation of services and interaction with customers (for example, business meetings).

Hybrid regions   While previously the salespersons had a lower prestige compared to engineers, sales work now became more prestigious. The so-called business meetings, which were a 'hybrid region' where customer needs and service offerings could be discussed, and documentation studies could be defined and negotiated, became more important. The management of Letter Denmark implemented a user-centric logic in its organisational structures by using such business meetings for knowledge-sharing across organisational boundaries inside and outside its organisation, transferring, translating and transforming knowledge about customer needs and service innovations to employees and customers. Critical to the success of this hybridisation of the organisation is the question of achieving the right balance between the dominating logics of the organisation, illustrated by the recurrent reorganisation of the development and innovation unit (separation versus integration) in Letter Denmark, and the development of the necessary skills and qualifications of the sales personnel (changing a key account manager from a salesperson to a consultant).

Table 9.1   Comparison of three selected cases vignettes

	Life quality in nursing homes	Life quality in residential areas with many elderly	Post Denmark
Sectorial basis	Public	Public	Public
Type of hybridity	Shallow, embryonic	Networked	Entrenched, extensive
Hybrid logic/zone	Public organisation and servitisation	Public organisation and servitisation	Public organisation and servitisation
Hybrid region	Project context, learning workshops	Project context, learning workshops	Business meetings
Boundary concepts	'The good life', 'my life my day', 'residential democracy', 'homeliness', 'listen to users'	'Loneliness' (unwanted loneliness of citizens)	'Physical letter', 'customisation of services, 'documentation studies'
Skills and equipment	Care workers' skills, everyday experiences, simple information and communication technology (ICT) equipment, residential homes	Care workers' skills, civic society skills, skills of people working in and around the housing area	Logistics skills, salespersons' skills, infrastructure development

A Cross-Case Comparison

In Table 9.1, we compare the three cases with respect to the analyzed categories of hybrid region, the boundary concepts, and skills and equipment. To classify the cases more generally in relation to the theory framework we have added the three categories of sectoral basis, type of hybridity and hybrid logic/zone. Note that we add one form of hybridity to Billis's (2010) two forms (shallow and entrenched), which we call 'networked'. This is because one of the cases is built around a network of actors from different sectors, though it is still anchored in public service principles.

The three cases all combine a public administration logic and a servitisation logic in an innovation process, where elements from both sectors are negotiated and recombined to form new practices. A public administration logic is present in that services are intended to be reproduced across the municipality or across services, and these changes are policy-driven. The servitisation approach is manifested in the more user-centric approach to citizens. All cases evolve around boundary objects, which are integrated with existing skills and equipment, and hybrid regions of experimentation are created.

DISCUSSION

In this chapter we have discussed a framework for analysing how hybridity can lead to innovation by hybrid innovation. Hybrid innovation we defined as the process of combining elements from different institutional logics in the innovation process. The chapter suggested an agency-oriented and practice-based approach to hybrid innovation, where focus is on the connecting and integrating of diverse actions in the innovation process in order to form new practices that challenge old practices. Practices are nexuses of actions and routinised behaviours in which institutional structures become manifested. We introduced the notion of the boundary concept as something that can connect actions. Boundary concepts create a common direction and context for innovation between diverse actions, while also being plastic and interpretatively flexible. Yet boundary concepts must be connected and integrated with extant skills and equipment in order to form new practices that challenge old practices. In our model, this integration or connecting may take place in hybrid regions of organisations at the practical operational level where governance principles are relaxed. This means that employees and others have more autonomy to experiment with solutions and enact hybrid logics.

The three case vignettes were drawn from a Danish context of elderly care and postal services. Individuals and organisations experiment with new forms of welfare that combine a public administration logic and a servitisation logic. The servitisation logic introduces a more user-centric and market-like approach, which increases sector hybridity. The public administration logic focuses on universal and large-scale innovations that are policy-driven. In elderly care, there is a drive towards new forms of welfare that take citizens' individual lives and experiences more into consideration and invite service receivers to participate in service creation practices. These initiatives are at the same time anchored in policies and part of sector-wide development processes of large-scale welfare innovation. In postal services, there is a change of business model as a result of technological developments, which leads to new practices of customised services, which are combined with universal services.

Research finds that servitisation happens because of changes in citizens' resources, quality demands, changes in public sector technology and financial pressures on the public sector. Coping with servitisation as an institutional logic for public services can lead to more trust in public services, and robust services that become more user-friendly. Previously, public service development has mostly focused on large-scale innovation and internal control, and the potential for creating more user-friendly services has traditionally not been much emphasised. However, we have shown in this chapter that servitisation does not imply that previous service obligation disappears; rather, what come to the fore are paradoxes and tensions between different logics that may be transformed into innovation. Nevertheless, it may not always be easy to develop and maintain such hybridised logics. Employees and managers may still mostly be oriented towards public sector principles, and their skills and competences are intertwined with previous norms and ethics in the public sector that stress public ethos, fairness and universalism. To listen to users and deliver services according to individual choice is a major change of direction. Further, it can be difficult to organise top-down because it relies on the ability and willingness of frontline employees. It may also be difficult to organise bottom-up because employees may be faced with work dilemmas and paradoxes between the two logics.

What we have developed in this chapter is essentially a pragmatic approach to servitisation and hybridisation in public services. Employees and managers work with bold concepts that are sufficiently broad to cover both a public service logic and a servitisation logic. Employees and managers can contribute to filling them in with practical suggestions and lived experiences from different angles. The bold ideas can be worked out through sense-making processes that connect them with extant skills and equipment.

They can be taken to a higher level through learning workshops and interaction between employees and public managers who, in turn, are in close contact with politicians. The horizontal frameworks are convened, managed and facilitated by public managers, but hierarchical decision-making procedures and top-down decisions are present at the same time. A special contribution of the chapter is the notion of the 'hybrid region' at the organisational and practical level, which complements Billis's notion of hybrid zones (Billis, 2010).

All in all, we have shown how a practice-based and agency-oriented perspective can guide analysis of hybridised innovation. Hybridity, in this perspective, is something that can be worked out in a pragmatic way through interactions between public managers, employees, users and other stakeholders. The key issue in our model is integrating and connecting boundary concepts, skills and equipment. The analysis demonstrates in a preliminary way the usefulness of a model where practitioners, within a broad policy framework, such as 'Live Strong – The Whole Life', work out the premises of action such as boundary objects by connecting them to skills and equipment within an experimental hybrid region. More research will be needed to explain the complexities of this model and construct possible roadmaps of action.

REFERENCES

Akaka, M.A., Vargo, S.L., and Lusch, R.F. (2013). The complexity of context: A service ecosystems approach for international marketing. *Journal of International Marketing*, *21*(4), pp. 1–20.

Annisette, M., and Richardson, A.J. (2011). Justification and accounting: Applying sociology of worth to accounting research. *Accounting, Auditing and Accountability Journal*, *24*(2), pp. 229–249.

Baines, T.S., Lightfoot, H.W., Benedettini, O., and Kay, J.M. (2009). The servitization of manufacturing: A review of literature and reflection on future. *Journal of Manufacturing Technology Management*, *20*(5), pp. 547–567.

Barrett, M., and Oborn, E. (2010). Boundary object use in cross-cultural software development teams. *Human Relations*, *63*(8), pp. 1199–1221.

Battilana, J., and Lee, M. (2014). Advancing research on hybrid organizing: Insights from the study of social enterprises. *Academy of Management Annals*, *8*(1), pp. 397–441.

Billis, D. (2010). Towards a theory of hybrid organizations. In D. Billis (ed.), *Hybrid Organisations and the Third Sector: Challenges for Practice, Theory and Policy* (pp. 46–69). London: Palgrave Macmillan.

Boltanski, L., and Thévenot, L. (2006). *On Justification: Economies of Worth*. Princeton, NJ: Princeton University Press.

Carlile, P.R. (2004). Transferring, tranlating and transforming: An integrative framework for managing knowledge across boundaries. *Organization Science*, *15*(5), pp. 555–568.

Corradi, G., Gherardi, S., and Verzelloni, L. (2010). Through the practice lens: Where is the bandwagon of practice-based studies heading? *Management Learning*, *41*(3), pp. 265–283.

DiMaggio, P.J., and Powell, W.W. (1983). The iron cage revisited: Institutional isomorphism and collective rationality in organizational fields. *American Sociological Review*, *48*(2), pp. 147–160.

Fuglsang, L. (2015). *Public value and bricolage-work*. Paper presented at the Conference on Public Service Innovation and the Delivery of Effective Public Services, National University of Public Services, 5–16 October, 2015, Budapest.

Fuglsang, L. (2018). Towards a theory of a practice-based approach to service innovation within spheres of interaction. In A. Scupola and L. Fuglsang (eds), *Services, Experiences and Innovation: Integrating and Extending Research* (pp. 147–164). Cheltenham: Edward Elgar.

Fuglsang, L. (2019). Human-centric service coinnovation in public services from a practice-based perspective: A case of elderly care. In M. Toivonen and E. Saari (eds), *Human-Centered Digitalization and Services* (pp. 17–36). Singapore: Springer.

Fuglsang, L., and Eide, D. (2013). The experience turn as 'bandwagon': Understanding network formation and innovation as practice. *European Urban and Regional Studies*, *20*(4), pp. 418–435.

Fuglsang, L., and Møller, J.K. (2014). Framing innovation in postal services: Developing a hybrid organization.

In L. Fuglsang, R. Rønning and B. Enquist (eds), *Framing Innovation in Public Service Sectors* (pp. 112–129). New York: Routledge.

Fujimura, J. (1992). Crafting science: Standardised packages, boundary objects, and translation. In A. Pickering (ed.), *Science as Practice and Culture* (pp. 168–211). Chicago, IL: University of Chicago Press.

Gebauer, H., Ren, G.J., Valtakoski, A., and Reynoso, J. (2012). Service-driven manufacturing provision, evolution and financial impact of services in industrial firms. *Journal of Service Management*, *23*(1), pp. 120–136.

Gherardi, S. (2006). *Organizational Knowledge: The Texture of Workplace Learning*. Oxford: Blackwell.

Giddens, A. (1984). *The Constitution of Society Outline of the Theory of Structuration*. Cambridge: Polity Press.

Grönroos, C. (1994). From marketing mix to relationship marketing: Towards a paradigm shift in marketing. *Asia–Australia Marketing Journal*, *2*(August), pp. 9–29.

Hartley, J. (2005). Innovation in governance and public services: Past and present. *Public Money and Management*, *25*(1), pp. 27–34.

Jay, J. (2013). Navigating paradox as a mechanism of change and innovation in hybrid organizations. *Academy of Management Journal*, *56*(1), pp. 137–159.

Jensen, M.B., Johnson, B., Lorenz, E., and Lundvall, B.Å. (2007). Forms of knowledge and modes of innovation. *Research Policy*, *36*(5), pp. 680–693.

Københavns Kommune (2015). Lev stærkt – hele livet, Københavs ældrepolitik 2015–2018 (høringsudkast). Københavns Kommune, Sundheds- og Omsorgsforvaltningen, Center for Omsorg.

Kowalkowski, C., Kindstrom, D., Alejandro, T.B., Brege, S., and Biggemann, S. (2012). Service infusion as agile incrementalism in action. *Journal of Business Research*, *65*(6), pp. 765–772.

Kraatz, M.S., and Block, E.S. (2008). Organizational implications of institutional pluralism. In R. Greenwood, C. Oliver, K. Sahlin-Andersson and R. Suddaby (eds), *Handbook of Organizational Institutionalism* (pp. 243–275). London: SAGE.

Lindblom, C.E. (1979). Still muddling, not yet through. *Public Administration Review*, *39*(6), pp. 517–526.

Mailhot, C., Gagnon, S., Langley, A., and Binette, L.-F. (2016). Distributing leadership across people and objects in a collaborative research project. *Leadership*, *12*(1), pp. 53–85.

Miettinen, R. (2012). *Innovation, Human Capabilities and Democracy: Toward an Enabling Welfare State*. Oxford: Oxford University Press.

Oldenhof, L., Postma, J., and Putters, K. (2014). On justification work: How compromising enables public managers to deal with conflicting values. *Public Administration Review*, *74*(1), pp. 52–63.

Osborne, S.P. (2010). The (new) public governance. A suitable case for treatment? In S.P. Osborne (ed.), *The New Public Governance? Emerging Perspectives on the Theory and Practise of Public Governance* (pp. 1–16). London: Routledge.

Osborne, S.P., Radnor, Z., and Nasi, G. (2013). A new theory for public service management? Toward a (public) service-dominant approach. *American Review of Public Administration*, *43*(2), pp. 135–158.

Osborne, S.P., Radnor, Z., Kinder, T., and Vidal, I. (2015). The service framework: A public-service-dominant approach to sustainable public services. *British Journal of Management*, *26*(3), pp. 424–438.

Pantzar, M., and Shove, E. (2010). Understanding innovation in practice: a discussion of the production and re-production of Nordic walking. *Technology Analysis and Strategic Management*, *22*(4), pp. 447–461.

Pavitt, K. (1984). Sectoral patterns of technical change: Towards a taxonomy and a theory. *Research Policy*, *13*(6), pp. 343–373.

Pratt, M.G., and Foreman, P.O. (2000). Classifying managerial responses to multiple organizational identities. *Academy of Management Review*, *25*(1), pp. 18–42.

Reckwitz, A. (2002). Toward a theory of social practices: A development in culturalist theorizing. *European Journal of Social Theory*, *5*(2), pp. 243–263.

Rhodes, R.A.W., and Wanna, J. (2007). The limits to public value, or rescuing responsible government from the platonic guardians. *Australian Journal of Public Administration*, *66*(4), pp. 406–421.

Schatzki, T.R. (2002). *The Site of the Social: A Philosophical Account of the Constitution of Social Life and Change*. University Park, PA: Pennsylvania State University Press.

Siltaloppi, J. (2015). Framing service as ideology and practice: Cognitive underpinnings of service transformation in Finland's residential sector. PhD thesis, Aalto University School of Engineering, Helsinki. Aalto University publication series, Doctoral dissertations 186/2015.

Skålén, P., and Edvardsson, B. (2016). Transforming from the goods to the service-dominant logic. *Marketing Theory*, *16*(1), pp. 101–121.

Star, S.L., and Griesemer, J.R. (1989). Institutional ecology, 'translations,' and boundary objects: Amateurs and professionals in Berkeley's Museum of Vertebrate Zoology, 1907–1939. *Social Studies of Science*, *19*, pp. 387–420.

Stewart, J. (2006). Value conflict and policy change. *Review of Policy Research*, *23*(1), pp. 183–195.

Thacher, D., and Rein, M. (2004). Managing value conflict in public policy. *Governance – An International Journal of Policy and Administration*, *17*(4), pp. 457–486.

Thornton, P.H., Ocasio, W., and Lounsbury, M. (2012). *The Institutional Logics Perspective: A New Approach to Culture, Structure, and Process*. Oxford: Oxford University Press.

Vandermerwe, S., and Rada, J. (1989). Servitization of business: Adding value by adding services. *European Management Journal 6*(4), pp. 314–324.

Vargo, S.L., and Lusch, R.F. (2004). Evolving to a new dominant logic for marketing. *Journal of Marketing, 68*(1), pp. 1–17.

Vargo, S.L., and Lusch, R.F. (2008). Service-dominant logic: Continuing the evolution. *Journal of the Academy of Marketing Science, 36*(1), pp. 1–10.

Vargo, S.L., and Lusch, R.F. (2016). Institutions and axioms: An extension and update of service-dominant logic. *Journal of the Academy of Marketing Science, 44*(1), pp. 5–23.

Windrum, P. (2008). Innovation and entrepreneurship in public services. In P. Windrum and P. Koch (eds), *Innovation in Public Sector Services: Entrepreneurship, Creativity and Management* (pp. 3–20). Cheltenham, UK and Northampton, MA, USA: Edward Elgar Publishing.

10. Hybridity in higher education
Richard Winter and Richard Bolden

INTRODUCTION

Successive waves of higher education reform present complex challenges and tensions for staff employed in higher education institutions (HEIs). As governments increasingly position higher education in 'terms of the economic role it can fulfil' (McArthur, 2011, p. 737), 'unitary business values and practices originating in the private sector are "squeezing out" broader liberal education values and goals of the public university' (Winter and O'Donohue, 2012, pp. 565–566). Crucially, a key organisational challenge facing leaders in HEI is working out how to successfully graft a business culture onto a public sector and academic-oriented culture such that these competing values and ideals can coexist as 'hybrid' states and persist over time (Fethke and Policano, 2013; Mouwen, 2000; Tahar et al., 2011).

In this chapter, we identify some of the leadership and management challenges that arise from the changing context of higher education and consider their implications for managers and academic staff. In making this argument we describe HEI as 'multiple-identity' hybrid organisations made up of competing utilitarian (managerial) and normative (professional) beliefs and values systems that challenge the existence of any unitary, fixed or stable cultural identity (Foreman and Whetten, 2002). As core cognitive beliefs, values serve as guiding principles in our conceptualisation of academic and manager identities given that they shape academics' orientations towards teaching, research and business or community engagement (Billot, 2010; Churchman and King, 2009; Harley, 2002), and govern managers and academics' modes of thought of how they should or ought to behave in particular higher education contexts (Barry et al., 2006; Deem et al., 2008).

In establishing the disparate and fragmented aspects of organisational identity in HEI, we contrast the dynamic role of managerial values systems that give priority to the 'financial imperative' (Parker, 2013) of revenue generation and cost-efficiency with the stabilising role of academic and professional values systems that articulate ideals of tradition and autonomy, collegiate governance, learning and scholarship (Henkel, 2012). Our central argument is that the different values systems articulated by academics, managers and other occupational groups in HEI prevent a unitary and shared form of organisational identity emerging. Implicit in this proposition is the assertion that academics and managers, as members of distinct occupational groups (Deem and Brehony, 2005; Trowler et al., 2012), voice in thought and action different 'action-oriented beliefs' (values systems) of what aspects of work matter to them and their organisation (Trice, 1993, p. 48). Different values systems, we contend, mean that different institutional logics and meanings of work get mixed up as priorities for managers and professionals to follow.[1]

Since values systems are relatively enduring patterns of thought that transcend specific situations, we view them as playing a key role in binding occupational groups together and discouraging interaction with other groups (Anthony, 1977; Beyer, 1981). One important identity-affirming mechanism in HEI is the assignment of different social meanings to academic work and working relationships (for example, 'academics should serve students as customers'; 'managers, academics and professional staff should work together as a team'). By linking core beliefs to particular role identities within the organisation, values systems act to shape the perceived rights and wrongs of work behaviour, and in so doing, legitimate certain social action (Lok, 2010). For example, in HEI there exists the context for multiple logics and discourses to be voiced as to: '(1) the roles, rights, and obligations of academics (e.g. academics as autonomous professionals; academics as managed employees); and (2) the nature and purpose of the institution (e.g. a crucible of learning and scholarship; a profit-making enterprise)' (Winter, 2009, p. 124). Hence, a key identity challenge facing managers and staff in HEI is to find productive and sustainable ways of working whereby managerial, academic and professional occupational groups pursue and value different things at the same time whilst also contributing towards an overarching set of institutional objectives (Christopher, 2012; Ek et al., 2013).

To address this key identity challenge in higher education, our chapter is structured as follows. First, we consider the concept of hybridity in relation to the competing values systems that give rise to value conflicts and identity tensions in HEI. Second, we review literature relating to hybrid configurations of leadership as a way of balancing and/or combining different values systems and ways of working in HEI. Third, we offer some observations of how individuals, groups and/or organisations might (re)construct hybrid identities in HEI. We conclude by considering the potential contribution of a hybridity perspective on leadership and management in higher education.

HYBRIDITY TENSIONS AND CHALLENGES

The concept of hybridity refers to the 'state of being composed though the mixture of disparate parts' (Battilana and Lee, 2014, p. 400). Disparate parts in an organisational sense present paradoxes and tensions in the everyday life of hybrid organisations given that these interrelated parts 'exist simultaneously and persist over time' (Smith and Lewis, 2011, p. 382). Disparate parts of a multiple-identity hybrid organisation reflect competing beliefs, values and practices such that 'organisational actors have to cope with different interpretations of reality, different norms of appropriate behaviour and different success criteria' (Johansen et al., 2015, p. 2). For example, HEIs face competing identity challenges to deliver more corporate-focused services to students as customers (Barnett, 2011), to be professionally effective in teaching and education (Nixon, 2001), and to be socially relevant and responsive (McArthur, 2011). The challenge for hybrid organisations is to generate creative insights and find workable solutions to competing demands and expectations that do not easily fit together (Johansen et al., 2015).

Because HEIs consist of seemingly incompatible normative values systems (emphasising public service, professional autonomy, collegial practice, and traditions) and utilitarian values systems (characterised by profit-making, corporate management, customer service and change), the identity of the organisation fragments into multiple types such that the organisation 'considers itself (and others consider it), alternatively, or even simultaneously, to be different types of organisations' (Albert and Whetten, 1985, p. 270). Value conflicts and identity tensions are important features of HEI given that competing utilitarian and normative values play a key role in: (1) influencing 'resource allocation' priorities (Parker, 2012, 2013); (2) establishing the legitimacy of certain types of scholarship (Rolfe, 2013); and (3) shaping what groups of managers and professionals perceive the central work of the organisation to be in times of change and uncertainty (Deem et al., 2008; Henkel, 2005, 2012).

Different approaches to valuing work are clearly evident in Winter and O'Donohue's (2012) study of an Australian public university striving to 'combine and sustain competing and contradictory managerial (economic) and academic (professional) values systems' (ibid., p. 565). In responding to an online survey designed to provoke academics in teaching and research roles to reveal their values preferences, lecturers and professors indicated a deep-seated antipathy to managerial values 'that reduces higher education to a narrow economic function' (ibid., p. 565). Over 90 per cent of respondents in both lecturer and professorial groups professed a strong belief in universities being 'first and foremost learning institutions focused on intellectual rigour and scholarship' (ibid., p. 568). In respect to academics offering students 'greater product choice as consumers', only a minority of professors (19 per cent) and lecturers (9 per cent) indicated a preference for the university organising itself around student-as-consumer ideals (Furedi, 2011). Anti-business and anti-consumer comments expressed by individual academics echoed comments made by academics in earlier studies suggesting that identity tensions are firmly entrenched in the academic heartland of Australian public universities (Churchman, 2006; Churchman and King, 2009; Winter and Sarros, 2002).

MANAGING COMPETING VALUES SYSTEMS

Managing competing values systems is particularly difficult in HEIs given that uncertainty and interdependence represent two pervasive features of context that must be managed in tandem (Griffin et al., 2007). Uncertainty in HEI economic and social environments, as a result of reductions in government higher education expenditures in constant dollars per student terms (Pollitt and Bouckaert, 2011), has pressured HEIs and staff to engage in 'academic capitalism' (Slaughter and Rhoades, 2009) and to compete vigorously for fee-paying students and external grant income.[2]

However, the desirability of all academics and professional staff engaging in a capitalist mode of academic work has not gone unchallenged (Gonzales et al., 2014; Rolfe, 2013). Typically, academics and professional staff in a variety of management and teaching–research roles compete to organise academic work around their own set of assumptions, values and beliefs about what knowledge is important and valuable for students to understand and receive, as well as the norms for scholarship behaviour (Ek et al., 2013; Rolfe, 2013). In some cases, academics have openly questioned whether their own and the institution's research status and legitimacy is best represented by an instrumental logic that allocates monies and prestige on the basis of best publications, numbers of external research grants, and sensationalist research impact statements (Chubb and Watermeyer, 2017; Willmott, 2011).

Managing different values systems effectively means understanding the benefits and trade-offs of balancing competing goals and requirements so that efficiency (economic-business) and legitimacy (normative-professional) logics can be achieved simultaneously

(Johansen et al., 2015). However, taking account of different values systems and working practices is a difficult process to achieve in HEIs (de Boer and Goedegebuure, 2009). Often latent problems such as a lack of inter-departmental teamwork or poor student attendance at lectures cannot be openly addressed without causing controversies, irritations or denial. Two interrelated reasons account for this. Firstly, academic (so-called 'front office') and professional (so-called 'back office') functions differ fundamentally in the organisation structures of HEIs (Tahar et al., 2011). Typically, academic staff work in decentralised, loosely coupled systems (that is, discipline-based schools and departments), whilst administrative and support tasks are organised as hierarchical units with lines of authority to the Vice Chancellor and Registrar offices to facilitate centralised planning, budgeting, infrastructure and technology platforms.

Secondly, academics in discipline-oriented departments, and administrators and staff in professional support functions, have distinctly different cultures (Christopher, 2012; Trowler et al., 2012). Cultural variations are apparent in the differing responses to seeing the university as a corporate enterprise (Deem et al., 2008; Whitchurch and Gordon, 2010). For instance, academics often emphasise their respective professional identities by articulating values of collegiality, learning, and scholarship somewhat sheltered from the more hierarchical university environment (Teelken, 2015; Winter and O'Donohue, 2012). University executives, academic managers and professional staff tend to identify more with the corporate culture of performance accountability, research targets and student evaluation scores because they 'see their interests as represented by it' (Deem and Brehony, 2005, p. 226), and can use such measures as a proxy for quality in specialist areas that they are unable to assess directly. In essence, trying to unify university managers, professional staff and academics under one corporate vision is fraught with difficulty as members of each group identify 'more with members of their own subcultures rather than as members of the university' (Winter and O'Donohue, 2012, p. 566).

Different values systems, reflecting different discipline orientations and modes of practice, often become apparent as HEIs attempt to restructure their operations around unitary business ideals. Ek et al. (2013) present evidence from Sweden, where heads of discipline-oriented departments perceived the marketisation of higher education as a 'threat to the department's own educational culture' given that they believed 'academic knowledge and skills cannot always be captured in the model of management by objectives' (ibid., p. 6). To protect their autonomy as traditional academics, discipline-based heads responded to demands for more adjustment of education to market forces (that is, greater attention to student 'employability' and 'efficiency in training') by introducing 'so-called labour market days, to which companies were invited' (ibid., p. 7). Such 'safeguarding' action was seen as necessary by heads as it meant 'teachers at discipline-oriented departments could be liberated from any responsibility concerning employability' (ibid., p. 7) and therefore able to continue with their 'clear research focus' (ibid., p. 10).

Conversely, heads of professional-oriented departments responsible for preparing students for professions that require certification (for example, engineering, nursing) perceived the needs of students (and their roles) quite differently. Instead of sheltering academics and course programmes from market forces, they actively invited industry representatives to 'participate in training in various ways' and encouraged students to 'write their degree projects in collaboration with companies' (ibid., p. 7). Future employers' demands for practical skills were written into course materials as the market was perceived to 'not exist outside, but rather within education itself' (ibid., p. 8). As can be seen, traditional academic discipline and professional-oriented departments may have different teaching and research responses to market forces in HEIs. These responses are premised on the assumption that market (change) and professional (stability) logics and values systems do coexist and persist over time in hybrid organisations (Jay, 2013). Hence, a major challenge of hybridity is to match different leadership and management structures and processes to the different values systems and paradoxes that exist in hybrid contexts.

HYBRID CONFIGURATIONS OF LEADERSHIP

Hybridity research is currently an emerging field of inquiry. Although advances have occurred in understanding structural hybridity and corresponding shifts in market, hierarchy and networks modes of governance, little is known of the institutional dynamics of hybrids and the processes by which structures, systems and underpinning values interact, coexist or collapse over time in organisations (Denis et al., 2015). Of particular concern is the lack of knowledge relating to how individuals and groups collectively learn to perceive and manage different values systems in hybrid contexts. Indeed, in respect to leadership practice in HEIs, there exist few accounts of 'how leadership is accomplished through the interaction of vertical, horizontal, emergent and other forms of social influence' (Bolden and Petrov, 2014, p. 409).

Recent years have seen growing interest and investment in leadership development, practice and research in HEIs (see Lumby, 2013 and Dopson et al., 2016 for reviews). For the most part, however, attention has been focused on leadership by those in formal positions of authority in the pursuit of organisational aims and objectives. In accordance with our earlier argument, it seems that a managerialist logic and the promotion of an enterprise culture has come to dominate popular conceptions of leadership in higher education. Despite an increase in studies of 'academic leadership', the vast majority are concerned with the leadership of HEIs as businesses rather than the leadership of 'academic work' per se (Bolden et al., 2012, 2014). This problematic state of affairs may help to explain the high levels of occupational stress and dissatisfaction reported by academic staff in United Kingdom (UK) HEIs (Kinman and Wray, 2013; Parr, 2015) and the frustrations of professional managers and administrators within HEIs when trying to engage with and influence academics; an experience frequently compared to 'herding cats' (Garret and Davies, 2010; McCormack et al., 2014).

Whilst mainstream literature continues to promote the myth of the individual 'hero' leader, more recent work highlights the distributed nature of leadership in organisations (Bolden et al., 2015) and the significance of identity dynamics in terms of where, when and why people may be willing to follow the lead of others (Haslam et al., 2011). These perspectives have much to offer in cross-boundary contexts of HEIs where monodimensional representations fail to reflect the multifaceted and contested nature of power relations, influence and assessments of 'success'. Importantly, a distributed leadership perspective draws attention to the importance of context in determining who can lead others at a given time; suggesting, for example, that professional skills and expertise are equally as important as manager seniority (Spillane et al., 2004).

Whilst there are clear differences between HEIs depending on the relative complexities

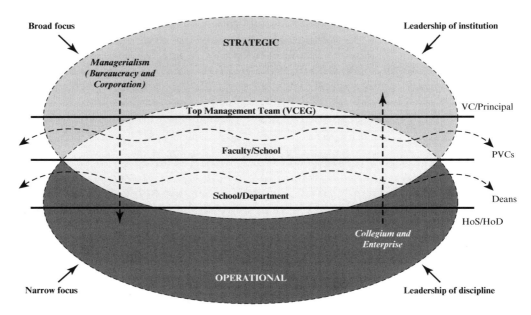

Note: VC = Vice Chancellor, VCEG = Vice Chancellor's Executive Group, PVC = Pro-Vice Chancellor, HoS = Head of School, HoD = Head of Department.

Source: Bolden et al. (2008, p. 21). Reproduced with the permission of the Leadership Foundation for Higher Education.

Figure 10.1   Leadership roles and approaches in UK HEI

of their structures, there are also significant differences between leadership functions at different levels, with some operating in a vertical, hierarchical structure, and others operating in a horizontal, boundary-spanning manner across different subgroups within the institution (Pearce, 2004). This blend of horizontal and vertical leadership is considered essential in such large, complex organisations but is rarely discussed in institutional documentation or the academic literature.

Figure 10.1, derived from an in-depth study of leadership in UK higher education (Bolden et al., 2008), illustrates a number of the key tensions between leadership functions and roles across HEIs. The top of the diagram represents the strategic priorities of university executive members, such as Vice Chancellors and Pro-Vice Chancellors, whose responsibility is for the running of the institution (that is, a more corporate perspective). At the centre of the diagram is the faculty space (where Deans and Associate Deans operate) that spans both strategic and operational domains.

Within the academic heartland of discipline units (that is, schools and departments) leadership processes focus mainly on operational issues and the development of the academic discipline. Key roles, such as Programme Director, Module Coordinator and Principal Investigator, tend to operate in a collegial rather than hierarchical manner, in which post-holders carry out responsibilities on behalf of the wider group. Formal accountability lies with the Head of Department, who is often the main budget-holder, line manager and point of contact with the faculty (Hancock, 2007), but who may well not be perceived as an 'academic leader' by colleagues (Bolden et al., 2012).

Whilst Figure 10.1 demonstrates a number of possible reasons why staff may experience a sense of disconnection between leadership of the institution and departments, it also hugely simplifies the complexity of context in HEIs. Alongside the academic roles illustrated runs a parallel professional services structure reporting to the Registrar (or equivalent head of administration) and, indeed, an emerging 'third space' (Whitchurch, 2008) that combines elements of both. There is also a requirement to combine an internal and external focus at all levels, leading processes and activities both within and beyond the institution, often in collaboration with professionals and organisations with very different cultures, values and ways of working. Time is another important factor, with institutional processes simultaneously following a number of different tracks: the annual cycle of academic programmes, alongside fixed-term and open research projects, consultancy, tailored short-courses, doctoral research and publication processes.

Within a hybrid education context, academic managers have multiple and divided loyalties and often find themselves working in very different ways, to different ends, at different times, and accountable to different people and communities (Deem et al., 2008; Noordegraaf and De Wit, 2012). For instance, Heads of Department are 'expected to act as agents of institutional management' whilst simultaneously acting as 'first among equals in a [academic] unit where all are engaged in a collective enterprise' (Middlehurst, 1993, p. 138). As agents of institutional management, Heads are expected to devote significant time to income generation but may not regard this activity as an important aspect of their role. In a survey of 233 UK professors (44 per cent of whom occupied hybrid roles, such as Head of Department, Dean or Pro-Vice Chancellor), professors 'ranked income generation activities as their least important role' but 'considered that it was second only to leadership in research as an institutional [role] expectation' (Macfarlane, 2011, p. 64).

Reconciling different and contradictory expectations presents intractable role identity problems for hybrid professionals such as Heads of Department. For instance, with which particular group (if any) should the loyalties of the Head of Department lie? Should the Head adopt a managerial approach since the Dean and institution is evaluating their performance primarily in economic terms? Or should the Head adopt more of a collegiate approach and align with members of their own department since it is here that they will continue working once their position as Head expires?[3] Or is it possible for the Head to adopt a hybrid approach that embraces both managerial and collegiate role expectations?

Assuming a 'one size fits all' approach to leadership in higher education environments, characterised by strong economic values and normative professional values, is clearly misguided and a more pluralistic approach is required (Denis et al., 2007). In support of distributed leadership, Jones et al. (2012, p. 68) argue for universities to build a more participative and collaborative approach that 'acknowledges the individual autonomy that underpins creative and innovative thinking'. Gronn (2009, 2011) suggests focusing on 'hybrid configurations of leadership' on the basis that successful university leadership is dependent on a combination of styles, roles and approaches, as summarized in the following quotation: 'A term such as hybrid would be a more accurate description of situational practice that includes both individual leaders and holistic leadership units working in tandem than distributed, because the notion of hybrid signals a mixture of types' (Gronn, 2009, p. 384).

Hybrid configurations of leadership place emphasis on 'maintaining an appropriate balance between top-down, bottom-up and lateral processes of communication and influence' (Bolden et al., 2008, p. 364). An important component of hybrid leadership is the ability of individuals to exercise different forms of social influence whereby they share experiences and ideas across administrative and professional domains of higher education. Hybrid leadership in practice translates into university leaders and academics finding different and innovative ways to integrate business ideals into the cultures of discipline-oriented and professional-oriented departments (Clegg and McAuley, 2009; Ek et al., 2013).

The analysis of 'hybrid professionalism' in UK higher education (Whitchurch, 2008; Whitchurch and Gordon, 2010) provides some guidelines for thinking about how individuals occupying management and professional roles may collaborate effectively by sharing their knowledge and expertise whilst working in large, corporate bureaucracies. As Nixon (2001) and Noordegraaf (2007) persuasively argue, reinterpreting professionalism in a changing service context opens up new professional and organisational theories and practices. For example, organising and managing large numbers of students under conditions of high uncertainty and interdependence can be seen as professional issues by linking discourses of autonomy and collaboration to education quality and student service delivery targets (Barnett, 2011; Nixon, 2001).

Working interdependently as hybrid professionals often requires individuals to think and act differently, to look at organisational issues through different lenses or 'two-way windows' (Croft et al., 2015), so that work matches the different role expectations of executives, academics, instructional designers, information technology (IT) experts, and employers (Jones et al., 2012). Hybrid scholarship terms such as 'engaged scholarship' (Van de Ven, 2007) and 'ambidextrous scholarship' (Corbett et al., 2014) may prove useful 'reframing' devices in helping individuals to rethink education, research and engagement as an interdependent nexus rather than as separate activities (Hughes et al., 2011; Jones, 2013).

Finally, creating different ways of working in hybrid HEIs requires leaders to synthesise, bridge and reconcile differences in values and logics so that individuals and groups see the benefits of collaboration and sharing a collective identity (Heffernan, 2014). According to Ernst and Chrobot-Mason (2011), successful collaboration requires individuals at all levels and functions to understand boundaries (real and imaginary) and feel valued for their contributions as part of a distinct group with a shared organisational identity. Two key sequential practices are necessary to help integrate individuals into a larger whole (the organisation) while respecting and validating key expertise and department affiliations (subgroups).

Firstly, *connecting* places importance on the skills of cultivating and utilising interpersonal relationships in order to support wider organisational communication, gain access to resources and support different routes to employer engagement (Bolden and Petrov, 2014; Hughes et al., 2011). Secondly, *mobilising* refers to those engagement conditions (for example, minimal use of hierarchy, interlinked project teams, open office spaces) that enable academic, professional and administrative groups to feel equally involved in organisation planning and decision-making. Engagement implies opportunities for academics to collaborate with different professional groups (for example, business managers, professional staff, practitioners) and discuss different ideas of teaching and research in forums (Whitchurch, 2008), conferences (Hughes et al., 2011), cross-disciplinary projects

(Jones, 2013), consultancy arrangements (Knights and Scarbrough, 2010) and research-based communities of practice (Ng and Pemberton, 2013).

(RE)CONSTRUCTING HYBRID IDENTITIES

Albert and Whetten (2004) demonstrate how the tensions between values-based (normative) and managerial (utilitarian) perspectives in HEIs can be traced to their history; initially through the monastic tradition and more recently in producing 'work-ready' graduates (McArthur, 2011). They suggest that universities should be considered as 'dual identity' organisations – a hybrid of both church and business – and that this dual identity provides insight into both the challenges for governance and leadership, and potential solutions. Utilitarian organisations, they argue, tend to have a 'multi-level, highly differentiated rank structure', whilst 'normative organisations tend not only to be comparatively egalitarian, but also stress the distinction between members and non-members, insiders ('believers') vs. outsiders ('heretics'), as the central status criterion, over any internal differentiations' (Albert and Whetten, 2004, p. 112). The key to being an effective and credible leader in such an organisation, they suggest, is to be able to bridge these two worlds:

> Effective leaders of dual identity organisations should personify and support both identities. University presidents who were never professors (ordained members of the priesthood) will always be considered managers, not leaders. This deficiency should impair their effectiveness during retrenchment when they must be perceived as the champion of the normative as well as the utilitarian values of the organisation (Albert and Whetten, 2004, p. 112).

Empirical evidence for a dual (hybrid) identity observation is provided by Goodall (2009), whose research shows a strong correlation between the personal research track record of Vice Chancellors and Deans and their organisation's performance in university league tables. Whilst such findings lend support to the claim that the best researchers make the best leaders, there is value in considering alternative lines of causality. Whilst it may be that the critical and analytical skills of research are useful when it comes to leadership in higher education, other possible explanations include: (1) that the most successful HEIs are able to recruit and retain the best researchers; (2) that academics are more likely to follow someone they see as a legitimate academic like themselves; and/or (3) that higher education leaders with a research background are less likely to engage in managerialist practices that erode the engagement and participation of academic staff.

The ambiguous and contested nature of leadership roles in HEIs is graphically illustrated in Martin Parker's (2004) autobiographical account of taking on the role of Head of Department and his struggle with the role identity tensions this created. Coming to terms with the role was an ongoing process of 'identity work' (Sveningsson and Alvesson, 2003) in which he navigated and experimented with multiple identities:

> I think that the most important distinction to be made is that I am a manager with an alternate 'professional' identity. Like other professionals in large organisations (doctors, engineers, lawyers) I have a somewhat divided series of identifications, some of which have little to do with my employer as such (Parker, 2004, p. 56).

Whilst this account does not offer a solution to identity tensions (indeed, it suggests it may not be possible to resolve them), it does encourage the possibility of embracing a 'much more polymorphous [approach] than one best way market managerialism might assume' (ibid., p. 55). In a sector where professionalism is associated with being critical, analytical and reflective it is perhaps unsurprising that academics are skeptical of explicit attempts to 'manage' or 'lead' them. As Oakley and Selwood (2010, p. 6) argue: 'The culture of academics is, if anything, distrustful of overt organisational leadership. This appears to be partly about not wanting to swap their professional expertise for what is perceived as the more banal role of management, but also about a more deep-seated resistance to the language of leadership.'

Indeed, it is not uncommon to observe people within universities engaged in activities that they do not call leadership, but that have a significant influence on the attitudes and behaviours of others. Likewise, there are many activities undertaken by those in positions of formal authority that are not regarded by others as leadership. It seems, perhaps, that a unitary concept of 'leadership' is inadequate in such contexts of hybridity.

Recognising the existence and value of hybridity within higher education requires a more nuanced approach to both leadership practice and development. Macfarlane's work, for example, highlights the need for a broader conceptualisation of the forms of leadership that can be provided by senior academics, including acting as role models, mentors, advocates, guardians and ambassadors (Macfarlane, 2011, 2012). Whilst such functions may be supported through formal roles, both within and beyond the institution, they should not be constrained by such structures and, indeed, may benefit from a wider set of performance metrics for their recognition and development (Franco-Santos et al., 2014).

Evans (2015) takes a follower-centric perspective on the leadership role of professors, identifying three main expectations from 'the led': *distinction* (as a person of renown in their field), *knowledge* (as subject expert) and *relationality* (as approachable, well-connected and supportive of colleagues and students). She concludes that there is 'no such thing as the (singular) UK-based professor' and that 'the most we should perhaps hope for are multiple delineations of multiple roles, purposes and professionalisms' (ibid., p. 682). This is another illustration of hybridity in action, and one that results in the strange situation where neither professors nor those appointing them are exactly clear about the nature and purpose of their role (see also Rayner et al., 2010).

Embracing a more inclusive and pluralistic approach to leadership and management in higher education requires creativity and debate: in opening up spaces and opportunities for collective conversations around the benefits of thinking differently about the academic enterprise (Bolden et al., 2014; Hardy et al., 2005). Sewerin and Holmberg (2017) suggest the idea of 'rooms' as a way of dealing with the paradoxes of university leadership by foregrounding different professional identities and facilitating a shared understanding between people about priorities at a given time. For example, a 'room' where people come together as researchers or educators is likely to feel quite different to one where they come together as employees or managers. Following our earlier argument, whilst both are important, within an increasingly marketised and managerialist environment the latter tends to dominate, marginalising and disengaging those with different values and identities.

By recognising how to adapt their behaviours to the diverse forms of professional life that exists in higher education, academics and managers not only interpret their skills of influence and persuasion more actively, but they also learn how to move laterally across discipline and organisational boundaries to create new professional spaces, knowledge and social relationships (Whitchurch, 2008; Whitchurch and Gordon, 2010). Schön's (1983) classic work *The Reflective Practitioner* reminds us that professionals and managers are more able to work constructively with competing knowledge claims when they do not hold onto singular logics of technical rationality, but instead look for multiple interpretations and meanings of relationships and roles that mirror a changed situation.

Asking university leaders, academic managers and professional staff in HEIs to practice hybridity and do different and potentially contradictory things simultaneously is a big ask. HEIs, like all bureaucracies, have relatively enduring structural features (for example, policy instruments, rules, norms of behaviour) that contribute to order and stability (Jungblut and Vukasovic, 2013). Change, if it happens at all, tends to proceed incrementally and through layering of new rules on top of old ones (Musselin, 2005). By this account, if hybridity is to 'stick' successfully in an institution, it may well need to work within and around existing policies and processes rather than attempting to displace them outright.[4]

CONCLUSION

By making explicit the competing utilitarian (managerial) and normative (professional) values systems that exist in higher education, our intention has been to challenge the notion that leaders in HEIs can manage hybridity effectively (that is, combine and/or balance different values systems simultaneously) in a unitary and unified way. Competing values systems, we suggest, contribute to value conflicts and identity tensions in HEIs by attributing different meanings and institutional logics to academic work (Winter, 2017), manager–academic working relationships (Deem et al., 2008), resource allocation issues (Parker, 2012), the nature and legitimacy of types of scholarship (Rolfe, 2013), and responses to change and continuity in times of economic uncertainty (Henkel, 2012).

In response to these identity tensions and value conflicts in HEIs, we have reviewed the literature relating to hybrid configurations of leadership to see whether there are effective ways of managing competing values systems so that they exist simultaneously and endure over time. Our review found little evidence of the institutional dynamics by which managers and professionals learn to recognise and respond to the challenges of efficiency, legitimacy and meaning across different levels and functions of the hybrid organisation (Johansen et al., 2015). Hybridity, and the pluralistic and paradoxical modes of thinking underpinning it (Denis et al., 2007; Jay, 2013), is clearly not embedded in the reported practices of institutional leaders in HEIs. The lack of hybrid forms of thinking and action perhaps reflects the dominance of managerial values systems that give priority to an economic mode of thought and an assumptive academic world which is difficult to challenge or refute (Parker, 2013; Trowler, 2010).

Simultaneously embracing continuity (that is, professional ideals of education and scholarship quality) and change (that is, innovation ideals of responding to student and employer demands in an environment of diminishing public funding) requires institutional leaders to be skilled at 'navigating paradox' (Jay, 2013; Smith and Lewis, 2011). Navigating paradox means constructing working patterns and goals that reflect a myriad of different manager and professional staff relationships within and beyond the academic world (Henkel, 2012; Whitchurch and Gordon, 2010).

Importantly, academic and professional staff will need to work interdependently with university managers, students and industry practitioners in order to generate research income, facilitate knowledge exchange and engage in 'scholarship that matters' to different external and internal stakeholders (Hughes et al., 2011). Without some degree of collaboration across managerial, academic and professional systems, hybrid HEIs will find it difficult to create the engagement conditions by which occupational groups share knowledge, respond proactively to funding shortfalls, and think and talk differently about the academic enterprise (Ek et al., 2013; Hardy et al., 2005). Similarly, too much reliance on competition over collaboration may weaken the social ties crucial to professional relationships and continuity in academic life (Gersick et al., 2000; Winter, 2017).

Clearly, a key challenge of hybridity remains in HEIs: how to devise multiple-identity governance structures and leadership and management processes for orienting academic work around change and enterprise ideals, whilst simultaneously enabling academics and professional staff to retain their professional identities, act autonomously, but still do different and creative work activities that staff and institutional leaders value (Fulton, 2003; Henkel, 2012; Musselin, 2005). We suggest that the hybridity paradox is more likely to be 'lived with' (Bolden et al., 2016) when leaders in management and professional roles open up spaces for collective conversation: spaces where individuals and groups are permitted to think differently about the academic enterprise and the kinds of values, processes and systems needed to make hybrid organisations efficient, legitimate and meaningful.

Finally, our chapter acknowledges the lack of evidence around how different occupational groups manage and balance competing values systems in higher education. In respect to hybrid leadership practices, there are few empirical accounts of how business enterprise concepts are successfully integrated into universities whilst respecting and retaining existing academic and professional values and identities. Understanding the social conditions by which hybridity occurs in HEIs requires more in-depth studies of the institutional dynamics of hybrids and the 'hybrid configurations of leadership' that enable and facilitate pluralistic ways of working (Gronn, 2009, 2011).

One possible focus for research might be the collaborative processes by which multiple-identity individuals and groups find workable norms of appropriate behaviour for values systems that do not easily fit together. Other valuable areas for enquiry include exploring the hybrid spaces in which universities collaborate and work alongside external partners, such as business, public sector, voluntary sector, community groups, government, and professional and trade associations. Hybridity encourages a focus on diversity and inclusion and hence could also serve as a useful entrée to research around gender, race, language, power and other important areas of difference, as well as consideration of the temporal and spatial aspects of leadership and academic work over varying durations and geographies.

NOTES

1. Our conception of an HEI's organisational identity is based on a social constructionist perspective (Berger and Luckmann, 1967) of what different individuals and occupational groups interpret the central work of the organisation to be (or what it should be) at a particular time, and in a given cultural context (Deem et

al., 2008; Garcia and Hardy, 2007). Organisational identity is not understood as a direct property by itself, as organisations do not have ideals, purposes or goals like people do. That is, HEIs as distinct entities do not make decisions to organise themselves as hybrids. Rather, senior managers, academics and professional staff make those decisions; 'individual human beings' acting and interpreting their roles in a dynamic work context (Kenny et al., 2011, p. 125).

2. Our analysis is focused mainly on HEIs in Westernised economies, such as Australia, New Zealand, the United States, Canada, the UK and continental Europe, where there is a strong tradition of academic independence and an emphasis on the three pillars of education, research and engagement. Whilst the arguments may not be directly transferrable to other contexts, given the globalisation of the higher education sector the market-based rationale of economic performance is becoming pervasive even within developing higher education systems (Bentley et al., 2013).

3. This observation assumes a fixed-term, rotating model of academic management that, whilst still present in many universities, is increasingly being replaced by permanent, executive appointments. Both models have their benefits and limitations but, in terms of hybridity, the former is more likely to require post-holders to simultaneously balance multiple professional and managerial values and identities, and the latter is more likely to promote a separation of academic and managerial values and identities.

4. For example, no matter how disconnected academics may feel from performance-related metrics, these still represent an important part of the higher education landscape, with a significant influence on academic labour markets, student recruitment and research funding.

REFERENCES

Albert, S., and Whetten, D.A. (1985). Organizational identity. In Cummings, L.L., and Staw, M.M. (eds), *Research in Organizational Behavior*, Vol. 7 (pp. 263–295). Greenwich, CT: JAI Press.

Albert, S., and Whetten, D. (2004). Organizational identity. In Hatch, M.J., and Schultz, M. (eds), *Organizational Identity: A Reader* (pp. 89–118). Oxford: Oxford University Press.

Anthony, P.D. (1977). *The Ideology of Work*. London: Tavistock Publications.

Barnett, R. (2011). The marketised university: Defending the indefensible. In Molesworth, M., Scullion, R., and Nixon, E. (eds), *The Marketisation of Higher Education and the Student as Consumer* (pp. 39–51). London: Routledge.

Barry, J., Berg, E., and Chandler, J. (2006). Academic shape shifting: Gender, management and identities in Sweden and England. *Organization*, 13(2), pp. 275–298.

Battilana, J., and Lee, M. (2014). Advancing research on hybrid organizing – insights from the study of social enterprises. *Academy of Management Annals*, 8(1), pp. 397–441.

Bentley, P.J., Coates, H., Dobson, I., Goedegebuure, L., and Meek, V.L. (2013). Academic job satisfaction from an international comparative perspective: Factors associated with satisfaction across 12 countries. In Bentley, P.J., Coates, H., Dobson, I., Goedegebuure, L., and Meek, V.L. (eds), *Job Satisfaction Around the Academic World, The Changing Academy – the Changing Academic Profession in International Comparative Perspective*, Vol. 7 (pp. 1–23). Dordrecht: Springer.

Berger, P., and Luckmann, T. (1967). *The Social Construction of Reality*. New York: Anchor.

Beyer, J.M. (1981). Ideologies, values, and decision making in organizations. In Nystrom, P.C., and Starbuck, W.H. (eds), *Handbook of Organizational Design*, Volume 2 (pp. 166–202). New York: Oxford University Press.

Billot, J. (2010). The imagined and the real: Identifying the tensions for academic identity. *Higher Education Research and Development*, 29(6), pp. 709–721.

Bolden, R., and Petrov, G. (2014). Hybrid configurations of leadership in higher education employer engagement. *Journal of Higher Education Policy and Management*, 36(4), pp. 408–417.

Bolden, R., Gosling, J., and O'Brien, A. (2014). Citizens of the academic community: A societal perspective on leadership in UK higher education. *Studies in Higher Education*, 39(5), pp. 754–770.

Bolden, R., Gosling, J., O'Brien, A., Peters, K., Ryan, M., and Haslam, S.A. (2012). *Academic Leadership: Changing Conceptions, Identities and Experiences in UK Higher Education*. London: Leadership Foundation for Higher Education.

Bolden, R., Jones, S., Davis, H., and Gentle, P. (2015). *Developing and Sustaining Shared Leadership in Higher Education: Stimulus Paper*. London: Leadership Foundation for Higher Education, in collaboration with LH Martin Institute.

Bolden, R., Petrov, G., and Gosling, J. (2008). *Developing Collective Leadership in Higher Education: Final Report*. London: Leadership Foundation for Higher Education.

Bolden, R., Witzel, M., and Linacre, N. (2016). *Leadership Paradoxes: Rethinking Leadership for an Uncertain World*. London: Routledge.

Christopher, J. (2012). Tension between the corporate and collegial cultures of Australian public universities: The current status. *Critical Perspectives on Accounting*, 23, pp. 556–571.

Chubb, J., and Watermeyer, R. (2017). Artifice or integrity in the marketization of research impact? Investigating the moral economy of (pathways to) impact statements within research funding proposals in the UK and Australia. *Studies in Higher Education*, 42(12), pp. 2360–2372.

Churchman, D. (2006). Institutional commitments, individual compromises: Identity-related responses to compromise in an Australian university. *Journal of Higher Education Policy and Management*, 28(1), pp. 3–15.

Churchman, D., and King, S. (2009). Academic practice in transition: Hidden stories of academic identities. *Teaching in Higher Education*, 14(5), pp. 507–516.

Clegg, S., and McAuley, J. (2009). Conceptualising middle management in higher education: A multifaceted discourse. *Journal of Higher Education Policy and Management*, 27(1), pp. 19–34.

Corbett, A., Cornelissen, J., Delios. A., and Harley, B. (2014). Variety, novelty, and perceptions of scholarship in research on management and organizations: An appeal for ambidextrous scholarship. *Journal of Management Studies*, 51(1), pp. 3–18.

Croft, C., Currie, G., and Lockett, A. (2015). Broken 'two-way windows'? An exploration of professional hybrids. *Public Administration*, 93(2), pp. 380–394.

De Boer, H., and Goedegebuure, L. (2009). The changing nature of the academic deanship. *Leadership*, 5(3), pp. 347–364.

Deem, R., and Brehony, K.J. (2005). Management as ideology: The case of 'new managerialism' in higher education. *Oxford Review of Education*, 31(2), pp. 217–235.

Deem, R., Hillyard, S., and Reed, M. (2008). *Knowledge, Higher Education, and the New Managerialism: The Changing Management of UK Universities*. Oxford: Oxford University Press.

Denis, J.L., Ferlie, E., and Van Gestel, N. (2015). Understanding hybridity in public organizations. *Public Administration*, 93(2), pp. 273–289.

Denis, J.L., Langley, A., and Rouleau, J. (2007). Strategizing in pluralistic contexts: Rethinking theoretical frames. *Human Relations*, 60, pp. 179–215.

Dopson, S., Ferlie, E., McGivern, G., Fischer, M.D., Ledger, J., et al. (2016). *The Impact of Leadership and Leadership Development in Higher Education: A Review of the Literature and Evidence*. London: Leadership Foundation for Higher Education.

Ek, A.C., Ideland, M., Jönsson, S., and Malmberg, C. (2013). The tension between marketisation and academisation in higher education. *Studies in Higher Education*, 38(9), pp. 1305–1318.

Ernst, C., and Chrobot-Mason, D. (2011). *Boundary-Spanning Leadership: Six Practices for Solving Problems, Driving Innovation, and Transforming Organisations*. New York: McGraw Hill.

Evans, L. (2015). A changing role for university professors? Professorial academic leadership as it is perceived by 'the led'. *British Educational Research Journal*, 41(4), pp. 666–685.

Fethke, G.C., and Policano, A.J. (2013). Public no more universities: Subsidy to self-reliance. *Journal of Management Development*, 32(5), pp. 525–536.

Foreman, P., and Whetten, D.A. (2002). Members' identification with multiple-identity organizations. *Organization Science*, 13(6), pp. 618–635.

Franco-Santos, M., Rivera, P., and Bourne, M. (2014). *Performance Management in UK Higher Education Institutions: The need for a hybrid approach*. Research and Development Series, 3 (Pub. 8.1). London: Leadership Foundation for Higher Education and Cranfield University School of Management.

Fulton, O. (2003). Managerialism in UK universities: Unstable hybridity and the complications of implementation. In Amaral, A., Meek, V.L., and Larsen, I.M. (eds), *The Higher Education Managerial Revolution?* (pp. 155–178). Dordrecht: Kluwer Academic Publishers.

Furedi, F. (2011). Introduction to the marketisation of higher education and the student as consumer. In Molesworth, M., Scullion, R., and Nixon, E. (eds), *The Marketisation of Higher Education and the Student as Consumer* (pp. 1–7). London: Routledge.

Garcia, P., and Hardy, C. (2007). Positioning, similarity and difference: Narratives of individual and organizational identities in an Australian university. *Scandinavian Journal of Management*, 23, pp. 363–383.

Garret, G., and Davies, G. (2010). *Herding Cats: Being Advice to Aspiring Academic and Research Leaders*. Axminster: Triarchy Press.

Gersick, C.J.G., Bartunek, J.M., and Dutton, J.E. (2000). Learning from academia: The importance of relationships in professional life. *Academy of Management Journal*, 43, pp. 1026–1044.

Gonzales, L.D., Martinez, E., and Ordu, C. (2014). Exploring faculty experiences in a striving university through the lens of academic capitalism. *Studies in Higher Education*, 39(7), pp. 1097–1115.

Goodall, A. (2009). *Socrates in the Boardroom: Why Research Universities Should Be Led by Top Scholars*. Princeton, NJ: Princeton University Press.

Griffin, M.A., Neal, A., and Parker, S.K. (2007). A new model of work role performance: Positive behavior in uncertain and interdependent contexts. *Academy of Management Journal*, 50(2), pp. 327–347.

Gronn, P. (2009). Leadership configurations. *Leadership*, 5, pp. 381–394.

Gronn, P. (2011). Hybrid configurations of leadership. In Bryman, A. Collinson, D., Grint, K., Jackson, B., and Uhl-Bien, M. (eds), *SAGE Handbook of Leadership* (pp. 435–452). London: SAGE.

Hancock, T.M. (2007). The business of universities and the role of department chair. *International Journal of Educational Management*, 21(4), pp. 306–314.

Hardy, C., Lawrence, T.B., and Grant, D. (2005). Discourse and collaboration: The role of conversations and collective identity. *Academy of Management Review*, 30, pp. 58–77.

Harley, S. (2002). The impact of research selectivity on academic work and identity in UK universities. *Studies in Higher Education*, 27(2), pp. 187–205.

Haslam, S.A., Reicher, S.D., and Platow, M.J. (2011). *The New Psychology of Leadership: Identity, Influence and Power*. Basingstoke: Routledge.

Heffernan, M. (2014). *A Bigger Prize: How We Can Do Better Than the Competition*. New York: Public Affairs.

Henkel, M. (2005). Academic identity and autonomy in a changing policy environment. *Higher Education*, 49, pp. 155–176.

Henkel, M. (2012). Introduction: Change and continuity in academic and professional identities. In Gordon, G., and Whitchurch, C. (eds), *Academic and Professional Identities in Higher Education* (pp. 3–12). New York: Routledge.

Hughes, T., Bence, D., Grisoni, L., O'Regan, N., and Wornham, D. (2011). Scholarship that matters: Academic–practitioner engagement in business and management. *Academy of Management Learning and Education*, 10(1), pp. 40–57.

Jay, J. (2013). Navigating paradox as a mechanism of change and innovation in hybrid organizations. *Academy of Management Journal*, 56, pp. 137–159.

Johansen, S.T., Olsen, T.H., Solstad, E., and Torsteinsen, H. (2015). An insider view of the hybrid organisation: How managers respond to challenges of efficiency, legitimacy and meaning. *Journal of Management and Organization*, 21(6), pp. 725–740.

Jones, S. (2013). Beyond the teaching–research nexus: The scholarship teaching–action–research (STAR) conceptual framework. *Higher Education Research and Development*, 32(3), pp. 381–391.

Jones, S., Lefoe, G., Harvey, M., and Ryland, K. (2012). Distributed leadership: A collaborative framework for academics, executives and professionals in higher education. *Journal of Higher Education Policy and Management*, 34(1), pp. 67–78.

Jungblut, J., and Vukasovic, M. (2013). And now for something completely different? Re-examining hybrid steering approaches in higher education. *Higher Education Policy*, 26, pp. 447–461.

Kenny, K., Whittle, A., and Willmott, H. (2011). *Understanding Identity and Organizations*. Los Angeles, CA: SAGE.

Kinman, G., and Wray, S. (2013). Higher stress: A survey of stress and wellbeing among staff in higher education. University and College Union (UCU). http://www.ucu.org.uk/media/pdf/4/5/HE_stress_report_July_2013.pdf.

Knights, D., and Scarbrough, H. (2010). In search of relevance: Perspectives on the contribution of academic–practitioner networks. *Organization Studies*, 31, pp. 1287–1309.

Lok, J. (2010). Institutional logics as identity projects. *Academy of Management Journal*, 53(6), pp. 1305–1335.

Lumby, J. (2013). *What do We Know about Leadership in Higher Education?* London: Leadership Foundation for Higher Education.

Macfarlane, B. (2011). Professors as intellectual leaders: Formation, identity and role. *Studies in Higher Education*, 36(1), pp. 57–73.

Macfarlane, B. (2012). *Intellectual Leadership in Higher Education: Renewing the Role of the University Professor*. Abingdon: Routledge.

McArthur, J. (2011). Reconsidering the social and economic purposes of higher education. *Higher Education Research and Development*, 30(6), pp. 737–749.

McCormack, J., Propper, C., and Smith, S. (2014). Herding cats? Management and university performance. *Economic Journal*, 124 (578), pp. 534–564.

Middlehurst, R. (1993). *Leading Academics*. Buckingham: Society for Research into Higher Education and Open University Press.

Mouwen, K. (2000). Strategy, structure and culture of the hybrid university: Towards the university of the 21st century. *Tertiary Education and Management*, 6(1), pp. 47–56.

Musselin, C. (2005). Change or continuity in higher education governance? In Bleiklie, I., and Henkel, M. (eds), *Governing Knowledge* (pp. 65–79). Dordrecht: Springer.

Ng, L.L., and Pemberton, J. (2013). Research-based communities of practice in UK higher education. *Studies in Higher Education*, 38(10), pp. 1522–1539.

Nixon, J. (2001). 'Not without dust and heat': The moral bases of the 'new' academic professionalism. *British Journal of Educational Studies*, 49(2), pp. 173–186.

Noordegraaf, M. (2007). From 'pure' to 'hybrid' professionalism: Present-day professionalism in ambiguous public domains. *Administration and Society*, 39(6), pp. 761–785.

Noordegraaf, M., and De Wit, B. (2012). Responses to managerialism: How management pressures affect managerial relations and loyalties in education. *Public Administration*, 90(4), pp. 957–973.

Oakley, K., and Selwood, S. (2010). *Conversations and Collaborations: The Leadership of Collaborative Projects between Higher Education and the Arts and Cultural Sector: Final Report*. London: Leadership Foundation for Higher Education.

Parker, L. (2012). From privatized to hybrid corporatised higher education: A global financial management discourse. *Financial Accountability and Management*, 28(3), pp. 247–268.

Parker, L. (2013). Contemporary university strategising: The financial imperative. *Financial Accountability and Management*, 29(1), pp. 1–25.

Parker, M. (2004). Becoming manager – or, the werewolf looks anxiously in the mirror, checking for unusual facial hair. *Management Learning*, 35(1), pp. 45–59.

Parr, C. (2015). Best university workplace survey 2015: Results and analysis. *Times Higher Education*, 5 February. http://www.timeshighereducation.co.uk/features/best-university-workplace-survey-2015-results-and-analysis/2018272.article.

Pearce, C. (2004). The future of leadership: Combining vertical and shared leadership to transform knowledge work. *Academy of Management Executive*, 18, pp. 47–57.

Pollitt, C., and Bouckaert, G. (2011). *Public Management Reform: A Comparative Analysis – New Public Management, Governance, and the Neo-Weberian State*, 3rd edition. Oxford: Oxford University Press.

Rayner, S., Fuller, M., McEwen, L., and Roberts, H. (2010). Managing leadership in the UK university: A case for researching the missing professoriate? *Studies in Higher Education*, 35(6), pp. 617–631.

Rolfe, G. (2013). *The University in Dissent: Scholarship in the Corporate University*. London: Routledge and the Society for Research into Higher Education.

Schön, D.A. (1983). *The Reflective Practitioner: How Professionals Think in Action*. London: Temple Smith.

Sewerin, T., and Holmberg, R. (2017). Contextualizing distributed leadership in higher education. *Higher Education Research & Development*, 36(6), pp. 1280–1294.

Slaughter, S., and Rhoades, G. (2009). *Academic Capitalism and the New Economy: Markets, State, and Higher Education*. Baltimore, MD: Johns Hopkins University Press.

Smith, W.K., and Lewis, M.W. (2011). Toward a theory of paradox: A dynamic equilibrium model of organizing. *Academy of Management Review*, 36, pp. 391–403.

Spillane, J.P., Halverson, R., and Diamond, J.B. (2004). Toward a theory of leadership practice: A distributed practice. *Journal of Curriculum Studies*, 36(1), pp. 3–34.

Sveningsson, S., and Alvesson, M. (2003). Managing managerial identities: Organizational fragmentation, discourse and identity struggle. *Human Relations*, 56(10), pp. 1163–1193.

Tahar, S., Niemeyer, C., and Boutellier, R. (2011). Transferral of business management concepts to universities as ambidextrous organisations. *Tertiary Education and Management*, 17(4), pp. 289–308.

Teelken, C. (2015). Hybridity, coping mechanisms, and academic performance management: Comparing three countries. *Public Administration*, 93(2), pp. 307–323.

Trice, H.M. (1993). *Occupational Subcultures in the Workplace*. Ithaca, NY: ILR Press.

Trowler, P. (2010). UK higher education: Captured by new managerialist ideology? In Meek, L.V., Goedegebuure, L., Santiago, R., and Carvalho, T. (eds), *The Changing Dynamics of Higher Education Middle Management* (pp. 197–211). London: Springer.

Trowler, P., Saunders, M., and Bamber, V. (2012). *Tribes and Territories in the 21st Century: Rethinking the Significance of Disciplines in Higher Education*. London: Routledge.

Van de Ven, A.H. (2007). *Engaged Scholarship: A Guide for Organizational and Social Research*. New York: Oxford University Press.

Whitchurch, C. (2008). Shifting identities and blurring boundaries: The emergence of 'third space professionals' in UK Higher Education. *Higher Education Quarterly*, 62(4), pp. 377–396.

Whitchurch, C., and Gordon, G. (2010). Diversifying academic and professional identities in higher education: Some management challenges. *Tertiary Education and Management*, 16(2), pp. 129–144.

Willmott, H. (2011). Journal list fetishism and the perversion of scholarship: Reactivity and the ABS list. *Organization*, 18, pp. 429–442.

Winter, R.P. (2009). Academic manager or managed academic? Academic identity schisms in higher education. *Journal of Higher Education Policy and Management*, 3(2), pp. 121–131.

Winter, R.P. (2017). *Managing Academics: A Question of Perspective*. Cheltenham: Edward Elgar Publishing.

Winter, R.P., and O'Donohue, W. (2012). Academic identity tensions in the public university: Which values really matter? *Journal of Higher Education Policy and Management*, 34(5), pp. 569–577.

Winter, R.P., and Sarros, J.C. (2002). Corporate reforms to Australian universities: Views from the academic heartland. *Journal of Institutional Research*, 11(2), pp. 92–104.

PART II

PRIVATE SECTOR HYBRIDS

11. The rise of the Dutch East India Company
Patrick A. M. Vermeulen and Arlette Cindy van Lint

INTRODUCTION

Our study focuses on one of the first organisations to combine state and commercial logics: the Dutch East India Company (Verenigde Oost-Indische Compagnie, or VOC) which existed from 1602 to 1799. In 1670 the former director of the VOC, Coenraad van Beuningen, wrote that the VOC was a company 'not just of commerce but also of state' (Gaastra, 2013, p. 58). This had already been the case since 1602 when the VOC established itself as a national trading company assembled out of a variety of former trading companies to create a Dutch monopoly of trade from the East adopted by the state and using investments from shareholders (Gaastra, 2013). Thus, from the first day on, the VOC needed to secure the support from different internal and external parties: the directors of the VOC, the shareholders and the States General. Gelderblom et al. (2010, p. 16) confirm the VOC's hybrid character from its foundation onwards: 'The charter and the preamble . . . highlight the VOC's character as a hybrid: a private commercial company with superimposed public responsibilities'. Never before had a company organised itself this way. As a result the VOC could not follow a 'ready-to-wear' model to deal with the tensions between the logics the company had to combine (see Battilana and Dorado, 2010). 'The contradiction between merchant and king, which had characterized the VOC from the beginning, became more and more pressing' (Gaastra, 2013, p. 59). Hence our first research question is: how did the VOC respond to the conflicting logics of state and commerce? We address this question in the research findings below.

The most important assumption of this study, then, is that the Dutch East India Company was a hybrid organisation. The overview undertaken by the Dutch historian Gaastra (2013) provides a clear indication for this. As a 'new hybrid' it had to develop and maintain its hybrid nature itself over a long period of time under enduring conflicting demands. Hybrid organisations are gaining prevalence in today's societies (Battilana and Lee, 2014). These hybrid organisations can be found in a broad range of sectors, for example in healthcare, elderly care, education, social housing, microfinance, transport and waste management (Brandsen and Karré, 2011). A key feature of hybrid organisations is that they 'belong' to 'overlapping sectoral segments' (Seibel, 2015, p. 697). As such, they are not exclusively part of the private sector or public sector but are governed by the 'principles' of multiple sectors (Billis, 2010). As a result, hybrid organisations often 'involve a variety of stakeholders, pursue multiple and often conflicting goals and engage in divergent or inconsistent activities' (Mair et al., 2015, p. 713). Our historical analysis can serve to reflect on how ideas about hybridity help to understand the VOC history, an issue to which we return in the discussion section of this chapter.

RELEVANT LITERATURE

Recently the interest in hybrid organisations has increased strongly (Billis, 2010). The blurring of public and private sectors which has been taking shape for the last few decades can be seen as creating a continuum, with governmental agencies on the one hand and private companies on the other (Dahl and Lindblom, 1953; Lan and Rainey, 1992). Despite distinctions between these two sectors in terms of ownership, governance, operational priorities, and human and other types of resources (Billis, 2010), there are also similarities and interrelations. These have led in part to the emergence of hybrid forms of organisations, blending public and private aspects (Lan and Rainey, 1992). Brandsen and Karré (2011, p. 828) state that hybridity always symbolises the process and product of a mixture of essentially contradictory and conflicting elements. As such, hybrids need to find ways to deal with the multiple demands to which they are exposed, and they may have to incorporate practices that may not easily work together (Pache and Santos, 2013). Hybrids have to manage these external tensions and have to be careful not to lose their legitimacy in the eyes of important institutional actors (D'Aunno et al., 1991). In doing so, they have to create an integrated strategy to realise unfamiliar combinations of activities and avoid 'mission drift' (Battilana et al., 2012) to maintain their hybrid nature over time.

Following recent studies in neo-institutional theory, we define hybrids as organisations that incorporate elements from different institutional logics (Battilana and Dorado, 2010; Pache and Santos, 2013). An institutional logic can be defined as: 'an overarching set of principles that prescribes how to interpret organisational reality, what constitutes appropriate behaviour, and how to succeed' (Thornton, 2004, p. 70). Hence, hybrid organisations are 'confronted with incompatible prescriptions from multiple constituents holding different institutional logics' (Greenwood et al., 2010, p. 317). Social enterprises, for instance, whose goal it is to achieve a social mission through commercial activities, are caught between the competing demands of the market logic of making profits and the social welfare logic of achieving a social mission. These social enterprises have to make choices. Should they incorporate for-profit and not-for-profit entities? Should they distribute profit to their owners or reinvest in their social mission? (Pache and Santos, 2013). As a result, hybrids have to make decisions as to what demands they should prioritise, satisfy, alter or neglect in order to secure support and survival (Greenwood et al., 2010; Pache and Santos, 2010). However, incompatible prescriptions of different logics generate challenges and tensions for hybrid organisations that are exposed to them, and can make them 'highly unstable and unlikely to retain their hybrid nature over time' (Battilana and Dorado, 2010, p. 1419). 'Because adopting elements prescribed by a given logic often requires defying demands of the other logics, hybrid organizations may potentially jeopardize their legitimacy with regard to important institutional referents' (Pache and Santos, 2013, p. 973). Incorporating elements from different logics creates the potential for incoherence and conflict (Kraatz and Block, 2008). Because of these difficulties it is interesting to investigate how hybrids actually respond to conflicting demands and how they retain their hybrid nature over time.

Institutional logics originate from societal sectors, such as professions, the market, the state, family and religion (Dunn and Jones, 2010; Friedland and Alford, 1991; Thornton, 2004). Each of these sectors is associated with a central institutional logic, providing

Table 11.1　State and market logics of the VOC

Characteristics	State logic	Market logic
Economic system	A strong VOC fleet to protect state interests overseas	A strong trading and shipping network to establish profitable trade relationships
Raison d'être	The VOC as a powerful force to consolidate the interests of the state	The VOC as an economic force, creating strong trade positions
Strategy	Capturing of enemy ships for lucrative and political reasons	Create value for shareholders
Logic of investment	Build a strong fleet to create political and military influence	Build relations and networks to expand overseas territory

organisations with different guidelines on how to interpret and function in social situations (Greenwood et al., 2010). In the case of the VOC two central logics competed for influence: the commercial logic and the state logic (see Table 11.1). Each of these logics 'distinguishes unique organising principles, practices, and symbols that influence individual and organisational behaviour' (Thornton et al., 2012, p. 51). Thornton (2004) was the first to formulate a theoretical model, which includes building blocks that specify the appropriate organising principles and behaviours belonging to each societal sector and its central logic (Thornton, et al., 2012). According to her, an organisation following the state logic gains legitimacy by democratic participation, gains authority through bureaucratic domination, values citizenship and membership, focuses on its status as an 'interest group', aims to increase the community good, uses backroom politics as an informal control mechanism and views the economic system as one of welfare capitalism (Thornton, 2004). Jay (2013) further argues that, according to the state logic, an ideal organisation would be a government bureaucracy that focuses on providing public services, policy implementation and serving constituents. An organisation following the state logic is guided by principles of public benefit and collective choice, is owned by the citizens and the state, and is resourced through taxation (Doherty et al., 2014). It also has the power to coordinate public resources, to make rules and laws and to enforce these. It is constrained by the law and it has to be publicly transparent (Jay, 2013).

An organisation following market or commercial logic gains legitimacy by its share price, gains authority by shareholder activism, values self-interest, focuses on its status in the market, aims to increase its profits, uses industry analyses as an informal control system and views the economic system as one of market capitalism (Thornton, 2004). Central to the commercial logic is a focus on the private financial gain of the organisation, the purpose of which is to create value for its owners and shareholders through the sales of goods and services (Ebrahim et al., 2014). Following the commercial logic an ideal type of organisation would be a business firm that values client service, revenue, profit and value creation. It has the power of salesmanship and the power of delivering service and product. It is constrained by the rules of the game, scarce client attention and resources, and its fiduciary responsibility to financiers (Jay, 2013). Organisations following the commercial logic are guided by market forces (Doherty et al., 2014), are resourced through equity (by the sale of shares and earnings on the marketplace) and debts (Battilana et al., 2012; Brandsen and Karré, 2011), and their missions are to build a competitive position

(Thornton and Ocasio, 1999). Because of this, commercial logic rewards efficiency and control (D'Aunno et al., 2000, in Pache and Santos, 2013) and organisational performances are measured using quantitative evaluation and performance criteria (Ebrahim et al., 2014).

Logics guide organisational behaviour within an organisational field (Scott, 2001). Multiple institutional logics are available, and interact and compete for influence within such a field (Greenwood et al., 2011). Subsequently, organisations face a trade-off of how to respond to these conflicting institutional demands. Oliver (1991) was the first to create a response model showing that organisations are not just passive adapters of external demands. Instead they can actually choose from a range of creative strategies in response to external pressures, varying from passive acquiescence to active resistance. She identified five possible responses to institutional pressures: acquiescence, compromise, avoidance, defiance and manipulation. Acquiescence refers to a situation where organisations obey institutional requirements. Organisations could, for example, attempt to compromise with important institutional referents and adopt elements prescribed by a certain logic in a slightly altered form (Oliver, 1991), or choose to selectively couple intact elements prescribed by different external constituents (see also Pache and Santos, 2013) and use an avoidance strategy to escape institutional rules. More active forms of resistance can be found when organisations defy or actively challenge institutional requirements. Finally, manipulation refers to rather opportunistic attempts to change the content or source of the pressure. Building on Oliver's work, several scholars have started to explore how organisations respond to the presence of multiple institutional constituents with conflicting demands, that is, conflicting logics (Greenwood et al., 2011; Kodeih and Greenwood, 2014; Kraatz and Block, 2008; Pache and Santos, 2010; Vermeulen et al., 2014; Zilber, 2011). In Table 11.2 we provide an overview of different strategies identified in the literature that can provide responses to conflicting institutional demands.

THE RESEARCH CONTEXT

The foundation of the VOC was a direct result of an increased level of trade in Asian markets. Shortly after the first Dutch expedition in 1595, trade companies were established in various Dutch cities (Parthesius, 2010). The success of Dutch vessels in outcompeting Portuguese and Spanish ships further increased the popularity of trading in Asia, and served as a stepping-stone for creating a strong international trading and shipping network. Importantly, the funds that were generated by this lucrative network were much needed to fund wars against other European nations. The competitive position and growth of the Netherlands was at stake and this required international expansion beyond European borders.

The foundation of the VOC required the support of three key actors. The first of them was the directors of the earlier companies (the 'Heren XVII') out of which the new VOC would be created. Secondly, support was needed from the States General who had to grant the VOC its trade monopoly and suzerain rights in the East. This would ensure the success of the company by preventing other Dutch companies from undermining its competitive position. In also meant that the number of ships needed could be deceased and the character of the Asian trade could be changed: 'no longer just existing out of

Table 11.2   Overview of different organisational responses to conflicting external demands

Response	Definition	Illustration
Compromise	The attempt by organisations to enact institutional prescriptions in a slightly altered form, crafting an acceptable balance between the conflicting expectations of external constituents	Conforming to the minimum expected standards, crafting a new behaviour bringing together elements of the conflicting demands, bargaining with institutional referents so that they alter their demands (Pache and Santos, 2013)
Avoidance	The organisational attempt to preclude the necessity of conformity	Concealing their nonconformity, buffering themselves from institutional pressures, or escaping from institutional rules or expectations (Oliver, 1991) Decoupling: the ceremonial espousal of a prescribed practice with no actual enactment; organisations decouple their formal from their operational structure (Meyer and Rowan, 1977)
Defiance	More active form of resistance: explicit rejection of at least one of the institutional demands	Ignoring institutional rules and values or assault and denounce institutionalised values and the external constituents that express them (Oliver, 1991)
Manipulation	Active intent to use institutional processes and relations opportunistically, to co-opt and neutralize institutional constituents, to shape and redefine institutionalised norms and external criteria of evaluation, and to control or dominate the source, allocation, or expression of social approval and legitimation	Joining the organisation or its board of directors that exert pressure on the company to strategically influence the standards by which the company is evaluated (Oliver, 1991)
Selective coupling	Selectively coupling of intact elements prescribed by each logic	Using a profit destination model (prescribed by the social welfare logic), but also invest in a strong national brand (a practice promoted by the commercial logic) (Pache and Santos, 2013)

returning fleets, but including own settlements in East India to monopolise the spice trade' (Witteveen, 2002, p. 49). Thirdly, the support of external shareholders was needed since they had to provide the VOC with capital.

It was no easy task to secure the support of these three actors in order to establish the VOC as they (and especially the directors of the pre-companies and the States General) had their own requirements for the way in which the new company operated. In general, the demands of the States General were shaped by the logic of the state and the need for the States General to secure the military and economic position of the Dutch Republic and the welfare of all its inhabitants (Bruijn, 2002; Gaastra, 2013). 'It was mostly economic and not military motives that inspired the government and the state attorney of Holland, Johan van Oldenbarnevelt, to persuade the merchants to cooperate. However, when the "merger" was soon to be realised, the trade with Asia was also used more and more as an aggressive and military weapon against the Spaniards and Portuguese' (Gaastra, 2013, p. 19). 'Enemy Spain/Portugal owned a huge empire overseas, which the Republic wanted to conquer. Impairing this territory would weaken the enemy in its conduct of war and would increase the military and economic power of the Republic' (Bruijn, 2002, p. 51). Though the VOC directors also wanted to weaken the power of the Spaniards and Portuguese in the East, and it was clear that 'the VOC would engage in war overseas' (Gaastra, 2013, p. 30), 'the scale of the operations which the Estates General demanded went much further than anticipated. Consequently these demands created serious friction' (Gelderblom et al., 2010, p. 28).

Furthermore, it was difficult to combine the demands of the States General and those of the shareholders. The shareholders were aligned with commercial logic. For them it was most important that the VOC realised profits as quickly and as high as possible, profits that would subsequently be passed on to the shareholders in the form of dividends (Gaastra, 2013). Unlike the States General they opposed the idea of using the VOC as instrument of war for the Republic in the East. Some shareholders were opposed to the use of excessive violence for religious reasons; others were just concerned about the commercial effects of this policy (Gelderblom et al., 2010). The starting point for the conflict of interests between the VOC directors and the shareholders was the founding of the VOC on 20 March 1602 and its coercion by the States General. 'Particularly in the initial period, the Heren XVII acted on their own behalf, instead of acting in the interests of the legal entity and the shareholders' (Gepken-Jager and Ebeldina, 2005, p. 80).

In addition, a solution had to be found for the conflicting demands of the directors of the different pre-companies. 'Negotiations between the Dutch companies took a long time because of conflicting demands' (Gelderblom et al., 2010, p. 14). 'The relationship between the Zeeuwen and Hollanders had always been difficult, especially in the last months of 1601' (Witteveen, 2002, p. 50). Although all three actors supported the economic rationale for founding the VOC, the States General focused more on it as an aggressive and military weapon in favour of the Republic than the directors themselves (Gaastra, 2013). The shareholders did not want the VOC to be used as a war instrument of the Republic at all (Gelderblom et al., 2010). The shareholders wanted to receive as much dividend as possible but, on the other hand, the directors wanted to keep financial gains for themselves (Gepken-Jager and Ebeldina, 2005). In addition, the directors from the pre-companies distrusted each other, making the foundation of a single monopolised trading organisation even more difficult (Parthesius, 2010).

RESEARCH FINDINGS

Our case study focuses on the strategy of the VOC as a hybrid organisation in the Dutch Republic (where it was founded and where its highest executive board the Heren XVII was settled). We selected three points in time from which to examine the VOC's responses to conflicting institutional demands. The first of these, the foundation of the VOC in 1602, concerns the combination of state and commercial logics and the way the conflicting demands of all three actors were taken into account: the States General, the shareholders and the VOC directors. The second period of time, characterised by protesting shareholders (1609–23), is mainly concerned with the conflicting demands of the VOC directors and its shareholders. And the third period, featuring the Anglo-Dutch Wars and the role of the VOC (1652–1784), is concerned with the conflicting demands of the VOC directors and the States General.

From the moment it was founded in 1602 until its definitive downfall in 1799, the VOC struggled with the conflicting demands exerted on the company by its own directors, by the States General and by its shareholders. As a result, the VOC took on different roles throughout its existence, sometimes behaving more like a trading company and sometimes more like a military company or even a territorial ruler. Figure 11.1 provides a summary of the ways in which the VOC responded to these changing demands.

Foundation of the VOC (1602): Creating a Hybrid Organisation through Negotiation

The first response to conflicting external demands was the result of years of negotiations between representatives of the Republic and the Dutch trading companies. This ultimately led to the creation of a hybrid company with an internal and external balance of power defined in the charter of foundation in 1602. Shareholders were excluded from these negotiations. Between August 1599 and October 1601 it was the States of Holland (the most powerful province represented in the States General) that laid the foundations for a merger of the Dutch trading companies, fiercely supported by the powerful trading company of Amsterdam (Witteveen, 2002). The first commission to explore a merger between different merchants was made up of governmental representatives from different cities who concluded that regulation of the trade with Asia was desirable, but that more information was needed about the intentions of the merchants and what they were willing to give the Republic if such a monopoly was granted (Witteveen, 2002). No real efforts were made, however, to address these questions.

In May 1601 a new commission of governmental representatives decided it was necessary for all the companies to be merged into one new trading company that would be granted a monopoly and suzerain rights in the East (Witteveen, 2002). Merchants from Amsterdam had put pressure on the States of Holland to grant their trading company a monopoly in order to avoid the destruction of their trade as the result of the entry of newcomers to the market. Their company, they argued, would serve the whole of the Republic because all of its inhabitants would be offered the possibility of becoming shareholders in the company (Gaastra, 2013). This arrangement established a foundation for the principle of participation in any new company (and part of the logic of the state) that was agreed and was not discussed any further. The Amsterdam company did not receive the monopoly it had asked for but the States General agreed to discuss the content of a charter of foundation with merchants of all the existing East India trading companies in the Republic. Representatives of the States General and merchants of the different trading companies undertook negotiations in November and December 1601. The company of Amsterdam put pressure on the States General to take responsibility for a merger, arguing that without this the situation would harm not only the companies but also the reputation of the Republic (Witteveen, 2002). The States General and the merchants all agreed that a single merger was desirable and, following proposals from

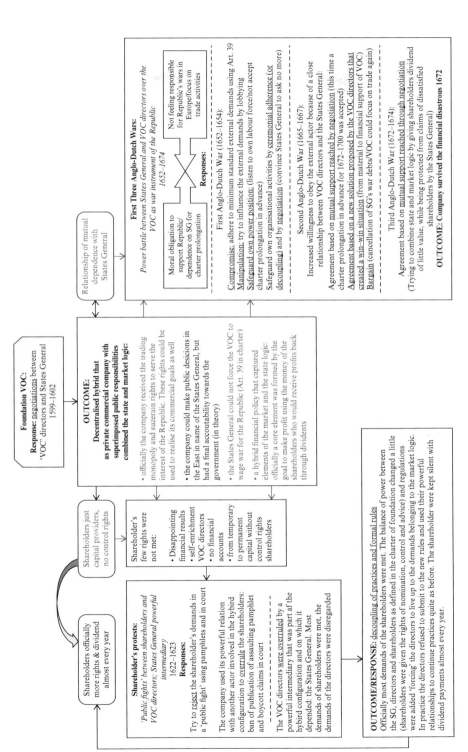

Figure 11.1 Overview of response strategies

all of the companies, the proposal put forward by Amsterdam was adopted for further negotiations which mostly concerned the internal balance of power between directors from Amsterdam and from Zeeland (and the other smaller companies) who would form the executive board or Heren XVII. Zeeland was the only company not willing to approve Amsterdam's proposal, and the delegates all went home (Witteveen, 2002).

The States General did not accept this deadlock and summoned the representatives of the companies and its own delegates to return to The Hague in January 1602. State attorney Van Oldenbarnevelt urged the merchants to come to an agreement, stating that those delaying the merger were actually enemies of the Republic as they were not helping to weaken the Spanish enemy and strengthen the Republic (Witteveen, 2002). An agreement had to be realised (Bruijn, 2002). Within a week internal agreement was reached on the most important points of the merger, which included the internal balance of power between the pre-companies, the relationship between the Republic and the company, and the liability of the directors (Witteveen, 2002). The final vote over the charter of foundation originally planned for 11 February 1602 was postponed due to internal conflicts within the States of Zeeland which wanted to be sure that the merger would only be temporary. On 9 March, the States of Holland tried to stop the States of Zeeland from arguing about details in the charter, stating that even within the States of Holland not all articles were discussed separately. The trade was important and a merger was necessary, so all representatives simply had to vote in favour of the advantageous charter. They argued that: 'the trade was profitable and created a lot of work in the Republic. The Spanish enemy would also be weakened and the Republic would not even have to pay for all this' (Witteveen, 2002, p. 56). Still, the States of Zeeland did not give in and even after His Highness Prince Maurits tried to force Zeeland into an agreement, Zeeland did not obey (Witteveen, 2002). In the end, the governmental representatives of the cities Vlissingen and Veere were excluded from the debate, and Joachimi, the highest representative from the States of Zeeland, and representatives from the States of Holland and the merchants, came to an agreement that the States General would now close the deal (Witteveen, 2002). On 20 March 1602 the States General granted a charter for 21 years to the VOC.

The outcome of these years of negotiation was a merger of six pre-companies with a decentralised organisational structure consisting of one general board of directors – the Heren XVII – and six more or less independent chambers that were established in the cities of the former pre-companies. This central board was composed of eight directors from Amsterdam, four from Zeeland and one from each of the other four chambers. The seventeenth position would be filled in turn by a representative from one of the chambers, except for Amsterdam. As the Heren XVII made their decisions by majority vote, Amsterdam was thus prevented from overruling all other chambers on its own (as Zeeland had so fiercely tried to prevent) (Bruijn, 2002). Further, the directors of the pre-companies had ensured that there should be limits on the power of the Heren XVII by confining it to some fundamental coordinating tasks, thereby safeguarding the chambers' independent management of day-to-day activities (Heijer, 2005). This organisational structure was an acceptable solution to the internal conflicts between the merchants and the governmental representatives from different cities. The new hybrid company was now challenged to combine the logics of the state and the market.

To deal with conflicting demands from three different actors the charter established a clear balance of power between the VOC directors, the States General and the shareholders to regulate how much influence each actor would have on the company's course of affairs. The directors were responsible for running their share of the joint operations from their respective ports: equipping ships, recruiting labour, selling produce and paying bills; whereas the States General made sure to officially keep final authority over the VOC (Gelderblom et al., 2010, p. 1055). While the relationship between the VOC directors and the States General was based on mutual dependence, the position of the shareholders was limited to that of providers of capital, without any authority or rights to control (Jongh, 2011). 'Shareholders were no party to the charter; this was a contract between the directors and the States General. The shareholders put their name under the preamble, thereby agreeing to put their money in the company for a period of ten years and to submit to its subscription conditions' (Gelderblom et al., 2010, p. 16). This meant that in 1612 and 1622 (once every ten years) the Heren XVII would have to present 'a financial balance and report' of the company (Gepken-Jager and Ebeldina, 2005, p. 74). After this general audit the shareholders had the right to withdraw their money from the company. In the meantime they could freely transfer their shares on the emerged stock market (Jongh, 2011). The charter further defined that there had to be a distribution to the shareholders when sales of goods had reached 5 per cent of the original capital (Gepken-Jager and Ebeldina, 2005, p. 63). To make sure that the directors would take the demands of the shareholders into account, it was decided that 'one of the criteria for appointment to the function of director was that a contribution of 6000 or 3000 guilders (for the smaller chambers) had to be made' (Gepken-Jager and Ebeldina, 2005, p. 55). These regulations meant that the VOC directors had to act at least partly according to the logic of the market

While some regulations set out in the charter clearly supported either the state or the market logic, others supported both. 'The charter and the preamble highlight the VOC's character as a hybrid: a private commercial company (mostly supported by the VOC directors and shareholders) with superimposed public responsibilities (supported by the States General)' (Gelderblom et al., 2010, p. 16). The preamble, for example, showed that the States General gave the VOC its trade monopoly and suzerain rights to serve the interests of the Republic and all its inhabitants. Of course the VOC directors could also use these rights to realise its commercial goals, thereby holding on to the commercial logic. The fact that all inhabitants were permitted to be shareholders, regardless of the amount of money, justified the government in transferring these rights to the VOC (Bruijn, 2002). The hybrid character was also clearly visible in the VOC's unique financial policy that supported both the commercial and the state logic. 'The financial policy of the VOC was based on the principles of the pre-companies, that were formed for the duration of a single voyage, after which the proceeds were divided and the company liquidated' (Jongh, 2011, pp. 64–65). The core element of this policy was formed by the goal to make profit using the money of the shareholders, who would receive profits back through dividends, which supports the market logic. Because these companies were temporary, 'most investors in the pre-companies were not interested in control rights', given the expected profits (Heijer, 2005, p. 810). The market logic was further shaped by the VOC due to the fact that the VOC was 'a legal entity with rights and obligations' (Gepken-Jager and Ebeldina, 2005, p. 50), and by the fact that directors were not personally liable for the company's debts (only for the amount of their own share, like the shareholders) (Gaastra, 2013). These were fundamental differences compared to the organisation of the pre-companies. Jacobs

(2002, pp. 526–527) even states that this way of organising, including a 'more or less permanent capital of the VOC turned the VOC into the first modern joint-stock company'. In this way the VOC directors could gain access to capital exceeding 6 million guilders for at least ten years without the obligation of giving the shareholders any control rights.

Although the VOC was founded as a trading company, the States General also wanted to use the VOC as an aggressive military weapon in the East to weaken the Republic's enemies, the Spaniards and Portuguese (Gaastra, 2013, p. 19). In the end, however, the articles about the VOC as an instrument of war proposed by the Admiralties had not been included in the company's charter (Somers, 2001). And although war beyond the Cape of Good Hope was a matter for the company to decide (Bruijn, 2002), Article 39 stipulated that the States General could never force the VOC to wage war for the Republic, but always had to ask the VOC for military support. So the VOC had the power to negotiate over these demands and had the right to refuse them (Staarman, 1996). This way, the state logic could not force the VOC to put goals of war above goals that were aligned with the market logic. However, in the end, the VOC knew that it needed the States General's support to prolong the company's necessary trade monopoly and suzerain rights. This caused fierce discussions between the States General and the VOC directors during the Anglo-Dutch Wars.

Protesting Shareholders (1609–23): Enduring Conflicts, Rejection and Decoupling Strategies

In the first 20 years of the VOC's existence the VOC directors converted the shareholders' capital from a temporary investment into a permanent one, while refusing to give an insight into the financial policy of the company, which had so far realised disappointing financial results. This led to demands from protesting shareholders that the VOC directors should take more serious account of their demands. In 1662, the publication of a series of pamphlets attacking the VOC directors instigated a 'battle of pamphlets' in which the directors defended the status quo (Jongh, 2011). The Heren XVII tried to explain the lower-than-expected earnings by mentioning mitigating circumstances (Jongh, 2011). While promising to produce a financial audit the following year, they explained how complicated it was to prepare this (Jongh, 2011), and they also emphasised that as a semi-public company involved in the battle against Spain, the VOC could not publish better financial details, in order to protect the national interest (Robertson and Funnell, 2012). Following market logic, they had a responsibility towards the financiers of the company (Jay, 2013) while, on the other hand, the logic of the state meant that the national interest had to be protected. Apparently the VOC considered the latter more important than adhering to the market logic.

Moreover, the Heren XVII tried to reject the institutional claims of the shareholders. They attemped, for example, to damage the image of the protesting shareholders by calling them 'impudent', 'cheeky enough to account their own masters' (Bruijn, 2002, p. 75) and 'just as greedy as they accused their masters of being' (Jongh, 2011, p. 72). The directors also denied abusing their position (Jongh, 2011) and stated that the charter did not expressly forbid them from trading with the company (Robertson and Funnell, 2012). Last but not least, the VOC threatened that its shareholders would not receive dividend for seven years if they continued their protests (Jongh, 2011). In that case the balance between the adherence to the logics of the market and state would be further disrupted, as the VOC directors would no longer accept the core demand of market logic.

Many VOC directors had close links with the States of Holland and some of them were even members of this powerful public authority. Because of this, the States of Holland supported the VOC by banning the publication of a hostile pamphlet (Jongh, 2011) and by instructing the courts of Holland (which had jurisdiction over five of the six chambers) 'not to acknowledge or deal with any matter relating to the shareholders' claims' (Roberson and Funnel, 2012, p. 354). The representatives of the other provinces in the States General, however, were more receptive to the shareholders' complaints (Jongh, 2011). The continued existence of the company depended on an extension to the period covered by the charter and so shareholders exerted pressure on the VOC directors through the States General in negotiations about the charter's extension (Gaastra, 2013). On 22 December 1622 the States General decided not to liquidate the VOC, but to prolong the charter for 21 years, acknowledging for the first time 'that shareholders were more than just the financiers of the company' (Jongh, 2011, p. 62). This was a critical decision: the States General who had mainly adhered to state logic now gave more power to actors who pursued the logic of the market. It overruled the directors of the VOC and put them under pressure to incorporate more practices that would follow the logic of the market. The stance taken by the States General reflected the article of the charter that enabled all inhabitants of the Republic to be shareholders and which, therefore, ensured that the protection of the shareholders' rights would adhere to both commercial and state logics.

Without final agreement having been reached between the VOC directors and the shareholders, the States General announced that the balance of power would be adjusted in the new charter. The principal shareholders were granted more rights, and some restrictions were imposed on the VOC directors (Parthesius, 2010). Representatives of the principal shareholders gained some rights to influence the financial policy of the company, the election of new directors, and decisions that were made by important VOC committees (Gaastra, 2013; Jongh, 2011; Rietbergen, 2012). Some rules were introduced to restrict the self-enrichment of the directors. As of 1623, the directors had to swear an oath in line with the logic of the market, promising 'to be a loyal servant of the VOC, not to accept slush money or to enrich themselves at the cost of the company' (Heijer, 2005, p. 83). Furthermore, the directors no longer had the right to purchase goods from the company (Heijer, 2005); they could only deliver goods to the VOC after approval from governmental officials (Jongh, 2011; Robertson and Funnell, 2012), and their system of remuneration was adjusted (Heijer, 2005; Jongh, 2011). In addition, the shareholders were promised, in principle, to receive dividends every year (Jongh, 2011) as long as 'the company's debts, liabilities and working capital were adequately covered' (Robertson and Funnell, 2012, p. 355). In 1625 the strong shareholders' protests finally faded away, indicating that the manner in which the VOC directors from now on had to adhere to the logic of the market was finally to the satisfaction of the shareholders (Jongh, 2011). As the VOC depended on the States General for the necessary prolongation of the charter (and with that the VOC's trading monopoly and suzerain rights), the directors had no choice but to approve the concessions given to the shareholders. The shareholders' influence nonetheless remained limited (they had the right to control the books, the right of nomination and the right of advice) and their role was restricted to that of the principal shareholders (Gepken-Jager and Ebeldina, 2005).

In practice, the VOC directors responded to conflicting demands by decoupling their formal organisational rules from their actual operational practices. They refused to submit to the new rules and only finally presented on 14 October 1628 an inadequate oral account of their administration for the period 1602–23 without any supporting documents (Robertson and Funnel, 2012; Gepken-Jager and Ebeldina, 2005). Nepotism was also still common practice (Bruijn, 2002). The official rules for the appointment of new directors were ignored and directors continued to act as suppliers of the company just as before (Jongh, 2005). The one thing that did change from 1623 onwards was that the shareholders generally received a satisfying level of dividends (Heijer, 2005). This was the most important reason why the charter's amendments did not in practice lead to critical supervision of the directors and the conduct of the affairs of the VOC by the shareholders (Gaastra, 2002; Heijer, 2005). As long as the shareholders received dividends (the most important demand following commercial logic) they remained quite silent (Bruijn, 2002).

Anglo-Dutch Wars (1652–1784): Towards a Settlement through Compromise, Ceremonial Conformity and Collaboration

After the start of the First Anglo-Dutch War in May 1652, the VOC directors had to deal with repeated requests from the States General for maritime support. In July 1652, the States General first asked for returning VOC ships to be made available to the Republic's war fleet. Only part of the Heren XVII gathered to find a solution that would at the same time 'serve the country and harm the company the least'. 'As the VOC needed the support of the States General to safeguard the charter prolongation, the Heren XVII could not simply reject this request, though the charter's Article 39 suggested this' (Heijer, 2005, p. 155). They did, however, use the right given by this article to set conditions when promising to make four ships ready for maritime war (Heijer, 2005). The Heren XVII considered these conditions to be moderate and praised themselves by stating that 'the VOC would not charge any rent for its ships, presenting itself as good patriots of the State'. These conditions were accepted by the States General. The VOC had thus responded to this situation of conflicting demands by compromising, and by using its own position of power defined in the founding charter to find a solution that balanced the interests of the two different actors. The company thereby adhered to the minimum expected standards of the States General and the logic of the state, while still maintaining a sufficient number of ships to pursue its profitable business.

While in 1652 the Heren XVII were initially willing to support the States General, at least in part, they withdrew their support in the following year. However, their attempt to convince the Mayor of Amsterdam to make the States General lower the demands failed (Staarman, 1996), which meant that he did not lobby for the VOC at the highest governmental level of the Republic. Meanwhile the States General tried to persuade the Heren XVII to deliver maritime support by offering to extend the life of the charter 19 years in advance (Heijer, 2005), but they rejected this offer. They were afraid that bargaining over a charter prolongation so far in advance would increase the States General's position of power. Furthermore, the Heren XVII were not prepared to increase the VOC's debts to support the Republic in already difficult times (Heijer, 2005; Staarman, 1996). So the VOC directors tried to protect the company's own position of power by not giving in to the States General's demands. The States General reacted to this denial by threatening to claim the returning ships without the VOC's permission. The Heren XVII were barely impressed by this threat, although they promised to lend out some ships for the Republic's fleet. In reality, however, the Heren XVII sent their ships back to Asia as soon as they could (Heijer, 2005). 'The States General was furious as in practice the promised support was an empty promise the VOC only made on paper' (Heijer, 2005, p. 155). The VOC directors had only complied with the demands of the States General in a ceremonial way, without really enacting their promises. Once more they used a decoupling strategy to deal with the conflicting demands. In a reaction to this, 'an angry States General demanded a delegation of the VOC to come to The Hague and account for this behaviour' (Staarman, 1996, p. 8). This delegation convinced the States General of the difficult position the VOC was in, as the company already waged war in Asia against local Asian people and the Portuguese. 'Not to endanger the trading activities of the VOC any further, the States General could ask no more support of the VOC' (Staarman, 1996, p. 8). Finally, following the different strategic responses by the VOC directors during the First Anglo-Dutch War, the States General now recognised 'that asking the VOC for more support would indeed be useless' (Staarman, 1996, p. 8).

At the beginning of the Second Anglo-Dutch War in 1665 the relationship between the representatives of the Republic and the VOC directors was much closer. Due to family ties, 'a good relationship with Grand Pensionary Johan De Witt (the most important representative of the Republic) was important for the VOC directors' (from Amsterdam) political careers' (Staarman, 1996, p. 10). This could explain why the VOC directors were now more willing to cooperate with the States General, and gave them a better position from which to negotiate. Negotiations in 1665 resulted in the Heren XVII accepting a 'free' charter prolongation in advance (from 1672 to 1700) in exchange for a remission of 635 000 guilders (the amount the States General owed the VOC) and the delivery of 20 ships (at the full risk of the VOC) to support the Republic (Gaastra, 2002; Heijer, 2005). On the other hand, the governmental admiralties rather than the VOC would take full responsibility for the safe return of the VOC's returning fleet (Bruijn, 2002; Knaap and Teitler, 2002).

However, in June 1665 the Republic had already lost 20 ships, among which were three from the VOC. The States General demanded the VOC should replace these three ships as soon as possible, while the VOC found itself in financial trouble and tried to postpone this (Staarman, 1996). 'What followed looked a lot like what happened during the First Anglo-Dutch War: repeated requests of the States General and unwilling VOC directors stating that the VOC could not deliver any support' (Staarman, 1996, p. 13). In order not to endanger the trading activities of the company any further, the Heren XVII proposed that the old contract should be dissolved and replaced by a new agreement (Staarman, 1996). According to this agreement the VOC would pay the Admiralties from their profits, allowing 'the Admiralties to spend the VOC's money to equip real war ships and the VOC could use its ships again for its trading activities' (Staarman, 1996, p. 16). The States General and the VOC also agreed that the Republic's debt to the VOC from the First Anglo-Dutch War would be written off if the war was over within 12 months. As the war ended in July 1667, this bargain was to the advantage of the States General (Staarman, 1996), but also enabled the VOC to focus once more on its trade with Asia.

Because the Provincial States, including the powerful State of Holland, were convinced of the VOC's moral obligation to support the Republic in 1672 at the beginning of the

Third Anglo-Dutch War, the Heren XVII had no choice but to come to an agreement with the States General (Staarman, 1996). 'The question was if the company should deliver material or financial support or both' (Staarman, 1996, p. 17). The States General decided not to force the VOC to loan them 2 million guilders, but to discuss the matter with the VOC directors in the hope of an agreement based on their 'willingness'. 'The Heren XVII did not simply comply to the demand, but did not protest to the hilt either' (Blussé and Ooms, 2002, p. 60). Support for the VOC from the Republic was achieved more smoothly than had been the case in 1652 or 1665 (Staarman, 1996, p. 18). This could be explained by the bad experiences of both actors in the past when the VOC was pushed to deliver material support.

This time it was easier to realise financial support through a loan. On 29 December 1672 the chamber of Amsterdam accepted the need to reach agreement and the VOC promised to lend the Republic 2 million guilders (Blussé and Ooms, 2002). In exchange for this loan the VOC received non-negotiable bonds with an interest rate of 4 per cent and the government promised to protect the VOC from claims from dissatisfied creditors (Heijer, 2005). In the 'disastrous' year of 1672 the Heren XVII decided not to pay any redemption or interest over its bonds, which were then passed on to the shareholders as dividends (Gaastra, 2002; Heijer, 2005). 'This solution of the VOC directors was at the costs of the shareholders, who suffered considerable loss' (Staarman, 1996, p. 18). Due to the precarious financial position of the Republic the worth of these state obligations decreased, which made them practically impossible to sell. Because the VOC could neglect the claims of creditors (with the protection of the States General), the shareholders' power had once again turned out to be minimal. Yet, the VOC directors tried to balance market and state logic in order to satisfy the conflicting demands from multiple actors. By protecting the VOC from creditors' claims and by passing on the debt from the States General to the VOC to a debt from the States General to the shareholders, it seemed that the Heren XVII mostly adhered to the demands of the VOC itself while trying to combine both logics.

DISCUSSION

Our longitudinal case study on the VOC investigates the repertoire of responses a hybrid company could use to deal with conflicting institutional demands over time. The strategies used by the VOC were designed to achieve compromises through negotiations, ceremonial adherence or decoupling, defiance and manipulation. These approaches ultimately convinced the States General to lower its demands during the Anglo-Dutch Wars. Furthermore, the case study illustrates clearly how, on the one hand, hybrids are constrained by the need for legitimacy in the eyes of the external actors on which they depend for critical recourses, while on the other, they have the ability to work around institutional constraints and use them to their advantage, and this demonstrates that they have a significant degree of agency (Pache and Santos, 2013). The most important reason why the VOC was able to comply to a certain extent with the demands of the shareholders and the States General was that it depended on the shareholders as capital providers and on the States General as providers of the Dutch trading monopoly and suzerain rights in the East. Indeed, the reason for the VOC becoming a hybrid organisation in the first place and combining state and commercial logics from 1602 onwards was to safeguard the support of both these external actors and to use the resources they had secured for the company's advantage. While the hybrid nature of the company meant that it was constrained to some extent, the directors of the company had been able to use their powers to employ different strategies for responding to the conflicting demands and finding appropriate ways of dealing with them

We have argued that the VOC has sometimes struggled to maintain its hybrid nature despite enduring conflicting demands over a long period of time. Our analysis has served to reflect how ideas about hybridity have helped us to understand the history of the VOC. According to Mair et al. (2015, p. 713), hybrid organisations often 'involve a variety of stakeholders, pursue multiple and often conflicting goals and engage in divergent or inconsistent activities'.

In the case of the VOC, three main stakeholders were identified: the States General, the VOC directors and the shareholders. Each of these stakeholders adhered to a different type of logic or emphasised different elements of the logic of the state or the market. The combination of these different logics at the core of the organisation meant that a hybrid organisation like the VOC would face conflicting demands and would have to find ways through which to gain and maintain the institutional support of the different external and internal actors on which their survival depended. Understanding how hybrid organisations balance these conflicting demands is of growing importance, because the number of hybrids is rapidly increasing and they are becoming increasingly important actors on the organisational landscape. Nowadays organisations can no longer simply be categorised into private, public or non-profit organisations (Battilana and Lee, 2014; Ebrahim et al., 2014). Instead, hybrid organisations that cross these 'traditional borders' and combine different logics at their core are found in a wide range of fields of activity within our society. While these hybrids may well enjoy strategic advantages, they also face strategic challenges that may prevent them from thriving (Battilana et al., 2012; Vermeulen et al., 2014).

Our longitudinal case study of the VOC, a hybrid organisation that combined the logic of the state and commercial logic from its foundation in 1602 to its bankruptcy in 1799, aimed to increase our understanding of how hybrids could respond to the conflicting demands of external actors. It also explored the ways in which this hybrid organisation could use agency to develop and adapt its hybrid strategy along the way, and choose the most fitting responses to situations created by conflicting demands. Strategies that create a 'win–win' situation for the hybrid company itself and the external actors are likely to prove the most enduring ones. 'The combination of private and public and the implementation of an innovative policy that used the advantages and protection offered by the charter (which also stimulated a long-term commercial policy) gave the VOC a decisive lead in the Europe–Asia trade' (Blussé and Ooms, 2002, p. 59). The VOC's innovative financial strategy was based on its possession of its own permanent capital rather than of raising capital for each single voyage, as had generally been the case with the pre-companies. This made possible the realisation of its key success factors (trade monopolies and a powerful position within the intra-Asiatic trading network) (Bruijn, 2002) and by using smart trading strategies in the intra-Asiatic trade the VOC became the most powerful merchant in Asia.

Nonetheless, the company directors faced difficulties in placing the demands of the hybrid entity above and beyond the demands of the individual actors within it. A hybrid organisation needed to safeguard its own position of power and to avoid dependence on any one external actor. And it was important that it continued to monitor the extent to which its strategy continued to meet the needs of its institutional environment, and that it continued to lead to profitable organisational outcomes. The directors of the VOC in the Republic and the servants of the company in Asia had already begun to doubt the consequences of territorial expansion of the VOC in 1761: 'If only the Company would have stayed a merchant and never pushed the boundaries . . . And what did the Company receive for all its expenses?' (Remmelink, 1988, quoted in Gaastra, 2013, p. 70). The VOC directors had failed to adapt the company's hybrid strategy at the end of the 18th century; they had not increased the company's share capital and had tended to appease the shareholders by paying high dividends. As a result the VOC had to finance most of its activities from short-term loans as it did not possess an adequate level of directly available assets. The costs of maintaining its hybrid strategy eventually exceeded the company's income and the VOC was on the edge of bankruptcy after losing the support of private capital providers; and even the powerful States General could not save the hybrid from bankruptcy in 1799.

While the VOC could probably not have prevented some events that led to the decrease in the company's income, it was due to its own hybrid business strategy that the costs of continuing its organisational activities became untenable in the long term. The costs of maintaining its spice monopolies and its powerful position in Asia became too high, while the company's hybrid strategy of trading, fighting and ruling exceeded the company's income. At the same time, the military position of the VOC had become weak compared to strong competitors such as the (British) East India Company. The weak financial position of the company at the start of the Fourth Anglo-Dutch War led to the loss of the support of its shareholders and other creditors. As the company needed private capital providers to survive, this was the start of an irreversible downfall. Due to its dependence on external actors (shareholders and States General) and its expensive hybrid organisational activities, together with the failure of the Heren XVII themselves to take action, the company went bankrupt.

CONCLUSION

Our study has contributed to the recent stream of publications that have emphasised the existence of multiple logics as a more or less permanent phenomenon (Mair et al., 2015). However, earlier studies have disregarded the possibility of temporary adjustments to the same institutional pressures (Greenwood et al., 2011; Jay, 2013; Vermeulen et al., 2014). The different strategies adopted in response by the VOC could generally be seen as part of an ongoing process. In 1602 the VOC attempted to secure the essential support of two external actors in the Republic, the States General (supporting the logic of the state logic) and the shareholders (supporting commercial logic), by founding the VOC as 'a private commercial company with superimposed public responsibilities (Gelderblom et al., 2010, p. 16). While the States General remained the final authority, the VOC exercised the power of making decisions in its name. The shareholders, however, were very dissatisfied with the way in which power was allocated between the three actors, and the approach taken by the VOC directors in putting into practice the combination of the logic of the state and commercial logic. As a result the directors had to accept changes to the company's charter to secure the support required by the shareholders. Similarly, during the first three Anglo-Dutch Wars between 1652 and 1674, the directors had to secure the support of the States General by supporting the Republic in its European wars, and thus live up to the logic of the state. The responses of the VOC directors to these conflicting demands were necessary to secure the survival of the company and to be able to carry out its organisational activities in Asia.

Looking at the process by which the VOC maintained its hybrid nature over time, it seems as though the company did not have one 'master plan' in mind. Instead, its hybrid strategy unfolded in the actions and responses it carried out along the way. Every time the VOC was faced with conflicting demands, the directors searched for a new matching response. At the same time, the VOC directors sought to secure the company's position of power and prevent the external parties from gaining any direct influence over the affairs of the company. The articles requiring the VOC to wage war for the Republic were not included in the charter, and shareholders were only given formal rights of control over the company after huge pressure from both the external actors, and even then without a complete enactment of these rights. But the VOC could not prevent its being overruled by the powerful States General during these shareholder protests.

Our study has demonstrated that hybrid organisations can have a long history, and we call for more research into historical organisations. The possibility of exploring them over time holds great promise for the study of hybrid organisations. Whereas we focused on the responses that hybrid organisations deploy when confronted with conflicting demands, future research could also focus more on the consequences of different response strategies. As our study shows, the hybrid character that once made the company so powerful also caused its downfall.

REFERENCES

Battilana, J. and Dorado, S. (2010). 'Building sustainable hybrid organisations: the case of commercial microfinance organisations'. *Academy of Management Journal*, 53(6), 1419–1440.

Battilana, J. and Lee, M. (2014). 'Advancing research on hybrid organizing – insights from the study of social enterprises'. *Academy of Management Annals*, 8(1), 397–441.

Battilana, J., Lee, M., Walker, J. and Dorsey, C. (2012). 'In search of the hybrid ideal'. *Stanford Social Innovation Review*, 10(3), 51–55.

Billis, D. (2010). 'Towards a theory of hybrid organizations'. In D. Billis (ed.), *Hybrid Organizations and the Third Sector* (pp. 46–69). Basingstoke: Palgrave Macmillan.

Blussé, J.L. and Ooms, I. (2002). *Kennis en Compagnie: de Verenigde Oost-Indische Compagnie en de moderne wetenschap*. Amsterdam: Balans.

Brandsen, T. and Karré, M. (2011). 'Hybrid organisations: no cause for concern?' *Journal of Public Administration*, 34, 827–836.

Bruijn, J.R. (2002). *Roemrucht verleden: de Staten-Generaal en de VOC*. Den Haag: Tweede Kamer der Staten-Generaal.

Dahl, R.A. and Lindblom, C.E. (1953). *Politics, Economics and Welfare: Planning and Politico-Economic Systems, Resolved into Basic Processes*. Chicago, IL: University of Chicago Press.

D'Aunno, T., Sutton, R.I. and Price, R.H. (1991). 'Isomorphism and external support in conflicting institutional environments: a study of drug abuse treatment units'. *Academy of Management Journal*, 14, 636–661.

Doherty, B., Haugh, H. and Lyon, F. (2014). 'Social enterprises as hybrid organizations: a review and research agenda'. *International Journal of Management Reviews*, 16(4), 417–436.

Dunn, M.B. and Jones, C. (2010). 'Institutional logics and institutional pluralism: the contestation of care and science logics in medical education, 1967–2005'. *Administrative Science Quarterly*, 55, 114–149.

Ebrahim, A., Battilana, J. and Mair, J. (2014). 'The governance of social enterprises: mission drift and account-ability challenges in hybrid organisations'. *Research in Organisational Behavior*, 34, 81–100.

Friedland, R. and Alford, R.R. (1991). 'Bringing society back in: symbols, practices, and institutional contradic-tions'. In Powell, W.W. and DiMaggio, P.J. (eds), *The New Institutionalism in Organisational Analysis* (pp. 232–266). Chicago, IL: University of Chicago Press.

Gaastra, F.S. (2002). 'De neerslag van een jubileumjaar: VOC 2002'. *BMGN Low Countries Historical Review*, 120(4), 546–561.

Gaastra, F.S. (2013). *Geschiedenis van de VOC, opkomst bloei en ondergang*. Walburg: Walburg Pers B.V.

Gelderblom, O., de Jong, A. and de Jonker, J. (2010). *An Admiralty for Asia: Isaac le Maire and conflicting conceptions about the corporate governance of the VOC*. ERIM: ERS-2010-026-F&A.

Gepken-Jager, E. and Ebeldina, E. (2005). 'Verenigde Oost-Indische Compagnie (VOC): the Dutch East India Company'. In Gepken-Jager, E., Sollinge, G. van and Timmerman, L. (eds), *VOC 1602–2002: 400 Years of Company Law* (pp. 41–81). Deventer: Kluwer Legal Publishers.

Greenwood, R., Diaz, A.M., Li, S.X. and Lorente, J.C. (2010). 'The multiplicity of institutional logics and the heterogeneity of organisational responses'. *Organisation Science*, 21(2), 521–539.

Greenwood, R., Raynard, M., Kodeih, F., Micelotta, E.R. and Lounsbury, M. (2011). 'Institutional complexity and organisational responses'. *Academy of Management Annals*, 5(1), 317–371.

Heijer, H. den (2005). *De geoctrooieerde compagnie: de VOC en de WIC als voorlopers van de naamloze ven-nootschap*. Amsterdam: Stichting tot Bevordering der Notariële Wetenschap.

Jacobs, E.M. (2002). 'De Verenigde Oost-Indische Compagnie: een veelkantig handelsbedrijf'. *Tijdschrift voor Geschiedenis*, 115(4), 525–543.

Jay, J. (2013). 'Navigating paradox as a mechanism of change and innovation in hybrid organisations'. *Academy of Management Journal*, 56(1), 137–159.

Jongh, J.M. de (2011). 'Shareholder activists avant la lettre, the "complaining participants" in the Dutch East India Company, 1622–1625'. In Koppell, J.G.S. (ed.), *Origins of Shareholder Advocacy* (pp. 61–88). New York: Palgrave Macmillan.

Knaap, G. and Teitler, G. (2002). *De Verenigde Oost-Indische Compagnie: tussen oorlog en diplomatie*. Leiden: KITLV Uitgeverij.

Kodeih, F. and Greenwood, R. (2014). 'Responding to institutional complexity: the role of identity'. *Organisational Studies*, 35(1), 7–39.

Kraatz, M.S. and Block, E.S. (2008). 'Organisational implications of institutional pluralism'. In Greenwood, R., Oliver, C., Sahlin, K. and Suddaby, R. (eds), *The SAGE Handbook of Organisational Institutionalism* (pp. 243–275). London: SAGE.

Lan, Z. and Rainey, H.G. (1992). 'Goals, rules, and effectiveness in public, private, and hybrid organizations: more evidence on frequent assertions about differences'. *Journal of Public Administration Research and Theory*, 2(1), 5–28.

Mair, J., Mayer, J. and Lutz, E. (2015). 'Navigating institutional plurality: organizational governance in hybrid organizations'. *Organization Studies*, 36(6), 713–739.

Meyer, J.W. and Rowan, B. (1977). 'Institutionalized organisations: formal structure as myth and ceremony'. *American Journal of Sociology*, 83, 340–363.

Oliver, C. (1991). 'Strategic responses to institutional processes'. *Academy of Management Review*, 16, 145–179.

Pache, A. and Santos, F. (2010). 'When worlds collide: the internal dynamics of organisational responses to conflicting institutional demands'. *Academy of Management Review*, 35(3), 455–476.

Pache, A.C. and Santos, F. (2013). 'Inside the hybrid organisation: selective coupling as a response to competing institutional logics'. *Academy of Management Journal*, 56 (4), 972–1001.

Parthesius, R. (2010). *Dutch Ships in Tropical Waters: The Development of the Dutch East India Company (VOC) Shipping Network in Asia 1595–1660*. Amsterdam: Amsterdam University Press.

Rietbergen, P.J. (2012). *De Verenigde Oost-Indische Compagnie, 1602–1795: 's werelds eerste multinational tussen commercie en cultuur*. Amersfoort: Bekking & Blitz.

Robertson, J. and Funnell, W. (2012). 'The Dutch East-India Company and accounting for social capital at the dawn of modern capitalism 1602–1623'. *Accounting, Organisations and Society*, 37(5), 342–360.

Scott, W.R. (2001). *Institutions and Organisations*, 2nd edn. Thousand Oaks, CA: SAGE.

Seibel, W. (2015). 'Studying hybrids: sectors and mechanisms'. *Organization Studies*, 36(6), 697–712.

Somers, J.A. (2001). *De VOC als volkenrechterlijke actor*. Hilversum: Verloren.

Staarman, A. (1996). 'De VOC en de Staten-Generaal in de Engelse Oorlogen; Een ongemakkelijk bondsge-nootschap'. *Tijdschrift voor Zeegeschiedenis*, 15, 3–24.

Thornton, P.H. (2004). *Markets from Culture: Institutional Logics and Organisational Decisions in Higher Education Publishing*. Stanford, CA: Stanford University Press.

Thornton, P.H. and Ocasio, W. (1999). 'Institutional logics and the historical contingency of power in organisa-tions: executive succession in the higher education publishing industry, 1958–1990'. *American Journal of Sociology*, 105, 801–843.

Thornton, P.H., Ocasio, W. and Lounsbury, M. (2012). *The Institutional Logics Perspective: A New Approach to Culture, Structure and Process*. Oxford: Oxford University Press.

Vermeulen, P., Zietsma, C. and Greenwood, R. (2014). 'Special issue of *Strategic Organisation*: strategic responses to institutional complexity'. *Strategic Organisation*, 12(1), 79–82.

Witteveen, M. (2002). *Een onderneming van landsbelang: de oprichting van de Verenigde Oost-Indische Compagnie in 1602*. Amsterdam: Amsterdam University Press.

Zilber, T. (2011). 'Institutional multiplicity in practice: a tale of two high-tech conferences in Israel'. *Organisation Science*, 22, 1539–1559.

12. Social enterprise and the dilemmas of hybrid organisations
Curtis Child

INTRODUCTION

This chapter surveys the literature on social enterprises in order to understand the tensions that they face as hybrid organisations. I show that there are three classes of concerns about social enterprises – what I call consonance, trustworthiness and morality concerns – and argue that scholars have been more successful at addressing the first two than the last. I conclude that, although social enterprise might be characterised as a flawed proposition, it is not hopelessly so, and recent scholarship provides insights into how the challenges inherent to social enterprise might be addressed.

A social enterprise is a unique kind of hybrid organisation. For the purposes of this chapter, hybrids are organisations that combine different organisational elements under the same metaphorical roof (Galaskiewicz and Barringer, 2012; Mair et al., 2015). These elements might be practices, internal structures, goals or cultural logics embedded within organisations that do not typically coexist in the same organisation. Following Battilana et al. (2015, p. 3), social enterprises are a special case of hybrid that 'pursue a social mission while engaging in commercial activities to sustain their operations'. As the definition implies, this chapter takes seriously the possibility that there are, indeed, commercial organisations with genuinely prosocial ambitions.

Social enterprises are complicated by the fact that organisations with commercial goals and practices, and organisations with social mission-oriented goals and practices, tend to operate in separate sectors of the economy. Businesses in the private for-profit sector typically work to increase shareholder value. Nonprofit organisations in the private charitable sector are obligated to advance a charitable cause. True, conventional businesses have corporate responsibility (or similar) programmes, and traditional nonprofits benefit from earned (rather than donated) income (Child, 2011), but organisations for which the pursuit of a social mission is their *raison d'être* and that generate support through commercial means are a rarer case.

Social enterprises are increasingly common, however. Many social enterprises exist as unique members of conventional for-profit industries. But recent decades have also been witness to the emergence of a number of entire social enterprise industries: work integration, fair trade, socially responsible investing, microcredit, and the like (Child, 2016; Cooney and Shanks, 2010; Kerlin and Gagnaire, 2009; Nyssens, 2006).

For advocates, there is a lot to like about social enterprise (Brinckerhoff, 2000; Cooney and Shanks, 2010; Dees, 1998; Ellis, 2010; Frances and Cuskelly, 2008), and market-based solutions to social problems have gained wide popularity in international development and other circles (Polak and Warwick, 2013; Prahalad, 2004; Yunus, 2008; Yunus and Weber, 2010). Relying on commercial revenues provides access to resources in a way that feels more controllable, and perhaps even more authentic, to practitioners than relying on donations or charitable gifts (Child et al., 2015). Advocates argue that working according to market principles makes their efforts efficient and sustainable (Polak and Warwick, 2013).

Much of the popular excitement about social enterprise, however, overlooks the challenges inherent to it. Some scholarship does so as well. The remainder of this chapter documents these challenges and notes how they might be addressed. I draw selectively on illustrations from my own research in the fair trade industry as well as other scholarship.

The fair trade movement, which has its roots in activism during the mid-1900s, is organised around the goal of developing ethical trading relationships between organisations (primarily) in the Global North and farmers and artisans (primarily) in the Global South (Fridell, 2007; Jaffee, 2007; Raynolds and Bennett, 2015; Raynolds and Long, 2007). Organisations that operate within the fair trade paradigm work to reduce inequalities by participating in direct, transparent trade relationships. In the coffee industry, fair trade businesses are committed to supporting farmers by importing, roasting and selling coffee beans according to high ethical standards. By 'pursu[ing] a social mission while engaging in commercial activities to sustain their operations' (Battilana et al., 2015), fair trade businesses in the Global North are social enterprises par excellence.

THREE CLASSES OF CONCERNS

Concerns about social enterprises stem primarily from the fact that they are hybrid organisations. It might be argued that all hybrid organisations face challenges related to their hybrid natures, but the specific combination of commercial and prosocial values in social enterprise ventures makes the challenges particularly vexing.

There are three classes of concerns: consonance, trustworthiness and morality. Consonance concerns are those that relate to the internal functioning of the organisation. They are issues about which managers might be concerned, or they are issues that principals or stakeholders might have that relate to the management of the organisation. Whereas consonance concerns are internal to an organisation, trustworthiness concerns are about the organisational form generally and come from the perspective of actors external to the organisation. No doubt, the two concerns are related, but I separate them to highlight broader concerns about the social enterprise field beyond what might be happening within the walls of any one organisation. Key here are questions by external stakeholders about whether social enterprises can be regarded as trustworthy in their pursuits of a social mission. Finally, moral concerns are those that deal with the moral and ethical consequences of merging commercial and social goals and values in society. As much the purview of philosophers as social scientists, I address these concerns because they have so far been dealt with only peripherally, if at all, by scholars of social enterprise.

CONSONANCE

The Concern

Perhaps the most well-documented concern about social enterprises is that holding tightly both to commercial and to prosocial values will pull an organisation in different directions. Social enterprises could, in a word, promote disconsonance within organisations, or disagreement and discord, resulting in unproductive tensions.

Disconsonance within organisations results partly from social enterprises' hybrid natures. From an institutional logics perspective (Friedland and Alford, 1991; Thornton et al., 2012), social enterprises try to reconcile two different logics: that of the market and that of social welfare. Thus, although the rhetoric of social enterprise suggests that reconciling commercial and social values is easy (Child, forthcoming), win–win or double- and triple-bottom-line approaches to business can be quite challenging. Indeed, the day-to-day practices associated with 'doing well' and 'doing good' can be very much at odds with each other. The logic of the market and the logic of social welfare are each defined by different goals – respectively, financial or social value – and different means of achieving them. Because these goals are to some extent in conflict, since pursuing one often comes at the cost of pursuing the other (see Battilana et al., 2015), the methods of accomplishing them – that is, the day-to-day practices of actors – can be at cross-purposes, thus opening the door to disconsonance.

To illustrate the types of complications that can arise out of competing logics, consider the fair trade industry (Child, forthcoming). A coffee-importing business will favour the logic of the market if it sources from well-established, stable co-operatives in developing nations. Doing so produces a limited social impact even though it is a prudent financial strategy. Alternatively, the business will favour the logic of social welfare if it works with newly established, potentially needier co-operatives. This is a riskier financial move but the social impact could be greater. Both outcomes – low financial risk and high social impact – cannot be achieved simultaneously. Likewise, an importing business will favour the logic of the market if it sells fairly traded lines of coffee alongside conventional lines that were sourced according to suspect ethical standards. The business will benefit financially from the appearance of being socially responsible even if its actions (selling conventional lines of coffee) indicate that its commitment to the fair trade cause is weak. Alternatively, the importing business will follow the logic of social welfare by importing and selling only those coffees sourced according to the highest ethical guidelines, although doing so might not be as financially lucrative as supplementing those lines with higher-margin, conventional coffees. Again, both outcomes – in this case, increasing revenues by selling conventional lines of coffee, and staying true to fair trade ideals by selling only fairly traded coffees – are to a significant degree contradictory.

There are two specific worries when it comes to consonance. The first is that constituencies might develop along the lines of the logics (Besharov and Smith, 2014; Reay and Hinings, 2009), with some members of the social enterprise concerned primarily with its commercial success and other members concerned primarily with its mission-oriented success. If the two goals are in conflict with each other, members of the organisation might find themselves working at cross-purposes, resulting in internal turmoil. Cooney (2006) reports exactly this in her case study of a nonprofit hybrid organisation whose purpose was to provide welfare recipients with work opportunities in its in-house business venture. She notes that: 'the need for each side [i.e. the commercial side and the social services side] of the organisation to respond to demands from external forces in the field and concurrently act in tandem to provide integrated social service provision create[d] an operating model that [was] rife with tension' (ibid., p. 152). Among other things, the need for competitive and efficient business production conflicted at times with an interest in tailoring programmes to meet client needs. The result was that 'contradictions exist[ed] side by side, pulling the organisation in different directions, until the organisational terrain [was] full of built-up tension' (ibid., p. 154).

The second worry regarding disconsonance is related to the first. More than internal tension within the organisation, the concern here is that social enterprises might lose the focus on their social missions as the commercial needs of the enterprise exert themselves. This is commonly referred to in the literature as 'mission drift' and has been a (perhaps 'the') major preoccupation of scholars of social enterprise (Battilana and Lee, 2014; Cornforth, 2014; Dees and Anderson, 2003; Ebrahim et al., 2014; Edwards, 2008, 2010; Santos et al., 2015).

The assumption undergirding the mission drift argument is that the two logics prevailing in social enterprise – commercial and social welfare – are not on an equal footing. The demands of the market are more readily present, the rewards and punishments for aligning with them more readily felt, than are the demands of social welfare. So, if one logic must give way to the other, then it will likely be the commercial demands of the organisation that prevail. Left unchecked, the social enterprise will drift away from its mission and towards the market.

What Can Be Done?

For many scholars, the solution to concerns about consonance resides in developing accountability structures that are unique to social enterprise hybrids. For Ebrahim et al. (2014), the key to doing so is found in monitoring and in aligning stakeholder interests. The relationship between social and commercial activities must be continuously monitored, Ebrahim et al. argue, as should the agents who work in social enterprise contexts. Aligning stakeholder interests occurs through identifying accountability mechanisms that will help the organisation give due attention to its commercial and social goals; not only to those who invest in or otherwise support the organisation, but also to those who are its beneficiaries. Encouraging accountability to the former is straightforward; powerful stakeholders such as investors and funders can withdraw financial support if they feel that the social enterprise is not meeting its goals. Accountability to clients and beneficiaries is more challenging, however, because clients and beneficiaries may not have the power of exit or voice because of their marginalised or vulnerable positions. The solutions that Ebrahim et al. propose include ensuring that beneficiaries are an important part of the social enterprise's target market, or allowing beneficiaries a seat on the social enterprise's governing board.

How these strategies for aligning stakeholder interests, as well as for monitoring the social enterprise, play out depends critically on the type of hybrid in question. In integrated hybrids, the social and commercial activities of the organisation are one and the same (Battilana and Lee, 2014). For example, microcredit organisations are integrated in that making small loans to low-income borrowers is in line with both the social and commercial purposes of the organisation. In differentiated hybrids, by contrast, they are not. Work integration social enterprises, for example, hire marginalised individuals in order to equip them with the experience they need to be productive members of the workforce. Typically, the social enterprise also provides counselling and other job-related or life-skills training – activities that are not required for the commercial success of the organisation – which introduce the possibility of tensions between pursuing financial goals and social mission-oriented ones. Thus, although the spectre of mission drift hangs over both, and the broad types of solutions are applicable to all social enterprises, integrated or differentiated hybrids will require strategies sensitive to each.

Like Ebrahim et al. (2014), Santos et al. (2015) see governance mechanisms as key to addressing the challenges inherent in social enterprises. And, like Ebrahim et al., Santos et al. argue that the implementation of specific governance mechanisms should be dependent on the nature of the social enterprise in question. For Santos et al., the question is not only whether the clients are also the beneficiaries, but also whether a social enterprise's activities generate automatic social value spillovers or whether value spillovers are contingent on additional interventions. Automatic value spillovers occur when there are positive benefits that accrue to the buyer and their community simply because the product or service is purchased and used. When kerosene lamps are replaced by LED-based rechargeable lamps, for example, there is a benefit to the family that uses the lamp as well as to the broader community in the form of reduced toxic fumes. These benefits are achieved through no additional action on the part of the seller, making them automatic. The spillover values of some products and services, however, are contingent on additional efforts made by the organisation that provides them.

These two dimensions – whether the clients are also the beneficiaries, and whether there are automatic or contingent value spillovers – create a 2 × 2 typology, which Santos et al. use to identify four different types of social enterprise hybrids. Each is at a different risk of mission drift and each should implement a governance structure unique to it. For example, a work integration social enterprise, where the client (the customer) is not necessarily the beneficiary (e.g., an unemployed individual in need of interventions such as training and counselling), is difficult to sustain and is at a high risk of mission drift. Governance should thus focus on ensuring that the commercial needs of the firm do not take precedence over its social mission. Inviting advocates of the beneficiaries to help govern the enterprise is one strategy that would help to make this possible.

Beyond governance mechanisms, scholars point to a variety of other strategies, some structural and some cultural, that may help to address the consonance concerns raised above (see, e.g., Greenwood et al., 2011; Kraatz and Block, 2008, for general overviews). For instance, strategies such as structural differentiation could help to alleviate some of the tensions in social enterprises (Battilana and Lee, 2014; Cooney, 2006; Santos et al., 2015). Separating the commercial side of the organisation from the social mission-oriented side, or creating differently purposed subunits, might allow each to flourish as much as possible in a hybrid venture (Battilana and Lee, 2014; Santos et al., 2015). Scholars also point to cultural strategies to resolve consonance concerns. Battilana and Dorado (2010), for example, argue that purposefully socialising members of the enterprise or strategically hiring employees who are not yet committed to one logic or another help to build a common organisational identity that respects both logics and prevents subgroup identities. Other strategies include selectively choosing which organisational elements to match to the institutional logic (Mair et al., 2015; Pache and Santos, 2010), creating 'spaces of negotiation' where grievances might be settled and courses of action planned out (Battilana et al., 2015), or accepting paradox as a managerial strategy (Smith and Lewis, 2011).

Thus consonance concerns are those primarily internal to the organisation. Internal turmoil from different factions within the organisation or favouring one logic over another might stand in the way of social enterprise organisations accomplishing their commercial and social mission-oriented goals. Scholars of social enterprise, however, have suggested various governance mechanisms and structural and cultural strategies that might be effective in addressing these concerns.

TRUSTWORTHINESS

The Concern

A second and related class of concerns has to do with the trustworthiness of social enterprises from the perspective of actors external to the organisations. I distinguish between two types of trust, drawing loosely on the *New Oxford American Dictionary*'s definition of the word. The first, trust as believability, refers to the extent to which actors external to the organisation can trust the organisation's claims. The second, trust as reliability, refers to whether actors external to the organisation know what to expect from the organisation. I address them in turn.

Regarding the first, trust as believability, outside actors might have difficulty determining whether the enterprise makes good on its joint commitment to commercial and prosocial goals. True, members of the social enterprise may represent themselves as committed to both, but talk is easy and consumers or other external stakeholders could be forgiven for their scepticism. One need not look far to find examples of organisations that belie their verbalised commitments to social welfare with practices that seem counter to it. This creates challenges for all social enterprises, as the fair trade coffee industry illustrates.

The fair trade coffee movement has its ancestry in religious and social activist movements of the 20th century (Child, 2015), but the movement's authenticity has been challenged by the increasing prevalence of conventional coffee firms that market fairly traded coffee. The original fair trade organisations were dedicated to their social missions, demonstrated by their exclusive interest in fairly traded goods. Soon, however, conventional firms such as Starbucks, Costco and Walmart started selling fairly traded lines of coffee as well. While it is impossible to know their motives for doing so, it is clear that these firms did not abandon their conventional lines of coffee, which raises questions about their loyalty to the fair trade cause. For audiences, this casts doubt on the authenticity of the businesses' commitments, a scepticism that is then generalised to all fair trade organisations, even those totally committed to fair trade ideals which cannot compete with major corporations and which worry that the movement's original ideals are becoming diluted (Jaffee, 2012).

The fair trade case thus demonstrates some of the challenges that social enterprises face when trying to convince audiences of their believability. For-profits have traditionally been understood as operating to maximise profits. It is therefore difficult for businesses with social missions to persuade stakeholders that they are different, especially when they face competition from other for-profit organisations that sell what appear to be very similar products or services.

The second type of trust, trust as reliability, likewise presents problems for social enterprise organisations. At issue is whether the organisation is aligned with others' expectations of what the organisation is and what it should be. This, then, is a matter of legitimacy, which is achieved when the actions of an organisation are perceived as 'desirable, proper, or appropriate within some socially constructed system of norms, values, beliefs, and definitions' (Suchman, 1995, p. 574). Even if an organisation is trustworthy in the first sense – that its claims are believable – it may not be regarded as an appropriate organisation given the social context. It becomes trustworthy in this second sense only when there are socially defined expectations that the organisation fulfils in the eyes of its stakeholders.

The legitimacy problem is not necessarily the result of counterfeit organisations in social enterprise fields, as is the case for the trust-as-believability problem. Trust as reliability becomes a concern when the hybrid nature of social enterprises makes them difficult to categorise, which in turn renders them difficult to value (Zuckerman, 1999). External stakeholders may not necessarily know what social enterprises are, because the organisations such as the profit-seeking charity or the mission-driven business do not fit nicely into conventional categories.

The practical consequences of not meeting expectations reliably are many (Galaskiewicz and Barringer, 2012). Perhaps most worrisome for the organisation is that its hybrid nature might make it hard for the organisation to acquire the funding that it needs to grow (Battilana and Lee, 2014). Potential consumers and regulators might fail to value social enterprises accurately because they do not operate within better-understood categories, with the result that it is difficult for organisations to survive.

What Can Be Done?

Trustworthiness – trust as believability and trust as reliability – has been long sought after by organisations whose interests are in promoting social welfare, and different types of organisations have evolved different ways of promoting it. Governments, for example, are required by law to operate on behalf of the common good. They are also subject to public scrutiny, and the existence of popular elections, transparency requirements, oversight officials, separations of power and the like all help to keep governments in check and to allow for corrections to their course, thus building trust with their publics.

As private organisations, for-profit businesses lack the basic mechanisms that governments use to instil confidence in audiences. Indeed, one of the primary theoretical justifications for a nonprofit sector hinges precisely on this issue. Hansmann (1980), a legal scholar, argues that the reason for the existence of nonprofit organisations in modern economies is that they resolve information asymmetries between prosocial organisations and their stakeholders. '[D]ue either to the circumstances under which the product is purchased and consumed or to the nature of the product itself,' Hansmann writes, 'consumers may be incapable of accurately evaluating the goods promised or delivered' (ibid., p. 843). Because of nonprofits' legal obligations to operate as mission-driven organisations, however, external stakeholders can take confidence in the services or goods being provided them. Thus, although '[t]he nonprofit producer, like its for-profit counterpart, has the capacity to raise prices and cut quality . . . it lacks the incentive to do so because those in charge are barred from taking home any resulting profits' (ibid., p. 835).

So it is that two organisational sectors have evolved methods for instilling trust in stakeholders. What, then, of for-profit organisations that try to pursue a social mission? How might they be perceived as trustworthy? Of course they will represent themselves as such. But rhetoric can only go so far, as discursive representations can justify a wide range of actions, some of which are not necessarily prosocial (Child, forthcoming).

Two developments are noteworthy when it comes to making sense of how for-profit organisations are able to generate trust and legitimacy. First, legal scholars and social enterprise advocates have taken steps to create new legal categories that give social enterprises and social enterprise-like organisations a recognisable legal status and, in turn, shelter the organisations within these categories from the full pressures of the market. Examples include the low-profit limited liability company (L3C), the community interest company (CIC), and the benefit corporation.

Briefly (see Reiser, 2010, 2011), the L3C is an innovation of the Vermont legislature in the United States, which pioneered the form as a modified limited liability company (LLC). Unlike conventional LLCs, the L3C must be formed for educational and charitable purposes. It is different from charities, however, in that generating and distributing profits to owners is not prohibited. The CIC, an invention of the United Kingdom, likewise operates as a social purpose business, but there are restrictions on how profits can be distributed and how assets are divided upon dissolution. Finally, several states in the United States have statutes that allow for the existence of benefit corporations (or other types of similar hybrids; Tyler et al., 2015), which are legally different from standard corporate forms and, like L3Cs and CICs, are required to pursue a goal beyond profit-making.

In theory, new legal categories such as these should make social enterprises at once more legitimate and more trustworthy. Their legitimacy would increase as the forms become codified in law and, eventually, popularised. As Tyler et al. (2015, p. 243) write, using the example of the L3C: 'With the intentional incorporation of branding in naming the L3C entity, customers, employees, investors, creditors, and others for the first time can know, rather than merely suspect, from the name that the enterprise has charitable purposes as a statutory priority and that it de-emphasizes distributable profits.' Their trustworthiness would increase as the legal obligations of social enterprises (operating as L3Cs, CICs, and so on) are clearly defined and regulators – either independent parties or governments themselves – are able to monitor their performance.

A second and related development that might contribute to overcoming trustworthiness problems is the rise of private certification and labelling initiatives (Raynolds and Bennett, 2015). This new mode of regulation – that is, regulation by standards – is notable because it diverges sharply from the state-led, command-and-control types of regulation so common throughout much of modern and ancient history (Bartley, 2007; Schneiberg and Bartley, 2008). Regulation by standards provides a way for businesses to certify their credibility even when governments – by establishing new legal forms, for example – cannot or do not. Trustworthiness is established, ideally, by third parties whose own trustworthiness is more secure, not least because the certifiers themselves are nonprofit organisations or sanctioned by governments.

Of course, with the proliferation of certifications and labels comes a worry that their value might ultimately be diluted (Jaffee, 2012). In the fair trade industry, for instance, there is intense debate about which labels signify true commitment to the fair trade cause and which are merely window-dressing. The stakes are high, as fair trade advocates worry that consumers are not savvy about the differences. It is too easy for products to bear a 'fairly traded' or 'ethically sourced' label even if those products were not produced under high fair trade standards (Child, 2015).

MORALITY

The Concern

The third and final class of concerns has to do with the morality of initiatives such as social enterprise. Social enterprise organisations use the amoral business form to achieve a moral end. But what if, in doing so, they produce undesirable, unexpected consequences? Specifically, the concern here is that the pursuit of social value could be limited by the tools of the market upon which, by definition, social enterprises rely. Like business entities, markets are amoral in and of themselves, so it is easy to think that using them towards moral ends can only turn out well. But it is possible – some say likely – that efforts to address social problems are not best governed by the tools of capitalism, and that efforts to make them do moral things might have an adverse effect.

Concerns of this sort are not necessarily new, but Sandel (2012) provides a language with which to make sense of them. Although he does not speak of social enterprise specifically, Sandel sees a world that is increasingly becoming monetised, and he is concerned that monetising things changes them for the worse. (In this, he espouses the 'commodified nightmare' view discussed by Fourcade and Healy, 2007.) There is a 'degrading effect of market valuation and exchange on certain goods and practices', Sandel (2012, p.111) writes. Perhaps most importantly, financial practices and incentives might have the unintended consequence of crowding out public spiritedness. Paying people to act in charitable, prosocial ways, for example, replaces the norms of sympathy, generosity and thoughtfulness with the norms of the market. Markets do have norms, such as efficiency, but these norms are not those typically relied upon to promote and to govern prosocial activity.

To illustrate, it may be easier to turn down a neighbour's invitation to help paint their fence if they offer me monetary compensation for doing so. By offering payment, they have invoked the norms of the market. My neighbour and I are now in an exchange relationship, and I am left to assess whether my time is worth the amount of money they have offered to pay me for it, which it very well may not be. If, however, my neighbour asks me to help paint their fence simply because we are neighbours, then they invoke a different set of norms: those of community and neighbourly attentiveness. Under these circumstances, even if painting the fence does not make financial sense, I feel morally obligated to help and I am thus, Sandel would argue, more likely to do so.

How does this apply to the social enterprise context, if at all? To be sure, the concern here is not only that of consonance, addressed above, although the two are closely related. Mission drift might plague social enterprises, but Sandel's contention is different.

It is that there is something objectionable to taking issues out of the realm of morality, where we try to resolve social problems because it is right and good to do so, and placing them in a market realm where we address them because and to the extent that they can have market value. The moral corruption that takes place, therefore, is not just that of mission drift; that is, what takes place inside the organisation. It is that social enterprise works against the public-spiritedness that ought to govern how we address the problems that vex us.

Considering again the fair trade industry, Sandel's argument in the social enterprise context might be thus: Global inequality is a moral concern as much as it is an economic one. The fair trade movement aims to address poverty in the Global South by using the mechanisms of the market – buying, roasting and selling coffee, for example – in the Global North. In doing so, fair trade may well fail to motivate citizens of the Global North as much as it could by relying on non-market mechanisms (i.e., by appealing to notions of justice and compassion). This is because fair trade relies very much on the same capitalist system that permitted gross global inequalities, which calls into question its ability to produce systemic change. A complicated set of social relations is thus reduced to a simple economic purchase. Whether the consumer drinks coffee, enjoys the particular blend or roast, or has easy access to fairly traded beans all interfere with – perhaps to the point of distracting from – the larger moral issue. And while it may be easy to turn down the economic purchase – much like turning down a neighbour's offer of payment for painting their fence – it may be more difficult to turn away from the humanity of impoverished farmers outside of an exchange relationship. Fair trade, Sandel might argue, summons the wrong set of norms and fails to energise the latent support that might be obtained had other norms been invoked.

What Can Be Done?

Of course, Sandel's is not the final word on this issue. Zelizer (2000), an economic sociologist, argues against what she calls the 'hostile worlds' approach—a phrase she uses to describe the popular view that the economic and intimate (we might say, social) spheres are totally incompatible. It is the view that economic relations ruin intimate ones, and that intimate relations interfere with economic productivity. Writ large, it is the argument that money and market activity corrupt meaningful, relational social life. To the contrary, Zelizer (1978) observes that people actually use money to make social life meaningful and to solidify relationships. They imbue money and exchange with meaning and use them to build and value social relationships. In her classic study of the development of life insurance, she writes:

> The monetary evaluation of death did not desacralize it; far from 'profaning' life and death, money became ritualized by its association with them. Life insurance took on symbolic values quite distinct from its utilitarian function, emerging as a new form of ritual with which to face death and a processing of the dead by those kin left behind. (ibid., p. 594)

Clearly, this way of thinking is at odds with Sandel's. For him, money and market activities crowd out prosocial values; they are at odds with public spiritedness and intimate relations. For Zelizer (1978), however, money is used to create, define and affirm social relations. 'Exchange,' Reich (2014, p. 1583) summarises, 'not only may be made possible by social ties or institutionalized rules but may be one of the mechanisms through which ties are maintained and strengthened.'

In my own research looking at individuals who have established and manage fair trade social enterprise businesses, I found traces of Zelizer's (1978) point of view as I listened to entrepreneurs evangelise the rightness of their work. Far from a morally corrupting activity, some regarded running a social enterprise business as a business as the morally honourable way to do it. They referred to establishing and operating a for-profit organisation as 'empowering', a 'ministry', an 'expression of one's ethics' and a way to 'glorify God' (Child et al., 2015, p. 842; 2016, p. 219). Using the business form to address social problems was given special meaning. In contrast to Sandel (2012), for them it did not imply a corruption at all, but rather a morally worthwhile activity.

CONCLUSIONS

Although much has been written about social enterprise in recent years, I argue that a large portion of the scholarship can be reduced to a few central themes. First, many people are enamoured of social enterprise, thus much of the writing – especially the popular writing – about social enterprise simply documents its development and praises its virtues. Social enterprise is regarded by advocates as an efficient, nimble and sustainable alternative to bureaucratic government and resource-deprived nonprofit solutions.

Second, despite the excitement about them, many scholars observe that social enterprises face significant challenges. Although all hybrids might face unique challenges simply by virtue of being hybrid organisations, social enterprise hybrids face an additional set of concerns, rendering them in some ways fundamentally problematic because the particular elements that are combined in social enterprise hybrids – the commercial and the social – are in so many ways at odds with each other.

Third, there are three classes of concerns about social enterprise that stem primarily from their hybrid natures. The first, consonance, has to do with the social enterprise organisation itself. What burdens, if any, do these organisations carry as social enterprise hybrids? And how are they dealt with? The second, trustworthiness, is related to the first but the focus is on external stakeholders and publics. That is, how might consonance concerns impact how others view social enterprises, and with what consequences? And what, then, can they do to address these concerns? The third class of concerns has to do with the morality of social enterprise and similar initiatives. Above and beyond managerial and legitimacy concerns, is there something morally problematic about using markets to address social problems?

The fourth theme is that social scientists, legal scholars, practitioners, ethicists, and the like are responding to the three classes of concerns. Different types of concerns warrant different types of responses. Consonance concerns call for governance and other structural and cultural strategies that address issues such as mission drift. Trustworthiness concerns require efforts to assure stakeholders and observers that social enterprises' claims are warranted. This is needed even if consonance concerns are not present. External audiences may find it hard to evaluate social enterprises' claims, so strategies – such as legal innovations and certification or labelling regimes – must be developed to appease their potential scepticism. And morality concerns call for reasoned debate and empirical scholarship to understand the moral consequences of social enterprise developments.

Looking forward, the research is far from settled when it comes to understanding social enterprises and the challenges that they face as hybrid organisations. Social enterprise itself is a fast-moving target which makes research in this area both exciting and difficult. The most promising scholarship on social enterprises is that which recognises different kinds of social enterprises and tailors diagnoses of problems (and their solutions) accordingly. Like 'nonprofit' or 'business', the term 'social enterprise' does not do justice to the diversity of organisations that adopt the label, and future research will do well to be sensitive to this fact. Future research will also benefit from continually adding empirical studies to the body of work. Much of the writing on social enterprise is conceptual. This is no doubt important, but our theories and concepts must be tethered to data if they are to be useful. One area in particular that needs more research is the extent to which trustworthiness really is a concern for social enterprises and, if so, how they deal with it. Research on certification regimes and legal forms especially could help us better understand how social enterprise hybrids deal with these problems. And, finally, it would seem appropriate for social enterprise scholars to think more deeply about the moral consequences of social enterprise and similar activities. In the excitement to understand this new type of hybrid and to figure out how it might productively manage the tensions inherent to it, it is constructive to reflect critically on whether encouraging social enterprise is ultimately a worthy pursuit.

REFERENCES

Bartley, T. (2007), 'Institutional emergence in an era of globalization: the rise of transnational private regulation of labor and environmental conditions', *American Journal of Sociology*, Vol. 113, pp. 297–351.

Battilana, J. and Dorado, S. (2010), 'Building sustainable hybrid organizations: the case of commercial microfinance organizations', *Academy of Management Journal*, Vol. 53, pp. 1419–1440.

Battilana, J. and Lee, M. (2014), 'Advancing research on hybrid organizing – insights from the study of social enterprises', *Academy of Management Annals*, Vol. 8, pp. 397–441.

Battilana, J., Sengul, M., Pache, A.-C. and Model, J. (2015), 'Harnessing productive tensions in hybrid organizations: the case of work integration social enterprises', *Academy of Management Journal*, Vol. 58, pp. 1658–1685.

Besharov, M.L. and Smith, W.K. (2014), 'Multiple institutional logics in organizations: explaining their varied nature and implications', *Academy of Management Review*, Vol. 39, pp. 364–381.

Brinckerhoff, P.C. (2000), *Social Entrepreneurship: The Art of Mission-Based Venture Development*, Wiley, New York.

Child, C. (2011), 'Whither the turn? The ambiguous nature of nonprofits' commercial revenue', *Social Forces*, Vol. 89, pp. 145–161.

Child, C. (2015), 'Mainstreaming and its discontents: fair trade, socially responsible investing, and industry trajectories', *Journal of Business Ethics*, Vol. 130, pp. 601–618.

Child, C. (2016), 'Tip of the iceberg: the nonprofit underpinnings of for-profit social enterprise', *Nonprofit and Voluntary Sector Quarterly*, Vol. 45, pp. 217–237.

Child, C. (forthcoming), 'Whence paradox? Framing away the potential challenges of doing well by doing good in social enterprise organizations', *Organization Studies*.

Child, C., Witesman, E.M. and Braudt, D.B. (2015), 'Sector choice: how fair trade entrepreneurs choose between nonprofit and for-profit forms', *Nonprofit and Voluntary Sector Quarterly*, Vol. 44, pp. 832–851.

Cooney, K. (2006), 'The institutional and technical structuring of nonprofit ventures: case study of a US hybrid organization caught between two fields', *Voluntas*, Vol. 17, pp. 143–161.

Cooney, K. and Shanks, T.R.W. (2010), 'New approaches to old problems: market-based strategies for poverty alleviation', *Social Service Review*, Vol. 84, pp. 29–55.

Cornforth, C. (2014), 'Understanding and combating mission drift in social enterprises', *Social Enterprise Journal*, Vol. 10, pp. 3–20.

Dees, J.G. (1998), 'Enterprising nonprofits', *Harvard Business Review*, Vol. 76, pp. 54–67.

Dees, J.G. and Anderson, B. (2003), 'Sector-bending: blurring lines between nonprofit and for-profit', *Society*, Vol. 40, pp. 16–27.

Ebrahim, A., Barttilano, J. and Mair, J. (2014), 'The governance of social enterprises: mission drift and accountability challenges in hybrid organizations', *Research in Organizational Behavior*, Vol. 34, pp. 81–100.

Edwards, M. (2008), *Just Another Emperor? The Myths and Realities of Philanthrocapitalism*, Demos, New York.

Edwards, M. (2010), *Small Change: Why Business Won't Save the World*, Berrett-Koehler Publishers, San Francisco, CA.

Ellis, T. (2010), *The New Pioneers: Sustainable Business Success through Social Innovation and Social Entrepreneurship*, John Wiley & Sons, New York.

Fourcade, M. and Healy, K. (2007), 'Moral views of market society', *Annual Review of Sociology*, Vol. 33, pp. 285–311.

Frances, N. and Cuskelly, M. (2008), *The End of Charity: Time for Social Enterprise*, Allen & Unwin, Crows Nest, Australia.

Fridell, G. (2007), *Fair Trade Coffee: The Prospects and Pitfalls of Market-Driven Social Justice*, University of Toronto Press, Toronto.

Friedland, R. and Alford, R.R. (1991), 'Bringing society back in: symbols, practices, and institutional contradictions', in Powell, W.W. and DiMaggio, P.J. (eds), *The New Institutionalism in Organizational Analysis*, University of Chicago Press, Chicago, IL.

Galaskiewicz, J. and Barringer, S.N. (2012), 'Social enterprises and social categories', in Gidron, B. and Hasenfeld, Y. (eds), *Social Enterprises: An Organizational Perspective*, Palgrave Macmillan, New York.

Greenwood, R., Raynard, M., Kodeih, F., Micelotta, E.R. and Lounsbur, M. (2011), 'Institutional complexity and organizational responses', *Academy of Management Annals*, Vol. 5, pp. 317–371.

Hansmann, H.B. (1980), 'The role of nonprofit enterprise', *Yale Law Journal*, Vol. 89, pp. 835–901.

Jaffee, D. (2007), *Brewing Justice: Fair Trade Coffee, Sustainability, and Survival*, University of California Press, Berkeley, CA.

Jaffee, D. (2012), 'Weak coffee: certification and co-optation in the fair trade movement', *Social Problems*, Vol. 59, pp. 94–116.

Kerlin, J.A. and Gagnaire, K. (2009), 'United States', in Kerlin, J.A. (ed.), *Social Enterprise: A Global Comparison*, Tufts University Press, Lebanon, NH.

Kraatz, M.S. and Block, E.S. (2008), 'Organizational implications of institutional pluralism', in Greenwood, R., Oliver, C., Suddaby, R. and Sahlin, K. (eds), *The SAGE Handbook of Organizational Institutionalism*, SAGE Publications, Los Angeles, CA.

Mair, J., Mayer, J. and Lutz, E. (2015), 'Navigating institutional plurality: organizational governance in hybrid organizations', *Organization Studies*, Vol. 36, pp. 713–739.

Nyssens, M. (2006), *Social Enterprise: At the Crossroads of Market, Public Policies and Civil Society*, Routledge, New York.

Pache, A.-C. and Santos, F. (2010), 'When worlds collide: the internal dynamics of organizational responses to conflicting institutional demands', *Academy of Management Review*, Vol. 35, pp. 455–476.

Polak, P. and Warwick, M. (2013), *The Business Solution to Poverty*, Berrett-Koehler Publishers, San Francisco, CA.

Prahalad, C.K. (2004), *The Fortune at the Bottom of the Pyramid: Eradicating Poverty Through Profits*, Wharton School Publishing, Upper Saddle River, NJ.

Raynolds, L.T. and Bennett, E.A. (2015), 'Introduction to research on fair trade', in Raynolds, L.T. and Bennett, E.A. (eds), *Handbook of Research on Fair Trade*, Edward Elgar Publishing, Cheltenham, UK and Northampton, MA, USA.

Raynolds, L.T. and Long, M.A. (2007), 'Fair/alternative trade: historical and empirical dimensions', in Murray, D.L., Wilkinson, J. and Raynolds, L.T. (eds), *Fair Trade: The Challenges of Transforming Globalization*, Routledge, New York.

Reay, T. and Hinings, C.R. (2009), 'Managing the rivalry of competing institutional logics', *Organization Studies*, Vol. 30, pp. 629–652.

Reich, A.D. (2014), 'Contradictions in the commodification of hospital care', *American Journal of Sociology*, Vol. 119, pp. 1576–1628.

Reiser, D.B. (2010), 'Blended enterprise and the dual mission dilemma', *Vermont Law Review*, Vol. 35, pp. 105–116.

Reiser, D.B. (2011), 'Benefit corporations – a sustainable form of organization', *Wake Forest Law Review*, Vol. 46, pp. 591–625.

Sandel, M.J. (2012), *What Money Can't Buy: The Moral Limits of Markets*, Macmillan, New York.

Santos, F., Pache, A.-C. and Birkholz, C. (2015), 'Making hybrids work: aligning business models and organizational design for social enterprises', *California Management Review*, Vol. 57, pp. 36–58.

Schneiberg, M. and Bartley, T. (2008), 'Organizations, regulation, and economic behavior: regulatory dynamics and forms from the nineteenth to twenty-first century', *Annual Review of Law and Social Science*, Vol. 4, pp. 31–61.

Smith, W.K. and Lewis, M.W. (2011), 'Toward a theory of paradox: a dynamic equilibrium model of organizing', *Academy of Management Review*, Vol. 36, pp. 381–403.

Suchman, M.C. (1995), 'Managing legitimacy: strategic and institutional approaches', *Academy of Management Review*, Vol. 20, pp. 571–610.

Thornton, P.H., Ocasio, W. and Lounsbury, M. (2012), *The Institutional Logics Perspective: A New Approach to Culture, Structure, and Process*, Oxford University Press, Oxford.

Tyler, J.E., Luppino, A.J., Absher, E. and Garman, K. (2015), 'Producing better mileage: advancing the design and usefulness of hybrid vehicles for social business ventures', *Quinnipiac Law Review*, Vol. 33, pp. 235–337.

Yunus, M. (2008), *Creating a World Without Poverty: Social Business and the Future of Capitalism*, Public Affairs, New York.

Yunus, M. and Weber, K. (2010), *Building Social Business: The New Kind of Capitalism That Serves Humanity's Most Pressing Needs*, Public Affairs, New York.

Zelizer, V.A. (1978), 'Human values and the market: the case of life insurance and death in 19th-century America', *American Journal of Sociology*, Vol. 84, pp. 591–610.

Zelizer, V.A. (2000), 'The purchase of intimacy', *Law and Social Inquiry*, Vol. 25, pp. 817–848.

Zuckermann, E.W. (1999), 'The categorical imperative: securities analysts and the illegitimacy discount', *American Journal of Sociology*, Vol. 104, pp. 1398–1438.

13. The governance of hybrid organisations
Chris Cornforth

INTRODUCTION

In an era when the recent financial crisis has raised questions about the morality and sustainability of the economic system, and austerity measures have led to funding challenges for many charitable and voluntary organisations, hybrid organisational forms such as social enterprise offer a promising alternative: an ethical form of business able to address social issues and reduce the dependence on donations and government funding. However, history suggests that it can be difficult for social enterprises to maintain their social goals in the face of commercial pressures and that consequently they may succumb to mission drift. Organisational governance is important in helping to manage these competing pressures, and this chapter examines some of the main choices and challenges that social enterprises face in designing their governance structures, systems and processes.

One of the challenges facing hybrid organisations, such as social enterprises, is how to combine different logics; for example, many social enterprises have to combine a commercial logic necessary for operating in the market with a 'charitable'[1] logic of pursuing a social mission (Ebrahim et al., 2014). It has been suggested that combining different logics can result in long-term instability, where one logic comes to dominate (Young et al., 2012). Indeed, traditional left-wing critiques of co-operatives and other forms of employee ownership suggested that these organisations would simply degenerate into being no different from capitalist forms of business as they succumbed to pressures from the marketplace (Mandel, 1975). This process whereby an organisation gradually loses its social mission is often called mission creep or mission drift (Minkoff and Powell, 2006; Jones, 2007). While social enterprises are not the only types of organisation to be susceptible to mission drift, they face the particular challenge of trying to manage being both a business and pursuing a social mission.

Empirical evidence on whether social enterprises can sustain their social missions suggests a mixed picture. While there are examples of mission drift (e.g., Augsburga and Fouillet, 2010), there are also examples where social enterprises have found ways of successfully combining different logics (e.g., Battilana and Dorado, 2010). Young (2012) argues that some combinations of characteristics of hybrid organisations, such as legal forms, governance and sources of finance, are likely to be more stable than others. Ebrahim et al. (2014) suggest that organisational governance and governing boards are of particular importance in attempting to manage conflicting logics and priorities in order to avoid mission drift, but this aspect of governance in social enterprises has been little studied.

This chapter helps to address that gap and focuses on the governance of social enterprises. It examines the question: what choices and challenges do social enterprises face in designing their governance structures, systems and processes in order to manage competing institutional logics and avoid mission drift? It argues that the various options have different advantages and disadvantages, which need to be weighed up when deciding what is appropriate for a particular organisation. The aim then is to examine some of the choices that practitioners are likely to face when considering how their social enterprise is governed, and drawing on extant research to identify some of the important factors and challenges that they should consider in making their choices.

The chapter proceeds as follows. First it examines different ways of understanding organisational hybridity, highlighting the importance of both competing institutional logics and the path-dependent nature of hybridity. Then, drawing on the literature on institutional logics (Friedland and Alford, 1991; Kraatz and Block, 2008; Skelcher and Smith, 2014), it examines some of the different ways in which hybrid organisations can adapt to the demands of plural institutional environments. This analytical framework is then used to consider how governance structures, systems and processes can be designed to help social enterprises manage competing logics and avoid mission drift.

UNDERSTANDING ORGANISATIONAL HYBRIDITY

As Skelcher and Smith (2014, p. 3) note, hybridity and hybrid organisation are 'slippery concepts with inexact empirical referents', and a variety of different approaches have been taken to conceptualising them. One approach has been to define hybrid organisations in terms of a continuum. So, for example, Alter (2007, p. 14) suggests that one way of thinking about social enterprises is as hybrid organisations that lie on a continuum between traditional voluntary or non-profit organisations and traditional for-profit businesses. He further distinguishes social enterprises from socially responsible businesses that pursue social goals, but whose primary purpose is still to make a profit for shareholders, and voluntary and non-profit organisations that establish trading activities as a way of raising additional funds. While this approach may be useful heuristically it lacks precision, and there has been a good deal of debate about at what point an organisation can be called a social enterprise.

A second approach has conceptualised hybridity in terms of the space between three primary or ideal sectors of the market, state and community (Pestoff, 1998). In this formulation the third sector as a whole is conceptualised as a hybrid space between the three primary sectors (Rhodes and Donnelly-Cox, 2014). All third sector organisations, including voluntary organisations and social enterprises, are seen as hybrid organisations combining characteristics from the other sectors. Again, this approach offers no very clear way of distinguishing between different types of hybrid organisation except perhaps in terms of proximity to the three main sectors.

A third, related but somewhat different approach, has been put forward by Billis (2010). In his model the third sector itself is seen as a primary sector with its own ideal characteristics. He defines hybrid organisations with regard to the core principles underlying three ideal sectors: the private sector, the public sector and the third sector. The core principles of each sector include ownership, governance, operational priorities, distinctive human resources, and what he calls distinctive other resources, essentially how they generate income. In his approach the ideal-typical third sector organisation is the voluntary membership association, that is 'owned' by its members who elect the governing body in order to pursue a distinctive social mission, rely on donations to fund the organisation, and on volunteers and members to carry out its work. For Billis, hybridity occurs when an organisation 'moves away' from its primary sector by adopting some of the characteristics of other sectors, but he suggests that organisations will retain a primary adherence to the sector in which they had their origins. This enables Billis to identify nine types of hybrid organisation depending on the transition an organisation makes from its primary sector. For instance, an example of a public–third sector–private hybrid is a recreation service that has spun out of a local authority as a charitable trust but that is partly funded by clients' fees. This approach has the advantage of specifying in more detail at least some of the distinctive characteristics of organisations in different sectors, highlighting different types of hybrid organisation and the path-dependent nature of organisational hybridity. It suggests that the origins of the organisation and the path it takes will influence the sort of hybrid it becomes, and that hybridisation is a dynamic process.

A fourth approach, and the one adopted in this chapter, draws on the theory of institutional logics (Friedland and Alford, 1991; Kraatz and Block, 2008; Thornton and Ocasio, 2008). This suggests that within society there exist plural institutional orders with their own central logics, consisting of normative symbolic constructions and material practices (Friedland and Alford, 1991) that give meaning and identity to individuals and organisations (Skelcher and Smith, 2014). Kraatz and Block (2008) suggest that they can be thought of as the 'rules of the game' that both shape and constrain organisational behaviour. The fact that organisations may be subject to different and potentially conflicting institutional logics opens up the possibility of strategic choice and change. Skelcher and Smith (2014) theorise hybrid organisations as combining different institutional logics. They argue that such an approach puts the study of hybrid organisations on a strong theoretical footing, and a number of authors have used the idea of competing institutional logics to help explain the dynamics within hybrid organisations, such as social enterprises (see, e.g., Mullins, 2006; Battilana and Dorado, 2010; Pache and Santos, 2010, 2013; Cornforth, 2014). Organisations may respond to the demands of competing institutional logics in different ways, as will be discussed next.

ADAPTING TO THE DEMANDS OF COMPETING INSTITUTIONAL LOGICS

Kraatz and Block (2008) suggest four basic ways in which organisations may adapt to the demands of plural institutional environments. First, an organisation may adapt by consciously or unconsciously trying to eliminate pluralism by challenging or not acknowledging the legitimacy of certain claims, while supporting others. This may result in mission drift when, for example, an organisation gives priority to business success at the expense of its broader social mission, or vice versa to business failure as priority is given to its social mission at the expense of commercial considerations.

A second approach is to 'compartmentalize' the different identities and logics in the organisation, so that the different parts of the organisation contain the separate institutional logics and attend to different institutional demands. Skelcher and Smith (2014) suggest that this may take two forms: the 'segmented hybrid' where compartmentalisation is performed within a single organisation, for example by separating functions with different logics into separate departments; or the 'segregated hybrid' where activities are divided into separate organisations, for example when a charity sets up a separate trading subsidiary to do commercial work, or when a social enterprise establishes an affiliated foundation to undertake charitable work.

In contrast to the second approach the third and fourth approaches aim at integrating rather than separating the different logics within the organisation. The third approach concerns trying to manage competing demands and logics. Strategies may range from playing off one constituency against another, to more cooperative solutions, such as trying to get the different constituencies to recognise their mutual dependence and the need for balance. This approach may involve reaching a compromise between conflicting views and logics, so that the different parties recognise the legitimacy of each other's views and practices even if they do not necessarily agree. However, Kraatz and Block (2008) suggest that these compromises are often uneasy and that tensions are still likely to remain between different groups.

Fourthly, organisations may attempt to forge a new identity that combines the different institutional logics, which gains wider legitimacy and begins to create a new organisational field. This may be what is happening in social enterprise fields such as fair trade, which has gained widespread legitimacy and acceptance. Much of the work of social enterprise associations, such as the Social Enterprise Coalition in the United Kingdom (UK),[2] is about trying to gain this legitimacy. Kraatz and Block (2008) suggest that in some cases an organisation may become an 'institution in its own right', and become a 'valued end in its own right and thus become capable of legitimating its own actions'. A few well-known social enterprises such as the *Big Issue*, a magazine sold by the homeless to provide them with an income, may have achieved this status.

However, as will be argued below when considering organisational governance, these strategies are not necessarily mutually exclusive; so even if, for example, a social enterprise chooses a strategy of segmentation, it may still need to adopt integrative strategies and reinforce its identity as a social enterprise.

GOVERNANCE STRATEGIES FOR MANAGING COMPETING LOGICS IN SOCIAL ENTERPRISES

Organisational governance is defined as 'the structures, systems and processes concerned with ensuring the overall direction, control and accountability of an organisation' (Cornforth, 2004; Cornforth and Spear, 2010). It includes the legal form that an organisation takes and accompanying regulatory requirements; any voluntary accreditation requirements; the internal governance structure and systems of accountability; board composition, and the performance management and control systems established by board. The chapter will now go on to examine each of these in turn, outlining some of the main challenges and choices that social enterprises face in designing their governance systems to manage competing logics and avoid the dangers of mission drift. It first examines how governance structures, systems and processes can be used to help integrate conflicting institutional logics. As will be discussed below, these integrative governance strategies may also help to create and maintain the identity of the social enterprise, and so these strategies will be discussed together. Then the chapter will examine governance structures that attempt to manage competing logics through compartmentalization.

INTEGRATIVE GOVERNANCE STRATEGIES

Legal Structures and Regulation

One of the most important decisions a new social enterprise has to make is deciding what legal form to adopt, because a poor choice and lack of appropriate advice can lead to future problems (Spear et al., 2007, 2009). There has been a concern that traditional legal forms that businesses commonly adopt do not provide adequate protection for a social enterprise's social mission, leave them vulnerable to takeover by other businesses that do not share their social mission, and provide inadequate means of accountability to other stakeholders beyond owners or shareholders. In the UK the demutualisation and takeover of many building societies by private sector banks is a classic example (Marshall et al., 2003). In the United States (US) the takeover of Ben & Jerry's by Unilever is another high-profile example. The typical legal structures for charities, voluntary organisations and mutual organisations, such as the company limited by guarantee or the industrial and provident society in UK law, while offering some safeguards for the organisations' social mission, limit their ability to raise external capital, which may limit their ability to grow and develop.

While in some jurisdictions it may be possible to build safeguards into traditional legal structures for businesses to address some of these concerns (Page and Katz, 2012), there have been efforts to develop new legal structures that are more suitable for enterprises that pursue a social mission. In the US these include the low-profit limited liability company, the benefit corporation and the flexible purpose corporation (Battilana et al., 2012; Cooney, 2012). In the UK the community interest company (CIC) has been developed; this was designed to enable people to establish a business for the benefit of the community and not purely for private gain, and is overseen by the Regulator of Community Interest Companies.[3]

A key concern in developing these new legal forms has been how to balance an organisation's 'charitable' logic of pursuing a social mission with a business logic of operating in the marketplace and enabling better access to external finance. In the UK the CIC legal form attempts to protect a social enterprise's mission through a 'community interest test' to ascertain that the purpose of the organisation is of benefit to the community, and an 'asset lock' that prevents the assets of the organisation being used for other than their designated purpose. On dissolution any surplus assets of a CIC have to be transferred to another organisation with an asset lock, so that its assets cannot be sold off for financial gain. CICs have greater freedoms to raise external finance than companies limited by guarantee, the legal form commonly adopted by many charities and voluntary organisations in the UK. If a CIC's constitution allows, it can pay a dividend on equity investments, but a cap is placed on the amount of dividends and interest that can be paid. There has been a good deal of debate about whether these restrictions are too severe and discourage equity investments, or whether loosening the cap would endanger an enterprise's social mission. A consultation carried out by the regulator did lead to the loosening of restrictions on dividend and interest payments in 2009 (Regulator for Community Interest Companies, 2010) and then again in 2014, but debate is likely to continue about the appropriateness of these changes and whether further reform is required (De Grave, 2013; Spreckley, 2014).

The CIC form provides a number of mechanisms besides the asset lock to try to protect an organisation's social mission. When a company registers to become a CIC it must satisfy the regulator that its primary purpose is to benefit the community by passing a community interest test. It must also file an annual report with the regulator saying how it is meeting the community interest test and how it consulted with those affected by its activities (Regulator for Community Interest Companies, 2013). The Regulator also has the power to change the directors of the CIC or close it down if the community interest is not being met. However, it is intended that the regulation is light touch.

While there are likely to be continuing debates over the relative merits of these new legal forms compared to traditional legal forms in balancing social benefits and the freedoms to raise external capital, there may also be less tangible symbolic benefits. They may help to increase the legitimacy of social enterprises by signalling to external stakeholders that the organisation's primary purpose is to benefit the community rather than benefit its owners or shareholders (Page and Katz, 2012). In this way, adopting a new legal form may be one part of a strategy to integrate different institutional logics by reinforcing the organisation's identity as a social enterprise and increasing external legitimacy. However, this is likely to be at the expense of certain restrictions on raising external capital.

In summary, the advantage of traditional legal forms, such as a company limited by shares, is that they are readily understood by potential external investors and offer the ability to raise capital from external shareholders; the disadvantage is that they can leave an organisation's social mission vulnerable to commercial pressures or takeovers. In contrast, new legal forms such as CICs have the advantage of offering some protection for an organisation's social mission and reinforcing its special identity but have the disadvantage that they can make raising external capital more difficult. As a result, in thinking about what legal form to adopt a social enterprise will need to weigh up a number of questions. On the one hand, how important will access to external equity investments be for the development of the enterprise, and will potential external investors be put off by an asset lock and limits on dividend payments? On the other hand, how important is it to have legal safeguards to protect the organisation's social mission, and will this help to reinforce the identity of the social enterprise and increase its legitimacy?

External Accreditation

Official regulation of businesses is often relatively 'light touch' and regulators will usually only investigate an organisation if allegations of a serious breach of regulations are received, so the ability to protect a social enterprise's social mission is limited. Another integrative strategy a social enterprise may choose to adopt in trying to maintain and signal its distinctive mission and identity is voluntary, external accreditation of standards. In the US the B Corporation certification process is one example. B Corporations can take a variety of legal forms but the process certifies that they meet certain minimum social and environmental standards and that their articles of incorporation include the consideration of stakeholder interests (Cooney, 2006, 2012). Another example in the UK is the Social Enterprise Mark.[4] In the absence of a legal definition of a social enterprise in the UK it sets out various criteria that social enterprises should meet. To meet these criteria a social enterprise must have: social/environmental aims and demonstrate social value; at least 50 per cent of revenue coming from trading; at least 50 per cent of profits being used for social/environmental aims; its own constitution and governance; and any residual assets distributed for social/environmental aims if the organisation is dissolved. In order to receive accreditation a social enterprise has to demonstrate how it meets these standards. Organisations may also be subject to periodic inspections to assess compliance.

However, while external validation of standards offers some reassurance against mission drift there is no guarantee that compliance with standards will not gradually change over time, or that external assessment and enforcement will be adequate. There has also been debate over what are the appropriate standards or criteria that should be used to define a social enterprise; for example, there have been different views over the percentage of revenues that should come from trading (Teasdale et al., 2013). As well as helping to safeguard against mission drift the value of external accreditation also depends on how widely the mark is recognised and valued by the organisation's stakeholders and the wider public. So far, the Social Enterprise Mark in the UK has not been able to achieve the level of public recognition as, say, the Fairtrade Mark. When deciding whether to go down this route social enterprises need to consider whether the potential benefits of accreditation outweigh the costs.

Membership and Board Composition

Decisions concerning the membership of an organisation and the composition of its board can have an important influence on how it is governed. An organisation's governing document[5] sets out who the organisation's members or owners are and how the organisation plans to work and govern itself, including how the members select the governing body or board. The board is responsible for overseeing the day-to-day operations of the organisation and is expected to account to the members at the annual general meeting, or any extraordinary general meetings that are called to agree major issues, such as constitutional change. Organisations can then be thought of as having a two-tier governance structure consisting of the membership and the board, except in those cases where membership is restricted to board members, and the board is essentially self-selecting.

The board or governing body of a social enterprise has the ultimate responsibility for trying to ensure that the organisation achieves its mission and remains financially viable. As a result, it has the responsibility for managing any tensions between commercial or financial imperatives and the organisation's social goals. How the membership is defined and the composition of the board can be an important integrative mechanism in trying to manage these tensions and again be used to signal the distinctive identity of the social enterprise. For example, organisations may decide to include on their boards people with different interests and competences, so that their membership is made up of people with commercial skills and people with expertise relevant to the organisation's social mission. Some organisations may want to go further and establish multi-stakeholder boards including representatives of various stakeholder groups, such as staff, funders, and beneficiaries or users, or establish advisory or consultative groups to represent the community interest (Young, 2011).

How do people get to serve on a governing body? There are three main methods of selection. Some organisations are constituted as membership associations, where the governing body is elected by the membership of the organisation. In others, new governing body members are appointed by the existing governing body; what I will call 'board appointed'. In yet others, some external stakeholders may have the right to appoint some of the governing body members; what I will call 'stakeholder appointed'. The different methods of selecting governing body members have contrasting advantages and disadvantages.

Elections can promote member participation and involvement in the organisation. They may also enhance the legitimacy of the governing body or board through its democratic accountability. However, it can be difficult with elections to ensure that the board has all the necessary competences to be effective. In a study of mutual organisations that have spun out of the public sector, Davies and Yeoman (2013) note what they call the dilemma of expertise. Members elected to the boards of mutual organisations may not have the commercial and financial expertise necessary to exercise their duties as board members, and may be poorly equipped to hold management to account. They also suggest that the added burden of getting a mutual board to work can add to costs and reduce efficiency. Another challenge is the difficulty of maintaining an active membership and the danger of oligarchic tendencies, where the organisation becomes dominated by a small 'elite' group of active members (Michels, 1949).

By contrast, governing bodies that appoint their own members have the opportunity to recruit people with the specific skills the governing body needs. However, the danger is that self-selecting boards can become self-serving and lack external accountability with no wider membership to hold them to account. It may also reduce the board's openness to new people and ideas as the board chooses new board members who are like themselves. This lack of diversity can reduce the effectiveness of boards.

Stakeholder appointments may help to bring in new perspectives and increase external accountability and influence. The decision to include different stakeholders on the board may be influenced by the particular origins and development path of the social enterprise. For example, some social enterprises in the UK that have spun out of the public sector have multi-stakeholder boards embodying a variety of different interests, often including staff, users, and trade union and local authority nominated members. One of the reasons for this is to try to reassure stakeholders that their interests will be protected in the spin-out (Spear et al., 2007, pp. 51–54).

However, including multiple stakeholders on boards is not without its own potential challenges, which need to be weighed up when decisions are made about appropriate governance structures. Spear et al. (2007, 2009) highlight the problem of what one interviewee in their study called 'delegate syndrome', where board members act as if they are delegates for the particular stakeholder group they come from rather than acting in the best interests of the organisation as a whole. Pache and Santos (2010) also note that the internal representation of multiple institutional demands in organisations can lead to conflict and manipulation. They suggest that the more even the power balance between stakeholder representatives, the more likely is the outcome of organisational paralysis or break-up. They also note that conflicting institutional demands on organisations are likely to be particularly prevalent in enterprises providing public and social services.

Table 13.1 presents a summary of the potential advantages and disadvantages of different methods of board selection. In choosing their legal form and deciding on their governing document, organisations need to weigh up the advantages and disadvantages of different methods of board selection. In addition, boards need to keep their methods of board recruitment and selection under review and consider how they can address any

Table 13.1   A comparison of the advantages and disadvantages of different methods of selecting governing body members

Method of selection	Potential advantages	Potential disadvantages
Board appointed	1. Can select on the basis of expertise and experience. 2. Can choose people to fill gaps in governing body skills, and balance commercial and 'social' expertise.	1. Narrow, self-selecting governing body that lacks diversity can mean needs of some important stakeholders are not met. 2. Lack of openness and external accountability.
Stakeholder appointed	1. Can bring an external perspective. 2. Can increase external influence and accountability. 3. Can help balance interests of different stakeholders.	1. May lead governing body members to have divided loyalties. 2. Diversity may increase conflict and make it difficult to make decisions.
Elected	1. Greater openness and accountability. 2. Greater legitimacy. 3. May enhance user/community empowerment. 4. Encourages active membership.	1. Governing body members may lack expertise. 2. Questionable representativeness because of low participation in elections. 3. Responsibility without expertise can lead to failure/disempowerment.

weaknesses that arise. For example, organisations with elected boards may want to use co-options to fill important gaps in skills and experience on the board. Self-selecting boards may reserve some places on their boards for important stakeholders, such as users, to ensure that their voices are heard at board level. Alternatively, they might want to set up other mechanisms, such as consultative forums, to make sure the views of users or other important stakeholders are considered. Open advertising and recruitment procedures can be used to bring in new perspectives and skills and make selection processes more open and transparent. In addition, organisations need to provide induction, training and other forms of support to better equip new board members for their role.

Control Systems and Performance Management

The governing body or board of an organisation has overall responsibility for maintaining the mission of the organisation and ensuring that it performs satisfactorily. To do this the board, with the assistance of management, needs to put in place control systems to manage the performance of the organisation and oversee the work of management. One of the main challenges the board of a social enterprise faces is how to balance social and financial performance and avoid the attendant danger of mission drift.

What makes this particularly difficult is that assessing social performance is very different from assessing financial performance. As Ebrahim et al. (2014) discuss, there are well-established, standardised and quantifiable ways of measuring the financial performance and sustainability of a business, such as profit and loss statements, budgetary performance, return on investments, cash flow and, if the organisation's shares are traded, then various market measures such as share price or market value. This makes it easier to assess the financial performance of an organisation over time and to compare it with other similar organisations. The same is not true for social performance. For social performance there are no commonly accepted, standardised measures of performance that boards can rely upon, making comparison of performance between organisations difficult.

In evaluation studies it is usual to distinguish between the immediate outputs of an organisation's activities, for example the number of beneficiaries that have been helped, and the longer-term outcomes and social impacts the organisation is aiming to achieve. It is usually much easier to measure outputs than outcomes and impacts. For example, in an organisation that is aiming to rehabilitate drug users it is relatively easy to measure certain outputs, such as how many people complete the programme; it is much harder to measure how many of those stay drug-free for longer periods, the extent to which their quality of life has improved and the wider social impacts this may have, for example on reducing crime. While a good deal of research has gone into improving evaluation research it can often be complex, expensive and long term. Research in the US by Liket et al. (2014) also suggests that non-profit organisations struggle to carry out and make good use of evaluation studies. Evaluations are often undertaken to meet the external accountability requirements of funders or the public, and have limited relevance to non-profits' strategic decision-making.

In the UK, the charity think-tank New Philanthropy Capital[6] has campaigned vigorously for voluntary organisations to develop their own systems of measuring outcomes and impact, and has developed methods to help organisations do this (e.g., Kazimirski and Pritchard, 2014). However, these methods assume that organisations can accurately identify cause-and-effect chains between what they do, the outcomes that they want to achieve and wider social impacts. This can often be very difficult to do as a variety of other contextual factors may also influence the outcomes and impacts the organisation is trying to achieve, and make it difficult to disentangle what has actually caused the impact.

If social performance is difficult to measure and interpret, the danger is that boards and managers of social enterprises will focus more strongly on financial performance and commercial objectives. This can lead to mission drift as financial performance becomes the focus of attention rather than a means to achieving social goals. The challenge then for social enterprises is to try to find cost-effective ways to meaningfully assess their social performance, while recognising that financial performance is a means to an end rather than an end in itself.

In contrast to integrative governance strategies discussed above, compartmentalising governance strategies try to manage competing logics by containing them in different parts of the organisation. These strategies are examined next.

COMPARTMENTALISING GOVERNANCE STRATEGIES

Segregation

One of the common ways in which some social enterprises manage the financial risks of engaging in commercial activities and the risk of mission drift is through segregating or separating their charitable and commercial activities into legally distinct, but connected organisations (Skelcher and Smith, 2014). The origins of the organisation and its path to hybridity may affect this choice of strategy. Many organisations established as charities in the UK have subsequently established trading activities as part of their fundraising strategies. A common example is charity shops selling donated goods. For many charities, separating the commercial from non-commercial parts of the organisations is a legal requirement in the UK (Cornforth and Spear, 2010). If a charity wants to engage in significant trading activities that do not directly further its charitable objects it is required by law to establish a trading subsidiary. Charities may also decide to set up trading subsidiaries as a way of protecting their charitable assets from commercial risks and for tax reasons (Sladden, 2008). Whatever the reasons this is one important way of trying to protect an organisation's social mission while benefiting from trading activity. The longevity of many charities that also have trading subsidiaries suggests that this can also have the advantage of being a relatively stable form of hybridity (Young, 2012).

Interestingly there have also been moves in the opposite direction, where social enterprises that were first established to trade commercially have subsequently established charitable subsidiaries or foundations where they have social goals that qualify as charitable. This has the advantage again of helping to protect the organisation's social mission and means that their charitable activities are better able to attract donations, grants and tax relief (Social Enterprise Coalition, 2007, p. 15). An example is the *Big Issue* magazine.[7] This social enterprise was established to produce a magazine that homeless vendors could sell in order to give them a source of income. Later the Big Issue Foundation was established as a charity to provide additional support to homeless vendors.

Another potential advantage of separating trading from social activities is that it can make it easier for the respective boards of the separate organisations to establish performance management systems, with the trading organisation concentrating on commercial performance and the 'charitable' part of the organisation concentrating on social performance. However, this does not necessarily remove all tensions. Chew (2010) carried out comparative case study research on the strategic positioning of four social enterprises set up as subsidiaries of UK charities. She found that the charities have 'strong strategic positions . . . anchored in their charitable missions' that helped to prevent mission drift as they developed commercial activities. This constrained the subsidiaries from developing their own distinctive identities. In addition, there were cultural differences that led to emerging tensions. The charities had an operational culture that emphasised control, policies and processes, whereas the social enterprises had a more enterprising culture.

Similarly, Spear et al. (2007) also reveal tensions in trading charities. For example, in one children's charity there were regular discussions about putting up fees for services because of concerns about low reserves. However, the charitable side of the organisation resisted these proposals because of the likely negative impact on some of the charity's main beneficiaries. Another example concerns the merger of local Age Concern charities in the UK with a national body, Age UK. One of the ways Age UK raises funds for its charitable activities is through a commercial subsidiary that sells products, such as insurance, through commercial tie-ups with companies. A number of local Age Concerns were concerned about the ethics of these commercial arrangements and decided against merging with the national body (Sharman, 2016). Subsequently Age UK was criticised in the press because it was claimed that some of these products did not offer good value to Age UK's beneficiaries.

What may happen then in segregated organisations is that tensions emerge at a higher level at the parent board, where decisions have to be made concerning, for example, how much to invest in a trading subsidiary, how the organisation's beneficiaries will benefit from the trading activities, what identity the trading subsidiary should have and what sort of returns should be expected from its activities. As a result, there may also be a need for integrative strategies at a higher organisational level to address tensions arising from conflicting logics.

A potential disadvantage of a strategy of segregation is the cost of creating separate legal organisations, servicing separate boards and meeting regulatory requirements such as producing annual reports and accounts. An interesting example is the case of UK housing associations (HAs), where many organisations followed a strategy of segregation only later to reintegrate in order to reduce costs and achieve increased economies of scale. HAs are the main providers of low-cost social housing in the UK. They can be regarded as hybrid organisations as they receive public subsidies and are required to house households with low incomes or special needs, but are also increasingly reliant on private finance and other commercial activities. Most were originally established to provide housing in a particular locality, often with a strong ethos of local accountability. Since the late 1990s a period of rationalisation has occurred, stimulated by changes in the regulatory and funding environments, that led organisations to seek economies of scale through mergers between organisations (Mullins, 2006, 2010). In order to keep a degree of local account-ability and control this was often done through the creation of group structures, where the different HAs become subsidiaries of the group, but keep their own boards. Mullins (2006) highlights how there were frequent governance and management challenges during the life cycle of these group structures, with key stakeholders often having quite different perceptions of the balance between retaining independence with local boards and accountability, and the need for further consolidation to achieve economies of scale, greater efficiency, clearer lines of leadership and competitive advantage. As a result of these pressures, many groups have moved to integrate the HA subsidiaries into a unitary organisation (Mullins, 2010, 2014).

Segmentation

Rather than compartmentalisation by establishing linked but legally separate organisa-tions, segmentation involves separating parts of the organisation with different logics within the same organisation, for example by setting up separate divisions or departments. This may be preferable to full segregation as it avoids the costs associated with establish-ing separate legal organisations, and servicing two or more boards and meeting separate regulatory requirements.

Again, while segmentation may enable the different parts of the organisation to operate in a way that is consistent with the underlying logic, there is no guarantee that there will not be tensions between the different parts of the organisation. This is more likely to be the case where the different parts of the social enterprise are highly interdependent. Cooney (2006) provides an example in a detailed case study of a non-profit human ser-vices organisation in the US that created separate divisions for business and social service units with their own separate goals, budgets and operating procedures. The social service division was part-funded by government and foundations, and by profits from the

Table 13.2   A comparison of the advantages and disadvantages of segregation and segmentation

Method of compartmentalisation	Potential advantages	Potential disadvantages
Segregation	1. Each organisation can focus on its primary purpose. 2. May enable one organisation to have charitable status with related tax and funding advantages. 3. Enables 'charitable' assets to be protected from commercial risk. 4. Relatively stable form of organisation.	1. More complex governance structure with the added cost of servicing multiple boards and regulatory requirements. 2. May be more difficult to create a coherent identity for the organisation. 3. Tensions may still arise which need to be resolved at a higher level.
Segmentation	Enables different parts of the organisation to focus on its primary purpose, without the added cost of establishing separate organisations.	When the activities are highly interdependent it can be difficult to insulate social mission from commercial pressures and risks, with the attendant danger of goal displacement and mission drift.

business units. However, this segmentation failed to prevent tensions between these highly interdependent divisions. The organisation provided 'welfare to work' services, where the social services division recruited, case-managed and monitored the flow of clients of the business divisions for vocational training and rehabilitation. Tensions arose because of the different pressures the units faced from external stakeholders in their fields. It was difficult to match the requirements of the businesses, such as the need for skilled labour or fluctuating demand, with the need to meet enrolment and training targets for clients set by grant funders. The difficulty of reconciling these conflicting demands led to a degree of goal displacement or mission drift as the training of clients suffered.

Table 13.2 summarises the advantages and disadvantages of segregation compared with segmentation that need to be considered if a strategy of compartmentalisation is being pursued. However, as discussed, neither segmentation or segregation strategies will necessarily eliminate tensions arising from conflicting logics and external demands, which may need to be addressed at a higher organisational level. As a result, integrative and compartmentalising governance strategies should not necessarily be regarded as mutually exclusive and different aspects of both strategies may need to be combined.

CONCLUSIONS

Hybrid organisations, such as social enterprises, can be characterised as having to combine different institutional logics. However, combining different logics can lead to internal conflict and instability, with the danger that one logic may come to dominate; a social enterprise may succeed commercially but gradually lose its social mission or, conversely, the social mission may dominate at the risk of commercial failure. Institutional theorists have argued that organisations may adopt different strategies in order to manage conflicting institutional logics, through segregation, segmentation, integration and forming a new identity (Kratz and Block, 2008; Skelcher and Smith, 2014). This chapter has used that framework to examine how governance systems can be designed to help manage conflicting logics in hybrid organisations such as social enterprises.

How an organisation is governed is one important means of trying to manage potentially conflicting logics and priorities, but has been little explored in the research literature (Ebrahim et al., 2014). The variety of social enterprises and the different circumstances in which they are formed and develop means that there is no one ideal form of governance that can help to preserve the balance between social and commercial goals. In designing their governance structures, systems and processes, organisations need to consider a variety of issues, including: what legal form to adopt and how they will meet associated regulatory requirements; whether to pursue any voluntary external accreditation; their internal governance structure, board composition and accountability; and what performance management and control systems to establish. In considering these issues practitioners face what can seem like a bewildering variety of options and choices. In order to assist practitioners in navigating this terrain and making informed choices the chapter has set out some of the main options and their advantages and disadvantages.

Young (2012) has suggested that some combinations of the characteristics of social enterprises, including legal forms and governance, are likely to be more stable than others. The longevity of many hybrid organisations that have adopted segregated structures, such as charities that establish linked, but legally separate commercial subsidiaries, suggest that this is one form of social enterprise that is relatively stable. However, empirical research shows that these organisations may still experience tensions between their commercial priorities and their social mission that have to be resolved at a higher level.

This type of segregated structure is unlikely to be appropriate for social enterprises where their social and commercial activities are closely interrelated. In this case it may be possible to separate commercial and social mission activities through segmentation into separate divisions or departments, but as Cooney (2006) shows, where the activities are interdependent and there are conflicting demands from external stakeholders there is always a danger of goal displacement and mission drift over time. Integrative governance strategies are likely to be of particular importance in these unitary social enterprises in helping to reconcile and keep a balance between commercial and social priorities, and to reinforce the organisation's identity as a social enterprise.

In setting out the advantages and disadvantages of some of the main options that social enterprises face in designing their governance systems to help manage their commercial and social goals, it has only been possible to draw on a limited range of empirical studies. There is a growing need for more empirical research that systematically examines how different aspects of an organisation's governance system can help to reconcile potentially competing expectations, pressures and goals. In particular, there is a need to examine what influences social entrepreneurs to choose particular legal forms and governance structures for their social enterprises. More research is also needed into the advantages and disadvantages of new legal forms of organisation. How do these new legal forms affect a social enterprise's ability to maintain its social goals and raise external capital? Do they help to create and maintain the social enterprise's distinctive identity?

Goal displacement and mission drift are processes that occur over time. It will be particularly important therefore to carry out more longitudinal and historical studies that examine how social enterprises perform over time, and the role that governance structures, systems and processes play in attempting to manage competing priorities. For example, Blundel and Lyon (2014) demonstrate the value of taking a historical approach to studying the long-term growth and performance of social enterprises, showing how the organisations they studied responded to changes in their environment. Existing empirical research suggests that how social enterprises are formed and the field of activity they operate in can influence the governance structures and processes they adopt and the challenges they face. It will also be important therefore to conduct comparative research examining the governance of social enterprises operating in different fields, in order to examine the influence of contextual factors such as different funding and regulatory regimes.

NOTES

1. 'Charitable' is used here in the broad sense to indicate the purpose of the organisation is intended to achieve some wider social, environmental or community benefit, which may not necessarily meet the legal definition of charity.
2. http://www.socialenterprise.org.uk/.
3. www.gov.uk/government/organisations/office-of-the-regulator-of-community-interest-companies.
4. http://www.socialenterprisemark.org.uk/.
5. The governing document is called different things in different legal forms of organisation. For example, in UK companies it is called the 'memorandum and articles of association', and in unincorporated associations the 'constitution'.
6. http://www.thinknpc.org/.
7. https://www.bigissue.org.uk/.

REFERENCES

Alter, K. (2007) 'Social Enterprise Typology', Virtue Ventures LLC. www.virtueventures.com/typology (accessed November 2007).
Augsburga, B. and Fouillet, C. (2010) 'Profit Empowerment: The Microfinance Institution's Mission Drift', *Perspectives on Global Development and Technology*, 9, pp. 327–355.
Battilana, J. and Dorado, S. (2010) 'Building Sustainable Hybrid Organisations: The Case of Microfinance Organisations', *Academy of Management Journal*, 53, 6, pp. 1419–1440.
Battilana, J., Lee, M., Walker, J. and Dorsey, C. (2012) 'In Search of the Hybrid Ideal', *Stanford Social Innovation Review*, Summer, pp. 51–55.
Billis, D. (2010) 'Towards a Theory of Hybrid Organizations', in D. Billis (ed.), *Hybrid Organizations and the Third Sector: Challenges for Practice, Theory and Policy*, Basingstoke: Palgrave Macmillan.
Blundel, R. and Lyon, F. (2014) 'Towards a "Long View": Historical Perspectives on Scaling and Replication of Social Ventures', *Journal of Social Entrepreneurship*, online early. DOI: 10.1080/19420676.2014.954258.
Chew, C. (2010) 'Strategic Positioning and Organizational Adaptation in Social Enterprise Subsidiaries of Voluntary Organizations', *Public Management Review*, 12, 5, pp. 609–634.
Cooney, K. (2006) 'The Institutional and Technical Structuring of Nonprofit Ventures: Case Study of a US Hybrid Organisation Caught Between Two Fields', *Voluntas*, 17, pp. 143–161.
Cooney, K. (2012) 'Mission Control: Examining the Institutionalization of New Legal Forms of Social Enterprise in Different Strategic Action Fields', in B. Gidron and Y. Hasenfeld (eds), *Social Enterprises: An Organisational Perspective*, Basingstoke: Palgrave Macmillan.
Cornforth, C. (2004) *Governance and Participation Development Toolkit*, Manchester: Co-operatives UK.
Cornforth, C. (2014) 'Understanding and Combating Mission Drift in Social Enterprises', *Social Enterprise Journal*, 10, 1, pp. 3–20.
Cornforth, C. and Spear, R. (2010) 'The Governance of Hybrid Organisations', in D. Billis (ed.), *Hybrid*

Organisations and the Third Sector: Challenges for Practice, Theory and Policy, Basingstoke: Palgrave Macmillan.

Davies, W. and Yeoman, R. (2013) 'Becoming a Public Service Mutual: Understanding Transition and Change', Oxford Centre for Mutual and Employee-Owned Business, Kellogg College, University of Oxford.

De Grave, I. (2013) 'New Rules could "Open the Investment Floodgates" for Community Interest Companies', Pioneers Post. www.pioneerspost.com/news/20131211/newrules-could-open-the-investment-floodgates-community-interest-companies (accessed 27 January 2014).

Ebrahim, A., Battilana, J. and Mair, J. (2014) 'The Governance of Social Enterprises: Mission Drift and Accountability Challenges in Hybrid Organisations', *Research in Organisational Behavior*. http://dx.doi.org/10.1016/j.riob.2014.09.001.

Friedland, R. and Alford, R.R. (1991) 'Bringing Society Back In', in W.W. Powell and P.J. DiMaggio (eds), *The New Institutionalism in Organisational Analysis*, Chicago, IL: University of Chicago Press.

Jones, M.B. (2007) 'The Multiple Sources of Mission Drift', *Nonprofit and Voluntary Sector Quarterly*, 36, 2, pp. 299–307.

Kazimirski, A. and Pritchard, D. (2014) 'Building Your Measurement Framework: NPC's Four Pillars Approach', London: New Philanthropy Capital. http://www.thinknpc.org/publications/npcs-four-pillar-approach/ (accessed 31 March 2015).

Kraatz, M.S. and Block, E.S. (2008) 'Organisational Implications of Institutional Pluralism', in R. Greenwood, C. Oliver, K. Sahlin-Andersson and R. Suddaby (eds), *The SAGE Handbook of Organisational Institutionalism*, Thousand Oaks, CA: SAGE Publications.

Liket, K., Rey-Garcia, M. and Maas, K. (2014) 'Why Aren't Evaluations Working and What To Do About It: A Framework for Negotiating Meaningful Evaluations for Nonprofits', *American Journal of Evaluation*, 35, 2, pp. 171–188.

Mandel, E. (1975) 'Self-Management Dangers and Possibilities', *International*, 2, 4, pp. 3–9.

Marshall, J.N., Willis, R. and Richardson, R. (2003) 'Demutualisation, Strategic Choice, and Social Responsibility', *Environment and Planning C: Government and Policy*, 21, 5, pp. 735–760.

Michels, R. (1949) *Political Parties: A Sociological Study of Oligarchical Tendencies of Modern Democracy*, New York: Free Press.

Minkoff, D.C. and Powell, W.W. (2006) 'Nonprofit Mission: Constancy, Responsiveness and Deflection', in W.W. Powell and R. Steinberg (eds), *The Non-Profit Sector: A Research Handbook*, 2nd edition, New Haven, CT: Yale University Press.

Mullins, D. (2006) 'Competing Institutional Logics? Local Accountability and Scale and Efficiency in an Expanding Nonprofit Housing Sector', *Public Policy and Administration*, 21, 3, pp. 6–24.

Mullins, D. (2010) 'Housing Associations', Working Paper 16, Third Sector Research Centre, University of Birmingham, UK.

Mullins, D. (2014) 'The Evolution of Corporate Governance Structures and Relationships in English Housing Associations', in C. Cornforth and W. Brown (eds), *Nonprofit Governance: Innovative Perspectives and Approaches*, Abingdon: Routledge.

Pache, A. and Santos, F. (2010) 'When Worlds Collide: The Internal Dynamics of Organisational Responses to Conflicting Institutional Demands', *Academy of Management Review*, 35, 3, pp. 455–476.

Pache, A. and Santos, F. (2013) 'Inside the Hybrid Organisation: Selective Coupling as a Response to Competing Institutional Logics', *Academy of Management Journal*, 56, 4, pp. 972–1001.

Page, A. and Katz, R.A. (2012) 'The Truth About Ben and Jerry's', *Social Innovation Review*, Fall, pp. 39–43.

Pestoff, V. (1998) *Beyond the Market and State: Civil Democracy and Social Enterprises in a Welfare Society*, Aldershot, UK and Brookfield, VT, USA: Ashgate.

Regulator for Community Interest Companies (2010) 'Response to the Consultation on the Dividend and Interest Caps', Department of Business Innovation and Skills. http:// .bis.gov.uk/assets/cicregulator/docs/consultations/10-1386-community-interest-companies-consultation-caps-response.pdf (accessed 9 May 2013).

Regulator for Community Interest Companies (2013) Chapter 9 'Corporate Governance', Community Interest Companies: Guidance Chapters, Department of Business Innovation and Skills, UK. https://www.gov.uk/government/publications/community-interest-companies-how-to-form-a-cic (accessed 25 March 2015).

Rhodes, M.L. and Donnelly-Cox, G. (2014) 'Hybridity and Social Entrepreneurship in Social Housing in Ireland', *Voluntas*, 25, 6, pp. 1630–1647.

Sharman, A. (2016) 'Age Concern charities criticise Age UK over commercial deals', *Civil Society News*, 9 February. https://www.civilsociety.co.uk/news/age-concern-charities-criticise-age-uk-over-commercial-deals.html.

Skelcher, C. and Smith, S.R. (2014) 'Theorizing Hybridity: Institutional Logics, Complex Organisations and Actor Identities: The Case of Nonprofits', *Public Administration*, Online early. DOI: 10.1111/padm.12105.

Sladden, N. (2008) 'Trading Places?', *Caritas*, April, pp. 7–8.

Social Enterprise Coalition (2007) *Keeping it Legal: A Guide to Legal Forms for Social Enterprises*, London: Social Enterprise Coalition.

Spear, R., Cornforth, C. and Aiken, M. (2007) 'For Love and Money: Governance and Social Enterprise', London: Governance Hub, National Council for Voluntary Organisations. http://oro.open.ac.uk/view/person/cjc9.html (accessed 27 January 2014).

Spear, R., Cornforth, C. and Aiken, M. (2009) 'The Governance Challenges of Social Enterprises: Evidence from a UK Empirical Study', *Annals of Public and Cooperative Economics*, 80, 2, pp. 247–273.

Spreckley, F. (2014) 'Danger! Socially Incompetent Enterprises Ahead', *Pioneers Post*. http://www.pioneerspost.com/comment/20140121/danger-socially-incompetent-enterprises-ahead (accessed 27 January 2014).

Teasdale, S., Lyon, F. and Baldock, R. (2013), 'Playing with Numbers: A Methodological Critique of the Social Enterprise Growth Myth', *Journal of Social Entrepreneurship*, 4, 2, pp. 113–131.

Thornton, P.H. and Ocasio, W. (2008) 'Institutional Logics', in R. Greenwood, C. Oliver, K. Sahlin-Andersson and R. Suddaby (eds), *The SAGE Handbook of Organisational Institutionalism*, Thousand Oaks, CA: SAGE Publications.

Young, D.R. (2011) 'The Prospective Role of Economic Stakeholders in the Governance of Nonprofit Organisations', *Voluntas*, 22, 4, pp. 566–586.

Young, D.R. (2012) 'The State of Theory and Research on Social Enterprises', in B. Gidron and Y. Hasenfeld (eds), *Social Enterprises: An Organisational Perspective*, Basingstoke: Palgrave Macmillan.

Young, D.R., Kerlin, J.A., Teasdale, S. and Soh, J. (2012) 'The Dynamics and Long Term Stability of Social Enterprise', in J. Kickul and S. Bacq (eds), *Patterns in Social Entrepreneurship Research*, Cheltenham, UK and Northampton, MA, USA: Edward Elgar Publishing.

14. Strategic management tensions in hybrid organisations
Bob Doherty, Helen Haugh and Fergus Lyon

INTRODUCTION

The pursuit of commercial, social and environmental goals makes social enterprise hybrids an ideal setting in which to investigate organisational hybridity. Social enterprise hybrids bridge the public, private and non-profit sectors and are found in a range of industries and locations. They differ from other forms of enterprise as they prioritise the achievement of social and environmental objectives above commercial goals, and they differ from other forms of non-profits as they generate income from trading activity (Doherty et al., 2014; Pache and Santos, 2013; Zahra et al., 2009). Research concerning how social enterprise hybrids are managed, however, is still in its infancy. This chapter explores the strategic management tensions encountered when seeking to balance commercial, social and environmental objectives, and presents a conceptual framework to advance our understanding of the management of social enterprise strategic management tensions.

We define strategic management as the fundamental decisions that shape the course of a firm (Eisenhardt and Zbaracki, 1992), and it is of particular interest to leaders of social enterprise hybrids when seeking to scale up impact or scale out delivery (Lyon and Fernandez, 2012; Vickers and Lyon, 2013). There has been a growing societal interest in the scaling of social enterprise hybrids as people search for alternatives to the conventional divisions between public, private and charitable organisations in order to find ways to increase well-being, prosperity and sustainable development (Mair and Martí, 2006; Ridley-Duff and Bull, 2011). A fundamental element of social enterprise strategic management is the ability to respond to the conflicting demands to achieve commercial, social and environmental objectives.

The strategic prioritisation of goals other than revenue growth and profitability distinguishes social enterprises from organisations in the private sector (Mair and Martí, 2006; Lumpkin et al., 2013). Social goals are broadly construed to include serving the needs of the disadvantaged (Defourny and Nyssens, 2006), unemployed (Pache and Santos, 2013), homeless (Teasdale, 2012) and poor (Battilana and Dorado, 2010; Seelos and Mair, 2005). Environmental objectives include responding to climate change, biodiversity loss and pollution (Austin et al., 2006; Vickers and Lyon, 2013) through initiatives such as leadership development and recycling (Vickers and Lyon, 2013).

To achieve sustainable outcomes in all three domains, social enterprises adopt business models that encompass commercial trading as well as creating social and environmental impacts. This is achieved by blending practices from organisations in the private, public and non-profit sectors (Doherty et al., 2014). Although deviation from the institutional conventions anchored in each sector of the economy might appear to be a risk-laden strategy, the outcome has been the development of an increasing population of social enterprises that strive to generate social change (Mair and Martí, 2006).

Social enterprises are perceived to be a discrete category of hybrid organisations since they are not aligned with the organisational conventions of traditional economic sectors (Battilana and Lee, 2014; Billis, 2010). Although distinguishing between public, private and non-profit sector organisations is a useful categorisation technique, it is based on the assumption that organisations manifest generic structural features and characteristics that are in some way 'pure' and representative of a distinct and recognisable group of organisations (Billis, 2010; Crittenden and Crittenden, 1997; Haigh and Hoffman, 2012; Somerville and McElwee, 2011). On this view categories are presented as idealised structures from which organisations derive legitimacy from alignment with categorical logics and discourse (Zuckerman, 1999). To elaborate, Billis (2010) presents organisational templates for the categories of private, public and non-profit organisations. Thus private sector organisations are guided by market forces to maximise financial return, owned by shareholders, governed according to size of share ownership, and generate revenue from sales and fees. Organisations in the public sector are characterised as guided by the principles of public benefit and collective choice, owned by citizens and the state, and resourced through taxation. Finally, non-profit sector organisations pursue social and environmental goals, are owned by members, governed by private election of representatives, staffed by a combination of employees and volunteers, and generate revenue from membership fees, donations and legacies. Specifically, non-profit distributing organisations are legally prohibited from distributing any residual earnings to those with a managerial or ownership interest (Hansmann, 1980).

Organisational forms that do not fit neatly into the institutionalised categories outlined above are labelled hybrids and are found in a range of constellations including, private–public, private–non-profit and public–non-profit. Social enterprise hybrids are 'not aligned with the idealized categorical characteristics' of the private, public or non-profit sectors (Doherty et al., 2014, p. 3), and by pursuing the achievement of commercial, social and environmental objectives are thus a classic hybrid organisational form (Battilana and Lee, 2014; Dees and Elias, 1998; Defourny and Nyssens, 2006; Billis, 2010).

This chapter reviews the institutional origins of conflicting demands and their impact on the strategic management of social enterprise hybrids (Jay, 2013; Smith et al., 2010). By bridging institutional sectors (Phillips et al., 2011) social enterprise hybrids draw on multiple institutional values and practices. We examine the tensions arising from competing commercial, social and environmental goals and explore four strategic management tensions related to conflicting demands. We present four short case studies to shed light on the outcomes of resisting and responding positively to conflicting demands. This is followed by a new conceptual framework for analysing social enterprise responses to strategic management tensions both within the organisation and with external relationships. The chapter concludes by suggesting areas for future research.

STRATEGIC MANAGEMENT AND SOCIAL ENTERPRISE

Aims of Strategic Management

The aims of strategic management are to elicit the medium- and long-term goals of an organisation and then devise, implement and control a plan for achieving these goals (Brown and Iverson, 2004; Moore, 2000). The tangible output of strategic management is the development of a strategic plan in which the business model for achieving the medium- and long-terms goals is outlined. Since strategic management decisions have important implications for the future resource needs and revenue of an organisation, they tend to be complex and infrequently made (Eisenhardt and Zbaracki, 1992). Effective strategic management is important for organisational sustainability and is associated with improved performance (Brown and Iverson, 2004; Siciliano, 1997; Stone et al., 1999). Originating from organisations in the private sector, strategic management tools and techniques have been adopted by organisations in the non-profit sector to improve the performance of organisations that pursue social and environmental goal achievement (Crittenden and Crittenden, 1997; Dees et al., 2002; Frumkin and Andre-Clark, 2000). The diffusion of strategic management models across economic sectors, however, has been criticised by scholars concerned about the implications of the divergent value systems characteristic of each sector (Teasdale, 2012).

In addition, approaches to strategic management vary in terms of economic conditions, legal form and social philosophy (Ridley-Duff and Bull, 2011). For example, in times of recession and public sector austerity, organisations face resource constraints that are likely to impact on strategy and goals. Second, strategic choices are shaped by the legislation concerning specific organisational forms, for example, legal constraints concerning income generation and charities and the tax implications of different legal forms. Third, ideologies vary between different nation states (Hall and Soskice, 2004) and these in turn influence strategy and goals. For example, in the United States (US) social enterprises are framed as a mechanism for stimulating entrepreneurship in the non-profit sector (Dees et al., 2002). An alternative discourse dominant in mainland Europe frames social enterprise as an alternative to the dominance of capitalist organisations (Defourny and Nyssens, 2006). In the United Kingdom (UK) the dominant political discourse frames social entrepreneurship as part of the neoliberal discourse of the free market, rising individual interest in entrepreneurship and self-determination, and part of the safety net for those excluded or marginalised from the benefits of capitalism (Sonnino and Griggs-Trevarthen, 2013).

The aim of strategic management is to create a shared plan for action for the organisation, as this is believed to confer benefits in that everyone is clear about their roles and how they fit into the organisation, resources are used more effectively, knowledge builds commitment and motivation, and diverse stakeholders act cooperatively. Collective approaches to strategic management bring people together to make decisions and implement strategic plans. The strategic management process might be simple and easily managed, or extraordinarily (and potentially unnecessarily) complex. In social entrepreneurship the challenge is to craft a strategy that is sensitive to the environmental context (Battilana and Lee, 2014), responsive to conflicting demands (Pache and Santos, 2013) and forms the foundation of a sustainable business model. Social enterprise strategic management therefore is likely to be characterised by input from multiple stakeholders informed by a range of underlying social values.

Strategic Management Tensions

The strategic management tensions faced by social enterprise leaders arise from the conflicting demands of pursuing viable commercial markets at the same time as generating social and environmental value (Austin et al., 2006; Pache and Santos, 2013; Smith et al., 2013; Wilson and Post, 2013). For example, in a study of social enterprises established to serve the needs of the homeless it was found that the implementation of strategies to achieve commercial sustainability was at the expense of social mission achievement (Teasdale, 2012). Although the commercial focus of the strategy increased the productivity of the social enterprise, it was associated with neglecting individuals who were perceived to be the most difficult to place in employment. In the next two sections we discuss four strategic management tensions and two solutions from practice for responding to conflicting demands.

Mobilising financial resources

The acquisition of financial resources is fundamental to opportunity exploitation and, for social enterprise hybrids, the tension between dual mission achievement is manifest in two ways. First, the dual missions have the potential to impact negatively on the acquisition of financial resources (Austin et al., 2006; Dacin et al., 2010). Research has noted that social enterprise hybrids have access to fewer sources of finance than commercial ventures, particularly where those controlling resources (such as investors) are uncertain about how the organisation will combine the social objectives with a financial return (Austin et al., 2006; Hansmann, 1980; Seelos and Mair, 2005). Further, revenue generation from commercial trading may crowd out philanthropy and donations because donors perceive that the funds are no longer needed (Kingman, 1995). To respond to the negative impact of the social mission on access to finance, social enterprise strategies draw on novel resource acquisition strategies such as bricolage (Desa and Basu, 2013; Di Domenico et al., 2010), where social enterprises make do by combining a range of existing but undervalued resources.

Second, the impact of dual missions on strategic management tensions is played out in the allocation of resources to commercial and social mission achievement (Battilana and Lee, 2014; Doherty et al., 2014). Although social and environmental goals are prioritised above the commercial mission (Mair and Martí, 2006), the relationship between the competing goals varies on a continuum from complementary to oppositional (Stevens et al., 2015). In business models where the dual missions are complementary, the allocation of resources is likely to be less controversial than when the dual missions are in competition with each other (Moizer and Tracey, 2010).

We identify four strategies for accessing financial resources to achieve commercial and social missions. First, leveraging the social mission to achieve commercial goals; for example, fair trade product certification in which the product brand and commercial market development activities rely on certification of the social value created for producers of raw materials in the supply chain (Doherty et al., 2015). Second, accessing sources of funds designated for advancing social innovation; for example, Comic Relief and the National

Endowment for Science and Technology (NESTA) in the UK. Third, accessing repayable finance to support social entrepreneurship; for example, loans from ethical banks such as Triodos Bank. Finally, the internal movement of resources between different functions; for example, the transfer of the surplus from commercial activity to the achievement of the social mission (Alter, 2007).

Mobilising human resources

Strategic tensions are also present in how social enterprise leaders manage human resources, and influence employee recruitment, remuneration and volunteer management. First, employee recruitment is shaped by the skills requirements of the social enterprise (B.R. Smith et al., 2012). For example, in work integration social enterprises, different groups of people are employed to generate income when compared to those employed to deliver services to beneficiaries (Pache and Santos, 2013). Battilana and Dorado (2010) found that social enterprise hybrids are recruiting people with the values and culture needed to meet both social and commercial objectives.

Second, hybridity also affects strategic decisions to determine salaries and wages. Previous research has noted how remuneration in the non-profit sector is lower than comparable employment in the private sector (for a review, see Bell and Haugh, 2014). In a study of employment and motivation in community finance organisations in the UK it was found that employees who had previously worked in private sector finance accepted reduced remuneration in exchange for a personal desire to work for an organisation that provides benefits for society (Bell and Haugh, 2014).

The third influence on mobilising human resources concerns the role of volunteers in social enterprise hybrids (Borzaga and Solari, 2001). The unpaid supply of labour provided by volunteers is a valuable resource and means that full labour costs are not included in the cost structure of the social enterprise. The reliance on volunteers for service delivery, however, means that the full economic cost of running the social enterprise is not accounted for. The long-term implication is that social enterprise sustainability is reliant on a risky strategy of subsidising labour costs by volunteers.

Organisations making a transition from a purely voluntary organisation to one with a trading element need to find ways of coping with the specific tensions related to cultural change and more commercial orientations. However, with the shift to a more social enterprising orientation, the relationship with volunteers can change. Volunteers may be motivated by the intrinsic rewards of job satisfaction and community impact, while a more commercial orientation can lead to greater managerial direction, with volunteers withdrawing labour if they disapprove of such strategic directions.

Mobilising social alliances

Turning now to the strategic management of external relationships in social enterprise, the development of social alliances with partners is an important strategy for acquiring resources, gaining access to markets and serving the needs of beneficiaries more easily than fulfilling these tasks in-house (Austin, 2010). Social alliances range from formal cooperative structures such as joint ventures, partnerships, licensing (Austin, 2010) and social franchising (Tracey and Jarvis, 2007), to less formal mechanisms such as sharing ideas freely and allowing others to scale up an innovative approach (Lyon and Fernandez, 2012). The outcomes of effective social alliances include asset accumulation, market expansion and wider social impact, which in turn foster greater mission fulfilment. The choice of partner in a social alliance is extremely important, however, as legitimacy with stakeholders is influenced by the reputation of the partner (Austin et al., 2006; Moizer and Tracey, 2010).

Previous research has noted the benefits of social alliances between partners within and across sectoral boundaries (Austin, 2010; Gillett et al., 2016). Hybrids are well placed to collaborate with non-profits and with the private sector corporates (Di Domenico et al., 2010). Amin et al. (2002) found social enterprises using alliances with smaller private sector businesses that were willing to absorb trainees who had been supported on social enterprise employment programmes.

Alliances are also important when bidding for public service delivery contracts (Lyon, 2012). When the resource requirements of large service delivery contracts are beyond those of individual social enterprise hybrids, alliances provide a structure for pooling complementary skills and resources.

Mobilising stakeholders
Finally, mobilising stakeholders has emerged as an important strategy to enable social enterprises to achieve their commercial and social missions (Doherty et al., 2014). A stakeholder is defined as any individual or group who is affected by or who can affect an organisation's ability to achieve its objectives (Freeman, 1984). Social enterprise hybrids are responsible to a wider array of external stakeholders than commercial ventures (Low, 2006; Lumpkin et al., 2013) since they cater to interests in both commercial and social performance. Responding appropriately to the demands of different stakeholder groups (Battilana and Dorado, 2010; Low, 2006) has been associated with strategic effectiveness (Brown and Iverson, 2004). The demands of stakeholder groups are also likely to vary in terms of expectations and clarity. For example, co-operative models allow stakeholders to own the enterprise and have a right to a share of any surplus. The strategic management of co-operatives can be challenging as it requires attention to the democratic processes, while also allowing for swift decision-making. The expectations of stakeholders with financial interests in the social enterprise, such as formal lenders and investors, will be specified in contractual terms and conditions. These investors can play a considerable role in shaping strategic management, which in turn can create greater tensions between the social and commercial objectives.

The expectations of community members and philanthropic funders may be more focused on social impacts. These stakeholders may be expecting accountability through forms of social accounting and reporting. However, despite advances in measuring social performance (Darby and Jenkins, 2006), social impact and outcomes continue to be more difficult to specify. There are a wide range of approaches, resulting in inconsistent measurement and difficulties in comparing one organisation with another (Arvidson and Lyon, 2013), and even when similar approaches are used there is a degree of discretion, allowing evaluators to make different assumptions or interpretations of impacts (Arvidson et al., 2013).

In summary, this section has shown that social enterprise hybrids have to address a range of challenges related to their strategic management. In addition to delivering their services and maximising their social impacts, their hybrid nature creates specific challenges within the organisation related to how they mobilise both their financial and their human resources. There are also specific challenges related to external relationships. We group these into challenges related to social alliances and challenges related to mobilising stakeholders. The next section looks at how social enterprise hybrids respond to these tensions.

RESPONSES OF SOCIAL ENTERPRISES TO STRATEGIC MANAGEMENT TENSIONS

In this section we examine responses to strategic management tensions (Alter, 2007; Battilana et al., 2012; Moizer and Tracey, 2010; Santos, 2012; Short et al., 2009). To begin, we consider what happens when strategic management tensions are resisted. We then identify two principal strategies for responding to conflicting demands. The first is mission separation, in which dual missions are mutually exclusive and achieved by the internal structuring of work into responsibility for the achievement of either social or commercial goals. The second is mission integration, in which a dual mission is achieved through combining the pursuit of both social and commercial goals.

Resisting or Tuning Out of Strategic Tensions

Although we might assume that not responding to conflicting demands would be damaging to the sustainability and survival of social enterprise hybrids, empirical studies of the impact of resisting conflicting demands are few. Insights into the impact of failure to achieve a balance between commercial and social objectives, however, can be gleaned from a small group of studies (Battilana and Dorado, 2010; Frumkin and Andre-Clark, 2000; Phillips et al., 2011; Teasdale, 2012). An in-depth qualitative analysis of two microfinance organisations found that intractable identity conflicts between banking and development logics led to 'an impasse which made it impossible to operate effectively' (Battilana and Dorado, 2010, p. 1427). The impasse was resolved after staff resignations, dismissals and strategic reorientation. Research that explored non-profit employment service organisations found that attending to the needs of the most job-ready compromised the achievement of the social mission and risked negative attention from stakeholders in the media and local community (Frumkin and Andre-Clark, 2000; Teasdale, 2012). Finally, in a study of a mail order catalogue distribution by a social enterprise franchise (Phillips et al., 2011), the demise of Aspire was attributed to prioritisation of the social mission above commercial sustainability. A case study from our own research also sheds light on the impacts of failing to manage the achievement of both commercial and social goals.

Liberation Nuts (a community interest company or CIC) was established in 2007 as the first Fair Trade nut company in the UK. The CIC is part owned by the International Nut Producers Cooperative (INPC) which consists of 12 nut co-operatives across Africa, South America and Asia. The mission of Liberation Nuts is to be run for the benefit of the community of interest, that is, smallholder nut-gatherers in developing countries. The initial financial investment was provided by social investors and Liberation Nuts invested the money in marketing campaigns at music festivals and other events, at the expense of a focus on commercial imperatives such as achieving retail distribution of the products. The marketing strategy was successful in raising consumer awareness and intention to purchase, but lack of availability of the products in retail outlets meant that sales revenue was insufficient. A former board member explained that: 'Liberation in the first few years was being run with semi-donor logic without enough financial control and the board was not bringing the management team to account.' The failure to generate sufficient revenue was compounded by the external global financial crisis in 2007/08 and Liberation Nuts ran into serious commercial difficulty. Action to resolve the crisis included replacing the managing director and chair of the board, and the appointment of a sales manager. Liberation Nuts thus responded to the tension and ultimately secured contracts with major retail outlets and built a sustainable business model.

Mission Separation

Mission separation involves the structuring of responsibility for the achievement of commercial and social objectives into different functional units. Mission separation separates the customers and beneficiaries of the social enterprise into different stakeholder groups, and the key challenge is to manage the conflicting demands of both stakeholder groups. For example, in the retailing of Christmas cards by the charity Oxfam, the Christmas cards are sold by the trading arm of Oxfam and the services to the disadvantaged in developing countries are delivered by the charity. The sustainability of the commercial retail arm generates surpluses which are then gifted to the charity. The strategic management tension lies in the extent of resources directed to the different functional units which may in practice compete with each other for resources. To invest too much in the achievement of social objectives ultimately threatens the long-term survival of the commercial arm and the organisation.

In a mission separation strategy the commercial venture is either aligned to the social mission – strategic coupling – or distinct – strategic decoupling, also referred to as compartmentalisation (Costanzo et al., 2014). Strategic decoupling may impact negatively on stakeholder perceptions of legitimacy (Moss et al., 2011). Two examples from our own research illustrate the impact of coupled mission separation and decoupled mission separation on the achievement of dual missions.

The social enterprise Can Cook (Liverpool) has adopted the strategy of coupled mission separation. The commercial trading arm of Can Cook comprises the Cookery and Dine Kitchen studio which sells master chef workshops and team-building training to corporations. The surplus generated from the Cookery and Dine Kitchen Studio is invested in raising awareness of the benefits of cooking with fresh food to people living in deprived areas of the city. In 2015 a new initiative, 'Share your Lunch', was launched to provide fresh food to local families to replace processed and canned food.

The strategy of Shoreditch Trust (London) illustrates decoupled mission separation. In 2002 the senior management team at Shoreditch Trust agreed to invest in the purchase and renovation of physical assets to create workspaces to be rented out to generate income. The workspaces are leased by all types of businesses, not just social enterprises. The strategy generates revenue which provides the Trust with financial security as well as funds to invest in more challenging social initiatives. For example, the Trust supports two innovative social enterprises: Blue Marble Training, which identifies, trains and pastorally supports ex-offenders and care leavers to gain catering skills, qualifications and work experience; and Bump Buddies, a maternity peer-to-peer support and education programme.

Mission Integration

The strategy of mission integration is based on striving to generate income and social value through an integrated business model in which all business functions support the achievement of the dual mission. This strategy is found in mission-driven organisations such as fair trade organisations, and affirmative businesses such as work integration social enterprises (WISE). The focus of strategic management is to balance the tensions between the achievement of commercial and social objectives. Previous research has identified two strategies for integrating dual mission. First, temporal management by switching focus from the social mission to the commercial mission at different times, for example on a project-by-project basis (Battilana and Dorado, 2010); and partial integration through alignment on a subset of functions (Pache and Santos, 2013). A final example from our own research is presented below to illustrate mission integration.

Divine Chocolate Ltd is an international social enterprise hybrid with offices in London and the United States. Divine Chocolate Ltd is a fair trade farmer-owned business in which cocoa farmer representatives of the farmers' co-operative Kuapa Kokoo (Ghana) have two seats on the board. Mission integration is achieved in two ways: first, from Fairtrade certification of cocoa beans supplied by the farmers; and second, from the company's own Producer Support and Development Programme. For every tonne of cocoa bought by Divine, the Kuapa Kokoo receives the Fairtrade premium per tonne of cocoa plus the social premium of $250 per tonne. In addition, dependent on the annual performance of Divine, the farmers also receive a dividend plus funds for producer capacity-building projects. During the period 2007–09 investments in new product development and distribution were prioritised at Divine by working with Innovate UK on a knowledge transfer partnership. The temporal prioritisation of commercial objectives enabled revenues to be built internationally, thus increasing the amount of surplus invested in Kuapa Kokoo.

In summary, we can see how social enterprises can respond to tensions. Some may ignore the tensions and this can lead to considerable threats to the sustainability of the organisation. There are two distinct strategies that social enterprise hybrids are found to be drawing on. Mission separation allows different parts of the organisation to separate the social and commercial objectives. By contrast, mission integration strategies allow the organisation to combine the social goals and commercial objectives in specific activities. In distinguishing these different strategies, we can develop a conceptual framework related to the strategic management of hybrids.

A CONCEPTUAL FRAMEWORK FOR RESPONDING TO CONFLICTING DEMANDS

The conceptual framework for responding to conflicting demands presented in Table 14.1 is anchored in the four social enterprise strategic management tensions and practical solutions discussed above. Consider, first, the strategic management tensions associated with the coupling of commercial and social missions. Strategies that focus on coupled mission integration employ related commercial income to subsidise the achievement of the social mission and employ staff with expertise in both commercial and social task performance. In addition, social alliances and relationships with stakeholders are built

Table 14.1　A framework for analysing social enterprise strategic management tensions

		Mission separation		Mission integration	
		Coupled	Decoupled	Constant	Temporal sequencing
Internal relationships	Mobilising financial resources	Subsidisation of social mission from related commercial income	Subsidisation of social mission from unrelated commercial income	Long-term alignment of commercial and social missions	Prioritisation of commercial mission and then social mission (and vice versa)
	Mobilising human resources	Employee expertise in both commercial and social task performance	Employee expertise in either commercial or social task performance	Employees and beneficiaries can be the same stakeholder group	Project-based recruitment of human resources and volunteers
External relationships	Mobilising social alliances	Social alliance partners committed to commercial and social missions	Social alliance partners committed to either commercial or social mission	Long-term social alliances to achieve commercial and social missions	Project-based social alliances
	Mobilising stakeholders	Stakeholders committed to commercial and social missions	Stakeholders committed to either commercial or social mission	Long-term stakeholder engagement in commercial and social missions	Project-based stakeholder engagement

on commitment to an integrated commercial and social mission. For example, strategic management at Can Cook (Liverpool) seeks to integrate the achievement of commercial and social missions across all activities, and recruits employees and volunteers skilled in both commercial and social task performance.

Second, strategic management tensions associated with decoupled commercial and social missions are managed by strategies in which the financial and human resources, as well as social alliances and stakeholder relationships, are committed to either the commercial or the social mission. For example, at Shoreditch Trust the strategies to generate income for the social mission include asset-based strategies to generate rental income. Employees skilled in property management manage the buildings, and skills in social care are required for employment in Blue Marble Training.

Third, strategic management tensions that arise when commercial and social missions are constantly integrated, are responded to in strategies that seek to find routes to align the conflicting demands, when clients and beneficiaries are the same. Furthermore, long-term social alliances and relationships with stakeholders are invested in to support the achievement of both commercial and social missions. For example, Fairtrade-certified social enterprises such as Divine Ltd integrate the achievement of commercial and social missions throughout the organisation.

Finally, when mission integration is achieved through temporal sequencing, financial and human resources, as well as social alliances and stakeholder relationships, are mobilised on a project-by-project basis. This was illustrated in the example of Liberation Nuts when sustainability was compromised by failure to respond effectively to the commercial performance of the organisation.

The selection between the alternative strategic options outlined in Table 14.1 will be influenced by opportunity recognition, resource availability, plus stakeholder perceptions and legitimacy. Opportunity recognition will determine whether the achievement of a dual mission is practical and achievable (W.K. Smith et al., 2012). Resource availability will also influence the extent to which strategies are feasible and viable (Foster and Bradach, 2005). Finally, when stakeholders' expectations are not met by the strategies adopted, this is likely to impact negatively on the perceived identity and legitimacy of social enterprise hybrids (Dart, 2004; Smith et al., 2010).

CONCLUSION

This chapter has identified four strategic management tensions arising from the conflicting demands inherent to the management of social enterprise hybrids. These relate to mobilising financial resources, human resources, social alliances and mobilising other stakeholders. Using case studies from practice we then reviewed the practical response strategies adopted by social enterprise hybrids. To summarise the conflicting demands we presented a conceptual framework (see Table 14.1) of social enterprise responses to strategic management tensions. This distinguishes the challenges in managing internal and external relations. The framework helps social enterprise managers to develop their own strategies to deal with hybridity. Some aim to maximise social impacts through separating their social mission from trading activity, while others aim to integrate their social and commercial mission by generating trading revenue in activities that also meet their social objectives.

In contrast to the deliberate strategic management found in organisations in the for-profit sector (Mintzberg and Waters, 1985), social enterprise strategic management has typically been less formal and emergent (Stone et al., 1999). However, in light of the constrained resource contexts in which social enterprise hybrids typically work, the need for careful and considered attention to the best use of resources suggests that social enterprise strategic management is too complex to be left to emergence. The framework we present provides a useful guide to the alternative strategic options available to social enterprise hybrids. The framework makes explicit the tensions inherent in the mobilisation of internal financial and human resources and the development of relationships with partners and stakeholders external to the organisation.

Using this framework as a strategic management tool can help social enterprises to set clear objectives and to communicate these objectives with a range of stakeholders. Social enterprises are often found to draw on more democratic forms of decision-making and strategy development compared to the private and public sectors. This is particularly important for co-operative models. In such contexts, the explicit articulation of different strategic options is particularly important.

This chapter has identified the emerging literature on strategic management for hybridity, although this subject area has not been explored in detail in previous literature. There are therefore opportunities for further exploration and understanding of strategies being used in different contexts. In particular there is a need for more research on human resources within organisations, and the relationships outside of the social enterprise. More attention has been given to mobilising financial resources, but in a rapidly changing world there are knowledge gaps related to novel forms of finance and new income-generating opportunities.

Social enterprises operate in range of industries and sectors. While there has been much research on employment support, health and education, there has been less attention to the strategic management tensions found in other sectors such as culture, arts and leisure. Environmental pressures, and particularly climate change, also present new challenges and there is a need for hybrid forms to present alternatives that lead to both sustainability and well-being.

REFERENCES

Alter, K. (2007). Social enterprise typology. *Virtue Ventures LLC*, 12(2007), 1–124.

Amin, A., Cameron, A. and Hudson, R. (2002). *Placing the Social Economy*. London: Routledge.

Arvidson, M. and Lyon, F. (2013). Social impact measurement and non-profit organisations: Compliance, resistance, and promotion. *Voluntas: International Journal of Voluntary and Nonprofit Organisations* 25(4), 869–886.

Arvidson, M., Lyon, F., McKay, S. and Moro, D. (2013). Valuing the social? The nature and controversies of measuring social return on investment (SROI). *Voluntary Sector Review*, 4(1), 3–18.

Austin, J. (2010). *The Collaboration Challenge: How Non-Profits and Businesses Succeed Though Strategic Alliances*. San Francisco, CA: Jossey Bass.

Austin, J., Stevenson, H. and Wei-Skillern, J. (2006). Social and commercial entrepreneurship: Same, different or both? *Entrepreneurship Theory and Practice*, 30(1), 1–22.

Battilana, J. and Dorado, S. (2010). Building sustainable hybrid organisations: The case of commercial micro-finance organisations. *Academy of Management Journal*, 53(6), 1419–1440.

Battilana, J. and Lee, M. (2014). Advancing research on hybrid organising: Insights from the study of social enterprises. *Academy of Management Annals*, 8, 397–441.

Battilana, J., Lee, M., Walker, J. and Dorcey, C. (2012). In search of the hybrid ideal. *Stanford Social Innovation Review*, Summer, 51–55.

Bell, B. and Haugh, H. (2014) Working for a social enterprise: An exploration of employee rewards and remuneration. In *Social Enterprise: Accountability and Evaluation around the World*, edited by Simon Denny and Frederick Seddon. London: Routledge, pp. 67–84.

Billis, D. (2010). *Hybrid Organisations for the Third Sector. Challenges for Practice, Theory, and Policy*. London: Palgrave Macmillan.

Borzaga, C. and Solari, L. (2001). Management challenges for social enterprises. In *The Emergence of Social Enterprise*, edited by C. Borzaga and J. Defourny. London, UK and New York, USA: Routledge, pp. 333–349.

Brown, W.A. and Iverson, J.O. (2004). Exploring strategy and board structure in non-profit organizations. *Non-profit and Voluntary Sector Quarterly*, 33(3), 377–400.

Costanzo, L.A., Vurro, C., Foster, D., Servato, F. and Perrini, F. (2014). Management in social entrepreneurship: Qualitative evidence from social firms in the United Kingdom. *Journal of Small Business Management*, 52(4), 655–677.

Crittenden, W.F. and Crittenden, V.L. (1997). Strategic planning in third-sector organisations. *Journal of Managerial Issues*, 9(1), 86–103.

Dacin, P.A., Dacin, M.T. and Matear, M. (2010). Social entrepreneurship: Why we don't need a new theory and how we move forward from here. *Academy of Management Perspectives*, 24(3), 37–57.

Darby, L. and Jenkins, H. (2006). Applying sustainability indicators to the social enterprise business model. *International Journal of Social Economics*, 33(5/6), 411–431.

Dart, R. (2004). The legitimacy of social enterprise. *Nonprofit Management and Leadership*, 14(4), 411–424.

Dees, J.G. and Elias, J. (1998). The challenges of combining social and commercial enterprise. *Business Ethics Quarterly*, 8(1), 165–178.

Dees, J.G., Emerson, J. and Economy, P. (2002). *Enterprising Non-Profits: A Tool Kit for Social Entrepreneurs*. Chichester: Wiley.

Defourny, J. and Nyssens, M. (2006). Conceptions of social enterprise in Europe and the United States: Convergences and divergences. *Social Enterprise Journal*, 1(1), 32–53.

Desa, G. and Basu, S. (2013). Optimization or bricolage? Overcoming resource constraints in global social entrepreneurship. *Strategic Entrepreneurship Journal*, 7(1), 26–49.

Di Domenico, M.-L., Haugh, H. and Tracey, P. (2010). Social bricolage: Theorizing social value creation in social enterprises. *Entrepreneurship Theory and Practice*, 34(4), 681–703.

Doherty, B., Haugh, H. and Lyon, F. (2014). Social enterprises as hybrid organisations: A review and research agenda. *International Journal of Management Reviews*, 16(4), 417–436.

Doherty, B., Smith, A. and Parker, S. (2015). Fair trade market creation and marketing in the global south. *Geoforum*, 67, 158–171.

Eisenhardt, K.M. and Zbaracki, M.J. (1992). Strategic decision making. *Strategic Management Journal*, 17(Winter), 17–37.

Foster, W. and Bradach, J. (2005). Should non-profits seek profits? *Harvard Business Review*, 83(February), 92–100.

Freeman, R.E. (1984). *Strategic Management: A Stakeholder Perspective*. Boston, MA: Pitman.

Frumkin, P. and Andre-Clark, A. (2000). When missions, markets and politics collide: Values and strategy in the non-profit human services. *Non-profit and Voluntary Sector Quarterly*, 29(1), 141–163.

Gillett, A., Doherty, B., Loader, K. and Scott, J. (2016). Multi-organisational cross-sectoral collaboration: Empirical evidence from an 'Empty Homes' project. *Public Money and Management*, 36(1), 15–22.

Haigh, N. and Hoffman, A.J. (2012). Hybrid organisations. *Organisational Dynamics*, 41(2), 126–134.

Hall, P.A. and Soskice, D. (2004). *Varieties of Capitalism and Institutional Complementarities*. London: Springer.

Hansmann, H.B. (1980). The role of non-profit enterprise. *Yale Law Journal*, 89, 835–898.

Jay, J. (2013). Navigating paradox as a mechanism of change and innovation in hybrid organisations. *Academy of Management Journal*, 56(1), 137–159.

Kingman, B.R. (1995). Do profits crowd our donations or vice versa? The impact of revenues from sales on donations to local chapters of the American Red Cross. *Non Profit Management and Leadership*, 6(10), 21–38.

Low, C. (2006). A framework for the governance of social enterprises. *International Journal of Social Economics*, 33(5/6), 376–385.

Lumpkin, G.T., Moss, T.W., Gras, D.M., Kato, S. and Amezcua, A.S. (2013). Entrepreneurial processes in social contexts: How are they different, if at all? *Small Business Economics*, 40(3), 761–783.

Lyon, F. (2012). Social innovation, co-operation and competition: Inter-organisational relations for social enterprises in the delivery of public services. In *Social Innovation: Blurring Boundaries to Reconfigure Markets*, edited by A. Nicholls and A. Murdock. Basingstoke: Palgrave Macmillan, pp. 139–161.

Lyon, F. and Fernandez, H. (2012). Strategies for scaling up social enterprise: Lessons from early years providers. *Social Enterprise Journal*, 8(1), 63–77.

Mair, J. and Marti, I. (2006). Social entrepreneurship research: A source of explanation, prediction and delight. *Journal of World Business*, 41(1), 36–44.

Mintzberg, H. and Waters, J.A. (1985). Of strategies, deliberate and emergent. *Strategic Management Journal*, 6, 257–272.

Moizer, J. and Tracey, P. (2010). Strategy making in social enterprise: The role of resource allocation and its effects on organisational sustainability. *Systems Research and Behavioural Science*, 27(3), 252–266.

Moore, M.H. (2000). Managing for value: Organisational strategy in for-profit, non-profit and governmental organisations. *Non-Profit and Voluntary Sector Quarterly*, 29(1), 183–204.

Moss, T.W., Short, J.C., Payne, G.T. and Lumpkin, G.T. (2011). Dual identities in social ventures: An exploratory study. *Entrepreneurship Theory and Practice*, 35(4), 805–830.

Pache, A.C. and Santos, F. (2013). Inside the hybrid organisation: Selective coupling as a response to competing institutional logics. *Academy of Management Journal*, 56(40), 972–1001.

Phillips, N., Tracey, P. and Jarvis, O. (2011). Bridging institutional entrepreneurship and the creation of new organisational forms: A multilevel model. *Organisation Science*, 22(1), 60–80.

Ridley-Duff, R. and Bull, M. (2011). *Conceptualizing Social Enterprise: Theory and Practice*. London: SAGE.

Santos, F.M. (2012). A positive theory of social entrepreneurship. *Journal of Business Ethics*, 111(3), 335–351.

Seelos, C. and Mair, J. (2005). Social entrepreneurship: Creating new business models to serve the poor. *Business Horizons*, 48(3), 241–246.

Short, J.C., Moss, T.W. and Lumpkin, G.T. (2009). Research in social entrepreneurship: Past contributions and future opportunities. *Strategic Entrepreneurship Journal*, 3(2), 161–194.

Siciliano, J. (1997). The relationship between formal planning and performance in non-profit organisations. *Non-Profit Management and Leadership*, 7(4), 387–403.

Smith, B.R., Cronley, M.L. and Barr, T.F. (2012). Funding implications of social enterprise: The role of mission consistency, entrepreneurial competence and attitude toward social enterprise donor behaviour. *Journal of Public Policy and Marketing*, 31(1), 142–157.

Smith, B.R., Knapp, J., Barr, T.F., Stevens, C.E. and Cannatelli, B. (2010). Social enterprises and the timing of conception: Organisational identity tension, management and marketing. *Journal of Non Profit and Public Sector Marketing*, 22(2), 108–134.

Smith, W.K., Besharov, M., Wessels, A. and Chertok, M. (2012). A paradoxical leadership model for social entrepreneurs: Challenges, leadership skills, and pedagogical tools for managing social and commercial demands. *Academy of Management Learning and Education*, 11(3), 463–478.

Smith, W.K, Gonin, M. and Besharov, M.L. (2013). Managing social–business tensions: A review and research agenda. *Business Ethics Quarterly*, 23(3), 407–442.

Somerville, P. and McElwee, G. (2011). Situating community enterprise: A theoretical explanation. *Entrepreneurship and Regional Development*, 23(5/6), 317–330.

Sonnino, R. and Griggs-Trevarthen, C. (2013). A resilient social economy? Insights from the community food sector in the UK. *Entrepreneurship and Regional Development*, 25(3/4), 272–292.

Stevens, R., Moray, N. and Bruneel, J. (2015). The social and economic mission of social enterprises: Dimensions, measurement, validation and relation. *Entrepreneurship Theory and Practice*, 39(5), 1051–1082.

Stone, M.M., Bigelow, B. and Crittenden, W. (1999). Research on strategic management in non-profit organisations: Synthesis, analysis and future directions. *Administration and Society*, 31(3), 378–423.

Teasdale, S. (2012). Negotiating tensions: How do social enterprises in the homelessness field balance social and commercial tensions? *Housing Studies*, 27(4), 514–532.

Tracey, P. and Jarvis, O. (2007). Toward a theory of social venture franchising. *Entrepreneurship Theory and Practice*, 31(5), 668–685.

Vickers, I. and Lyon, F. (2013). Beyond green niches? Growth strategies of environmentally-motivated social enterprises. *International Small Business Journal*, 32(4), 449–470.

Wilson, F. and Post, J.E. (2013). Business models for people, planet (and profit): Exploring the phenomena of social business, a market-based approach to social value creation. *Small Business Economics*, 40(3), 715–737.

Zahra, S.A., Gedajlovic, E., Neubaum, D.O. and Shulman, J.M. (2009). A typology of social entrepreneurs: Motives, search processes and ethical challenges. *Journal of Business Venturing*, 24(5), 519–532.

Zuckerman, E. (1999). The categorical imperative: Securities analysts and the illegitimacy discount. *American Journal of Sociology*, 104(5), 1398–1438.

15. Increasing social impact among social enterprises and traditional firms

Elena Dowin Kennedy, Erynn Beaton and Nardia Haigh

INTRODUCTION

Social enterprises have developed unique governance structures and practices to balance the needs of beneficiaries, communities, employees, shareholders and funders, while also balancing their own dual social–business objectives (Ebrahim et al., 2014). They may therefore offer insights into how traditional firms (that is, regular for-profit companies) as well as other social enterprises might better complement positive financial returns with positive social impacts. Conversely, the well-established body of corporate governance knowledge that guides traditional firms may also benefit social enterprises. In this chapter, we utilise studies of corporate governance practices among traditional firms (and where possible, social enterprises) to identify common corporate governance issues and practices to answer the question: how might social enterprises and traditional firms increase their social impact through governance practices?

We draw on three bodies of literature: on corporate governance, hybrid organisations and social enterprises. We briefly review relevant key concepts of these literatures below, before outlining the structure of the chapter, and reviewing the literatures in more detail in the body of the chapter as we undertake our analysis.

Corporate Governance

Corporate governance is a well-established field of scholarship and practice with the goal of addressing the agency relationship between executives and shareholders, and its practice has progressed to a point where international principles have been established (and are updated periodically) by the Organisation for Economic Co-operation and Development (OECD) (G20 and OECD, 2015). We adopt the OECD's broad definition of corporate governance, and utilise its principles to frame our analysis:

> Corporate governance involves a set of relationships between a company's management, its board, its shareholders and other stakeholders. Corporate governance also provides the structure through which the objectives of the company are set, and the means of attaining those objectives and monitoring performance are determined. (ibid., p. 9)

Historically, corporate governance has been viewed through the lens of economic theories – commonly, agency theory – which assume self-interest (Jensen and Meckling, 1976), thus corporate governance structures were established to protect the interests of owners, while impacts upon other stakeholders, such as communities, vulnerable people and nature, were considered externalities. However, over time, corporate sustainability efforts and calls for transparency have driven corporate governance to include a broader set of stakeholders (Freeman and Reed, 1983; Kolk, 2008), and the two are increasingly related.

Corporate sustainability describes strategies to engage positively with society and nature (Haigh and Hoffman, 2014). Evidence of the rising importance of corporate sustainability to corporate governance includes the expansion of corporate governance codes to emphasise social and environmental responsibility (Money and Schepers, 2007; Ayuso et al., 2014), combining or complementing corporate governance and corporate sustainability mechanisms (Harjoto and Jo, 2011), and the correlation of favourable corporate governance ratings with corporate sustainability disclosures (Chan et al., 2014). The rise in the importance of corporate sustainability to corporate governance demonstrates that firms are motivated to create positive social impacts, but also challenges the self-interest assumption. This has led the current landscape to be described as:

> polarized between a shareholder perspective and a stakeholder perspective . . . On one side is the traditional shareholding model that regards the corporation as a legal instrument for shareholders to maximize their own interests . . . On the other side is the relatively new stakeholding approach that views the corporation as a locus of responsibility in relation to wider stakeholders' interests rather than merely in relation to shareholders' wealth. (Ayuso et al., 2014, p. 415)

The turn of corporate governance toward corporate sustainability, and its corresponding social–business duality, demonstrate the competing perspectives, principles and logics that exist within organisations, and which have led over recent decades to the emergence of literature examining organisational 'hybridity' and 'hybrid organisations'.

The Constellation of Hybrid Organisations

Hybrid organisations have been defined as: 'organisations that possess "significant" characteristics of more than one sector (public, private and third)' (Billis, 2010a, p. 3). They include public–private organisations such as Fannie Mae, private–third sector organisations such as the John Lewis Partnership, and public–third sector organisations such as the National Health Service (NHS) Foundation Trusts in England (Billis, 2010b). The literature on organisational hybridity is significant and growing and increasingly represents the inherent complexity of hybrid organisations. To date, significant contributions in this literature have included detailed historical accounts and definitions of hybrid organisations (Billis, 2010b; Seibel, 2015), the relevance of hybridisation to specific sectors (Billis, 2010a; Cabral et al., 2010; Heijden, 2011; McDermott et al., 2015; York et al., 2016) and changing forms of hybrid organisations (Haigh et al., 2015). Other key contributions include illuminating the ways in which hybrids experience and manage tensions between different institutional logics or different stakeholder demands (Besharov and Smith, 2014; Battilana et al., 2015), and the potential consequences of not managing those tensions well enough, such as drifting away from one set of stakeholder demands to meet others (Battilana et al., 2012; Jay, 2013; Pache and Santos, 2013; Gras and Mendoza-Abarca, 2014). Some have also provided critical insights into the potential for hybrid organising to have a dark side that may see hybrid organisations undermine third sector organisations (Dart, 2004), or examine how hybrids might address the symptoms of social issues rather than their underlying societal, policy or other causes (Westley and Antadze, 2010; Jáuregui Casanueva, 2013). Finally, there is a budding interest in the governance of hybrid organisations (Ebrahim et al., 2013; Mair et al., 2015), to which this chapter contributes.

As is evident in the work cited above, many of these topics are examined in this *Handbook*. The ownership, governance, priorities and resources of hybrid organisations are also explained in Billis's (2010b) theory of hybrid organisations, which defines the 'hybrid zones' that form as organisations blend the three sectors of society. For the purposes of this chapter, we are concerned with hybrids in the private–third zone between traditional for-profit firms and third sector organisations, which is where social enterprises reside.

Social Enterprise

Social enterprises are a type of hybrid organisation (Billis, 2010a) that sit within the 'polarised' landscape outlined above by Ayuso et al. (2014), where the needs of a broad group of stakeholders need to be balanced. Scholars have sometimes struggled to clearly and consistently define social enterprises (Dacin et al., 2011), and others have argued that social enterprise remains a contested concept (Choi and Majumdar, 2014). Doherty et al. (2014, p. 417) found that 'pursuit of the dual mission of financial sustainability and social purpose' was the 'defining characteristic' of social enterprises, and we adopt this as a basic definition, while focusing on for-profit social enterprises. Figure 15.1 illustrates the position of the social enterprises upon which we focus within the broader constellation of hybrid organisations.

Despite definitional issues, there is one thing upon which authors (and we) have a consensus, which is that their main goal is to create positive social impact (Dacin et al., 2010; Santos, 2012). Social enterprises complement practices associated with traditional for-profit firms (for example, selling goods and services) with practices associated with

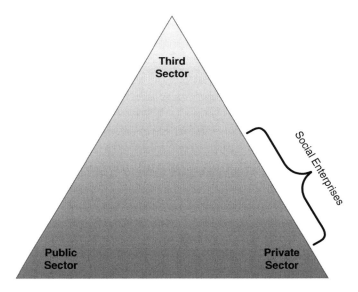

Figure 15.1   Social enterprises within the constellation of hybrids

third sector organisations (for example, employing the homeless, or providing subsidised or free goods and services) to meet social impact and business goals (Battilana et al., 2012; Gidron and Hasenfeld, 2012). Social impact refers to 'the societal and environmental changes created by activities and investments' (Epstein and Yuthas, 2014, p. 15), and social enterprises have sought to create a wide range of social impacts such as improving livelihoods, health and nutrition (Desa and Koch, 2014; Ebrahim and Rangan, 2014).

Like the growing collection of work on hybrid organisations, there is a burgeoning literature on social enterprises (some of which is found in this *Handbook*) addressing topics such as their emergence (Gidron and Hasenfeld, 2012; Kickul and Lyons, 2012) and evolution (Millar, 2012), and their relationship to hybrid organisations and organisational theory (Battilana and Lee, 2014). Other work examines the nature of social entrepreneurs and their founding of social enterprises (Santos, 2012), and ways in which strategies are developed (Joldersma and Winter, 2002) and resources managed (Doherty et al., 2014) through business models designed to solve social issues through commerce (Wilson and Post, 2013). Social enterprise literature has sought to understand how they are managed and how they juggle the demands of competing goals (Battilana et al., 2015; Hockerts, 2015), the solutions they provide, and their potential to create negative as well as positive impacts (Ridley-Duff and Bull, 2011; Gidron and Hasenfeld, 2012; Kickul and Lyons, 2012). There is also a growing focus on examining how social enterprises measure social impact (Bagnoli and Megali, 2009; Cooney and Lynch-Cerullo, 2014).

The private and third sector practices that social enterprises mix are often chosen based on the operating environment and the founder's background (Pache and Santos, 2013), which means that social enterprises are often designed without clear models to follow, and social entrepreneurs are often left to make operational decisions with little understanding of best or even effective practices (Battilana et al., 2012). This is particularly true in the case of social enterprise governance practices, where with few exceptions (e.g., Ebrahim et al., 2014; Larner and Mason, 2014) there is a dearth of research, and it is our hope to begin to remedy this situation.

Summary and Guide to the Chapter

To answer our guiding question about how social enterprises and traditional firms might increase their social impact through corporate governance practices, we compare the corporate governance practices of social enterprise and traditional firms on each of the OECD's six corporate governance principles (G20 and OECD, 2015). Social enterprises are a recent addition to the corporate governance literature and little is published about their corporate governance practices compared to what is known about the practices of traditional firms; therefore, we proceed knowing the risk of not being able to develop a perfect answer to our question. However, we feel that it is a worthy pursuit, and in lieu of sufficient literature on social enterprise governance, we draw on 14 examples of social enterprises to provide examples of social enterprise governance practices.

Based on our comparison of corporate governance practices among traditional firms and social enterprises, we develop hypotheses about specific practices that could enhance social impact, such as seeking out socially responsible investors and adopting a broad definition of stakeholders. These hypotheses may serve as practical advice, or as the basis for studying how corporate governance practices affect social impact. Our analysis reveals that traditional firms would likely increase their social impact were they to adopt social enterprise governance practices, and that both traditional firms and social enterprises would likely increase their social impact were they to adhere more strictly to OECD corporate governance principles. We also suggest changes to wording of the OECD corporate governance principles that would further support increased social impact by both social enterprises and traditional firms. In what follows, we first explain our selection of social enterprise examples, then review social enterprise and traditional firm practices in relation to each OECD principle, and finally discuss our results and draw conclusions.

SELECTING SOCIAL ENTERPRISE EXEMPLAR CASES

Social enterprises are somewhat difficult to study, because there is no single register or database of them (Bromberger, 2011; Haigh et al., 2015). However, an increasing number of social enterprises are becoming certified by B Lab (a non-profit that certifies companies as 'B Corporations' or 'B Corps'; B Lab, 2016). With a dearth of literature on the governance practices of social enterprises and the lack of a register of them, we selected our examples from those certified by B Lab. To become a certified B Corp, companies must complete the B Lab Impact Assessment and achieve a minimum score across five 'impact areas', which are defined in Figure 15.2.

One of the greatest current challenges in social enterprise literature is measuring social impact, because impact often occurs long after the exchange between social enterprise and beneficiary, and can be reliant on a constellation of other factors in addition to the social enterprise's work (Dowin Kennedy, 2016). Comparing impacts across social enterprises is even more complicated because of their unique missions and theories of

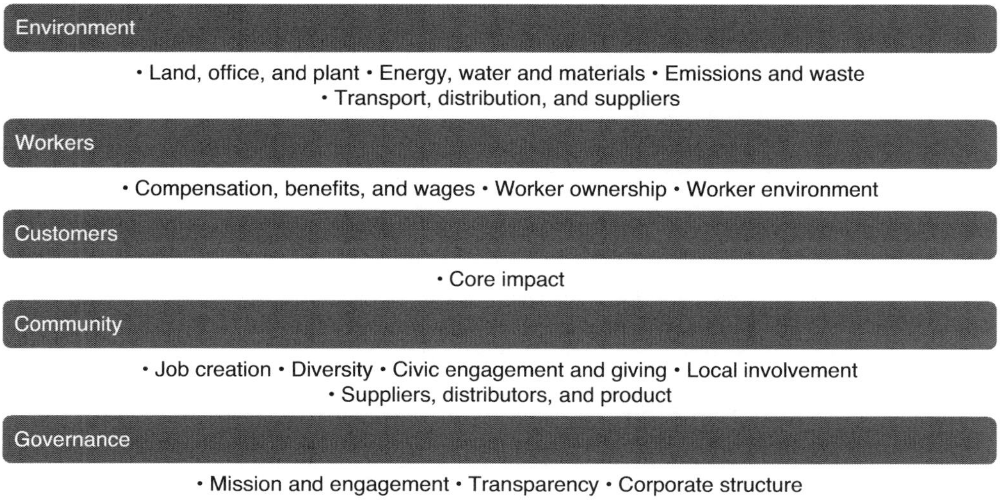

Environment
· Land, office, and plant · Energy, water and materials · Emissions and waste
· Transport, distribution, and suppliers

Workers
· Compensation, benefits, and wages · Worker ownership · Worker environment

Customers
· Core impact

Community
· Job creation · Diversity · Civic engagement and giving · Local involvement
· Suppliers, distributors, and product

Governance
· Mission and engagement · Transparency · Corporate structure

Source: Adapted from Honeyman (2014).

Figure 15.2 B-Lab impact area descriptions

change (Kickul and Lyons, 2012). The B Lab Impact Assessment tracks, verifies and allows for comparison between firms, sectors and social missions across a standardised list of social impact metrics for B Lab's five impact areas (Honeyman, 2014). Given the rigour of the B Lab assessment, we believe that certified B Corps can legitimately be called social enterprises.

In search of social enterprises with model governance practices, we chose a theoretical sample of certified B Corporations that scored above average on their Impact Assessment (cases were selected and data collected in January 2016). We assumed these companies might be more likely to have publicly available data even if privately held, which would be advantageous from a data collection standpoint. We compiled information about the companies from B Lab (www.BCorporation.net), company websites, annual reports, press releases, media coverage, and company and analyst databases such as Morningstar, Bloomberg and PrivCo. Our examples range in age and mission, and many are considered pioneers of the social enterprise field. Some have championed social enterprise business models, become early adopters of new legal categories and innovative legal structures, or have created strong employee ownership plans. Table 15.1 provides a brief overview of these organisations.

CORPORATE PRINCIPLES, COMMON ISSUES, AND SOCIAL ENTERPRISE PRACTICES

Table 15.2 details corporate governance principles as set out by the OECD. While these principles were developed by an international agency for application at the country level, each can readily de scaled down to the level of the firm. In each section below we introduce an OECD corporate governance principle and then highlight a common issue found from research on traditional firms. Then, drawing from social enterprise literature (where available) and our examples, we examine social enterprise practices in relation to the issue. We use the practices of traditional firms and social enterprises to identify hypotheses about how they both might enhance their social impact.

Principle 1: Ensuring the Basis for an Effective Corporate Governance Framework

The OECD encourages an effective legal framework that supports an efficient and transparent market and corporate governance frameworks that are lawful and fair (G20 and OECD, 2015). This overarching principle is primarily concerned with controlling the principal–agent relationship to ensure shareholders' interests are protected through profit maximisation (Jensen and Meckling, 1976; Daily et al., 2003).

Social missions and legal jeopardy

While effective corporate governance frameworks enhance a firm's social performance (Kolk, 2008; Ntim and Soobaroyen, 2013), under many current frameworks the pursuit of a social mission can lead to legal issues, as Bromberger (2011) notes: 'For-profit businesses have a fiduciary duty to maximise shareholder return, and if pursuit of a social mission interferes with the primary duty, the directors and officers can face legal jeopardy' (Bromberger, 2011, p. 50).

Table 15.1   Social enterprise examples

Social enterprise	Social impact initiatives
Ben & Jerry's	Opposes the use of recombinant bovine growth hormone. Promotes community development, fair trade, lesbian, gay, bisexual and transgender (LGBT) equality, and genetically modified organisation (GMO) labelling.
Cabot Creamery	Promotes local ownership, fair wage employment, and sustainable agriculture.
Dansko	Promotes environmental restoration, helping underprivileged community members and employee ownership.
Etsy	Supports local economies by helping local craft people reach a global audience.
Greyston Bakery	Provides employment for people with a history of incarceration, substance abuse or homelessness.
King Arthur Flour	Provides a living wage and health care benefits for all employees. Promotes local environmental sustainability through recycling, composting, energy efficiency. Supports communities through paid employee volunteerism.
Klean Kanteen	Committed to responsible sourcing, ethical production, waste minimisation and environmental preservation.
method	Committed to sourcing from green suppliers, utilizing renewable energy, and converting its fleet to biodiesel.
New Belgium Brewing Co.	Committed to reducing carbon emissions, waste and water use. Awards grants to non-profits relating to youth environmental education, sustainable agriculture, bike advocacy and water stewardship.
Numi Organic Tea	Promotes fair labour practices, direct sourcing and environmental sustainability. Foundation funds a global awareness curriculum, community development and clean water sourcing in developing countries.
Patagonia	Committed to environmental health, fair trade and waste reduction.
Seventh Generation	Develops cleaning products that are safer and healthier for people, their pets and their homes. Committed to increasing corporate transparency in the cleaning industry.
The Honest Company	Develops non-toxic, eco-friendly diapers, cleaning, feeding and personal care products. Funds research into and education about the healthy development of children, nutrition and youth skills training.
Warby Parker	Committed to improving the accessibility and affordability of prescription eyewear for all.

All firms potentially face legal jeopardy if pursuing social initiatives that do not maximise shareholder return; however, the overt dual social–business goals to which for-profit social enterprises subscribe that lead them to develop governance structures described as 'stewardship' or 'social welfare' approaches (Low, 2006; Mason et al., 2007; Peattie and Morley, 2008) can leave them vulnerable when viewed through a shareholder maximisation lens. The legal jeopardy faced by social enterprises has led to the development of two solutions that enable the pursuit of dual social–business goals without legal risk. One response has been to lobby for new legislation, and the other to create mixed-entity social enterprises. We discuss each below.

Table 15.2   OECD principles of corporate governance

Principle	Details
Ensuring the basis for an effective corporate governance framework	'The corporate governance framework should promote transparent and fair markets, and the efficient allocation of resources. It should be consistent with the rule of law and support effective supervision and enforcement' (G20 and OECD, 2015, p. 13)
The rights and equitable treatment of shareholders and key ownership functions	'The corporate governance framework should protect and facilitate the exercise of shareholders' rights and ensure the equitable treatment of all shareholders, including minority and foreign shareholders. All shareholders should have the opportunity to obtain effective redress for violation of their rights' (G20 and OECD, 2015, p. 19)
Institutional investors, stock markets and other intermediaries	'The corporate governance framework should provide sound incentives throughout the investment chain and provide for stock markets to function in a way that contributes to good corporate governance' (G20 and OECD, 2015, p. 31)
The role of stakeholders in corporate governance	'The corporate governance framework should recognise the rights of stakeholders established by law or through mutual agreements and encourage active co-operation between corporations and stakeholders in creating wealth, jobs, and the sustainability of financially sound enterprises' (G20 and OECD, 2015, p. 37)
Disclosure and transparency	'The corporate governance framework should ensure that timely and accurate disclosure is made on all material matters regarding the corporation, including the financial situation, performance, ownership, and governance of the company' (G20 and OECD, 2015, p. 41)
The responsibilities of the board	'The corporate governance framework should ensure the strategic guidance of the company, the effective monitoring of management by the board, and the board's accountability to the company and the shareholders' (G20 and OECD, 2015, p. 51)

Source: Adapted from G20 and OECD (2015).

Social enterprise inspired legislation protects the pursuit of a social mission
In response to social enterprise advocacy, new for-profit legal categories are being developed to protect firms with dual social–business goals. In the United States (US), many states have enacted new legal categories in response to pressure from entrepreneurs (Rawhouser et al., 2015). The new legal categories are variations of existing for-profits, such as the US-based categories public benefit corporation, benefit corporation, benefit limited liability company (benefit LLC), and L3C (low-profit LLC), and in the UK, the community interest company (CIC) designation. These new categories enable companies to pursue their social mission without fear of legal reprisal. For instance, benefit corporations 'must pursue a general public benefit (and may pursue a specific public benefit) in addition to profit' (Rawhouser et al., 2015, p. 16).

Several of our social enterprise examples changed their legal category to promote their commitment to social and environmental impacts. King Arthur Flour, Patagonia and method all became early adopters of new legal categories. By adopting the new category early, these companies protected their social and environmental commitments and paved the way for others considering the same. Given that effective corporate governance frameworks facilitate better social performance among traditional firms, new legal categories protecting the pursuit of social impacts may be useful to both social enterprises and traditional firms wanting to enhance their social impacts.

Mixed-entity social enterprises protect the pursuit of a social impact
For social enterprises registered in regions where new legislation is not available, or those that choose not to utilise it, creating a mixed-entity venture is another option. Mixed-entity social enterprises work around the limitations of traditional legal categories by maintaining independent for-profit and non-profit entities and linking the two through licensing or distribution contracts, ownership or donations (Haigh et al., 2015).

Four of our social enterprise examples had mixed-entity models, where the non-profit facilitated social commitments that were typically funded by the for-profit entity. Ben & Jerry's pursues a social mission focused on product excellence, sustainable financial growth and improving quality of life locally, nationally and globally. At the time of its initial stock offering in 1985, Ben & Jerry's created Ben & Jerry's Foundation and committed to it 7.5 per cent of the company's annual pre-tax profits. The foundation engages employees in philanthropy, supports Vermont communities, and aids social justice and grassroots organisations. Ben & Jerry's employees make grant decisions. This structure allows the foundation to support the social mission, while the company focuses on product excellence and sustainable financial growth.

Following the advent of new legal forms and mixed-entity structures to support the pursuit of dual social–business goals, we hypothesise that:

Hypothesis 1: Social enterprises and traditional firms will enhance their social impact if they adopt new legal forms or mixed-entity structures supporting dual social–business goals.

Principle 2: The Rights and Equitable Treatment of Shareholders and Key Ownership Functions

Owners of an enterprise influence the objectives of that enterprise, and ownership is determined by shareholding, of which there are different types (preference shares versus ordinary shares). Shareholders have differing amounts and types of shares, which can create inequity. In particular, shareholder votes are a powerful means of influencing firms (Bebchuk, 2005; Mallin and Melis, 2012). The OECD advocates for the protection and facilitation of shareholders' rights so that all shareholders are treated equitably (G20 and OECD, 2015). Studies of traditional firms have found that the ability of shareholders to vote or otherwise influence companies positively affects corporate performance: raising firm value, profits and sales growth, and reducing costs (Gompers et al., 2003).

The influence of ownership concentration
One particular issue that affects the equitable influence of shareholders is ownership concentration, which is defined by the number of large-block shareholders (those that own 5 per cent or more of the company's shares) and the percentage of shares they hold (Hitt et al., 2014). Ownership concentration may have positive or negative effects. Large-block shareholders are increasingly active in using their influence to mitigate

managerial self-interest (Goranova et al., 2010) and can promote stronger monitoring controls (for example, avoiding overdiversification) (Connelly et al., 2010). However, large-block shareholders can also expropriate the value of minority shareholders (Morck et al., 1988).

Social enterprises are open to the same positive and negative effects of concentrated ownership experienced by traditional firms. However, in addition to its effects on goals and the value of minority shareholdings, concentrated ownership also creates more potential for social enterprises to be pulled further towards their desired social impacts (potentially risking financial viability) or, in the case of 'mission drift' (Smith et al., 2013), away from their social impacts in favour of increasing profits. As is the case with traditional firms, social enterprises maintain a variety of models of ownership (Laville and Nyssens, 2001), and this is reflected in our examples. Questions about ownership and the ability to maintain the social mission have been raised when a social enterprise is acquired or publicly listed. For instance, Ben & Jerry's was acquired as a wholly owned subsidiary of Unilever in 2001 amidst heated debate about whether the takeover would destroy its social mission (Austin and Leonard, 2008; Mirvis, 2008).

Social enterprises often choose privately held models

Twelve of our examples are privately held companies or co-ops, including two family-owned companies (Numi Tea, Patagonia) and three employee-owned companies (Dansko, King Arthur Flour, New Belgium Brewing). Although privately held companies that are controlled by a small group or one person have potential for ownership concentration problems (Morck et al., 1988; Bozec and Bozec, 2007), ownership concentration in our examples seem to be supporting their creation of positive social impacts without jeopardising their financial standing. Further, our three employee-owned examples are particularly interesting given their potential for increasing social impact.

Once thought of as a fringe movement, an increasing number of companies are becoming employee-owned, which has the potential for 'significant and positive impacts on employee well-being, employee wealth accumulation, firm productivity, and long-term firm stability and growth' (Carberry, 2011, p. 1). Employee well-being and wealth accumulation potentially create positive social impacts, and employee-owned companies are also argued to have greater commitment to the local community, and stand in opposition to income inequality (Honeyman, 2014). King Arthur Flour, Dansko and New Belgium Brewing Company all converted to become employee-owned. Typical of the transition, Dansko's founders created an employee stock ownership programme (ESOP) and sold their shares to the ESOP prior to retiring, which allowed Dansko to maintain its commitment to employees after the founders left. Having ownership concentrated in the employees can protect a company against takeovers and safeguard the interests of employees by giving them voting rights (Paranque and Willmott, 2014). In these respects, the employee-owned companies appear well positioned to make positive social impacts.

In sum, protecting shareholder rights by warding against the negative potential of ownership concentration and encouraging shareholder equity and engagement (with one option being employee ownership) not only correlate with better company performance, but also appear to have the potential to support the creation of positive social impacts for both social enterprises and traditional firms. This leads to hypothesis 2:

Hypothesis 2: Social enterprises and traditional firms will enhance their social impact if they encourage shareholder equity and engagement.

Principle 3: Institutional Investors, Stock Markets and Other Intermediaries

Institutional investors include pension funds, investment banks, mutual funds and other institutions that manage investments on behalf of clients. Institutional investors have recently replaced individuals as large-block shareholders, and are the major holders of publicly traded stock (Pozen, 2015). This OECD principle acknowledges the power held by institutional investors, and the importance of providing appropriate incentives throughout the investment chain to minimise conflicts of interest between investors voting in a fiduciary capacity and their clients who are the beneficial owners (G20 and OECD, 2015).

Short-termism among institutional investors

The pursuit of social impact requires patience and, although institutional investors carry the responsibility to grow their clients' wealth (Cheng et al., 2014), principal–agent issues are often present because institutional investors are influenced by managerial incentives prompting them to seek short-term gains (Lok, 2010) even though they are likely to underperform in the long term (Cheng et al., 2014) and are at odds with clients' goals (Opazo et al., 2015). Mutual funds and investment banks are particularly likely to take a short-term view of their investments (Johnson and Greening, 1999), as are pension funds (Opazo et al., 2015), while venture capitalists have been shown to hold especially short-term horizons (Cadman and Sunder, 2014).

Short-termism is a problem for companies wanting to create positive social impacts because institutional investors with a short-term focus are less likely to support corporate sustainability efforts (Johnson and Greening, 1999). With the weight of their large stockholding, institutional investors can make corporate sustainability a priority, but in countries where short-term investing is common, they tend to have a negative impact on corporate sustainability outcomes (Aguilera et al., 2006).

In response to short-termism within the institutional investing world, there has been a steady rise in socially responsible investing (SRI) where institutional investors screen potential investments on the basis of performance on such issues as human rights, environmental management and social justice (Haigh and Hoffman, 2012; Hernandez and Hugger, 2016). In 2009, 12 per cent of US managed funds were invested according to SRI principles (US SIF, 2010) and in 2014 it was 17 per cent (Hernandez and Hugger, 2016).

Social enterprises seek impact investors to curb short-termism and facilitate social impact

More closely related to social enterprises, SRI is known as the parent of 'impact investing', a trend where investors screen potential investments with the intent of investing in companies aiming to make a particular social or environmental impact as well as gaining financial returns (Hernandez and Hugger, 2016). Impact investors are important for social enterprises, because they provide 'patient capital' or 'below market-rate' financing to facilitate long-term growth and social impact goals, and they understand that longer time horizons are needed to create sustainable social impacts (Kickul and Lyons, 2012).

Several of our social enterprise examples avoided institutional investors (or ensured they had only minority interests), or sought SRI and/or impact investor capital. One example is Numi Organic Tea, which accepted venture capital from Triple Bottom Line Capital. Upon receiving funding, chief executive officer (CEO) and co-founder Ahmed Rahim stated publicly that he was happy to be in partnership with Triple Bottom Line Capital because of its understanding of the Numi business model and agreement with the prioritisation of Numi's social objectives. Founders such as Ahmed Rahim have made concerted efforts toward raising capital only from impact investors.

Research suggesting that traditional institutional investors are more likely to suffer short-termism and be less likely to implement significant corporate sustainability measures (Johnson and Greening, 1999; Aguilera et al., 2006), the rise of SRI and impact investing, and social enterprises such as Numi that take on only investors that are supportive of their social goals lead us to hypothesise:

Hypothesis 3: Social enterprises and traditional firms have the potential to enhance their social impact if they are able to attract SRI or impact investors.

Principle 4: The Role of Stakeholders in Corporate Governance

Stakeholder groups are often defined by the economic function they play within organisations, such as customers, employees and suppliers (White, 2009; Crane and Ruebottom, 2011), and this OECD principle places merit on the participation of (predominantly economic) stakeholders in governance structures. The dominant historical perspective is one of placing shareholders as the top priority because managers have a fiduciary duty to maximise shareholder return (Bromberger, 2011). It has been argued that expanding to a broader definition of stakeholders would increase the demands on already limited resources, and create conflicting claims between social and economic stakeholders (Smith et al., 2013) which will reduce margins, and result in firms avoiding conflict by manipulating stakeholders (Fiss and Zajac, 2006).

However, the expansion of corporate governance mechanisms to include social and environmental responsibility signals an expanding definition of stakeholders. Stakeholder theorists argue that managers are accountable to a wide range of groups that may be affected by the actions of a firm (Freeman, 1984), with some arguing that stakeholders include groups not traditionally recognised as having an economic function (Haigh and Griffiths, 2009).

Social enterprises often define stakeholders broadly

It is common for social enterprises to define stakeholders broadly to include both economic and non-economic actors and even to design their business models around alleviating particular issues faced by communities or other beneficiaries (Miller et al., 2012). The legal forms noted earlier are often chosen by social enterprises because they explicitly require the board to define stakeholders broadly (Ebrahim et al., 2014).

Social enterprises employ a variety of mechanisms to include a broad range of stakeholders within governance practices (Larner and Mason, 2014). One mechanism consistent across all our social enterprise examples is online stakeholder feedback. For instance, The Honest Company encourages stakeholder feedback – through a phone line, online contact form and live chat – not only about its products and marketing but also about its 'social goodness'. In addition, many of our examples prioritise employees as decision-makers (for example, among the employee-owned firms) or as recipients of programmes to address employee priorities in others. Utilising stakeholder knowledge on dedicated boards, such as Greyston Bakery's Wisdom Council, were also important practices that increased stakeholder voices.

The inclusion of a broad range of stakeholders within governance mechanisms, the design of models to assist people not traditionally viewed as stakeholders, and the propensity to ensure that many stakeholders have a voice, all suggest that going beyond a narrow view of stakeholders will support the creation of positive social impacts; prompting us to hypothesise:

Hypothesis 4: Social enterprises and traditional firms will enhance their social impact if they define stakeholders broadly and engage with all stakeholders.

Principle 5: Disclosure and Transparency

Information asymmetries between managers and stakeholders can cause governance breakdowns because, in order for owners, intermediaries and other stakeholders to participate in governance, they must have knowledge of a firm's position, strategies and operations (Healy and Palepu, 2001). This OECD principle addresses the need for companies to be transparent in communicating material information, such as financial results, objectives, the identity of major shareholders, the names of board members and any other information that would affect stakeholder decisions. Disclosing results also has the effect of making companies accountable for their impacts on stakeholders, and exposing them to normative responses. The OECD advocates that some of this information (for example, financial results) should be independently audited, and that all material information should be accessible and updated regularly (G20 and OECD, 2015).

Selective disclosure and disclosure timing

In most countries, there are regulations that ensure a minimum level of transparency. However, even where transparency is regulated, firms vary widely in the information they disclose and some fail to comply with regulation. For instance, one study of firms in Central and Eastern Europe found many firms were not meeting minimum reporting requirements due to a lack of enforcement (Berglöf and Pajuste, 2005). Other motivations for evading transparency include the costs associated with reporting and fear of transparency negatively affecting firm value (Healy and Palepu, 2001).

When corporations do make disclosures, research suggests that it can be for instrumental, even manipulative, purposes (Healy and Palepu, 2001). For instance, executives have been found to purposefully disclose voluntary information about six months prior to a stock offering to 'hype the stock' (Lang and Lundholm, 2000) and use disclosures for personal advantage when stock option compensation awards are imminent (Aboody and Kasznik, 2000).

Reporting on social and environmental impacts has become a widespread practice, and many companies produce corporate sustainability or corporate social responsibility reports, or report through the Carbon Disclosure Project (2017) and/or the Global

Reporting Initiative (2016). However, the same issues surrounding selective disclosure and timing of disclosures may apply to these companies, as suggested by a study by Dhaliwal et al. (2011) that found corporate sustainability reports are published in anticipation that they will reduce the cost of capital.

Social enterprises also practice selective disclosure

Although many of the social enterprises we examined were not legally required to report their financial or sustainability results due to being privately held, they all stated significant social or environmental impact goals, so it is difficult to rule out the likelihood of selective reporting among them. Only three of our example social enterprises voluntarily disclosed financial information on an ongoing basis, and sustainability reporting ranged from thorough to product-based information and basic infographics summarising sustainability measures. Even fewer of our examples voluntarily disclosed financial and social impact information on a regular basis, which inhibits the ability of stakeholders to determine their progress on dual social–business goals. Our examples reported information to varying degrees in sustainability reports, on their webpage or through the Global Reporting Initiative. For instance, Greyston Bakery provides a summary of its audited financial statements showing total sales and expenses; the New Belgian Brewing Company produces a short annual reflection on achievements and lessons related to sustainability; Numi Organic Tea prints an eco-responsibility audit on the bottom panel of each product in lieu of publishing a company sustainability report; and Cabot Creamery assesses its sustainability according to its own sustainability index but does not produce a report.

From our review of the literature and examination of examples, it appears that both social enterprises and traditional firms might increase their social impact if they disclosed more material information. Given that disclosing sustainability results appears to have a positive impact on how businesses are perceived among investors, and that social enterprises focus on making a social impact, we expected more transparency among them, even though disclosing more information on negative impacts would mean exposure to negative responses and influence from stakeholders. In sum, our examination emphasises the OECD's argument that all companies need to be transparent in disclosing material information to benefit stakeholder decision-making, and we hypothesise that such transparency will also increase social impacts:

Hypothesis 5: Social enterprises and traditional firms will enhance their social impact if they are more transparent in disclosing material information.

Principle 6: The Responsibilities of the Board

Boards provide an interface between corporations, their owners and their external environment, and play a crucial role in corporate governance (Ebrahim et al., 2014). Leading up to the 1980s there was concern that CEOs were acting in their own self-interest and running firms as personal empires rather than acting as agents of the owners (Lok, 2010). Today, the oversight of executives and their performance is a primary responsibility of the board, and this OECD principle advocates for a board that monitors executives while being accountable to shareholders (G20 and OECD, 2015). An inefficient board can be 'costly to companies and, in turn, to society as a whole' (de Andres et al., 2005, p. 197), and boards have begun to supervise corporate sustainability responsibilities such as environmental regulatory compliance, ethics issues and external verification of sustainability performance (Kolk, 2008).

Lack of board independence: insiders versus outsiders, and CEOs serving as chair

One governance issue that garners much attention is lack of board independence. To fulfil their duties, boards 'must be able to exercise objective and independent judgement' (G20 and OECD, 2015, p. 51). Board independence focuses both on the degree to which the board is composed of internal (insiders) versus external (outsiders/independent) members, and the relationship of the CEO to the board. Board reform research has suggested that having independent board members and ensuring that different people serve in CEO and chairperson positions can ensure that stakeholder interests are met (Shipilov et al., 2010).

On the point of insiders versus outsiders, Baysinger and Butler (1985) found that a mix of insiders, outsiders and expert specialists (lawyers, financiers and consultants) performs best for the interests of shareholders, and that having at least one outsider is necessary for the board to be effective. A board with insiders and outsiders also increases corporate sustainability performance (Johnson and Greening, 1999), which suggests that addressing board independence would support the creation of positive social impacts.

Social enterprises often have outsiders on their boards

Like the boards of traditional firms, a good social enterprise board is said to include representation from multiple stakeholders (Spear et al., 2009) and broad expertise (Below and Tripp, 2010). Social enterprise boards are accountable for dual social–business performance objectives, so it is important that members have a strong understanding and commitment to both sets of goals. Typically, this entails being accountable to multiple stakeholders, such as investors, funders and beneficiaries (Ebrahim et al., 2014).

Most of our social enterprise examples showed a commitment to board independence and had more than one outsider on the board, with many having multiple outsiders. Many of our examples also reported that their boards were composed of members from 'previously excluded populations' or 'underrepresented populations'. For example, Greyston Bakery's management and board has over 40 per cent representation of people from previously excluded populations including women, minorities and individuals with barriers to employment. The board has also elected members with significant ties to community organisations in Yonkers, New York (where it is headquartered), such as the Yonkers Council of Parent Teacher Association and the Westchester County Board of Legislators, to ensure the community's needs influence decision-making. Ben & Jerry's sought to maintain an independent board of directors following its acquisition by Unilever. The board has a number of members with expertise in community development, environmental activism and impact investing, in addition to those with financial and industry expertise. These measures appear to hold much potential for positive social impacts.

Social enterprise CEOs sometimes serve as chairperson

Having the same person occupy both the CEO and the chairperson positions undermines the agency relationship by enabling CEOs to leverage information asymmetries for their self-interest (Joseph et al., 2014). Having different individuals in CEO and chairperson positions distributes power and allows the board to oversee CEO conduct and provide regular performance reviews (Lipton and Lorsch, 1992). Among our example social enterprises, it was common for the CEO to sit on the board (at least seven companies, according to available information). In three of our examples (Dansko, Etsy and Klean Kanteen) the CEO also served as chairperson, which places pressure on the agency relationship and requires a well-chosen leader who is competent at meeting dual social–business objectives.

In summary, it appears that social enterprises address the issue of lacking board independence to some degree (by having outsiders on the board), but (as is the case among traditional firms) there is room for improvement in relation to having different people serve in CEO and chairperson positions. Given prior research which indicates that appropriately structured boards can increase sustainability performance and our observations that some social enterprises could improve their board independence, we hypothesise that:

Hypothesis 6: Social enterprises and traditional firms will enhance their social impact if they structure their boards with a balance of insiders and outsiders and refrain from having the CEO simultaneously serve as chairperson.

DISCUSSION AND CONCLUDING REMARKS

In this chapter, we have used the OECD principles of corporate governance as a backdrop for identifying common corporate governance issues among traditional firms and social enterprises, and their potential implications for social impact. We then developed a set of hypotheses suggesting governance practices that both traditional firms and social enterprises might adopt to enhance their social impact, or which scholars might use as a basis for studying such phenomena. Corporate governance practices have long been based on the assumption of self-interest; however, as sustainability has become more important to stakeholders, corporate governance has begun to evolve and we suggest that social enterprises may offer assistance in the evolution.

On one hand, social enterprises are designed to create positive social impacts, but on the other hand they are relatively new in contrast to traditional firms (and even in contrast to other hybrid organisations) and there is still much we do not know about them. We have shown how the literature on corporate governance, covering years of scholarly work, can add value for social enterprises; while traditional firms seeking to increase their social impact might benefit by adopting some of the new governance practices that social enterprises have developed. The OECD highlighted six principles of governance that we have explored through this chapter, leading to hypotheses suggesting what governance mechanisms social enterprises and traditional firms might adopt or change to enhance their social impact. Table 15.3 summarises our main points.

In our exploration, we revealed ways that traditional firms and social enterprises can enhance their social impact. In particular, social enterprises may further enhance their social impact by moderating their level of ownership concentration, by disclosing more material information, and by ensuring that they avoid having the CEO simultaneously serve as chairperson. Traditional firms may enhance their social impact by adopting new legal or mixed-entity forms, attracting socially responsible investors, defining stakeholders more broadly, and ensuring the representation of stakeholders on the board. Each of our

Table 15.3 Practices to enhance social impact

OECD principles	Traditional corporate principles	Emerging social enterprise principles	Proposed practices to enhance social impact
Basic governance framework	Traditional corporate legal structure has a governance framework that controls principal–agent issues	New (and mixed entity) legal structures offer governance frameworks that protect dual social–business goals	**Adopt new legal forms or mixed entity social enterprise forms**
Treatment of shareholders	Ownership is increasingly concentrated in the hands of large-block shareholders	Ownership is concentrated in the hands of founders, and sometimes employees	**Encourage shareholder equity and engagement**
Investors	Institutional investors seek to influence strategic decision-making in the firm to protect their financial interests	Attract impact investment capital to avoid conflict between investor interests and social impact goals	**Seek to attract socially responsible investors**
Stakeholders	Recognise economic actors as primary stakeholders with an emphasis on the interests of shareholders	Acknowledge the interests of a broader group of stakeholders including community, beneficiaries and nature	**Adopt a broad view of stakeholders and actively engage them**
Disclosure and transparency	Engage legally required reporting and some selective voluntary reporting	Engage legally required reporting and some selective reporting	**Increase disclosure and transparency**
Board responsibilities	Common to have few outsiders, and for CEO to serve as chairperson	Common to have many outsiders, but also for CEO to serve as chairperson	**Have internal and external board members and avoid CEO being chairperson**

hypotheses suggests directions for future research into corporate governance for increased social impact, and testing them will ultimately reveal best practices for increasing social impact that are useful to each type of organisation.

Taken together, our examples and review of corporate governance literature for social enterprises and traditional firms have shown much room for improvement in governance practices to support dual social–business goals and, ultimately, social impact. We believe that continuing to improve the OECD principles would promote greater attention to creating positive social impacts. To that end, in Table 15.4 we suggest changes to wording that would enable the OECD principles to guide social enterprises and traditional firms as they continue to move toward creating positive social impacts. In Table 15.4 we have added underscoring to the text we would add in comparison to the existing OECD principles, and have added strikethroughs to text that we would delete from the existing principles.

In conclusion, the corporate governance literature has historically driven firms to maximise profits and define stakeholders narrowly. Our examination of social enterprises suggests there are stakeholder interests that firms can meet, and positive social impacts that firms can create, without jeopardising financial interests. There is still much to be

Table 15.4   Principles of corporate governance to enhance social impact

Principle	Details
Ensuring the basis for an effective corporate governance framework	The corporate governance framework should promote transparent and fair markets, and the efficient allocation of resources. It should be consistent with the rule of law, <u>improve society and nature,</u> and support effective supervision and enforcement.
The rights and equitable treatment of shareholders and key ownership functions	The corporate governance framework should protect and facilitate the exercise of shareholders' rights and ensure the equitable treatment of all shareholders, including minority and foreign shareholders. All shareholders should have the opportunity to obtain effective redress for violation of their rights.
Institutional investors, stock markets, and other intermediaries	The corporate governance framework should provide sound incentives throughout the investment chain and provide for stock markets to function in a way that contributes to good corporate governance, <u>society and nature.</u>
The role of stakeholders in corporate governance	The corporate governance framework should recognise the rights of stakeholder, <u>defined as any individual or group that can affect or is affected by the business (Freeman, 1984)</u> ~~established by law or through mutual agreements and encourage active co-operation between corporations and stakeholders in creating wealth, jobs, and the sustainability of financially sound enterprises.~~
Disclosure and transparency	The corporate governance framework should ensure that timely and accurate disclosure is made on all material matters regarding the corporation, including the financial situation, performance, ownership, <u>impacts on society and nature,</u> and governance of the company
The responsibilities of the board	The corporate governance framework should ensure the strategic guidance of the company, the effective monitoring of management by the board, and the board's accountability to the company and <u>its stakeholders</u> ~~the shareholders~~.

Source: Based on G20 and OECD (2015).

understood about social enterprise governance, and we suggest that social enterprises and traditional firms have much to learn from one another and from corporate governance principles. Ultimately, we hope that the literature will converge on principles of governance that will lead social enterprises and traditional firms to positive social impacts.

REFERENCES

Aboody, D. and R. Kasznik (2000). CEO stock option awards and the timing of corporate voluntary disclosures. *Journal of Accounting and Economics*, 29(1): 73–100.

Aguilera, R.V., C.A. Williams, J.M. Conley and D. Rupp (2006). Corporate governance and social responsibility: a comparative analysis of the UK and the US. *Corporate Governance: An International Review*, 14(3): 147–158.

Austin, J.E. and H.B.D. Leonard (2008). Can the virtuous mouse and the wealthy elephant live happily ever after? *California Management Review*, 51(1): 77–102.

Ayuso, S., M.A. Rodriguez, R. Garcia-Castro and M.A. Arino (2014). Maximizing stakeholders' interests: an empirical analysis of the stakeholder appoach to corporate governance. *Business and Society*, 53(3): 414–439.

B Lab (2016). Retrieved 3 January 2016, from http://bcorporation.net/.

Bagnoli, L. and C. Megali (2009). Measuring performance in social enterprises. *Nonprofit and Voluntary Sector Quarterly*, 40(1): 149–165.

Battilana, J. and M. Lee (2014). Advancing research on hybrid-organizing: insights from the study of social enterprises. *Academy of Management Annals*, 8(1): 397–441.

Battilana, J., M. Lee, J. Walker and C. Dorsey (2012). In search of the hybrid ideal. *Stanford Social Innovation Review*, 10: 51–55.

Battilana, J., M. Sengul, A.-C. Pache and J. Model (2015). Harnessing productive tensions in hybrid organizations: the case of work integration social enterprises. *Academy of Management Journal*, 58(6): 1658–1665.

Baysinger, B.D. and H.N. Butler (1985). Corporate governance and the board of directors: performance effects of changes in board composition. *Journal of Law, Economics, and Organization*, 1(1): 101–124.

Bebchuk, L. (2005). The case for increasing shareholder power. *Harvard Law Review*, 118(3): 835–914.

Below, C.L. and K.D. Tripp (2010). Freeing the social entrepreneur. *Stanford Social Innovation Review*, 8(4): 36–41.

Berglöf, E. and A. Pajuste (2005). What do firms disclose and why? Enforcing corporate governance and transparency in Central and Eastern Europe. *Oxford Review of Economic Policy*, 21(1): 178–197.

Besharov, M.L. and W.K. Smith (2014). Multiple institutional logics in organizations: explaining their varied nature and implications. *Academy of Management Review*, 39(3): 364–381.

Billis, D. (2010a). From welfare bureacracies to welfare hybrids. In *Hybrid Organizations and the Third Sector: Challenges for Practice, Theory, and Policy*. D. Billis (ed.). New York: Palgrave Macmillan, pp. 3–23.

Billis, D. (2010b). Towards a Theory of Hybrid Organizations. In *Hybrid Organizations and the Third Sector: Challenges for Practice, Theory, and Policy*. D. Billis (ed.). New York: Palgrave Macmillan, pp. 46–69.

Bozec, Y. and R. Bozec (2007). Ownership concentration and corporate governance practices: substitution or expropriation effects? *Canadian Journal of Administrative Sciences*, 24(3): 182–195.

Bromberger, A.R. (2011). A new type of hybrid. *Stanford Social Innovation Review*, 9: 49–53.

Cabral, S., S.G. Lazzarini and P.F. de Azevedo (2010). Private operation with public supervision: evidence of hybrid modes of governance in prisons. *Public Choice*, 145: 281–293.

Cadman, B. and J. Sunder (2014). Investor horizon and CEO horizon incentives. *Accounting Review*, 89(4): 1299–1328.

Carberry, E.J. (ed.) (2011). *Employee Ownership and Shared Capitalism: New Directions and Debates*. Ithaca, NY: Cornell University Press.

Carbon Disclosure Project (2017). CDP Open Data Portal. Carbon Disclosure Project. Retrieved 3 December 2017 from https://data.cdp.net/.

Chan, M., J. Watson and D. Woodliff (2014). Corporate governance quality and CSR disclosures. *Journal of Business Ethics*, 125(1): 59–73.

Cheng, L.-Y., M.-C. Wang and K.-C. Chen (2014). Institutional investment horizons and the stock performance of private equity placements: evidence from the Taiwanese listed firms. *Review of Pacific Basin Financial Markets and Policies*, 17(2): 1–30.

Choi, N. and S. Majumdar (2014). Social entrepreneurship as an essentially contested concept: opening a new avenue for systemic future research. *Journal of Business Venturing*, 29: 363–376.

Connelly, B.L., R.E. Hoskisson, L. Tihanyi and S.T. Certo (2010). Ownership as a form of corporate governance. *Journal of Management Studies*, 47(8): 1561–1589.

Cooney, K. and K. Lynch-Cerullo (2014). Measuring the social returns of nonprofits and social enterprises: the promise and perils of the SROI. *Nonprofit Policy Forum*, 5(2): 367–393.

Crane, A. and T. Ruebottom (2011). Stakeholder theory and social identity: rethinking stakeholder identification. *Journal of Business Ethics*, 102: 77–87.

Dacin, M.T., P.A. Dacin and P. Tracey (2011). Social entrepreneurship: a critique and future directions. *Organization Science*, 22(5): 1203–1213.

Dacin, P.A., M.T. Dacin and M. Matear (2010). Social entrepreneurship: why we don't need a new theory and how we move forward from here. *Academy of Management Perspective*, 24(3): 37–57.

Daily, C.M., D.R. Dalton and A.A. Cannella (2003). Corporate governance: decades of dialogue and data. *Academy of Management Review*, 28(3): 371–382.

Dart, R. (2004). The legitimacy of social enterprise. *Nonprofit Management and Leadership*, 14(4): 411–424.

de Andres, P., V. Azofra and F. Lopez (2005). Corporate boards in OECD countries: size, composition, functioning and effectiveness. *Corporate Governance: An International Review*, 13(2): 197–210.

Desa, G. and J.L. Koch (2014). Scaling social impact: building sustainable social ventures at the base-of-the-pyramid. *Journal of Social Entrepreneurship*, 5(2): 146–174.

Dhaliwal, D.S., O.Z. Li, A. Tsang and Y.G. Yang (2011). Voluntary nonfinancial disclosure and the cost of equity capital: the initiation of corporate social responsibility reporting. *Accounting Review*, 86(1): 59–100.

Doherty, B., H. Haugh and F. Lyon (2014). Social enterprises as hybrid organizations: a review and research agenda. *International Journal of Management Reviews*, 16(4): 417–436.

Dowin Kennedy, E. (2016). Positioning the beneficiary: the role of entwinement in social enterprise impact and performance management. College of Management, University of Massachusetts, Boston, MA.

Ebrahim, A. and V.K. Rangan (2014). What impact? A framework for measuring the scale and scope of social performance. *California Management Review*, 56(3): 118–141.

Ebrahim, A., J. Battilana and J. Mair (2013). Neither fish nor flesh: governance challenges within hybrid organizations. Unpublished working paper, Harvard Business School.

Ebrahim, A., J. Battilana and J. Mair (2014). The governance of social enterprises: mission drift and accountability challenges in hybrid organizations. *Research in Organizational Behavior*, 34: 81–100.

Epstein, M.J. and K. Yuthas (2014). *Measuring and Improving Social Impacts: A Guide for Nonprofits, Companies, and Impact Investors*. Abingdon: Greenleaf Publishing.

Fiss, P.C. and E.J. Zajac (2006). The symbolic management of strategic change: sensegiving via framing and decoupling. *Academy of Management Journal*, 49(6): 1173–1193.

Freeman, R.E. (1984). *Strategic Management: A Stakeholder Approach*. Boston, MA: Pitman.

Freeman, R.E. and D.L. Reed (1983). Stockholders and stakeholders: a new perspective on corporate governance. *California Management Review*, 25(3): 93–94.

G20 and OECD (2015). *Principles of Corporate Governance*. Ankara: OECD.

Gidron, B. and Y. Hasenfeld (eds) (2012). *Social Enterprises: An Organizational Perspective*. Houndmills: Palgrave Macmillan.

Global Reporting Initiative (2016). Sustainability Disclosure Database. Global Reporting Initiative. Retrieved 15 December 2017, from http://database.globalreporting.org/.

Gompers, P.A., J.L. Ishii and A. Metrick (2003). Corporate governance and equity prices. *Quarterly Journal of Economics*, 118(1): 107–155.

Goranova, M., R. Dharwadkar and P. Brandes (2010). Owners on both sides of the deal: mergers and acquisitions and overlapp. ing institutional ownership. *Strategic Management Journal*, 31(10): 1114–1135.

Gras, D. and K.I. Mendoza-Abarca (2014). Risky business? The survival implications of exploiting commercial opportunities by nonprofits. *Journal of Business Venturing*, 29(3): 392–404.

Haigh, N.L. and A. Griffiths (2009). The natural environment as primary stakeholder: the case of climate change. *Business Strategy and the Environment*, 18(6): 347–359.

Haigh, N. and A.J. Hoffman (2012). Hybrid organizations: the next chapter of sustainable business. *Organizational Dynamics*, 41: 126–134.

Haigh, N. and A. Hoffman (2014). The new heretics: hybrid organizations and the challenges they present to corporate sustainability. *Organization and Environment*, 27(3): 223–241.

Haigh, N., E. Dowin Kennedy and J. Walker (2015). Hybrid organizations as shape-shifters: altering legal structure for strategic gain. *California Management Review*, 57(3): 59–82.

Harjoto, M. and H. Jo (2011). Corporate governance and CSR nexus. *Journal of Business Ethics*, 100(1): 45–67.

Healy, P.M. and K.G. Palepu (2001). Information asymmetry, corporate disclosure, and the capital markets: a review of the empirical disclosure literature. *Journal of Accounting and Economics*, 31(1): 405–440.

Heijden, J. van der (2011). Friends, enemies, or strangers? On relationships between public and private sector service providers in hybrid forms of governance. *Law and Policy*, 33(3): 367–390.

Hernandez, D. and C. Hugger (2016). Creating social impact through responsible investing. *Benefits Magazine*, 53(2): 14–22.

Hitt, M.A., R.D. Ireland and R.E. Hoskisson (2014). *Strategic Management: Competitiveness and Globalization*. Stamford, CT: Cengage Learning.

Hockerts, K. (2015). How hybrid organizations turn antagonistic assets into complementarities. *California Management Review*, 57(3): 83–106.

Honeyman, R. (2014). *The B Corp Handbook: How to Use Business as a Force for Good*. San Francisco, CA: Berrett-Koehler Publishers.

Jáuregui Casanueva, L.M. (2013). Money is never enough. *Stanford Social Innovation Review*, 11(2): 20–22.

Jay, J. (2013). Navigating paradox as a mechanism of change and innovation in hybrid organizations. *Academy of Management Journal*, 56(1): 137–159.

Jensen, M.C. and W.H. Meckling (1976). Theory of the firm: managerial behavior, agency costs, and ownership structure. *Journal of Financial Economics*, 3(4): 305–360.

Johnson, R.A. and D.W. Greening (1999). The effects of corporate governance and institutional ownership types on corporate social performance. *Academy of Management Journal*, 42(5): 564–576.

Joldersma, C. and V. Winter (2002). Strategic management in hybrid organizations. *Public Management Review*, 4(1): 83–99.

Joseph, J., W. Ocasio and M.-H. McDonnell (2014). The structural elaboration of board independence: executive power, institutional logics, and the adoption of CEO-only board structures in US corporate governance. *Academy of Management Journal*, 57(6): 1834–1858.

Kickul, J. and T.S. Lyons (2012). *Understanding Social Entrepreneurship: The Relentless Pursuit of Mission in an Ever Changing World*. New York: Routledge.

Kolk, A. (2008). Sustainability, accountability and corporate governance: exploring multinationals' reporting practices. *Business Strategy and the Environment*, 17(1): 1–15.

Lang, M.H. and R.J. Lundholm (2000). Voluntary disclosure and equity offerings: reducing information asymmetry or hyping the stock? *Contemporary Accounting Research*, 17(4): 623–662.

Larner, J. and C. Mason (2014). Beyond box-ticking: a study of stakeholder involvement in social enterprise governance. *Corporate Governance: The International Journal of Effective Board Performance*, 14(2): 181–196.

Laville, J.-L. and M. Nyssens (2001). The social enterprise: towards a theoretical socio-economic approach. In *The Emergence of Social Enterprise*, C. Borzaga, J. Defourny, S. Adam and J. Callaghan (eds). London: Routledge, pp. 312–332.

Lipton, M. and J.W. Lorsch (1992). A modest proposal for improved corporate governance. *Business Lawyer*, 48(1): 59–77.

Lok, J. (2010). Institutional logics as identity projects. *Academy of Management Journal*, 53(6): 1305–1335.

Low, C. (2006). A framework for the governance of social enterprise. *International Journal of Social Economics*, 33(5/6): 376–385.

Mair, J., J. Mayer and E. Lutz (2015). Navigating institutional plurality: organizational governance in hybrid organizations. *Organization Studies*, 36(6): 713–739.

Mallin, C. and A. Melis (2012). Shareholder rights, shareholder voting, and corporate performance. *Journal of Management and Governance*, 16(2): 171–176.

Mason, C., J. Kirkbride and D. Bryde (2007). From stakeholders to institutions: the changing face of social enterprise governance theory. *Management Decision*, 45(2): 284–301.

McDermott, A.M., L.M. Hamel, D. Steel, P.C. Flood and L. McKee (2015). Hybrid healthcare governance for improvement? Combining top-down and bottom-up approaches to public sector regulation. *Public Administration*, 93(2): 324–344.

Millar, R. (2012). Social enterprise in health organisation and management: hybridity or homogeneity? *Journal of Health Organization and Management*, 26(2): 143–148.

Miller, T.L., M.G. Grimes, J.S. McMullen and T.J. Vogus (2012). Venturing for others with heart and head: how compassion encourages social entrepreneurship. *Academy of Management Review*, 37(4): 616–640.

Mirvis, P. (2008). Can you buy CSR? *California Management Review*, 51(1): 109–116.

Money, K. and H. Schepers (2007). Are CSR and corporate governance converging? A view from boardroom directors and company secretaries in FTSE100 companies in the UK. *Journal of General Management*, 33(2): 1–11.

Morck, R.K., A. Shleifer and R.W. Vishny (1988). Management ownership and market valuation: an empirical analysis. *Journal of Financial Economics*, 20: 293–315.

Ntim, C.G. and T. Soobaroyen (2013). Corporate governance and performance in socially responsible corporations: new empirical insights from a neo-institutional framework. *Corporate Governance: An International Review*, 21(5): 468–494.

Opazo, L., C. Raddatz and S.L. Schmukler (2015). Institutional investors and long-term investment: evidence from Chile. *World Bank Economic Review*, 29(3): 479–522.

Pache, A.-C. and F.M. Santos (2013). Inside the hybrid organization: selective coupling as a response to competing institutional logics. *Academy of Management Journal*, 56: 972–1001.

Paranque, B. and H. Willmott (2014). Cooperatives – saviours or gravediggers of capitalism? Critical performativity and the John Lewis Partnership. *Organization*, 21(5): 604–625.

Peattie, K. and A. Morley (2008). Eight paradoxes of the social enterprise research agenda. *Social Enterprise Journal*, 4(2): 91–107.

Pozen, R.C. (2015). How to curb short-termism in corporate America. *Business Economics*, 50(1): 20–24.

Rawhouser, H., M. Cummings and A. Crane (2015). Benefit corporation legislation and the emergence of a social hybrid category. *California Management Review*, 57(3): 13–35.

Ridley-Duff, R. and M. Bull (2011). *Understanding Social Enterprise: Theory and Practice*. London: SAGE.

Santos, F.M. (2012). A positive theory of social entreprenuership. *Journal of Business Ethics*, 111: 335–351.

Seibel, W. (2015). Studying hybrids: sectors and mechanisms. *Organization Studies*, 36(6): 697–712.

Shipilov, A.V., H.R. Greve and T.J. Rowley (2010). When do interlocks matter? Institutional logics and the diffusion of multiple corporate governance practices. *Academy of Management Journal*, 53(4): 846–864.

Smith, W.K., M. Gonin and M.L. Besharov (2013). Managing social-business tensions: a review and research agenda for social enterprise. *Business Ethics Quarterly*, 23(3): 407–442.

Spear, R., C. Cornforth and M. Aiken (2009). The governance challenges of social enterprises: evidence from a UK empirical study. *Annals of Public and Cooperative Economics*, 80(2): 247–273.

US SIF (2010). Report: socially responsible investing assets in US top $3 trillion; nearly 1 out of every 8 dollars under professional management. Forum for Sustainable and Responsible Management. Retrieved 12 August 2011, from http://ussif.org/news/releases/pressrelease.cfm?id=168.

Westley, F. and N. Antadze (2010). Making a difference: strategies for scaling social innovation for greater impact. *Innovation Journal*, 15(2): 1–19.

White, A.L. (2009). Confessions of a CSR champion. *Stanford Social Innovation Review*, 7(1): 31–31.
Wilson, F. and J.E. Post (2013). Business models for people, planet (and profits): exploring the phenomena of social business, a market-based approach to social value creation. *Small Business Economics*, 40(3): 715–737.
York, J.G., T.J. Hargrave and D.F. Pacheco (2016). Converging winds: logic hybridization in the Colorado wind energy field. *Academy of Management Journal*, 50(2): 579–610.

16. Organisational hybridity in affordable housing finance
*Anita Blessing and David Mullins**

INTRODUCTION

In the wake of the recent global financial crisis, social vulnerability is on the increase in Europe. Yet in the globalising housing markets of European urban cultural and financial centres, there is a growing shortage of affordable rental housing for low- and middle-income groups. Implications are broad, spanning social justice, socio-spatial cohesion and urban competitive advantage (Habitat for Humanity, 2015). As both a public good demanding state involvement and a market commodity, housing is never a pure product of either state policy or competitive market dynamics but rather an ongoing co-production of these forces, wherein respective roles shift over time (Bengtsson, 2001). Moreover, the spatially grounded nature of housing in specific neighbourhoods makes it a key resource for local communities and civil society organisations (CSOs), who may become important actors in contesting both shifts in state policy and competitive market pressures through various forms of political participation and activism.

Questions regarding the role of local actors in housing have gained particular salience amongst recent neoliberal reforms that mirror earlier ones in the United States (US). State support for affordable rental housing has been cut back and targeted to encourage the growth of private providers that can access private development capital. Use of state-backed mission-oriented financial institutions has in some cases been curbed, based on claims that this distorts property markets. Affordable rental housing provision has come to involve increasing inter- and intra-organisational complexity, with both mission-oriented and commercial actors in key decision-making roles. Reforms promoting localism envision 'local participatory governance' as a means of negotiating new housing supply, despite asymmetrical power relationships between housing market actors and tensions between the goals of profit and affordability (Lawson et al., 2015; Swyngedouw, 2005). Within this changed development context, the decisions of banks, pension funds and other mainstream financial institutions that manage local savings wield particular power over access to debt and equity finance.

So-called 'institutional investment' in affordable rental housing, on terms that support and sustain affordability, has been described as the Holy Grail of housing policy, framed alternately as a sought-after prize, and as an unattainable goal or chimera (Pawson and Milligan, 2013). While low interest rates are currently enhancing the appeal of debt investment in affordable rentals, efforts to motivate sustained flows of institutional investment have often failed to yield expected results (Blessing and Gilmour, 2011). In Europe there is a notable disconnect between different debates over how such investment might be encouraged. While politicians make moral arguments for pension funds and other profit-oriented investors to finance affordable rental housing in the communities

273

where they do business, academic and policy studies tend to assume a purely commercial orientation, and to focus on financial incentive tools (see Oxley, 2013). Meanwhile, CSOs active in affordable housing are beginning to connect to broader societal debates about how environmental, social and governance concerns might legitimately be integrated into investors' fiduciary duties, and to market affordable rental housing as a social impact investment (Sullivan, 2015; Carroll and Shabana, 2010; Clark, 2000).

Within these debates, relatively little is known about how investment opportunities in affordable rental housing connect with contemporary investors' organisational structures and goals. In this chapter we set out to help fill this gap by utilising ideas from theories of hybridity. To date, studies of social and public housing reform in the Netherlands, Sweden, the United Kingdom (UK), Australia and the US have used conceptual frameworks based on hybridity to explain and classify new organisational forms and practices emerging under neoliberal reforms (Morrison, 2016; Nguyen et al., 2012; Mullins, 2006; Blessing, 2012; Czischke et al., 2012). Mission-oriented housing providers responding to these market-oriented reforms have commanded most attention. Examples of providers cultivating commercial traits, partnering with commercial developers and investors, and in some cases moving away from civil society roots, have made for compelling studies of organisational hybridisation, leading to debates about their regulation.

We aim to complement these studies of mission-oriented providers responding to market signals with insights into how profit-oriented investors respond to state and civic governance mechanisms for encouraging societally beneficial investments in affordable rental housing. While we acknowledge that commercial investors will be guided by the profit motive, we view all housing market actors as embedded in reciprocal societal relations and thus regulated by formal and informal social norms. This includes formal state policy and legislative structures on which we focus our attention. Previous studies on motivating institutional investment in affordable rental housing have noted the potential for high-level financial regulations such as Basel III, a global regulatory agreement on bank capital adequacy, to impact on investor demand (see Milligan et al., 2013). However, the rise of the localism agenda, which devolves responsibility to local communities, prompts equal attention to how local and civic sector participation in financial regulation might drive demand for local societally beneficial investments, including affordable rental housing.

To provide a case within which to explore these issues, we turn to the US, and to the relatively larger body of experience that US housing actors have in financing affordable housing under localism. We examine a state policy programme based on tax incentives, widely described as the most significant resource for financing affordable rental housing in the US. We also consider a legal Act originating from civic activism that has been flagged in previous academic studies as helping to drive demand for local societally beneficial investments (see Schwartz, 2012; Blessing and Gilmour, 2011). While both structures are federal, implementation and compliance activities span multiple scales of action, with important roles for local municipal actors and CSOs. To reflect this, we draw on grey literature and academic studies as well as similar secondary data specific to New York City. We supplement this with informed stakeholder perspectives from interviews with experts in the local affordable housing industry during late 2016. While not representative of other US settings, New York City's rental markets are subject to pressures characteristic of other global financial and cultural centres. Tough local housing conditions have also driven strong developments in housing and community development advocacy.

Using organisational hybridity as a conceptual lens, we consider how these policy initiatives and legislative structures, and the governance mechanisms that they employ, impact on the organisational structures and practices of investors and, where relevant, those of other key actors in the field. While this is not a comparative study, we follow Bengtsson and Hertting's (2014) approach of generalising from single cases, which enables us to consider structural dimensions such as social norms and power relations. Thus viewed, single cases provide grounds for 'rationalistic mechanism-oriented generalisations' based on the assumption of 'thin rationality' (that actors usually do things for a reason). Observations of interaction between constellations of actors in US affordable rental housing provision are used here to identify ideal-typical social mechanisms that may help to connect housing projects with finance. This provides a basis for further discussions regarding whether similar mechanisms used amongst similar constellations of actors could produce similar results in very high-demand European urban rental markets. Insights into US affordable rental housing finance are also timely, given recent UK interest in adapting tax credits, and EU policy debates on incentive instruments (see Oxley, 2013).

This chapter first elaborates on our approach and develops the concept of organisational hybridity for our discussion, drawing on previous studies that use hybridity to explain and classify shifts in organisational structures and practices. Next, it presents our examples of state policy measures and legislative structures in order to identify the relevant incentive and regulatory mechanisms that they employ and to make clear how they motivate target investors. It then draws on the concept of hybridity to describe and explain several types of inter- and intra-organisational change associated with these structures and governance mechanisms. This shows how they help to connect investment opportunities with investors' organisational structures and goals, and how resulting investment patterns drive organisational change amongst other key actors in the field. Next, the chapter draws out some mechanism-oriented generalisations about the urban governance challenge of motivating institutional investment in affordable rental housing. These are then related back to the contexts of European urban governance, both to address interest in policy transfer and to raise questions for further research on motivating institutional investment in affordable rental housing.

While 'affordable rental housing' remains a contested term, it is useful in international comparative research where terms such as 'social' or 'public' housing have limited travelling power. Here it provides a general descriptor for various kinds of sub-market rental housing, both within and outside traditional social housing systems. Used increasingly in the US, Australia, Canada, the UK and continental Europe to describe various forms of state-supported rental housing, the term 'affordable rental housing' may denote rents set below local market rates or to a percentage of personal or median area income. The extent to which rents allow households to meet other basic costs sustainably is a further widely accepted measurement of affordability. While affordable rental housing projects may provide profitable investments, they are rarely profit-maximising in high-demand markets, since alternative uses of these assets will often yield higher returns even after allowing for several layers of subsidy (Blessing, 2016).

ORGANISATIONAL HYBRIDITY AND INSTITUTIONAL CHANGE

In this discussion, we take an institutional approach to enable us to capture some of the societal and political dynamics that impact on urban affordable rental housing finance (Dart, 2004). This provides for a more nuanced understanding of how both regulatory and incentive mechanisms work than we might otherwise gain through an economic rationalist perspective focusing solely on the (financial) business case for investment. While we assume that investors will be driven by profit, and may thus need to be financially incentivised towards non-profit-maximising ventures, we pay attention to how the 'business case' for investment is shaped by other drivers that may be overlooked in international comparative studies, such as state policy and legislation, civic activism, societal expectations and related issues of organisational legitimacy (Carroll and Shabana, 2010). We thus give consideration to the power of institutional norms: the general principles, or socio-cultural rules of conduct, both informal and formalised in policy and law, that regulate organisational behaviour and convey certain power relations (Salet, 2002).

In studies of institutional and organisational change, socio-cultural rules of conduct are seen as loosely coupled in a causal sense with organisational structures and practices, with each potentially shaping the other (Salet, 2002). Following Suchman (1995), Dart (2004) explains the regulatory power of these norms in terms of managers following environmental cues to ensure that organisations meet societal expectations, thereby attaining legitimacy, from which critical benefits and resources flow. While the 'pragmatic' variety of organisational legitimacy is obtained by meeting stakeholder needs, moral legitimacy depends on a given organisational form or activity being seen as the 'right thing'. A third more basic variety, 'cognitive legitimacy', flows from the comprehensibility and taken-for-grantedness of an organisation's societal role. Once attained, organisational legitimacy may again be lost, raising challenges of repair and maintenance (see Suchman, 1995; Dart, 2004).

While neoliberal ideology is based on the premise that states and markets are run separately, actually existing neoliberal reforms have introduced competitive market principles into the running of universities, hospitals, municipalities, state housing agencies and other not-for-profit sector organisations with societal tasks (Crouch, 2012). The rising popularity of 'mixed economy' models of delivery has resulted in organisations themselves becoming 'mixed', leading to what has been described as 'a period of intense organisational hybridity' (Billis, 2010, p. 46). Recent studies of institutional and organisational change in housing and other areas of social assistance have found the concept of organisational hybridity useful in explaining trajectories of change and associated problems of organisational legitimacy, and in classifying new organisational forms (Blessing, 2012).

A term used across fields as diverse as biology, mythology, popular culture and design, 'hybridity' has gathered multiple meanings. Fundamentally, it signals 'heterogeneous arrangements, characterised by mixtures of pure and incongruous origins' (Brandsen et al., 2005). In this chapter we use Billis's definition of an organisational hybrid as one that exhibits significant characteristics associated with more than one of the public sector, the private sector or the private not-for-profit (voluntary) sector, such as a state-subsidised charity that provides certain goods or services on a commercial basis in order to fund a social mission. We also follow Billis's call for attention to the 'inherent, contradictory, distinctive and conflicting' nature of the 'rules of the game' that regulate elements of each sector, including ownership, governance and decision-making, organisational priorities and resources. These different sets of principles are central to understanding hybrid organisational identity, with Billis finding that hybrids tend to adhere primarily to the principles of a single sector (Billis, 2010, pp.55, 56). As a further core condition of organisational hybridity, we assume the ongoing presence of multiple stakeholder configurations and thus multiple accountabilities that relate to the principles of more than one sector (see Anheier, 2011).

Previous studies of housing provision have highlighted the explanatory powers of hybridity in helping to reveal the mechanisms behind dynamic processes of organisational change (Mullins et al., 2012; Mullins and Pawson, 2010). Morrison's (2016) recent study of English housing associations uses hybridity to analyse their diversification into commercial rental in response to reductions in public subsidy and uncertainty over future sources of finance. Blessing (2012) explores the conflict between the different sets of principles that govern not-for-profit housing providers. She finds that, while the hybrid status of large and entrepreneurial social housing providers may confer advantages in the housing market, it also renders them susceptible to problems of organisational legitimacy. Efforts to meet the expectations of commercial stakeholder groups may transgress those of the constituents that these mission-oriented providers serve.

One example of how organisational hybridity can lead to problems of legitimacy is found in the Netherlands. Dutch social housing associations achieved a pragmatic legitimacy over the post war decades as state support and the appreciation of their assets enabled them to boost housing supply. In the mid-2000s, complaints by commercial investors that this unfairly advantaged them in the property market, together with public anger over incidents of mismanagement and private inurement, as well as low housing output, soon led to a crisis of moral legitimacy. Public sector stakeholders demanded that their social and commercial functions be split; and their organisational hybridity thereby diminished (Blessing, 2012, 2015). In England, during the same period, efforts to scale up housing associations through mergers were seen as compromising local accountability, leading to reputational problems (Mullins, 2006). Significantly for this discussion, commercially oriented investors making socially beneficial investments may face similar problems of legitimacy unless the business case for their actions is clear to stakeholders (Carroll and Shabana, 2010). In 2015, stakeholders in housing provision asked English local government pension funds to make a positive social impact in their members' communities by committing 3 per cent of capital to local affordable housing projects. Funds cited potential conflicts with their fiduciary duties as grounds for declining (Apps, 2015).

In this discussion, we also draw upon hybridity as a classificatory tool, applied not just to organisations, but to other institutional structures and relationships, such as hybrid financial dependencies, hybrid governance structures, and hybrid programmes and services (Mullins et al., 2012). We follow Nguyen et al. in using the term 'inter-organisational' hybridity to capture services and programmes that rely on ongoing collaboration across sectors to achieve a social mission. Rather than one-off cross-sectoral collaborations, the term is reserved for ongoing initiatives wherein 'mixed public, private, and non-profit organisations are working together to provide goods and services' (Nguyen et al., 2012, p. 459). A further term, 'programmatic hybridity', captures the expansion and diversification of services provided by single organisations (ibid., p. 460). We also make use of Billis's classificatory distinction between degrees of organisational hybridity, with 'shallow' forms occurring only when hybrid qualities do not call into question the basic identity and function of the organisation or construct, and more 'entrenched' forms manifesting when relevant hybrid qualities are essential to its continued functioning (Billis, 2010).

CARROTS AND STICKS: USING INCENTIVES AND REGULATORY POWERS TO CREATE MARKETS FOR INVESTMENT IN AFFORDABLE RENTAL HOUSING

In this section, we examine examples of US state policy initiatives and legislative structures credited with motivating financial institutions to invest in affordable rental housing. In view of the growing policy reliance on civic participation as state support is reduced in European cities, we pay attention to the role of civic activism in helping to create and to implement these structures. We explore related impacts on the organisational identities and practices of investors and other key actors in the field, asking whether organisational hybridisation occurs, and to what potential effects. As cases, we focus on a tax incentive scheme and a federal Act mandating socially beneficial community reinvestments. While separate, these two institutional constructs have been described as working in tandem to motivate significant investment in US affordable rental housing and to catalyse the development of an affordable rental housing industry (Guthrie, 2004).

Affordable Rental Housing in the US

Long typified as the archetypal liberal welfare state (Esping-Andersen, 2013), the US has also been described as a 'heartland' of neoliberalism, an original site of its discursive production (see Peck and Tickell, 2002, p. 381). In European commentaries, the US is often portrayed as having an ultra-capitalistic marketised economy. Yet it is also home to countertendencies to neoliberalism. Peck and Tickell argue that to be effective in 'deliberalising' spatial relations, these countertendencies must somehow be made translocal through 'the remaking of extra local rule systems in fields like trade, finance (and) labour' (Peck and Tickell, 2002, p. 399). In the context of international neoliberal policy transfer, US affordable housing finance provides a site within which to explore these countertendencies.

The liberal welfare state is characterised as 'residual' in nature with minimum levels of means-tested assistance for the households in greatest need (Esping-Andersen, 2013; Harloe, 1995). While its roots lie in the 1930s 'New Deal' programme of Keynesian economic stimulus, by the early 1950s US public housing was effectively 'residualised'. Initially opposed by the real-estate lobby as an inhibitor of fair competition, the first US federal public housing legislation system evolved with a low maximum tenant income, and a low maximum cost per unit that resulted in sub-market standards, precluding competition with for-profit landlords (Schwartz, 2012). Although the character of public housing was influenced by the private real-estate lobby, it has been described as 'a public endeavour involving federal, state, and local governments' that was 'decidedly un-hybrid' in nature (Nguyen et al., 2012, p. 460).

In the early 1970s, the construction of new public housing was suspended, beginning an era characterised by neoliberalism, funding cuts and the decentralisation of power (ibid.). This phase of development, however, deviated from the residual welfare state model. From the 1980s, US welfare spending on middle-income groups rose, while spending on the poorest households fell and income polarisation grew (Rosen, 2014). This shift in policy may be partially explained by Crouch's theory of privatised Keynesianism, which describes a need within neoliberal systems predicated on the growth of financial markets to enable the middle class and working poor to continue spending and amassing debt. Individual spending enabled by government policy and private credit facilities thus partially replaces state spending as a form of economic stimulus (Crouch, 2009; Blessing, 2016).

Accordingly, US public housing was supplemented by multiple programmes for privately financed 'affordable' rental housing that were often targeted at low- to moderate-income working households in tight rental markets, rather than welfare recipients. Currently, public housing comprises less than 1 per cent of all dwellings, having been surpassed in quantity by affordable rentals with rents linked to area median incomes or local market rates. Added to public housing, these subtypes amount to around 5 per cent of all housing or 15 per cent of the rental sector overall (Schwartz, 2011). In large cities, concentrations of affordable rentals are higher. In New York City, around 8 per cent of rental dwellings are in public tenure, with roughly another 10 per cent comprising privately owned, but government-subsidised affordable dwellings (Ellen and Weselcouch, 2015). When rent-controlled or rent-stabilised units are included, nearly 50 per cent of rental dwellings are subject to an affordability mechanism. Despite this, affordability problems remain severe.

The participation of neighbourhood-based not-for-profit community development corporations (CDCs) has been pivotal to the supply of affordable rental housing, especially in urban areas. Not-for-profits accommodated more than 1.5 million households around the US by 2009 (Bratt, 2009). As in other liberal welfare states, the majority of US state financial support for housing targets homeowners. In major cities, however, where many people rent, demand-side rental assistance is also significant.

Financial Incentives for Institutional Investment in Affordable Housing

The most significant resource for financing affordable housing is a tradable federal tax credit. The 1986 Low Income Housing Tax Credit (LIHTC) programme (see Table 16.1), run at an annual cost of around US$8 billion, has yielded over 2.7 million privately provided affordable rental dwellings, more than now exist in public housing (HUD, 2017). Previous studies have examined this programme as a driver of hybridity, describing it as a hybrid structure (Blessing, 2015), and as driving the hybridisation of public housing by enabling mixed-income development (Nguyen et al., 2012).

LIHTCs take the form of federal tax exemptions that can be set against the tax liabilities of organisations and which are paid annually over a ten-year period. Allocated annually to state governments on a per capita basis, the credits are then awarded via competitive tender for affordable housing proposals that best fulfil national and local assessment

Table 16.1   Acronym guide: US community development and affordable housing finance terms

Acronym	Explanation
LIHTC	Low Income Housing Tax Credit: federal programme and major instrument for US affordable rental housing finance
CRA	Community Reinvestment Act: 1977 US federal legislation requiring regulated banks to demonstrate that they serve the credit needs of low- and moderate-income constituents in areas where they accept deposits
AMI	Average median income: the average gross household income within the local area; a measurement used to determine affordable rents within US federal government-supported housing programmes
CDC	Community development corporation: neighbourhood-based not-for-profits active around the US in providing affordable rental housing and related services
CDFI	Community development financial institution: general term for financial institutions that provide financial services to underserved markets; CDFIs may take not-for-profit or for-profit forms, which include community development banks, credit unions, loan funds and venture capital funds

criteria. Proposals may be submitted by not-for-profits, for-profit developers or mixed consortia. Once a developer has won tax credits for a designated scheme, they may retain them for direct use, but will typically trade them via a syndicator in return for development capital. Having met a significant proportion of project development costs, developers may then source the remaining funds needed from loans. Syndicators, many of which are not-for-profits, then sell credits to investors.

LIHTCs were originally aimed at individual property owners, but community development professionals soon began to market them to corporate investors. Favourably structured deals that involved property depreciation benefits in addition to the tax credits mobilised investors (McQuarrie and Guthrie, 2007). Large financial institutions, primarily banks, now make up the majority of investors. By contrast pension funds, as tax-exempt organisations, tend to choose another route by providing long-term debt investment, encouraged in some instances by state guarantees.

Under the LIHTC programme rents are geared to the (gross) local average median income (AMI). An initial 15-year 'compliance period' wherein rents were capped at 30 per cent of AMI was later extended to 30 years. After this, investors may exit, potentially resulting in the withdrawal of properties from the affordable housing sector. With increasing numbers of LIHTC schemes now approaching the end of 30-year terms, tenant displacement is a growing concern, especially where properties are in for-profit ownership. The programme enables mixed-income developments, but allocates credits only for units designated for tenants earning up to either 50 per cent or 60 per cent of AMI, depending on the architecture of the scheme. Tenants with rising incomes are not evicted, and the marketised nature of programme rent-setting may incentivise developers to target 'the high end of the low-income category . . . a position that is occupied by the working poor' (McQuarrie and Guthrie, 2007, p.258). The proliferation of LIHTC projects and the simultaneous scaling back of public housing raises concerns regarding future options for very low-income or unemployed households (ibid.).

Investors do not necessarily pay the syndicator a full dollar for each dollar of tax credits lost to the public purse. During the financial crisis, appetite for credits fell and stalled projects prompted government intervention. Early in the scheme, less than half of each tax dollar foregone went into new housing, while 2006 saw close to full dollar returns, which have returned in recent years. Significantly for this discussion, credits may trade at rates higher than a full dollar depending on local market conditions; a point to which we shall return later (Kimura, 2014; Schwartz, 2012). A late 2016 local industry estimate of LIHTC pricing in New York City was $1.10–$1.15 for a dollar of tax credit; however by early 2017, the Trump administration's plans to reduce corporate taxes had already negatively impacted LIHTC markets around the nation (Riquier, 2017).

By allocating credits via competitive tenders based on both federal and local selection criteria, the LIHTC programme encourages quality and innovation while enabling solutions to be tailored to local needs. As tradable credits of value to not-for-profits and for-profits alike, LIHTCs appear to encourage collaboration between mission-oriented organisations and commercial developers and investors. This raises the question as to how these different groups of actors may behave at key points in projects, such as near the end of the 30-year term, when use requirements expire. The credits' tradability and the role of syndication enables both large- and small-scale, as well as mixed-tenure, investments. However, small affordable projects tend to be more difficult to finance.

The LIHTC programme has attracted significant international policy interest as a successful construct that pursues a publicly defined mission in a commercial market context (see Oxley, 2013). As a marketised scheme that evades the radar of traditional measures of state expenditure, it fits neatly into neoliberal reform agendas. The US government has described the market for tax credits as being 'as complex and sophisticated as the market for stocks and bonds' (Blessing and Gilmour, 2011, p. 465), and although the intricate LIHTC programme may appear to be driving this market, New York City affordable housing developers stress that it is not a stand-alone programme.

State Regulatory Stimuli for Investment in Affordable Housing

Leading US scholars explain the apparent anomaly of tax credits trading above their value in terms of 'non-financial considerations' (Schwartz and Meléndez, 2008, p. 267). Certain types of banks, the main investor group, purchase LIHTCs to meet some of the more challenging requirements of the federal Community Reinvestment Act (CRA), 1977. The CRA emerged as civic activists from a number of cities collectively sought to counter 'redlining': systemic discrimination in the form of geographically based exclusion from mortgage finance and other forms of investment. 'Redlining' refers to the practice of colour-coding maps, with red indicating perceived high credit risk, prompting lenders to withhold, or to increase the price of, local credit even where individual applicants were credit-worthy. Begun in the private sector, and institutionalised in the 1934 Federal Housing Act, redlining patterns typically reflected the race or ethnicity of residents, with the result that certain communities, including many in New York City, experienced catastrophic disinvestment during the 1970s economic slowdown. While redlining was formally institutionalised in the US, similar exclusionary practices have been observed in Europe (Aalbers, 2009).

The CRA applies to all banks classified as 'holding companies'; typically retail banks that take deposits. However, wholesale banks also have responsibilities under the Act that relate to community development. The Act states that 'depository institutions have a continuing affirmative obligation to meet the credit needs of the communities in which they operate, including low- and moderate-income neighborhoods, consistent with safe and sound operation' (Federal Reserve Bank, 2014). It works in tandem with the 1975 Home Mortgage Disclosure Act, which requires banks to make public their lending patterns, with online data broken down by neighbourhood, income and race. Signalled by the phrase 'safe and sound operations', CRA assessment criteria incentivise safer forms of credit and penalise loans deemed deceptive (Taylor and Silver, 2009).

Described by civil sector organisations as a 'greenlining' mechanism, the CRA is enforced through public examinations that grade banks' reinvestment performance against those of others nearby. For larger banks, they occur every two years and are carried out by relevant federal financial agencies. Covering both qualitative and quantitative assessment criteria, these examinations have evolved into a sophisticated source of data for community groups and activists. The mechanism of disclosing results publicly, along with the participation of local civil sector stakeholders, is thus key to CRA enforcement. In New York City, the membership organisation for community development corporations (CDCs) participates by monitoring and reporting on local bank reinvestment activities. Accordingly, New York City industry participants describe the Act itself as 'necessary but not sufficient' for channelling investment into affordable rental housing.

Regulated financial institutions are required to demonstrate adequate reinvestment within lending, community development, and 'service' (adequate bank branches and automated teller machines, ATMs). The community development test, which covers goods with a societal purpose such as affordable housing, is challenging to comply with, and purchasing LIHTCs provides a simple means. Accordingly, the CRA drives demand for tax credits amongst regulated investors, which purchase the majority (Lindsey, 2009; Kimura, 2014). Lending to community development financial institutions (CDFIs), explored in the next section, also attracts CRA credit, as do certain forms of financial support for CDCs. Bank performance is graded relative to other local CRA regulated banks.

As opposed to relying on reputational gains, the CRA has been described as having 'real (regulatory) teeth' (McQuarrie and Guthrie, 2007, p. 251). Banks with inadequate ratings risk being denied approval by the Federal Reserve to undertake proposed mergers or acquisitions. CRA enforcement is to some extent triangular, in the sense that it provides community groups, often highly organised advocates, with the opportunity to comment on performance and to challenge major corporate plans. Many banks pursue high CRA ratings by pledging and making local investments. While CRA commitments inevitably include some investments that would occur anyway, they are highly significant to urban community development. The value of CRA local area investment plans made between 1977 and 2009 is estimated at over US$6 trillion, with single bank pledges running well into the billions (Lindsey, 2009; Schwartz, 2012; Taylor and Silver, 2009).

As a form of market intervention, the Community Reinvestment Act has attracted controversy as a 'monstrous' hybrid that contributed to the financial crisis (Lindsey, 2009). Recent studies, however, have found that only around 6 per cent of subprime loans were made by CRA-covered lenders to CRA targeted borrowers and neighbourhoods, due to the requirement to follow 'sound lending practices' (Aalbers, 2009). Most subprime lending targeted middle- or higher-income households, with delinquency rates fairly consistent across all groups (FCIC, 2011; Canner and Bhutta, 2008).

The Carrot and the Stick

Not-for-profit affordable housing developers emphasise the importance of the CRA in driving demand for LIHTCs (Blessing and Gilmour, 2011; ANHD, 2014). However, some describe a synergistic effect; albeit one that was unplanned by the designers of the two separate institutional structures. While both structures took time to take effect, the CRA alone motivated little institutional investment in urban housing and community development until the launch of the LIHTC programme (McQuarrie and Guthrie, 2007). From the late 1980s, the mutually reinforcing effect of the two instruments – the 'stick' of federal legislation and the 'carrot' of the tax credit – gave significant momentum to bank involvement in low-income housing markets, and 'brought banks, corporations, community developers, and local governments together to build the market for low-income housing' (ibid., p. 250).

The CRA has been widely credited for turning around patterns of neighbourhood decline in US cities and improving banks' dealings with low-income communities (McQuarrie and Guthrie, 2007; Olsen et al., 2009). Given its role in stimulating markets for local societal investments, its effect may best be understood in terms of 'quasi-market' forces. Arguably, its 'regulatory teeth' threaten lost market opportunities in the sense that poor ratings or objections by CSOs to proposed bank mergers or acquisitions may delay or even block these plans. Disclosure of CRA examination results and requirements to consider comments from community groups during merger approval processes help to connect bank performances to evolving societal expectations by enlisting actors involved in state policy, civic activism and commerce around the cause of community development. Although the Act is rarely used to block corporate plans, the threat is substantial and CRA compliance is arguably a prerequisite for maintaining organisational legitimacy of both its moral and its pragmatic varieties (Dart, 2004). Significant post-financial crisis increases in some bank CRA commitments highlight the importance of repairing and maintaining organisational legitimacy, as critics question the finance industry's role in society (Baer, 2013).

An 'oft-cited rationale' for the CRA is 'quid pro quo' (Olsen et al., 2009). Civil sector commentators describe a social compact between the state and the banks that provide crucial economic and community services. Banks receive various taxpayer-funded benefits including deposit insurance and access to emergency lines of finance. Recent research has shown that implicit government backing gives larger banks a market edge in allowing them to pay out lower interest on large deposits (ANHD, 2014). Based on this 'quid pro quo' reading of the CRA, proposals have been made to extend it to other financial institutions and industries that enjoy taxpayer support (Olsen et al., 2009). The idea of reciprocal obligations between commercial investors and the communities where they do business raises questions about organisational hybridity. Do CRA-regulated banks hybridise internally as they fulfil reinvestment requirements? Alternatively, is the CRA more of a driver of inter-organisational hybridity by enabling banks to comply by supporting not-for-profits?

Using the mechanisms of public disclosure, voluntary local monitoring and regulatory power, the CRA activates both competition and collaboration between regulated banks. It also encourages regulated banks to fund and work with not-for-profit financial institutions and developers. Key roles in implementing the CRA are played by state agencies including departments of the Federal Reserve Bank, state housing finance agencies and federal tax agencies (Schwartz and Meléndez, 2008). It is likely that the quasi-government bodies Fannie Mae and Freddie Mac provided opportunities to securitise CRA-related loans during the financial crisis. Given the sheer volume of CRA-related lending, the Act is also likely to have driven organisational hybridisation amongst the civil sector actors involved in monitoring bank reinvestment performance by providing new sources of funding that encourage professionalisation. As they monitor large banks with national community reinvestment programmes, these not-for-profit actors have also begun networking and advocating nationally (Seidman, 2005).

A further story could be told about the impact of the LIHTC and the Community Reinvestment Act on stimulating the growth of the for-profit developers that carry out around half of LIHTC developments, sometimes in partnership with community development corporations. Questions arise as to how these actors build solid reputations in a semi-social market, and whether their motives impact on housing outcomes at critical decision-making points, such as when partnership agreements are formed, or affordability requirements expire. However, we limit our discussion to the organisational impacts of the CRA–LIHTC-related synergy on mission-oriented housing development and finance organisations, and on CRA-regulated banks, giving consideration to both intra- and inter-organisational hybridity.

DESCRIBING ORGANISATIONAL CHANGE: COMMUNITY DEVELOPMENT CORPORATIONS AND FINANCIAL INSTITUTIONS

CDCs

In addition to providing affordable housing, not-for-profit community development corporations in US cities participate in urban redevelopment, job training, healthcare, small business development and other activities. In this sense, they display programmatic hybridity that is partially facilitated by government contracts for these services (Andrews, 2001; Nguyen et al., 2012). As charities governed by conditional exemptions within the US tax code, they are subject to regulations that define the terms of their organisational legitimacy, and they must demonstrate compliance through annual publicly filed tax statements.

CRA and LIHTC-related streams of investment have been described as significant drivers of growth, empowerment and organisational hybridisation in CDCs. They stimulate partnerships with CRA-regulated banks and for-profit developers, putting CDCs 'at the table with corporate and financial institutions' (McQuarrie and Guthrie, 2007). By enlarging flows of resources for their activities, these structures have boosted the pragmatic legitimacy of CDCs, enabling them to meet stakeholder needs. In New York City, many CDCs emerged from grassroots voluntary origins in the context of severe urban decline during the late 1960s and 1970s. During these periods and into the 1980s, the city took possession of more than 100 000 distressed units from landlords in tax arrears. This provided significant land and building stock for new affordable housing and helped these groups to develop.

Over recent decades, the structural hybridity within both the LIHTC programme and the CRA has supported professionalisation within CDCs, which have stepped into both developer and manager roles within LIHTC projects (Glickman and Servon, 1998). As an indicator of deepening organisational hybridity, commercial risks assumed by CDCs in early LIHTC partnerships prompted warnings from the federal tax authority that they could lose their charitable status (Blessing, 2016). Spurred by the need to develop economies of scale, some CDCs have merged and expanded their geographical reach. Most have remained small and are seen as accountable to a single neighbourhood community (Blessing and Gilmour, 2011; Andrews, 2001). In New York City, 11 of the largest local CDCs have pooled their assets into a new joint ownership entity (JOE), in order to reap economies of scale in asset management and development.

CDFIs

As the capital needs of CDCs have grown in complexity, financial intermediaries have developed to serve these needs, led by foundations and socially motivated insurance companies that provided loans (Andrews, 2001). These community development financial institutions (CDFIs) have brought benefits of scale and efficiency. They are hybrids in the sense that they help to bridge the gap between small CDCs and large for-profit institutional investors. While banks used to make face-to-face loans in local communities, CDFIs have stepped into this role, drawing on local knowledge and providing ongoing expertise to support funded projects. This enables them to make certain loans outside mainstream risk parameters (LISC, 2016).

US CDFIs, which have been likened to UK community development finance associations, include community development banks, credit unions, loan funds and venture capital funds. They are defined as non-governmental financing entities with community development missions that serve target markets, and they are seen as accountable to local communities. Amongst them are not-for-profit variants of Low Income Housing Tax Credit syndicators (Schwartz and Meléndez, 2008). By 2001, community development financial institutions had amassed resources of US$6 billion, which had grown to approximately $29.6 billion by 2012 in the CDFI banking industry alone (Narain et al., 2012). While their activities may be profitable, they are not profit-maximising (Andrews, 2001). Significantly, CRA-regulated banks investing in CDFIs receive credit towards the CRA investment examination which has helped to stimulate the growth and diversification of CDFIs. In 1994, CDFIs were officially recognised under US federal law. Simultaneously, a federal fund was established to help finance 'certified' CDFIs (Barr, 2005).

As mission-oriented organisations committed to servicing low- and moderate-income communities, the various types of CDFIs drive inter-organisational hybridity, bringing together not-for-profit and for-profit actors and connecting affordable housing projects with finance. While some larger CDFI loan funds have received private credit ratings, the sector as a whole faces limitations. Many CDFIs are capitalised only in the short term, enabling only short-term loans. While CDFI venture capital funds may make long-term equity investments, requirements for returns may preclude investments that reach very low-income groups. Furthermore, the social missions of CDFIs work against their building up substantial reserves (Andrews, 2001).

CRA-Regulated Banks

While other investors can and do invest in the LIHTC programme, regulated banks are motivated by the Community Reinvestment Act (McQuarrie and Guthrie, 2007). Monitoring of bank CRA performance in New York City shows that considerable local reinvestment responsibilities apply to both large retail and wholesale banks of US origin such as Capital One, Bank of America and Citibank, and US-based affiliates of European banks such as Santander, Deutsche Bank and HSBC (ANHD, 2014). While commercial investment firms have not traditionally fallen under the jurisdiction of the CRA, some, including Goldman Sachs and Morgan Stanley, took on holding company status in 2008 in order to gain access to emergency state relief funds. This move afforded them significant privileges, but also pulled them into the jurisdiction of the CRA and other regulatory provisions.

By grading reinvestment performances against those of other regulated banks in the same assessment area, the CRA activates competition. The service test, comprising 25 per cent of the CRA examination, analyses 'the extent and innovativeness of (a bank's) community development services' in relation to the local 'performance context'. This includes 'economic and market factors; the bank's capacities, constraints, and business plans' and 'the performance of similarly situated lenders' (Barr, 2005). As well as driving inter-bank competition, the imperative of CRA compliance encourages coordination between banks to reduce costs associated with the compliance process. This has spurred the development of multi-bank community development corporations and loan consortia to develop best practice. Potentially problematically, banks also get CRA consideration for originating and purchasing loans and loan securities, creating a trading system and secondary market that has increased liquidity (Barr, 2005).

Industry peak bodies enhance competition by publishing detailed quantitative and qualitative monitoring of bank reinvestment activities, and by promoting strong performers as industry standard-setters. The peak body for New York City CDCs, for example, recommends reinvesting 5 per cent or more of local deposits in 'targeted, strategic reinvestment lending' (ANHD, 2014). Bank self-promotion of outstanding ratings in mainstream media is widespread, indicating that ratings do actively connect to banks' ability to maintain organisational legitimacy (Taylor and Silver, 2009; Willis, 2009). While driving competition amongst banks has helped to increase lending volumes, to add liquidity to local markets and, potentially, to decrease the risk of individual loans, it has also been criticised for pouring investment into communities too suddenly and driving gentrification (Lindsey, 2009).

A 1999 Federal Reserve Bank survey of CRA-related lending activities of the 500 largest retail banking organisations (Avery et al., 2000) showed that many had already established distinct units or departments for CRA-related activities. Amongst large banks, over 70 per cent had developed such a unit. Due to the tendency amongst large banks to encompass national or multi-state markets, some operate their CRA programmes at similar scales of action (Seidman, 2005, p. 199). However, local expertise is still needed in order to engage community actors, and to develop appropriate loan products and risk mitigation procedures, such as enhanced monitoring of local repayment patterns and early intervention procedures. CRA examinations reward banks for foreclosure prevention efforts, as well as for counselling, modifying loans and investing in funds that finance loan modification (Taylor and Silver, 2009).

These activities require ongoing collaboration between relevant branches or subsidiaries of the banks on the one hand, and local mission-oriented actors on the other. This leads to considerable inter-organisational hybridity in Nguyen et al.'s (2012) sense of the term, as well as driving 'intra-organisational hybridity' within individual banks through structural and policy adaptations. Within these activities, members of banks' staff straddle multiple stakeholder requirements. While specialised units have been associated with strong CRA performance and innovation, changes to assessment procedures, including stronger reliance on quantitative data, have discouraged their establishment.

Within their broader organisations, CRA compliance units tend to absorb the development costs of new products that may later go mainstream and to face profitability challenges because their loans are smaller and more complex. Here, tensions of intra-organisational hybridity arise that may be addressed by justifying non-profit-maximising activities in terms of CRA compliance (Willis, 2009). Regulated banks may also establish tax-advantaged charitable foundations to carry out philanthropic grant-making activities or establish revolving credit facilities. While CRA-specific units and their staffing patterns are indications of organisational hybridity, this is hybridity of a relatively 'shallow' nature as described by Billis (2010). CRA-specific units or foundations may be associated with best practice, but they are not crucial to the core functioning of the entire organisation. Reinvestment options such as funding local mission-oriented organisations enable basic compliance through inter-organisational hybridisation without the need for significant intra-organisational hybridisation within the banking sector.

A further variety of organisational hybridisation lies in the possibility that CRA-stimulated organisational transformations of regulated banks, including the growth of specialised urban development units, may release isomorphic pressures that encourage similar behaviour amongst non-CRA regulated banks. Questions arise as to whether regulation encourages a local culture of publicly visible programmes of corporate social responsibility, and whether banks realise profits from integrating themselves into local property markets.

CONCLUSIONS

The Community Reinvestment Act and the Low Income Housing Tax Credit programme, both federal policy and legal structures, have been credited with creating a cross-sectoral organisational field around the cause of affordable rental housing. We considered how these two constructs help to connect local opportunities for investment in affordable rental projects with investors' organisational structures and goals, and asked whether the incentive and regulatory mechanisms they employ drive organisational hybridity amongst the actors in the field.

With respect to CRA-regulated banks, our analysis revealed visible organisational changes. The development of specialised reinvestment units that rationalise their actions in terms of CRA compliance has helped to connect local societally beneficial investment classes to the goal of profit. While significant for local community development, this organisational hybridity appeared to be of a shallow variety, with commercial goals and functions retaining primacy. A more significant conceptual key to understanding the organisational impacts of the governance framework on banks proved to be 'inter-organisational hybridity'. While the tax credit programme is 'sector-agnostic' in that credits are awarded to not-for-profits and for-profits alike, it has driven significant growth and hybridisation of not-for-profit CDCs, and brought for-profit developers into social projects. Awarding CRA credit to banks that fund and partner local mission-oriented developers and financial institutions has stimulated their growth and professionalisation. This may explain why intra-organisational hybridity in banks, where present at all, remained shallow, while inter-organisational hybridity was core to their community reinvestment activities, including affordable housing finance.

The CRA is a small part of financial regulation that neither radically challenges the societal power of financial institutions nor corrects serious societal injustices associated with financial markets. Yet it finds power in the mechanisms of public disclosure through periodic public assessments with local civil sector organisation input, and in the regulatory muscle to frustrate plans for major corporate moves. Disclosure provisions empower CSOs and other local actors to participate in regulation. While enforcement in New York City may be stronger than in other areas, local enforcement of the CRA has helped to maintain significant ongoing streams of local societal investments, including funds for affordable rental housing. Arguably, the CRA provides an example of how state legislation can support local countertendencies to neoliberal reforms by empowering local stakeholders (Peck and Tickell, 2002, p. 399).

The CRA arose from local patterns of civic activism in response to systematic race- and space-based discrimination around access to finance. Its interaction with the LIHTC programme, while successful in financing housing, was unplanned. The 'quasi' market forces unleashed by this synergy were slow to gather momentum as new actors mobilised around the cause of affordable rental housing. Any lessons to be drawn from our case regarding opportunities for direct international policy transfer are therefore likely to be negative ones. Incentive tools for institutional investment in affordable rental housing may not work in settings lacking the 'stick' of community reinvestment laws.

International lessons may also be negative in the sense that LIHTC affordable housing outcomes are weaker than traditional social or public housing outcomes. There is growing concern about the time-limited nature of affordability requirements and the potential for commercial developers to realise significant gains by exiting the scheme when they expire. Mission-oriented CDCs, with a default position to refinance and extend projects to maintain affordability, have important roles to play. While for-profits may choose to extend affordability, asset sales where values have appreciated or conversion to market rents may prove more attractive, threatening existing residents with displacement. Another policy premise that our exploration of hybrid financing has debunked is the idea of straight substitution of public subsidy with private finance and private sector risk. In practice, LIHTC schemes often have multiple layers of investment, subsidised by the state in one form or another, and the strong hand of the state remains key to monitoring and compliance.

Moving to a higher level of abstraction, and taking a rationalistic, mechanism-oriented perspective, our case can still yield tentative findings of interest to European policymakers. Under the guise of UK localism and the Big Society, the Dutch *participatiestaat*, or German *bürgerbeteiligung*, political emphasis on stronger collaborative roles between commercial actors and civic groups as the state retreats creates relational choreographies of participation that are newer in Europe than in the US. Emerging power asymmetries call for effective models of participatory governance (Peck and Tickell, 2002). The CRA–LIHTC synergy provides one example that illustrates how state policy and legislation could activate similar mechanisms amongst similar constellations of actors in other settings.

While Europe needs to consider how to motivate a range of potential investors, including pension funds, projected shortfalls in retirement income make 'required' societal investments on the part of these giant firms highly morally problematic. However, emerging EU debates on integrating environmental, social and governance (ESG) frameworks into investor decision-making raise the question as to whether the mechanism of public disclosure may offer solutions, if coupled with incentives (EU, 2013). Particularly within newer pension plans that offer member choice over portfolio contents, the benefits of circulating local savings within local economies may prove attractive in the post-financial crisis environment. There is also a strong potential for ongoing partnerships between pension funds and other investors and mission-oriented housing associations.

As Europe neoliberalises, its policy-makers are coming to grips with the inability of competitive markets to address issues of long-term sustainability, including housing provision. Our case study of US governance raises the prospect of affirmatively creating markets for socially beneficial investments such as affordable rental housing using state policy and regulatory power. While European studies highlight the dependence of financial firms on the high-amenity urban environments in which they do business, these firms often enjoy favourable tax conditions, or government support such as guarantees and access to emergency lines of taxpayer-funded credit (Engelen and Musterd, 2010). The conditionality attached to such support in the US appears to be missing in the European Union, where the Economic and Monetary Union (EMU) treats investors as pure market actors (Crouch, 2012). With this contribution, we highlight the potential value of renewing attention to the societal role of mainstream financial institutions, and re-establishing their hybridity as both market and social actors that enjoy benefits, but also have obligations. This may prove to be an important step towards more socially productive and inclusive forms of governance beyond the state.

NOTE

* Research for this chapter was enabled by a Marie Skoldowska Curie European Fellowship 661659. The authors thank the following organisations and people for their generosity in speaking to us about their work in New York City Affordable Housing Provision: the New York Housing Authority; the Association of Neighbourhood and Housing Development; the Local Initiatives Support Corporation; Enterprise Community Partners; JOE NYC and Mr M. Jahr; Professor A. Schwartz.

REFERENCES

Aalbers, M.B. (2009) Why the Community Reinvestment Act cannot be blamed for the subprime crisis. *City and Community*, 8(3), pp. 346–350.
Andrews, N. (2001) Equity with a twist. Brookings Institute. http://www.brookings.edu/research/articles/2001/04/community-development-andrews.
ANHD (2014) The state of bank reinvestment in New York City. http://www.anhd.org/wp-content/uploads/2011/07/2014-REPORT-Single_Page-NoBleed_FINAL.pdf.

Anheier, H. (2011) Governance and leadership in hybrid organisations: comparative and interdisciplinary perspectives. Background paper, Centre for Social Investment, University of Heidelberg.

Apps, P. (2015) Council pension funds reject 3% challenge. *Inside Housing.* http://www.insidehousing.co.uk/council-pension-funds-reject-3-challenge/7008089.article.

Avery, R.B., R.W. Bostic and G.B. Canner (2000) The performance and profitability of CRA-related lending. *Economic Commentary*, November. https://ideas.repec.org/a/fip/fedcec/y2000inov.html.

Baer, J. (2013) Goldman Sachs wheels to a top grade. *Wall Street Journal*, 31 October. http://www.wsj.com/articles/SB10001424052702303843104579170113203418016 (accessed 6 October 2016).

Barr, M. (2005) 'Credit where it counts', maintaining a strong Community Reinvestment Act. Brookings Institution, Research Brief. https://www.brookings.edu/wp-content/uploads/2016/06/20050503_cra.pdf.

Bengtsson, B. (2001) Housing as a social right: implications for welfare state theory. *Scandinavian Political Studies*, 24(4), pp. 255–275.

Bengtsson, B. and N. Hertting (2014) Generalization by mechanism: thin rationality and ideal-type analysis in case study research. *Philosophy of the Social Sciences*, 44(6), pp. 707–732.

Billis, D. (ed.) (2010) *Hybrid Organizations and the Third Sector: Challenges for Practice, Theory and Policy.* Basingstoke: Palgrave Macmillan.

Blessing, A. (2012) Magical or monstrous? Hybridity in social housing governance. *Housing Studies*, 27(2), pp. 189–207.

Blessing, A. (2015) Public, private, or in-between? The legitimacy of social enterprises in the housing market. *VOLUNTAS: International Journal of Voluntary and Nonprofit Organizations*, 26(1), pp. 198–221.

Blessing, A. (2016) Repacking the poor? Conceptualising neoliberal reforms of social rental housing. *Housing Studies*, 31(2), pp. 149–172.

Blessing A. and T. Gilmour (2011) The invisible hand? Using tax credits to encourage institutional investment in social housing. *International Journal of Housing Policy*, 11(4), pp. 453–468.

Brandsen, T., W. Van de Donk and K. Putters (2005) Griffins or chameleons? Hybridity as a permanent and inevitable characteristic of the third sector. *International Journal of Public Administration*, 28(9/10), pp. 749–765.

Bratt, R.G. (2009) Challenges for nonprofit housing organizations created by the private housing market. *Journal of Urban Affairs*, 31(1), pp. 67–96.

Canner, G. and N. Bhutta (2008) Staff analysis of the relationship between the CRA and the subprime crisis. Memorandum, Board of Governors of the Federal Reserve System.

Carroll, A.B. and K.M. Shabana (2010) The business case for corporate social responsibility: a review of concepts, research and practice. *International Journal of Management Reviews*, 12(1), pp. 85–105.

Clark, G.L. (2000) Moral sentiments and reciprocal obligations: the case for pension fund investment in community development. *Ethics, Place and Environment*, 3(1), pp. 7–24.

Crouch, C. (2009) Privatised Keynesianism: an unacknowledged policy regime. *British Journal of Politics and International Relations*, 11(3), pp. 382–399.

Crouch, C. (2012) Sustainability, neoliberalism, and the moral quality of capitalism. *Business and Professional Ethics Journal*, 31(2), pp. 363–374.

Czischke, D., V. Gruis and D. Mullins (2012) Conceptualising social enterprise in housing organisations. *Housing Studies*, 27(4), pp. 418–437.

Dart, R. (2004) The legitimacy of social enterprise. *Nonprofit Management and Leadership*, 14(4), pp. 411–424.

Ellen, I. and M. Weselcouch (2015) Housing, neighborhoods, and opportunity: the location of New York City's subsidized affordable housing. New York: NYU Furman Center. http://furmancenter.org/files/NYUFurmanCenter_HousingNeighborhoodsOpp_Jan2015. pdf.

Engelen, E. and S. Musterd (2010) Amsterdam in crisis: how the (local) state buffers and suffers. *International Journal of Urban and Regional Research*, 34(3), pp. 701–708.

Esping-Andersen, G. (2013) *The Three Worlds of Welfare Capitalism*. Hoboken, NJ: John Wiley & Sons.

European Union (EU) (2013) Green Paper on the long-term financing of the European economy. https://eur-lex.europa.eu/legal-content/en/TXT/?uri=celex%3A52013DC0150.

Federal Reserve Bank (2014) About the Community Reinvestment Act. https//www.federalreserve.gov/consumercommunities/cra_about.htm (accessed 2 September 2018).

Financial Crisis Inquiry Commission (FCIC) (2011) *The financial crisis inquiry report: Final report of the national commission on the causes of the financial and economic crisis in the United States.* Washington, DC: Author. https://www.govinfo.gov/content/pkg/GPO-FCIC/pdf/GPO-FCIC.pdf.

Glickman, N.J. and L.J. Servon (1998) More than bricks and sticks: five components of community development corporation capacity. *Housing Policy Debate*, 9(3), pp. 497–539.

Guthrie, D. (2004) An accidental good: how savvy social entrepreneurs seized on a tax loophole to raise billions of corporate dollars for affordable housing. *Stanford Social Innovation Review*, 34, pp. 34–42.

Habitat for Humanity (2015) Affordability, Sustainability, Liveability: Housing Review, 2015. https://www.habitatforhumanity.org.uk/who-we-are/where-money-goes/.

Harloe, M. (1995) *The People's Home? Social Rented Housing in Europe and America*. Oxford: Blackwell.

HUD (2017) The US Department of Housing and Urban Development, Office of Policy Development and Research, Low Income Housing Credit Dataset. https://www.huduser.gov/portal/datasets/lihtc.html.

Kimura, D. (2014) How long can current LIHTC prices last? *Affordable Housing Finance*, 22 April. http://www.housingfinance.com/finance/how-long-can-current-lihtc-priceslast_o (accessed 1 September 2018).

Lawson, J., M. Berry and H. Pawson (2015) Guaranteeing investment in affordable rental housing. *Housing Finance International*, Winter, pp. 38–43.

Lindsey, L.B. (2009) The CRA as a means to provide public goods. In P. Chakrabarti, D. Erickson, R.S. Essene, I. Galloway and J. Olso (eds), *Revisiting the CRA: Perspectives on the Future of the Community Reinvestment Act*. Federal Reserve Banks of Boston and New York, pp. 160–166.

Local Initiatives Support Corporation (LISC) (2016) Affordable housing – the cornerstone of our work. http://www.lisc.org/our-initiatives/affordable-housing/.

McQuarrie, M. and D. Guthrie (2007) Houses for the poor and new business for banks: the creation of a market for affordable housing. In J. Quelch, A. Rangan, V. Kashturin, H. Gustavo and B. Barton (eds), *Business Solutions for the Global Poor: Creating Social and Economic Value*. Hoboken, USA: Jossey-Bass, pp. 249–258.

Milligan, V., J. Yates, I. Wiesel and H. Pawson (2013) Financing rental housing through institutional investment – Volume 1. AHURI Final Report (202). Sydney, NSW.

Morrison, N. (2016) Institutional logics and organisational hybridity: English housing associations' diversification into the private rented sector. *Housing Studies*, 31(8), pp. 897–915.

Mullins, D. (2006) Competing institutional logics? Local accountability and scale and efficiency in an expanding non-profit housing sector. *Public Policy and Administration*, 21(3), pp. 6–24.

Mullins, D. and H. Pawson (2010) Housing associations: agents of policy or profits in disguise. In D. Billis (ed.), *Hybrid Organizations and the Third Sector: Challenges for Practice, Theory and Policy*. Basingstoke: Palgrave Macmillan, pp. 197–218.

Mullins, D., D. Czischke and G. van Bortel (2012) Exploring the meaning of hybridity and social enterprise in housing organisations. *Housing Studies*, 27(4), pp. 405–417.

Narain, S., J. Schmidt and J. Ferrari (2012) The CDFI banking sector: 2011 annual report on financial and social performance. Chicago, IL: National Community Investment Fund.

Nguyen, M.T., W.M Rohe and S.M. Cowan (2012) Entrenched hybridity in public housing agencies in the USA. *Housing Studies*, 27(4), pp. 457–475.

Olson, J., P. Chakrabarti and R. Essene (2009) A framework for revisiting the CRA. In P. Chakrabarti, D. Erickson, R.S. Essene, I. Galloway and J. Olson (eds), *Revisiting the CRA: Perspectives on the Future of the Community Reinvestment Act*. Federal Reserve New York: Banks of Boston and New York.

Oxley, M. (2013) How America and France increased affordable housing supply. *Guardian*. https://www.theguardian.com/housing-network/2013/dec/09/lessons-abroad-affordable-housing-tax-breaks.

Pawson, H. and V. Milligan (2013) New dawn or chimera? Can institutional financing transform rental housing? *International Journal of Housing Policy*, 13(4), pp. 335–357.

Peck, J. and A. Tickell (2002) Neoliberalizing space. *Antipode*, 34(3), pp. 380–404.

Riquier, A. (2017) Trump tax plan, not even on drawing board, is already roiling rental housing. *Market Watch*, 1 March. http://www.marketwatch.com/story/trump-tax-plan-not-even-on-drawing-board-is-already-roiling-rental-housing-2017-02-28.

Rosen, J. (2014) US welfare spending up – but help for the neediest down. Johns Hopkins University, Media Release, 6 May. http://releases.jhu.edu/2014/05/06/u-s-welfare-spendingup-but-help-for-the-neediest-down/ (accessed April 2015).

Salet, W.G. (2002) Evolving institutions: an international exploration into planning and law. *Journal of Planning Education and Research*, 22(1), pp. 26–35.

Schwartz, A. (2011) The credit crunch and subsidized low-income housing: the UK and US experience compared. *Journal of Housing and the Built Environment*, 26(3), 353–374.

Schwartz, A. (2012) *Housing Policy in the United States*. New York: Routledge.

Schwartz, A. and E. Meléndez (2008) After year 15: challenges to the preservation of housing financed with low-income housing tax credits. *Housing Policy Debate*, 19(2), pp. 261–294.

Seidman, K.F. (2005) *Economic Development Finance*. Newbury Park, CA: SAGE.

Suchman, M. (1995) Managing legitimacy: strategic and institutional approaches. *Academy of Management Review*, 20(3), 571–610.

Sullivan, R. (2015) Fiduciary duty in the 21st century. London School of Economics. https://papers.ssrn.com/sol3/papers.cfm?abstract_id=2724866.

Swyngedouw, E. (2005) Governance innovation and the citizen: the Janus face of governance-beyond-the-state. *Urban Studies*, 42(11), pp. 1991–2006.

Taylor, J. and J. Silver (2009) The Community Reinvestment Act: 30 years of wealth building and what we must do to finish the job. In P. Chakrabarti, D. Erickson, R.S. Essene, I. Galloway and J. Olson (eds), *Revisiting the CRA: Perspectives on the Future of the Community Reinvestment Act*. New York: Federal Reserve Banks of Boston and New York, pp. 148–159.

Willis, M. (2009) It's the rating, stupid: a banker's perspective on the CRA. In P. Chakrabarti, D. Erickson, R.S. Essene, I. Galloway and J. Olson (eds) *Revisiting the CRA: Perspectives on the Future of the Community Reinvestment Act*. New York: Federal Reserve Banks of Boston and New York, pp. 59–70.

PART III

THIRD SECTOR HYBRIDS

17. Third sector hybrid organisations: two different approaches
Adalbert Evers

INTRODUCTION

Debates often evolve around central topics and labels that have a conjuncture. For more than a decade, 'hybrids' and processes of 'hybridisation' have been such a topic. Beyond the sphere of academic research this topic has reached some popularity as a background notion in the debate on social enterprises and social entrepreneurship (*The Economist*, 2009; *European Business Review*, 2013). And in this context there has been a move from an earlier conceptual stage to contributions on procedural and organisational questions (see the overview in Doherty et al., 2014).

This chapter, however, focuses on conceptual issues. The main reason is that the conceptual debate about hybrids and hybridisation has pushed aside some dimensions of hybridity that could allow for a broader perspective than one in which hybridisation in practical and political terms is narrowed down to issues of social entrepreneurship. It will be argued that there are two very different concepts of hybridity that exist separately, each of them pointing in a different direction for research and practice.

The chapter first sketches out these two concepts. The first concept is often seen as the only interpretation of hybridity. Here hybrids represent a kind of intra-organisational intertwining of usually separated institutional logics and organisational fields. As well as this concept, however, there is another stream in the debate which has had far less attention. Here hybrids appear as organisational forms that combine distinct purposes, such as service provision and advocacy, value change and mutual help. This kind of traditionally given hybridity is seen as essential for the vitality of a third sector and of many organisations therein that cannot rely on one unique background principle.

These approaches must not be seen as mutually exclusive. They do, however, direct attention and debate in different directions. The first one mostly leads to concerns with variations of a special organisational form in relation to the production of goods and services. The second one raises broader issues concerning the rationale not only of individual organisations but also of the whole broader domain in the civil society, the third sector, for which it is essential to intertwine and balance various purposes. Hence it seems useful to look at complementarities between the two concepts and perspectives. What does it mean when services, so far embedded in a multipurpose context, are increasingly shaped by the logics prevailing in the state and/or market sector?

With respect to the question of how 'inter-sectoral' and 'multipurpose' hybridity might interact, this chapter then suggests a kind of research that is oriented more to history and contexts. First of all, rather than relating hybridity to the rivalry between 'eternal' institutional logics, for example of 'the state' and 'the market', it recommends looking at the impact of discourses and the way in which such sector logics are intertwined and interpreted. Being more affiliated to the state, for example, will mean different things depending on the prevailing discourses. Secondly, this approach gives special attention to those goals and tasks of multipurpose hybrids that might be lost sight of once the focus is on better, somehow 'more social', products and services: it focuses on issues such as the link with movements and values and its own tasks in advocacy and campaigning, so important for the distinctiveness of the third sector and for cross-sector alliances in civil society.

DEBATES ON HYBRIDITY: MAPPING THE FIELD

Merging Sector Logics and Rationalities: Inter-Sectoral Hybridity

Putting it in simple terms, hybrids mix and intertwine features that are mostly separate, be it on the level of organisations or sectors where similar organisations and foundational rationalities prevail. Debates and research about hybridisation have focused very much on the third sector, an organisational field marked by a great diversity of organisational tasks and a plurality of values and normative orientations. Diversity was developed by trends such as the progress of professional and administrative logics in what were traditionally called voluntary organisations, or the fact that many organisations that basically operated for other reasons than profit-making were concerned with making a surplus or had to operate on social markets, alongside private business. Later on, with the growth of multiculturalism, for example, there was a great deal of overlapping between semi-formal community organising on grounds of shared, binding cultural or religious traditions on the one hand, and formal organisations with voluntary membership on the other.

For a while this could be dealt with as a marginal phenomenon, occurring only at the fringes of the sectoral lines between state, market, community and the third sector. However, there came a point where third sector organisations and their rationales themselves became understood as being hybrid. This kind of understanding was the shared perspective in the early contributions of Brandsen et al. (2005) and Evers (2005).

Evers's contribution was built on his previous work in the field of welfare studies that situated the sector – thought of then as being largely the same as the civil society – within a triangular tension field, constituted by the basic institutions of the market, the state and the community or family sphere (Evers, 1995). It was argued that this sector and its organisations represented an intermediary field of public opinion-building, negotiation and service provision between the competing and rivalling basic logics of state (hierarchical authority) market (for-profit competition) and community (with its binding ties for more or less 'involuntary' members). This laid the grounds for a conceptual model of the third sector/civil society sphere as a constituency which was clearly defined by its pluralism and its ways of linking orientations such as free association, solidarity and civic action with values dominating in the other sectors, such as administrative professionalism, the search for profits in competition, or the cultivation of bonding ties. In one way or another the intermingling of these norms also gave leeway to organisations that represented inter-sectoral compromises. On the level of organisations, Evers (2005, p. 741) observed three dimensions of hybridisation. The first of these involved mixing not only material and financial resources but also those derived from the social capital of trust relationships and civic commitment. The second dimension was related to the intertwining of sector-specific goals and steering mechanisms with public-good and group-specific local orientations, with state regulation and participatory elements brought in by various stakeholders. And the third dimension was related to kinds of corporate identity expressed in labels such as 'social enterprise'. Hybridisation was introduced as an ambiguous issue, a chance and a challenge: 'There is the chance to constitute a complex agenda made up by the various goals, but also the challenge to balance and keep the diversity of goals compatible' (ibid., p. 742)

In a similar vein Brandsen et al. (2005) argued that we should not see organisations in the third sector as 'griffins' – strange figures composed of elements that are supposed to belong to different entities – but should think of third sector organisations as 'chameleons', conceiving 'the third sector as a central area of society wherein tensions between competing values and methods of coordination are exacerbated or resolved, in a more or less complex portfolio that inevitably has to combine the various rationalities and mechanisms relevant for the production of social services and goods' (ibid., p.761). In a similar vein to Evers, who takes the weakening of the distinct profiles of the state, market and community sectors as trends that are alleviating a hybridisation in the third sector, Brandsen et al. describe respective tendencies such as the marketising of public services and the emergence of quasi-markets. But they radicalise this observation up to the point where they question to what degree it is at all justifiable to use ideal one-dimensional rationalities and organisational domains in contrast to a hybrid third sector. With respect to the identity and distinctiveness of a third sector that is 'miscellaneous and fuzzy' (Brandsen et al., 2005, p. 751), they propose two different hypotheses. The first one argues that there is a third sector wherever it is needed to get to arrangements that 'combine more successfully with some products and services than others' (ibid., p. 761), such as 'care for others on a voluntary basis, directed at a more or less defined and exclusive "other"' (ibid., p. 751). The second one goes much further in the direction of stating that there is a world of different chameleons in all sectors, even so more in the 'third' sector than in the others.

Among the various publications that followed later in this foundational stage of theorising hybridity, the collection edited by Billis (2010) is notable. In the first place it differentiated and further developed observations like those mentioned above. Billis described different 'hybrid zones' which resulted from areas of overlapping what he called the public, the private and the third sector, and suggested that some third sector organisations were significantly co-shaped either by the public or the private (market) sector, or simultaneously by both. Furthermore, in a historical perspective, Billis described different dynamics and types of hybridity that are illustrated later on in various contributions to the book. These include the concept of a 'shallow' and an 'entrenched' hybridity (Billis, 2010, pp. 58–61), with the first being more in the nature of a minor addendum to a persisting third sector core, and the second becoming (by means of government boards, a high degree of professionalism and other influences) a co-feature of the organisation. He also differentiates between 'organic' and 'enacted' hybrids (ibid., p. 61); hybridity of the first type results from the steady accumulation of external resources; hybridity of the second type results from a decisive step toward kinds of inter-sectoral organisational partnership.

It should be noted that Billis's model of three sectors that are partially overlapping seems to subsume the community sector within his concept of a third sector. The second difference in Billis's concept compared to other contributions of the kind sketched out formerly derives from the fact that he argues that there is a central distinctive hallmark of the third sector. With respect to the often raised question of whether hybridity is a special case or the hallmark of all third sector organisations (TSOs) (Glänzel and Schmitz, 2012), he concludes:

> that the positive attributes most frequently claimed for the sector were found in their most pristine form in the archetypal association . . . Placing the association and its claimed virtues at the heart of the third sector is comparable to the powerful ideal models of the public and private sectors under whose own general *principles* can be found equally diverse groups of institutions. (Billis, 2010, p. 64)

In all of these contributions one finds – despite notable differences concerning the nature of the distinctiveness of the third sector – a shared concept of hybridity as an inter-sectoral phenomenon. And one finds links with the theoretical approach of the new institutionalism (for its basics, see Friedland and Alford, 1991) that conceives organisations as units that belong to different domains and sectors, sharing with them a logic that is dominant in the respective organisational field. It also suggests that change is possible within these frameworks since these constructs are embedded in changing historical contexts.

The contribution made by Skelcher and Smith in 2014 is among the first that theorizes hybridity by an explicit reference to and use of the institutional logics approach as a feature of the new institutionalism. Here, organisations are a medium between institutional logics and the agency of actors. A mix of different logics can influence organisational development and likewise the kind of identity of the actors in the respective organisations, be they managers, workers or volunteers. With some degree of autonomy, they can argue and act as citizens, employees or professionals to various degrees with a 'multiple identity' (Foreman and Whetten, 2002). The important point, then, is that institutional logics (such as a for-profit market logic or a community logic) are not bound to a sector and its organisations, but can be influential in different sectors. 'It is the plurality of institutional logics and their availability for utilization by actors within organizations that makes this theory highly relevant' (Skelcher and Smith, 2014, p. 439). The relationships between institutional orders, organisations within those orders and the individuals within those organisations are seen as interdependent, but only loosely coupled. Given organisational forms can be seen as being supported, questioned or shifted by the institutional logics they are related to. A voluntary organisation, for example, can come under pressure when a managerial logic is increasingly shaping its action grounds, reducing the impact of the community logic that has prevailed so far; reforms imposing new administrative proceedings that question its former amateurism may follow, assuming that the actors (such as the staff and the users) are willing at least to tolerate such changes.

On the level of the descriptions of types of hybrids that Skelcher and Smith offer, there is not really a great deal of difference from the findings of other authors quoted before, such as Billis: here as well, a market function can be 'segmented' and 'segregated', which means that a for-profit organisation can be compartmentalised within or become associated with a larger third sector organisation; it can be 'assimilated' as a subdominant feature and it may finally be 'blended' with others in a way where it is hard to attach the respective organisation to the persisting classical order of institutional sectors.

The contribution of Skelcher and Smith makes a difference, first of all, by emphasising actorship and its relative autonomy. In the version of the new institutionalism used by them, actors are not seen to be mere followers of prescribed institutional and organisational logics and their shifts. It is possible to think of the involvement of deviance, resistance or counter-strategies. These things did not play much of a role in the early notions of neo-institutionalism where organisations and actors seemed to be condemned altogether to kinds of institutional isomorphism (DiMaggio and Powell, 1983): the stronger organisational culture and domain always causes a process of assimilation in the weaker sectors. This kind of hybridity is then due to the structural opportunism of the actors to be found there.

The second interesting element in Skelcher and Smith's approach is that they present more than the usual three ideal-typical logics which are referred to in third sector debates, and which have a fairly clear domain: family/community, state and market. In a table, they give a number of other special logics including religion, profession and corporation (Skelcher and Smith, 2014, p. 438). It is, however, a pity that they make little use of this enrichment. This would make it possible to conceive of more dimensions of hybridity: for example, in the way that the logics of a religious community could intermesh its faith-based organisation with public and third sector services. One can also state that the more rationalities are considered that have no sectoral home domain, such as religion or profession, the more questionable becomes the sectoral concept of a state–market–community triangle as a sole reference point. Rivalling and merging rationalities are hard to conceive without the notion of a public sphere and a civil society wherein, for example, ideas are born, concepts deliberated and finally consented to in rules for a 'good professional', or with respect to the influence religion should have in public life and its various organisational fields.

Summing up, despite some controversial questions such as whether or not one can define principles that define the third sector, the various versions of conceptualising a kind of 'inter-sectoral' hybridity have much in common:

- They state that principles that are clearly dominant in an institutional order can likewise become influential to different degrees and in different combinations in other fields, such as the third sector.
- This kind of co-presence of different logics has an impact on organisational forms, even leading to clusters across sectoral lines, or to various kind of blending within associational forms that allow for it.
- This may change the kind of goods and services, the concept of cooperation, and the degree to which the respective organisation is mirroring what makes up the core of the domain and institutional order it belongs to. And there is much diversity beyond the third sector; there may be, for example, different degrees of community links in the worlds of markets or contributions of local associations to public services such as schools.

It should, however, be noted that to some degrees all the approaches share a selective perspective when it comes to the kind of third sector organisations (TSOs) they look at. These are always the kind of organisation where service provision is the prevailing activity; given that they take on board some market logics they may all be called and analysed as 'social enterprises' (as in Battilana et al., 2012). Yet it is common wisdom that many of the organisations in the third sector, such as advocacy and interest groups and associations of professionals, are either not at all concerned with service provision or only engaged in it to a minor degree.

Organisations and Networks in the Third Sector: Multipurpose Hybridity

Some of the literature we have discussed so far notes a publication by Minkoff as an early contribution to the debate on hybridity. However, Minkoff herself explicitly states that her study on 'The emergence of hybrid organizational forms' (Minkoff, 2002) 'differs from the usage of the term in the literature on non-profits, where it tends to refer to a combination of different sectoral forms in one organization' (ibid., p. 382). Her focus was on 'a hybrid organizational form that combines advocacy and service provision as its core identity' (ibid., p. 377), and her case studies looked at organisations in the United States (US) that had the 'dual commitment to promoting the interests of women and racial or ethnic minorities through both service provision and advocacy' (ibid., p. 377). She discussed the emergence of this kind of new organisational form as part of the social and democratic politics linked to civil rights movements in response to increasingly restrictive state politics that, by the 1980s under the Reagan administration, was opposed to further civil rights advances. Within the national organisations for women and minorities there was then a rapid expansion of advocacy organisations related to some extent to service organisations, but also a substantial number of organisations that combined advocacy and campaigning with a commitment to providing resources and services. Minkoff showed that the new hybrid forms emerging borrowed 'self-consciously from both traditional and newly emergent social movement organisational forms' (ibid., p. 381).

In 2005, Hasenfeld and Gidron addressed the issue of 'Understanding multi-purpose hybrid voluntary organizations' as part of a discussion of the 'contributions of theories on civil society, social movements and non-profit organizations' (Hasenfeld and Gidron, 2005, p. 205). The kind of hybridity they were concerned with was – like those studied by Minkoff – related to the interplay of movements and organisations that 'set out as their mission to uphold and promote cultural values that are typically at variant with dominant and institutionalized values'. Against that background:

> they evolve into hybrid organizations by having multiple purposes – combining to various degrees goals of value change, service provision and mutual-aid . . . offering services to members and the public that express distinct values, using services as a model and catalyst for social change. In addition to their instrumental goals, they aim to meet the expressive and social identity needs of their members by promoting a collective identity. (Hasenfeld and Gidron, 2005, p. 97)

One can say, in a way, that the kind of hybrids Minkoff studied, and the multiplicity of purposes within society, the third sector and many of its organisations that Hasenfeld and Gidron addressed, had a long history. They could be traced back to older social movements, such as labour, popular or peasant movements, where in the milieu of 'working people' inspiration, values, loyalties were shared between parties, trade unions, co-operatives and mutual self-help associations. There was organisational differentiation, but there were also shared goals and perspectives across the different organisational borders. Voluntary organisations and charities and their nationwide associations have been service providers, but they were also involved as advocacy and campaigning organisations. That made – and still makes – a difference from public services or for-profit service providers. Readers may know of similar forms of this kind of hybridity from their own countries which have had a history where both 'old' and 'new' social movements have shaped various kinds of third sector organisations. What comes to the foreground in that case is the pioneering and innovative role of the respective organisations and movements. These have not only resulted in new services and arrangements but have also helped to shape new democratic forms of statehood and governance and have contributed to the turn towards forms of welfare state which have taken up and integrated to different degrees parts of the third sector organisations and their concepts which were at their beginnings of minority interest.

In their 2005 study, Hasenfeld and Gidron made use of the opportunities that the new institutionalism was opening up. They tried to embed the study of organisations into an understanding of historical social contexts, the role of collective actors, power structures, and controversies in the making of different organisational fields with typical institutional patterns, such as the democratic welfare state and the third sector. They looked back on a history where, along with social movements, one can find various ways to combine civic activism, volunteer-run association building and the creation of social services and mutual social support. By an experimental interrelating of civil society, social movement and non-profit sector studies they tried to articulate what was separated when the field of the third sector was reduced to a field where civic action, social protest and a different kind of social service provision were studied separately and not with a view to their interrelation. The kind of hybridity they described, with an explicit reference to Minkoff, could be found not only in networks and alliances in and across the sector but also in 'multi-purpose hybrid organizations . . . combining to various degrees goals of value change, service provision and mutual aid . . . and a deliberate mix of organizational forms borrowed from volunteer run associations, social movements and non-profit service organisations' (Hasenfeld and Gidron, 2005, p. 98).

It is important then to get a clearer picture on the ways in which multipurpose hybridity is developing these days. No systematic research so far has followed the paths laid out by Minkoff, Hasenfeld and Gidron. Yet some observations can be made.

Many of those third sector organisations that used to combine advocacy, service provision and the preservation of a culture that invited commitment seem to have lost much of this former hybridity as a result of the other – 'intersectoral' – hybridity that has resulted from the increasing entrenchment of state and market logics and their organisational counterparts. Rochester argues that: 'The concentration on service delivery as the main or sole purpose of voluntary action has undesirable effects. It relegates other historical functions of voluntary organisations, such as self-help, mutual aid, community development and campaigning, or advocacy roles, to the margin' (Rochester, 2013, p. 77). The ways in which many third sector organisations have been tied into subcontracts with state agencies that focus on their service performance, instead of receiving support from open grants to the organisation along with all of its various purposes, has weakened their impact as advocates for what Knight (1993) once called a 'vision based approach'. Furthermore, they are less and less likely to receive support from a firm foundation of shared values such as was found in the historical milieu of the working classes that enabled them to play an additional role as agencies for socialising, or in a middle-class and bourgeois milieu of 'good citizens' who felt obliged to join a body where volunteering played an important role. Bode (2010) has described this weakening of what is discussed here as 'multipurpose hybridity', in terms of what happened to the big and central area of welfare associations in Germany which have won impact as service providers in close cooperation with markets and politics, and have lost impact as socio-political bodies that intervened as advocates and campaigning organisations in ways that were different from the operational style of lobby organisations. In a piece of research based on case studies, Aiken (2014, p. 26) has demonstrated that those organisations 'seeking to combine services with advocacy . . . were facing severe strain. There were also indications that some larger voluntary sector groups – particularly those that were "contract heavy" and directly delivering social welfare services – were less interested (or less forthright) in campaign work'.

On the other hand, the last few decades have seen the emergence of a multitude of rather small groups and initiatives active around issues such as health and lifestyle, micro-solidarities on a local level and in the community, or environmental concerns. Mostly they are not established in a clearly structured and organised supportive environment of organisations with which they can build a clear division of tasks and roles. For many projects and organised initiatives that means intra-organisational hybridity. The multiple purposes of trying out a new service concept, creating a cooperative and inviting atmosphere, building a committed community advocating for their goals and concerns on local and global levels, and winning allies, have to be undertaken largely by and within the individual organisation (for an overview on such innovative initiatives and organisational forms, see Evers et al., 2014).

In the context of this research on innovative initiatives and projects for fostering social inclusion in urban contexts, Evers and Brandsen (2016) have conceptualised social innovations as having a double character that points to the kind of multipurpose hybridity under discussion. They represent solutions that have to work here and now but also involve 'messages' about the wider concerns and utopias that activate the respective organisation and its volunteers, engaged professionals and/or social entrepreneurs. What is a special task for a distinct group of employees in a mainstream organisation – marketing – is here a foundational dimension of the appropriate social innovation project and initiative. And while some of these initiatives may aim only at maintaining their local project, others look for ways of extending and solidifying the mission, networking with individual and corporate allies and hoping for sensibility and support from public state and municipal bodies or partners in the business sector. The nudges of projects and milieus that generate innovative services and try to promote wider aspirations and utopias, 'acting local' and 'thinking global', constitute an archetype of multipurpose hybridity. Unconventional hybrid features with regard to resources, staff and the tasks of popularising one's innovation have to do with a situation where one is not part of an agreed and mainstreamed intra- or cross-sectional division of labour (as many big voluntary service providers are) or organisations specialising in one major purpose.

Against this background, the differences between the first debate on hybrids as organisations that merge principles from different sectors, and this debate on hybrids as organisations that are merging multiple purposes, can be subsumed under three points:

- While in the first approach hybridity means to adopt and integrate in various ways, and to various degrees, logics and organisational items from other fields or sectors, the second approach focuses on the hybridisation of the multitude of purposes that help to uphold many third sector organisations and the kind of 'social ecology' of this domain.

- While the first approach focuses on the impact of hybridisation on organisations that are usually mainly concerned with service provision, the second one, by taking into account the multipurpose character of TSOs, gives attention as well to other organisations such as social movements or non-governmental organisations (NGOs), which may be mainly concerned with the cultivation of identities and values and involvement in deliberation and decision-making processes.
- The first approach articulates the principles that may guide stakeholders and decision-makers when developing strategies of organisational change in fairly abstract and singularised points of reference (market versus state logics, logics of association, professional logics, and so on); the second approach makes reference to concerns and narratives that are richer, less single-focused, but also more fuzzy and complex, such as those of cultural and social movements, or of milieus where innovative experiments are tried out.

EXPLORING THE INTERACTION OF TWO KINDS OF HYBRIDITY: SUGGESTIONS FOR THE FURTHER STUDY OF HYBRIDISATION

There are forms of inter-sectoral hybridisation that can often be seen as mere isomorphism. This is the case when hybridisation results from some kind of reactive adaption to the activities of organisational fields with a stronger role and a higher status. However, opting for this kind of hybridisation can also be the result of reflected coping strategies that try to make the best out of a difficult situation.

Take a local public school, for example. Changed state regulations may foresee that parents are allowed to inscribe their child at any school in the local area; and moreover the public money may now come as a budget, giving some autonomy to the school on how to spend it. Market elements make themselves increasingly felt. One way of reacting could be purely managerial reforms, trying to save as much of the given services with a smaller budget; such a way of reacting would result in a kind of hybridisation that is in fact an isomorphism of adapting to a more competitive environment. It might, however, also be possible to strengthen public and community support for the respective school, founding a support association of parents; using the room opened up by the budgets in order to adapt the services better to the needs of local pupils and families; enlarging school offers by cooperation with local associations in fields such as sport or culture; and finally, to network with other schools under similar pressure, building some community support and advocating by means of this network for a different policy of the authorities, which allows for a kind of differentiated allocation of state financing that takes account of the special challenges schools in difficult districts have to face.

On both roads 'hybridisation' takes place. But the intention and ability for the purpose of organising community support and advocacy makes a difference for the kind of inter-sectoral hybridity that will finally take shape. However, as long as hybridisation is conceived as a process wherein purposes such as active community-building and campaigning for policy changes have no place, things look different. This example may illustrate that the character of inter-sectoral hybridity depends on the impact of multipurpose hybridity, and vice versa. One should be aware of this when arguing for hybridisation and recommending it as a strategy.

With regard to campaigning and advocacy and their key role in a multipurpose set, one has to consider that third sector organisations are characterised by a kind of basic double loyalty. First of all, there is loyalty to the community, allies and networks of organisations, professionals with similar perspectives, and so on, with which one shares convictions and tasks. Then there is loyalty to the public authorities which guarantee the legal and fairly consented framework of operation, such as by laws on free association, and opinion-building, and tax deductions for the non-profit status. The conditions for navigating in these tension fields, looking for synergies between inter-sectoral and multipurpose hybridity, will vary greatly between times and places. In much of the second half of the last century, for example, a state such as Sweden made it quite easy to integrate both kinds of loyalty, with a welfare state on the one hand and a strong organised society on the other hand, building on generally agreed principles. Today, however, where the values and strategies of many governments are shaped by managerialism and marketisation, it is very difficult to develop a strategy that can synergise both kinds of hybridity: one that is about inter-sectoral bridging, and the other that is about a distinctive multipurpose culture. Today, entering into a service contract that seems essential for ensuring an organisation can make an impact may easily make it less and less possible for it to stay with its allies and to advocate (with them) for its own goals and ways of operation (a nice case study of this kind of impact on hybridity is provided by Hustinx and De Waele, 2015). Hybridisation may then mean co-optation.

With an eye on these challenges of balancing a kind of hybridity that is mainly about trans-sectoral cooperation and kinds of assimilation, and a hybridity that is mainly about the ability of organisations to retain a degree of difference and autonomy, I suggest a research and policy perspective that concentrates on two intertwined levels. The key words are 'discourse' and 'context'.

First of all, taking up the idea of a loose coupling of multiple and competing institutional logics, the logics of actors and stakeholders and organisational change, I suggest looking at the level where such logics take more concrete forms: as discourses. They are defined here as a combination of views, concepts and practices that may even crystallise in a strategy (Schmidt, 2010). What are the main overarching discourses in which tasks and priorities for our societies become visible, and what are their implications for the third sector, and the impact on both inter-sectoral and multipurpose hybridity?

Secondly, I would recommend case studies of hybridisation processes that – in different policy fields and settings – represent tendencies, that deviate to some degree or even counter the overall mainstream course of developments. One should look at examples of inter-sectoral hybridisation that take account of the local context, the kind of constellation of actor coalitions, their discursive orientations and the multipurpose hybridity to be found there. This would enable us to provide evidence that other ways and policy choices are possible both for leaders of organisations and for political actors.

The Impact of Discourses on the Third Sector and Hybridisation

Discourses rank in between the analytical level of institutional logics (market logic, or state-bureaucratic logic of top-down steering and regulation, logics of association and solidarism) and the real world of individual or collective actors with their convictions, interests and self-made strategies. They can be defined as historical concepts that link convictions, guidelines and narratives with strategy and practical action. Popular examples include the neoliberal discourse or the social-democratic welfare discourse. Such discourses have an impact on – or even drive – social actors as well as the direction taken by a third sector and hybrid organisation.

The suggestion that discourses provide an important reference point adds impetus to the task of overcoming thinking in terms of a strict triptych, where state, market and community represent the sole and rather invariant points of reference. Instead, a discourse, unlike the employment of a mix of single logics or principles (as in the new institutionalism, used by Skelcher and Smith), constitutes itself as a complex narrative that tries to give a role at once to the state, the market and the third sector in a historical context. This is exemplified in concepts of a 'social market' order or in concepts that define the welfare state as a 'social investment' state which establish a better link between economic and public-good logics. Once 'the state' is seen not only in terms of representing an institutional logic but also as an area where different discourses may prevail, hybridisation by assimilation of a third sector agency to a public service administration can mean very different things for welfare and for the rights of citizens. There is a state logic, but state action can represent very different discourses and orientations. The history of assimilative hybridisation by welfare states that have taken up the impulses of third sector organisations illustrates that.

Given the fact that a neoliberal discourse has prevailed for several decades in many welfare states, this might lead to the assumption that each merger with public administrations and units will probably mean a weakening of third sector organisations in terms of the impact of their distinctive multipurpose character. In a plural society, however, such a discourse is not the only game in town.

In an earlier study, Evers (2010) has tried to sort out various coexisting and rivalling discourses on welfare and social services, focusing on the role played in them by civicness and civility. He describes how in each of them the third sector and its organisations are given a different role:

- In 'traditional welfarism', TSOs were seen to have both a complementary and an innovative part, strengthening a welfare ethos and nudging new services; their assimilation in corporatist settings could be seen as a kind of historical compromise that worked quite well over a long time, challenging but not inevitably damaging the multipurpose hybridity of so many voluntary organisations.
- In the discourse on 'empowerment and participation', whose birth-pangs Evers associates with the new social movements, TSOs were taking part more than before through advocacy, voice and the kinds of provision that were reshaped and tailored for new needs; the type of hybridity described by Minkoff took shape in the heyday of this discourse.
- In the discourse on 'consumerism', some TSOs are meant to create more service choice as a special kind of providers, while others could gain increasing legitimacy

as consumer advocates; in this vein, the third sector is foremost giving a perspective for organisations of citizen-consumers, extending choice but also providing a public realm for consumer advocacy with respect to private and public goods.

- In the discourse on the 'activating social investment state', the general orientation is for better managed and streamlined services that should result not only in cost containment but also in developing the kinds of services that help to create better human capital, fit for a more competitive environment. One can easily imagine that, within the broad arrays of TSOs, opinions would be divided about such a course. It might give TSOs an intermediary role of special importance when it comes to contacting population groups that are hard to reach and include in such a perspective. But it might raise questions about the extent to which public policies can overcome an instrumental approach focusing exclusively on the service role of the relevant TSOs.

In a recent book, and an article based on it, Salamon (2015a, 2015b) has analysed the impact for the US of these kinds of overarching discourses. He starts by stating that a former long-lasting and widely accepted compromise over the roles of the third sector has eroded. More recently, according to his analysis, there are four especially significant 'impulses', each using its own 'ideological prism' (his labels for what is here called 'discourse'), which have implications for the features of the non-profit sector and – as one might conclude – on hybridisation. Besides the impulses labelled by him as 'civic activism' and 'commercialism/managerialism' which describe in similar ways the treatment of 'empowerment/participation' and 'activating social investment' in the approach in the work of Evers set out above, Salamon points at two other discourses and the ways in which they influence third sector organisations and their degree of assimilation and distinctiveness:

- According to him, the 'voluntarism' discourse as it appears in the USA these days often offers a kind of simplistic folklore of a sector that stands on its own and whose primary role is to express and cultivate values, operating in a paternalistic style that is centred on volunteering. From the point of view of the concerns of this chapter one could conclude that in such a view inter-sectoral hybridisation will be seen as an unnecessary or unwelcome tendency.
- The impulse of 'professionalism' that, according to Salamon, predated the expansion of government activities in the fields where non-profits were active, puts the focus on bureaucratic, professional rule-bound operation. From the point of view of the current topic one could assume that such a perspective might, for good or bad reasons, work against one kind of hybridisation that is focusing on managerial strategies for getting third sector organisations contracted as tightly managed aids of government, concerned with increasing effectiveness and productivity.

Obviously, one may debate to what degree these two pictures of four important discourses sketched here reflect reality. And one may also ask about possibilities of discursive mergers. Why not imagine, for example, that the civic activism, participation and empowerment discourse, and a new professionalism that opts for a more dialogic co-producing kind of service action, could enhance each other, giving room and renewing a volunteer discourse that is (as described by Salamon) so far still under conservative domination? But beyond such speculation, one can only agree with Salamon that, in view of the impulses he describes, the 'resilience' of the third or non-profit sector will be hard to safeguard since it 'is lacking the firm anchor of a single clear, dominant raison d'etre [*sic*]' (Salamon 2015a, p. 6). Its multipurpose hybridity might then be seen as a central asset.

In conclusion, future research should not only target hybridisation in terms of challenges on the level of single organisations as some kind of social enterprise. It should also be discussed as an issue for public policy and for debates in society as a challenge to the profile and vitality of the third sector at large; that is, a central element of a civil society. If one wants to do so, understanding discourses of actors and specific alliances across sectors, and the room they leave for different concepts and practices, is central. This emphasis on studying social and political actors and the discourses they rely on is not to say that the tendencies and constraints from the economy, new social cleavages, lifestyles and labour market changes in society would be of secondary importance. It means rather that, after more than a century of welfare states and organised civil societies, more and more of these challenges have become highly intermingled with collective political actions, concepts and strategies: a new kind of 'political economy'. That is what makes discourses matter so much.

Different Settings, Constellations of Discourses and Actors: Their Meanings for Hybridisation

Balances of discourses and actor constellations vary between different places and different policy fields. Managerial logics may be very strong, for example, in labour market politics, but count to a lesser degree in urban policies. Then again, an active civic society, with a supporting discourse aiming at more participatory and empowering politics, may have much more impact in one locality compared to another. Against this background one and the same item such as a cooperation between a work integration social enterprise and local partners may look and develop differently. It would therefore be useful to study the two kinds of hybridity identified here in different contexts, where state, third sector and market can then mean different things. In such a vein one can possibly find more typical trends than those described as 'shallow' and 'entrenched' (Billis) or 'assimilated' or 'blended' (Skelcher and Smith). A few examples can be given with respect to developments in Germany.

Segmentation and segregation

In Germany one of the big nationwide welfare associations, the Arbeiterwohlfahrt (AWO, Workers Welfare) that developed alongside the social-democratic movement for nearly 100 years carried out a major organisational reform some years ago. The mighty service branch of the AWO is no longer run by individual members who sat on the boards of the AWO associations that ran their services, but have been hived off and run along mainly managerial lines with the intention of making a decent surplus from contracts with public financing institutions (such as care insurance).

Apart from that there persist local small AWO associations for the usually elderly AWO members that offer small-scale services on a community basis that work as casual add-ons to the fairly professionalised core services. While the organisational and legal status of the AWO as a whole remains that of a non-profit organisation keeping the respective tax advantages, the bigger part of it has become a conglomeration of service enterprises, while the smaller part continues to cultivate the traditions of workers' community life. A multipurpose hybrid has changed into two rather single-purpose sections.

Friendly domination towards clientelism
For decades in Germany associations that organised services such as institutional and ambulant elderly care or child care facilities were members of big nationwide welfare associations. As member organisations they were part of a local network that operated within a special milieu (for example, Caritas was linked with Catholic parishes, and Diakonie with the Protestant church). For some decades, however, there has been an increase in the number of small-scale associations promoting service and community-building aims which are no longer rooted in such milieus, nor operating under nation-wide umbrella organisations. They negotiate with their public partners the conditions for regulating and co-financing the operations of their member organisations. The former kind of multipurpose hybridity where umbrella organisations were able to promote community-building, cultivating identity and values, and have a strong organised voice to speak out for the small groups and help to decide the conditions of public co-financing, has given way to a new scenario. Small and often precarious local associations without strong advocates have to negotiate the conditions for their activities with comparatively powerful public bodies; this creates a kind of clientelism, with its typical servile conduct that leaves little room for purposes such as cultivating relationships with others or even for open dissent.

Clusters with uncertain futures
In recent decades the public schools in Germany have seen an enormous increase in the numbers of support associations which take different kinds of members; while the membership of some is restricted to the parents of the pupils, others also include organisations such as representatives of local businesses (as corporate citizens and future employers). So far they have mainly helped by means of the additional finances they collect, enhancing the resources the school can build on. In the meantime, however, they have also become more important through organising a process of opening up the schools to the local communities and helping them to cope better with the challenge of developing full-day instead of the traditional half-day provision. In the process they raise the profile and not just the budget of the school. In the meantime, these school support associations have founded a nationwide network; discussions among professionals, teachers and academics have promoted the guiding image of a more autonomous and locally networked kind of school. These kinds of hybrid clusters, with the traditional public school logic still in the centre but also involving additional partners from local associations and business, have the potential to strengthen inter-sectoral and multipurpose hybridity alike.

Investments into multipurpose hybridity
In several areas on the fringes of mainstream politics, at local, federal and regional level, small-scale special programmes have developed that aim at co-financing, supporting and cooperating with third sector organisations such as:

- volunteer centres that define themselves as development agencies for a more vital local culture of volunteering and participation;
- community centres (called 'multigeneration houses') that aim to support all kind of initiatives that strengthen the intergenerational caring potential and economic, cultural and social revitalising of neighbourhoods at risk; and
- programmes such as 'the Engaged City' where for a limited time seed money is given for the kind of activities that help to reshape horizontal networks among organisations from local civil society as well as building new channels for cooperation and participation with the local political administration.

All these initiatives entail some support for multipurpose hybridity where issues are addressed not by single organisations such as a volunteer centre, but by local third sector organisations at large. And they are seen not only as service providers but also as facilitators for more convivial lifestyles and improved conditions, and as partners for debates on the future of the city.

The four small case stories summarised here should point towards a kind of research that looks at the different ways in which two things co-shape inter-sectoral hybridisation. Firstly, there is the degree to which a single organisation, cooperating in a joint inter-sectoral service project, is respected for its own multipurpose quality and/or can count on the multipurpose nature of its environment. Secondly, one needs to look at the impact of competing discourses as frames of references for actor coalitions that usually cross-cut sectoral borderlines.

SUMMARY

It has been argued that, when reviewing studies on hybridisation and hybridity, two different understandings can be reached. On the one hand there is a dominant debate that defines hybridity as an inter-sectoral phenomenon, a tight organisational knitting together of principles from different sectors, including third sector organisations. Furthermore, this debate is addressed throughout organisations where service provision is central. On the other hand, one finds contributions where hybridity is seen as a hallmark of multipurpose organisations that tie together such different things as service provision and campaigning. This is something to be found especially in the third sector, on both the organisational and the sector level, marked by the co-evolution of movements and organisations. In this debate, a richer variety of organisations comes into focus and service provision will not be the most important feature.

The study of hybridisation processes, it has been suggested, should look at the interaction of both kinds of hybridity. Multipurpose hybridity, the availability and cultivation of elements that help to strengthen the identity, values and claims that a third sector organisation and its service activities are relying on, will have a major influence on the character of inter-sectoral hybridisation, and the kind of mission drift it will imply.

With an eye on further studies of hybridity that take into account both kinds of hybridisation, two suggestions have been made. In the first place, discourses and their constellations should serve as a point of reference when studying hybridisation rather than invariant institutional logics. The former's complex, historical and less abstract character, and the fact that their adherents can be found throughout society, will help to think across sector borders and to analyse the direction and meaning of hybridisation processes. This is where discursive and historical institutionalism can meet. Secondly, case studies could provide the visibility needed for looking at a wider spectrum of different, or even opposing, developments that can stretch from a de facto dissolution of third sector organisations formerly based on multipurpose hybridity, to public policies that invest into these kinds of organisational and sector-wide qualities. Such an approach will facilitate the kind of research on hybridity that avoids replicating the narrow perspective on social enterprises and services that prevails in public policies, and instead addresses issues that concern the vitality of civil society, the third sector and the rich variety of its organisations.

REFERENCES

Aiken, M. (2014): Voluntary services and campaigning in austerity UK: saying less and doing more. National Coalition for Independent Action, Working Paper No. 16. http://www.independentaction.net/wp-content/uploads/2015/01/Say-less-do-more-final.pdf.

Battilana, J., Lee, M., Walker, J., Dorsey, C. (2012): In search of the hybrid ideal. *Stanford Social Innovation Review*, pp. 51–55. http://ssir.org/articles/entry/in_search_of_the_hybrid_ideal.

Billis, D. (2010): Towards a theory of hybrid organizations. In: Billis, D. (ed.), *Hybrid Organizations and the Third Sector: Challenges for Practice, Theory and Policy*, Basingstoke: Palgrave Macmillan, pp. 46–69.

Bode, I. (2010): Thinking beyond borderlines: a 'German gaze' on a changing interface between society and the voluntary sector. *Voluntary Sector Review*, 1 (2), pp. 139–161.

Brandsen, T., van de Donk, W., Putters, K. (2005): Griffins or chameleons? Hybridity as a permanent and inevitable characteristic of the Third Sector. *International Journal of Public Administration*, 28 (9/10), pp. 749–766.

DiMaggio, P.J., Powell, W.W. (1983): The iron cage revisited: institutional isomorphism and collective rationality in organizational fields. *American Sociological Review*, 48 (2), pp. 147–160.

Doherty, B., Haugh, H., Lyon, F. (2014): Social enterprises as hybrid organizations: a review and research agenda. *International Journal of Management Reviews*, 16, pp. 417–436.

The Economist (2009): The rise of the hybrid company. http://www.economist.com/node/15011307.

European Business Review (2013): Best of all worlds: hybrid models of public-service delivery. http://www.europeanbusinessreview.com/?p=1219.

Evers, A. (1995): Part of the welfare mix: the third sector as an intermediate area. *Voluntas*, 6 (2), pp. 119–139.

Evers, A. (2005): Mixed welfare systems and hybrid organizations: changes in the governance and provision of social services. *International Journal of Public Administration*, 28 (9/10), pp. 737–748.

Evers, A. (2010): Civicness, civility and their meanings for social services. In: Brandsen, T., Dekker, P., Evers, A. (eds), *Civicness in the Governance and Delivery of Social Services*, London, UK and New York, USA: Routledge, pp. 41–66.

Evers, A., Brandsen, T. (2016): Social innovations as messages: democratic experimentation in local welfare systems. In: Brandsen, T., Cattacin, S., Evers, A., Zimmer, A. (eds), *Social Innovations in the Urban Context*, New York: Springer, pp. 161–180.

Evers, A., Ewert, B., Brandsen, T. (eds) (2014): Social innovations for social cohesion: transnational patterns and approaches from 20 European cities (an E-reader). WILCO project, Brussels. http://www.wilcoproject.eu/ereader-wilco/.

Foreman, P., Whetten, D.A. (2002): Members' identification with multiple-identity organizations. *Organization Science*, 13 (6), pp. 618–635.

Friedland, R., Alford, R.R. (1991): Bringing society back in: symbols, practices and institutional contradictions. In: Powell, W.D., DiMaggio, P.J. (eds), *New Institutionalism in Organizational Analysis*, Chicago, IL USA and London, UK: University of Chicago Press, pp. 232–266.

Glänzel, G., Schmitz, B. (2012): Hybride Organisationen – Spezial- oder Regelfall? In: Anheier, H.K., Schröer, A., Then, V. (eds), *Soziale Investitionen. Interdisziplinäre Perspektiven*, Wiesbaden: Springer, pp. 181–203.

Hasenfeld, Y., Gidron, B. (2005): Understanding multi-purpose hybrid voluntary organizations: the contributions of theories on civil society, social movements and non-profit organizations. *Journal of Civil Society*, 1 (2), pp. 97–112.

Hustinx, L., De Waele, E. (2015): Managing hybridity in a changing welfare mix: everyday practices in an entrepreneurial non-profit in Belgium. *Voluntas*, 26 (5), pp. 1666–1689.

Knight, B. (1993): *Voluntary Action*, London: Centris.

Minkoff, D.C. (2002): The emergence of hybrid organizational forms: combining identity-based service provision and political action. *Nonprofiit and Voluntary Sector Quarterly*, 31 (3), pp. 377–401.

Rochester, C. (2013): *Rediscovering Voluntary Action. The Beat of a Different Drum*, Basingstoke: Palgrave Macmillan.

Salamon, L.M. (2015a): The four impulses of nonprofits and what they each create. *Nonprofit Quarterly*. https://nonprofitquarterly.org/2015/10/12/the-four-impulses-of-nonprofits-and-what-they-each-create/.

Salamon, L.M. (2015b): *The Resilient Sector Revisited: The New Challenge to Nonprofit America*, Washington, DC: Brookings Institution Press.

Schmidt, V.A. (2010): Taking ideas and discourse seriously: explaining change through discursive institutionalism as the fourth 'new institutionalism'. *European Political Science Review*, 2 (1), pp. 1–25.

Skelcher, C., Smith, S.R. (2014): Theorizing hybridity: institutional logics, complex organizations, and actor identities: the case of nonprofits. *Public Administration*, 93 (2), pp. 433–448.

18. Public administration regimes and co-production in hybrid organisations
Victor Pestoff

INTRODUCTION

This chapter analyses the impact of public administration regimes (PARs) and co-production on hybrid organisations. The study of both PARs and co-production is a relatively new academic phenomenon, so there is still little systematic knowledge on how they impact on hybridity, and in particular how they impact on third sector organisations (TSOs). Yet, TSOs often work closely with public sector organisations, sometimes in partnership, so important changes in the way the public sector works have clear implications for TSOs and other hybrid organisations. For example, a major shift in the function and operation of traditional public administration occurred in the early 1980s that had clear and far-reaching ramifications for both the private and the third sectors. The growth and spread of a market ideology in the management of public services that later became known as New Public Management (NPM) brought with it a new focus and mode of operating, particularly in relation to the private and third sector providers of public services. So, it is impossible to ignore such sweeping changes in the public sector when considering hybridity and the third sector.

Therefore, the purpose of this chapter is to clarify the impact of public administration regimes and co-production on hybridity, in particular in the third sector. This will be achieved in part by comparing and contrasting the values and goals of four PARs, with a focus on the role played by service users and professionals in the provision of publicly financed social services. The development of new PARs, such as New Public Management, contributes significantly to the complexity and hybridity facing the leaders of third sector providers of publicly financed services. The concept of co-production furthers the study with its focus on the mix of activities that both public agents and citizens contribute to the provision of public services. It also adds to the complexity and hybridity facing the leaders of third sector providers of publicly financed services. How these two concepts interact with each other and with hybridity are also explored in the following pages.

Hybridity is considered as the overlap between the third sector and other major social sectors, such as the state, market and community, illustrated by the welfare triangle discussed below. Co-production is the mix of activities that both public service agents and citizens contribute to the provision of public services. Public administration regimes can be distinguished by a combination of elements, including their theoretical roots, value base and key concepts, as well as the role attributed to citizens, service professionals and the third sector. Changes in public administration regimes help to set the parameters for the activity and focus of third sector organisations and their leaders, as well as to set the limits for citizen participation and co-production. This in turn can determine the type of hybridity that develops in third sector organisations, such as 'shallow' or 'entrenched' and perhaps even 'enforced' or coerced forms of hybridity.

Elinor Ostrom (2009) advised against promoting and pursuing overly simple models of human behaviour, particularly ones that focus solely on self-interest. We need to embrace the challenges for the third sector and its leaders posed by the development of different public administration regimes, each with its own values and focus, and by the spread of co-production in the provision of public services. The complexity posed by public administration regimes and co-production has now become part of the contemporary environment of the third sector in most European countries, but it poses some new challenges for its leaders. They will need to understand it better in order for them to achieve their goals and operate more successfully and sustainably. Providing a better understanding of these new complexities is the main purpose of this chapter.

The chapter begins by employing a mixed sectoral approach to understanding the hybrid nature of study of many TSOs, particularly when they operate in the overlapping area with other major social sectors, such as the state, market and community. It continues in the following section by introducing the ideas of public administration regimes (PARs) and briefly presents four of them. It argues that each of them is based on different values, and they have different logics. PARs also attribute different roles to citizens, the professional staff and third sector organisations as providers of publicly financed services, which has some implications for hybridity. The chapter then discusses the relationship between PARs and hybridity. After that, the next section introduces the complexities of co-production along with different levels of citizen participation in the provision of public services. This is followed by a section which analyses PARs, co-production and hybrid TSOs together. Finally, the chapter presents a summary and reaches some conclusions about the impact of PARs and co-production on hybrid TSOs.

A MIXED SECTORAL APPROACH TO UNDERSTANDING THE HYBRIDITY OF THE THIRD SECTOR

This section presents a mixed sector approach to understanding the hybridity of the third sector. Several European scholars have adopted a mixed sectoral approach to analysing the role of the third sector in the growing mix of service providers by employing a welfare triangle to help understand the relations between sectors (Evers, 1993, 1995; Laville, 1992, 1994; Evers and Laville, 2004; Pestoff, 1992, 1998, 2008; Defourny et al., 2014; Defourny and Pestoff, 2015). Similarly, the Centre for Social Investment has defined hybrid organisations as entities that straddle the border between the public and private, as well as between the for-profit and non-profit, sectors that often combine the logics of the seemingly distinct spheres of the market, state and civil society (Anheier, 2011).

The welfare mix approach utilised here can be considered from both a theoretical and an empirical perspective. At the theoretical level, the idea of the welfare mix expresses variations in the importance attributed to the four major social sectors of community, market, state and associations, as well as the values associated with each of them (Streeck and Schmitter, 1995; Billis, 2010). Note, however, that sectoral divisions can shift over time and also vary between countries. Thus, much of the debate in recent decades concerns the dividing line between the state and market, or the public and private sectors,

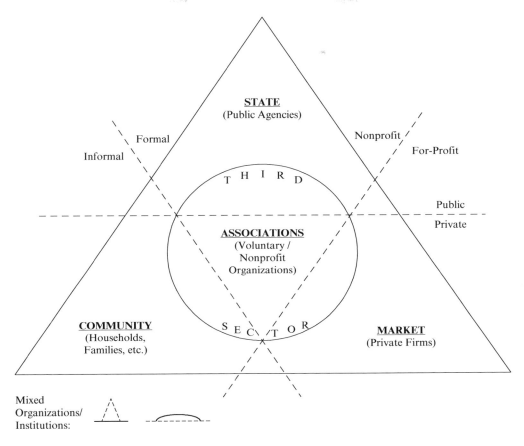

Source: Pestoff (1998, 2008).

Figure 18.1 *The third sector and the welfare triangle*

and where the division between them lies or should lie. By contrast, the third sector and households have received much less attention both in the public debate and in academic discourse.

At the empirical level, the welfare triangle (set out in Figure 18.1) helps to emphasise the shifting role played by various sectors in delivering social welfare services, and how such changes contribute to the current blurring of the third sector's borders (Brandsen et al., 2003). Moreover, actors within the smaller inverted triangle can express varying degrees of privateness/publicness, non-profitness/for-profitness and formality/informality, placing them closer to one of the other three social sectors (Van Der Meer et al., 2009). Note that many third sector organisations also overlap with the other social sectors. Thus, we should expect to find a higher degree of hybridity and clearer hybrid forms in the parts of the third sector circle that overlap with other social sectors.

The overlap between the community and the third sector provides numerous examples of hybrid organisations that operate with different logics, such as self-help groups that provide mutual aid and comfort to their own members as well as support to others in the community, regardless of their formal membership status. For example, most HIV/AIDS groups serve both the interest of their members and those of the community (Marin and Kenis, 1997; Walden-Laing and Pestoff, 1997).

In the next area of the circle we find organisations in the overlap between the state and the third sector that include the increasingly important partnerships between TSOs and public authorities. This is illustrated by the growth of public–private partnerships (PPPs) in recent decades and third sector compacts in many European countries.

The final overlapping area between the market and the third sector suggests that some third sector enterprises operate in the market and seek a surplus, but that they do not adopt rules that are typical of capitalist companies, that is, shareholders only receive a limited return on their capital and decision-making power can be distributed equally among members, often on the basis of one member, one vote (Defourny et al., 2014). Anheier (2005) considers the overlap between the third sector and the market to be an important source of hybridity that poses challenges to TSOs and their leaders. Hybrid organisations of this kind attempt to combine business and non-profit elements in relation to their objectives, orientation, outputs, and so forth (ibid., p. 184). Consumer and agricultural co-operatives constitute a classical example of this category, but they also illustrate the dangers inherent in such intermediary positions. They often face a serious challenge of goal displacement or organisational atrophy associated with pursuing multiple and sometimes conflicting goals (Pestoff, 1991). Their leaders must learn to balance the various conflicting demands of their stakeholders in order to survive and remain true to their original purpose (Pestoff, 2011; Pestoff et al., 2017).

TSOs operating in these overlapping areas are subject to a greater degree of hybridity than those not doing so. However, in the long run these hybrid areas can become their 'comfort zone', since TSOs and their leaders learn to adjust and accommodate themselves to a particular type of hybridity. However, if they leave one area of overlap and move to another, they will expose themselves to a new type of hybridity with new 'rules of the game' and new tensions stemming from such changes.

Billis (2010) distinguished between 'shallow' and 'entrenched' hybridity in TSOs. The former is typically found when a TSO wants to expand its operations by engaging in commercial activities, sometimes referred to as 'social entrepreneurship', or more simply, by using commercial means to promote its social mission. However, if the shallow form of hybridity continues over time, it can eventually lead to an 'entrenched' form of hybridity that impacts upon both the governance and the operational levels of a TSO (ibid., p. 60). In the latter case, professionals become more dominant in managing the TSO and goal deflection can become a serious challenge. Moreover, Billis has argued that hybridity can either develop in an 'organic' or an 'enacted' fashion. The former represents a more gradual development, while the latter expresses more sudden change found in today's 'frenzied' organisational experiments (ibid.). The development of public administration regimes discussed below provide a good illustration of the latter type of development. However, they also suggest the existence of a further category, called 'enforced' or 'coerced' hybridity, seen most clearly in New Public Management. The latter serves to illustrate one of the main theses of this chapter: that PARs have different values and focuses that can impact on third sector organisations, complicate their environment and increase their degree of hybridity.

Co-production also introduces important ramifications for understanding hybridity, since it opens new areas for collaboration between the public sector and third sector organisations that provide services. Such service provision not only involves professional staff and volunteers in third sector provision but also includes service users as co-producers of services. So, a new kind of stakeholder is involved which leads to greater complexity and more hybridity. The co-production of public services will be considered below in terms of its potential impact on the governance and leadership of hybrid organisations. It offers both new opportunities and challenges for collective solutions to growing problems for the provision of social services in Europe. However, greater citizen participation in, and more third sector provision of, social services can encounter hurdles in both traditional public administration and New Public Management (NPM), each of which is based on a separate logic of its own. However, the extent to which greater citizen participation and co-production of public services poses new leadership challenges for TSOs also depends on the nature of the third sector provider, as noted below. Increased hybridity may seem inevitable given the growing complexity of today's societies. Yet, it is argued below that TSOs and their leaders do not have to orient themselves toward the type of hybridity represented by a greater overlap between the third sector and market, under a New Public Management regime that promotes 'entrenched' hybridity. Instead they can pursue the social values associated with co-production and New Public Governance (NPG).

PUBLIC ADMINISTRATION REGIMES

This section introduces the concept of public administrations regimes and briefly presents four of them: traditional public administration, New Public Management, New Public Governance and a communitarian regime. Changes in public administration regimes can set the parameters for the activity of third sector organisations and the focus of their leaders, particularly those providing publicly funded services. They can also set limits for citizen participation and the co-production of public services. It is therefore important to compare PARs and understand how they differ in terms of their values and focus. Such differences will help to determine the type of hybridity that develops in third sector organisations: shallow, entrenched, or, perhaps, enforced or coerced forms of hybridity. The purpose of this section is to explore the possible ramifications of different public administration regimes, while the next section discusses the relationship between PARs and hybridity.

In the immediate post-Second World War period, citizens faced a rapidly expanding, yet basically traditional, public administration with its hierarchical chain of command, where citizens were primarily viewed as passive clients or beneficiaries of mostly public services. Later, in the 1980s and 1990s, with the spread of New Public Management, citizens were expected to become consumers and to exercise more choice between various providers of publicly financed services, whether public, private for-profit or non-profit. In NPM, the market replaces the state as the main mechanism for governing the expression of citizens' preferences. At the turn of the century we can witness the spread of network governance (Hartley, 2005) or New Public Governance (Osborne, 2006, 2010). NPG implies a more plural and pluralist model of providing and governing welfare services, based on public–private networks. Citizens are expected to play a more active role as co-producers of some aspects of the services they demand and have come to depend upon in their daily life.

It is therefore necessary to explore how changes in the public sector and the development of new public administration regimes impact on the relationship between the third sector and the public sector in general, how they impact on the complexity facing the third sector and its leaders as a provider of publicly financed social services, and how they contribute to their hybridity. Much more could, of course, be said about these four PARs but neither time nor space allow for that here. Some of the core elements of each public administration regime are found in Figure 18.2. It summarises some of the main points about PARs, including their theoretical roots, value base and some of the key concepts of each administrative regime.

Figure 18.2 depicts these four PARs in terms of two important analytical dimensions: the level of citizen participation in service delivery, and the degree of individual or collective responsibility for the provision of such services. The first variable is fairly straightforward and ranges from low to high. The second is more complex and reflects the institutionalisation of public versus private responsibility for providing services to citizens. Healthcare or childcare can used to illustrate this difference. Is it a universal service provided to everyone in a given territory, or is it mainly dependent on individual initiative, where access to service often depends on the ability to control various private assets? In the former case there is a collective responsibility for providing a service, with certain limits or eligibility criteria; while in the latter case the responsibility for accessing services is primarily with the individual. This variable thus ranges from individual to collective. One can note some striking contrasts between different PARs in Figure 18.2.

Both communitarian and New Public Governance regimes require a high degree of citizen participation in the provision of social services but they are found at different

Figure 18.2   Public administration regimes: citizen participation and responsibility

ends of the continuum from individual to collective service provision. Similarly, neither traditional public administration nor New Public Management provide much room for citizens to participate actively in service delivery compared to NPG and communitarian regimes, but they too reflect different degrees of individual and collective actions in the provision of public services.

I will begin my presentation of these four PARs from a historical perspective, starting with traditional public administration seen during most of the 20th century; followed by New Public Management, starting in the 1980s; and then, more recently, the newly emerging paradigm of New Public Governance at the turn of the century, based on ideas of network governance (Hartley, 2005; Osborne, 2006). I conclude this overview with an account of a potential new regime which has coalesced from ideas of communitarianism and volunteerism in the United Kingdom, Japan and elsewhere. This brief summary also mentions some important features related to the principal agents in co-production, the users/citizens and the professional service providers, as well as the role of TSOs as service providers in each PAR. While these four regimes differ in many important aspects, they also share some common features.

Although each PAR may be linked to a particular ideology or historical period, they can also be conceived as 'layered realities' that coexist with one another (Hartley, 2005; Osborne, 2010). Thus, rather than one PAR simply replacing the other, we can find more than one regime coexisting at any given time, operating in different service sectors where one PAR may dominate in one of them while another does so in another. They can, moreover, shift over time through the spread and ascent of a new public administration regime. These characteristics help to identify some of the crucial aspects of different PARs and provide similar insights into the ideas of different welfare regimes (Esping-Andersen, 1990) and different production regimes (Kitschelt et al., 1999). As noted before, PARs also attribute quite different degrees of weight or importance to the role of citizens and the third sector in the provision of public services, while their perspective on the role of professionals in providing services and their view on service quality guarantees also varies considerably. The chapter will therefore consider these differences in greater detail below. It will argue that co-production develops in different directions in different PARs, with quite different roles attributed to its key actors, the users and professionals, and to the third sector.

Traditional Public Administration

Traditional public administration has its theoretical roots in sociology, political science and public policy. It is based on a hierarchical model of command and control, stemming from the ideas of Max Weber, with clear lines of vertical authority and responsibility. Weber's ideas were later developed and expanded by President Woodrow Wilson (Ostrom and Ostrom, 1971 [1999]). The value base of traditional public administration is found in the public sector ethos of serving the public, and its key concept is the idea of public goods that are provided by public or civil servants, who place a heavy emphasis on the professional implementation of policy and meeting the bureaucratic norms of the equal treatment of all citizens.

New Public Management

NPM's theoretical roots were found in the growing criticism in the 1980s of the inefficiencies of traditional public administration that were clearly articulated in public choice theory and management studies. It promoted ideas about the marketisation and commercialisation of public services in order to rectify these shortcomings and improve the efficiency and productivity of public sector services. Its value base stems from industry, and it promotes a manufacturing logic that emphasises service inputs and outputs rather than a service logic that focuses on outcomes (Osborne et al., 2013). Its key concepts are freedom of choice for consumers and competition between various providers in order to ensure better service quality.

New Public Governance

The theoretical roots of New Public Governance stem from sociology and network theory, and its value base is considered by some to be 'participatory democracy' (Pestoff, 2009) and by others to be 'neo-corporatist' (Osborne, 2010). NPG is based on a logic of production that focuses on service processes and outcomes, where public value is a key concept (Denhardt and Denhardt, 2008). It governs through networks and partnerships where the third sector and social enterprises can play an important role and citizens are active co-producers of public services.

A Communitarian Regime?

The following is an early approximation at best of an emerging PAR, although some clues have been gleaned by earlier work from Brundy and England (1983), Horne and Shirley (2009) and Bovaird and Löffler (2012). The Coalition Government that ruled the United Kingdom after 2010 introduced a programme called the Big Society to promote community empowerment by reorganising public services and facilitating social action (Hudson, 2012; Slocock, 2015). Its value base comes from volunteering, philanthropy and charity. During Prime Minister David Cameron's administration this policy was reflected in massive budget cuts for public services, while families, communities and the third sector were encouraged to fill the vacuum. It remains to be seen how this approach will fare under Brexit. Similar policies are surfacing elsewhere: in Japan, under the guise of 'Integrated Community Care'; as a growing attachment to voluntarism in Thailand (Ungsuchaval, 2016); and in Europe, including Denmark (*Politiken*, 21 October 2015) and the Netherlands (Nederhand and Van Meerkerk, 2017), under the label of 'co-production and/or co-creation' (ibid.). I have gathered these diverse expressions of policy together under the heading of a 'communitarian regime' in this chapter. Under this regime government retains responsibility for the design of service delivery, while citizens become co-producers, since they are now responsible for implementing public services, particularly in the provision of welfare and care services (ibid.; Agenosono et al., 2014; Tabata, 2014; Tsutsui, 2013).

Thus, we find that each public administration regime has separate theoretical roots, value base and key concepts, as well as involving different roles for citizens, professionals and the third sector. Together they result in a unique constellation that helps to distinguish one

PAR from another. These differences have clear implications for hybridity, co-production and the third sector, which are explored in the sections below on the relationship between PARs and hybridity and the relationship between co-production and PARs.

THE RELATIONSHIP BETWEEN PARs AND HYBRIDITY

A new perspective can be found when hybridity is put into the political context of public sector reforms. Rapid changes brought on by shifts in political discourse at the macro level can have a significant impact on work of TSOs and their leaders, opening up new ways of operating and constraining or closing old ones. They can also have an impact on the ways in which public administration operates by facilitating the development of a new regime, as was seen in the growth and spread of New Public Management in the 1980s. This can result in a situation where TSOs that usually operate in one area of overlap in the welfare triangle, for example with the state, must shift rapidly or substantially to another area of overlap, with the market for example. TSO leaders may be unprepared to cope with the challenges and demands of their new environment and the new 'rules of the game'. This can expose them to increasing levels of hybridity, and the uncertainty this involves. Thus, with the introduction of New Public Management across Europe, many TSOs lost their previously cosy relations with public authorities that had recognised their inherent social value added and financed their activities primarily through public grants. Once governments began to privatise the provision of public services, competition and efficiency became the principal criteria for distributing public funds and this cosy relationship ended. TSOs have had to adapt to and operate in a new, highly competitive and insecure environment; one, moreover, where many of their earlier partners or collaborators are now their competitors, who have joined many new entries in the form of private for-profit firms, including multinational companies and venture capitalists. This process of adaption, however, can take time and require resources.

The development of a New Public Management regime forced many TSOs to change their role as service providers working in partnership with the government, often together with other TSOs as close allies, to one of preparing competitive tenders, where some of their previous collaborators were now their main competitors. The transition from the earlier regime of traditional public administration was not necessarily an expression of their preference or something they chose to do of their own free will. Rather, it was something they had to do in order to survive. Hence it seems reasonable to refer to this as 'enforced' or 'coerced' hybridity. Today, the continued funding of TSOs depends on winning tenders for providing services, but in order to succeed in this competitive environment they need to become more 'professional'. In fact, their very survival in the competitive NPM environment demands greater professionalisation and this, in turn, introduces a new stakeholder into the management of a TSO in the form of its professional staff. The staff can contribute to a greater degree of 'entrenched' hybridity as they develop interests that are separate and sometimes different from those of the board and/ or the clients of a TSO.

Furthermore, professionalisation can take the form of promoting different types or sets of professional competencies, including those that emphasise command and control, competition, or collaboration and negotiation. One public administration regime may emphasise one set of competencies, while another will give priority to a different set. In addition, the new rules of the game are often very complex and demanding, and may well subject TSOs to new and sometimes contradictory logics, thus enhancing the extent of their hybrid nature. From a political perspective there are potential status inconsistencies when TSOs leave their comfort zone as trusted and reliable partners of the public sector and become competitors among many others for a public service contract, where the price of and professionalism in preparing a proposal are the main criteria of success. TSOs must now shift their operations to new and uncharted waters. Thus, a high degree of enforced hybridity might imply the need for a TSO to overcome even more challenges and hurdles that might divert attention from the organisation's original mission and that could have an impact on its ability to survive in a new and highly competitive environment.

Recent developments both in Europe and in the United States of America (USA) suggest that TSOs often lose out to private for-profit actors that have more resources to promote their interests and understand better the rules of the competitive game. In fact, the preliminary evidence paints a bleak picture concerning the ability of the third sector as a whole to adapt and adjust to the new competitive environment as providers of publicly funded social services. In Denmark, Germany, Sweden and the USA two trends have been notable in the past decade: first, the dramatic growth of private for-profit providers of welfare services; and second, the marginalisation of the third sector. This in turn reflects, to a large extent, the growing complexity of the bidding processes adopted by most New Public Management regimes, along with the heavy emphasis on competition and efficiency. Here large actors, often international venture capitalists, appear to have a competitive advantage, particularly when strict financial criteria are applied to the bidding process and little, if any, consideration is given to social criteria and service quality (Henriksen et al., 2012; Shekarabi, 2012; Statistiska Meddelanden, 2012; Sivesind, 2016; Baturina et al., 2016). Some argue that TSOs must become more 'business-like' and make more professional bids in order to be more competitive although this may conflict with their social goals. Thus, the increasing overlap between the third sector and market logic, particularly in a NPM regime, will result in greater enforced and entrenched hybridity; greatly increased levels of complexity; and both internal and external tensions. Many TSOs may find it difficult to cope with these challenges.

CO-PRODUCTION AND ITS RELATION TO PUBLIC ADMINISTRATION REGIMES

The concept of co-production was developed by Nobel laureate Elinor Ostrom and her colleagues in the 1970s to describe and delimit the involvement of ordinary citizens in the production of public services (Ostrom, 1996 [1999]). Their research led them to realise that it was difficult to produce services, in contrast to producing goods, without the active participation of those persons receiving the service (ibid.). They developed the term 'co-production' to describe 'the potential relationship that could exist between the "regular producer" (street-level police officers, schoolteachers, or health workers) and their clients who wanted to be transformed by the service into safer, better-educated or healthier persons' (Parks et al., 1981 [1999]). Co-production, therefore, can be seen as 'the mix of activities that both public service agents and citizens contribute to the provision of public services. The former are involved as professionals or "regular producers", while "citizen production" is based on voluntary efforts of individuals or groups to enhance the quality and/or quantity of services they receive' (ibid.).

Co-production was overshadowed in the 1980s and 1990s by NPM, but gained renewed interest during the first decade of the 21st century, as witnessed by the growing number of academic conferences and publications devoted to the subject (Alford, 2002, 2009; Pestoff and Brandsen, 2006 [2009]; Bovaird, 2007; Pestoff, 2008; Pestoff et al., 2012). Studies of co-production have expanded rapidly across different disciplines, especially those focusing on public services and/or the third sector. It has been used to analyse the role of voluntary and community organisations (VCOs) in the provision of public services in the United Kingdom (UK) (Osborne and McLaughlin, 2004) and to explore its use in more mundane public services in Australia, the USA and the UK (Alford, 2009), including the use of post or zip codes on letters and completing and returning annual income tax forms. I will consider below some central aspects of co-production found in two studies of childcare in Europe: the role of the central actors in co-production; the involvement of users and professionals in different PARs; ways of determining service quality in different PARs; and the relationship between co-production and PARs.

Central Aspects of Co-production Found in Two Studies of Childcare in Europe

Two recent comparative studies of parent participation in preschool services in Europe provide further insights into how co-production works in different countries and with different providers which enables us to compare service providers from different sectors. The TSFEPS Project[1] examined the relationship between parent participation in the provision and governance of childcare in eight European Union (EU) countries (Pestoff, 2006 [2009]). It found different levels of parent participation in different countries, and in different forms of provision, that is, public, private for-profit and third sector childcare. The highest levels of parent participation were found in third sector providers, such as parent associations in France, parent initiatives in Germany, and parent co-operatives in Sweden. The project also noted the existence of different kinds of parent participation. It distinguishes between three different kinds of participation, that is, economic (donating supplies, paying fees and working for the organisation), political (decision-making), and social (arranging social events, such as the spring party). All three kinds of participation were readily evident in third sector providers of childcare services, while both economic and political participation were much more restricted in municipal and private for-profit services.

A follow-up study by Vamstad (2007) focused on the politics of diversity, parent participation and service quality in Swedish childcare. It compared parent and worker co-ops, municipal services and small for-profit firms providing childcare in two regions of Sweden: Stockholm and Östersund. Both these studies demonstrate that parent co-ops in Sweden provided parents with unique possibilities for active participation in the management and running of their children's childcare facility and becoming active co-producers of high-quality childcare services for their children.

Turning to issues of parent and staff influence, Vamstad noted that participation and influence did not necessarily mean the same thing. So he asked parents and staff at childcare facilities how much influence they currently had and whether they wanted more. Parental influence was greatest in parent co-ops and least in small for-profit firms.

This is an expected result, and nearly nine out of ten parents in parent co-ops claimed much influence, which was twice as high as in municipal services. Half of the parents in worker co-ops also claimed much influence, while only one in eight parents claimed much influence in small for-profit firms. Turning to their desire for more influence, he found the expected pattern of answers, which inversely reflects how much influence they currently experienced. Very few parents in parent co-ops wanted more influence, while nearly three out of five did so in small for-profit firms. In between these two types came the worker co-ops, where more than one in four wanted more influence; and municipal childcare, where more than one in three parents wanted more influence (Vamstad, 2007).

Shifting to the staff of childcare facilities, once again the logically expected pattern of influence can be noted, where the staff in worker co-ops claimed the most influence and the staff in municipal facilities claimed the least influence. Nearly nine out of ten staff members claimed large or very large influence in worker co-op childcare, while only a third did so in municipal facilities. Nearly three out of five members of staff claimed much influence in parent co-ops, while half of them did so in small for-profit firms. Again, the proportion of the staff desiring more influence inversely reflected the proportion claiming much influence. Few wanted more influence in either the worker or parent co-ops, while the opposite was true of the staff in the other two types of childcare providers. Nearly three out of five wanted more influence in municipal childcare, and three out of four did so in small for-profit firms (ibid.).

This suggests the existence of a 'glass ceiling' in public and private for-profit childcare services. Public policies can either crowd-in or crowd-out desired behaviour by citizens. Co-production is not an exception to this rule. These findings lead to three clear conclusions. First, there are different forms of citizen participation in the provision of publicly financed social services such as childcare: that is, economic, social and political participation. Second, a higher level of citizen participation was noted for third sector providers of publicly financed social services, since it was based on collective action and direct client participation in service provision, as illustrated by parent co-op childcare in France, Germany and Sweden. Third, more limited citizen participation was noted for public provision of welfare services, where citizens were allowed to participate sporadically or in a limited fashion, such as contributing to the Christmas or spring party in municipal childcare. But they were seldom given the opportunity to play a major role, to take charge of the service provision, or given decision-making rights and responsibility for the economy of the service provider. (Parents manage the preschool facility, keep the books and undertake the maintenance. If it spends more than it earns, it can go bankrupt. Thus, they bear the economic responsibility if it fails and suffer the consequences if it closes its doors.) This leads to the question of what role users and service professionals play in different PARs and in determining service quality.

The Role of Users and Service Quality

The role of the users of public services varies considerably in different PARs where they can become 'enforced agents', citizens, beneficiaries or consumers of such services, as noted in Figure 18.2. Each of these will be commented on briefly below and this review will be followed by a discussion of the role of service providers, which also varies notably between PARs.

Traditional public administration tends to be perceived as paternalistic by many since it is achieved through the 'professional gift' model of service provision. Here citizens are considered to be the beneficiaries of public services, but with a clearly passive role as recipients of services. There are no exit or voice options available to users. Their only recourse or channel of influence is found in the electoral system that, at best, can provide indirect, intermittent representation of their interests, given the outcome of an election. In addition, service professionalism supposedly provides a guarantee of service quality in a command and control system, while third sector organisations are supposed to function as advocates and/or service providers, for which they receive public grants.

New Public Management often attempts to achieve its goals by using a 'carrot and stick' approach to incentives designed to discourage or reward different behaviour by the providers and users of services. Here citizens are considered customers with some limited choice, but little voice and no representation. Users can choose between pre-existing packages or offers, but they have little influence on the content or features of such services. Service quality is guaranteed through competition, making the role of professionals highly competitive. Moreover, third sector organisations are expected to become social enterprises that provide services in competition with each other and with private for-profit firms, since they no longer qualify for the public grants that have become a thing of the past.

New Public Governance is based on ideas of establishing a partnership between citizens and the government, where citizens are considered co-producers of public services. This not only gives them both choice and voice, but can even provide them with direct representation, giving users greater influence than in either traditional public administration or NPM. Service quality is guaranteed by user participation in the delivery of public services, while the role of professionals is collaborative. Here the third sector becomes a partner with the state, in collaboration with other providers of public services, including public bodies, TSOs, social enterprises and for-profit firms.

Finally, in a communitarian regime the role of service users is to provide many public services by and for themselves, with little or no public support, sometimes alongside, but often instead of the professionals, turning users into enforced or constrained co-producers (Fotaki, 2011). Here they and/or their loved ones and neighbours become informal caregivers or service providers, while professionals are transformed into back-up agents who only intervene when the informal care provided proves insufficient. Determination of service quality becomes more like patchwork, since access depends on the availability, willingness and capacity of informal caregivers or service providers, which can vary considerably. In addition, the role of the third sector is relegated to fend for itself by creating consortia or becoming social businesses that can compete on the market with other consortia or private firms, in order to earn their income, rather than depend on grants from the state.

The Role of Professionals in Determining Service Quality

Traditional public administration relies heavily, if not exclusively, on training and professionalism to guarantee service quality (Vamstad, 2012); thus, professionals alone decide on and prescribe appropriate measures, based on their professional knowledge, experience and insights. New Public Management places heavy emphasis on competition and consumer choice. It is therefore not surprising that professionals, regardless of whether public, private or non-profit, should focus strongly on competition between providers. NPM assumes that service quality is guaranteed by consumer choice, where the best-quality providers will attract more customers than those with inferior products or services. New Public Governance, by contrast, emphasises collaboration and negotiation between various partners, public, private and/or non-profit (Vidal, 2013). Here greater user participation and mutual dialogue between users and professionals replaces professionalism or competition as the main guarantee of service quality. The main focus of professionals is on promoting collaboration and negotiation rather than on command and control or competition. Finally, the perspective of a communitarian regime in terms of professionalism and service quality remain largely undeveloped in this respect, but professionals can complement informal care provision, mainly by steering users and caregivers to available resources in the community or voluntary organisations. However, the consequences of this for service quality or availability for different groups of users and caregivers remains to be seen.

Thus, co-production or citizen participation can develop in several different directions, with a different content and meaning in each PAR. Each of these directions implies different roles for service users and the professional staff. This clearly poses challenges for the leaders of TSOs, complicates their situation and increases the degree of hybridity in their organisations. They need to understand these differences and what the implications of following one path of development means in relation to following another. Moreover, taken together, the growth of divergent PARs implies a more plural and pluralist world where TSOs and their leaders must learn to navigate between competing views and visions and choose to follow one that best encompasses their values and their aspirations for the future.

Co-production and Public Administration Regimes

Brandsen and Pestoff (2006 [2009]) have expanded the scope of the concept of co-production to explicitly include the third sector as a provider of publicly financed services, and they proposed a rudimentary typology for studying this phenomenon, based on the existence of different venues for citizen participation in public policy-making. They suggested that citizen participation in the delivery of public services should be contrasted with co-management, or formalised coordination between public, private and third sector actors providing public services in a given territory; as well as with co-governance, or third sector participation in public policy-making (ibid.). Such a multi-level perspective provides a more nuanced understanding than a singular focus on co-production at the micro level or using the same term for various phenomena at different levels. This multifaceted approach encourages a more comprehensive view of the different roles the third sector may have within the complex structure of public service provision. It also promotes comparisons of the role of the third sector across the entire policy cycle, not just on advocacy or service provision, but on both the input and output sides of the political system (Easton, 1965). It should be noted, however, that although these three concepts are not mutually exclusive there are some potential trade-offs between co-production, co-management and co-governance (Pestoff et al., 2006 [2009]) that may contribute to greater hybridity.

It is also important to distinguish between individual and collective co-production (Pestoff, 2012). For example, Hudson (2012) sketches three phases in the shift from mass production to mass collaboration in the UK's National Health Service (NHS). First, in mass production, professionals design and deliver services to their patients who are passive recipients of healthcare. This corresponds with the traditional view of public administration. Then, in today's mass customisation and personalisation of services, professionals and patients may jointly design the services, but professionals take a clear lead in the implementation, by prescribing the appropriate treatments. Patients can become individual co-producers of such customised and personalised services, resulting in a patient-consumer model that fits well with a New Public Management perspective. By contrast, in mass collaboration and participatory healthcare patients, TSOs and communities are central in both the design and delivery of health services (ibid.), bringing it closer to ideas related to New Public Governance.

Moreover, issues of hybridity also become evident here. Co-governance can be seen as a core element for modernising public services since it provides a means of bringing the views of TSOs and public service users into the design, management and delivery of welfare services, as promoted by NPG. A recent study of the challenges faced by one major TSO in the UK in trying to facilitate more user influence in the National Health Service pilot programme illustrated the tensions this created with its advocacy role (Martin, 2011). The researcher concluded that sooner or later TSOs might discover that traditional management concerns outweighed those of newer participants in such public service networks. Rather than giving weight to TSO and user views, participation in these governance networks tended to co-opt them (ibid.). Furthermore, TSOs may experience a conflict of interest between divergent goals that can include: (1) increasing their own influence in a current project (co-management); (2) securing their role as a service provider in the next round of funding (co-production); and/or (3) promoting the development of institutions for greater user participation and influence (co-governance). Thus, TSOs often find their own values marginalised when governments compile lists of standard service providers that should compete with each other for funding (ibid.) according to the managerial and economic criteria used by NPM.

DISCUSSION: ANALYSING PARs, CO-PRODUCTION AND HYBRID TSOs

The two studies of childcare in Europe which we looked at earlier in the chapter threw some light on the relationship between co-production and PARs. In the first of the two studies it was clear that co-production was common in the provision of childcare in France, Germany and Sweden; while co-management and co-governance were found in France and Germany, but not in Sweden. Parent participation was limited to the site of service delivery in Sweden but French and German parents also had some influence in the overall management of local childcare services and the development of childcare policy in general. Both studies of childcare also illustrate the coexistence of several different layers of public administration regime in the same service sector and country, as Hartley (2005) and Osborne (2006) have suggested. In Sweden, for example, most preschool services are provided by municipalities in a traditional top-down public administration fashion, while private for-profit preschool services are inspired by the ideas of greater consumer choice related to NPM. Parent co-ops contain some elements of NPG, such as an obligation for parents, who also manage these facilities, to work in them. This makes parents active co-producers of their own childcare. This suggests that different public administration regimes produce different ideas of hybridity and a different mix of logics. Thus, a higher degree of citizen participation and co-production in third sector services appears more compatible with NPG than with NPM or traditional public administration.

Moreover, these three levels of TSO participation in delivering public services – co-production, co-management and co-governance – may lead to competing expectations, both internally and externally, about the role of TSOs and what their distinctive contribution is, or should be. The professional staff may argue for toning down traditional values while emphasising their professionalism or their competitive advantage as service providers, in order to gain continued funding. Such competing expectations and stakeholder conflicts need to be understood and balanced by the leaders of TSOs. Coerced participation in competitive tenders and market-like arrangements will often result in greater enforced hybridity for TSOs and their leaders. Thus, TSO participation in various aspects of co-production can augment hybridity and goal conflict, in particular in an NPM regime.

Furthermore, this introduces yet another dimension to this study of hybridity, namely that of internal decision-making in TSOs. Not all third sector providers of publicly financed services are able to facilitate client and/or staff participation to the same degree or in the same fashion. Some TSOs practice democracy in their internal affairs, while others depend on something more like a corporate governance model to guide their activities. Whether or not TSOs can facilitate greater client and/or staff participation will depend, at least in part, on the degree of democracy in their own decision-making. Basically, those third sector organisations that are membership organisations and practise some form of democratic decision-making will probably facilitate and encourage greater citizen participation and more collective co-production of public services than those governed by a corporate model. By contrast, those TSOs that are not membership-based organisations may face clear difficulties participating in programmes, services and/or networks based on greater citizen participation and co-production. They would have to introduce new, often foreign, elements or structures into their organisation. This can result in new challenges and will take time and effort. Moreover, the benefits of such changes may appear vague or illusiory in relation to an organisation's goals. Thus, whether or not NPG implies clear advantages for TSOs as service providers depends in part on the values and internal structures of the TSOs concerned.

SUMMARY AND CONCLUSIONS

This chapter has considered hybridity to be the overlap between the third sector and other major social sectors, such as the state, market and community. Co-production is the mix of activities that both public service agents and citizens contribute to the provision of public services. Public administration regimes can be distinguished by a combination of elements, including their theoretical roots, value base and key concepts, as well as the role attributed to citizens, service professionals and the third sector. Together each results in a unique constellation that distinguishes one PAR from another. These differences have clear implications for hybridity, co-production and the third sector, and the major changes in the character of PARs that began in the 1980s provide a political perspective on hybridity.

This chapter has argued that changes in public administration regimes set the parameters for activity of TSOs and determined the focus of their leaders. One public administration regime may emphasise one set of competences, while another will give priority to another. Moreover, the new rules of the game are often very complex and demanding, subjecting TSOs to new and sometimes contradictory logics, sometimes enhancing the extent of their hybrid nature. A more political perspective would, therefore, emphasise the potential status inconsistencies facing a TSO when it leaves its comfort zone and shifts its operations to new and uncharted waters, where different professional competencies may be required if the TSO is to survive.

This, in turn, is reflected in the growing complexity of the bidding processes adopted by most New Public Management regimes, along with their heavy emphasis on competition and efficiency. Here it has been noted that large actors, often international venture capitalists, appear to have a competitive advantage, particularly when strict financial criteria are applied to the bidding process and little, if any, consideration is given to social criteria and service quality. Some would therefore argue that TSOs must become more 'business-like' and make more professional bids in order to become or remain competitive. On the other hand, this approach may lead to conflict with their social goals.

Changes between PARs will in turn help to determine the type of hybridity that develops in third sector organisations; whether shallow or entrenched, or perhaps an enforced or coerced form of hybridity. The rapid and sweeping changes under NPM seem more likely to bring about enforced or coerced hybridity rather than the organic or enacted types suggested by Billis (2010). Thus, the increasing overlap between the third sector and market logic, particularly in a NPM regime, will probably result in greater enforced and entrenched hybridity, complexity, and both internal and external tensions that many TSOs may find difficult to cope with.

PARs also have a clear impact on co-production and set limits for citizen participation. Two empirical studies reviewed here lead to three conclusions. First, citizen participation can take one or more forms: that is, economic, social and political. Second, third sector providers of publicly financed social services were associated with higher level of citizen participation. Third, more limited citizen participation was associated with public providers of welfare services, where citizens were allowed to participate only sporadically or in a limited fashion. Co-production can also develop in several different directions, with a different content and meaning for each PAR. Furthermore, each of these directions implies different roles for service users and the professional staff. This clearly poses challenges for the leaders of TSOs, makes their situation more complicated and increases the degree of their hybridity in their organisation. They need to attempt to understand these differences and what the implications of following one path of development means in relation to another. Moreover, taken together, the growth of divergent PARs implies a more plural and pluralist world where TSOs and their leaders have to learn to navigate between competing views and visions and to choose to follow one that best encompasses their values and aspirations for the future.

The existence of layered or mixed reality, with different PARs in different social services, suggests that hybridity will probably become increasingly common as the provision of public services becomes more pluralistic and more fragmented, and as the difference between NPM and NPG develops and becomes clearer. This will contribute to the growing complexity facing TSOs and subject their leaders to greater challenges. A shift in PARs can either promote more competition and commercialisation of the delivery of publicly financed services, in an NPM regime; or it will result in greater citizen involvement in the provision of public services, through co-production, co-management and co-governance, in an NPG regime.

The development of shallow hybridity will lead to fewer far-reaching changes in a TSO's structures and operations and can therefore be corrected and compensated more easily than entrenched hybridity. However, membership-based TSOs may adapt and adjust more easily to NPG and co-production than non-membership TSOs. Thus, the former TSOs will survive more readily in a NPG regime, while the latter will do so more easily in a NPM regime. So, different types of TSOs will probably orient themselves to different types of public administration regime. Moreover, promoting co-production and new governance techniques can also pose some new challenges to the management of hybrid organisations in its own right. It can expose them to additional institutional and organisational forces and therefore increase the risks of failing to balance multiple goals and/or the interests of various stakeholders in a sustainable fashion (Pestoff, 2015).

TSOs and their leaders, therefore, can choose at least to some degree which type of hybridity they want to adopt or pursue. Those TSOs that orient themselves toward greater market competition and NPM will have to learn to navigate both the pull and the push from the overlapping and sometimes competing logics of the third sector and the market. In order to cope with this type of hybridity they will need to increase their professionalisation, promote their competitive advantage(s) and improve their efficiency. This, however, may come at the price of their traditional values and goals, particularly if shallow hybridity is allowed to turn into the entrenched form. By contrast, those TSOs that want to retain more of their traditional social values and distinctiveness may opt to pursue an NPG vision by participating in service networks that emphasise co-production, co-management and co-governance. This may promote a different kind of hybridity, one with greater overlap with both the public sector and the community sector, and it will bring its own challenges. It can prove risky for some TSOs, particularly for those that lack well-developed participatory institutions for democratic decision-making that provide them with legitimacy, to embrace greater citizen participation or co-production of public services involved in an NPM-dominated regime and/or service sector.

In order to embrace more fully the complexities posed by the spread of different public administration regimes and co-production for the third sector and its leaders, we should perhaps remember the concluding words of Elinor Ostrom's Nobel Prize speech in Stockholm:

> Designing institutions to force or nudge entirely self-interested individuals to achieve better outcomes has been a major policy prescription for more than half a century, yet it has failed miserably . . . When the world we are trying to explain and improve is not well described by a simple model, we must continue to improve our frameworks and theories to be able to understand complexity and not simply reject it. (Ostrom, 2009, p. 436)

Including public administration regimes and co-production in our models of organisational behaviour, particularly for third sector organisations and their leaders, is an important step for improving our framework and understanding the complexities facing TSOs in the contemporary environment. These two concepts also go a long way towards grasping the challenges that growing hybridity poses to third sector organisations and their leaders.

NOTE

1. The TSFEPS Project, Changing Family Structures and Social Policy: Childcare Services as Sources of Social Cohesion, took place in eight European countries between 2002 and 2004. They were: Belgium, Bulgaria, England, France, Germany, Italy, Spain and Sweden. See www.emes.net for more details and the reports.

REFERENCES

Agenosono, Y., S. Kamazawa and T. Hori (2014). Japan's next care system: how do communities participate? 3rd International Conference on Evidence-Based Policy in Long-Term Care, London.
Alford, J. (2002). Why do public sector clients co-produce? Towards a contingency theory. *Administration and Society*, 34(1): pp. 32–56.
Alford, J. (2009). *Engaging Public Sector Clients: From Service Delivery to Co-production*. Houndmills, UK and New York, USA: Palgrave Macmillan.
Anheier, H. (2005). *Nonprofit Organizations: Theory, Management, Policy*. London, UK and New York, USA: Routledge.
Anheier, H. (2011). Governance and leadership in hybrid organizations: comparative and interdisciplinary perspectives. draft background paper, Centre for Social Investment, University of Heidelberg.
Baturina, D., T. Brandsen, R. Chaves Ávila, J. Matančević, J.B. Pahl, et al. (2016). Transforming policy environments and third sector development in Europe. ISTR Conference paper, Stockholm.
Billis, D. (2010). Towards a theory of hybrid organizations. In *Hybrid Organizations and the Third Sector. Challenges for Practice, Theory and Policy*, D. Billis (ed.). New York, USA and London, UK: Palgrave.
Bovaird, T. (2007). Beyond engagement and participation: user and community co-production of public services. *Public Administration Review*, 67(5): pp. 846–860.
Bovaird, T. and E. Löffler (2012). From engagement to co-production: how users and communities contribute to public services. In *New Public Governance, the Third Sector and Co-Production*, V. Pestoff, T. Brandsen and B. Vereschuere (eds). London, UK and New York, USA: Routledge.
Brandsen, T. and V. Pestoff (2006 [2009]). Co-production, the third sector and the delivery of public services: an introduction. In *Co-production: The Third Sector and the Delivery of Public Services*, Victor Pestoff and Taco Brandsen (eds). London, UK and New York, USA: Routledge.
Brandsen, T., W. van der Donk and K. Putters (2003). Griffins or chameleons? Hybridity as a permanent and inevitable characteristic of the third sector. *International Journal of Public Administration*, 28(9/10): pp. 749–765.
Brundy, J. and R. England (1983). Towards a definition of the coproduction concept. *Public Administration Review*, 43(1): pp. 59–65.
Defourny, J. and V. Pestoff (2015). Towards a European conceptualization of the third sector. In *Accountability and Social Accounting for NPOs, NGOs, Cooperatives and Social Enterprises*, M. Andreaus, E. Costa and L. Parker (eds). Cheltenham, UK and Northampton, MA, USA: Edward Elgar Publishing.
Defourny, J., L. Hulgård and V. Pestoff (2014). Introduction. In *Social Enterprise and the Third Sector: Changing European Landscapes in a Comparative Perspective*, J. Defourny, L. Hulgård and V. Pestoff (eds). London, UK and New York, USA: Routledge.
Denhardt, J. and R. Denhardt (2008). *The New Public Service: Serving not Steering*. Armok, NY, USA and London, UK: M.E. Sharpe.
Easton, D. (1965). *A Systems Analysis of Political Life*. New York: J. Wiley & Sons.
Esping-Andersen, G. (1990). *The Three Worlds of Welfare Capitalism*. Cambridge: B. Blackwell, Polity Press.
Evers, A. (1993). The welfare mix approach: understanding the pluralism of welfare systems. CIES conference paper, Barcelona.
Evers, A. (1995). Part of the welfare mix: the third sector as an intermediate area. *Voluntas*, 6(2): pp. 119–139.
Evers, A. and J.-L. Laville (2004). Defining the third sector in Europe. In *The Third Sector in Europe*, A. Evers and J.-L. Laville (eds). Cheltenham, UK and Northampton, MA, USA: Edward Elgar Publishing.

Fotaki, M. (2011). Towards developing new partnerships in public services: users as consumers, citizens and/or co-producers driving improvements in health and social care in the UK and Sweden. *Public Administration*, 89(3): pp. 933–995.
Hartley, J. (2005). Innovation in governance and public services: past and present. *Public Money and Management*, 25(1): pp. 27–34.
Henriksen, L.S., S. Rathgeb Smith and A. Zimmer (2012). At the eve of convergence? Transformations of social service provision in Denmark, Germany and the United States. *Voluntas*, 23: pp. 458–501.
Horne, M. and T. Shirley (2009). Co-production in public services: a new partnership with citizens. Cabinet Office, Strategy Unit. London: HM Government.
Hudson, B. (2012). Competition or co-production? Which way for governance of health and wellbeing. In *Making Health and Social Care Personal and Local: Moving from Mass Production to Co-Production*, E. Loeffler, David Taylor-Gooby, Tony Bovaird, Frankie Hine-Hughes and Laura Wilkes (eds). London: Governance International and LGiU, Local Government Information Unit.
Kitschelt, H., P. Lange, G. Marks and J.D. Stephens (eds) (1999). *Continuity and Change in Contemporary Capitalism*. Cambridge, UK and New York, USA: Cambridge University Press.
Laville, J-L. (1992). *Les services de proximite en Europe*. Paris: Syros Alternative.
Laville, J-L. (1994). *L'economie solidare Une perspective internationale*. Paris: Desclee de Bauwer.
Marin, B. and P. Kenis (1997). *Managing AIDS: Organizational Responses in Six European Countries*. Aldershot, UK and Brookfield, NJ, USA: Ashgate.
Martin, G. (2011). The third sector, user involvement and public service reform: a case study in the co-governance of health care provision. *Public Administration*, 89(3): pp. 909–932.
Nederhand, M.J. and I.F. Van Meerkerk (2017). Activating citizens in Dutch welfare reforms: framing new co-production roles and competencies for citizens and professionals. *Policy and Politics*. DOI: 10.1332/0305 57317X15035697297906.
Osborne, S.P. (2006). The New Public Governance. *Public Management Review*, 8(3): pp. 377–387.
Osborne, S.P. (2010). The (New) Public Governance: a suitable case for treatment? In *The New Public Governance? Emerging Perspectives on the Theory and Practice of Public Governance*, S.P. Osborne (ed.). London, UK and New York, USA: Routledge.
Osborne, S.P. and K. McLaughlin (2004). The cross-cutting review of the voluntary sector: what next for local government voluntary sector relationships. *Regional Studies*, 38(5): pp. 573–582.
Osborne, S.P., Z. Radnor and G. Nasi (2013). A new theory for public service management? Towards a (public) service dominant approach. *American Review of Public Administration Review*, 43(2): pp. 135–158.
Ostrom, E. (1996 [1999]). Crossing the great divide: coproduction, synergy, and development. *World Development*, 24(6): pp. 1073–1087. Reprinted 1999 in *Polycentric Governance and Development. Readings from the Workshop in Political Theory and Policy Analysis*, Michael D. McGinnis (ed.). Ann Arbor, MI: University of Michigan Press.
Ostrom, E. (2009). Beyond markets and states: polycentric governance of complex economic systems. Nobel Prize Lecture 8 December, Stockholm, Sweden.
Ostrom, E. and V. Ostrom (1971 [1999]). Public choice: a different approach to the study of public administration. *Public Administration Review*, March/April: 203–216. Reprinted 1999 in *Polycentric Games and Institutions*, M. McGinnis (ed.). Ann Arbor, MI: University of Michigan Press.
Parks, R.B., P.C. Baker, L. Kiser, R. Oakerson, E. Ostrom, et al. (eds) (1981 [1999]). Consumers as co-producers of public services: some economic and institutional considerations. *Policy Studies Journal*, 9: pp. 1001–1011. Reprinted 1999 in *Local Public Economies. Readings from the Workshop in Political Theory and Policy Analysis*, Michael D. McGinnis (ed.). Ann Arbor, MI: University of Michigan Press.
Pestoff, V. (1991). *Between Markets and Politics: Cooperatives in Sweden*. Frankfurt, Germany and Boulder, CO, USA: Campus Verlag and Westview Press.
Pestoff, V. (1992). Third sector and cooperative social services – an alternative to privatization. *Journal of Consumer Policy*, 15(1): pp. 27–45.
Pestoff, V. (1998). *Beyond the Market and State. Civil Democracy and Social Enterprises in a Welfare Society*. Aldershot, UK and Brookfield, VT, USA: Ashgate.
Pestoff, V. (2006 [2009]). Citizens as co-producers of welfare services: preschool services in eight European countries. *Public Management Review*, 8(4): pp. 503–520. Reprinted 2009 in *Co-production: The Third Sector and the Delivery of Public Services*, Victor Pestoff and Taco Brandsen (eds). London, UK and New York, USA: Routledge.
Pestoff, V. (2008). *A Democratic Architecture for the Welfare State*. London, UK and New York, USA: Routledge.
Pestoff, V. (2009). Towards a paradigm of democratic governance: citizen participation and co-production of personal social services in Sweden. *Annals of Public and Cooperative Economy*, 80(2): pp. 197–224.
Pestoff, V. (2011). Cooperatives and democracy in Scandinavia – the Swedish case. In *Nordic Civil Society at a Cross-Roads: Transforming the Popular Movement Tradition*, F. Wijkstrom and A. Zimmer (eds). Baden Baden: Nomos.

Pestoff, V. (2012). Co-production and third sector social services in Europe: some concepts and evidence. *Voluntas*, 23: pp. 1102–1118.

Pestoff, V. (2015). Collective action and the sustainability of co-production. *Public Management Review*, 16(3): pp. 383–401.

Pestoff, V. and T. Brandsen (2006 [2009]). *Public Management Review*, 8 (Thematic Issue on Co-production). Reprinted 2009 as *Co-production: The Third Sector and the Delivery of Public Services*. London, UK and New York, USA: Routledge.

Pestoff, V., T. Brandsen and S. Osborne (2006 [2009]). Patterns of co-production in public services: some concluding thoughts. *Public Management Review*, 8(4): pp. 591–595. Reprinted 2009 in *Co-production: The Third Sector and the Delivery of Public Services*, Victor Pestoff and Taco Brandsen (eds). London, UK and New York, USA: Routledge.

Pestoff, V., T. Brandsen and V. Verscheure (eds) (2012). *New Public Governance, the Third Sector and Co-Production*. London, UK and New York, USA: Routledge.

Pestoff, V., A. Kurimoto, C. Gijselinckx, A. Hoyt and M. Vuotto (2017). Volunteering in consumer and service cooperatives. In *The Palgrave Handbook of Volunteering, Civic Participation, and Nonprofit Associations*, D. Horton Smith, R.A. Stebbings and J. Grotz (eds). Houndmills, UK and New York, USA: Palgrave Macmillan.

Shekarabi, A. (2012). Vinst och den offentliga tjanstemarknad. Arena ide, Ny Tid Rapport 15, Stockholm.

Sivesind, K-H. (2016). The changing role of for-profit and nonprofit welfare provision in Norway, Sweden and Denmark and consequences for the Scandinavian model. Oslo: Institute for Social Research.

Slocock, C. (2015). *Whose Society? The Final Big Society Audit*. London: Civil Change.

Statistiska Meddelanden (2012). *Finansiarer och utforare inom vord och omsorg 2010*. Stockholm: SCB, Sveriges Officella Statistik. OE 29 SM 1201.

Streeck, W. and P. Schmitter (1995). Community, market, state – and associations? *Private Interest Government – Beyond Market and State*. Beverly Hills, CA, USA and London, UK: SAGE.

Tabata, K. (2014). Health and welfare policy in Japan: toward the establishment of 'integrated community care system'. Paper presented at the CIREC 30th Congress, Buenos Aires.

Tsutsui, T. (2013). Implementation process and challenges for the community-based integrated care system in Japan. *International Journal of Integrated Care*. PMCID: 3905786.

Ungsuchaval, T. (2016). NGOization of civil society as unintended consequence? Premises on the Thai Health Promotion Foundation and its pressures toward NGOs in Thailand. ISTR conference, Stockholm.

Vamstad, J. (2007). Governing welfare: the third sector and the challenges to the Swedish welfare state. PhD thesis, No. 37, Östersund.

Vamstad, J. (2012). Co-production and service quality: a new perspective for the Swedish welfare state. In *New Public Governance, the Third Sector and Co-Production*, V. Pestoff, T. Brandsen and V. Verscheure (eds). London, UK and New York, USA: Routledge.

Van Der Meer, T., M. Te Grotenhuis and P. Scheelers (2009). Three types of voluntary associations in comparative perspective: the importance of studying associational involvement through a typology of associations in 21 European countries. *Journal of Civil Society*, 5(3): pp. 227–242.

Vidal, I. (2013). Governance of social enterprises as producers of public services. In *Organisational Innovation in Public Services. Forms and Governance*, P. Valkama, S. Bailey and A.-V. Anttiroiko (eds). New York, USA and London, UK: Palgrave.

Walden-Laing, D. and V. Pestoff (1997). The role of nonprofit organizations in managing HIV/AIDS in Sweden. In *Managing: Organizational Responses in Six European Countries*, B. Marin and P. Kenis (eds). Aldershot, UK and Brookfield, VT, USA: Ashgate.

19. The hybridisation of Russian non-profit organisations
Sergej Ljubownikow and Jo Crotty

INTRODUCTION

In this chapter, we look at the impact of the system of 'managed democracy' on non-profit organisations (NPOs) in the Russian Federation and focus on the way in which the lines between them and the agencies of the state have become increasingly blurred. This development is part of the widespread growth in the creation of hybrid organisations on an international scale (Billis, 2010). Hybridity is the result of organisations crossing sectoral boundaries (Pache and Santos, 2013) to form a combination of the characteristics of two or more sectors.

One of the more common forms of hybrid organisation blurs the boundaries between NPOs and the state as the former engages in the delivery of public services that had previously been the role of statutory agencies (Billis, 2010). This blurring of sectoral boundaries between NPOs and state is not simply a transfer of practices but involves more fundamental changes to the way organisations operate (Bromley and Meyer, 2017). It means that organisations attempt to adhere to different, if not competing, institutional logics; the 'rules' that govern the various sectors (Battilana and Lee, 2014; Brandsen et al., 2005; Doherty et al., 2014; Pache and Santos, 2010). NPOs might, for example, attempt to marry a third sector logic based on collective ownership, engaging constituencies, altruism, provision of free support and/or democratic leadership with a state bureaucracy logic based on centralised control, rule-based mechanisms for service provision and/or hierarchical structures.

As a result, the expectations that NPOs represent some kind of panacea that is able to offset neoliberal-inspired changes to welfare provisions and facilitate accountability and increased public participation in policy are increasingly questioned. In Russia, we found that its NPOs have integrated more closely with the public sector and this has led to blurred sectoral boundaries. The resulting hybridity is driven by – and is a key feature of – Russia's system of managed democracy. We find that, as a result, NPOs focus less on encouraging public participation, engagement in advocacy or holding the state to account. We draw on qualitative data collected from health and education NPOs and environmental organisations in a variety of Russian industrial regions. We have focused on organisations in the regions because they operate in the industrial areas where the majority of Russians live. The data used have been collected via semi-structured interviews and observations in a variety of different research projects that have studied the activities of NPOs in the Russian context.

We draw on these data to explore how macro-institutional forces have encouraged these organisations to focus on building vertical ties with state authorities rather than with the public. We show how NPOs are involved in the blurring of boundaries both by engaging and building ties with state authorities and by accessing resources from the state. This has the result of turning NPOs into hybrid organisations: part agents of the third sector and part agents of the state. But we begin by establishing the context for the studies by presenting an overview of the development of the third sector in the Russian Federation.

THE DEVELOPMENT OF NPOs IN THE RUSSIAN FEDERATION

The break-up of the Soviet Union and the establishment of the Russian Federation as an independent state led to a process of democratisation (Choudry and Kapoor, 2013) that stimulated the setting up and growth of NPOs. This development was not, however, the result of action by the Russian state. In the 1990s it largely ignored NPOs (Pickvance, 1998) and provided limited resources to them. Instead, NPOs relied on donations from overseas (Henderson, 2002). Much of this overseas funding was allocated through a process of competitive tendering which meant that, in order to be eligible to access these resources, Russian NPOs needed to adopt the agenda of donors rather than reflect the needs and demands of the Russian public (Jakobson and Sanovich, 2010; Javeline and Lindemann-Komarova, 2010). At the same time, NPOs also became adept at developing vertical ties (that is, agency relationships) with their donors (Salmenniemi, 2008) rather than focusing on building horizontal ties with other organisations to form coalitions or collaborations.

This early stage in the development of Russian NPOs was also influenced by the continuing mistrust between the public and governing elites that characterised Soviet culture (Howard, 2002). The Russian public extended this mistrust to NPOs, which saw their public support dwindle and resulted in persistently low rates of participation in NPOs (Kamerade et al., 2016). This was not helped by the continuing dominance of Soviet cultural values in political institutions (Hedlund, 2006) as well as in social organisations such as NPOs (Spencer, 2011), which meant that the majority of Russian NPOs remained parochial and inward-looking (Crotty, 2006; Mendelson and Gerber, 2007; Spencer, 2011) and were themselves uninterested in engaging the wider public.

The ascendance to power of President Putin led to the emergence of a system termed 'managed democracy' in which the state controlled all significant areas of societal activity (Wegren and Konitzer, 2007). As part of this process, the Russian state attempted to renationalise the third sector and its agents (Ljubownikow et al., 2013; Robertson, 2009), taking advantage of the propensity of NPOs to rely on vertical ties to their resource providers. Funding and other resources are now made available to NPOs via the Civic Chamber of the Russian Federation (Richter, 2009). Persistently low donations per head (only 6 per cent of the Russian population made a donation to charity in 2013; CAF Russia, 2014) means that resources provided by the Civic Chamber are an important source of income for Russian NPOs.

In addition, the Russian state has adopted a regulatory framework that involves the scrutiny of NPO activity and membership (Crotty et al., 2014; Ljubownikow and Crotty, 2014), and it has placed restrictions on the receipt of overseas funds (Machleder, 2006). NPOs engaged in what can be loosely defined as political activity and receiving overseas funding are now considered to be foreign agents (Bennetts, 2012). NPOs have also been affected by further regulatory changes including the imposition of heavy fines for unofficial demonstrations (Bryanski, 2012), the criminalisation of libel and an increase in internet censorship (Lewis, 2013). These changes have made it difficult for NPOs to access funding to foreign donors and have also limited their scope for playing the third sector's important role of representing and protecting the interests of their constituents.

At the same time, the Russian state paid more direct attention to NPOs (Salamon et al., 2015) and used the structures of the Civic Chamber to stimulate state–NPO interaction (Richter, 2009). The Civic Chamber and its regional and local offshoots were presented as an open but institutionalised platform on which NPOs could raise concerns and represent the interests of their constituencies (Ljubownikow and Crotty, 2016), and hence hold the state to account (Richter, 2009). The impact of this system was to control and constrain advocacy by NPOs and close down any attempts at open dissent. In this way, it encouraged Russian NPOs to build vertical ties with their new donor (the Russian state; Ljubownikow and Crotty, 2014).

This 'carrot and stick' approach to the management of third sector agents has been termed (by Daucé, 2015) the 'duality of coercion'. On the one hand the state used regulatory powers to suppress NPO activity – in particular (horizontal) domestic or international cooperation for advocacy or protest purposes and for holding the state to account – and on the other hand it simultaneously encouraged NPOs to contribute to what is presented as the amelioration of social ills (Krasnopolskaya et al., 2015; Salamon et al., 2015). Having been ignored by the state in the 1990s, NPOs were now taking up the more recent opportunities for interacting with the state and had become reliant on ties with ruling and governing elites to access resources and help to navigate this complex environment. As a result, they were becoming hybrid organisations that blurred the lines between the third sector and the state by becoming in part agents of the third sector and in part agents of the state. In the next two sections of the chapter, we explore empirical data from two kinds of Russian NPOs: those engaged in health and education on the one hand, and those concerned with the environment on the other.

BLURRING THE LINES BY BUILDING VERTICAL TIES: HEALTH AND EDUCATION NPOs

In this section, we draw on data collected from 80 non-profit organisations engaged in health and education-related causes (hereafter termed 'heNPOs') across three industrial regions in Russia: Yekaterinburg, Samara and Perm. Details of the organisations included in this part of our study are in set out in Appendix A. They were engaged in a wide range of activities relating to health and education such as the provision of health services or the provision of afternoon children's clubs with an educational focus. The majority of them were small in size (for example, in terms of members or staff) although some organisations listed in Table 19A.1 in the Appendix had high levels of membership and staff. They tended to be led by middle-aged women in line with the feminine nature of Russian human service NPOs observed by Salmenniemi (2005). Many of these organisations operated on minimal financial resources or none at all, and only a few of them had been able to gain funding from the Civic Chamber. Several of the older heNPOs, primarily the ones that existed in the 1990s, had received foreign funding in the past but this had dried up post-2006 (Ljubownikow and Crotty, 2014).

The institutionalisation of state–NPO interaction has resulted in the establishment of a myriad of roundtables (*kruglyye stoly*) or committees (Richter, 2009). Involvement in these can be seen as a means of reducing the ability of NPOs to challenge the activities of state authorities, but it also provides them with access to state structures for the first time since the demise of the Soviet Union. This provided them with the opportunity to build 'vertical ties' with governing elites through the state's role as a key resource provider, and provided key individuals or key organisational human resources in heNPOs with the incentive for services delivery and to carry out other work on behalf of the state. This led to the development of an overlap between the roles and responsibilities of individuals active in heNPOs and those working within the agencies of the state that blurred the line between where the responsibilities of the state end and the work of heNPOs takes over. In previous work, we had highlighted the role of the individuals at the centre of these developments who have the responsibility of managing the boundary between the third sector and the state authorities (Ljubownikow and Crotty, 2017). In effect, they are in responsible for negotiating, coordinating and/or filtering the logics (Lee and Lounsbury, 2015; Smets et al., 2015) governing these two different sectors. We term this process 'sucking in' (Ljubownikow and Crotty, 2017). In order to explore these developments empirically, we now turn our attention to the ways in which individuals within heNPOs have built, understood and utilised their ties with state authorities and/or governing and ruling elites.

Respondents from our dataset highlighted the fact that they had been 'sucked in' to 'work for the state' as a consequence of attending roundtables and committees (Respondents 49, 51, 61, 62). Examples included the acquisition of 'a desk in the state administration' (Respondent 51), acting as regular consultants or as 'an expert with the department of education' (Respondent 52), providing 'advice as an expert' (Respondent 49), and working in close physical proximity with state agencies: 'our office is down the corridor from the department of social protection' (Respondent 75). A further benefit of these arrangements was the provision of access to resources such as 'office space' (Respondents 1, 2, 3, 14, 23). Respondents also highlighted their use of emerging vertical ties as a means of securing government 'support' (Respondent 60), without which 'it will be difficult for us to do our work' (Respondent 81) or 'talk to the people that could help [them do their work]' (Respondent 64). Similarly, Respondent 52 told us that her government role meant that she could access premises from which to run her heNPO: 'many old nursery buildings were in decay, [and subsequently] we were given this building here [by the state], which we refurbished with money from sponsors and the state'. Her heNPO now used this building as a base for its work with children with mental health needs. Another respondent reported that her organisation had been unable to pay staff a wage. As a result of her participation in state-run committees, however, she had been able to convince state authorities to 'hire me and the organisation's other employees' (Respondent 65). Now all its staff were employed full-time by the state to run their heNPO, which promoted physical activity amongst children with learning difficulties. Both organisations were insistent that without these ties they would not have been 'helping all these children' (Respondent 52) or continuing the work of 'enabling such children to do physical activity' (Respondent 65). Respondents thus illustrated how they had been 'sucked in' to work for the state through direct state access and resources.

In addition to direct support and resources, collaboration with state authorities was also considered to be an important benefit of these vertical ties. It enabled heNPOs to work 'closely together with the government authorities' (Respondent 5) and find a 'good way to collaborate with the state' (Respondent 51). As a result, heNPOs had closer 'contact to the department' (Respondent 15) and an increased ability to 'cooperate with the state' (Respondent 3) or to 'work with state institutions' (Respondent 22). Respondents also felt that building cross-sector partnerships or collaborations were greatly aided by the sucking in of key decision-makers within heNPOs: 'Without between sector interactions, you would not survive a day, so we build good relations with the regional powers. These relations are constructive because we offer services and programs, which they [the state] accept and support' (Respondent 1).

These closer ties provided individuals with opportunities to engage with policy-makers which highlighted not only how they were sucked in or co-opted, but also how they were able to negotiate and manage the boundary between the state and the third sector. HeNPOs could thus utilise vertical ties with the state to support their work. They also perceived being sucked in as a way of engaging with the state; the state now 'listen(ed) to our problems' (Respondent 15) and showed 'appreciation' (Respondent 9, 19). Hence, collaborative work enabled heNPOs to 'make friends in the administration' (Respondent 79) as well as in delivering services, helping constituencies, or more generally engaging in day-to-day activities. Engaging in these activities was seen as 'always a win–win' situation (Respondent 52). HeNPOs, therefore, were able to utilise emergent vertical ties for their advantage as well as successfully redrawing or managing the boundary between the state and their sector.

Not all respondents, however, took such a positive view of the blurring of the boundaries between the state and NPOs. One perceived disadvantage of this development was the nature of the relationship between an heNPO and the state. Rather than being seen as a genuine collaboration between the two parties, this was restricted to the targeted co-option by the state of specific individuals who possessed some specific human capital or expertise: 'They [the authorities] look for the key decision makers in the third sector and then work with us to develop the third sector so it can do what it needs too' (Respondent 45).

This was a sentiment shared by respondents that had not been sucked in. Their view was that 'the administration only works with the organisations they like' (Respondent 31), and it specifically targeted those organisations that did not explicitly challenge the state. As a result, some respondents feared that the third sector would be divided into two groups: those organisations which were able to interact with the state, and the others that would be sidelined: 'I think the danger is that an elite of HENPOs is emerging. As a result, the state will only interact with them and other organisations will have no chance to work with the state' (Respondent 37). The views of other heNPOs resonated with this statement. They feared that sucking in was a double-edged sword, positive for those that were able to establish vertical ties and access resources, but negative for those that missed out on them.

Our informal probing of the respondents tended to suggest that heNPOs working with children or disabled people were more likely to benefit positively from their contacts with state organisations and were more likely to be sucked in than those which dealt with HIV/AIDS or drug abuse (Respondents 25, 30, 37, 43, 45, 48). The organisations that had access to the state tended to be viewed as part of the state structure and so had lost their 'connection with the public' (Respondent 42). This division of agents into what the state considered to be appropriate third sector actors and what they did not is important as it was the former organisations that were undergoing hybridisation. The boundary between the state and the Russian third sector became even more blurred when the respondents highlighted the extent to which they observed the overlap between how they defined the role of the government and the way they identified the objectives of their organisation. Respondent 51's role, for example, included the responsibility for overseeing on behalf of the local state the regulations for accessibility to public buildings throughout the city. This overlapped with the key objective of her organisation to promote and ensure accessibility to public buildings and spaces. Similarly, Respondent 19 was responsible for the implementation of the city's youth programme and policies as part of her role as an agent of the state: 'I do not work here [in this heNPO] all the time. I work for the state and I focus on the development of youth policy' (Respondent 19). The mission statement of her organisation was to 'improv[e] the life of children'.

As key sucked-in individuals from third sector organisations played these kinds of roles they became supporters or legitimisers of state policy (Cook and Vinogradova, 2006) and lost their ability to criticise or oppose it. In the process, these heNPOs had become hybrid organisations with characteristics of both the third sector and the state. Thus, as observed in other similar contexts, this contributes to the legitimacy of current power arrangements rather than challenging them (Hsu, 2010; Lewis, 2013). Hence hybridisation on NPOs in the Russian context is as much an outcome of organisational necessities (as elsewhere) as it is an outcome of current power arrangements.

BLURRING THE LINES THROUGH RESOURCE PROVISION: ENVIRONMENTAL NPOs

For this section of the chapter, we draw on data from 26 environmental NPOs (eNPOs) situated in the Samara and Volgograd Oblasts and in Stavropol Krai. Like the heNPOS discussed above, these organisations tended to be small in size, but unlike them, they had in the main a longer history. Their activities included the preservation of a local national park, the protection of animals, and environmental education of the public (fuller details are set out in Table 19A.2 in the Appendix). They operated on minimal or no existing financial resources; many of the organisations had received foreign funding in the past but had yet to find a way to offset its disappearance by securing replacements from domestic sources.

The data collected from eNPOs identifies a different kind of hybridisation from that experienced in the heNPOs discussed earlier. Rather than developing vertical ties that led to boundary-crossing between state and third sector, hybridisation was driven by access to the resources which influenced the kinds of activity undertaken by eNPOs. The majority of them had orientated their campaigning activity to that which was perceived as acceptable to the state and they had now focused on non-confrontational, apolitical activities. By focusing on activities such as environmental education and conservation, eNPOs have supplemented the work of the state even if they have stopped short of crossing the boundary into it. Discussions with eNPO leaders revealed just how closely linked organisational identity had become to the prevailing funding context. The presence of the Civic Chamber and the need for groups to align their objectives to those of the state in order to secure funding dominated the data. eNPOs were split into two groups: those at risk of being institutionalised (Tarrow, 1989) which felt it was necessary to have a strong public image in particular vis-à-vis the state (in order to access funding), and those risking isolation which tried to remain independent (rejecting state funding).

Public image and reputation were perceived by many groups as paramount if their organisation and activities were to have both 'influence' (1.9) and access to state funds. It was important for them to have a 'good reputation' (1.10), to ensure 'more chances to cooperate' (1.10). Interviewees also spoke of the need to have 'acceptance in the funding community' (1.7), to 'prove' (1.2) themselves, and to be 'well known' (1.6) in order to 'collaborate with the authorities' (1.6). Given the lack of anonymity within this process (Richter, 2009), the better the image of the eNPO then the greater chance that funding applications to the Civic Chamber would be viewed favourably. Those eNPOs working with the Civic Chamber described groups outside of this structure as 'amateurs' (1.7) or 'not professional' (2.2) because they did not have the capabilities to develop a relevant public image and reputation. The requirement to align organisations with state priorities was the major driver of hybridisation amongst eNPOs.

Within the prevailing political environment (McCarthy and Zald, 1977; Tarrow, 1988) eNPOs faced a funding dilemma (Melucci, 1989). Seeking state funding via competitive grants from the Civic Chamber and thus adopting the state's 'interests' required some degree of institutionalisation (Tarrow, 1989) and involved the development of a hybrid form of organisation. The alternative strategy – to attempt to raise money themselves and set their own campaigning agenda – would lead them to remain a more 'pure' third sector actor. Many groups recognised that the former approach would result in the subjugation of individual group interests to those of the state, as indicated by the following extracts:

> If you want to win grants and be active then you can win these grants, but your actions will be totally controlled by the powers that be. (3.1)

> The state will only provide financing for 'their' NPOs, groups of people who have surrendered their independence and simply carry out the orders of their political masters . . . Now the grants are simply 'bought' for those organisations which are willing to play the game and will allow the grant-giving bodies to 'dictate' the frameworks in which they will operate. (3.3)

Those which had secured funding also acknowledged the tension between individual and state interests, but – unsurprisingly – viewed relationships with the state in a positive way: 'When we carry out a project using the government financing, and if the Ministry is interested in business participating in the project, it may become a joint project, and thus it strengthens the project and minimizes the expenditures' (1.7).

Without guaranteed sources of income outside of those provided by the state, the primary concern of the Russian environmental movement had become finance (or the lack of it). Funding, rather than environmental concerns, had become the key issue. This reflects the work of Piven and Cloward (1977) who asserted that, over time, groups might become more concerned with their survival than with their original goals. The prioritisation of funding goals is also frequently associated with the hybridisation of NPOs in other contexts (Billis, 2010).

As a result, the experience of eNPOs was similar to that of the heNPOs discussed above. Although eNPOs lacked the close integration with state structures displayed by heNPOs, most of the eNPOs in our dataset engaged in activity that could be described as cooperational or 'safe', focusing on educational and children's projects (1.3, 1.6, 1.11, 1.12, 1.14, 1.16, 2.2), conservation (1.12, 1.14, 2.3), and hosting or attending conferences and exhibitions (1.2, 1.6, 1.8, 2.1, 3.1). Thus, while not crossing the boundary into activity undertaken by the state, many groups were supplementing it by their work, particularly in the spheres of education and conservation, and took on some of the aspects of hybridisation as a result. Those in receipt of state funding were unlikely to engage in activity that was not supportive of the state. Similarly, eNPOs that had close links and funding from industrial enterprises (1.13, 1.16, 3.4) were also unlikely to engage in critical or oppositional relationships with them.

Many organisations also failed to express their core environmental interests through their activities. It was commonplace for them to engage in broad activities such as the education of children, conservation and attending conferences without addressing any prescribed environmental purpose or objective. As a result, there were very few instances of confrontational mobilisation on environmental issues and the Russian environmental movement did not aspire to become a mass movement (Weiner, 2002), focusing instead on 'safe' campaigning issues with a view to maximising agency within the restrictions of the new Russian political landscape. This, in turn, shaped the scope and content of groups' networks (Tilly and Wood, 2013). Those working with the state described the networks that included the 'Governor, the vice-Governor' (1.6), 'presidents of big companies' (1.7) or 'a wide range of relationships in different economic and political spheres' (2.2). These offered a direct channel to networks that were both formal and resource-rich (Eesley and Lenox, 2006).

A small minority of eNPOs sought to maintain their independence and their ability to express their concerns by looking for other sources of funding and resources. Those eNPOs, usually smaller, grassroots organisations, were keen to stress their 'independent' (1.1, 1.8, 1.9, 3.2, 3.3, 3.6) nature. They asserted their independence of Civic Chamber funding in order to give them the freedom to pursue interests of their own choosing, as one participant articulated: 'There are many who think it's vital to support the authority and they are well financed. [1.1] is not sponsored (funded by the state) but on the other hand, we are not afraid to express our attitude' (1.1).

In demarcating themselves from the majority of eNPOs that aligned themselves with the state, eNPOs in this group described the former as 'puppet' organisations (1.9) or 'not real' (3.1). The difference was also reflected in their description of the networks they maintained to realise their work as 'friends' (1.3) that had come together because they had 'similar opinions' (1.3) and 'similar objectives' (1.3). Only one respondent (1.16) mentioned their access to industrial and regional elites, while the rest of them described their relationship with elites as non-existent, as 3.3 and 3.6 explained:

> Previously, we had positive relations with many of the major factories in Volgograd region. Now these relations are very strained. We have virtually no interaction with them now. They are not interested in listening to us and co-operating with us. (3.3)

> We have spoken or tried to speak to the local councillors on numerous occasions, but our efforts fell on deaf ears. (3.6)

With limited access to both industrial and governing elites, independent eNPOs had little access to resources that could be secured through such networks and this further entrenched the disparities and inconsistencies between eNPOs and their ability to mobilise (Routledge, 2003). They gained access to resources by engaging with the logic of state bureaucracy. This took place at the expense of the logic of the third sector as hybridisation facilitated institutionalisation and favoured organisational survival as the priority for NPOs in Russia's managed democracy. While eNPOs stopped short of becoming boundary crossers in the way that their heNPOs counterparts had, their organisational goals had become more focused on the acquisition of resources and this, in turn, brought them closer to the state's environmental objectives than their own. At the same time, many of their activities supplemented the work of the state in areas such as education and conservation. Our study of the two kinds of organisation – heNPOs and eNPOs – has highlighted how they followed two different paths towards becoming hybrid organisations. In the concluding section of the chapter, we discuss the commonalities of the trends and pressures that led them in this direction.

DISCUSSION AND CONCLUSION

In this chapter, we have highlighted two different paths that hybridisation has taken in the context of the Russian Federation. The eNPOs experienced comparatively indirect and informal drivers to hybridity. The curtailment of political opportunity (McCarthy and Zald, 1977) and restricted access to resources made the Civic Chamber the primary funding source for the Russian environmental movement (Crotty et al., 2014). In turn, eNPOs limited their aims and activities to ensure that they were perceived to be eligible for obtaining resources. Groups not wishing to engage with the Chamber could only rely on their own personal resources or the funds they could raise in a difficult philanthropic environment (Sundstrom, 2005). As a result, eNPOs were forced to make a choice between 'institutionalisation [or] isolation' (Tarrow, 1989, p. 138) which in turn determined the scope and nature of their activity. Many eNPOs pursued 'safe', apolitical activities and chose not to engage with the more contentious socio-economic environmental consequences of both Soviet and Russian economic policy. We did not see the Russian environmental movement making strategic decisions about changes to policy, cultural codes or ways of thinking about contentious environmental issues on a wider scale (Melucci, 1989). Instead, the great majority of the eNPOs we studied had presented themselves in ways that made them acceptable to the state and located them as hybrids between the third sector and the state.

The experience of heNPOs, on the other hand, suggests that hybridisation in the Russian context is not only a response to resource dependency which is indirect or informal in nature, but also takes on more formalised ways of organising. The 'sucking in' narrative of heNPO respondents and their lack of engagement with the emerging vertical ties for dissent represented a formal route to hybridisation for this part of the Russian third sector. Significantly, respondents did not regard this process as co-option but as collaboration: a way of aligning the objectives of their organisations with those of the state. They understood themselves as occupying a dual role, spanning and indeed managing the boundary between the aspirations of the third sector and the responsibilities of the state, rather than achieving full insider status by shaping state policy. While organisations were enabled to engage with the state and thus create potential opportunities for influence, this approach reduced the potential for NPOs to criticise the activities of the state or oppose formal power arrangements (Ray, 1999). It was difficult for a Russian heNPO to protest openly about a state policy it had been a part of delivering. The possibility of raising questions or issues about the actions of the state was also constrained by the way in which hybridisation took place. It tended to be driven by individuals rather than by organisations and their causes. The process of sucking in increased the opportunities for individuals to undertake informal advocacy for causes at the same time as it reduced the opportunities for organisations to protest formally. The quiet (or silent) and private approach to protest conducted by the sucking-in narrative has also been observed elsewhere as part of the professionalisation and institutionalisation of social action that has been termed 'NGOisation' (Alvarez et al., 1998; Choudry and Kapoor, 2013; Lang, 1997).

Our findings reveal that the drive towards the institutionalisation of access to state authorities and power-holders has been largely the result of the development of incentives for key individuals from within Russian NPOs to deploy their activities within state agencies, and for the NGOs to tailor their activities to those which are seen to be acceptable to the state and those that supplement state activity. These key individuals play the role described by Lewis as 'boundary crossers' who, while engaged in one sector (state or NPO) at a time, move 'backwards and forwards across [sector] boundaries' (Lewis, 2008, p. 572) Their frequent movements between sectors enables them to 'oil the relationship between government and third sector [NPOs]' (ibid.). In the Russian context, individuals are responsible for managing the boundary between the third sector or what their organisation does and the activities of the state in their organisation's area of activity. Many of them still consider themselves (and the NPOs with which they work) as agents of the third sector but they have increasingly also become seen as agents of the state. Those who manage the boundaries of the two sectors may now find opportunities for NPOs to be heard by the government; to access resources from the state, and to achieve the kind of legitimacy that they were missing during the political and economic turmoil of the 1990s.

We argue that the effects of hybridisation by integration with the state changes the third sector logic of activism or holding the state to account into one of serving the greater social good as determined by the state. In the short term, the managed democracy of the Russian Federation means that, although NPOs may become varying forms of hybrid, they tend to be aligned closely with the state's logic of control and minimising dissent. But in the longer term, their role of managing the boundary between third sector and the state may lead them to become institutional entrepreneurs who can stimulate change from within. Thus boundary managers may in future be able to carve out broader campaigning opportunities for their organisations (Newman, 2012). This is, of course, speculative; what we can say with any certainty at the moment is that the boundaries between the state and the third sector in Russia have become increasingly blurred, and the future lines between them will continue to shift over time as the processes of hybridisation continues to develop.

ACKNOWLEDGEMENTS

For parts of this chapter, we draw on our previous published work. In particular, we draw on our publication Ljubownikow, S. and Crotty, J. (2017) Managing Boundaries: The Role of Non-profit Organizations in Russia's Managed Democracy, *Sociology* 51(5), http://doi.org/10.1177/0038038515608111, to illustrate the blurring lines by heNPOs. For eNPOs we draw on data collected for the United Kingdom Economic and Social Research Council Grant RES-061-25-0002-A, extracts from which were published in Crotty, J. and Hall, S.M. (2013) Environmental Responsibility in a Transition Context, *Environment and Planning C: Government and Policy* 31(4): 667–681.

REFERENCES

Alvarez, S.E., Dagnino, E. and Escobar, A. (1998) Introduction: The Cultural and the Political in Latin American Social Movements. In: *Cultures of Politics Politics of Cultures: Re-Visioning Latin American Social Movements*. Boulder, CO: Westview Press, pp. 1–29.

Battilana, J. and Lee, M. (2014) Advancing Research on Hybrid Organizing: Insights from the Study of Social Enterprises. *Academy of Management Annals* 8(1): 397–441.

Bennetts, M. (2012) Russian Parliament Approves NGO 'Foreign Agents' Law. *RIA Novosti*. http://en.rian.ru/russia/20120706/174436993.html (accessed 6 July 2012).

Billis, D. (2010) Towards a Theory of Welfare Hybrids. In: Billis D (ed.), *Hybrid Organizations and the Third Sector: Challenges for Practice, Theory and Policy*. London: Palgrave Macmillan, pp. 46–69.

Brandsen, T., Van de Donk, W. and Putters, K. (2005) Griffins or Chameleons? Hybridity as a Permanent and Inevitable Characteristic of the Third Sector. *International Journal of Public Administration* 28(9/10): 749–765.

Bromley, P. and Meyer, J.W. (2017) 'They Are All Organizations' The Cultural Roots of Blurring Between the Nonprofit, Business, and Government Sectors. *Administration and Society* 49(7), 939–966.

Bryanski, G. (2012) Russia's Putin Signs Anti-Protest Law before Rally. *Reuters*, 8 June. http://www.reuters.com/article/2012/06/08/us-russia-protests-idUSBRE8570ZH20120608 (accessed 23 July 2012).

CAF Russia (2014) *Russia Giving: Research on Individual Giving in Russia*. Moscow: Charities Aid Foundation Russia. https://www.cafonline.org/PDF/CAF_Russia_GivingReport_ENG_final_web.pdf (accessed 10 December 2014).

Choudry, A. and Kapoor, D. (2013) *NGO-ization: Complicity, Contradictions and Prospects*. London: Zed Books.

Cook, L. and Vinogradova, E. (2006) NGOs and Social-Policy Making in Russia's Regions. *Problems of Post-Communism* 53(5): 28–41.

Crotty, J. (2006) Reshaping the Hourglass? The Environmental Movement and Civil Society Development in the Russian Federation. *Organization Studies* 27(9): 1319–1338.

Crotty, J., Hall, S.M. and Ljubownikow, S. (2014) Post-Soviet Civil Society Development in the Russian Federation: The Impact of the NGO Law. *Europe–Asia Studies* 66(8): 1253–1269.

Daucé, F. (2015) The Duality of Coercion in Russia: Cracking Down on 'Foreign Agents'. *Demokratizatsiya* 23(1): 57–75.

Doherty, B., Haugh, H. and Lyon, F. (2014) Social Enterprises as Hybrid Organizations: A Review and Research Agenda. *International Journal of Management Reviews* 16(4): 417–436.

Eesley, C. and Lenox, M.J. (2006) Firm responses to secondary stakeholder action. *Strategic Management Journal* 27(8): 765–781.

Hedlund, S. (2006) Vladimir the Great, Grand Prince of Muscovy: Resurrecting the Russian Service State. *Europe–Asia Studies* 58(5): 775–801.

Henderson, S.L. (2002) Selling Civil Society: Western Aid and the Nongovernmental Organization Sector in Russia. *Comparative Political Studies* 35(2): 139–167.

Howard, M.M. (2002) Postcommunist Civil Society in Comparative Perspective. *Demokratizatsiya* 10(3): 285–305.

Hsu, C. (2010) Beyond Civil Society: An Organizational Perspective on State–NGO – Relations in the People's Republic of China. *Journal of Civil Society* 6(3): 259–277.

Jakobson, L. and Sanovich, S. (2010) The Changing Models of the Russian Third Sector: Import Substitution Phase. *Journal of Civil Society* 6(3): 279–300.

Javeline, D. and Lindemann-Komarova, S. (2010) A Balanced Assessment of Russian Civil Society. *Journal of International Affairs* 63(2): 171–188.

Kamerade, D., Crotty, J. and Ljubownikow, S. (2016) Civil liberties and Volunteering in Six Former Soviet Union Countries. *Nonprofit and Voluntary Sector Quarterly*. http://nvs.sagepub.com/cgi/doi/10.1177/0899764016649689 (accessed 26 May 2016).

Krasnopolskaya, I., Skokova, Y. and Pape, U. (2015) Government-Nonprofit Relations in Russia's Regions: An Exploratory Analysis. *VOLUNTAS: International Journal of Voluntary and Nonprofit Organizations* 26(6): 1–29.

Lang, S. (1997) The NGOization of Feminism: Institutionalisation and Institution Building within the German women's movement. In: Scott, J., Kaplan, C. and Keates, D. (eds), *Transitions, Environments, Translation*, New York: Routledge, pp. 101–120.

Lee, M.-D.P. and Lounsbury, M. (2015) Filtering Institutional Logics: Community Logic Variation and Differential Responses to the Institutional Complexity of Toxic Waste. *Organization Science* 26(3): 847–866.

Lewis, D. (2008) Using Life Histories in Social Policy Research: The Case of Third Sector/Public Sector Boundary Crossing. *Journal of Social Policy* 37(4): 559–578.

Lewis, D. (2013) Civil Society and the Authoritarian State: Cooperation, Contestation and Discourse. *Journal of Civil Society* 9(3): 325–340.

Ljubownikow, S. and Crotty, J. (2014) Civil Society in a Transitional Context: The Response of Health and Educational NGOs to Legislative Changes in Russia's Industrialized Regions. *Nonprofit and Voluntary Sector Quarterly* 43(4): 759–776.

Ljubownikow, S. and Crotty, J. (2016) Nonprofit Influence on Public Policy Exploring Nonprofit Advocacy in Russia. *Nonprofit and Voluntary Sector Quarterly* 45(2): 314–332.

Ljubownikow, S. and Crotty, J. (2017) Managing Boundaries: The Role of Non-profit Organisations in Russia's Managed Democracy. *Sociology* 51(5): 940–956.

Ljubownikow, S., Crotty, J. and Rodgers, P. (2013) The State and Civil Society in Post-Soviet Russia: The Development of a Russian Style Civil Society. *Progress in Development Studies* 13(2): 153–166.

Machleder, J. (2006) Contextual and Legislative Analysis of the Russian Law on NGOs. Discussion Paper, INDEM Foundation, Moscow. http://www.indem.ru/en/publicat/Russian_NGO_Law_03252006.pdf (accessed 7 December 2010).

McCarthy, J.D. and Zald, M.N. (1977) Resource Mobilization and Social Movements: A Partial Theory. *American Journal of Sociology* 82(6): 1212–1241.

Melucci, A. (1989) *Nomads of the Present*. Philadelphia, PA: Temple University Press.

Mendelson, S.E. and Gerber, T. (2007) Activist Culture and Transnational Diffusion: Social Marketing and Human Rights Groups in Russia. *Post-Soviet Affairs* 23(1): 50–750.

Newman, J. (2012) *Working the Spaces of Power: Activism, Neoliberalism and Gendered Labour*. London, UK and New York, USA: Bloomsbury Academic.

Pache, A.-C. and Santos, F. (2010) When Worlds Collide: The Internal Dynamics of Organizational Responses to Conflicting Institutional Demands. *Academy of Management Review* 35(3): 455–476.

Pache, A.-C. and Santos, F. (2013) Inside the Hybrid Organization: Selective Coupling as a Response to Competing Institutional Logics. *Academy of Management Journal* 56(4): 972–1001.

Pickvance, K. (1998) Democracy and Grassroots Opposition in Eastern Europe: Hungary and Russia Compared. *Sociological Review* 46(2): 187–207.

Piven, F.F. and Cloward, R.A. (1977) *Poor People's Movements: Why They Succeed, How They Fail*. New York: Random House.

Ray, R. (1999) *Fields of Protest: Women's Movements in India*. Social Movements, Protest, and Contention series, Minneapolis, MN: University of Minnesota Press.

Richter, J. (2009) The Ministry of Civil Society? *Problems of Post-Communism* 56(6): 7–20.

Robertson, G.B. (2009) Managing Society: Protest, Civil Society, and Regime in Putin's Russia. *Slavic Review* 68(3): 528–547.

Routledge, P. (2003) Convergence Space: Process Geographies of Grassroots Globalization Networks. *Transactions of the Institute of British Geographers* 28(3): 333–349.

Salamon, L.M., Benevolenski, V.B. and Jakobson, L.I. (2015) Penetrating the Dual Realities of Government–Nonprofit Relations in Russia. *VOLUNTAS: International Journal of Voluntary and Nonprofit Organizations* 26(6): 2178–2214.

Salmenniemi, S. (2005) Civic Activity – Feminine Activity?: Gender, Civil Society and Citizenship in Post-Soviet Russia. *Sociology* 39(4): 735–753.

Salmenniemi, S. (2008) *Democratization and Gender in Contemporary Russia*. London: Routledge.

Smets, M., Jarzabkowski, P., Burke, G.T., et al. (2015) Reinsurance Trading in Lloyd's of London: Balancing Conflicting-yet-Complementary Logics in Practice. *Academy of Management Journal* 58(3): 932–970.

Spencer, S.B. (2011) Culture as Structure in Emerging Civic Organizations in Russia. *Nonprofit and Voluntary Sector Quarterly* 40(6): 1073–1091.

Sundstrom, L.M. (2005) Foreign Assistance, International Norms, and NGO Development: Lessons from the Russian Campaign. *International Organization* 59(2): 419–449.

Tarrow, S. (1988) National Politics and Collective Action: Recent Theory and Research in Western Europe and the United States. *Annual Review of Sociology* 14: 421–440.

Tarrow, S. (1989) *Struggle, Politics, and Reform: Collective Action, Social Movements and Cycles of Protest*. Ithaca, NY: Center for International Studies, Cornell University.

Tilly, C. and Wood, L.J. (2013) *Social Movements 1768–2012*, 3rd edition. Boulder, CO: Routledge.

Wegren, S. and Konitzer A. (2007) Prospects for Managed Democracy in Russia. *Europe–Asia Studies* 59(6): 1025–1047.

Weiner, D.R. (2002) *A Little Corner of Freedom: Russian Nature Protection from Stalin to Gorbachev*. Berkeley, CA: University of California Press.

APPENDIX

Table 19A.1   List of health and education NPOs

Organisational code	Date established, size of organisation (staff and/or membership)	Main objective(s)
Org01Sam	1991, 8 staff	Third sector development
Org02Sam	2001, 1 staff	Promoting educational techniques
Org03Sam	2007, 6 staff	Charitable programmes
Org04Sam	2000, 2 staff	Educating volunteers
Org05Sam	1992 (1918), c. 3000 members	Youth programmes
Org06Sam	1991, 2 staff	Deaf education
Org07Sam	2003, c. 20 members	Disability support
Org08Sam	2000, 3 staff	Folklore education
Org09Sam	1997 (1993), 3 staff	Legal education
Org10Sam	2001, 60 staff	Drug addiction and HIV/AIDS support
Org11Sam	2002, 3 staff	Language education
Org12Sam	2003, 100 members	Assisting families of Down's Syndrome children
Org13Sam	1998, c. 15 members	Healthy lifestyle promotion
Org14Sam	(1924–33) 1987, 5 staff	Humanitarian aid for children
Org15Sam	1999, 7 staff	HIV/AIDS support
Org16Sam	2005 (1988), 2 staff	Disability support
Org17Sam	1998, 23 staff	Disability rights
Org18Sam	1985, 5 staff	Healthy lifestyle promotion
Org19Sam	2005, c. 4 staff	Organising youth exchanges and volunteers
Org20Sam	2007, 3 staff	HIV/AIDS support
Org21Sam	1992, 3 staff	Children's rights
Org22Sam	1999, 3 staff	HIV/AIDS education
Org23Sam	1998, 1 staff, c. 10 members	Child health promotion
Org24Sam	2000, c. 60 members	Assisting the families of autistic children
Org01Per	1999, 3 members	Drug rehabilitation and education
Org02Per	1868, 12 staff	Health services
Org03Per	1999, c. 20 staff	Disability employment
Org04Per	1995, 6 staff	Promoting and organising paralympic sport
Org05Per	1938, 38 staff	Advocacy for the blind
Org06Per	2006, n/a	Youth education
Org07Per	1993, 4 staff	Disability rights
Org08Per	1926, 22 staff	Advocacy for the deaf
Org09Per	1997, n/a	Disability rehabilitation
Org10Per	1998, 4 staff	Promoting children's rights
Org11Per	1992, c. 18 staff	Running museum and human rights education
Org12Per	1998, 4 staff	Human rights education
Org13Per	2000, 60 members	Disability rights
Org14Per	c. 1997, 70 members	Assisting the families of autistic children
Org15Per	1994, 50 members	Hospice
Org16Per	2005, 10 members	Election monitoring and democracy education
Org17Per	2006, 4 staff	Drug rehabilitation
Org18Per	1996, 16 staff	Assisting TSOs with marketing and legal advice

Table 19A.1 (continued)

Organisational code	Date established, size of organisation (staff and/or membership)	Main objective(s)
Org19Per	2005, 9 members	Housing rights education
Org20Per	2003, 20 members	Citizenship education
Org21Per	1994, 11 staff	Health rights education
Org22Per	1998, 3 staff	Supporting and implementing social projects
Org01Yek	1988, c. 15 staff	Disability rights
Org02Yek	2003, 5 staff	Supporting new mothers
Org03Yek	c. 2005, 1 staff	Disability rights
Org04Yek	1999, 1 staff	Disability rights
Org05Yek	c. 2000, 5 staff	Respite care for the families of disabled children
Org06Yek	2001, 10 staff	Healthy lifestyle promotion
Org07Yek	2001, c. 5 members	Disability rights
Org08Yek	2002, c. 30 members	Disability rights
Org09Yek	c. 2000, 20 staff	Drug rehabilitation
Org10Yek	1996, 0	Disability rights – dissolved
Org11Yek	2000, 7/8 staff	Children's rights
Org12Yek	1918, 10 staff, c. 7000 members	Advocacy for the blind
Org13Yek	1998, 1 staff	Aid to children in poverty
Org14Yek	2004, 1 staff	After school education
Org15Yek	2003, 20 members	Disability rights
Org16Yek	1999, 22 staff	Providing support to families of those with HIV/AIDS
Org17Yek	1995, 2 staff	Organizing special Olympics
Org18Yek	2002, 9 members	Learning disability rights
Org19Yek	2007, 6 members	Education for peace
Org20Yek	1992, 32 members	Support for children's homes
Org21Yek	1999, c. 30 members	Respite for the families of children with cancer – dissolved
Org22Yek	1992, 8 staff	Disability rehabilitation
Org23Yek	1996, 2 members	Assisting for children with disabilities
Org24Yek	1998, 3 staff	Education of deaf children
Org25Yek	1999, c. 10 staff	Student's rights education
Org26Yek	1992 (1918), c. 17000 members/c. 25 staff	Youth education activities
Org27Yek	1988, 5 staff	Disability rights
Org28Yek	1961, 4 staff	After school clubs
Org29Yek	1998, c. 40 staff	Drug rehabilitation
Org30Yek	2003, c. 450 members	Support MS sufferers
Org31Yek	2004, c. 3 staff	Migrant rights education
Org32Yek	2005, c. 20 staff	Disability rights education
Org33Yek	2000, 1 staff	Addiction education

Table 19A.2   List of environmental NPOs

Organisational code	Date established, size of organisation (staff and/or membership)	Main objective(s)
1.1	1998, 50–100 staff	Preservation of national parks
1.2	2005, 2 members	Animal protection
1.3	1973, 2 staff, 10–15 volunteers staff	Workshops and education for children on animals and nature
1.4	1996, 3 members	Cultural heritage; assisting other groups with grant applications
1.5	1996, 20 staff	Share intellectual and practical knowledge about the environment. Establish ecological legislation Defend ecological rights of the population
1.6	1999, 50 organisational members, 100 individual members	Professional assessment of environmental situation in Samara
1.8	2006	Public education Engagement with roundtables
1.9	1998, 57 members	Stated aims are to improve ecological culture and politics
1.10	1998, 15 members	Coordinate ecological activity across the region and overseas organisations Contract work for state Award grants on behalf of the Public Chamber
1.11	1988, 10 organisational members, 360 individual members	Children's activities in the national park Annual residential in the park for school children
1.14	2000	Seeks donors for local projects, including environmental Acts as an agent for firms and the state fund public organisations
1.16	2002, 500 members	Annual rally to promote the uniqueness of the nature reserve Children's activities and education
2.1	2004	Established by President Putin Assessment of the environmental situation in Russia; campaigning for specific improvements
2.2	2007	Independent monitoring of radiation levels; ground and surface water
2.3	20 members	Children's projects including education, cleaning projects, festivals
3.1	Late 1980s	Campaign for environmental improvements through engagements with local authorities and politics; participate in roundtables and field candidates for local and state dumas

Table 19A.2   (continued)

Organisational code	Date established, size of organisation (staff and/or membership)	Main objective(s)
		Had 12 elected local deputies during the El'tsin period, no elected representatives currently
3.2	1990, 57 members across 15 regions	Publish papers, debate and attempt to highlight environmental issues to the wider population and government
3.3	1993	Communicating environmental issues through own newspaper
		Environmental monitoring and assessment
3.4	1999	To 'improve the environmental situation in Volgograd'
3.5	n/a	Commentator through eco-press and other outlets
3.6	Soviet Union	Focused on raising awareness and campaigning for an improved environment around the Red October Steelworks and district
		Demonstrations and meetings
3.7	Soviet Union	Communicating environmental issues to the state

20. The development of civil society organisations in the transitional economy of the Czech Republic

Gabriela Vaceková, Hana Lipovská and Jana Soukopová

INTRODUCTION

The theoretical relevance and practical importance of the development of hybrid organisations around the world has been experienced, among others, by the post-communist economies. The trend towards emerging hybridisation in the transitional economies of Central and Eastern Europe (CEE) has grown significantly in recent years. The process of spanning sectoral boundaries (Billis, 2010; Dees and Anderson, 2003; Laville and Nyssens, 2001) is 'now perhaps accelerating' (Donnelly-Cox, 2015), especially with the development of social enterprises that seem to transcend sectors (Dees and Anderson, 2003). To date, however, we lack the means of reflecting in detail on the specific nature of hybridity in a transitional context as well as on the kinds of current public debates and policy-making discourses within which it takes place. This chapter intends to try to fill this gap.

The chapter does not attempt to do justice to the considerable heterogeneity of transitional economies but focuses on the Czech Republic in an attempt to present a comprehensive picture of the way in which civil society was transformed in this one country. From the early years of the transition from communist rule, public services were seen as being delivered by hybrid organisations operating in the intersection of the market, the civil society and the public sector.

There are different types of hybrid organisations; for example, Grossi and Thomasson (2015) distinguish between:

> Mixed public and private commercial (for-profit) enterprises – these are corporations with both public and private commercial owners operating in the public interest (the 'mixed economy'); and
> Mixed public and private not-for-profit organisations, in which a public sector entity has strong influence (via funding and regulation) but a private not-for-profit organisation delivers public services.

In reviewing the nature of the changes in the historical configuration of civil society, we have highlighted the emergence of two types of hybrid organisation which are of special interest in the Czech Republic: public–private partnerships (PPPs) and social enterprises. Taking into account the definition of hybrid organisations as those that combine the characteristics of at least two of the public, private and third sectors, the chapter focuses especially on social enterprises that can be defined as private and third sector hybrids.

While there is a great deal of relevant research devoted to hybridity in the scientific literature worldwide, unfortunately this does not hold true for the transitional CEE countries. This chapter looks at the broad opportunities offered by hybridity but focuses on the challenges and potentials of social enterprises, while noting PPPs as part of the context in which social enterprises operate. This, we argue, provides an illustrative example of the role of hybrid organisations in the Czech Republic which has a wider relevance for, and possibilities of application to, the other transitional economies of Central and Eastern Europe.

THE TRANSFORMATION OF CENTRALLY PLANNED ECONOMIES: LESSONS FROM THE CZECH REPUBLIC

The 'transitional economies' constitute a varied mixture of 27 countries, predominantly from the CEE but complemented by the republics of the former Soviet Union situated to the south of the Caucasus and in Central Asia. The concept of the transitional economy came into existence at the end of the 1980s when all these countries were gradually abandoning the path towards socialism that they had followed under the leadership of the Communist Party. Instead they were setting out on a phase of transition from a state-controlled economy to one that was driven by the market, a change that was seen as the general goal of economic transformation. While it can be argued that some elements of the market economy also existed in a centrally commanded economy (just as the state might have intervened in the market), the key feature of the communist regime was the way in which the economy was controlled or planned by the state and not driven by market forces. In 1989 and 1990, citizen movements were decisive in overturning the political order and, with it, the economic configuration in CEE countries (Strachwitz, 2015). The process of transition has had its setbacks, but overall the changes since 1989 have been regarded as an outstanding success in implementing a new economic regime (Shleifer and Treisman, 2014).

There are big differences in the extent to which individual countries have implemented the development of market economies and the growth of democratic institutions that are seen as complementary to them. Even under socialism there were significant differences between the transitional countries and they embarked on the process of transition from different starting points – and with considerable misgivings: 'The worst thing about communism,' quipped the Polish newspaper editor and anti-communist dissident Adam Michnik, 'is what comes after' (Shleifer and Treisman, 2014, p. 92). Today the transition to the market economy of the post-communist countries is seen to be far from complete, but generally typical of states at similar stages of economic development.

When it comes to economic transformation, the obvious winner among the group of post-socialist countries in the current ranking of the richest European Union (EU) countries is the Czech Republic. This is the finding of the Eurostat rankings (Table 20.1) which compares the economic development of each of the EU countries on the basis of their gross domestic product (GDP) and the purchasing power of their population.

The degree of transformation in individual countries depends on a number of baseline conditions. One of these is the size of the economy. A distinction has been made by Baldwin and Wyplosz (2012) between groups of large countries with populations of above 35 million inhabitants, medium-sized countries with 8–11 million inhabitants, and small states which are comparable to the metropolitan cities. Using this division, the Czech Republic belongs to the category of medium-sized countries. A second variable

Table 20.1   GDP per capita (index, EU28 = 100)

	2004	2005	2006	2007	2008	2009	2010	2011	2012	2013	2014	2015
Bulgaria	35	37*	38	42	45	46	45	45	46	46	47	46
Czech Republic	79	80*	81	83	81	83	81	83	82	83	84	85
Estonia	55	59*	64	68	68	62	63	69	74	75	76	74
Croatia	57	58*	58	61	63	61	59	59	60	59	59	58
Latvia	47	51*	55	60	60	52	52	56	60	62	64	64
Lithuania	50	53*	56	60	63	56	60	65	70	73	75	74
Hungary	62	62*	62	61	63	64	65	65	65	66	68	68
Poland	49	50*	50	53	54	59	62	64	66	67	68	69
Romania	34	34*	38	41	48	49	50	51	54	54	55	57
Slovenia	85	86*	86	87	89	85	83	82	81	80	82	83
Slovakia	56	59*	62	67	71	71	73	73	74	76	77	77

Note: * = break in time series.

Source: Data from Eurostat, http://ec.europa.eu/eurostat.

was the extent to which national economies had been linked with the other members of the Soviet-led economic association of the Council for Mutual Economic Assistance (COMECON) where the Czech Republic was rated one of the most integrated. And, thirdly, the starting point for the transformation of each economy depended on the size of its private sector and the extent to which aspects of the market economy were found within centrally commanded systems. In the case of the Czech Republic these features were negligible. An overview on mixed enterprises (MEs) in selected post-communist countries is shown in Table 20.2.

Over the last 26 years, the Czech economy has undergone a deep transformation in its shift from a centrally commanded economy to one driven by the market. This transformation has involved systemic, institutional and structural changes (Lašek, 1998) and it has led to some negative consequences such as unemployment and social exclusion. The Czech transformation process is often criticised for not being consistently secured through institutional changes. The lack of a clear understanding of the hybridisation phenomena on the micro level is also implicitly related to this criticism, which is a result of competition between economists and lawyers. Theoretical economists outside the transitive countries (especially consultants from the International Monetary Fund) were fervent proponents of the ideal (but hardly ever feasible) immediate implementation of the rule of law. According to a prominent critic of the Czech economic transition, Joseph Stiglitz, the rule of law means well-defined and enforced property rights, broad access to these rights, and predictable rules for resolving property rights disputes, in contrary to the non-existing protection of investors' returns from the confiscation of minority shareholders from 'tunnelling', that is, asset-stripping typically conducted by the former socialist managers (Hoff and Stiglitz, 2002, p. 4). Such critics claimed that 'the economists had overtaken lawyers' (Pick, 2000) or that 'the transformers turned off the lights for a while to make embezzling easier' (Stránský, 2013).

Table 20.2   Mixed enterprises (MEs) in selected post-communist countries

	Czech Republic	Slovakia	Poland
Number of MEs	6	44	401
MEs with >50% public ownership	4	14	13
MEs with <50% public ownership	2	30	87
Major sectors	infrastructure, trade, energy, agriculture	infrastructure, transportation, communication	n/a
Dominant legal forms	JSC	JSC	JSC
Trends of MEs in last 10 years	n/a	n/a	n/a
Local level			
Number of MEs	115	7	800
MEs with >50% public ownership	n/a	n/a	n/a
MEs with <50% public ownership	n/a	n/a	n/a
Major sectors	water, waste, energy	energy, waste	utilities, construction, real estate
Dominant legal forms	n/a	n/a	n/a
Trends of MEs in last 10 years	n/a	n/a	n/a

Source: Based on Reichard (2016).

These arguments are valid only from a purely theoretical point of view. There has never been an easy way of implementing a new legal code overnight. The economic transition was not conducted in a vacuum, it reflected existing legislation and it needed to be done in a very short time scale if it was to avoid the Hungarian approach to 'managerial capitalism' that was connected to asset-stripping (Žídek, 2014). Moreover, as Tříska (1999) mentions, even if the Czech (or Czechoslovak) legislative system was completely perfect, its courts were not perfect, as the judges were exponents of the Communist Party regime. Moreover, as the case of East Germany clearly shows, neither is a ready-made legal system the way to an easy, direct and effective economic transition. As Sepp and Frear (2011) notice, informal institutions were different in East and West Germany. Yet, informal institutions were one of the biggest problems during Czech transition. While the formal institutions such as the banking system or Commercial Code could be – and indeed were – implemented fairly quickly, the change in informal institutions (people's attitudes towards the political parties, elections, corruption, accuracy and punctuality) are taking decades to be transformed. According to Dahrendorf (2005) such change needs at least 60 years.

At the macro level, the transformation of the Czech economy has included changes to its structure: in terms of different sectors, industries, branch specialisations and products; in terms of the size of corporations; and in the nature of foreign trade. The restructuring of former large state-owned corporations has been a persistent problem. The accession of the Czech Republic to the EU in 2004 has involved the complete transformation of the former command economy to one based on the market, a process shared with virtually all the economies of the former socialist CEE countries. And the transformation of the economy was the precondition for a radical change in the political system to create a capitalist social system, a process that was much broader than changes to the economy.

CIVIL SOCIETY IN THE TRANSITIONAL CONTEXT: A REALITY CHECK FROM THE CZECH REPUBLIC

While the concept of a transitional economy has always been a kind of simplification or abstraction, all of the economies concerned, even after more than 25 years of transformation, share certain characteristics essentially because the institutions of their democracies and their market economies are not fully developed. This lack of development also holds true for civil society. The term 'civil society' is ubiquitous in research on democratisation, especially in the context of the collapse of Communist Party rule (Weigle and Butterfield, 1992; Linz and Stepan, 1996; Ekiert and Kubik, 1997; Green, 1999). It is an increasingly common term, but it is also increasingly difficult to define it; the borders are becoming more blurred, and hybridity and change are permanent features (Brandsen et al., 2005). In the case of the Czech transition the battle to define civic society was determined by the struggle between the group of pro-market conservative economists around Václav Klaus and the group of progressives around Václav Havel. At the heart of this dispute was the wide gap between civic society as a governing elite and as the society of civilians (Klaus, 2012).

Arguably civil society's finest hour (Strachwitz, 2015) came in 1989 and 1990 when the Velvet Revolution in the Vysegrád Four (V4) countries of Czechoslovakia (now the Czech Republic and Slovakia), Poland and Hungary was decisive in overturning the political order in CEE. What has happened in CEE more than a quarter of a century after 1989? The abolition of the Communist Party's monopoly of power created a tremendous upsurge in civil society (Frič et al., 1999) and, not surprisingly, the number of civil society organisations (CSOs) mushroomed after the transition in all four countries. This change of regime was largely perceived by citizens as an opportunity for founding new CSOs and for getting involved in the civil society sector (Navrátil and Pospíšil, 2014). Today, 'the picture is quite diverse, both by country and by field of activity' (Strachwitz, 2015: 1). Poland was able to build on a stronger civic tradition than the Czech Republic and Hungary. Where service provision was the main activity, CSOs relied on government funding and were widely seen as government agencies. Where this was not the case, they faced a struggle to survive. Slovak CSOs are comparatively strong in education; community development and housing are stronger in Hungary; and culture, religion, and health and social services are stronger in the Czech Republic. The activities of Polish CSOs are more evenly balanced across these areas. The main concern in all four countries is capacity-building; CSOs need help to be able to fulfil their roles as watchdogs, change agents and a political force (ibid.).

In the Czech Republic over the past 25 years, the nonprofit sector has experienced a dramatic transformation during the change from a totalitarian regime to a parliamentary democracy, but one which remains in transition: 'The field of the Czech civil society and the nonprofit sector is still largely terra incognita, or one large gap. The whole field remains in statu nascendi' (Pospíšil et al., 2014). We can, however, identify some specific features (Frič and Goulli, 2001; Pospíšil, 2006; Pospíšil et al., 2012).

In the first place, Czech civil society is informed by two influential traditions. The first of these is that of Czech National Revival; a considerable number of nonprofit organisations (NPOs) base their work and mission on the model of selfless sacrifice for a patriotic cause. The second is the tradition of the first Czechoslovak Republic; the pre-Second

World War Czechoslovakia is seen as the golden age of civil society and the desire to restart its successful institutions and to copy its successful models has been very strong.

By contrast, Czech civil society has struggled with legacies from the totalitarian years. The experience of totalitarianism has meant that people continue to mistrust nonprofit institutions. The legacy of corruption and clientelism through which the system of nepotism and informal networks has survived the fall of communism continues to pose a serious challenge to any attempt to introduce the rule of law and standard procedures even in the nonprofit sector. And there is a specific legacy of mistrust in the form of a deep divide that exists between 'old' and 'new' organisations. This makes concerted action by the whole sector difficult and means that the sector cannot provide trustworthy representatives for negotiations with the state whenever they are needed. Another distinctive characteristic of Czech civil society is the position of the churches, which have been finding it very hard to recover from the devastation inflicted on them by the Communist Party regime.

And, finally, we can highlight the important legacy of the 'nanny state'. The paternalistic communist state was a monopoly provider of all educational, cultural, social, health and other services (Brhlíková, 2004). It had a purpose-built centralised system of organisations that provided a state nonprofit sector of its own. The public sector has been finding it very hard to accept the loss of its monopoly in public services after 1989, to recognise the existence of an independent nonprofit sector, and to change its former role of providing public services into the new role of securing their provision (Frič, 2000). In the field of public services the dominance of the state and state-run organisations is still clearly visible. This is not only typical of the Czech Republic: it seems to be a general 'post-communist' pattern of providing public services (Hyánek and Pospíšil, 2009). Civil society in the Czech Republic is nonetheless increasingly thought of in positive terms (Frič et al., 1999):

> The civil society is . . . the best safeguard against authoritative powers that always ask for the floor when a society feels shaken or considers its future to be uncertain; of course, the conditions for them to dominate the country are getting the better the more power remains in the center. Communists knew very well why they needed to dominate, manipulate and bring under their control every beekeeper's club. (Havel, 1999)

THE PHENOMENON OF HYBRIDITY: 'BLURRING THE BOUNDARIES' IN THE CZECH REPUBLIC

More than a quarter of a century after the *annus mirabilis* of 1989, the study of post-communist countries has shifted from the question of democratic transition to the question of democratic consolidation (Green, 2002). There is a broad consensus that the Czech transformation was completed by 2004, the year of full Czech membership of the EU (Žídek, 2006). The literature on transition has moved away from a focus on public or private to a study of the various forms of public and private that are now emerging in the provision of public services (Swarts and Warner, 2014). The development of the transitional CEE economies has been influenced by ideas on New Public Management (NPM) (Pollit and Bouckaert, 2011) and, in the wake of NPM, it has become common for public services to be delivered by organisations operating at the intersection of the market and public sectors (Grossi and Thomasson, 2015). The implementation of these reforms differs from country to country (Thomasson, 2009), but what is common with these developments is the emergence of a new type of organisation that is a hybrid governed by the key principles of more than one sector. Typically these include combinations of the public and private commercial sectors, or hybrids drawing on the features of both the public and the private nonprofit sector. These hybrids do not simply combine any mixture of mixture of features from different sectors but involve 'fundamental and distinctly different governance and operational principles in each sector' (Billis, 2010).

In the history of the Czech Republic and other post-communist countries, many examples of hybrid arrangements can be found, especially in the transitional phases of their economic development. These combine public features and features generally associated with market logic; it appears far easier to find arrangements that are hybrid than those approximating ideal-typical notions (Brandsen et al., 2005). One of the key developments during the period of transition has been the emergence of mixed ownership concepts and the implementation of public–private partnerships (PPPs). Mixed (PPP) companies consist of joint ventures between public sector entities on one side and private operators and/or financial investors on the other. Nowadays, mixed companies are used by local governments all over the world, although with special incidence in Europe, mainly in Italy, Spain, France, Germany and Portugal (Verdier et al., 2004); and South America, especially in Colombia, but also in Cuba and Mexico (Marin, 2009); see also da Cruz et al. (2014).

PPP also represents one of the most common hybrid forms in the post-communist countries of CEE. The implementation of this concept into the public service system in post-communist countries, including the Czech Republic, and the growth of PPP projects reflects a somewhat uncritical perception of PPP as a kind of universal panacea that is seen – wrongly – as a completely new approach in the provision of public services (Řežuchová, 2010). While a number of advantages are attributed to PPP – for example, the use of mixed companies should place a relatively high degree of control over the performance of services on the public sector side (Grossi, 2007; da Cruz et al., 2014) – it has also raised a number of concerns. These include higher costs for PPP projects and the lack of a clear legal and regulatory framework (da Cruz and Marques, 2012; Hodge and Greve, 2010; Marques and Berg, 2010; McQuaid and Scherrer, 2010).

But the development of mixed ownership is not the whole story and the concept of hybridity is still undeveloped in the transition economies (Denis et al., 2015). A systematic review in the V4 countries (Tranfield et al., 2003) revealed a complete absence of scientific articles and papers that addressed the phenomenon of hybridisation in relation to civil society. Few, if any, studies go beyond recognising PPP. The literature seldom explains how hybrid organisations arise or what forms they take, and it does not take into account other forms such as the reorganisation of properties after the privatisation process. An important part of the complex process of privatisation that took place after 1992 involved the speedy transfer of property rights through 'voucher privatisation' which enabled Czech citizens to buy books of vouchers that could be invested in shares and other forms of privatised funds (Žídek, 2017). As a result numerous Czech organisations were owned by dozens of small investors who had their vouchers stored by the investment funds. Those funds were usually controlled by the commercial banks, and in the 1990s these banks were significantly under the influence of the Czech state as the important owner of banking shares (so-called 'recombined ownership'; Mlčoch, 1996). The managerial management of such companies was more complex than in purely private or purely state companies. One kind of organisation in the Czech Republic that is seen as possessing significant characteristics of more than one sector is the social enterprise. This is seen as a typical hybrid organisation that combines a market orientation with a social mission. Although hybridity is a relatively new subject of study, there is a considerable amount of literature on social enterprises in Europe (Valentinov, 2015) which shows that there are clear differences in the approach to social enterprise in different countries including differences among the (post-)transitional economies. We can, however, identify some significant determinants of social enterprise development in (post-)transitional economies that might not be found in developed economies (see Korimová and Vaceková, 2011).

In the first place, businesses with a social attribute are perceived quite negatively, politically and socially, as they are seen as reminiscent of socialism. Secondly, a characteristic of the Czech Republic, as in other former transition countries, is a high percentage of long-term and generational unemployed people. They were socially excluded and some have been reluctant to assume a mainstream way of life. Finally, there were important differences between the circumstances in which social enterprises developed. In developed economies, social economics and social enterprises were promoted organically through experience and drawing on established partnership networks with the nonprofit sector. In the transition economies, by contrast, the nonprofit sector has only recently been established and is still finding its feet. One result of this delay is that a variety of organisations – and not only NPOs – have been gradually entering the process of establishing social enterprises.

This implies that the development of social enterprises cannot be supported simply by importing Western European approaches. Unless the approaches are embedded in the circumstances found in the transitional economies, social enterprises will just be 'replications of formulas that will last only as long as they are fashionable' (Gidron and Hasenfeld, 2012). The concept of social enterprise is still new; it was almost unknown some 20 years ago (ibid.). In the last decade it has become a subject of discussion on both sides of the Atlantic including the CEE countries, and it is important to be clear about the distinctive ways in which developments have taken place in the different regions of Western and Eastern Europe.

The importance of the social economy in the former centrally planned economies was due to the enormous increase in unemployment and social exclusion created by the process of transformation and change to their national economic structures. Specific causes were: inertia in thinking, reliance on high standards of social state guarantees, low qualification of the workforce and low productivity, restructuring of the national economy, loss of sales in soft foreign markets, low competitiveness of products, new labour market demands for jobs with high added value, work process inefficiency, technological advances in production, and labour market rigidity in comparison to developed economies. All these factors created a specific historical, socio-economic, and political environment that differed from those found in Western Europe (Vaceková et al., 2015). By contrast, Western European social enterprises 'tend to be based in a social cooperative model and tend to be narrowly targeted on work integration efforts' (Gidron and Hasenfeld, 2012). The Western European approach also emphasises 'the participatory aspect of social enterprises' (ibid.), a characteristic that has received relatively little attention in the (post-)transitional countries so far.

THE EMERGENCE OF SOCIAL ENTERPRISES IN THE CZECH REPUBLIC

The history of nonprofit organisations in the territory of what is now the Czech Republic has been long and eventful. Many charitable organisations and societies promoting patriotism, science and the arts were established as early as the 19th century. These charitable societies – which included informal student groups – were recognised by the Freedom of Association Act (*Zákon o právě spolčovacím*) of 1867. During the reign of Joseph II many monasteries were abolished and their assets transferred to secular foundations and charities that had been established primarily for humanitarian purposes. The end of the First World War provided an impetus for the establishment of charitable organisations to mitigate the consequences of the war, and was followed by the foundation of the Czechoslovak Republic with a constitution that safeguarded the right to the freedom of assembly and association. These developments were brought to an end by the coming to power in 1948 of the Communist Party regime which carried out a series of purges and led to the closing down of charities whose activities were seen as inappropriate. No new legislative regulation was enacted until after 1989 (Dohnalová, 2006).

The first *družstva* (co-operatives) were established in the 1840s, with the first Cooperatives Act coming into force in the 1870s, when production co-operatives came to be established in large numbers. The first co-operative on the territory of the Czech Republic was established in 1847 and was called Pražské potravní a spořitelní (the Prague Food and Saving Society). The expansion of the co-operatives made it necessary to create a legislative framework for them, which was enacted during the Austro-Hungarian Empire. The system of co-operatives reached its peak in then-Czechoslovakia in the interwar period. By 1937, around 15 000 democratic economic benefit co-operatives were active in Czechoslovakia, employing about a quarter of the population (Dohnalová and Průša, 2011). After the Second World War the production of many co-operatives slowed, and after 1989 their number decreased rapidly (Hunčová, 2007).

Another feature of the social economy were the *spolky* (societies) which began to emerge at the time of the national revival and led to their legal registration in 1867. The first of these societies was Oul, the workers' benefit society, which was founded in 1868. These philanthropic organisations were formed to support patriotism, science and art, and they also included informal students' associations. The end of the First World War provided an incentive for founding charitable 'societies' to mitigate the consequences of the war. The most prosperous period for the societies was the period between the world wars (Dohnalová and Anderle, 2002). In 1951 the activities of these societies was effectively brought to an end by the passage of Act No. 68/1951 on voluntary associations and societies. Those that were not wound up were reformed and operated under the association of political parties of the National Front led by the Communist Party of Czechoslovakia. In 1989 a number of societies that had been in existence at the time of the national revival were re-established (Dohnalová and Průša, 2011).

Mutual aid movements based on solidarity and self-help emerged in the mid-19th century in order to support sole traders and small entrepreneurs. At much the same time Kampeličky (co-operative savings societies known as Raiffeisen after their founding father Friedrich Wilhelm Raiffeisen) developed, in order to lend money first to their own members in the form of short-term personal credit, and later to others. The first co-operative savings society was Občanská záložna (the Civic Savings Bank), founded in 1858 in Vlašim. Later, insurance companies developed protection against adverse life situations and the Imperial Letters Patent issued in 1819 permitted the establishment of private insurance companies in the Habsburg Monarchy. Insurance companies were not allowed to become public-law institutions until 1821. The first Czech mutual insurance company was established in Prague in 1827. It collected finances from its members and created insurance funds from them, managing and disposing of them according to predetermined rules.

Social enterprises emerged in CEE as a result of the fall of communism and the need to address some of the demands of economic transformation. Accentuated by the economic recession of 1970, the impact of structural changes to their economies led to high rates of unemployment and social distress at the same time that the state's role in addressing socio-economic problems was seriously curtailed, while the development of a nonprofit sector was sluggish. This created a gap into which social enterprises could develop. These 'exemplars of hybrid forms which intertwine within one organisation the different components and rationales of market, state and civil society' (Evers, 2005) remain relatively underdeveloped in the transitional economies of the CEE in terms of legal and institutional definitions (Poon, 2011). Across Europe more widely, however, the interest in social enterprises has increased and various forms of social enterprises have spread (Gidron and Hasenfeld, 2012). What is now needed is an understanding of the current state of social enterprise in the context of the transitional economies and, in particular, in the Czech Republic.

SOCIAL ENTERPRISE DOMAINS: EVIDENCE FROM THE CZECH REPUBLIC

In the Czech Republic, social enterprises have been much discussed but little understood. They tend to be found in many different sizes and a variety of legal forms, but are usually small or medium-sized companies and they include co-operatives. They are seen as innovative in terms of the diversity of their goals and sources of income; new approaches to job creation; and demonstrating new types of entrepreneurial behaviour that enable them to accommodate risk. Overall they need to balance the need to survive as businesses with their mission to make a social contribution. The orientation and character of a social enterprise is continuously influenced by financial possibilities and environmental pressure (Vaceková et al., 2015). The social enterprise is not intended primarily for profit but is designed to deliver activities for public benefit, and its contribution may be seen as including in the labour market people who are in some way disadvantaged. In the Czech Republic there has so far been a lack of legislation which would provide a clear framework for the operation of social enterprises.

The Czech Republic does, however, have a definition of one form of social enterprise – the social co-operative – which was set out in the 2014 Business Corporations Act:

> The social cooperative is a cooperative that systematically develops beneficial activities in support of social cohesion, for the purpose of labor and social integration of disadvantaged persons into society, with a priority to meet local needs and use local resources according to the place

where a social cooperative has its seat and the sphere of its authority, in particular in the area of job creation, social services and health care, education, housing, and sustainable development. (Act No. 90/2012 Coll.)

This definition of the social cooperative highlights the importance of its purpose of achieving social integration by including disadvantaged people as part of the general labour market. But there are other more general social enterprises that do not employ disadvantaged people but develop 'beneficial activities in support of social cohesion' and 'use local resources . . . in the area of job creation, social services and health care, education, housing, and sustainable development' (Hunčová, 2007). These social undertakings operate in the market at their own risk and finance themselves from the revenues of their own business. They are thus more likely to be social enterprises than some co-operatives which are not strongly profit-oriented, as Hunčová (2007) has suggested.

In the absence of specific legislation, social enterprises in the Czech Republic that do not qualify as social co-operatives use a variety of legal forms to define their activities. There have been a number of suggestions for legal regulation based on foreign adaptations of the idea of social enterprise that are not seen to be suitable for entrepreneurial activities because they are unduly rigid. These suggested adaptations include the use of an 'asset lock': a legal clause that prevents the assets of a company being used for private gain or distribution to its members rather than used only for the stated purposes of the organisation. What Czech social enterprises believe they need, however, is the development of a more appropriate and flexible regulatory framework.

In the absence of a legal definition of social enterprises in the Czech Republic and the lack of agreed criteria for defining them, we cannot find a single list or directory that would record all the social enterprises in the Republic. We have therefore drawn on a number of sources. The first of these is the list of social enterprises created under the Thematic Network for Social Economy (TESSEA) project. The TESSEA project was funded from the Operational Programme for Human Resources and Employment and the state budget of the Czech Republic, and started on 1 June 2009 and ended on 30 November 2011. The main purpose of the project was to provide support to public authorities in the Czech Republic in implementing social entrepreneurship by the means of TESSEA activities based on sharing experience and knowledge with transnational partners.

Statistics

An analysis of the development of social enterprises (Figure 20.1) shows that there has been a rapid increase in their number in the last decade (Vaceková and Murray Svidroňová, 2016). The first four were established in 1992, and there was little additional development until a further nine emerged in 2007 and 2008; then, once the economic crisis of 2008–09 had been weathered, the number of new social enterprises continued to grow. From 2009 until the first quarter of 2014, grants were available from the European Social Fund (ESF) and the European Regional Development Fund (ERDF) and, as a result, the number of social enterprises increased rapidly, with a record number of 45 new organisations established in 2012. The end of the entitlement to these subsidies meant that the number of newly established enterprises became fewer and only 10 came into existence in 2014. By December 2015 the total number of registered social enterprises was 211.

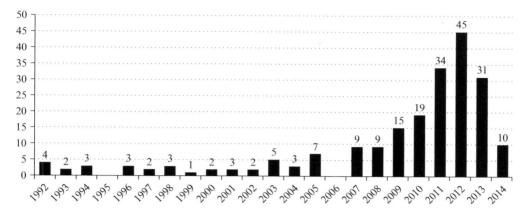

Source: Vaceková and Murray Svidroňová (2016).

Figure 20.1 *Development of the number of social enterprises in the Czech Republic*

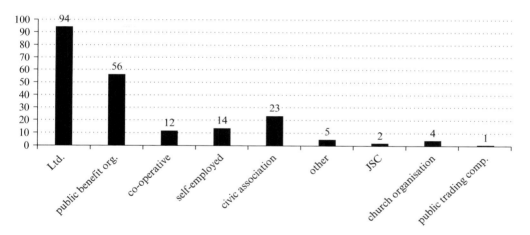

Note: JSC = joint stock company.

Source: Vaceková and Murray Svidroňová (2016).

Figure 20.2 *Social enterprises in the Czech Republic classified by their legal form*

Legal Status

The directory of social enterprises showed that the most common legal form for Czech social enterprises was the limited liability company (in the Czech legislative system called 's.r.o.') with 94 of them registered in this form towards the end of 2014 (Figure 20.2). The second most numerous group at this time – with 56 – were registered as publicly beneficial corporations but, since then, this legal status has been abolished and they will need to adopt an alternative form. Twenty-three social enterprises had adopted the form

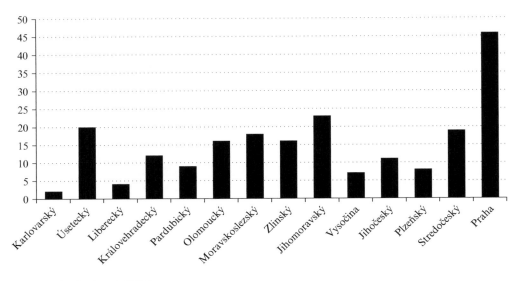

Source: Vaceková et al. (2015).

Figure 20.3   Social enterprises in the Czech Republic classified by their territorial scope

of a civil association ('o.s.'), 14 were self-employed and 12 were co-operatives. Of the five social enterprises that marked their legal form as 'Other' two were 'social co-operatives' a term which had not been included in the Directory at this stage.

Regional Variations

The majority of social enterprises operate in Prague (Praha): a total of 46 (Figure 20.3). The South-Moravian (Jihomoravský) region takes second place, with 23 social enterprises, followed closely by the Ústí nad Labem (Ústecký) region, where there are 20. The numbers of social enterprises in the Central Bohemia (Středočeský), Moravia-Silesia (Moravskoslezský), Zlín (Zlínský) and Hradec Kralové (Královehradecký) regions are almost identical. The lowest number of social enterprise activity was recorded in the Karlovy Vary (Karlovarský) region, where only two have been established. Social entrepreneurship in the Liberec (Liberecký) region is similarly underdeveloped: currently there are four businesses that are considered to be social.

Fields of Activity

It is difficult to obtain a clear picture of the various fields of activity covered by Czech social enterprises especially as many of specify more than one area of concern. The number of enterprises most often listed in the directory (47) operates in the area of horticultural services, landscaping, property maintenance, and cleaning work (Figure 20.4). The second most frequently chosen is, unhelpfully, the 'other' category. Some of these enterprises have selected a specific field of operation and then added the 'other' category. For example, one company that sells and rents ships states that its line of business is 'transport, transport

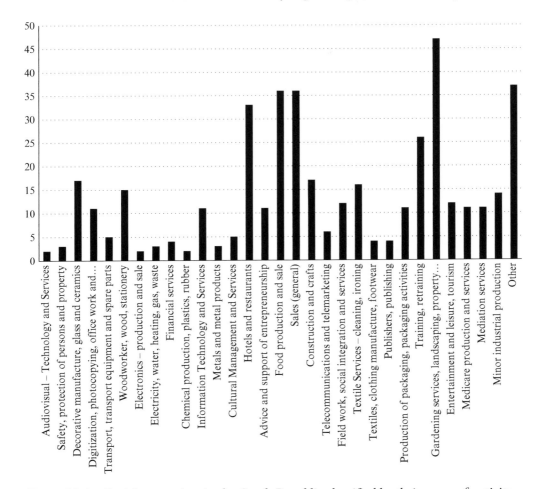

Figure 20.4   Social enterprises in the Czech Republic classified by their areas of activity

equipment and spare parts' and also marked the 'other' line of business. Many of the fields of activity described as 'other' are difficult to define, and enterprises chose this category if they had the impression that the specific areas listed on the directory would not completely cover their areas of operation. The least-represented areas of activity were the categories of 'audiovisual – technology and services' and 'electronics – production and sale'.

Public Benefit

The kinds of public benefits most often claimed as the result of the activities of social enterprises are equal opportunities (employment of socially or physically disadvantaged people) and a focus on the environment and ecology, development of local communities, and social or cultural areas. Figure 20.5 shows that 192 enterprises claim to be advancing equal opportunities, 120 are involved in the development of their local community, a total

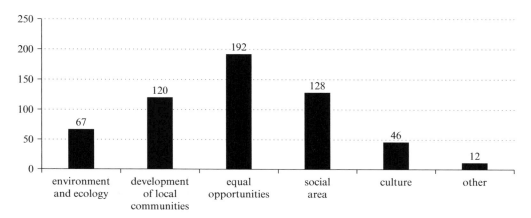

Source: Vaceková and Murray Svidroňová (2016).

Figure 20.5   Social enterprises in the Czech Republic classified by kinds of public benefit

of 128 social enterprises in total are involved in providing social counselling and social assistance services, and 46 identified cultural activities as their area of public benefit. Data from the Directory of Social Enterprises does not specify the proportions of employees with social or physical disadvantages needed to meet the requirements of a social integration enterprise.

Target Groups

The largest target group specified within the area of equal employment opportunities is people with disabilities (Figure 20.6). This group is targeted by a total of 143 enterprises. The second-largest group is the long-term unemployed: 68 enterprises focus on employing these socially disadvantaged people. The lowest number of social enterprises focuses on the integration of people with addictions into the current job market.

LESSONS AND IMPLICATIONS: CHALLENGES FOR SOCIAL ENTERPRISES IN THE CZECH REPUBLIC

We can identify a number of issues in the Czech social enterprise field which suggest that some lessons can be learned if social enterprises are to develop further.

The Need for Legislation

The transitional economies of CEE are acknowledged as encountering problems with gaps in legislation and the weak enforcement of existing laws (Brhlíková, 2004). This holds true especially for nonprofit laws, which do not provide sufficient protection against the misuse of the nonprofit status (Frič et al., 1999), and hence attract for-profits 'in disguise' (Weisbrod, 2004). They are lured into the nonprofit sector by the tax and subsidy advan-

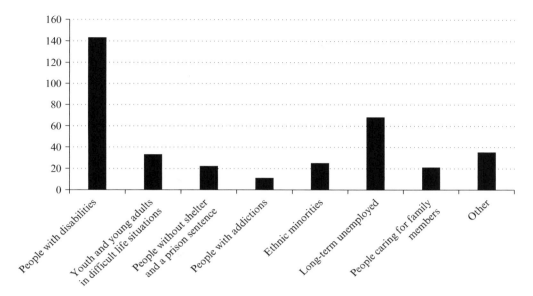

Figure 20.6   *The number of social enterprises in the Czech Republic classified by target groups*

tages that they gain (James, 2000). Among the members of the EU, the Czech Republic gives the least attention to social enterprises and lacks a legal definition for them. Other transitional economies, notably Poland and Slovakia, have developed very differently and offer models of good practice that the Czech Republic could learn from. In Italy, the United Kingdom, the United States of America, Belgium and Finland there are also policy initiatives to support this type of business.

The need for a clear legislative framework for social enterprise in the Czech Republic has been recognised in a forthcoming bill. This will be based on the definitions developed as part of the Thematic Network for Social Economy (TESSEA) and those currently being developed at the European level. The legal framework will probably be tied into existing Acts on employment and public procurement and the tax laws (Vyskočil, 2014). The bill is expected to draw on the criteria that have set out the definition of the social co-operative in the Business Corporation Act, but to strengthen the ways in which it is regulated. This means, for example, that, while the registration of a social co-operative by the Ministry is a once-and-for-all decision, the registration of a social enterprise will be seen as a continuous process that also allows for evolution over time. Failure to implement such a plan would lead to the withdrawal of social enterprise status (Fiala, 2014).

Drawing a Line between Social Enterprises and Purely Commercial Concerns

There is a clear need to draw a dividing line between social enterprises and 'regular businesses' or purely commercial concerns. This can be achieved by establishing a set of clear and binding indicators and using them to determine the extent to which the criteria used by them are met. The development of the indicators needs to be coordinated with the views of the stakeholders and then subjected to a pilot test before implementation. In the Czech Republic, a set of 14 indicators commissioned by the Ministry of Labour and Social Affairs (MoLSA) and prepared by the P3 Company has been tested yet still not implemented. What is then needed is a form on which social enterprises could enter their responses and demonstrate the degree to which they have met the criteria for acceptance as well as explaining any failures to meet them. This would form a basis for deciding whether or not the enterprise can be accepted as 'social'.

The Need for a More Secure Funding Base

During the period 2009 to 2013 social enterprises were able to secure funding for their activities from the European Social Fund (ESF) and the European Regional Development Fund (ERDF); for example, the integrated regional operational programme on the support of social entrepreneurs run under the Ministry of Regional Development in 2016–17. Under this programme about 130 million CZK was granted. Similarly, the Ministry of Labour and Social Affairs ran an ESF programme on the Support of Social Entrepreneurs which provided 100 million CZK for the development of the work of social entrepreneurs and as a contribution to active inclusion. Most of these grants, however, were provided for the implementation of specific projects with limited time-scales, which meant that social enterprises depended on assistance from the state for more general and longer-term funding. In order to develop these businesses further it is necessary to create a stable economic and political environment that will enable them to thrive and encourage them to develop.

Social enterprises need to fulfil the condition of 'nonprofit distribution'. These institutions share a crucial characteristic that makes it feasible to differentiate them from for-profit enterprises: the fact that they are prohibited from distributing any surplus they generate to their investors, directors or stakeholders, and that they therefore are presumably serving some broader public interest other than profit. When social enterprises increase their turnover they more or less inevitably become liable to pay value-added tax (VAT) which, in the Czech Republic, is charged at 21 per cent. In this, and in other ways, the state puts social enterprises on an equal footing with ordinary businesses. As a result, these enterprises are treated by the general public – and by many of the agencies of local government – as conventional businesses. According to the Chamber of the Social Entrepreneurs (KSP) the work of social entrepreneurs is based on the following principles:

- meeting public needs;
- democratic decision-making in the company;
- running activities which benefit society in general, or handicapped or socially disadvantaged people;
- being independent of public and private institutions;
- investing profits into the further development of the enterprise;
- promoting the environmental aspects of the business; and
- supporting local needs.

A key aim of the forthcoming law on social entrepreneurship is to ensure that the social entrepreneur uses at least 50 per cent of its profit on a socially beneficial activity or its further development. And those social entrepreneurs which employ at least 30 per cent of disadvantaged people will receive further benefits in the form of grants.

Lack of Interest on the Part of Local Government

In the Czech Republic social enterprises do not receive much financial support from local government. It is true that, like any other small organisation, a social enterprise can obtain support from the local public administration, but this is limited to 20 000 CZK (c. €730). Social enterprises do make efforts to promote themselves by participating in events organised by municipalities, but these do not bring any special treatment; they have to pay the same rates for rental fees as those required from ordinary businesses, and they are not allowed to advertise free of charge. In the Czech Republic, there are ways in which municipal budgets can be used to support the work of social enterprises but there is no commitment on the part of the authorities to implement them. Several Czech towns, however, do support social entrepreneurs through special partnership or the promotion of their activities. This may include awarding contracts to them, providing funds and creating other helpful financial and labour conditions for them. It is, however, important that any support from the municipal budget should not generate a negative impact on those businesses seen as competitors of the social enterprises. At the same time, social enterprises need to support any request for grants with evidence of the public benefits they provide in the community where they operate their business, in order to enhance the credibility of their activities.

Evaluating the Impact of Social Enterprises

The evaluation of social enterprises as hybrid organisations that combine entrepreneurial orientation with the pursuit of a social mission raises important issues. One useful approach to developing useful evidence of their publicly beneficial activities is the social return on investment (SROI) analysis which provides a means of identifying both the financial and the non-financial benefits generated by an enterprise. Out of more than 40 approaches that have been developed for measuring social impact (Stevenson et al., 2010), SROI analysis is one of the most widespread (Maier et al., 2015). It is a mixed-method approach to assessing the social, economic and environmental impact of interventions (ibid.). Its most prominent feature is the SROI ratio. This ratio aims to determine how many dollars or euros, for example, worth of social value are created for $1/€1 invested in an intervention (ibid.; Kara, 2013). The merit of the SROI analysis is that it has been used increasingly all over the world and has developed an international network of contacts which have contributed to the sharing of indicators and guides on how to measure them.

Promoting Social Enterprises in the Form of Seminars and Workshops

There are currently a number of initiatives operating in the field of social economy in the Czech Republic. These promote social enterprises, provide consultation services, and organise workshops and seminars at which the enterprises can present their work. At the same time there are a number of efforts being made to monitor the current situation of social enterprises. For example, the Ministry of Labour and Social Affairs has organised a series of workshops dealing with social enterprises and dealing with topics such as, 'How do I trade when I'm a social enterprise?' Furthermore, the Ministry has commissioned a number of local consultants to help with the start of new social enterprises, create business plans and promote networking. They have also provided experts who give advice free of charge on communication and public relations, explain the principles of social enterprise and advise on strategic and crisis management and procurements. Last but not least, it offers internships in one of the 239 existing social enterprises which are receiving special payments paid by the Ministry for such help.

Regular participation in these activities by those who would benefit from their involvement is seriously limited. These limitations include the pressure of time and the fact that the workshops and seminars are usually held in Prague and thus not more widely accessible. What is needed is the gathering together of the experiences of effective social enterprise activity from across the whole of the Czech Republic, to spread the lessons that have been learned from them and make them available to a much greater number of people interested in promoting social enterprise. One example of good practice of this kind that contributes to the development of young people's knowledge is the 'Social Business Through the Eyes of Young People' project which was announced as part of the framework of European Youth Week. It was organised by the Czech Ministry of Education in 2015 and was aimed at promoting social entrepreneurial attitudes by creating youth initiatives in the framework of the Erasmus+: Youth in Action Programme in order encourage the active participation of young people in social entrepreneurship.

The Need to Raise Awareness Among the General Public

The development of social enterprises depends on an improved awareness among the public at large of the needs they can address. They need to understand that there are people who are disadvantaged in some ways but who want as much as possible to live ordinary lives, and that it is in the interest of the public to help these people integrate into the labour market. A better understanding of the role of social enterprises is a first step towards the gradual elimination of barriers between ordinary workers, socially or physically disadvantaged employees, and the general public.

The general public should also be made aware that the world of civil society organisations is becoming increasingly interesting (Donnelly-Cox, 2015). Even in the early years of the field of nonprofit studies, some voices were calling for a broader recognition of the blurred boundaries among sectors (Billis, 2010). The tripartite distinction between public, private and nonprofit could be problematic because this distinction concealed the interrelationships among the sectors. More recently, theoretical frameworks have emerged that are characterised by a blurry sectoral boundary view. These frameworks recognise that the sectors can overlap or mix (Dees and Anderson, 2003; Brandsen et al., 2005; Evers, 2005; Jones, 2007; Hwang and Powell, 2009; Brandsen and Karré, 2011; Donnelly-Cox, 2015; Salamon and Sokolowski, 2016). However, Nobel laureate Muhammad Yunus, founder of the Grameen Bank, warns against putting too much faith in hybrid organisations (see also Pestoff, 2012). 'In the real world it will be difficult to operate a business with two conflicting goals of profit-maximising and social benefits. The executives of these hybrid businesses will gradually inch toward the profit-maximisation goal, no matter how the company's mission is designed' (Pestoff, 2007, p. 33). Hence, hybridisation is being examined carefully (Donnelly-Cox, 2015) and with some concern for its positive effects (see, e.g., Dees and Anderson, 2003; Hwang and Powell, 2009; Jones, 2007). There is evidence that the benefits outweigh the risks (Brandsen and Karré, 2011) and that hybrids will come to represent the 'new normal' of civil society organisations (Brandsen et al., 2005; Evers, 2005; Donnelly-Cox, 2015).

CONCLUSION

Hybrid organisations have received increasing attention in the scientific literature worldwide. This literature, however, is largely Anglo-Saxon and it is not perfectly suited to a context of the transitional economies. The lack of relevant research on hybridity in the post-communist countries shows a considerable gap that strongly indicates the need for deeper insight. This chapter has aimed to contribute to the conversation by rethinking the existing literature in the context of transitional economies. It has provided a picture of the driving forces, challenges and potentials of social enterprises in the specific historical, socio-economic and political conditions of the Czech Republic in order to create a space for discussing critical implications and making suggestions for further research.

This chapter has concentrated its attention on one hybrid organisational form – the social enterprise – in one transitional economy, that of the Czech Republic. But the ongoing transformation of a variety of cross-sectoral linkages in the delivery of public services needs to be explored across the (post-)transitional economies of CEE. This would involve the study of a variety of providers (in, for example, the areas of education, health, water and energy management, and transport) and a range of hybrid models (purchaser–provider models, contracting out, outsourcing and commissioning, corporatisation and public–private partnerships) that raise problematic new issues that require systemic solutions at the theoretical and practical level. And it would be possible to assess the scale and scope of the work of hybrid organisations in selected sectors of the economy, and to examine the overall state of hybridisation in the national economies of the CEE.

REFERENCES

Baldwin, R.E. and Wyplosz, C. (2012) *The Economics of European Integration*. New York: McGraw-Hill Higher Education.

Billis, D. (ed.) (2010) *Hybrid Organizations and the Third Sector: Challenges for Practice, Theory and Policy*. London: Palgrave Macmillan.

Brandsen, T. and Karré, P.M. (2011) Hybrid organizations: no cause for concern? *International Journal of Public Administration*, 34(13), pp. 827–836.

Brandsen, T., Van de Donk, W. and Putters, K. (2005) Griffins or chameleons? Hybridity as a permanent and inevitable characteristic of the third sector. *International Journal of Public Administration*, 28(9/10), pp. 749–765.

Brhlíková, P. (2004) The nonprofit sector in the Czech Republic. CERGE-EI Discussion Papers Series, 128.

da Cruz, N.F. and Marques, R.C. (2012) Mixed companies and local governance: no man can serve two masters. *Public Administration*, 90(3), pp. 737–758.

da Cruz, N.F., Ferreira, S., Cabral, M., Simões, P. and Marques, R.C. (2014) Packaging waste recycling in Europe: is the industry paying for it? *Waste Management*, 34(2), pp. 298–308.

Dahrendorf, R. (2005) *Reflections on the Revolution in Europe*. New York: Routlege.

Dees, J.G. and Anderson, B.B. (2003) Sector-bending: blurring lines between nonprofit and for-profit. *Society*, 40(4), pp. 16–27.

Denis, J.L., Ferlie, E. and Van Gestel, N. (2015) Understanding hybridity in public organizations. *Public Administration*, 93(2), pp. 273–289.
Dohnalová, M. (2006) Sociální ekonomika v evropském kontextu. Brno: Nadace Universitas.
Dohnalová, M. and Anderle, P. (2002) Občanský sektor: Úvahy a souvislosti. Moravský Beroun: Moravská expedice.
Dohnalová, M. and Průša, L. (2011) *Sociální ekonomika*. Praha: Wolters Kluwer.
Donnelly-Cox, G. (2015) Civil society governance: civil society, the third sector and social enterprise. *Governance and Democracy*, 200, pp. 30–45.
Ekiert, G. and Kubik, J. (1997) Collective protest in post-communist Poland, 1989–1993: a research report. *Communist and Post-Communist Studies*, 31(2), pp. 91–117.
Evers, A. (2005) Mixed welfare systems and hybrid organizations: changes in the governance and provision of social services. *International Journal of Public Administration*, 28(9/10), pp. 737–748.
Fiala, Z. (2014) Sociální podnikání dostane zákon. http://www.parlamentnilisty.cz/arena/nazory-a-petice/Zbynek-Fiala-Socialni-podnikani-dostane-zakon-320926.
Frič, P. (2000) *Neziskové organizace a ovlivňování veřejné politiky: (rozhovory o neziskovém sektoru II)*. Brno: Agnes.
Frič, P. and Goulli, R. (2001) *Neziskový sektor v České republice*. Praha: Eurolex Bohemia.
Frič, P., Goulli, R., Toepler, S. and Salamon, L.M. (1999) The Czech Republic. In L.M. Salamon (ed.), *Global Civil Society: Dimensions of the Nonprofit Sector* (pp. 285–304). Baltimore, MD: Johns Hopkins Center for Civil Society Studies. http://ccss.jhu.edu/wp-content/uploads/downloads/2011/08/Global-Civil-Society-I.pdf.
Gidron, B. and Hasenfeld, Y. (2012) *Social Enterprises: An Organizational Perspective*. London: Palgrave Macmillan.
Green, A.T. (1999) Nonprofits and democratic development: lessons from the Czech Republic. *VOLUNTAS: International Journal of Voluntary and Nonprofit Organizations*, 10(3), pp. 217–235.
Green, A.T. (2002) Comparative development of post-Communist civil societies. *Europe–Asia Studies*, 54(3), pp. 455–471.
Grossi, G. (2007) Governance of public–private corporations in provision of local Italian utilities. *International Public Management Review*, 8(1), pp. 132–153.
Grossi, G. and Thomasson, A. (2015) Bridging the accountability gap in hybrid organizations: the case of Copenhagen Malmö Port. *International Review of Administrative Sciences*, 81(3), pp. 604–620.
Havel, V. (1999) Co je občanská společnost. Speech in Minneapolis, USA.
Hodge, G. and Greve, C. (2010) Public–private partnerships: governance scheme or language game? *Australian Journal of Public Administration*, 69(s1), pp. S8–S22.
Hoff, K. and Stiglitz, J. (2002) After the Big Bang? Obstacles for the emergence of the rule of law in post-communist societies. NBER WP 9282.
Hunčová, M. (2007) *Sociální ekonomika a sociální podnik*. Ústí nad Labem: UJEP.
Hwang, H. and Powell, W.W. (2009) The rationalization of charity: the influences of professionalism in the nonprofit sector. *Administrative Science Quarterly*, 54(2), pp. 268–298.
Hyánek, V. and Pospíšil, M. (2009) Country-specific situation of the nonprofit sector in the Czech Republic. Working paper. Brno: MU.
James, E. (2000) Commercialism among nonprofits: objectives, opportunities, and constraints. In B. Weisbrod (ed.), *To Profit or Not To Profit: The Commercial Transformation of the Nonprofit Sector* (pp. 271–286). Cambridge: Cambridge University Press.
Jones, M.B. (2007) The multiple sources of mission drift. *Nonprofit and Voluntary Sector Quarterly*, 36(2), pp. 299–307.
Kara, H. (2013) *Research and Evaluation for Busy Practitioners: A Time-saving Guide*. Chicago, IL: Policy Press.
Klaus, V. (2012) Koncept občanské společnosti. Praha: CEP 95/2012.
Korimová, G. and Vaceková, G. (2011) Social economics and social enterpreneurship in the context of transition economies and Slovakia. IRSPM conference. Dublin, Ireland.
Lašek, J. (1998) Structural aspects of Czech economy transformation. *Politická ekonomie*, 46(1), pp. 29–42.
Laville, J.L. and Nyssens, M. (2001) The social enterprise: towards a theoretical socio-economic approach. In Carlo Borzaga and Jacques Defourny (eds), *The Emergence of Social Enterprise* (pp. 324–344). London: Routledge.
Linz, J.J. and Stepan, A. (1996) *Problems of Democratic Transition and Consolidation: Southern Europe, South America, and Post-Communist Europe*. Baltimore, MD: Johns Hopkins University Press.
Maier, F., Schober, C., Simsa, R. and Millner, R. (2015) SROI as a method for evaluation research: understanding merits and limitations. *Voluntas*, 26(5), pp. 1805–1830.
Marin, P. (2009) *Public–Private Partnerships for Urban Water Utilities: A Review of Experiences in Developing Countries*. Washington, DC: World Bank Publications.
Marques, R.C. and Berg, S. (2010) Revisiting the strengths and limitations of regulatory contracts in infrastructure industries. *Journal of Infrastructure Systems*, 16(4), pp. 334–342.
McQuaid, R.W. and Scherrer, W. (2010) Changing reasons for public–private partnerships (PPPs). *Public Money and Management*, 30(1), pp. 27–34.

Mlčoch, L. (1996) *Chování československé podnikové sféry*. Praha: EÚ ČSAV.

Navrátil, J. and Pospíšil, M. (2014) *Dreams of Civil Society Two Decades Later: Civic Advocacy in the Czech Republic*. Brno: Masarykova univerzita.

Pestoff, V. (2007) Democratic governance: citizen participation and co-production in the provision of personal social services in Sweden. Third Sector Study Group of the European Group for Public Administration, Madrid.

Pestoff, V. (2012) Co-production and third sector social services in Europe: some concepts and evidence. *VOLUNTAS: International Journal of Voluntary and Nonprofit Organizations*, 23(4), pp. 1102–1118.

Pick, M. (2000) Východiskem je třetí cesta. CEP 6/2000 Ekonomika, právo, politika. Praha: CEP.

Pollitt, C. and Bouckaert, G. (2011) *Public Management Reform: A Comparative Analysis – New Public Management, Governance, and the Neo-Weberian State*. Oxford: Oxford University Press.

Poon, D. (2011) The emergence and development of social enterprise sectors. University of Pennsylvania, Scholarly Commons.

Pospíšil, M. (2006) Mapping the Czech nonprofit sector. *Civil Review*, 3(3/4), pp. 233–244.

Pospíšil, M., Navrátil, J. and Pejcal, J. (2014) Czech Republic. In Maecenata Institute (ed.), *Civil Society in the 'Visegrád Four': Data and Literature in the Czech Republic, Hungary, Poland and Slovakia* (pp. 48–93). Berlin: Maecenata Institut.

Pospíšil, M., Prouzová, Z., Škarabelová, S. and Almani Tůmová, K. (2012) Czech nonprofit sector twenty years after: current developments and challenges. *Civil Szemle*, 3, pp. 5–22.

Reichard, C. (2016) Gemischtwirtschaftliche Unternehmen im europäischen Vergleich. *Gemischtwirtschaftliche Unternehmen, 2016*, pp. 10–24. https://www.nomos-elibrary.de/10.5771/9783845276281-10/gemischtwirtschaftliche-unternehmen-im-europaeischen-vergleich?page=1.

Řežuchová, M. (2010) *Fenomén Public Private Partnerships a poskytování veřejných služeb*. Brno: Masarykova univerzita.

Salamon, L.M. and Sokolowski, S.W. (2016) Beyond nonprofits: re-conceptualizing the third sector. *VOLUNTAS: International Journal of Voluntary and Nonprofit Organizations*, 27(4), pp. 1515–1545.

Sepp, J. and Frear, D. (2011) *The Economy and Economics After Crisis*. Berlin: Berliner Wissenschafts-Verlag.

Shleifer, A. and Treisman, D. (2014) Normal countries: the East 25 years after communism. *Foreign Affairs*, 93, pp. 92–103.

Stevenson, N., Taylor, M., Lyon, F. and Rigby, M. (2010) Joining the dots: Social Impact Measurement, commissioning from the Third Sector and supporting Social Enterprise Development: mutual advantage, EEDA, Social Enterprise East of England, Improvement East, The Guild, Middlesex University.

Strachwitz, R. (2015) Introduction. In C. Schreier (ed.), *25 Years After: Mapping Civil Society in the Visegrad Countries* (pp. 1–2). Stuttgart: Lucius and Lucius Verlegsgesellschaft.

Stránský, J. (2013) Co Klaus sám necítí, nikdy neposlechne. Interview for *Hospodářské noviny*, 8 March.

Swarts, D. and Warner, M.E. (2014) Hybrid firms and transit delivery: the case of Berlin. *Annals of Public and Cooperative Economics*, 85(1), pp. 127–146.

Thomasson, A. (2009) Exploring the ambiguity of hybrid organisations: a stakeholder approach. *Financial Accountability and Management*, 25(3), pp. 353–366.

Tranfield, D.R., Denyer, D. and Smart, P. (2003) Towards a methodology for developing evidence-informed management knowledge by means of systematic review. *British Journal of Management*, 14, pp. 207–222.

Tříska, D. (1999) Česká ekonomika očima ekonomů střední generace. CEP seminar, Praha. http://cepin.cz/cze/pozvanka.php?ID=26.

Vaceková, G. and Murray Svidroňová, M. (2016) *NPOs in Selected CEE Countries: A Journey to Sustainability*. Radom: Spatium.

Vaceková, G., Soukopová, J. and Křenková, T. (2015) Social entrepreneurship in the Czech Republic: current trends in research on hybridity. *Scientific Papers of the University of Pardubice, Series D*, 22(35), pp. 161–172.

Valentinov, V. (2015) Value devolution in social enterprises. *Administration and Society*, 47(9), pp. 1126–1133.

Van Til, J. (1988) *Mapping the Third Sector: Voluntarism in a Changing Social Economy*. New York: Foundation Center.

Verdier, A., Martinez, S. and Hoorens, D. (2004) *Local Public Companies in the 25 Countries of the European Union*. Paris: Dexia Editions.

Vyskočil, M. (2014) Sociální podnikání – Dílčí studie ke Koncepci 2020. https://www.vlada.cz/assets/ppov/rnno/dokumenty/studie_vyskocil_pro_web.pdf

Weigle, M.A. and Butterfield, J. (1992) Civil society in reforming communist regimes: the logic of emergence. *Comparative Politics*, 25(1), pp. 1–23.

Weisbrod, B.A. (2004) The pitfalls of profits. *Stanford Social Innovation Review*, 2(3), pp. 40–47.

Žídek, L. (2006) *Transformace české ekonomiky: 1989–2004*. Praha: C.H. Beck.

Žídek, L. (2014) Evaluation of economic transformation in Hungary. *Review of Economic Perspectives*, 14(1), pp. 55–88.

Žídek, L. (2017) *From Central Planning to the Market: The Transformation of the Czech Economy, 1989–2004*. Budapest: CEU Press.

21. Housing third sector organisations in Australia
Vivienne Milligan and Kath Hulse

INTRODUCTION

While much of the literature on hybridity has emanated from Europe and North America, hybrid organisations can be found in many other countries which have qualitatively different welfare regimes (Esping-Andersen, 1990) and in which the respective roles of government, market and civil society (including both third sector organisations and family) may vary enormously (Hill, 2006). This chapter focuses on Australia where scholarship has been concerned primarily with the relationship between the third sector and government since governments began to contract out human services from the late 1980s (Considine, 2001; Lyons, 2001). In addition, there is growing interest in ideas around social enterprise, combining elements of third sector and market (Barraket and Collyer, 2010). Within this literature, however, there has been very little focus on what sorts of housing third sector organisations (HTSOs) are developing in an era in which Australian governments have decreased their direct involvement in social housing, and people in need of assistance with their housing turn increasingly to families, third sector organisations and the market.

The aim of this chapter, therefore, is to apply contemporary thinking about hybrid organisations to understand the development and organisational dynamics of the Australian housing third sector. It examines how a particular set of state, market and third sector influences, combined with the Australian housing third sector's history and organisational dynamics, have circumscribed the growth and potential social contribution of HTSOs in Australia. The chapter provides a worked example of the challenges faced by some of the larger HTSOs as they have become a distinctive group of hybrid organisations that combine elements of the public and private sectors with those of third sector organisations. We argue that this is a case of 'fragile hybridity' in which competing internal logics within broader political and market contexts can either constrain or enable innovation and scaling up of hybrid organisational models.

The chapter draws on a body of previous research involving the authors, along with various other published reports and publicly available documents concerned with the housing third sector in Australia. Central to the research evidence are two connected research studies (Milligan et al., 2013, 2015a) which surveyed and interviewed chief executive officers (CEOs) from half of all larger HTSOs about strategic business decisions that their organisations had made between 2008 and 2013, a seminal period in the development of Australian HTSOs, and how they were responding to exogenous and endogenous drivers of change in their organisations.

The rest of the chapter proceeds by:

1. Outlining contemporary thinking on the emergence of hybrid organisational forms in the third sector.

2. Examining recent attempts to deploy theory on hybrid organisations to enhance understanding of developments in the housing third sector internationally.
3. Introducing the Australian context for the development of hybrid housing third sector organisations.
4. Analysing types of hybridity and core organisational elements of larger Australian HTSOs.
5. Investigating government, market and third sector influences on the evolution and development paths of Australian HTSOs.
6. Concluding that HTSOs in Australia have exhibited 'fragile hybridity' due to a combination of government control, market power and weak connections to the broader third sector.

THE THIRD SECTOR AND HYBRID ORGANISATIONS

Although used in Europe and North America, albeit in somewhat different ways,[1] the term 'third sector' is relatively new in an Australian context, where other terms have usually been deployed (such as 'community sector', 'not-for-profit sector' or 'non-profit sector'). Indeed in the first Australian work specifically on the third sector, Lyons (2001, p. 5) argued that the first task of his book was 'to convince readers that there is a distinctive third sector'. A starting point for Lyons was that the third sector encompasses organisations that are not in the public or business sectors, recognising that these could encompass a wide range of small and large organisations with different ownership and governance structures and modus operandi. The diversity of the third sector in terms of organisational size, interests and policy influence has been well established in the literature both in Australia (e.g., Butcher, 2015) and elsewhere (Doherty et al., 2014).

This diversity notwithstanding, many authors have tried to identify the distinctive features of the third sector, rather than it being defined by default as not public and not private. Billis (2010, pp. 53–54), in reviewing this literature, argues that the key principles of an 'ideal type' third sector (in a Weberian sense) are based on an association model, that is, ownership by members, governance determined by private elections; commitment about a distinctive mission; human resources comprising members and volunteers; and resources coming from dues, donations and legacies. Lyons (2001, pp. 5–7) in his Australian work has a similar view, suggesting that the third sector consists of democratically controlled private organisations that are formed and sustained by groups of people acting voluntarily to provide benefits for others without personal profit.

Notwithstanding consideration of ideal types of organisations in a three-sector approach (market, government and third sector), it is recognised in the international literature that the third sector is dynamic and changing. It has been argued that change in the third sector is inextricably tied to restructuring of national welfare states, such that 'new circumstances and forces have served to redefine the character of national welfare systems and of the kind of social and political embeddedness of the third sector' (Evers and Laville, 2004, p. 29). In this context, the third sector in Australia (as elsewhere) has been shaped by trends such as 'contractualism' under the rubric of New Public Management (Considine, 2001), 'partnership arrangements' under new models of network governance (Carson and Kerr, 2014, pp. 112–118) and changing government funding from gifts and grants to a competitive tendering model (Lyons, 2001, pp. 183–190). It is also apparent that some third sector organisations themselves seek to make a bigger difference in achieving their social mission by scaling up their operations, which may require diversification of their revenues to include not only payment for services under government contracts but also seeking resources from other sources, such as private finance and fee-for-service arrangements in the private market.

In this process, some mixing or hybridity (using a metaphor from biology) occurs in which the elements of public, private and third sector organisations may be combined in different ways. A 'hybrid organisation', therefore, refers to the mixing of core elements of two of more these types of organisations, such as third sector–public or third sector–private. It is a point of contention in the literature whether a primary adherence to the principles of one sector remain notwithstanding some organisational decisions to cross sector boundaries (Billis, 2010), or whether hybridity has resulted in the evolution of a new, fourth, type of 'hybrid organisation' sector which is a feature of the contemporary welfare state (Brandsen et al., 2005; Evers, 2005). It is important to note that not all third sector housing organisations have features of hybridity, and in this chapter we are particularly concerned with the larger HTSOs in Australia that do appear to have elements of hybridity.

Whilst some of the literature appears permeated by a sense of 'loss' of traditional third sector organisations, such as replacement of volunteers with professional staff (Billis, 2010, p. 60) and concern about 'mission drift' (Considine et al., 2014), there is also an argument that hybrid organisations are an innovative organisational form that can be better placed to achieve their social mission than traditional third sector organisations. A number of authors argue that, whatever their origins and alignment, third sector hybrids have in common a social enterprise culture: creating social value through applying market methods (Peattie and Morley, 2008; Czischke et al., 2012; Ko and Kong, 2012). It is worth noting at this point that much of the narrative about loss of accountability associated with hybridity in third sector organisations stems from the Northern or Western European context. In the Australian context, the hybridity literature has been overshadowed by a growing literature on social enterprise which generally celebrates innovation in organisational forms and new models of activity (Barraket and Collyer, 2010; Douglas, 2015).

In brief, applying a hybridity lens enables investigation of organisations which have a distinct organisational logic that is responsive to both their social mission and modus operandi (essentially as self-governing, not-for-profit and social purpose agencies) and to an array of external drivers that derive from three competing spheres of influence: arising in the state, market and third sector realms (Brandsen et al., 2005; Evers, 2005). Managing the potentially competing logics or tensions generated by such forces becomes the normal work of hybrid organisations (Brandsen et al., 2005). The next section examines attempts to deploy these ideas more specifically to an enhanced understanding of the housing third sector.

HYBRID ORGANISATIONS AND THE HOUSING THIRD SECTOR

There has been a long-term international trend towards the development of third sector organisations that provide and manage social housing and deliver a range of other housing services. As elsewhere, concepts of hybridity and hybrid organisations have been evoked in the housing literature to explain the growth and maturation of this sector's role in diverse national settings (see, e.g., Mullins, 2006; Bratt, 2012; Gilmour and Milligan, 2012; Rhodes and Donnelly-Cox, 2014; Nieboer and Gruis, 2014; Mullins and Jones, 2015).[2] Employing a notion of intensifying hybridity, such national accounts often depict a historic shift through three distinct phases. The pre-welfare state era is typified by traditional small-scale, charitable organisational forms heavily reliant on voluntarism and philanthropy and anchored in or representative of their (usually local) community. The post-welfare state to late 20th century era is seen as one of housing third sector expansion and change stimulated by preferential public funding and policy. The most recent 'turn of the century' era has been epitomised by larger and more complex organisational entities with specialised directors and paid staff that embrace commercial business practices and strive for profitability and private financing to help deliver their social purpose, usually in the context of significant public policy retrenchment (Blessing, 2012). Examples of newer activities of third sector housing providers that have been noted in the national accounts referenced above have included shifts into home care, market housing provision (for rent and/or sale), neighbourhood and community development services, neighbourhood revitalisation, real estate services, energy efficiency programmes, and a variety of resident employment, training and education initiatives.

Developments in hybridity theory have generated new perspectives on the housing third sector and reflected some of the contention about hybrid organisations referred to earlier in this chapter. For example, there has been discussion of whether hybrid HTSOs in England and the Netherlands could be construed as 'for profits in disguise or as agents of public policy'; that is, either as hybrids in a private–third sector zone or as hybrids in a public–third sector zone (Mullins and Pawson, 2010, p. 197). Whilst the larger HTSOs in both countries displayed many comparable elements of hybrid governance, blended financing and diverse products, English housing associations were depicted as 'agents of public policy', as they identified strongly with public policy values, their growth was underpinned by continuing (though reducing) public subsidies, and they were subject to strong regulatory controls. In contrast, in the Netherlands, in the absence of new public funding (after 1995) and subject to considerably weaker public accountability rules, major housing associations self-identified, and were more widely portrayed, as private organisations (characterised by some as 'profits-in-disguise') largely as a result of the entrepreneurial endeavours of many to trade in their sizeable assets and to undertake large-scale commercial developments in order to create surpluses for reinvestment. Gruis (2008) has provided specific evidence of the ways in which individual HTSOs in the Netherlands managed the tension between social and commercial objectives. His analysis postulated that attributes of organisational culture were highly significant in explaining individual organisational responses to shared challenges and opportunities. While some Dutch social housing providers regarded themselves as traditional 'social landlords', others invested and innovated to generate more social return, whilst the remainder sought to maximise commercial return (Gruis, 2008, pp. 1080–1081).

Another contribution is Blessing's (2012) account of hybridity in the Dutch and Australian rental housing markets that conceptualises hybridity alternatively as 'a state of transformation' providing 'links between cultures', 'hybrid vigour' and 'magical solutions'; and as 'transgressing binary divides' between state and market. She concludes that 'social entrepreneurship is not a super-blend, but a balancing act' (Blessing, 2012, p. 205), involving compromises and trade-offs between competing institutional rules and norms. It is the dynamic interaction of these internal and external forces that shapes a third sector organisation's hybridity, and the vigour, skill and effectiveness with which it performs its core social task (Blessing, 2012).

Such depictions, however, also signal the susceptibility of hybrid organisational models to changes in external parameters and influences that can suddenly disrupt prevailing business models (Mullins et al., 2017). This became apparent, for instance, in the stalling of growth in both the English and the Dutch housing third sectors in the aftermath of the 2007 global financial crisis (GFC) as private financing dried up and the residential development market collapsed, disrupting the prevailing housing association 'cross-subsidy' business model (Milligan et al., 2015a).

As again evidenced recently in those two countries, changing fortunes for hybridised housing associations also play out in the political realm. Following objections made to the European Commission about their 'privileged' tax status stemming from private sector competitors, and, later, serious financial transgressions in a minority, Dutch housing associations were perceived to lose 'legitimacy' among politicians and in some of the media. Consequently, they were re-regulated by the Dutch government in 2015 to curtail their independence and restrict their activities to the 'service of general economic interest'; essentially, in their case, requiring a business focus on the provision of housing for low-income households (Priemus and Gruis, 2011; Boelhouwer and Priemus, 2014; Mullins et al., 2017). In England, a 2015 decision to reclassify housing associations from 'private' to 'public' organisations because of the extent of government control applying to them was subsequently reversed, following 2017 legislation to reduce regulatory powers. Returning associations to private status redressed a perceived threat to their ethos as independent organisations and placed checks on government controls (Hilditch, 2015; Office for National Statistics, 2015, 2017). These examples underscore the changeable nature of the relationship between governments and third sector players.

Drawing on seminal contributions in the international literature on hybridity and hybrid organisations, and informed by examples of their deployment to understanding HTSOs in England and the Netherlands, the rest of this chapter uses these ideas in investigating larger HTSOs in Australia. The next section provides important context for understanding the development of hybrid organisations in the Australian housing third sector.

THE AUSTRALIAN CONTEXT FOR THE DEVELOPMENT OF HYBRID HTSOs

Australia is among a small group of countries that has been characterised as having an archetypal liberal welfare regime, which erects and maintains an order of stratification that is based on market provision for the vast majority of people and government welfare for a minority (Esping-Andersen, 1990, p. 27). The Australian housing system is a classic example of this market orientation, with 95 per cent of all housing being in the market sector. Most Australian households buy (67 per cent) or rent (25 per cent) market housing. Established in the aftermath of the Second World War, the very small size of the non-market sector can be attributed to large-scale sale of public housing from the 1950s to the late 1970s to support home ownership (Hayward, 1996) and chronic underinvestment since the 1980s (Hall and Berry, 2007). Less than 5 per cent of Australia's 7.76 million households (366 063 households) lived in social housing in 2011, with provision dominated by eight large public landlord entities (one located in each Australian state or territory) (ABS, 2013). Australia's housing third sector provided an estimated 16 per cent of the social housing provision, which equates to less than 1 per cent all domestic housing (AIHW, 2014; Milligan et al., 2015a, p. 6). Perhaps as a consequence of their historically marginal role, it is also important to note that the position and function of HTSOs in the Australian housing system is more limited than those of their counterparts in a wide range of comparably developed countries that include, for example, England, Scotland, the Netherlands, France, Austria, the United States of America and Canada (Lawson and Milligan, 2007; Maclennan and Chisholm, 2013).

Within this general context, the development trajectory of the Australian housing third sector can be characterised as having been in an ongoing state of flux, with short expansionary periods followed by (usually longer) periods of stagnation. Across Australia's federated system of governance (with six states and two territories) and geographically diverse housing markets, growth opportunities for the third sector have varied temporally and spatially, resulting in a complex and fragmented 'cottage industry' which, while seemingly resilient, has never had an assured development and growth path. As one component of government intentions to expand and strengthen the accountability of the sector, new specialised regulation was introduced state by state from the mid-2000s and is gradually being harmonised across jurisdictions (Australian Government, 2010; NRSCH, 2014a). In March 2016, 323 non-government organisations providing social housing, and homelessness services were registered under the prevailing regulatory systems that applied to third sector housing providers (Milligan et al., 2016). Many of the registered organisations do not have the characteristics of hybrid organisations: being very small, having minimal staff, without any significant asset ownership or private financing and providing only housing management functions usually on behalf of state or territory governments (Milligan et al., 2016).

Over the last decade or so, however, and stimulated initially by public and private investment directed mainly to 'government-preferred' providers, a small number of larger HTSOs with operations in several locations have begun to dominate what provision exists (Gilmour and Milligan, 2012; Milligan et al., 2015a). Some 40 organisations could be considered as 'larger' in this context and as exhibiting elements of hybridity derived from the third, public and private sectors (as reflected by the higher regulatory status accorded to them under the regulatory risk assessment regime) (NRSCH, 2014a; Milligan et al., 2016). Our two recent empirical studies (see above), upon which discussion in this chapter is partly based, involved respectively 20 and 14 of these organisations chosen for their larger operational scale, professionalisation of governance and staff, and functional and geographic diversity. To give an indicative measure of their size, the 20 organisations surveyed owned and/or managed over 38 000 dwellings, representing nearly 60 per cent of the housing in the third sector and around 9 per cent of all social housing provision. Business metrics compiled for the selected organisations from 2012–13 annual reports indicated that, on average, they owned housing assets worth AUS$210 million (£101 million), had liabilities of AUS$45 million (£22 million) and annual rent revenues of AUS$14 million (£7 million) at that time (Milligan and Hulse, 2015). In the Australian market context the leading HTSOs could be described as 'small businesses'. The rest of this chapter focuses on these larger organisations.

TYPES AND ELEMENTS OF HYBRIDITY IN LARGER AUSTRALIAN HTSOs

In this section, we draw on hybrid organisation theory to examine the foundation and subsequent development of larger Australian HTSOs and to identify their core organisational elements: ownership and governance; mission and operational priorities; human resources and financial resources (adapted from Billis, 2010, p. 55). This is a precursor to examining how some of the competing internal logics associated with hybridity play out for this group of organisations.

Foundation and Organisational Development

The literature suggests that hybrid organisations in the third sector may develop organically from predecessor grassroots voluntary associations and/or be enacted by other organisations (from any of the public, private or third sectors) for a specific purpose. Foundational factors may lead to differences between organic and enacted hybrids in identity, ownership, governance, collaboration and accountability (Billis, 2010, p. 61). Organic organisations, in particular, may follow a pathway from shallow (less developed) to entrenched hybridity, as they respond to state and market-driven opportunities and acquire more resources. Enacted organisations may be created as hybrid from the start. While these often lack roots in the third sector, or past traditions, they could be expected to exhibit orientations and allegiances strongly shaped by their founders and owners.

Reviewing the history and core characteristics of the larger Australian HTSOs through the lens of hybridity, most are best classified as enacted hybrids, with organisational beginnings that can be traced to state government actions from the 1980s to initiate specialised transitional housing services (especially in Victoria and Western Australia), community-based tenancy management services (New South Wales and Queensland), housing co-operatives (Victoria and South Australia) and, later, property development entities using government resources (Bisset and Milligan, 2004; Milligan et al., 2009). These services can largely be seen as a means of managing demand for public housing by offering an alternative or supplementary service, either on a temporary or a longer-term basis.

A second, smaller, group of entities formed more independently within the third sector but also usually in response to public sector incentives. Of this group, some had their origins in the faith-based sector while others operated as discrete parts of long-established general charities and welfare conglomerates. More recently some had been founded to support constituent smaller members (housing co-operatives and housing associations) to build their capacity and influence (Gilmour and Milligan, 2012). These cases are exceptional, however, as Australian HTSOs generally do not have roots in the traditional charitable sector, as will be discussed later in the chapter.

In recent years as urban redevelopment has gathered pace, a small number of new special-purpose, legally discrete entities have been created. Reasons why such entities have been enacted revolve around delivering specialised services for their founding partners (for example, property development services or specialised management of affected communities and tenants in urban renewal processes) and to quarantine financial risks from the parent organisation (Milligan et al., 2015a, p. 15).

It is clear from the discussion above that there is considerable diversity amongst the relatively small number of larger HTSOs in Australia. Notwithstanding this diversity, there are common core organisational elements that help to define their hybrid character, as we describe next.

Ownership and Governance

The origins and hybrid development of leading Australian HTSOs are reflected in characteristic patterns of governance and effective ownership. To meet the highest national regulatory standard applying since 2014, HTSOs have to incorporate as a company limited by shares or a company limited by guarantee under the Australian Corporations Act 2001 (NRSCH, 2014a, p. 5). This has resulted in many switching from long-standing but less onerous forms of incorporation, such as associations or co-operatives. HTSOs are also registered charities. While they do not actively use this status to source significant levels of donations, charitable status confers on them a range of tax benefits that privileges their business operations over both private and public housing providers.

Strategic oversight and ensuring compliance with relevant legislation and regulations are in the hands of directors who have clear fiduciary responsibilities under company law and require requisite skills and qualifications to exercise those responsibilities. In the past, HTSOs were governed by voluntary boards whose members were typically representative of stakeholder groups and local communities. As organisations expanded and diversified, this model has been replaced by skills-based boards, members of an increasing number of which are being (modestly) remunerated (NSWFHA, 2016). Underpinning this approach, regulatory evidence guidelines refer to the knowledge and skills of governing body members including 'financial management, asset management, risk management, human resource management and housing management' (NRSCH, 2014b, p. 26). These regulatory requirements were introduced as larger HTSOs began taking on much higher levels of risk in terms of private rather than government financing, and housing development and purchase rather than housing management (see below).

Non-executive directors may be elected or appointed, usually by a membership. Membership is a matter for individual organisations: among surveyed organisations this was either narrowly based (for example, board directors and patrons only) or, where membership was more open and larger, its influence was limited (Milligan et al., 2015a, pp. 16–17). Notably, too, active involvement of residents has generally been less structured and more limited than for many HTSOs in other countries (mirroring the Australian public housing model in which resident involvement has traditionally also been rather weak), and there are no prescribed regulatory standards in this regard (Darcy, 1999; Milligan et al., 2009, p. 111).

Recently, there has been a trend among leading HTSOs towards the creation of affiliated entities, both for-profit and not-for-profit, with overlapping or identical boards of directors. In our surveys this strategy was seen primarily as a means of managing political, regulatory and commercial risks that could arise from business diversification (see below) (Milligan et al., 2015a, p. 16).

This pattern of ownership and accountability notwithstanding, since the imposition of sector regulation (see above) it could be argued that the 'principal owners' (Billis, 2010, p. 49) are state government entities that have the ultimate power to direct that any community housing assets (as defined in state law) be transferred to another similar entity in circumstances of serious and persistent organisational non-performance, if so advised by a community housing regulator (NRSCH, 2014c).

Mission and Operational Priorities

As discussed above, most Australian HTSOs were founded to pursue niche service roles that included responses to homelessness and transitional (time-limited) housing services, innovative housing forms (for example, housing co-operatives) and/or social housing for clients not traditionally housed in public housing (for example, youth and people with support needs). In this respect their core functions were supplementary to those of the much larger state housing authorities that have dominated non-market housing provision in Australia (Dalton, 2014). Although phrased in different ways, most of the organisations had explicit social missions to improve access to, and provide, housing for lower-income and vulnerable households whose needs were not being met in the market sector (Milligan et al., 2015a, pp. 17–18).

Evident from the 1990s, but only gaining momentum and scale from the mid-2000s (and especially during a period of expanded public funding from 2008 to 2013), has been a push to greater financial independence and business diversification among leading HTSOs (Blessing, 2012; Gilmour and Milligan, 2012; Milligan et al., 2015a). New business elements – mostly small in scale – have included the introduction of an 'affordable' rental housing product (that is, less subsidised than social housing and targeted to a broader range of income groups), a move into place-based services (in the context of urban renewal) and increasing the focus on fee-for-service activity, for example real estate and facilities management services for private owners. By 2010 most leading organisations had moved into commissioning housing development or procuring from the private sector, securing private finance to achieve this. Several had also made an initial foray into developing housing for sale (typically in a small to medium-sized mixed tenure development) in order to create more financial capacity outside of government funding regimes. A growing number had expanded their market reach into new state or territory jurisdictions to achieve scale and growth, and to manage political risk associated with reliance on the policies of a single state government (Milligan et al., 2015a, p. 21). Some merger activity had also occurred, especially to enhance resource capacity (balance sheet and staff), to seek economies-of-scale benefits and/or to establish footholds in new jurisdictions.

Applying hybridity theory, these developments could be construed as 'mission drift', yet many of the CEOs interviewed in our research viewed this type of expansion as a means of making the provision of core social housing services to those in highest need more viable (in the context of reduced public investment) (Milligan et al., 2015a). Nevertheless, when asked to describe their organisation's ethos on a scale between 'socially oriented' or 'business-oriented', there were some differences in response. Perhaps echoing differences in entrepreneurial zeal found across the Dutch sector (see above), some among those in our surveys felt strongly that social goals should never be compromised by business drivers, while others appeared to have a greater appetite to innovate and take on business risks in order to advance their social goals (Milligan et al., 2013, p. 39; 2015a, p. 18). The hybridity literature suggests that this more enterprising modus operandi, and the changing organisational culture that may result, could have longer-term implications for organisational identity, performance and perceived legitimacy (Billis, 2010, p. 251; Blessing, 2012).

Human Resources

Billis (2010, p. 59) suggests that one gauge of entrenched (rather than shallow) hybridity is when paid staff (not volunteers) dominate service delivery and a hierarchical management structure is developed. The larger HTSOs in Australia all operate with chief executive officers, who are responsible for overall organisational and business management, and paid operational staff, and have done for many years. As they have grown and diversified, however, they have adopted more hierarchical structures by introducing senior managers in finance, housing development, corporate services and business development, as well as traditional housing management functions. Employment of operational staff is generally regulated under a workforce management regime that is widely used in the local community services industry. At senior management levels, however, contract employment is more likely (NSWFHA, 2016).

In recent years several organisations in our surveys had found it necessary to pay higher salaries to attract finance and housing development specialists with market experience. This had reportedly caused some friction with other long-serving staff on lower pay rates (Milligan et al., 2013, p. 68). More fundamentally, diversification of organisational functions had brought about changes to organisational culture. In our interviews chief executive officers described how their organisations were becoming a blend of socially motivated housing managers, newer commercially savvy recruits from the private sector, and staff transferring from former public housing roles with a 'public service mindset'. In response to this development, most organisations had embarked on change management programmes to try and protect a culture in which there was a primary emphasis on social mission but in which staff understood the importance of operating in a more commercial way, particularly in respect of private financing and housing development and purchase (Milligan et al., 2013, pp. 69–71). This highlights the challenge in diversifying hybrids of safeguarding a mission-driven organisational culture.

Financial Resourcing

The financial resourcing of Australia's HTSOs also indicates entrenched hybridity. From the outset, Australian HTSOs were not funded by dues, donations and legacies associated with an ideal-typical third sector (Billis, 2010, p. 55), but through government grants for capital purposes, combined with internal (rent) revenue from residents and ongoing subsidies for some tenant cohorts, with the mix and level of these varying across programmes and groups housed, and by jurisdiction and over time (Milligan and Hulse, 2015).

Reflecting another widely evident characteristic of third sector hybridity (Doherty et al., 2014), there has been a strong push in recent years by policy-makers and sector players to mobilise private financing for affordable housing supply. Most leading HTSOs now have private financing arrangements with major financial institutions. One organisational consequence of this development is that HTSOs have been subject to detailed scrutiny from private lenders about their capacity to repay loans. Lender examination of HTSO governance, finance and operations is said to have exerted a considerable influence, described by one CEO in our studies as a 'quasi second Board of Directors' that gets to approve major strategic decisions (Milligan et al., 2013, p. 48). Stringent lending terms and conditions, at least partly attributable to lender unfamiliarity with the HTSO business model, had also curtailed capacity for further growth (Milligan et al., 2015a, p. 95).

These developments illustrate how market organisations can have powerful effects on third sector organisational decision-making. Additionally, financial viability issues are a key performance area for public sector regulatory scrutiny (NRSCH, 2014b, pp. 38–41), thus highlighting the multiple layers of accountability that HTSOs are faced with.

GOVERNMENT, MARKET AND THIRD SECTOR INFLUENCES ON THE EVOLUTION AND DEVELOPMENT PATHS OF AUSTRALIAN HTSOs

In this chapter, we have provided a high-level overview of the types of hybridity and core organisational elements of the larger Australian HTSOs. It is clear from the preceding discussion that these organisations have had to manage tensions between public, third and, increasingly, private sector organisational principles. In this section, we explore how each of these distinctive influences has helped to shape the ways in which larger Australian HTSOs have operated and adapted. The section adds to understanding of the power, fluidity and interplay of these external influences on the evolution and development of HTSOs.

Government Control

While largely government-initiated, provision of housing by third sector entities has never enjoyed consistent or sustained support from governments in Australia's federal system, and the policy purpose(s) of government engagement with HTSOs is commonly not well defined. In this section, we explore the main reasons behind that situation, and their consequences for HTSOs.

As discussed earlier, many of the HTSOs were enacted originally by state governments. Additional federal funding from 1984 (until 2008) that was intended to stimulate diversification and innovation via 'community housing' was administered by the same state agency that also supplied and managed public housing. This resulted in organisational tensions that have worked to stymie the growth and development of alternative providers (Mant, 1992). While state housing agencies may have allocated funds for community housing, this was often done in ways suited to their own agendas (Darcy, 1999). This principal–agent relationship circumscribed HTSO activities, stifling their independence and diminishing their capacity for self-generated growth (Milligan and Pawson, 2010). Even after the break-up of most dedicated housing authorities from the 1990s, such paternalistic and self-interested control has for the most part remained embedded in the culture and practices of successor agencies (Milligan et al., 2016).

A recent instance of bureaucratic obstruction was the failure to fulfil a combined Housing Ministers' objective to restructure the existing system of social housing provision so that third sector housing would comprise up to 35 per cent of social housing by 2014 (Housing Ministers Conference, 2009, p. 18). As public housing agencies grappled with the political, workforce and government balance sheet implications of the scale of transfers that would be necessary to reach this target (around 96 000 dwellings), only one small jurisdiction (Tasmania) came close to its achievement (Pawson et al., 2013). We have observed that an additional factor widely believed to have impeded implementation was the scepticism of key managerial actors about the capacities of successor landlords to deliver. A hands-off Australian (federal) government made no attempt to ensure that an adequate programme of transfers was planned and implemented, and there was no national legislation or official policy that specified precisely the goals and intended outcomes of such social housing diversification (Milligan and Pawson, 2010).

Notwithstanding some evidence of bureaucratic resistance to transfers of public housing, policy-makers and independent researchers have articulated other reasons for contesting such moves. Chief among these are the financial problems plaguing public housing in Australia, following decades of underfunding, which has resulted in poor-quality assets with a substantial maintenance backlog (Hall and Berry, 2007). Thus, while transferring public housing to HTSOs could deliver some financial benefits and possibly service improvements for tenants, financially sustainable longer-term social benefits are unlikely to be achieved without core changes to current policy, and funding arrangements to enable adequate investment in both modernisation and new supply (Pawson et al., 2013).

This quandary was well recognised by CEOs in our research, many of whom expressed a major concern with the tangible tensions their organisations faced between ensuring the commercial viability of the transfer deals on offer, living up to the political expectations of their sector, and achieving high-quality social outcomes (Milligan et al., 2015a, p. 71). While some had participated in recent transfer tender processes, others had withdrawn transfer bids or remained watchful for more suitable opportunities (ibid., p. 26). Nevertheless, by acknowledging that this was 'the only game in town', several CEOs reflected the pressure HTSOs felt to participate in transfer negotiations, especially in the absence of any other assured growth and development path, even though their organisations faced significant cultural and financial risks if they took responsibility for undermaintained public housing dwellings and a large increase in high-dependency tenants. Reflecting ongoing tensions between the public and third sectors, at the time of writing in 2017 the extent of, and terms and conditions for, large-scale public housing transfers in Australia varied considerably between state jurisdictions. In 2016 a 5000-dwelling transfer package was cancelled by the Queensland Government after three years of negotiation and planning with government-selected HTSOs (Pawson et al., 2016).

The financial problems facing the social housing system also led to political and bureaucratic overreach on opportunities for leveraging new funding sources via HTSOs (Milligan and Pawson, 2010). Several organisations in our study had reached peak debt or had depleted their modest surpluses due to the extent of leverage expected under past programme requirements, as noted by the Auditor General in the state of Victoria (Victorian Auditor General, 2010). This situation has required careful attention to ongoing revenue affecting day-to-day operations such as tenant selection, vacancy management and maintenance operations. In a local policy context where the rent paid by low-income social housing tenants is income-restricted, maintaining loan repayments by granting more tenancies to modest-income households has given rise to another area of contention with state governments that seek to narrowly target scarce resource to those 'most in need' (ibid.). Determining the 'right balance' between social and affordable housing tenancies so that priority needs were being met but financial viability was not impaired has thus posed an ongoing tension for HTSOs. CEOs in our surveys indicated, however, that it was impossible to remain solvent when housing only low-income households (Milligan et al., 2013, p. 42).

In the context of endeavours to increase affordable housing supply via HTSOs, while rhetorically attracted to private financing of social housing, government efforts to establish effective mechanisms and frameworks to support this have been short-lived or feeble. This reflects in part changing political priorities but also a domestic policy-maker failure to grasp the public policy requirements for attracting private finance to social and affordable housing at scale. The botched implementation and ultimate demise of the National Rental Affordability Scheme (NRAS) (2008–14), which aimed to create a new residential asset class in Australia via the provision of tax-privileged affordable rental housing, brought to light the lack of leadership, skills and stability within governments to initiate such strategies (Milligan and Tiernan, 2011; Milligan et al., 2015b).

Beyond the housing agencies of government, there has been a deeply embedded resistance in Treasury departments to investment in social housing, reflecting both an ideological preference for supplementing the income of high-need individuals (rather than supplying social housing) and the unevidenced assertion that, with such assistance, the market would provide affordable and appropriate housing (Hulse, 2007).

Overall, in Australia capricious government behaviour, bureaucratic inertia or, at times, resistance, and poor policy-making in the housing realm, have contributed to a difficult operating environment for larger HTSOs. The precariousness of HTSOs as housing developers has been underscored since 2014 after the abrupt cancellation of NRAS (despite massive oversubscription) and by foreshadowed public housing transfers in several jurisdictions that failed to materialise. Although strongly socially minded, most surveyed organisations were therefore uneasily searching for new business ventures that could protect their recently enhanced organisational capacities and generate revenue for independent growth. Among other possible directions this was expected to involve further shifts in tenant mix – moving away from an exclusive focus on the lowest-income groups to boost rental income – and obtaining more fee income from market-based, housing-related activities (Milligan et al., 2015a). If this tendency develops and deepens, future hybridity among Australian HTSOs may well be more private (than public) oriented. Consistent with this direction, and perhaps reflecting a stronger market orientation generally in Australia, HTSOs in the 2013–14 survey aligned themselves more with 'private sector values' than their much larger and more hybridised housing association counterparts in England and the Netherlands, which were surveyed in complementary research (Milligan et al., 2015a, p. 57).

Market Power

As discussed earlier, the vast majority of Australian housing is provided through the private market, a situation that has prevailed throughout Australia's post-colonial settlement (Berry, 1999; Troy, 2012). In their growth endeavours, therefore, HTSOs have had to contend with the substantial market power exercised by firmly entrenched and well-organised players. These include large and powerful land developers who have always resisted direct involvement of governments and quasi-government entities in land development. Developers have also stridently opposed planning policies such as inclusionary zoning for affordable housing, which are commonplace in other liberal welfare countries (Gurran et al., 2008; Gurran and Phibbs, 2015). In this context, larger HTSOs are insignificant players who are faced with paying market prices for land, over which they have no control. While some have become involved in joint ventures, these are dwarfed by public–private partnership arrangements, particularly applying in the redevelopment of older public housing estates and other renewal precincts controlled by government development agencies.

It has at times been easier for HTSOs to deal with residential builders who operate separately from land developers in Australia and are less antithetical to social housing. Industry associations representing the predominantly small firms which comprise the residential building sector have supported government investment in social housing, especially in times of cyclical market downturn to sustain their industry, and builders have been willing to do business with HTSOs, which represent additional demand for their services. However, with the rapidly changing structure of urban housing markets – shifting from the once ubiquitous detached houses produced by small builders to more complex multi-unit developments (Dalton et al., 2013) – big developers have become more dominant and influential in construction as well. Untested HTSOs are perceived as marginal and insignificant players in this space, unless there is a specific advantage of partnering with them, such as to access government incentives which, as we have discussed, have been few and far between.

There is also a concentration of market power in the housing finance sector. When this sector was deregulated as part of general financial deregulation from the mid-1980s, smaller lenders gradually disappeared or became banks (Hulse et al., 2012). The banks were reluctant to lend to HTSOs, a sector that they knew little about. In their 2008–09 response to the GFC, the Australian Government introduced a guarantee scheme for the major banks which further concentrated market power. Whilst the leading organisations have secured finance from the major banks (as discussed earlier in the chapter), the terms and conditions of lending are not generally optimal, reflecting lenders' perceptions of risk in the sector (Lawson et al., 2014). Other prospective institutional financiers consider the sector as a whole (and individual organisations) to be too small, with too few assets and weak cash flows, to support complex, large-scale fund-raising in capital markets, as has occurred in Europe and North America (Milligan et al., 2015b). These barriers are exacerbated by a situation where Australian governments have been unwilling to assist in matching returns required by institutional investors (that is, those comparable to alternate asset classes) to stimulate their investment in social and affordable housing developments (Ross, 2015).

In the face of the entrenched market power of large developers and financiers, the CEOs of HTSOs in our surveys considered that 'market pressures' and 'private sector collaboration' were two of the top four 'external' pressures affecting their organisations, and these two, together with finance costs, were the most important drivers of change in them (Milligan et al., 2013, p. 29; 2015a, p. 29). The ways in which leading HTSOs responded to these challenges shaped the type of organisational hybridity that developed. The organisations recruited new board directors and specialist staff with strong commercial skills in the housing development and procurement and finance areas. Their challenge was to negotiate with powerful private developers and financiers and not be seen as a 'soft option', while having a clear view of the social objectives that their organisation wanted to achieve. However, as discussed earlier, the resultant cultural changes in organisations may in the longer term reshape the core characteristics of HTSOs.

The market drivers outlined above in respect of housing development and procurement and private finance were overlaid on an existing government-controlled pathway which focused on housing management services. In response, leading HTSOs effectively attempted to reshape their organisations in ways that moved them from state–third sector hybridity to an entrenched form of state–third sector–market hybridity. Nevertheless considerable barriers to a privately financed housing supply model remained: most notably, the failure of governments to offer effective financial backing for the new model, and powerful market players which were resistant to changes in the planning system to mandate the provision of more affordable housing. The situation that has resulted illustrates important factors that, we contend, have contributed to the fragility of HTSO endeavours to expand.

Weak Third Sector Connections

As discussed above, most Australian HTSOs had very small beginnings and focused on serving specialised groups who were not well catered for by mainstream public housing. Although many gradually developed connections to their local communities, they did not have roots in and close connections with other third sector organisations, particularly those in the local welfare sector, which has a long and vibrant history (Productivity Commission, 2010; McClelland, 2014).

The Australian pattern of social protection established soon after Federation in 1901 differed from other developed countries, in that the primary instrument was wage regulation (the so-called 'wage earners' welfare state') rather than the social insurance or social expenditure systems laid down elsewhere (Castles, 1996, p. 91). This model of social protection was supported by organised labour that did not, as in other places, favour non-market housing models. Indeed, as the wage earners' welfare state was based on working life, housing came into the equation mainly through the promotion of home ownership so that, in older age (when outside of the workforce), people would own their own homes and have low housing outlays. As we have seen, housing policy, particularly post-Second World War, was directed at supporting people to own their own homes. This mass home ownership model worked effectively for a long time and the overwhelming majority of Australians were well housed (Dalton, 2014, p. 188).

The HTSOs of today did not therefore evolve from the larger and longer-established charitable organisations (although there are a few exceptions), nor were they the inheritors of a history of mutuality in housing finance provision which dated back to the 19th century (Lyons, 2001, Ch. 12). They were, as discussed earlier, mostly new organisations established from the 1980s as the wage earners' welfare state began to weaken and new groups, such as single parents, were found to be in poverty and housing disadvantage (Henderson, 1975).

As a result, many HTSO were not well connected to the broader third sector, particularly not to welfare agencies, which had developed strongly from the 1990s as governments adopted new public sector management ideas (Hilmer, 1993) and systematically outsourced much of what had previously been government services, such as job search and employment assistance (Considine et al., 2014), on a contract-for-service basis. While the broader welfare sector had established an influential peak organisation in the 1950s to represent its views and advocate to governments, this organisation focused almost exclusively on defending public housing. The small housing third sector was the province of very small state-based housing peak and advocacy groups which were heavily dependent on government funding and periodically defunded at the whim of governments (Milligan et al., 2016).

As leading HTSOs expanded their size and functions in response to opportunities described earlier, they sometimes encountered hostility from the welfare third sector which continued to see them as 'exit points' from homelessness services for people with specialised needs. Some also viewed HTSOs as the 'thin end of the wedge' in terms of the privatisation of public housing. Comparable to some government views (discussed earlier), a particular point of contention was moving to a greater mix of households and housing products, which was sometimes denigrated by the welfare third sector as 'cherry-picking' clients.

Identity as part of a cohesive 'community housing sector' (or more recently 'affordable housing industry') has been fostered by sector-led initiatives variously aimed at building and promoting sector influence, capacity and collaboration since the mid-1990s (Milligan et al., 2016). This advocacy can be seen partly as a sector response to HTSOs' sometimes weak connection with the powerful welfare lobby, and the hesitancy of governments to support them. There is some evidence, however, that this cohesion may be weakening. For instance, as competition for resources between organisations has intensified and competitive tendering for government resources (such as development sites) becomes the norm, HTSOs have had to negotiate to be part of consortia involving market players, often in direct competition with other consortia involving their peers, in order to succeed.

One consequence of this procurement approach was that some in our surveys were seeking acceptance in the housing industry as commercially astute enterprises rather than being identified as 'little known or understood' community housing providers (Milligan et al., 2015a, pp. 22–23). In a pragmatic sense, this may be consistent with the proposition that hybrid organisations may use different identities to maintain legitimacy with existing stakeholders or to achieve legitimacy in their dealings with new ones (Teasdale, 2009). However, it may also be a pointer to deeper changes in the core character and culture of these organisations. In this case, we consider that it is too soon in the process of HTSO transformation in Australia to assess what these organisations are evolving to, and the impacts on sector legitimacy.

'FRAGILE HYBRIDITY': TENSIONS AT THE INTERSECTION OF PUBLIC, THIRD SECTOR AND PRIVATE SECTORS

The aim of this chapter has been to apply contemporary thinking about hybrid organisations to interpreting the development and organisational dynamics of larger HTSOs in the Australian third sector. In so doing, the chapter has traced the development of hybrid organisations in a country and a policy domain that have attracted relatively little previous research.

In this final section, we conclude that state, market and third sector influences, combined with the Australian housing third sector's history and organisational dynamics, have circumscribed the growth of HTSOs in Australia. We term this 'fragile hybridity', finding that HTSOs have been in a continuous state of flux, substantially unable to achieve their ambitions to upscale and develop more affordable housing, and thus they remain as 'bit players' in Australia's housing system. The body of the chapter has explored some possible explanations for this situation, drawing both on Australia's position as an archetypical liberal welfare regime and on concepts of organisational hybridity that depict third sector organisations as facing competing internal logics that are forged by three sets of powerful and dynamic external drivers: those influenced by the state, market and civil society. In the case illustrated in this chapter, these poles of influence and their intersection appear to have thrown up persistent obstacles to a significant third sector contribution to addressing Australia's housing needs. This, we argue, is suggestive of a fragility associated with the hybrid third sector form.

First among the obstacles has been a market provision system that is dominated by the entrenched power of large-scale developers and their associated institutional forces. For these players, HTSOs are either insignificant or unknown. Moreover, leading housing developers have been trenchantly opposed to public policies – commonplace elsewhere – that support HTSO-sponsored affordable housing developments, especially in the planning policy realm. More broadly, the housing industry has invested considerable effort in protecting its own self-interest in market-based solutions to mounting housing affordability challenges, and has forcefully resisted reform of tax measures that privilege speculative investment in housing over consumer interests and, thereby, contribute to severe house price inflation and housing wealth inequality (Yates, 2010).

Market domination in turn has helped to set the tone for what has been an erratic relationship between federal and, particularly, state governments and HTSOs. While many HTSOs were founded by state government initiatives, the sector has never enjoyed lasting or consistent public policy support. Governments have instead provided long-standing support for home ownership and private property ownership more generally, leaving little space for non-market housing provision, with severely adverse implications for the role of social housing (and the viability of all social housing agencies) in Australia. This is despite the profound changes that have taken place in Australia's demography, economy and society since the mid-1970s that have both exacerbated and fundamentally reshaped housing needs. Even with local progression in outsourcing of public services since the 1990s, housing has remained 'the odd one out' in human services delivery, with market and government forces interacting to check the growth of a third sector model. This outcome is consistent with a deeply entrenched Australian society preference for home ownership and the embedded institutional arrangements that support this.

The third set of societal forces that shape hybridity potential appears to be a weak influence in the Australian housing context. For their part, leading HTSOs generally – with some exceptions – have not prioritised stakeholder and resident engagement. Moreover, as one of the consequences of their foundation largely outside the welfare sector, HTSOs have only loose connections to other parts of the third sector and their cause has largely not been promoted or defended there. Thus to the extent that political movements have grown up around Australia's affordable housing shortage, many third sector welfare organisations have positioned themselves as defenders of a public housing model rather than advocating for the growth of third sector housing organisations.

The historical core social purpose of Australia's HTSOs was to provide appropriate housing affordable to lower-income households, whose needs were not being met by a retracting public housing sector or through an inaccessible market. Most leading HTSOs (and many much smaller local non-profit entities across Australia) have been working to fulfil this mission for decades, largely by compiling a strong track record of housing management services, which has defined their core function and shaped organisational culture. Increasingly, however, there is recognition that the sector is too small and will never make more than a minor contribution to its core social purpose unless it finds innovative ways to upscale and grow.

Faced with entrenched opposition and few prospects for growth, a number of leading Australian HTSOs have, over the last decade or so, begun to develop some aspects of a commercial modus operandi to enable them to pursue aspirations for greater autonomy and self-generated growth, with the intention of benefiting more households in housing need. Consequential strategic decisions have included moves to expand their areas of operation beyond specific local communities or single target groups, moves to house households on modest market incomes (rather than purely welfare benefits), and new commercial endeavours entailing much greater engagement with private sector partners and professionals. It is unlikely, however, that such moves into more commercial operations and a market orientation can achieve much greater social returns without higher levels of public subsidy support (which have not been forthcoming), especially in view of current HTSO organisational scales and low levels of financial resources and assets. While yet to unfold, but evoked by recent difficulties experienced by Dutch and English housing associations, a shift in the balance of their social and commercial functions has the potential to alter their hybrid identity and to dilute their core third sector characteristics.

The main lesson arising from this worked example, however, concerns how historical antecedents, weak nation-state policy regimes, powerful alternative market institutions and vested interests can work to stifle the potential for success of hybrid third sector organisations. In the case of larger HTSOs in Australia, we have argued that it has been such exigencies – largely external to the organisations themselves – that have so far impeded the progression of a third sector hybrid model of affordable housing provision. The causal part played by context and history that is highlighted by this particular housing case study, therefore, may offer one explanation for divergence from trends in other places and realms.

ACKNOWLEDGEMENTS

We would like to thank the Australian Housing and Urban Research Institute Ltd (AHURI) for funding which supported a body of research (involving the authors and numerous colleagues) into Australia's leading HTSOs between 2004 and 2016, which we have drawn on extensively for the analysis presented in this chapter.

NOTES

1. A primary difference according to Evers and Laville (2004, p. 13) is that in the United States the principle of non-distribution of profits is key to definition of the third sector, whereas in Europe this is limited to private distribution of profits such that co-operatives and mutual societies are included in the definition of third sector. The latter practice is also adopted in Australia.
2. A special issue of the journal *Housing Studies* (27(4)) was published in 2012 on 'Social enterprise and hybridity in housing organisations'. This provides a number of contemporary perspectives on hybrid HTSOs.

REFERENCES

ABS (2013), *2011 Census Community Profiles, Census of Population and Housing*, Canberra: Australian Bureau of Statistics.
AIHW (2014), 'Housing assistance in Australia 2014', Cat. No. HOU 271, Canberra: Australian Institute of Health and Welfare.
Australian Government (2010), 'Regulation and growth of the not-for-profit housing sector', Discussion Paper, Canberra; Australian Government.
Barraket, J. and Collyer, N. (2010), 'Mapping social enterprise in Australia: conceptual debates and their operational implications', *Third Sector Review*, 16(2): 11–28.
Berry, M. (1999), 'Unravelling the Australian housing solution: the post-war years', *Housing, Theory and Society*, 16(3): 106–123.
Billis, D. (ed.) (2010), *Hybrid Organisations in the Third Sector: Challenges of Practice, Policy and Theory*, Basingstoke: Palgrave.
Bisset, H. and Milligan, V. (2004), *Risk Management in Community Housing: Managing the Challenges Posed by Growth in the Provision of Affordable Housing*, Sydney: National Community Housing Forum.
Blessing, A. (2012), 'Magical or monstrous? Hybridity in social housing governance', *Housing Studies*, 27(2): 189–207.
Boelhouwer, P. and Priemus, H. (2014), 'Demise of the Dutch social housing tradition: impact of budget cuts and political changes', *Journal of Housing and the Built Environment*, 29: 221–235.
Brandsen, T., van den Donk, W. and Putters, K. (2005), 'Griffins or chameleons? Hybridity as a permanent and inevitable characteristic of the third sector', *International Journal of Public Administration*, 28(9): 749–765.
Bratt, R. (2012), 'The quadruple bottom line and nonprofit housing organisations in the United States', *Housing Studies*, 27(4): 438–56.
Butcher, J. (2015), 'The third sector and government in Australia: not-for-profit reform under Labor, 2007–2013', *Australian Journal of Political Science*, 50(1): 148–163.
Carson, E. and Kerr, L. (2014), *Australian Social Policy and the Human Services*, Port Melbourne: Cambridge University Press.
Castles, F. (1996), 'Needs-Based Strategies of Social Protection in Australia and New Zealand', in G. Esping-Andersen (ed.), *Welfare States in Transition*, London: SAGE Publications, pp. 88–115.
Considine, M. (2001), *Enterprising States: The Public Management of Welfare-to-Work*, Cambridge: Cambridge University Press.
Considine, M., O'Sullivan, S. and Nguyen, P. (2014), 'Mission-drift? The third sector and the pressure to be business-like: evidence from Job Services Australia', *Third Sector Review*, 20(1): 87–107.
Czischke, D., Gruis, V. and Mullins, D. (2012), 'Conceptualising social enterprise in housing organisations', *Housing Studies*, 27(4): 418–437.
Dalton, T. (2014), 'Housing policy: changes and prospects', in A. McClelland and P. Smyth (eds), *Social Policy in Australia: Understanding for Action, Third Edition*, South Melbourne: Oxford University Press, pp. 172–189.
Dalton, T., Hurley, J., Gharaie, E., Wakefield, R. and Horne, R. (2013), *Australian Suburban House Building: Industry Organisation, Practices and Constraints*, Final Report No. 213, Melbourne: Australian Housing and Urban Research Institute.
Darcy, M. (1999), 'The discourse of community and the reinvention of social housing policy in Australia', *Urban Studies*, 36(1): 13–26.
Doherty, B., Haugh, H. and Lyon, F. (2014), 'Social enterprises as hybrid organizations: a review and research agenda', *International Journal of Management Reviews*, 16: 417–436.
Douglas, H. (2015), 'Embracing hybridity: a review of social entrepreneurship and enterprise in Australia and New Zealand', *Third Sector Review*, 21(1): 5–30.
Esping-Andersen, G. (1990), *The Three Worlds of Welfare Capitalism*, Cambridge: Polity Press.

Evers, A. (2005), 'Mixed welfare systems and hybrid organizations: changes in the governance and provision of social services', *International Journal of Public Administration*, 28(9): 737–748.

Evers, A. and Laville, J.-L. (2004), 'Defining the Third Sector in Europe', in A. Evers and J.-L. Laville (eds), *The Third Sector in Europe*, Cheltenham, UK and Northampton, MA, USA: Edward Elgar Publishing, pp. 11–37.

Gilmour, T. and Milligan, V. (2012), 'Let a hundred flowers bloom: innovation and diversity in Australian not-for-profit housing organisations', *Housing Studies*, 27(4): 476–494.

Gruis, V. (2008), 'Organisational archetypes for Dutch housing associations', *Environment and Planning C: Government and Policy*, 26(6): 1077–1092.

Gurran, N. and Phibbs, P. (2015), 'Are governments really interested in fixing the housing problem? Policy capture and busy work in Australia', *Housing Studies*, 30(5): 711–729.

Gurran, N., Milligan, V., Baker, D. Bugg, LB. and Christensen, S. (2008), *New Directions in Planning for Affordable Housing: Australian and International Evidence and Implications*, Final Report No. 120, Melbourne: Australian Housing and Urban Research Institute.

Hall, J. and Berry, M. (2007), *Operating Deficits and Public Housing: Policy Options for Reversing the Trend, 2005/06 Update*, Final Report No. 106, Melbourne: Australian Housing and Urban Research Institute.

Hayward, D. (1996), 'The reluctant landlords? A history of public housing in Australia', *Urban Policy and Research*, 14(1): 5–34.

Henderson, R. (1975), *Poverty in Australia*, Australian Government Commission of Inquiry into Poverty. First Main Report, Canberra: Australian Government Publishing Service.

Hilditch, S. (2015), 'Why are the Tories so sanguine about adding 60 billion to public debt?', *Redbrick* Blog, 2 November, accessed 12 November at https://redbrickblog.wordpress.com/2015/11/02/why-are-the-tories-so-sanguine-about-adding-60-billion-to-public-debt/.

Hill, M. (2006), *Social Policy in the Modern World, A Comparative Text*, Malden MA: Blackwell Publishing.

Hilmer, F. (1993), *National Competition Policy*, Report by the Independent Committee of Inquiry, Canberra: Australian Government Publishing Service.

Housing Ministers Conference (2009), 'Implementing the national housing reforms: a progress report to the Council of Australian Governments from Commonwealth, state and territory housing ministers', November.

Hulse, K. (2007), 'Housing allowances and the restructuring of the Australian welfare state', in P. Kemp (ed.), *Housing Allowances in Comparative Context*, Bristol: Policy Press, pp. 17–38.

Hulse, K., Burke, T., Ralston, L. and Stone, W. (2012), *The Australian Private Rental Sector: Changes and Challenges*, Positioning Paper No. 149, Melbourne: Australian Housing and Urban Research Institute.

Ko, S. and Kong, E. (2012), 'Prospects of social enterprises from a framing perspective', *International Journal of Interdisciplinary Social Sciences*, 6(4): 169–186.

Lawson, J. and Milligan, V. (2007), *International Trends in Housing and Policy Responses*, Final Report No. 110, Melbourne: Australian Housing and Urban Research Institute.

Lawson, J., Berry, M., Hamilton, C. and Pawson, H. (2014), *Enhancing Affordable Rental Housing Investment via an Intermediary and Guarantee*, Final Report No. 220, Melbourne: Australian Housing and Urban Research Institute.

Lyons, M. (2001), *Third Sector: The Contribution of Non-profit and Cooperative Enterprises in Australia*, Sydney: Allen & Unwin.

Maclennan, D. and Chisholm, S. (eds) (2013), *New Times, New Businesses: Housing Provision in Times of Austerity*, St Andrews: University of St Andrews.

Mant, J. (1992), 'Inquiry into the Department of Housing', Report of the Commissioner, Sydney.

McClelland, A. (2014), 'The institutional context of decisions and actions', in A. McClelland and P. Smyth (eds), *Social Policy in Australia: Understanding for Action, Third Edition*, South Melbourne: Oxford University Press, pp. 6–77.

Milligan, V. and Hulse, K. (2015), 'Hybridity in the housing third sector: interpreting recent developments in Australia', *Third Sector Review*, 21(2): 191–218.

Milligan V. and Pawson, H. (2010), 'Transforming social housing in Australia: challenges and options', paper presented to ENHR Conference, Urban Dynamics and Housing Change, Istanbul, 1–4 July.

Milligan, V. and Tiernan, A. (2011), 'No home for housing: the situation of the Commonwealth's housing policy advisory function', *Australian Journal of Public Administration*, 70(4): 391–407.

Milligan, V., Gurran, N., Lawson, J., Phibbs, P. and Phillips, R. (2009), *Innovation in Affordable Housing in Australia: Bringing Policy and Practice for Not-for-Profit Housing Organisations Together*, Final Report No. 134, Melbourne: Australian Housing and Urban Research Institute.

Milligan, V., Hulse, K. and Davison, G. (2013), *Understanding Leadership, Strategy and Organisational Dynamics in the Not-for-Profit Housing Sector*, Final Report No. 204, Melbourne: Australian Housing and Urban Research Institute.

Milligan, V., Hulse, K., Flatau, P. and Liu, E. (2015a), *Strategies of Australia's Leading Not-for-Profit Housing Providers: A National Study and International Comparison*, Final Report No. 237, Melbourne: Australian Housing and Urban Research Institute.

Milligan, V., Martin, C., Phillips, R., Liu, E., Pawson, H. and Spinney, A. (2016), *Profiling Australia's Affordable Housing Industry*, Final Report No. 268, Melbourne: Australian Housing and Urban Research Institute.
Milligan, V., Pawson, H., Williams, P. and Yates, J. (2015b), ''Next moves? Expanding affordable rental housing in Australia through institutional investment', City Futures Research Centre, UNSW, Sydney, accessed at http://www.be.unsw.edu.au/sites/default/files/upload/research/centres/cf/publications/cfprojectreports/Next%20moves_report_0.pdf.
Mullins, D. (2006), 'Competing institutional logics? Local accountability and scale and efficiency in an expanding non-profit housing sector', *Public Policy and Administration*, 21(3): 6–21.
Mullins, D. and Jones, T. (2015), 'From "contractors to the state" to "protectors of public value"? Relations between non-profit housing hybrids and the state in England', *Voluntary Sector Review*, online first at www.ingentaconnect.com/content/tpp/vsr/pre-prints;content-pp_VSR-D-15-00020R2.
Mullins, D. and Pawson, H. (2010), 'Social housing: agents of policy or profits in disguise?', in D. Billis (ed.), *Hybrid Organisations in the Third Sector: Challenges of Practice, Policy and Theory*, Basingstoke: Palgrave, pp. 197–218.
Mullins, D., Milligan, V. and Nieboer, N. (2017), 'State-directed hybridity? The relationship between non-profit housing organizations and the state in three national contexts', *Housing Studies*, 33(4): 565–588.
Nieboer, N. and Gruis, V. (2014), 'Shifting back – changing organisational strategies in Dutch social housing', *Journal of Housing and the Built Environment*, 29(1): 1–13.
NRSCH (2014a), 'Tier Guidelines', National Regulatory System for Community Housing Directorate, accessed 20 November 2015 at http://www.nrsch.gov.au/__data/assets/file/0004/284035/I_Tiers_Guidelines.
NRSCH (2014b), 'Evidence Guidelines', National Regulatory System for Community Housing Directorate, accessed 20 November 2015 at http://www.nrsch.gov.au/__data/assets/file/0008/288224/D_Evidence_Guidelines.
NRSCH (2014c), 'Enforcement Guidelines for Registrars', National Regulatory System for Community Housing Directorate, accessed 20 May 2016 at http://www.nrsch.gov.au/__data/assets/file/0003/288219/D_Enforcement_Guidelines.
NSWFHA (2016), 'House keys: workforce, aggregate report', NSW Federation of Housing Associations (with Q Shelter), May.
Office for National Statistics (2015), 'Classification announcement: "Private registered providers" of social housing in England', 30 October, accessed 12 November 2015 at http://www.ons.gov.uk/ons/rel/na-classification/national-accounts-sector-classification/classification-update---october-2015/index.html.
Office for National Statistics (2017), 'Statement on classification of English housing associations', November, accessed 27 November 2017 at https://www.ons.gov.uk/news/statementsandletters/statementonclassificationofenglishhousingassociationsnovember2017.
Pawson, H., Martin, C. Flanagan, K. and Phillips, R. (2016), *Recent Housing Transfer Experience in Australia: Implications for Industry Development*, Final Report No. 273, Melbourne: Australian Housing and Urban Research Institute.
Pawson, H., Milligan, V., Wiesel, I. and Hulse, K. (2013), *Public Housing Transfers: Past, Present and Prospective*, Final Report No. 215, Melbourne: Australian Housing and Urban Research Institute.
Peattie, R. and Morley, A. (2008), *Social Enterprise: Diversity and Dynamics, Contexts and Contributions*, London: Social Enterprise Coalition.
Priemus, H. and Gruis, V. (2011), 'Social housing and illegal state aid: the agreement between European Commission and Dutch government', *International Journal of Housing Policy*, 11(1): 81–96.
Productivity Commission (2010), *Contribution of the Not-for-Profit Sector*, Research Report, Canberra: Productivity Commission.
Rhodes, M. and Donnelly-Cox, G. (2014), 'Hybridity and social entrepreneurship in social housing in Ireland', *Voluntas*, 25(6): 1630–1647.
Ross, J. (2015), 'New approaches to financing', Presentation to NSW Community Housing Conference, Setting New Directions, 5–6 May, Sydney.
Teasdale, S. (2009), 'The contradictory faces of social enterprise: impression management as (social) entrepreneurial behaviour', Working Paper no. 23, Third Sector Research Centre. Birmingham: University of Birmingham.
Troy, P. (2012), *Accommodating Australians: Commonwealth Government Involvement in Housing*, Sydney: Federation Press.
Victorian Auditor General (2010), 'Access to social housing', Report, accessed 27 November 2015 at http://www.audit.vic.gov.au/reports__publications/reports_by_year/2009-10/20102306_social_housing.aspx.
Yates, J. (2010), 'Housing and tax: the triumph of politics over economics', in Evans, C., Krever, R. and Mellor, P. (eds), *Australia's Future Tax System: The Prospects After Henry*, Sydney: Thomson Reuters, pp. 233–265.

22. Strategic mission management in hybrid organisations
Karin Kreutzer and Claus Jacobs

INTRODUCTION

To a marked extent hybrid organisations are driven by, and committed to, their missions. Yet they seem to struggle with the challenge of finding a sustainable way of incorporating different institutional logics. One reason is that operating with multiple bottom lines creates paradoxical demands on the organisations' strategy (Smith and Tushman, 2005). The advantages and benefits offered by hybridity do not come without a cost and conflicting institutional demands are an increasingly common phenomenon (Pache and Santos, 2010).

A direct consequence of their hybrid nature is the risk posed by the fundamental strategic challenge of 'mission drift'. Internally this might induce a decrease in the coherence of their organisational identity while externally it can lead to a loss of legitimacy for relevant stakeholder groups. As a preventive antidote we suggest that a regular and systematic mission review could mitigate this risk of mission drift. Furthermore, we suggest that while hybridity has been mainly discussed and explored in terms of a strategic challenge, it can also be considered as a strategic resource. The systematic review of a mission statement can thus be used proactively to make use of an organisation's hybrid nature.

In this chapter we introduce an approach that we term the 'hybridity tensions positioning protocol'. This assumes that hybrid organisations in general and social enterprises in particular integrate commercial and social welfare logics. Based on the work of Smith and Lewis (2011) this form of hybridity manifests itself in four domains: performing, organising, belonging and learning. In each of these domains we can identify three or four major tensions that we can use to discuss and define the future positioning of the organisation. This positioning of these 'hybridity tensions' provides, we suggest, an effective, detailed and relevant structural skeleton for revising an organisation's mission statement in the light of the most prevalent and pertinent aspects of the impact on the stresses that result from an organisation's hybrid status. We begin the chapter by discussing the nature of the strategic challenge that mission drift poses for hybrid organisations; we then introduce the 'hybridity tensions positioning protocol' which, we argue, provides a means through which hybrid organisations can address mission drift; and we present a case study of the United Nations Children's Fund (UNICEF) Germany to illustrate the use of the protocol.

MISSION DRIFT AS A FUNDAMENTAL STRATEGIC CHALLENGE IN HYBRID ORGANISATIONS

Hybrid organisations have been defined as organisations that incorporate and combine different institutional logics, such as those associated with social welfare on the one hand

and the market on the other (Battilana and Lee, 2014; Battilana and Dorado, 2010; Pache and Santos, 2010). Because of the often competing or conflicting nature of the institutional logics operating in hybrids, they are 'by nature arenas of contradiction' (Pache and Santos, 2013, p. 972; see also Haigh and Hoffman, 2012; Dees, 2012). Being embedded in the social as well as in the business sector creates conflicting demands on the organisations' strategy (Smith and Tushman, 2005). Hybrids in general, and social enterprises in particular, have received a great deal of attention from scholars and practitioners alike due to their potential in addressing large social and environmental problems (see, e.g., Yunus et al., 2010). By developing and applying innovative entrepreneurial approaches to social problems, they typically set out to address social or environmental challenges by empowering beneficiaries, fighting poverty or environmental pollution, and delivering services to the elderly, disabled people, and families and children, in new and effective ways (Smith et al., 2013). Hybrid organisations operate in different parts of the world, in different industries, different value chains and varying degrees of hybridity. The following three organisations exemplify the width and breadth of hybrid organisations.

Dialogue Social Enterprise

Founded by Andreas Heinecke in 1998, the German-based Dialogue Social Enterprise (DSE) offers a cultural experience in the form of exhibitions where visitors are led by blind guides in groups through specially constructed dark rooms in which scent, sound, wind, temperature, and texture convey the characteristics of daily environments (Dialogue Social Enterprise, 2018). DSE is a limited company (established in 2008) with 150 employees and a turnover of €5 million in 2012. It forms the basis of an international franchise system that has brought the exhibition to more than 41 countries and more than 130 cities, has attracted more than 7 million visitors and has provided thousands of blind exhibition guides and trainers with a job. DSE operates exclusively on commercial revenues from entrance and franchise fees as well as from workshop and training fees. Thus, DSE empowers typically marginalised blind people to form part of a successful enterprise and thereby contributes to sensitising the public with respect to disability (Saerberg, 2007).

SEKEM

Based in the north-east of Cairo and founded in 1979 by Ibrahim Abouleish, SEKEM (from the ancient Egyptian 'vitality from the sun') is an Egyptian social enterprise which aims to improve the vitality of soil and food and promote the biodiversity of nature through sustainable, organic agriculture (SEKEM, 2018; Mair and Marti, 2006). Operating as a limited company, its commercial arm comprises biodynamic farming and the production and processing of food, medicinal herbs and organic cotton products. Its sister organisation, the SEKEM Development Foundation, supports a medical centre and several schools and a college as well as a research centre. Currently, SEKEM has over 1600 employees and in 2012 had a group turnover of €28 million. At least 10 per cent of the revenue co-finances the activities of the SEKEM foundation, which has 200 employees. In addition, the SEKEM foundation also operates on grants and donations most of which come from Europe and the US.

APOPO

Founded as a Belgium-based non-governmental organisation in 1998 by Bart Weetjens, APOPO (the Dutch acronym for Anti-Personnel Landmines Detection Product Development) deploys the exceptional olfactory sense of (widely available and inexpensive) African giant pouched rats for detecting landmines in countries such as Mozambique, Thailand and the Gaza Strip, as well as for identifying tuberculosis in Tanzania and elsewhere (APOPO, 2018; Poling et al., 2010). Due to their light weight, the rats can walk through minefields without activating the detonation mechanism. Having detected and destroyed thousands of landmines, APOPO has been able to return over 234 million square metres of land to the local population. With approximately 300 local employees, its revenues of €4 million in 2012 are based on grants from public authorities and charitable foundations, donations and corporate sponsorship.

Because of their divergent identities, goals, logics and practices (Santos et al., 2015), hybrid organisations face a variety of internal and external organisational tensions (Battilana and Lee, 2014; Besharov and Smith, 2013), if not latent paradoxes, that challenge their effective and efficient operation (Jay, 2013; Smith and Lewis, 2011; Jarzabkowski and Lê, 2017; Greenwood et al., 2011). Externally, hybrids face a variety of different stakeholders, who themselves often represent a specific institutional logic such as those connected with social welfare or the market. As organisations want to gain legitimacy towards their organisational environment (DiMaggio and Powell, 1983), this places different, if not competing, institutional demands on the organisation (Jay, 2013; Pache and Santos, 2010). SEKEM, for instance, given the identity of those who provide its resources, needs to comply with demands from both investing banks and the customers of their products (commercial logic) and with the expectations of its philanthropic donor base (social welfare logic).

Internally, hybrids have to contend with similar pressures and, alongside their external institutional demands, they have to manage the different organisational identity beliefs of their members (Kraatz and Block, 2008). Dialogue Social Enterprise, for instance, involves its beneficiaries directly in its service provision and is part of what is – legally speaking – a corporation. This has led to internal debates between organisational members about whether they conceive DSE as an enterprise or a social initiative. These different organisational identity beliefs are rooted more often than not in different professional backgrounds and roles that are biased towards distinct institutional logics (Battilana and Dorado, 2010; Pache and Santos, 2013). SEKEM, for instance, draws on professionals from marketing, finance and engineering on the one hand, and on educators, healthcare professionals and social workers on the other.

Last but not least, hybrid organisations typically simultaneously operate social value and business value chains that can be more or less aligned. The ways in which they produce social value for their beneficiaries can be integrated to varying degrees with the – distinct or related – ways in which they produce commercial value for their customers (Santos et al., 2015; Emerson, 2003; Fowler, 2000). One example of the ways in which the two value chains can be aligned appears to be DSE, where the business value for its customers is the result of the orchestration of a unique experience, while its intended social value – assisting blind people in leading an independent and integrated life – is achieved to a significant extent by including them in the provision of the 'dialogue in the dark' service. In this case, social and business value chains seem rather closely aligned. By contrast, APOPO operates on two distinct, slightly less aligned social and business value chains. While its donors provide the organisation with the necessary resources, the direct beneficiaries of its activities – prevention of the harm caused by land mines – are the local populations.

Over and above these general organisational issues, the fundamental strategic challenge for hybrid organisations consists of creating and maintaining coherence between the strategic goals that are the manifestations of their hybrid nature. Balancing different and often divergent goals – such as combining a specific social mission with the need for financial viability – defines this central strategic need. Striking such a balance is vital in order to avoid the imbalance between goals that can paralyse an organisation (Pache and Santos, 2010) as the result of intra-organisational conflict. (For vivid descriptions of such internal conflicts about organisational identity in non-profit organisations, see Glynn, 2000; Golden-Biddle and Rao, 1997). Overemphasising one logic can have serious consequences for the other (Pfeffer and Salancik, 1978). Giving priority to social welfare, for example, might jeopardise the long-term financial viability of the organisation. On the other hand, privileging market logic might result in mission drift: the perception by relevant stakeholders that the organisation overemphasises a business or market logic and corresponding practices at the expense of its social mission. There is some economic evidence about mission drift in microfinance institutions (Aubert et al., 2009). One prominent example of mission drift has been the case of the Mexican microfinance bank Compartamos, which set out to provide low-income earners with micro-loans to trigger local development but then – based on its financial success – did not realise that charging an interest rate of 79 per cent per year might sit awkwardly with its initial social mission (see Pache and Santos, 2010, for a close examination of the case).

Carefully balancing divergent strategic goals in an organisation's overall strategic orientation therefore seems to be a key success factor for hybrid organisations. In this respect, mission statements constitute a core component of the normative strategic framework of an organisation by aiming to provide 'employees and stakeholders with clarity about the overall purpose and *raison d'être* of the organisation' (Johnson et al., 2008, p. 165). A well-defined mission statement can communicate a sense of the direction and purpose of the organisation; it may serve as a control mechanism keeping the firm 'on track'; it can aid in making day-to-day decisions; and last but not least, it can inspire and motivate employees (for a systematic overview of the value of mission statements, see Bartkus et al., 2000). A strong commitment to a social mission means that a mission statement is crucial for hybrid organisations (Austin et al., 2006). To paraphrase Drucker (1990), mission seems mission-critical for hybrid organisations, since the mission statement serves as the central reference point in social organisations. It influences resource allocation, employee and volunteer motivation, and serves as an important point of reference for social impact measurement. Thus, a well-crafted and hybridity-sensitive mission statement that accounts adequately for different logics seems to be the key to providing a hybrid organisation with long-term strategic direction.

Given its strategic relevance for hybrid organisations, an effective mission statement can be seen as pivotal to the success of a hybrid organisation's accomplishment of its economic and non-economic goals. We believe that strategic mission management consists of two elements. First, any hybrid that faces the risk of mission drift because of its volatile internal and external environments seems well advised to review and, if necessary, revise its mission statement on a regular basis. This can be especially important in the case of 'mature' hybrids whose activities have achieved a level of strategic coherence and legitimacy and which may then face the risk of a kind of 'strategic myopia'. We suggest that a regular, systematic review of its mission statement will enable an organisation to remain responsive to any changes in its environment. Changes in the external environment, for example, could include increased competition in its fundraising market, the emergence of new players such as social impact investors, changes in customer needs, and the requirement for new legal regulations. For their part, changes in the internal environment could be changes in the composition of its staff, management or board team, or the adoption of new process and accounting principles.

The second core element for strategic mission management in our view is the ability to draw proactively on an organisation's hybrid characteristics when reviewing its mission statement. To date, most scholars have viewed hybridity primarily as a strategic challenge, but we believe that because of its essentially ambiguous and socially complex nature, hybridity can also be seen a strategic capability (see, e.g., Makadok, 2001), as DSE, SEKEM and APOPO have compellingly demonstrated. Actively exploring the tensions resulting from the hybrid nature of the organisation can be used as the means of reviewing – and if necessary revising – a hybrid organisation's mission statement and using it as an important way of establishing the normative positioning of the organisation.

The purpose of this chapter is thus to outline both the features of a design process that is central to a successful review of a hybrid organisation's mission statement, and the conceptual foundations of our approach. For the processes of review and development of a mission statement in hybrid organisations we offer a 'hybridity tensions positioning protocol' (HTPP). In the following sections we will briefly outline the conceptual foundations, the premises and the basic mechanisms of the HTPP, and then demonstrate how it has been successfully employed in UNICEF Germany's mission statement review process of 2008–09.

THE HYBRIDITY TENSIONS POSITIONING PROTOCOL

As we have argued above, two different logics – typically, the commercial and the social – are at play in hybrid organisations. Our approach is based on the view that these logics manifest themselves in, and can be tracked in terms of, four generic organisational tensions. The HTPP provides a means of enabling hybrid organisations to identify, surface and specify these tensions in a systematic and integrated manner. They can thus identify the current position of the organisation in each tension as well as reaching a decision on how they can aim at the organisation's future position with respect to each of them.

Hybrid organisations face – by design – several challenges at the organisational level and in terms of their strategic orientation. These challenges are rooted in the organisation's choice to incorporate different institutional logics and to adhere to the resulting – often divergent – institutional demands. These interrelated, simultaneous and persisting challenges have been conceptualised and catalogued in terms of four generic tensions manifested in organisational activities (Smith and Lewis, 2011; Smith et al., 2013):

- 'Performing tensions' are the result of the existence of competing goals and objectives for a pluralistic stakeholder base. Hybrid organisations typically pursue goals and objectives from commercial as well as social domains. These give rise to the prevalent tensions that are the result of an organisation's attempt to adhere to them simultaneously.
- 'Organising tensions' are the consequence of the choices made by hybrid organisations in designing the structures and processes they adopt as a means of pursuing their strategic goals. Since the organisational goals are often the cause of tensions, the resulting design choices are too.
- 'Belonging tensions' stem from different – and sometimes divergent – organisational identity beliefs which are the result not only of competing goals rooted in different institutional logics but also of the bias towards specific logics based on different professional backgrounds and commitments.
- 'Learning tensions' are the result of different priorities about time horizons for an organisation's knowledge base. Typically this is a choice between an emphasis on exploiting the existing knowledge base now and exploring and extending the knowledge base for tomorrow.

The HTPP operationalises the two logics as the inner and outer ring of concentric circles where the centre of the circle represents a pure social logic and the circle's maximum periphery represents a pure commercial logic (there are five intermediate options between these extreme endpoints). It also presents the four domains of the tensions listed above as the four quadrants of the circle. These key features are presented as Figure 22.1.

While we suggest that the two logics and the four tensions apply across the board, each organisation can define three to four tensions in each of the quadrants that are specific to

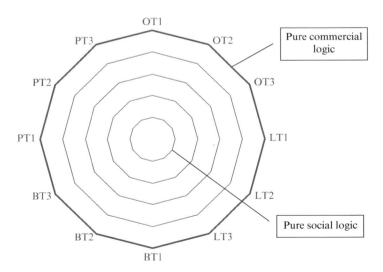

Note: PT = performing tension; OT = organising tension; BT = belonging tension; LT = learning tension.

Figure 22.1   Hybridity tensions: generic logic

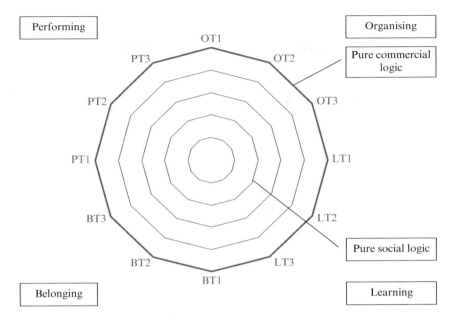

Figure 22.2   Hybridity tensions: four domains

that organisation. In this way, the HTPP enables organisational members to acknowledge, surface, identify and specify which three or four tensions are the most significant in each of the four domains (see Figure 22.2).

Once the hybridity tensions for the specific organisation have been identified, calibrated and localised, organisational members now decide on the organisation's future position-ing with respect to each tension. This positioning – either closer to the centre, and thus to the social logic, or closer to the peripheral ring, and thus to the commercial logic – could involve discussing and exploring all of the three or four most prevalent tensions in each of the four domains. The positioning will be facilitated by the use of the five intermedi-ate positions between the end points of each logic. The result of this process will be an organisation-specific hybridity 'map' which includes the future positioning aspiration for each of the tensions and quadrants (see Figure 22.3).

In order to carry out a review of the mission statement this positioning needs to take place in three steps:

- Firstly, the organisation can map its current positioning ('as is') on the localised hybridity tensions positioning protocol to gain a first round of review results and outcomes that will be manifested in an agreed and aggregated positioning of 'now'.
- Secondly, the organisation can then identify its future positioning ('to be') for each tension.
- Thirdly, the differences in current and future positioning can be clearly identified and can be used to revise the mission statement and/or take appropriate organisa-tional action to align current and future positioning.

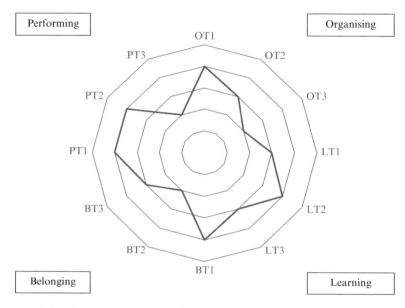

Figure 22.3   Hybridity tensions: example

Each future hybrid positioning choice (4x3 in our generic example in Figure 22.3) provides the basis for a corresponding paragraph in the revised mission statement that justifies and specifies this future positioning choice. Thus, the HTPP does not quasi-automatically produce a mission statement, but systematically explores the relevant hybridity tensions that in turn are then deployed as the backbone of an effective, relevant and actionable mission statement. In the next section, we will demonstrate the HTPP 'in action' by exemplifying how it has been employed in UNICEF Germany's mission statement review process of 2008–09.

THE HTPP IN ACTION: UNICEF GERMANY'S MISSION REVIEW PROCESS

In this section we demonstrate how the hybridity tensions positioning protocol (HTPP) has been effectively employed in the review process for the mission statement of UNICEF's National Committee in Germany (henceforth UNICEF Germany) in order to mitigate and guard against mission drift. UNICEF Germany is the local branch of the United Nations Children's Fund, a children's rights organisation which aims at leveraging political support and resources to improve the situation of children world-wide. On the one hand it strives to maximise financial resources through systematic and structured fundraising activities, corporate partnering and the sales of products such as greeting cards. On the other hand, it aims at engaging civil society at large and is an advocate of children's rights to the public. It has close to 90 employees in its Cologne-based headquarters and deploys 175 local volunteer teams. During Christmas peak time in 2012, 8000 volunteers generated a total turnover of €84 million (UNICEF Germany, 2018).

Although legally a charitable association, UNICEF Germany qualifies as a hybrid organisation. Since its foundation in the 1950s it has combined a strong commercial logic (raising funds, selling greeting cards, partnerships with corporations) with a social welfare logic (civil society engagement, advocating child rights to public and policy-makers). Furthermore, its hybridity is visible at various levels, for instance in the different practices of its three core business processes (marketing and fundraising; volunteer management; advocacy and information); in the composition of its top management team (the backgrounds of its five members include social work, journalism, management consultancy, marketing and accounting); and in the composition of its board (12 members with backgrounds including media, business, policy and legal experience).

The need for a substantive review of UNICEF Germany's mission statement occurred in 2007–08 when the then CEO and the then chair of the board disagreed on how to deal with a potential case of mission drift. The turnover of the organisation had grown substantially during the CEO's close to 20-year-long tenure and he had deployed several initiatives based on the practices of commercial logic. For her part, the chair of the board felt that these practices amounted to mission drift. A whistleblower passed the information about the internal disagreement on to the press, which scandalised those practices as misappropriation of funds. Even though an investigation by the management consultants KPMG and the public authorities did not find any legal misconduct, both the CEO and the chair resigned, and this paved the way for the appointment of a new CEO and the reconstitution of the board. But the damage had been done. Loss of external legitimacy as the result of media coverage of the disagreement had led to a net decrease in donations of 30 per cent for 2008. Damage to the organisation's legitimacy also led to internal repercussions, with both staff and volunteers seeking a reconciliation and reconfirmation of UNICEF Germany's *raison d'être*.

Within a broader team of pro bono consultants (including among others Roland Berger Strategy Consultants, Ernst & Young and Freshfields Legal Advisors), one of the authors of this chapter was mandated with the task of designing and delivering an inclusive mission statement review process that was considered the first building block of regaining internal and external legitimacy in UNICEF Germany's key constituencies. The other author acted as a non-participant observer to the process. Based on a mandate by the interim CEO and newly formed board, we started our analysis in September 2008 and carried out more than 25 interviews and a set of seven HTPP-based workshops with the board, top management team, staff and volunteers in order to provide the board with the draft of an HTPP-based map and mission statement in June 2009.

Using the HTPP we started by systematically identifying and surfacing the fundamental tensions within UNICEF Germany by interviewing all members of the top management team and the board as well as other selected members of the organisation. From this we identified a set of ten fundamental tensions validated by key organisational members that we deemed indicative of UNICEF's hybrid nature. These ten tensions were then grouped into four broad clusters (performing, organising, belonging and learning) and each tension was expressed in the form of a continuum with two endpoints, each representing either a pure commercial logic or a pure social welfare logic position. We then conducted HTPP workshops with each of the stakeholder groups (board plus top management; full-time staff; volunteers), in which we asked the participants to position the organisation with respect to each of these tensions. We asked them, firstly, how they perceived the current positions in the organisations; and secondly, how they would suggest the organisation needed to position itself in each tension in the future. Finally we integrated and consolidated the individual workshop results into a report to the board. This in turn went through the same exercise, but with the advantage of knowing how the other stakeholder groups had voted. The board then made the decision on how to position the organisation within each hybridity tension and took this finding as the basis for revising the mission statement accordingly.

In each of the workshops, participants were asked to discuss and then identify the organisation's current position in each tension. Then, in a second step, each group had to formulate a joint suggestion for how they wished to position the organisation in the future, again for each tension. Those discussions brought to the table not only explicit, but very often also implicit, assumptions about performing, organising, belonging and learning within UNICEF. In the final workshop with the board and top management, the results of all four stakeholder groups were presented to the top management team and the board. Not surprisingly, the positioning by the different groups varied quite substantially. The top management team and the board then took strategic decisions – based on the assessments of the different groups – about the current positioning ('Who are we now?') and the future positioning ('Who do we want to be in the future?') for each tension. In some cases, they followed the majority of votes but in other cases they made a decision based on their own positioning of the organisation.

Figure 22.4 provides an illustration of this final stage by showing how staff (triangle) and volunteers (square) wished to position the organisation in the future, and how subsequently and after a long discussion the board's decision was made (circle). Overall the board evaluated the current and future positioning of UNICEF Germany in the respective tensions as per Table 22.1.

The final figures portray the current (Figure 22.5) and future positioning (Figure 22.6) of UNICEF Germany within the four domains of hybridity tensions. As we have indicated above, they are to be read as follows: (1) the closer the organisation has been positioned towards the centre of the figure, the greater the emphasis it has attributed to

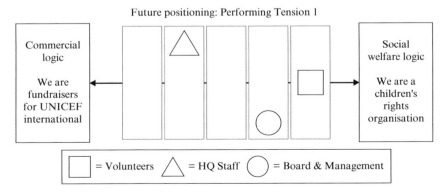

Figure 22.4   Single hybridity tension positioning across stakeholders in UNICEF (example)

Table 22.1   Hybridity tension positioning protocol as per UNICEF Germany's board in June 2009

Type/No. of tension	Hybridity tension statement (commercial vs. social logic)		Positioning by the board (today vs. future)	
	Commercial logic endpoint	Social logic endpoint	Today's position	Future position
Performing 1	We are fundraisers for UNICEF International	We are children's rights advocates	Balanced	. . . children's rights advocates (S>C)
Performing 2	We raise funds with every mean possible	We raise funds based on explicit ethical norms	Balanced	. . . strict ethical norms (S>C)
Belonging 1	Employees as means to reach organisational goals	Employees as co-activists	Balanced	. . . as co-activists (S>C)
Belonging 2	We are driven by full-time staff	We are driven by volunteers	. . . driven by full-time staff	Balanced
Belonging 3	Volunteers are our local sales channel	Volunteers are carriers of our social mission	. . . sales channel	Balanced
Organising 1	We invest in a professional infrastructure	We work very economically	Professional infrastructure	Professional infrastructure (C>S)
Organising 2	Decisions are made at the top	Decisions are made by all	Balanced	. . . at the top (C>S)
Organising 3	Board closely monitors operations	Board as overall 'guardian of its mission'	. . . closely monitors operations	Balanced
Organising 4	We inform in a measured and audience-oriented way	We inform with unlimited transparency	. . . with unlimited transparency	. . . in a measured way (C>S)
Learning 1	We seek new opportunities	We operate on established practices	. . . on established practices	. . . new opportunities (C>S)

social logic; and (2) the closer it has been positioned towards the peripheral rings, the greater the emphasis has been placed on commercial logic.

Overall, the table together with the current and future positioning within the hybridity tensions shown in Figures 22.5 and 22.6 indicates that UNICEF Germany's board has attempted to position the organisation in a way that has created a balance between the two logics, although not in a simple arithmetical formula. As the graphical representation clearly shows, for instance, they saw the need for moving closer to the social logic in terms of 'performing' and 'belonging', while retaining or extending the commercial logic in the 'organising' and 'learning' domains.

Drawing on the detailed ten-item hybridity tensions positioning outcome the board

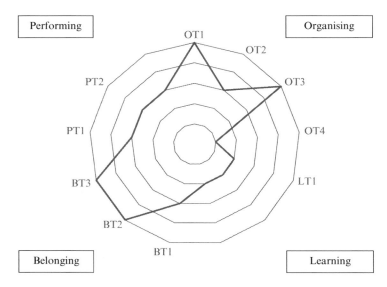

Figure 22.5   UNICEF current

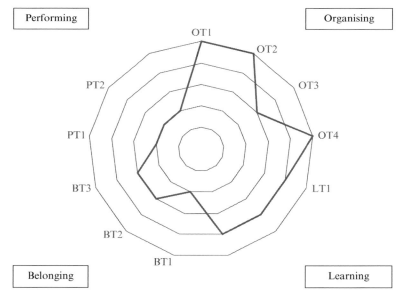

Figure 22.6   UNICEF future

used each positioning choice to formulate, justify and specify in a paragraph how and why this positioning would be crucial for the accomplishment of UNICEF Germany's mission. The effectiveness of the HTPP and the mission statement on which it had been formulated and implemented was validated by a survey in 2013 of 745 volunteers and 40 members of staff. More than 80 per cent of both groups reported that they identified with and were strongly inspired by the new mission statement. And the vast majority of the team leaders reported that the members of their teams knew of the statement and seemed to find it a source of guidance as they went about their daily tasks.

DISCUSSION AND CONCLUSION

We set out to explore how hybrid organisations could effectively guard against mission drift and the possibility of internal and external damage to the organisation; internal damage took the form of a loss of commitment to its members and their sense of coherence, while external damage took the form of risking a loss of legitimacy from key constituents and the consequent threat to provide the necessary resources. We observed that the fundamental challenge for hybrid organisations was to integrate different, often competing, institutional logics in the same organisation. This leads to struggles at various levels (Reay and Hinings, 2009). On a strategic level we found that a key characteristic of hybridity was the need for a mission that provides the normative framework for an organisation's *raison d'être*. Mission statements are crucial to the strategic development of hybrid organisations with their strong sense of social mission. They can help them to accomplish the overall achievement of the mission and thus assist the organisation to avoid – or, at least, mitigate – the problems of mission drift.

We propose a systematic review of a hybrid organisation's mission statement that proactively deploys its hybridity in general and its hybridity tensions in particular. We suggest that the hybridity tensions positioning protocol should be used as an instrument for effective guidance in a mission statement review process. Based on Smith and Lewis's (2011) typology of tensions (performing, organising, belonging and learning), the HTPP requires a hybrid organisation to identify and specify for each of these four domains the three to four most prevalent tensions that typically arise between a commercial and a social logic at play in hybrid organisations. Each of these tensions is to be assessed in terms of how organisational members evaluate its current position within each tension, followed by and juxtaposed with the way in which they aspire to a future position of them. The resulting HTPP maps the 10–12 most relevant future positioning tensions and serves as the structural backbone for the revision of the mission statement. Each future positioning decision is specified, justified and elaborated in a paragraph of the revised mission statement. We used the mission review process of UNICEF Germany 2008–09 as an example of this approach, and argue that using the HTPP has been effective and, according to a recent survey, sustainable.

The HTPP has both practical and conceptual advantages. Practically, it provides a theory-based but yet user-friendly framework to acknowledge, identify, surface, explore and systematically evaluate the relevant hybridity dimensions of a hybrid organisation. As one top manager from UNICEF Germany confirmed: 'just the fact to name, render visible and discussable our most pressing tensions was a contribution in and of itself'. Its easy-to-use appeal will help practitioners to produce usable outcomes. While the HTPP itself does not produce a revised mission statement, it can provide a much more nuanced, detailed and thus effective structural backbone for a mission statement, and one that is that is firmly rooted in the organisation's hybridity tensions as they are actually perceived by organisational members.

The HTPP operates on the basis of a general framework of tensions (Smith and Lewis, 2011; Smith et al., 2013) but is a context-sensitive framework that does not force any prefabricated categories onto the organisation. The four domains of tension (performing, organising, belonging and learning) are generic enough to be addressed through organisation-specific tensions and items that are deemed relevant to organisational members. And the fact that an organisation might identify few or no items in some of the four domains of tension can also provide a productive opportunity for critical reflection. In UNICEF Germany, for example, the aspect of learning and innovation had been somewhat neglected. As a result the organisation has made an effort to explore this dimension further and in more detail by allocating corresponding resources to product and service development initiatives.

As well as producing outcomes of this kind, the HTPP is also valuable as a means of addressing the value of its inclusive ethos. We found that it provided an effective and structured way of including the relevant stakeholders and constituencies of an organisation in exploring its tensions in a participatory process. The socialisation taking place between organisational members of different background played a central role for avoiding internal conflict and for rendering inherent tensions productive rather than destructive (Battilana et al., 2015). The brevity of the 8–10 month process used in UNICEF Germany might be seen as a limitation, but the systematic approach of the HTPP together with its participatory ethos, we argue, has had an effective and sustainable impact on the organisation.

The hybridity tensions positioning protocol is not only a practical tool but can also be employed conceptually to map the hybridity status of an organisation. Social impact advisors or impact investors, for example, might use the HTPP in their 'due diligence' to identify and classify the ways in which an organisation operates as a hybrid form, as well its ability to understand and acknowledge its hybrid nature. Both of these approaches could provide important insights for any decisions about the allocation of resources.

A final question for us refers not so much to the 'how' of the HTPP as to 'whether' or 'when' it might be deployed. Our view is that hybrids are well advised to engage in a process of regularly reviewing their mission. How often they should undertake a review of this kind depends on a number of factors. Firstly, we suggest that successful hybrids should review their mission statement sooner rather than later; success can gloss over the risk of mission drift, as the example of the microfinance institution Compartamos shows. And a hybrid that has been stable over a certain length of time might find it useful to draw on the HTPP to refresh the memory of its members and constituents about their organisation's *raisons d'être*. Secondly, there are different levels of hybridity in hybrid organisations and the value of a regular mission review process becomes greater as the degree of hybridity increases. Last but not least, the decision to engage in a structured mission review process is influenced by the volatility of an organisation's internal and external environments. As we saw in UNICEF Germany, what started out as an internal debate on the organisation's identity quickly turned into a public evaluation of the organisation's legitimacy.

Conceptually, the HTPP provides a translation and operationalisation of Smith and Lewis's theorised tensions (Smith and Lewis, 2011) for practical purposes. While Smith and Lewis propose a rather symmetrical model of organisational tensions, the HTPP also accounts for asymmetrical constellations which can be visualised (and potentially worked out). Thus, the HTPP process represents a 'space of negotiation', an arena of interaction allowing members to discover, picture and discuss the trade-offs that they face (Battilana et al., 2015). Such spaces of negotiation can – if used effectively – maintain a productive tension in hybrid organisations. The HTPP does not make tensions disappear but rather contributes to transforming potential conflict into productive tensions. Thus, if mobilised effectively, hybridity does not necessarily or exclusively imply a strategic challenge to an organisation. In fact, the social complexity and causal ambiguity of hybrid organisational arrangements can also provide them with aspects of a strategic capability. For example, such organisations might be able to strategically evoke and utilise different institutional logics in negotiations with different external stakeholders (banks, public authorities, charities, and so on) to reach their goals, since those logics are present in-house. Furthermore, a process that brings hidden and oftentimes neglected tensions to the surface might also spur an organisation's innovativeness. Organisational members with different professional backgrounds, from different organisational departments, who successfully negotiated a shared sense of 'who we are as an organisation' might be better able to jointly develop innovative solutions (for example, a technical solution to a social problem) compared to a homogenous workforce (Canales, 2014).

While we acknowledge the HTPP's limitations, we believe that it provides a conceptually grounded, context-sensitive and effective means of keeping track of a hybrid organisation's mission. Thus, the application of the HTPP not only effectively safeguards the organisation from risking mission drift, but it also it creates a mutual understanding which ideally contributes to avoiding internal conflict and helps to transform inherent structural tensions into strategic capabilities.

REFERENCES

APOPO (2018). Speeding up landmine detection. Retrieved 30 May 2018 from https://www.apopo.org/en/what-we-do/detecting-landmines-and-explosives/how-we-do-it.

Aubert, C., de Janvry, A., and Sadoulet, E. (2009). Designing credit agent incentives to prevent mission drift in pro-poor microfinance institutions. *Journal of Development Economics*, 90(1), 153–162.

Austin, J., Stevenson, H., and Wei-Skillern, J. (2006). Social and commercial entrepreneurship: same, different, or both? *Entrepreneurship Theory and Practice*, 30(1), 1–22.

Bartkus, D., Glassman, M., and Bruce McAfee, R. (2000). Mission statements: are they smoke and mirrors? *Business Horizons*, 43(6), 23–28.

Battilana, J., and Dorado, S. (2010). Building sustainable hybrid organisations: the case of commercial microfinance organisations. *Academy of Management Journal*, 53(6), 1419–1440.

Battilana, J., and Lee, M. (2014). Advancing research on hybrid organizing – insights from the study of social enterprises. *Academy of Management Annals*, 8(1), 397–441.

Battilana, J., Sengul, M., Pache, A.-C., and Model, J. (2015). Harnessing productive tensions in hybrid organizations: the case of work integration social enterprises. *Academy of Management Journal*, 58(6), 1658–1685. doi:10.5465/amj.2013.0903.

Besharov, M.L., and Smith, W.K. (2013). Multiple institutional logics in organizations: explaining their varied nature and implications. *Academy of Management Review*, 39(3), 364–381.

Canales, R. (2014). Weaving straw into gold: managing organizational tensions between standardization and flexibility in microfinance. *Organization Science*, 25(1), 1–28. doi:10.1287/orsc.2013.0831.

Dees, G.J. (2012). A tale of two cultures: charity, problem solving, and the future of social entrepreneurhip. *Journal of Business Ethics*, 111(3), 321–334.

Dialogue Social Enterprise (2018). About – Exhibition. Retrieved 30 May 2018 from http://www.dialogue-in-the-dark.com/about/exhibition/.

DiMaggio, P.J., and Powell, W.W. (1983). The iron cage revisited: institutional isomorphism and collective rationality in organizational fields. *American Sociological Review*, 48(2), 147–160.

Drucker, P.F. (1990). *Managing the Nonprofit Organisation*, New York: Harper-Collins.

Emerson, J. (2003). The blended value proposition: integrating social and financial returns. *California Management Review*, 45(4), 35–51.

Fowler, A. (2000). NGDOs as a moment in history: beyond aid to social entrepreneurship or civic innovation? *Third World Quarterly*, 21(4), 637–654.

Glynn, M.A. (2000). When cymbals become symbols: conflict over organisational identity within a symphony orchestra. *Organisation Science*, 11(3), 285–298.

Golden-Biddle, K., and Rao, H. (1997). Breaches in the board room: organisational identity and conflict of commitment in a non-profit organisation. *Organisation Science*, 8(6), 593–611.

Greenwood, R., Raynard, M., Kodeih, F., Micelotta, E.R., and Lounsbury, M. (2011). Institutional complexity and organizational responses. *Academy of Management Annals*, 5(1), 317–371.

Haigh, N., and Hoffman, A.J. (2012). Hybrid organisations: the next chapter of sustainable business. *Organisational Dynamics*, 41(2), 126–134.

Jarzabkowski, P., and Lê, J.K. (2017). Why we have to do this. *Organization Studies*, 38(3–4), 433–462.

Jay, J. (2013). Navigating paradox as a mechanism of change and innovation in hybrid organisations. *Academy of Management Journal*, 56(1), 137–159.

Johnson, G., Scholes, S., and Whittington, R. (2008). *Exploring Corporate Strategy*, Harlow: Pearson Education.

Kraatz, M.S., and Block, E.S. (2008). Organisational implications of institutional pluralism. In Greenwood, R., Oliver, C., Sahlin-Andersson, K., and Suddaby, R. (eds), *The Handbook of Organisational Institutionalism*, London: SAGE Publications.

Mair, J., and Martí, I. (2006). Social entrepreneurship research: a source of explanation, prediction, and delight. *Journal of World Business*, 41(1), 36–44. doi:10.1016/j.jwb.2005.09.002.

Makadok, R. (2001). Toward a synthesis of the resource-based and dynamic-capability views of rent creation. *Strategic Management Journal*, 22(5), 387–401.

Pache, A.-C., and Santos, F. (2010). When worlds collide: the internal dynamics of organisational responses to conflicting institutional demands. *Academy of Management Review*, 35(3), 455–476.

Pache, A.-C., and Santos, F. (2013). Inside the hybrid organisation: selective coupling as a response to competing institutional logics. *Academy of Management Journal*, 56(4), 972–1001.

Pfeffer, J., and Salancik, G.R. (1978). *The External Control of Organizations: A Resource Dependence Perspective*, New York: Harper & Row.

Poling, A., Weetjens, B.J., Cox, C., Mgode, G., Jubitana, M., Kazwala, R., et al. (2010). Using Giant African Pouched Rats to detect tuberculosis in human sputum samples: 2009 findings. *American Journal of Tropical Medicine and Hygiene*, 83(6), 1308–1310. doi:10.4269/ajtmh.2010.10-0180.

Reay, T., and Hinings, R.C.R. (2009). Managing the rivalry of competing institutional logics. *Organization Studies*, 30(6), 629–652.

Saerberg, S. (2007). The dining in the dark phenomenon. *Disability Studies Quarterly*, 27(3). http://dsq-sds.org/article/view/24/24.

Santos, F., Pache, A.C., and Birkholz, C. (2015). Making hybrids work: aligning business models and organizational design for social enterprises. *California Management Review*, 57(3), 36–58.

SEKEM (2018). The idea of holistic sustainable development. Retrieved 30 May 2018 from http://www.sekem.com/en/about/.

Smith, W.K., and Lewis, M.W. (2011). Toward a theory of paradox: a dynamic equilibrium model of organizing. *Academy of Management Review*, 36(2), 381–403.

Smith, W.K., and Tushman, M.L. (2005). Managing strategic contradictions: a top management model for managing innovation streams. *Organization Science*, 16(5), 522–536. doi:10.1287/orsc.1050.0134.

Smith, W.K., Gonin, M., and Besharov, M.L. (2013). Managing social–business tensions: a review and research agenda for social enterprise. *Business Ethics Quarterly*, 3(3), 407–442.

UNICEF Germany (2018). Über uns. Retrieved 30 May 2018 from https://www.unicef.de/informieren/ueber-uns/unicef-deutschland.

Yunus, M., Moingeon, B., and Lehmann-Ortega, L. (2010). Building social business models: lessons from the Grameen experience. *Long Range Planning*, 43(2/3), 308–325.

23. Building legitimacy for hybrid organisations
Benjamin Huybrechts, Julie Rijpens, Aurélie Soetens and Helen Haugh

INTRODUCTION AND CONTEXT

Hybrid organisations are 'organizations that combine institutional logics in unprecedented ways' (Battilana and Dorado, 2010, p. 1419; Scott, 2001); they thus bring together logics from different, and often conflicting, fields into a singular organisational form. Social enterprises, for example, are typical hybrids that combine economic, social and environmental goals (Battilana and Lee, 2014; Billis, 2010; Doherty et al., 2014) and have been found to operate successfully in diverse sectors such as microfinance (Battilana and Dorado, 2010), fair trade (Huybrechts, 2012) and work integration (Pache and Santos, 2013). Although exploiting business methods to address social or environmental problems might suggest an organisational model that combines the best of both worlds, categorical confusion has been found to limit an organisation's access to resources and negatively impact upon long-term survival (Tracey et al., 2011).

Hybridity in organisations is not a new phenomenon (Billis, 2010), but interest in innovative organisational models that facilitate the achievement of double, or triple, bottom lines has recently flourished in response to global sustainability challenges (Hoffman et al., 2012). Hybrid organisations, however, face legitimacy challenges in that they are: (1) difficult to categorise within established organisational taxonomies (Aldrich and Fiol, 1994; Suchman, 1995); and (2) held to account to multiple institutional demands by audiences that use different and possibly contradictory legitimation criteria (Kraatz and Block, 2008). In turn the credibility of their claims of commitment to different sets of standards may be deemed to be unconvincing. Securing the conferment of legitimacy from stakeholders is therefore an important challenge facing hybrid organisations. Previous research, however, has not investigated the activities required to build legitimacy when an organisational form bridges two or more institutional categories.

The empirical data used in this research is drawn from an analysis of the establishment of a network of community-owned renewable energy (RE) co-operatives across Europe: REScoop.eu. This chapter proceeds in four sections. The first reviews the literature relating to legitimacy and new hybrid organisations. The next section presents our methods and results. We then identify four legitimacy-building activities of hybrid organisations: critiquing, proposing, advocating and communicating. In the final section we discuss our model and its implications for practice.

SOME LITERATURE

Organisational Legitimacy

Legitimacy is a critical survival factor for organisations (Kraatz and Block, 2008) and is highly contingent on the institutional fields in which they operate (DiMaggio and Powell, 1983; Meyer and Rowan, 1977). Isomorphism explains how the environment in which organisations are embedded leads them to adopt dominant models of organising, processes and practices (DiMaggio and Powell, 1983; Meyer and Rowan, 1977). These dominant behaviours persist even when evidence of their efficacy is lacking (Meyer and Rowan, 1977) because they confer legitimacy on those organisations that follow the behavioural patterns of others in the field. Compliance with regulations, norms and taken-for-granted ways of doing business – that is, behaving as others do – leads to 'social acceptability and credibility' (Scott, 2001, p. 58). For example, as managers of corporations have a fiduciary responsibility to shareholders, the dominant norm in business is shareholder primacy, and corporations that do not comply with these rules and expectations face legitimacy challenges. Therefore, in order for new organisational forms to emerge they have to acquire legitimacy (Aldrich and Fiol, 1994), the crux of which is social acceptance and credibility.

Legitimacy has received an increasing amount of attention since the 1970s as scholars sought to understand how organisations emerge and survive in different environments (see Deephouse and Suchman, 2008, for a review). Suchman defines legitimacy as the 'generalized perception or assumption that the actions of an entity are desirable, proper, or appropriate within some socially constructed system of norms, values, beliefs, and definitions' (Suchman, 1995, p. 574). Several types of legitimacies can be distinguished: pragmatic (or regulative), normative (or moral) and cognitive.

Pragmatic (or regulative) legitimacy is secured by compliance with laws and rules (Scott, 2001; Suchman, 1995). For social enterprise hybrids the decision concerning the legal model to adopt (for example, charity, co-operative, business, and so on) has important implications for their access to capital and governance structure. In contrast to corporate structures, charities are barred from raising share capital and have stringent reporting responsibilities.

Normative (or moral) legitimacy is conferred when organisations comply with societal expectations about their behaviour (Scott, 2001; Suchman, 1995). Expectations about appropriate behaviour are less clear for new categories of organisations than for established categories (Lee and Pennings, 2002; McKendrick and Carroll, 2001; Fiol and Romanelli, 2012). Which organisational form is associated with, or 'morally favoured' for, the achievement of specific goals is made difficult when goals from more than one category are pursued by a single organisational type. By combining the goals and logics of different categories, social enterprise hybrids bridge existing categories in unprecedented ways and in so doing create categorical confusion. One type of normative legitimacy that is of particular interest here is structural legitimacy, when 'audiences see the organisation as valuable and worthy of support because its structural characteristics locate it within a morally favored taxonomic category' (Suchman, 1995, p. 581). Structural legitimacy signals that an organisation 'is acting on collectively valued purposes in a proper and adequate manner'. Structural characteristics are thus important signals in locating 'the organisation within a larger institutional ecology and thereby determining with whom it will compete and from whom it will draw support' (Suchman, 1995, p. 581). The struggle to achieve legitimacy is manifest in efforts to raise awareness of the distinctive characteristics of the new organisational form (Tracey et al., 2011).

Finally, cognitive legitimacy concerns how organisations draw on cultural understandings to make sense of their environment (Aldrich and Fiol, 1994; Scott, 2001; Suchman, 1995) and become embedded in the taken-for-granted assumptions about a category. To become taken-for-granted the characteristics and behaviours of organisations need to be understood by audiences that have the capacity to confer legitimacy. For example, investors need to understand the goals and functioning of an organisation to decide whether it is an adequate recipient of their investment objectives.

Hybrid Organisations

When new organisational models emerge they lack structural legitimacy and suffer from the liability of newness (Aldrich and Fiol, 1994). As their structural features are not aligned with existing taxonomies, new organisational models need to find ways to build their legitimacy in order to develop and survive (Aldrich and Fiol, 1994). According to Suchman, gaining legitimacy is achieved in three different ways: (1) by adapting to the immediate environment; (2) by choosing an environment in which the new organisational model fits; or (3) by manipulating the environment in a way that makes the new form more acceptable. For social enterprise hybrids, adapting to the immediate environment would involve focusing on either social purpose or financial sustainability and thus imply relinquishing their hybridity. Finding a new environment would also be problematical as their emergence is predicated on their position between existing domains. Therefore, influencing the environment in which they are located may be the only course of action available to build legitimacy in the long term.

Actively seeking to manipulate the environment to develop support for a new organisational form requires both entrepreneurial and innovative behaviour (Suchman, 1995) that blends existing frames into novel combinations. How this is achieved in practice leads to a paradoxical situation in which new organisational forms strive to manage both their inherent distinctiveness and at least some conformity with established institutional expectations (Navis and Glynn, 2011; Santos and Eisenhardt, 2009). New organisational forms may thus seek legitimacy by borrowing behaviours from existing institutional repertoires, creating new behaviours, or combining elements of both the old and the new (Lee and Pennings, 2002; McKendrick and Carroll, 2001; Fiol and Romanelli, 2012).

The challenge of gaining legitimacy is even more pressing for hybrid organisations that bridge different fields and thus combine logics and structural elements from different and contrasting organisational categories (Tracey et al., 2011). In addition to managing different logics within the organisation (Pache and Santos, 2013), hybrid organisations need to garner support, and secure legitimacy, from multiple external audiences (Kraatz and Block, 2008). Moreover, hybrid organisations often emerge in the context or at the intersection of emerging fields, which further exposes the ambiguity concerning appropriate patterns of behaviour (Santos and Eisenhardt, 2009). Hence, sources of legitimation are likely to be both multiple and weakly structured (Aldrich and Fiol, 1994; Navis and Glynn, 2011). Novel hybrid organisations thus face 'the double challenge of having to survive as new ventures while striking a delicate balance between the [different] logics they combine . . . so as to avoid mission drift' (Battilana and Dorado, 2010, p. 1419). As social enterprise hybrids do not naturally fit into the dominant categories of the socio-economic landscape (Battilana and Lee, 2014; Billis, 2010; Doherty et al., 2014), multi-level legitimation strategies and institutional work (Tracey et al., 2011) may be the only course of action to build legitimacy and become institutions in their own right (Kraatz and Block, 2008). This chapter examines the legitimacy-building efforts of a federation of renewable energy co-operatives established to promote the development of the REScoop model.

THE RESEARCH

REScoops and the REScoop.eu Federation

Renewable energy (RE) emerged within the domain of energy production in the 1970s (Sine and Lee, 2009). Since then the RE sector has developed rapidly due to technological improvements and public awareness of climate change. Since the opening of the energy production and supply markets, the landscape has diversified away from dominance by monopolistic public corporations to now include large corporations, small and medium-sized enterprises; public authorities at the local, regional and national levels; individual households; and citizen-based co-operatives.

Energy co-operatives have operated in Italy, Austria and the United States since the beginning of the 20th century; however, their engagement with RE is more recent (Weismeier-Sammer and Reiner, 2011). In Europe, RE co-operatives are known as REScoops (Renewable Energy Source co-operatives) and, as 'environmental social enterprises' (Huybrechts and Mertens, 2014; Vickers and Lyon, 2012), they can be seen as hybrid organisations combining economic, social and community, and environmental goals, and thus blending elements from different forms related to domains of business, community and environmental action. REScoops have been developing thanks to several factors (Huybrechts and Mertens, 2014): the response to the public suspicion that larger energy producers earn high profit margins from the sale of green energy; the willingness of consumers to control the source of the energy they consume; and the generation of 100 per cent 'green origin' energy, which has attracted support from both ecologically minded consumers and environmental non-governmental organisations (NGOs). In addition, through sharing ownership, decision-making and profit allocation among citizens, REScoops have been instrumental in reducing community resistance to RE generation facilities, typically seen in protests against the erection of onshore wind farms (Weismeier-Sammer and Reiner, 2011).

Despite the consumer, environmental and societal benefits of community-owned RE generation, REScoops face several barriers that hinder their growth, in particular difficult access to capital from members and bank loans, as well as low recognition by public authorities and RE stakeholders (Huybrechts and Mertens, 2014). For example, REScoops reported difficulties in securing funding from banks and investors (citizens) because of a perceived ambiguity of the REScoop form and associated practices such as the collective dimension of management and limits on profit distribution. Similarly, REScoops found themselves located in between some of the categories described in several legal texts. Because they were not profit-maximising shareholder-owned firms, they were not allowed to engage in certain activities (typically, electricity supply) in several countries. On the other hand, because they were engaged in economic activities, they often did not qualify as community-representing groups in the context of citizen consultations. In brief, all REScoop founders related detailed anecdotes of poor understanding of their multidimensional nature when seeking the support of given stakeholders. These barriers are indicative of regulatory, normative and cognitive legitimacy struggles that hinder the diffusion of the REScoop model.

To tackle this problem and advance the recognition and support (that is, the legitimacy) of REScoops, informal networking and experience sharing began in 2009, when individual REScoops and established co-operative groups collaborated to promote the REScoop model. The network was formalised in 2011 with the establishment of the REScoop.eu federation and its registration in 2013 as a Belgian non-profit organisation. At the founding in 2011, it brought together ten pioneer REScoops from different countries (Belgium, France, Italy, Germany, the United Kingdom and the Netherlands) and several national and European Union (EU)-level co-operative and RE-supporting structures. Membership of the federation has increased steadily since its inception. From 2011 to 2013, the founding group of ten pioneer REScoops was increased to more than 1500 organisations registered either directly or indirectly through their national federations. Moreover, 11 new REScoops were created directly in the context of the first project and 27 existing projects were scaled up.

In 2012, REScoop.eu secured EU funding for a three-year project called 'REScoop 20-20-20' aimed at promoting the REScoop model and supporting new citizen-led groups to set up co-operatives. Furthermore, REScoop.eu gradually gained endorsements from numerous RE stakeholders, for example environmental NGOs (such as Greenpeace), climate change and energy transition networks, local public authorities (such as the European 'Covenant of Mayors' network) and co-operative and social enterprise federations (including Cooperatives Europe). As a result of European funding and the support of Cooperatives Europe, the federation was able to hire two managers who had previously worked for a pioneer Belgian REScoop. The board of directors is made of representatives of the founding pioneers and also includes two associated networks.

Finally, there is tangible evidence of increasing recognition over time of REScoop.eu by public authorities, RE corporations and the media. Federation representatives have been invited to debates, seminars and meetings hosted by a broad array of stakeholders including the European Parliament, European Commission, environmental NGOs, co-operatives, and RE industry associations (such as the European Wind Energy Association, EWEA). Throughout the REScoop 20-20-20 project, federation representatives were received in an official capacity by five different EU commissioners, three members of the European Parliament and numerous administration officers. Increasingly recognised as a European-level representative federation, REScoop.eu has also been contacted by the EU Commission as part of its consultations with stakeholders of the RE field. In addition, since 2012 the federation has been featured in more than 120 television media reports and newspaper articles at both the national and European levels, such as Euronews.

Data

The data for our study relies on active participation, interviews and documentary analysis. The data were collected in the context of a broader study on the roles of networks in institutionalising new hybrid organisational forms (Huybrechts and Haugh, 2018). To gain a deeper understanding of how the federation operated, two of the authors participated in the REScoop 20-20-20 project between 2010 and 2013. This provided access to information about the day-to-day activities of the federation including meetings and events. Field notes were recorded and written up daily. Sixteen semi-structured interviews were conducted with informants from the federal organisation: federation members and key actors in the field of RE (see Table 23.1). Finally, all the documents produced by the federation between 2011 and 2013, as well as all the external reports on which the federation relied to advance its claims, were examined. Tables 23.1 and 23.2 provide details of the interviews and the documents forming the basis of the empirical analysis.

THE FINDINGS

Our analysis of the data demonstrates how the discourse employed by the REScoop.eu federation used language to build legitimacy for the social enterprise hybrid through four types of discourse: critiquing, proposing, advocating and communicating.

Critiquing the Dominant Patterns of the Field

When setting up REScoop.eu, the founder members of the federation undertook a joint analysis of the key actors in the RE field and their practices to diagnose the main

Table 23.1   List of interviewees

Type of organisation	Descriptor
REScoop representatives (involved in REScoop.eu)	2 interviews in pioneer Belgian REScoop with representatives now hired directly by REScoop.eu 1 interview in emerging Belgian REScoop 2 interviews in pioneer French REScoop 1 interview in pioneer German REScoop 1 interview in pioneer Dutch REScoop 1 interview in emerging Spanish REScoop 1 interview in pioneer British REScoop 1 interview in emerging British REScoop
Other networks and support organisations	1 interview in Belgian REScoop network 1 interview in UK co-operative network 1 interview in Italian co-operative network 1 interview with EU co-operative network 1 interview with EU renewable energy think tank 1 interview with EU Commission representative

Table 23.2   List of documents produced or used by the Federation

Sources	Documents
REScoop.eu documents	REScoop.eu (2011), 'Fostering citizen involvement to reach the EU 20-20 goals', federation of citizen groups and associations for renewable energy, Brussels. REScoop.eu (2012), 'REScoop.eu European Charter', Brussels. REScoop.eu (2012), 'Report on best practices across Europe', Brussels. REScoop.eu (2013), 'Report on REScoop business models in Europe', Brussels. REScoop.eu (2013), 'Report on REScoop financial models in Europe', Brussels. REScoop.eu (2013), 'Action guide for citizen engagement in renewable energy', Brussels. REScoop.eu (2013), 'Reaction to the EU Commission's consultation on its Green Paper proposal on renewable energy', Brussels.
Reports quoted by REScoop.eu in its documents	German Wind Energy Association (2012), 'Community wind power, local energy for local people'. Northwest Sustainable Energy for Economic Development (2006), 'Community wind: an Oregon guidebook'. Green European Foundation (2012), 'Common future of Europe – future of the commons in Europe', Green Academy Programme. The Cooperative Group (2012), 'Manifesto for a community energy revolution', part of the work of the Community Energy Coalition.

areas and gaps where REScoops offered a solution. Two principal groups of actors were identified: policy-makers responsible for the laws and policies that regulate and guide the RE industry; and organisations engaged in the supply and distribution of RE.

The federation considered that the public policies were dominated by economic and, to a lesser extent, environmental concerns and pointed to the fact that issues of citizen participation, local development and access to energy were, at best, little acknowledged in the policy texts and, at worst, seen as impediments to market competition. Informants further identified two themes that constrained the long-term sustainability of current European RE policy.

European laws and policies were interpreted as favouring corporate suppliers and placing barriers in the way of the development of community-owned and citizen-led RE initiatives. For example, the aim of the European 20-20-20 strategy is to reduce carbon emissions, develop renewable energy and increase energy efficiency by 20 per cent by 2020 (European Commission, 2009). However, according to the federation, no specific measures were taken to open the energy market to smaller players and encourage citizen participation. Both the EU and national governments were criticised for not ensuring that public goods were protected from commodification and exploitation by corporations. 'Why let others seize [the wind]? In which country are 97% of the revenues from a natural resource in the hands of private investors, often based abroad? That's what is happening here with wind energy' (REScoop manager, Belgium). The perceived privileges for corporations were criticised because they ignored and hindered the development of small producers and co-operatives that together played an increasingly important role both in the energy market and as mobilisers of social capital.

The dominant policy logic was considered by the network to have been unsuccessful in creating the conditions in which a fair and open market would meet long-term energy needs. 'EU member states' governments fail to reach the EU's objectives of liberalization in terms of competitive markets, fair prices and energy independence' (funding application made by the federation).

A major area of criticism by the federation, alongside public policies perceived as unfair, was the predominance of corporations and the difficulty for communities of competing on an equal footing. As many of the corporations were owned by foreign shareholders, the federation criticised the fact that the returns on investment were expatriated and not used to benefit the communities in which energy was generated. A recent short video produced by the federation has illustrated this point using the example of the island of Sifnos in Greece (see www.REScoop.eu). Corporations involved in RE generation and distribution were also criticised for not understanding the needs and priorities of communities in which they sought to build RE energy production facilities. This in turn was manifest in resistance to corporate investment in RE production facilities:

> These guys [the corporate staff promoting RE projects] are all engineers. They believe in numbers and don't understand the social mechanisms behind resistance to windmills. They come with their expensive reports on the benefits of windmills, but they don't speak the language of the citizens. Until we can explain this to [the corporate staff], they will fail over and over again. (REScoop Founder, France)

Critiquing the dominant logics of policy-makers and corporations in the RE field is therefore one of the legitimacy-building activities developed by the network. The REScoop.eu federation has tried to pave the way for the promotion of hybrid organisations that address the shortcomings of existing RE providers and suppliers by identifying, first, how current policy failed to acknowledge that the broader economic, social and environmental focus of community-owned RE initiatives might create superior benefits when compared to corporations; and second, how the focus and ownership of corporations failed to acknowledge the needs of communities.

Proposing a New Combination of Existing Logics Through the REScoop Model

Most documents produced by the federation started by critiquing the current logics of RE policy and corporations and then moved to propose and support the diffusion of a social enterprise hybrid that combined the logic of co-operative organisations with the principles and practices of RE. The federation argued that the appropriation of the logics from two different domains would deliver more than just a blend of the two: it would reorient the co-operative commitment to the community more generally (and therefore beyond its own members) and broaden the RE focus to include political activity. '[REScoops] are redefining the boundaries between private, public and the common, mapping a new political terrain in the struggle to transform political and social relations in Europe' (informant involved in the federation).

In proposing the REScoop model the federation actively sought to reframe the cognitive parameters of the existing RE field to accommodate a new social enterprise hybrid. The blueprint for the REScoop model is defined in the Charter of Principles established by REScoop.eu. The Charter identifies four challenges to which REScoops seek to respond:

the economic (that is, energy costs and market structure), the social-community (that is, consumer access to energy, local ownership and profit appropriation), the environmental (that is, climate change) and the political (that is, energy policy and the transition to a 'post-oil' society). By defining these common challenges, principles and practices to be adopted by individual REScoops, the Charter provides a mechanism for creating a shared identity and consistency between organisations that adopt a model which builds on the experience of the pioneers who have successfully experimented with it for several decades.

The Charter and other founding documents are inspired by the co-operative movement. When appropriating the logic of co-operatives, the REScoop.eu federation emphasised alignment with the history and principles of cooperative organisations. 'Our consortium supports cooperatives with economic, environmental, social and political objectives' (federation's statutes). Yet, at the same time, they have contributed to reinterpreting the co-operative model by following its most recent evolution towards a stronger community orientation and multi-stakeholdership (Huybrechts and Mertens, 2014).

A fundamental principle of the co-operative movement is that action is oriented towards the empowerment of individuals and communities through self-help and collective action. In common with private organisations, co-operatives are market-oriented, but they also focus on generating economic and social benefits for their members and, more widely, the community in which they operate. This stands in contrast to private enterprise in which the focus is on the maximisation of financial returns to shareholders. The combination of market and community orientation is enacted through REScoop policies to promote collective ownership of RE assets, consumer access to energy regardless of ability to pay, and reinvestment of profits to further the goals of the co-operative. 'There are also social and ethical benefits to this business model in that we're involved with fairness, we have a set of principles we work by such as investment by local people, equality, open membership, democratic control, information sharing, and concern for the local community' (informant from United Kingdom REScoop).

Another important element in the co-operative model is the principle of giving support to – and receiving support from – other co-operatives. This principle is central to strengthening the performance of individual co-operative organisations as well as diffusing the co-operative model more generally. By proposing the REScoop model the federation aimed to achieve both these goals. 'REScoops are a great opportunity to show the benefits of the cooperative model and contribute to boost the cooperative renewal' (Director, European co-operative network).

A broader goal of the co-operative movement is to bring about change in the way that property is owned and used: towards a lesser concern with private ownership for personal benefit, and a greater concern with collective ownership for the benefit of society. In relation to the REScoop.eu federation this ambition is met by a political project to raise awareness of societal needs and propose a solution for a 'post-oil' society in the future. '[REScoops are] key to the success of . . . energy transition. Here, we are not only talking about a technological . . . transition, but mainly a societal one. This is where [REScoops] play a crucial role' (report quoted in the federation's 'best practices' report).

The federation has promoted REScoops as citizen-based organisations, rooted in and serving the interests of local communities, and as a viable alternative to the perceived policy-favouring of corporations. At the same time, the federation has endorsed the principles of the RE industry to which committed organisations subscribe. The main goal of the RE industry is to reduce the emission of carbon dioxide, the achievement of which necessitates measuring and monitoring carbon dioxide production, measuring and assessing consumption of carbon dioxide, and developing new and sustainable sources of energy. These principles were adopted by REScoop.eu and promoted across initiatives such as REScoop 20-20-20. In addition, the RE industry raises awareness of strategies to reduce carbon dioxide consumption through providing information to stakeholders. The federation adopted this and included appropriate guidance in its Charter of Principles. In addition, REScoop.eu worked collaboratively with environmental NGOs such as Greenpeace and national consumer associations to promote energy-efficient and energy-reducing corporate and individual behaviour.

The consistent management of RE technologies and effective contribution to reducing carbon dioxide emissions is fundamental to the verification of organisational claims and accountability to stakeholders. On that account, REScoop.eu promotes technical expertise and accountability through its Charter of Principles as well as through the network of mentors. Mentors are founders of successful REScoops who coach newer members and help them to establish their own projects and solve specific challenges. Through the mentoring system, emerging initiatives can mobilise information and support from established co-operatives.

Promoting the social enterprise hybrid model was therefore another of the legitimacy-building activities undertaken by the federation as it sought to position REScoops as a viable alternative organisational model that could respond to the critiques of the dominant RE policy logic and its corporate actors. The REScoop.eu federation appropriated the logics of co-operative organisations and the RE industry and brought them together in a social enterprise hybrid organisational form. The combination of co-operative and RE logics in this hybrid model goes beyond simply combining them, by reinterpreting and enhancing the principles to strengthen community orientation and investment in solutions for a post-oil economy. This was achieved in three ways. First, by linking the traditions of co-operatives with the future-oriented RE industry the federation proposed a novel hybrid that captured the paradoxical qualities of a stable and experienced organisational form and a modern forward-looking industry. The establishment of the REScoop.eu federation was also an opportunity to show evidence of a resurgence of interest in co-operatives – the co-operative renewal heralded by the United Nations International Year of Cooperatives (2012) – from which other co-operative networks benefited. Second, by promoting community ownership the federation aims to disperse the distribution of power generation away from the dominant large and centralised power plants to include small-scale local production. In doing so, the federation expected REScoops to contribute to stabilising the grid system of power distribution, meet local demand, and reduce the need for the construction of wide and capital-intensive transmission systems. Finally, the federation encouraged members to consider energy production in the context of holistic and systemic sustainability. Thus members were supported to explore the wider environmental implications relating to how energy demands could be met in the long-term prospect of a post-oil future.

Advocating Advantages of Hybrid Organisations

To disseminate information about the social enterprise hybrid for locally owned RE generation the REScoop.eu federation made the case that REScoops were superior to other ownership models and better able to solve societal problems related to current and future access to energy. We suggest that, in advocating these qualities, the federation aimed to build both pragmatic and normative legitimacy for the REScoop model.

First, in terms of pragmatic legitimacy, the federation connected the hybrid nature of the REScoop model with a number of ways of providing solutions to a range of long-standing consumer, community and societal problems: 'It's ideally placed to address these energy challenges, reducing emissions, improving energy security, local competition against the big [corporations], addressing fuel poverty particularly through things like energy efficiency' (informant from UK REScoop).

To local citizens and communities, the federation emphasised that, with REScoops, ownership is held by the community in which energy is produced, in contrast with the corporate model in which citizens are excluded from decision-making and economic benefits. '[REScoops] can further concentrate the economic benefits of wind development in the local community, as local investors harvest the profits from power sales' (report quoted in federation's application to EU funding). The federation gathered data on job creation and local investments to document the pragmatic benefits of the model.

The federation also demonstrated how REScoops could solve issues of access to energy for communities located far from national grids, without access to natural energy sources, and lacking the capital to capture and distribute energy. For the mainstream customer, the '100 per cent renewable' origin of the energy and the traceability of the supply chain were emphasised as superior to those of large corporations. To document these claims, the federation mobilised the support of environmental NGOs (such as Greenpeace) and consumer associations.

To public authorities and the environmental movement, the federation also emphasised the ability of REScoops to overcome community resistance to wind farms. Community resistance to wind farms is well documented and is a major barrier to investments in RE production. Strategies to overcome community resistance tend to be lengthy, resource-intensive and uncertain in outcome. In several documents, such as the 'best practices' report, the federation attempts to document cases in which the community ownership model had strongly reduced community resistance. '[L]ocal acceptance is far greater when the wind farm is not just a project of out-of-town investors, but is locally owned. After all, active participation – from investments to input during planning and project management – leads people to identify with the wind farm project from the outset' (quoted in the federation's 'best practices' report).

Beyond pragmatic benefits, the federation emphasised the perceived normative superiority of the model. Informants commented that wind, water and solar energy resources were common resources that should be freely available. 'This is a public, natural resource . . . It is like oil that is blowing above our heads' (REScoop founder, Belgium). The statutes of the federation build on the open access property regime of natural resources and seek to ensure that the new property ownership regime of the REScoop model is designed to ensure that all benefit from these naturally available energy sources.

The federation's discourse also claimed that local democracy was strengthened by active community participation in formal consultations and the management of the REScoop. '[REScoops] democratize local energy supply. [T]hey bring together local people's ecological and economic interests, increasing the acceptance of [RE] in communities. [REScoops] turn citizens into green entrepreneurs . . . [REScoops] represent a democratic alternative to conventional power supply. Every citizen has input whenever decisions are made' (report quoted in federation's policy paper).

Finally, the federation anchored the normative superiority of the REScoop model within the broader movement towards a transition in the ways in which energy was employed. 'We need a global transition from a production-driven system owned by international power giants using . . . fossil or nuclear power, to a human economy with local actors that do not seek to maximize profits and engage consumers as responsible citizens' (federation's policy paper). Therefore, advocating the advantages of hybrid organisations is a third legitimacy-building activity relying on pragmatic and normative arguments in order to convince different types of audiences (including consumers, public authorities, investors and civil society actors).

Communication of New Practices of Hybrid Organisations

The final set of legitimacy-building activities by the federation involves sharing the new practices of the social enterprise hybrid model with stakeholders. Our interviewees described a wide range of activities that they had used to spread knowledge about the REScoop hybrid model: open access communications directed to a general audience and available through the federation website and disseminated in freely available publications; relational communications targeted at individuals and smaller groups, which involve personal interaction and exchange; and networking activities that seek to bring people together in open forums to share and learn from one another and create an active social movement.

The federation website is a repository of information about the origins and development of REScoops and provides resources for co-operatives that have adopted the model and for community groups seeking to explore it. Included on the website is information about 'best practices' identified among REScoops that are labelled 'success stories' in relation to achieving specific goals (such as economic success, strong environmental impact, lobbying capacity or community engagement) or achieving the multiple goals of the social enterprise hybrid. The case studies provide useful information sources for members to learn about how other members have managed the problems they currently face:

> So . . . when I get stuck with a problem, I turn back to REScoopB1 and ask myself: 'How did they solve this four years ago?' . . . and when I compare our evolution curves, well, they're quite similar, so I tell [the other co-op members] 'you see, we're going in the right direction, we can handle all these things together, and this [REScoopB1 situation] is how we're going to look like in four years' time. (REScoop board member, Netherlands)

The mentoring system established by the federation was also reported to be especially valuable in helping newer members to learn how to balance the achievement of multiple goals concerning economic efficiency, technical prowess, community engagement and political influence. 'The network is made of professionals who can explain to citizens and to communities the different dimensions of REScoop initiatives and present concrete cases where it works well' (REScoop founder, Belgium).

Finally, the federation arranged training workshops at which small groups of members could learn about REScoop processes and practices. The workshops addressed practical issues such as raising citizen and stakeholder interest in the community, accessing finance, organising group governance and overcoming legal barriers. These workshops enabled members to start or consolidate local dynamics and raise media attention.

DISCUSSION AND CONCLUSION

The purpose of our study was to explore how networks helped social enterprise hybrid organisations acquire legitimacy. To do this we examined a federation that was established with the objective of promoting a new social enterprise hybrid organisational model designed to assist communities in creating RE co-operatives. Our analysis identified four legitimacy-building discourses – critiquing, proposing, advocating and communicating – produced by the federation These four kinds of discourse were developed and communicated concurrently, although we present them in a sequence in order to clarify the ways in which they were employed.

The REScoop.eu federation delivered critiques of the current policy logics for RE and of the logic behind current energy suppliers. In the case of the hybrid organisations observed here, delegitimising these logics naturally preceded reframing the field to accommodate small-scale, co-operatively owned RE suppliers. The focus on profit maximisation and the limited, if any, attention given to communities by extant dominant actors served to highlight the potential benefits of hybrid organisations committed to supporting both community development and investment in RE. In doing so, the federation was instrumental in alerting stakeholders to the effects of corporate domination in at least two ways: fostering their ability to analyse the current arrangements and the possible alternatives for them, and exposing the contradictions between the stakeholders' potential goals and the extant institutional arrangements. This was particularly clear in the efforts of the federation to highlight the contradiction between the corporate appropriation of common goods and the collective (re)appropriation of common goods by communities.

Secondly, to overcome the shortcomings in the operation of the field, the federation invested in proposing a new social enterprise hybrid that could overcome the weaknesses they identified. In creating a novel hybrid to appeal to stakeholders the federation managed two contrasting forces, namely differentiation from and alignment with other forms. On the one hand, presenting the model as radically new created a risk of alienating risk-averse stakeholders who were likely to be concerned by the inability of the new model does to fit into existing categories of organisations. On the other hand, too close an alignment with existing models risked reducing stakeholder interest in investing resources in supporting alternative and innovative forms that could address the to the challenges of sustainable development. This paradox was managed by appropriating the logics of co-operatives and RE and combining them in a new hybrid model of RE co-operatives.

In parallel with designing the social enterprise hybrid model the federation sought to promote the viability of REScoops by advocating their distinctiveness in terms of socially and economically empowering communities and strengthening local democracy. These qualities were distinct from the logic of dominant actors (shareholder-owned corporations) that sought to maximise profit for shareholders. The federation also claimed the ethical superiority of REScoops in relation to protecting the common good for public benefit and adopting a longer-term sustainability agenda than was typical of corporations. At the same time as making the case for their optimal distinctiveness and

ethical superiority, the federation claimed that REScoops had the capacity to address key problems, by: their ability to provide access to green energy and energy at lower cost than that delivered by corporations; their capacity to work with communities to ensure that resistance to wind farms was understood and accommodated in REScoops; and their commitment to addressing the longer-term energy demands of society when finite energy sources were used up or too expensive to capture.

Concurrently, the federation invested in providing a forum for information about REScoops and sharing it with stakeholders via open access to information, relational learning and networking events. As well as providing information to members and potential members, the website was accessible to the public and its presence was an additional legitimacy-building activity. The provision of REScoop templates and toolkits for new members enabled emerging REScoops (the majority of the federation members) to situate and complete their own story more easily through building on the case studies of successful REScoops. The range of case studies also ensured that country-specific contexts and innovative methods could be shared with members.

Inevitably, the discourse and claims of the federation were heavily oriented towards demonstrating the adequacy and superiority of the REScoop model and should thus be treated with some caution. In the process, the benefits of the model as well as the critiques of corporations and public authorities were probably overstated. The discourse fed into the arguments supported by environmental NGOs and co-operative networks that were already convinced by the federation's diagnosis of the field's shortcomings and the proposed superiority of the REScoop model. For the environmental movement, REScoops were an opportunity to go beyond advocacy to tangible support for businesses geared towards environmental aims. For the co-operative movement, REScoops were an opportunity to engage in the RE field and with broader environmental issues and to show that co-operatives could go beyond the sole interests of their members and pursue general interest aims. The federation's discourse also resonated with consumer associations and local communities, although the enthusiasm was not generalised. Public authorities responded more ambiguously, encouraging community involvement in general but mainly refusing to provide direct support measures (except for countries such as Germany and Belgium). At the European level, the discourse of the EU Commission has clearly evolved during the research time span towards recognising and encouraging REScoops, but this had not (yet) been reflected in new EU rules. Finally, large corporations were obviously less receptive to the utility of REScoops and the arguments of the federation. However, some collaborations were observed, for example when large RE businesses worked with local REScoops to help gain the support of the community by including the latter into the RE projects.

There is clear empirical evidence from stakeholders that the federation has contributed to building legitimacy for REScoops as hybrid organisations. Regulative legitimacy has been built through influencing political action for legislation in favour of RE co-operatives. Favourable legislation has been passed, for example in Germany ('*Energiewende*') and in Wallonia, Belgium, but has proved to be much more difficult to introduce in other countries (such as Spain) and can be reversed at any time (as was the case in Denmark). Nevertheless, together with others, REScoop.eu has already managed to advance the issue of community-based RE on the EU agenda. Secondly, cognitive legitimacy has been built through raising awareness of the different types of RE supplier. Awareness has been raised in communities that have been seen as suppliers, and at policy level to ensure that hybrids are included in consultations about the development of RE. And finally, normative legitimacy has been built through the growing adoption and diffusion of the REScoop model across Europe, as described in the study reported in this chapter.

However, the progress is still fragile and, while the efforts of the federation have clearly advanced the case for the legitimacy of the model, there is still a long way to go to establish REScoops irreversibly as a legitimate actor in the RE field, and to garner active support from relevant stakeholders. There is a continuing need for further research which could assess to what extent different attempts at legitimation are successful in garnering legitimacy from different stakeholders and in different contexts. Indeed, while the federation acts as an advocate for the REScoop model at the European level, such advocacy may have different kinds of impact on individual countries and future research could highlight the factors that favour or hinder the legitimation of REScoops – and hybrids in general – at the local level. Finally, this study is only a first attempt to theorise legitimacy-building for hybrid organisations. Future studies could examine other types of hybrid and the role of other actors in building their legitimacy. Despite its limitations, nevertheless, we anticipate that our empirical analysis can make a contribution to the understanding of the challenges of legitimacy facing hybrid organisations, and more particularly for those that simultaneously deal with economic, environmental and social goals (Battilana and Lee, 2014; Billis, 2010; Doherty et al., 2014).

REFERENCES

Aldrich, H.E. and Fiol, C.M. (1994), 'Fools rush in? The institutional context of industry creation', *Organization Studies*, 19:4, pp. 645–670.
Battilana, J. and Dorado, S. (2010), 'Building sustainable hybrid organizations: The case of commercial microfinance organizations', *Academy of Management Journal*, 53:6, pp. 1419–1440.
Battilana, J. and Lee, M. (2014), 'Advancing research on hybrid organizing: Insights from the study of social enterprises', *Academy of Management Annals*, 8:1, pp. 397–441.
Billis, D. (2010), *Hybrid Organizations and the Third Sector: Challenges for Practice, Theory and Policy*, Palgrave Macmillan, New York.
Deephouse, D.L. and Suchman, M.C. (2008), 'Legitimacy in organizational institutionalism', in R. Greenwood, C. Oliver, K. Sahlin and R. Suddaby (eds), *The SAGE Handbook of Organizational Institutionalism*, SAGE, Los Angeles, CA, pp. 49–77.
DiMaggio, P. and Powell, W. (1983), 'The iron cage revisited: Institutional isomorphism and collective rationality in organizational fields', *American Sociological Review*, 48:2, pp. 147–160.
Doherty, B., Haugh, H. and Lyon, F. (2014), 'Social enterprises as hybrid organizations: A review and research agenda', *International Journal of Management Reviews*, 16:4, pp. 417–436.
European Commission (2009), *Directive 2009/28/EC of 23 April 2009 on the promotion of the use of energy from renewable sources*, Brussels.
Fiol, C.M. and Romanelli, E. (2012), 'Before identity: The emergence of new organizational forms', *Organization Science*, 23:3, pp. 597–611.
Hoffman, A., Gullo, K. and Haigh, N. (2012), 'Hybrid organizations as agents of positive social change: Bridging the for-profit and non-profit divide', in K. Golden-Biddle and J. Dutton (eds), *Exploring Positive Social Change and Organizations: Building and Theoretical and Research Foundation*, Routledge, New York, pp. 131–153.
Huybrechts, B. (2012), *Fair Trade Organizations and Social Enterprise. Social Innovation Through Hybrid Organization Models*, Routledge, New York.
Huybrechts, B. and Haugh, H. (2018), 'The roles of networks in institutionalizing new hybrid organizational forms: Insights from the European Renewable Energy Cooperative Network', *Organization Studies*, 39:8, pp. 1085–1108.

Huybrechts, B. and Mertens, S. (2014), 'The relevance of the cooperative model in the field of renewable energy', *Annals of Public and Cooperative Economics*, 85:2, pp. 193–212.

Kraatz, M.S. and Block, E.S. (2008), 'Organizational implications of institutional pluralism', in R. Greenwood, C. Oliver, R. Suddaby and K. Sahlin-Andersson (eds), *Handbook of Organizational Institutionalism*, SAGE, London, pp. 243–275.

Lee, K. and Pennings, J.M. (2002), 'Mimicry and the market: Adoption of a new organizational form', *Academy of Management Journal*, 45:1, pp. 144–162.

McKendrick, D.G. and Carroll, G.R. (2001), 'On the genesis of organizational forms: Evidence from the market for disk arrays', *Organization Science*, 12:6, pp. 661–682.

Meyer, J.W. and Rowan, B. (1977), 'Institutionalized organizations: Formal structure as myth and ceremony', *American Journal of Sociology*, 83:2, pp. 340–363.

Navis, C. and Glynn, M.A. (2011), 'Legitimate distinctiveness and the entrepreneurial identity: Influence on investor judgments of new venture plausibility', *Organization Studies*, 36:3, pp. 479–499.

Pache, A.-C. and Santos, F. (2013), 'Inside the hybrid organization: Selective coupling as a response to competing institutional logics', *Academy of Management Journal*, 56:4, pp. 972–1001.

Santos, F.M. and Eisenhardt, K.M. (2009), 'Constructing markets and shaping boundaries: Entrepreneurial power in nascent fields', *Academy of Management Journal*, 52:4, pp. 643–671.

Scott, W.R. (2001), *Institutions and Organizations*, SAGE, Thousand Oaks, CA.

Sine, W.D. and Lee, B.H. (2009), 'Tilting at windmills? The environmental movement and the emergence of the US wind energy sector', *Administrative Science Quarterly*, 54:1, pp. 123–155.

Suchman, M.C. (1995), 'Managing legitimacy: Strategic and institutional approaches', *Academy of Management Review*, 20:3, pp. 571–610.

Tracey, P., Phillips, N. and Jarvis, O. (2011), 'Bridging institutional entrepreneurship and the creation of new organizational forms: A multilevel model', *Organization Science*, 22:1, pp. 60–80.

Vickers, I. and Lyon, F. (2012), 'Beyond green niches? Growth strategies of environmentally-motivated social enterprises', *International Small Business Journal*, 32:4, pp. 449–470.

Weismeier-Sammer, D. and Reiner, E. (2011), 'Cooperative solutions for renewable energy production', RICC Working Paper, 2011/02, WU Vienna University of Economics and Business, Vienna.

PART IV

THE THREE SECTORS AND THEIR BOUNDARIES

24. Hybrid organisations and human problems: towards a New Organisational Reality
David Billis

INTRODUCTION

Human Problems and Formal Organisations

The background to this chapter is a period in which human problems are seemingly greater in scale and gravity than our ability to resolve them. The consequence is that it is has rarely been more important to increase our understanding of the relationship between human problems and formal organisations. It is a relationship which can be called symbiotic, since for organisations human problems are their lifeblood without which they cannot exist, whereas for those with problems the organisations often offer the hope of a solution.

The symbiotic relationship is not a balanced one. At times it seems that problems are always with us, apparently insolvable and overwhelming. It is not difficult to be pessimistic and we can all make our own lists of what is going wrong in the world. Nevertheless, influenced by the work of Karl Popper (discussed in the next section) I take the approach that humankind can continually, if often painfully, develop better theories to respond to problems. It is an optimistic approach which I attempt to follow in the search for an increased understanding of the nature of hybrid organisations and their own problems. The theory of authentic sectors and their associated concepts are presented as contributions in the search.

In this chapter it is formal organisations, with their public personas, their accountable structures and possessing sufficient resources to provide a systematic response, that take centre stage and provide the majority of organisational responses to human problems. I shall begin by arguing that these formal organisations can be aggregated and divided into ideal models of the three sectors (the public, private and third[1]) which possess their own distinctive principles. These principles are not accidental but reflect one of the three fundamental and different ways of responding to human problems that are not readily resolved by families, friends and the myriad of non-formal social interactions. The three sectors provide an ideal starting point for the development of organisational theory. And at the pinnacle of the pyramid of principles of each sector is decision-making accountable ownership, a central concept which is defined as those who are accountable for making the most critical organisational decisions.

But the chapter goes much further by questioning the centre-stage dominance of the Weberian ideal model of organisations and their sectors in response to human need. It does this by developing a theory of hybrid formal organisation, and replaces the ideal model of sectors by an authentic sector model that includes hybrid organisations. It concludes by proposing that we have entered a New Organisational Reality (NOR) that is partly theorised in this chapter. An introduction to these ideas is presented next.

Authentic Sectors and the New Organisational Reality

The growing recognition of the role of hybrid organisations has made it possible to move beyond the earlier conceptualisation of sectors as an aggregation of individual organisations with an undiluted adherence to one set of sector principles; what has previously been called the ideal model. In reality, the centre stage in the response to human problems is increasingly occupied by formal organisations that have become, to varying degrees, hybrid organisations. They have absorbed, or been set up to contain, some distinctive principles from one or both of the other sectors.

This leads to my proposition that there are authentic sectors that have been conceptualised by the development of the theory of hybrid organisations. The sectors are authentic because they reflect and confirm the existence of both 'pure' and hybrid organisations in the three sectors. This proposition needs to be explained more precisely. We have not entered a period of hybrid organisations only recently. Some of them have been around for centuries but have not been identified as such. It is the development of theory to catch up with practice that has now made it possible to discuss an authentic sector.

I will argue in this chapter that the identification of hybrid organisations, and the ability to analyse them, makes it possible to take a further major step forward in understanding the relationship between human problems and organisations and the growth of the NOR approach in practice and theory. Some speculative analysis will be undertaken in the conclusions. However, in order to get a fuller picture of the organisational response it will be necessary to confront some additional gaps in organisational theory. This will be further discussed in the conclusions and will be presented in more detail in Chapter 29. The best I can do is to explain that it goes beyond formal organisations and, based on research, takes the study of hybrid organisations into the overlapping territory between formal organisations and non-formal organisations that are rooted in the personal world of family and friends. This chapter takes the first steps into the NOR: an overarching approach to organisations. Having laid out some of the main themes, this introduction moves on to outline the chapter's main purposes and objectives, and the path to achieving them.

The Broad Purpose and the Objective of the Chapter

The broad purpose, the driving force, of this chapter is concern about the lack of understanding of the nature of hybrid formal organisations as important contributors in the response to human problems. More specifically, the objective is primarily to address the most important hurdle in understanding the organisational reality of the authentic organisations: maintaining transparent, accountable ownership when faced with the competing principles of the three sectors in their responses to human problems. Failure to secure clarity of ownership, which is at the top of the pyramid of organisational principles, can reverberate down through the entire organisation. It can have a destructive impact on the response to human problems, as will be illustrated in the case studies I present later.

The theoretical path to meeting the objective – achieving greater clarity of accountable ownership – is laid out below. I have, however, been more ambitious than addressing the problems of the authentic hybrid organisation, and in the final section of the chapter I attempt to reflect on the ways in which organisational reality has begun to move on to the era of the NOR.

The Path to Meet the Objectives

The path to the objectives builds on previous theory (Billis, 2010) and develops additional concepts, particularly the reappraisal of the 'ideal type' sector model and the introduction of the 'authentic sector'. I develop this path in the next five sections, which are summarised as follows:

1. The first of these sections discusses the research approach, introduces its theoretical basis and the problem-driven tentative theory of Karl Popper. Its concluding subsection utilises the work of Berger and Luckman in order to help our understanding of the symbiotic relationship between organisations and problems.
2. The next section presents the problem-driven ideal model of three sectors (public, private and third), each of which is an aggregation of individual formal organisations which share common principles of organisation. The principles of each of the sectors are distinctly different and conflict with the principles of the other sectors.
3. The third section presents the theoretical and practical heart of the chapter. In light of the new reality of hybrid organisations, it develops the theory of the authentic sector model which contains both ideal type organisations and their hybrids. This section continues by further developing the definition of the hybrid organisation and examines its significant features by utilising a suite of concepts to identify different states of hybridity.
4. The following section turns to the objective of the chapter by demonstrating the way in which the new concepts assist in understanding the problems of confused ownership in three case studies that provide examples of different levels of impact; global disaster, national uncertainty and local disturbance.
5. The concluding section looks ahead to the continued development of the ideas of the NOR approach and discusses the need to rethink the changing role of organisational theory.

THE RESEARCH APPROACH

The Problem-Driven Approach

The word 'problems' appears in the title of this chapter and reflects the influence of Karl Popper, the renowned philosopher of science whose work on the relationship between problems and theories and the concept of tentative theories have guided my methodological approach. Although infrequently used in organisational studies, several of his concepts are invaluable for research, teaching and practice. His schema (Popper, 1972, pp. 119–121; 1974, p. 222) provides the basis for the objectives and the framework of this chapter. In Figure 24.1, which is a much simplified version of the schema, Popper suggests that P1 represents a starting problem from which we can proceed to a tentative

$$P1 \longrightarrow TT \longrightarrow EE \longrightarrow P2$$

Figure 24.1   Popper's schema

solution or tentative theory (TT). This explanation might be (partly or wholly) mistaken; in any case, it will be subject to error elimination (EE). Writing about scientists, Popper argues that their trial and error consists of hypotheses which can be formulated in words, and often in writing. The attempt can then be made to find flaws in any of the hypotheses by criticism and experiment (Popper, 1972, p. 247). The schema continues with the next stage, which is when new problems arise 'from our own creative activity'. Then he suggests that, in this cycle, new problems arise (P2) – see Figure 24.1. In his autobiography Popper (1992, pp. 152–156) also suggests that theoretical development often starts from practical problems; and that these problems arise because something has gone wrong.

Most of the problems that I have analysed utilising this 'problem-driven' approach were of formal organisations and the individuals that work in them, and involved an understanding of the complex 'structure' of individual organisations. A definition of formal organisations is that they are set up to respond to human problems and comprise people who come together to respond systematically to their own, or other people's, problems. Their minimum requirements would be an accountable coordinator, agreement on the problems to be met, and a unique name in order to engage with society.

The use of the word 'structure' has a specific meaning for this research since it encompasses more than just the structure of accountable roles often represented (or misrepresented) in organisational charts. Rather, it is a more inclusive and critical approach which does not simply take for granted the individual roles that appear on the organisational chart. The inclusive structural approach goes beyond formal roles and apparent accountability. With their agreement, the people most closely involved in the problem being analysed will be confidentially interviewed in order to uncover their actual problem-solving work and real accountability. The early development of this approach is discussed in Billis (1984) and Billis and Rowbottom (1977).

The Symbiotic Relationship between Human Problems and Formal Organisations

The word 'problems' will continue to be used, although it was tempting to utilise 'need' in the title and in the narrative since 'need' has attracted a large body of influential literature. Foremost amongst these writings is the work of Abraham Maslow, whose hierarchy of needs I have used in relation to the response to social welfare problems (Billis, 1984). However, it proved to be less useful when the attempt was made to utilise them for the organisational purposes of this chapter. Any lingering doubts about utilising 'need' as the central theme of the chapter disappeared when encountering the authoritative book on *Understanding Human Need* by Dean (2010). The author begins with a 'not exhaustive' glossary of 30 definitions of the word, the usage of which is 'interpreted in a mind-boggling variety of ways' (ibid., p. 1), whilst at the same time being 'central to policy-making' (ibid., p. 10). I decided that 'need' carried too much intellectual baggage.

With relief I returned to the use of 'problems' and the work of Berger and Luckman (1971). In this seminal work they argue that, in a world consisting of multiple realities, by far the most important reality is that of 'everyday life', which is impossible to ignore because of its 'massive, urgent and intense manner' (ibid., p. 35). The authors suggest that this is 'an ordered reality' (ibid., p. 35) which is experienced in terms of different degrees of closeness and remoteness, of which the most directly accessible and dominant is the individual's world of work. They generalise their theory by proposing that the world of everyday life is shared as reality by many people, and that commonsense knowledge is a knowledge that is shared with others in the 'normal, self-evident routines of everyday life' (ibid., p. 37). The authors emphasise the importance of the world of work, which is also relevant for my own problem-driven approach to organisations.

At this point, the authors arrive at the main point of interest for this chapter. In their discussion of problems they declare that: 'as long as the routines of everyday life continue without interruption they are apprehended as unproblematic'. This unproblematic condition is interrupted 'by the appearance of a problem' (ibid., p. 38). Hence it follows that the logical conclusion from their narrative is that problems may be defined as interruptions to the routines of daily life.

This is an important starting point for some further comments about the symbiotic relationship. An important feature of the relationship is that, as human problems increase in complexity, so does the complexity of the required organisational response. Although the main concern of this chapter is with the organisational response, some minimal comments on the complexity of human problems are necessary.

For example, what appeared as a personal 'interruption' may only require a small, well-trodden path of response by the person themselves, perhaps with advice from family and friends. All that that might be needed is a good walk in the park, without the need for the services of a formal organisation such as a pharmacy. The problem may be well known, such as a headache, and the pharmacy may be an obvious solution. Should the problem increase in severity, more complex, organisations such as general practitioner (GP) doctors' partnerships and hospitals may be involved. Both the pharmacy and the hospital will be supported by a vast network, probably international, of research establishments and supply systems.

But individual problems can become more complicated in another way and, to echo Wright Mills, the private problem can become a public issue and enter the realm of formal organisations. By chance as I write this, yesterday was a national holiday in the United Kingdom, with packed beaches, on one of which an apparently authentic cloud slowly came closer. People discovered that their eyes were becoming painful. Rapidly it became obvious that this was not a personal problem, but a problem of the entire beach. Numerous governmental agencies soon arrived and the Royal National Lifeboat Institution (RNLI), a charity, sent lifeboats to search the coastal area. In more extreme cases such as natural disasters, a multi-organisational and multinational response, together with community and individual responses, may be required.

This brief consideration of the interdependence between human problems and formal organisations has segued from the personal, sometimes trivial interruptions in daily life, to global disasters. It begins to illustrate the dynamic and continuously changing nature of problems. In the search for responses, it is becoming increasingly evident that hybrid organisations can be identified as playing a vital role in the struggle to achieve a societally tolerable balance between the two sides of the symbiotic relationship. Assisting them to make a positive contribution to balancing the symbiotic relationship requires theories about their distinctive character and problems, above all the challenge of maintaining transparent accountability. The following section of the chapter presents the fundamental building blocks which eventually lead to a theory of hybrid organisations which responds to the challenge.

A PROBLEM-DRIVEN IDEAL TYPE OF THEORY OF SECTORS

Beginnings: A Personal Note

The original problem that led first to the theory of distinctive sectors, and later to this chapter's theory of hybridity, emerged in February 1979. I had invited ten voluntary sector staff from the area of health and welfare to Brunel University for a two-day workshop designed to discuss their work and the problems that they were encountering.[2] The inherited theoretical basis for the workshop was provided by Elliott Jacques whose corpus of work in the field of organisations was, and remains, influential. In common with the majority of organisational theorists Jacques was almost entirely concerned with the multilayered hierarchical public and private sectors which he carefully defined as bureaucracies, and his magnum opus was appropriately called *A General Theory of Bureaucracy* (Jacques, 1976). The inherited body of theories had proved effective when applied to the bureaucracies of the private sector, but less so when utilised in the public sector. In 1979, when confronted for the first time by a group of articulate and experienced participants from the voluntary sector, the inherited theories were found wanting.

I had presented the standard model of (all) organisations in which the governing body appointed, and was clearly separate from, the levels of paid staff. Towards the end of the day a participant gently declared that: 'your model does not fit the problems of voluntary organisations. There is no separation' between the two groups. I responded by drawing on the board a rough diagram of two incomplete overlapping circles. This crude depiction set in progress almost 40 years of continuous, but sometimes intermittent, development of endless Popperian cycles and numerous publications. Eventually, the use of 'ambiguity' and 'blurring' would be replaced by a theory of hybrid organisations, in turn itself dependent on a theory of sectors containing 'non-hybrid' organisations. The idea of a sector has already been introduced into the narrative in previous sections. The following subsection now discusses the nature of the sector in more detail.

The Ideal Models of the Three Sectors

As is so often the case, as was illustrated in the 1979 workshop, organisational problems can race ahead of available explanatory theories. At that time, the ubiquitous business-driven theory was inadequate when confronted by the specific problems faced by voluntary sector leaders. Also around this time, the search began by scholars to identify the distinctive features of each sector (Wamsley and Zald, 1976; Bozeman, 1987).

In the United States of America (USA) the issue of distinctive boundaries was the concern of several public administration scholars who, faced with the problematic relationship between government and the private sector, developed two-sector theories (Perry and Rainey, 1988; Koppell, 2003). Only with the recognition, still in progress, of the largely hidden importance of the third sector has it become possible to develop a more encompassing model which describes both the unique contribution of each sector and the interaction of those sectors in responding to human problems.

This section presents ideal models of each of the three sectors and illustrates in Table 24.1 how principles and structures are distinctly different in each sector. These interacting principles still provide powerful structural boundaries around the three

Table 24.1   Ideal models of the three sectors

Core elements	Private sector principles	Public sector principles	Third sector principles
1. Ownership	Shareholders	Citizens	Members
2. Governance	Share ownership size	Public elections	Private elections
3. Operational priorities	Market forces and individual choice	Public service and collective choice	Commitment about distinctive mission
4. Distinctive human resources	Paid employees in managerially controlled firm	Paid public servants in legally backed bureau	Members and volunteers in association
5. Distinctive other resources	Sales, fees	Taxes	Dues, donations, legacies

organisational ways of responding to human problems. As used here, boundaries are neither the walls of the prison nor the markings on a tennis court. The principles that comprise the boundaries are sufficiently broad to permit – up to a point – flexibility, innovation and change.

That point is arrived at when change threatens the internal coherence of the principles of the ideal model and the maintenance of transparent accountability. At that juncture, as will be discussed shortly, the ideal model as presented in Table 24.1 will requires rethinking and the new type of 'authentic model' is introduced in the next section. Before discussing this change, however, further comments are necessary on the ideal model itself and its continuing power.

An important point is that the 'sector', as utilised in this section, is a bottom-up concept which represents real formal organisations that can be aggregated and divided into ideal models of the three sectors. The inhabitants of each sector (the public, private, third) possess their own different and competing organisational principles, as presented in Table 24.1. These core elements and principles are logically interdependent and are held together by the concept of accountability.

With regard to accountability, Elliott Jacques (2002, p. 263) suggested that it is 'a situation where an individual can be called to account for his/her actions by another individual or body both to do so and to give recognition to the individual for those actions'. It still remains a powerful definition. Securing accountability at all every level of an organisation is one of the fundamental principles in a democratic society and one of its biggest challenges.

The importance for human problems is that these models of organisational governance and operations in Table 24.1 provide an accountable structure which is an essential prerequisite for democracy. Citizens with problems must know who to hold to account when things go wrong, be it a failure of care in public hospitals, car emissions, or a scandal in a local charity. There are a number of reasons why the ideal model of each sector remains influential.

Historic roots
The roots of the sector concept are so deep and important for hybridity theory that I will return to them again in the final discussion of the chapter. For the moment it will only

be noted that the awareness that there were several major organised responses to human problems is rooted in centuries of experience.

A relatively more recent example is Beveridge's (1948) report on *Voluntary Action*. In that report the difference between the role of the 'state'/'public authorities' and that of 'voluntary agencies' appears throughout his argument. His brief discussion of the Holloway societies (ibid., pp. 50–52) is particularly interesting. The first Holloway society was established in 1874 as part of the friendly society movement and combined insurance against sickness with personal saving. Beveridge recognises their successful role in 'meeting real needs', but is quick to point out, with implied displeasure, that 'the most successful of these societies present the aspect to-day rather of enterprising businesses than of associations with brotherly feeling' (ibid., p. 51). Doubtless, there are much earlier examples, but this is particularly relevant since it presents not only the idea of sectors with different attributes, but also that individual organisations within the Holloway societies have what Beveridge calls 'apparent complications'. In effect, he anticipates current discussions on hybrid organisations.

Continuing relevance

The power of the sector concepts is that the three distinctive principles represented by public, private and third sector organisations represent the most systematic ways of responding to human problems. Individuals, groups and communities with problems in many countries with different political, social and political conditions are highly likely to know, or to find out, which particular organisation they should turn to for help. Many individuals with problems have become what might be called 'experts by necessity' and are well aware of the likely responses from the different sectors.

When we turn to politics, elections and public policy, the concept of different sectors demonstrates its special utility. It is in these areas that sectors as aggregations of similar ideal type organisations prove their value. These ideal types have been for many decades more or less adequate enough to provide a major tool for policy-making, but will need rethinking in light of the arrival of the authentic sectors.

Flexibility

Each sector model provides a set of principles of governance and operations for the individual organisations that have a logical interdependence and that have proved their utility in the material world. Together, the principles provide an 'identity card' which clearly distinguishes the unique differences between the organisations in different sectors.

The organisational principles are flexible enough to allow for continuous change and improvement; they include, for example, the development of new ownership models for private sector organisations. Similar examples can be identified in both the public and third sectors. Nevertheless, the flexibility of the ideal model organisation is limited by the boundaries set by its primary organisational principles such as the private sector shareholders, shares and market forces (Table 24.1) which do not recognise hybrid organisations. And the sector, as an aggregation solely of ideal model organisation, is consequently a valuable but rather limited concept.

This ideal model is being challenged by the changing organisational reality, and the next section of this chapter will argue that this new reality requires a more sophisticated model of a sector. The new model acknowledges the continued strength of the ideal model, which still reflects the principles of the majority of individual organisations in all sectors. But it must now also take into account the emerging recognition of hybrid organisations.

HYBRID ORGANISATIONS IN THE AUTHENTIC SECTOR

In this section, the task is to reconsider the ideal model presented in Table 24.1 in light of the increasing recognition of hybrid organisations in all three sectors. It begins by discussing the development of a model that more accurately reflects these developments. This is followed by a discussion of two important features: shallow and entrenched hybridity. Finally, an explanation is presented of two key concepts that are essential to the achievement of accountable ownership: principal owners and prime sector adherence.

Developing an Authentic Model of Sectors

The models of sectors, as presented so far, are based on the aggregation of organisations that share common distinctive principles. As a straightforward mathematical exercise in addition, there was no dissonance between the individual (ideal type) organisations and their sector. And it remains the case, as best we can judge, that the majority of formal organisations abide by the principles of one sector and, even if often not perfect, strive for clarity of accountable structures. However, with the increasingly significant number of hybrids in all three sectors (Billis, 2013) it is time to revisit the function of aggregation. The increasing awareness of the nature of hybrid organisations, and the uncovering of many previously 'hidden' hybrids, changes the reality of the 'sector'. The reality is of sectors that are aggregations of ideal types plus hybrid organisations.

The consequence is that the inclusion of forms of organisation with different principles can no longer be encompassed within the Weberian ideal type. The sector has escaped from the inflexibility of the ideal type (Udy, 1959) and requires reconceptualisation and a name of its own. The ideal type model in Table 24.1 will be retained but its use will be restricted to individual non-hybrid organisations, and the sector will now be considered the 'authentic' sector.

In the main, these hybrid organisations do not often willingly abandon their prime allegiance to the most important principles of their parent sector: ownership, governance and operational priorities. The consequences of moving to a different sector and abandoning their roots, principles and established bases of legitimacy are uncertain, and are likely to be traumatic and may even prove terminal. However, to survive, they will require concepts that understand and can explain the nature and challenges of their existence as hybrid organisations. Organisational theories based on the 'traditional' pre-hybrid approach run the increasing risk of utilising incomplete concepts by failing to recognise the distinctive characteristics of hybrids. The discussion so far may suggest a rather dismal and negative approach to hybrid organisations by concentrating on their problems. This is not the case, since I am still holding firm to the positive Popperian approach of the problem-driven development of better theory. The next stage of this process is, as set out below, to put further flesh on the working definition of a hybrid organisation as one that incorporates 'significant' features of more than one of the three sectors that appear in Table 24.1.

What are Significant Features? Shallow and Entrenched Hybrid Organisations

This subsection develops and expands significant features of two states of hybrid organisations: shallow and entrenched (Billis, 2010, pp. 60–65). Both these states of hybridity can be either organic or enacted. The research suggests that each state is susceptible to different organisational problems with different impacts on the elements and principles set out in Table 24.1.

Shallow hybridity

Shallow organic hybridity occurs most frequently when organisations, often with strong sector principles and identity, adopt principles from other sectors. This organic hybridity signals a modest move into hybridity which may not arrive on the agenda of the ownership and governance bodies or impact on operational priorities. Hybridisation may, or may not, take place and can take many years or decades to arrive. Familiar examples from the third sector arise from the recruitment of paid staff (distinctive human resources of the private and public sectors) into the member- and volunteer-based association. This may well be very uncomfortable for a period of time, but as long as the paid staff do not have an impact on ownership, governance and operational principles the individual organisation can remain in shallow hybridity. Nevertheless, research projects based on an inclusive structural approach have demonstrated the human problems caused by the employment of the first paid staff. With some justification the members and volunteers are concerned about the conflict between the 'invasion' of different principles. Will their beliefs in a distinctive mission and service to clients be affected by the potential slide into the adoption of the principles of the private and public sectors?

Private sector organisations are not immune to hybridisation. Many make substantial efforts to support local and international charities and other third sector organisations. Large companies such as multinationals are likely to have dedicated staff charged with the responsibility to develop programmes and assist local communities. In multinationals the impact on the entire organisation may be modest and it is unrealistic to describe them as shallow hybrids. On the other hand, in small companies such as those collecting unwanted clothing, alliances with charities enable them to utilise the charity brand name in return for a percentage of the sales. This process has significantly influenced their operational priorities and they can then be considered shallow hybrids.

Shallow enacted hybrids are those that have been established from day one with conflicting sector principles. Some are created by different combinations of government, private sector and third sector principles. Often without the resources to establish sustainable organisations, 'they can collapse under the weight of conflicting expectations and commitments' (Howard and Taylor, 2010, p. 244). The enactment of a shallow hybrid, whilst it might eventually become a successful response to human problems, is, as these authors persuasively demonstrate, particularly susceptible to confusion. Those establishing a shallow hybrid confront the daunting challenge of building a new organisation not only with competing principles but also with limited resources. More importantly, the groundwork for enactment requires the necessary organisational knowledge and, above all else, the need to create an accountable and transparent organisational structure. Given that shallow hybridity is not central to the fundamental structure of the organisations, it is unlikely to appear for discussion in the process of planning and enacting the hybrid.

Entrenched hybridity

This occurs when the ownership, governance and operational priorities of responding to human problems of the organisation are consistently challenged by the conflicting principles of other sectors. Tensions arise about the operational priorities of the parent organisation: should they be driven by market forces, by governmental priorities, or by member-driven mission? Entrenched conflicting principles may arise organically or be enacted. Since the next section is almost entirely devoted to entrenched hybrids, they will only be briefly mentioned here.

Entrenched organic hybridity may reflect conflicting and embedded views in the ownership and governance structure. This may not have been planned, but may have developed organically. Many examples have been found in the third sector as a result of the steadily increasing dependence on market and governmental resources (Teasdale et al., 2013) with associated pressures for changes in operational priorities. It may also be accompanied by the growth of embedded structures of layers of staff whose employment is dependent on those external resources. This process can make a serious impact on those with problems. One example occurred when service recipients (parents of handicapped children) were removed from areas of decision-making in which they had previously participated. The result was that parents felt considerable anxiety about the future direction of the organisation for themselves and/or for their families.[3] Entrenchment that is enacted may also arise in a number of ways. One path might be the establishment of a new hybrid organisation with inbuilt competing principles of meeting human problems, such as nationalised industries which began their lives with the necessary resources to provide a sustainable response.

In addition to elaborating on the significant features of hybridity, this subsection has provided concepts to help us distinguish the different states of hybridity in different organisations. In the following subsection additional tools for understanding the structure of hybrid organisations are offered as the final step before presenting the authentic model.

Principal Owners and Prime Sector Adherence in Hybrid Organisations

It is a commonplace experience for those who research or work with organisations to find that it might require a severe problem before serious and objective analysis of the root causes is undertaken. In the case of hybrid organisations the serious problems that are causing persistent concern at the highest levels are likely to involve discussions of their basic identity. The tentative theories offered in this subsection provide greater substance to the meaning of ownership, the core element in the identification of different sectors, and their response to human problems. Drawing on an organisational approach to ownership and accountability), it utilises the concepts of principal owners and the prime sector approach (Billis, 2010).

Principal owners

Unfortunately, for a chapter covering all three sectors from an organisational perceptive, the great majority of research on ownership is firmly based on economic theory and mainly focuses on the for-profit firm. Typically, it concentrates on residual decision rights and the allocation of residual returns (Milgrom and Roberts, 1992). A good example is the influential paper by Grossman and Hart (1986), who begin by asking 'What is a firm?'

(ibid., p. 691). They then differentiate between two contractual rights: (1) specific rights which list all specific rights over assets; and (2) all the residual rights. For these authors the firm is defined as 'being composed of the assets (e.g., machines, inventories) that it owns'. And ownership is defined as 'the purchase of these residual rights of control' (ibid., p. 692).

By contrast, almost a decade earlier another influential paper, Fama and Jenson (1983), was also concerned with ownership but offered a different perspective. Whilst steeped in the economic literature, the authors draw on a broader disciplinary range and consider the issues both in corporations and in nonprofits. Their analysis is also critical of economists who 'tend to ignore analysis of the steps of the decision-making process'. They claim that the way organisations allocate the steps of that process across agents 'is important in explaining the survival of organisations' (ibid., p. 302).

The linkage of the decision-making process to the survival of organisations resonates with the theme of this section, with the difference that here a decision-making approach takes pride in exploring the nature of ownership itself. The argument for a decision-based definition of ownership runs as follows. In private and third sector organisations it is usual to find several distinct layers of decision-making groups: formal, active and principal. The formal or legal group is not involved in the organisation and has little interest in contributing to the hierarchy of decision-making. One example would be the large numbers who do not vote in elections. Of more interest is the category of active members who, for example, do vote in elections, and shareholder meetings when given the opportunity. Finally, the critical group for the analysis of hybridity is that of the principal owners. These are the members who in effect can make the most important organisational decisions; for example they can close the organisation down, amalgamate it with another organisation, or transfer it to another sector and change its mission. These are the real owners of the organisation.[4]

From a methodological and practical point of view the identification of the principal owners represents a critical step. Methodologically, clarification of the true state of ownership will necessitate organisational self-awareness that there is a problem and, in order to understand the reasons for the problem, external analytic assistance may be required. Practically, examining who can make the critical organisational life-and-death decisions is often a revealing process that challenges the myths of organisational decision-making.

Prime sector adherence
The proposition that organisations have primary adherence to the principles of one of the three sectors originated from early work with voluntary organisations and a frequent complaint that they 'were losing touch with their roots', or that there was 'an absence of roots' (Billis, 1991). At that time, utilising the dictionary definition which referred to them as drawing strength, inspiration and sustenance, the idea of 'roots' seemed to possess credibility in the world of organisations. Even today, referring to an organisation as 'possessing strong roots' will be readily understood. It still serves as useful shorthand for describing the more scholarly contention that each sector has distinctive interlocking principles.

The prime sector hypothesis is that hybrid organisations have roots and primary adherence to the principles of one sector. Of these principles, it is decision-making ownership that is the most powerful and determines organisational prime accountability. In good

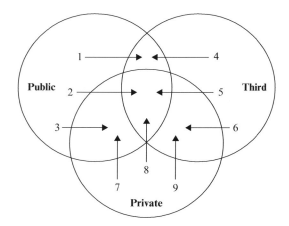

Key: The hybrid zones with principal owners underlined:
1. Public/Third
2. Public/Private/Third
3. Public/Private

4. Third/Public
5. Third/Public/Private
6. Third /Private

7. Private/Public
8. Private/Public/Third
9. Private/Third

Figure 24.2   The three authentic sectors

times the roots are below the surface, and organisational life carries on. In difficult times, as was noted in the discussion on shallow and entrenched hybridity, the increasing severity of the problem will be escalated to increasingly higher organisational levels. In times of crisis, when the future of the organisation is at risk, previously shadowy figures may materialise from the darkness. It may then become clear that these are the principal owners, and the harsh reality of who really owns the hybrid organisation may emerge.

Utilising the two principles of principal owners and prime sector adherence, it is now possible to present Figure 24.2, showing the three authentic models of sectors. Figure 24.2 presents an authentic model of the three sectors each with its own three types of hybrid organisation. Thus, the principal owners and prime accountability of the unambiguous organisations of each sector overlap with one or both of the other two sectors.

The presentation of the authentic model and the associated concepts now make it possible, in the next section, to return to the main ambitions of the chapter: to meet the challenge of maintaining transparent and accountable ownership in hybrid organisations.

REFLECTIONS ON ACCOUNTABLE OWNERSHIP

The objective of this chapter is to contribute to a better understanding of the problem of accountable ownership in hybrid organisations which, if not addressed, can have a destructive impact on the response to human problems in the symbiotic relationship. This section demonstrates the way in which concepts presented so far might assist in understanding the problems of confused ownership in three case studies. The three cases provide examples of different levels of impact: global disaster, national uncertainty and local disturbance.

The first case study is a notorious example of ownership confusion at global level in response to housing problems, and involves the private and public sectors. It is a study that is dependent on the research and insights of others. But the stakes are so high and the warnings of a potential reoccurrence of the disaster so persuasive, that I could not resist including some modest reflections.

The second case considers confused ownership at national level in response to health problems and involves all three sectors. My early research in the United Kingdom's (UK) National Health Service (NHS), a behemoth mostly impenetrable to organisational research, was as a young researcher and is now well out of date. Nonetheless I believe that the new ideas of hybridity will be helpful at organisational and public policy levels.

The final study involves the third and public sectors and discusses the illusion of accountable ownership and disturbance of the local level. I was involved for a period, and this is noted in the case study.

Global Disaster: Fannie and Freddie

There would appear to be little more to say about the most infamous example of hybrid ownership confusion: the case of Fannie Mae and Freddie Mac (see Koppell, 2003). In 1938, Fannie was established as a government agency to ensure the supply of mortgage funds, and in 1968 it was re-chartered by Congress as a company funded solely with private capital. In 1970, Freddie was established in order to end Fannie Mae's monopoly, and it went public in 1989. These two government-sponsored enterprises (GSEs) were key actors, and have often been seen as playing a pivotal role in the global financial crisis of 2008.

Other commentators have argued that, as Nielsen (2018) titled his brief analysis of the credit crisis, 'The US Congress is largely to blame'. Others have suggested that that GSEs were 'followers rather than leaders in the securitization of questionable and often fraudulent loans. That honor went to the private investment banks' (Baker, 2018). In 2008 *The Economist* summarised what it called the 'illusions'. It argued that: 'the giant twins [were] set up to provide liquidity for the housing market by buying mortgages from the banks. They repackaged the loans and used them as collateral for bonds called mortgage-backed securities that guaranteed buyers . . . against default'. They concluded that the model 'was based on the ability of investors to see through one illusion and boosted by their willingness to believe in another'. The view of *The Economist* was that investors saw through the illusion that the debt issued by the GSEs was not backed by the government: 'no one believe[d] this . . . They have just been proved right' (*The Economist*, 2008).

The power of what might be called the 'great illusion' is puzzling. Several decades earlier scholars had already expressed concern about the confused hybrid nature of many governmental organisations. Notable amongst these was Seidman (1988) who declared that 'today one can no longer determine whether an agency is government or non-governmental'. Indeed in one example, 'Congress has produced a hybrid that defied rational classification' (ibid., p. 23). Little progress has been made since then. The two companies (public companies owned by shareholders) were placed into conservatorship[5] and taken over by the Federal Housing Finance Agency (FHFA) in 2008. The US Treasury Secretary declared that policy-makers needed to decide whether the role of Fannie and Freddie 'is best played by private corporations, the government, or hybrids such as Fannie Mae or Freddie Mac' (Armour and Healey, 2008).

Nonetheless, more than a decade after the Congress report, the problem is still firmly on the agenda. Tom Forrester suggests that: 'the prevailing market view is that the $4 trillion of Fannie and Freddie mortgage-backed securities have an explicit federal guarantee. But they don't – hence the potential for trouble'. He foresees a 'potential market time bomb' (Forrester, 2010). The bomb may not have exploded, but the indecisiveness continues. In early 2018 another Treasury Secretary explained that that he would pursue bipartisan legislation to take the two mortgage giants out of the government's custody, but that would not happen in 2018 (Lawler, 2018).

Reflections

These few reflections explore how hybridity theory, with its decision-making definition of ownership, might have considered the market crash of 2008. It is an improbable scenario, given the political lack of appetite for clarity. Nevertheless, perhaps a better understanding of the nature of hybrid organisations might prove useful in what remains an unresolved problem. Both organisations are registered on the US stock market, are independent organisations, and are legally regarded as the owners of the companies. A problem-solving approach utilising the concepts of principal owners and prime sector adherence might have challenged the reality of this perception.

The main task would be to determine who could really make the critical organisational decisions which, as was also noted earlier, often appear at times of severe crisis. In this case the problem was evident long before the crash, and it would have been possible to uncover the principal owners much earlier. A forensic and independent analysis, supported by those who had the power to implement change, would need to identify and make transparent the real owners: those who can make the most important 'life-and-death' decisions. The concept of decision-making ownership is the most powerful organisational principle and determines organisational prime accountability, which proposes that organisations and their owners have prime adherence to the principles of just one sector.

For hybrid organisations, a conflict between competing sector principles of ownership could be, and in the case of Fannie and Freddie was, disastrous. As things stand, the main choices for the future of Fannie and Freddie appear to be: (1) following the traditional dichotomy of the ideal models, either public or private ownership; or (2) following the authentic model, either public–private hybrids or private–public hybrids.

In all four cases, transparent accountable ownership would be in the hands of either government or the private sector. For hybrid organisations, the degree to which other principles might be absorbed from either the public or private sectors would be a matter for the decision by the prime sector decision-making owners. The following subsection briefly considers the confusion regarding the ownership of many UK NHS Foundation Trusts and the negotiation of the confusion by a famous English hospital with a history of more than 150 years.

National Uncertainty: The Royal Marsden Foundation Trust

The Marsden Foundation Trust was founded by philanthropic funds in 1851 as the Free Cancer Hospital and in 1910 was granted its Royal Charter. Dating back to 1066, Charters are important as strong signals of legitimacy and as an indication of links with influential individuals. Philanthropy was not the only source of support for the Marsden. Payment by patients (important as early evidence of hybridity) has been tracked back to at least 1908. In 1948 it joined the NHS as a teaching hospital and in 2004 became one of the first Foundation Trusts.[6] Originally, foundation trusts were intended to be 'established in law as a new legally independent organisation with the duty to provide NHS services to NHS patients' (Department of Health, 2003). The NHS (NHS Foundation Trust Directory, 2018) declared that 'foundation trusts are not directed by government so have greater freedom to decide, with their governors and members, their own strategy and the way services are run'. This definition becomes more complicated in the following paragraph of the Directory when it is explained that Foundation Trusts are 'accountable to their local communities through their members and governors, their commissioners through contracts, and to Parliament, the Care Quality Commission and NHS Improvement' (ibid.). It is almost impossible to know what this might mean in practice, and it is a fine example of opaque, confused accountability. In the meantime, organisational life has continued. Some successful Foundation Trusts such as the Royal Marsden continued to consolidate their position as hybrid organisations, as discussed more conceptually in the following reflections.

Reflections

The concept of the Foundation Trust appears plagued by lack of clarity regarding its real ownership. The public policy discourse is largely framed within the constraints of the ideal model of sectors, and the future of the NHS is today seen as a straightforward choice between public or private ownership: to privatise or not to privatise? However, this is not the question that needs to be addressed. Reframing the discourse utilising the concept of the authentic sector unveils a more complex, but less constricting, picture that more accurately reflects the historic organisational path of the NHS and its hybrid organisations.

With the benefit of hindsight, the NHS itself can be analysed as having been enacted as a hybrid organisation, since the majority of general practitioners are self-employed independent contractors, and 'the partnership model of general practice has been at the heart of the NHS since 1948' (BMA, 2018). This model is a business in which profits are shared between the partners.

The organisational history of the Marsden reveals a hybrid organisation with a history stretching back more than 150 years. Although the Marsden had its roots and primary adherence to the principles of philanthropy and charity it also, as noted earlier, had a history of accepting private patients and now has a thriving Private Care department. It continues to have influential support, with members of the Royal Family as its patrons. Speculating, the Marsden appears to have been a third sector–private sector shallow hybrid almost since its foundation, and had moved slowly towards a more entrenched position by the time it became part of the National Health Service in 1948. At that point it would formally have become a government-owned organisation. However, later evidence suggests that hybridity had become entrenched. As the newly appointed Medical Director of Private Care noted on this appointment in 2015, 'the Royal Marsden has been able to maintain financial viability of growing the non-NHS work and cross subsidising the service'.[7] By 2017 the Marsden included a separate Department of Private Care, employed dedicated staff for its private work and was housed in separate buildings.

The evidence of entrenched hybridity with the third sector is evident in the important role of the Royal Marsden Cancer Charity. This is hardly surprising in view of the hospital's charitable roots that have never disappeared. Despite the entrenched hybridity, the Annual Report (Royal Marsden Cancer Charity, 2018) points out that the Foundation Trust receives 70 per cent of its income from the NHS and is insistent in its documents that it sees itself as an NHS (public sector) hospital.

The Royal Marsden is in a privileged but not unique position; other Foundation Trusts are in a similar position. They were, and continue to be, hybrid organisations but now the prime ownership has moved over to the public sector. Hybridity is likely to be a continuing feature and hybridity theory provides the organisational tools to achieve greater clarity of ownership and to decide how much hybridity is permissible in maintaining that clarity. The following, final case study returns to the grassroots, and returns to some of the early themes which have received only limited discussion.

Local Disturbance: A Case of Opaque Ownership

This final study is based on confidential, sensitive research now presented anonymously 15 years after the closure of the organisation concerned. It also illustrates the inclusive structural approach when hybridity theory was in the early stages of development. This chapter will utilise that and other material to revisit the case study utilising the concepts presented earlier

The organisation (here referred to as 'DIV'), a charity, provided services for deprived, isolated or vulnerable people and was affiliated to a national group of similar organisations. It operated in a local authority (LA) with a population of some 220 000 and served a target group of about 28 000. DIV had a total of approximately 26 staff divided into full-time and part-time employees, and supported by 50 volunteers. Importantly, at least 75 per cent of its income came from governmental sources: 60 per cent from the LA and 15 per cent from associated NHS sources. Non-governmental sources included 5 per cent from housing associations, 9 per cent from trusts, and 8 per cent from sales. Donations and fundraising accounted for 0.5 per cent of the total.

DIV had been founded as an amalgamation of three groups in the local area and had been in existence for 12 years. Although the organisation was well respected in the community, the director of DIV was aware that it had serious organisational problems and it rapidly became clear that it was a deeply dysfunctional organisation. As a result DIV commissioned a study that would involve an organisational review based on 20 individual confidential interviews with members of the executive committee, staff, volunteers and a member of the local authority. The project revealed that DIV was lacking three fundamental features: clear focus and strong roots; firm leadership and governance; and an accountable organisational structure. Each of these missing features was discussed in the three parts of the report of the review.

Thus, in part one, the report contained participants' comments such as: 'the organisation has lost its roots', 'we are just trundling along', 'we don't know where we are going', and 'there is confusion about core activities'. The discontent was widespread. In brief, DIV did not have a clearly identifiable core client group or area of expertise. This lack of focus and roots made it difficult to galvanise staff and volunteers, manage the organisation, build up expertise and develop a clear strategic policy.

Part two turned to the problems of governance and leadership. Again, the overwhelming response was dissatisfaction. Some of the comments were: 'there is lack of leadership', 'we need a board that does work', 'we haven't got around to have a membership, it just fell by the wayside', and 'I don't feel a part of DIV'. There was an absence of any sense of a common mission, or sense of a team. Board members and trustees were seen to be primarily interested in representing their specific personal interests or those of their own organisation, and were generally considered ineffective. This was evidently an important cause of the organisation's dysfunction.

Part three, the analysis of the organisational structure, completed the picture. The comments from different participants were deeply concerning: 'There is no sense of team', 'nothing gets done really well', 'there is unorganised chaos', 'there is a failure to delegate and take responsibility', 'there's a problem of overwork . . . and sickness', 'there's a lack of job boundaries which is a dangerous position', 'there is no supervision and also lack of fulfilment', 'we wear so many hats that we cannot focus and do one thing well', 'we are not managed very well', and 'the problem is the management structure at all levels'.

The critical comments were included anonymously in the final report, and the general consensus about the overwhelming scale of the problems provided an irresistible engine of change. It became clear that most of the problems stemmed from fundamental confusion regarding the roles of the board and the director, and their implementation. The final report contained 25 recommendations and reflected the changes that were required, including revised roles for the board and director. Most of the suggestions were in the process of implementation a year later. After that, contact was lost with DIV until I read of its closure 15 years later.

Reflections

In the period since this project the theory of hybrid organisations has been substantially developed and these reflections consider how the new concepts might have contributed to a better understanding of the problem of accountable ownership in DIV. Two confidential reports have been found from the time of the amalgamation that help to provide a better understanding of the organisational status of DIV. The first, written by the previous consultant to DIV, states that: 'the impetus for this amalgamation came neither from the local groups nor from the central organisation, but from the local authority, the major funder for all three groups'. It seems that at the same time their funding was substantially cut and half their staff were made redundant. The enforced closure of their shop had further cut their income. The consultant suggested that the LA was bringing together three very different autonomous groups and trying to create a coherent new organisation with an identity of its own. Soon after that report, DIV prepared its own detailed three-year Development Plan which helped to lay bare its dependency on the local authority: 'we are totally dependent on the local authority for funding'. The Plan was ambitious but, as it admitted, was 'contingent on factors outside our control'. The report contains a comparatively lengthy account of the severe problems faced by those in their client group and, on the other side, the limited resources of DIV. The symbiotic relationship was in the not unusual position of being unbalanced.

A major lesson from the project with DIV was that it was not an autonomous organisation. More realistically, it was enacted by the LA as a 'coerced enacted hybrid' without roots. The draconian cuts in staffing and the enforced closure of a shop culminated in the enactment of the new hybrid. The action of the LA was that of a principal owner with prime sector adherence to the ownership principles of the public sector. At the same time, because DIV was constituted as a charity, it was the governing body, the trustees, who were seen as the legal owners. Whilst the legal position was correct, it proved organisationally unhelpful when confronted with the real situation. Operating in the old organisational reality, the external world and the DIV board and staff regarded DIV as an autonomous voluntary sector organisation. And to a degree, it was. It could be argued that the board and staff made the operational decisions, in the way in which they responded to the problems of the clients, they chose which grants to chase, and they undertook some modest sales of services and fundraising. DIV was able to take decisions over short-term planning and implementation but was still largely dependent on the LA in the longer view.

In essence, principal ownership was opaque from the initial foundation of DIV. In large part the opaqueness resulted from the state of organisational knowledge at that time. The LA established the new organisation in good faith, by taking three financially dependent and troubled organisations and amalgamating them. It did not realise that, in so doing, it was making one of the most important decisions of a principal owner. Neither could it appreciate the fundamentally different principles of a public sector organisation and those of a third sector organisation that were exacerbated by the complexities of being a hybrid organisation.

The end product was the creation of a new organisation without its own accountable decision-making owner. Nor, after the amalgamation, did such a role exist in the local authority which, once it created DIV, was content to work on special issues and provide an annual grant. DIV was left with a gaping hole at the top of its pyramid of principles which it had found difficult to fill.

Neither side in the 'partnership' really appreciated that, despite their common interest in dealing with a particular range of problems, their core principles were basically different. The local authority was concerned to provide a level of public service that satisfied the voters and increased its chance of re-election. On the other hand, DIV was essentially interested in a specific group of people with problems, and in its close relationship with the LA, and its concern to ensure its grant. The latter may have been a factor in its failure to develop roots most relevant for a charitable third sector hybrid: membership was ignored, the number of volunteers was modest as were fundraising activities, and influential sponsors were not obtained.

The objective of this section of the chapter has been to demonstrate the value of the theory at the level of individual organisations. The following section, the conclusions, offers a reprise of the main argument in terms of the development of the ideal model and the authentic sectors. The rise of authentic sectors based on the amalgamation of both ideal model organisations and hybrid organisations is a major step into the NOR approach that will also be discussed.

CONCLUSIONS: TOWARDS A NEW ORGANISATIONAL REALITY

Reprise

Set against a background of the imbalance between human problems and the ability of formal organisations to respond to them, the concern of this chapter has been to explore the increasing role and challenges of accountability in hybrid organisations, principally that of achieving ownership. After first presenting the research approach, the argument may be seen as a process of building blocks in the development of theory.

The first stage comprised the linked concepts of the individual organisation and the ideal models of three sectors. As discussed in the following below, the formal organisations in these models draw their strength from the three historic organisational approaches: private, government and associational. Essential to this strength in a democracy are their distinctive pyramids of principles, and a transparency of accountability that flows down throughout the organisation.

The growing awareness of the presence of hybrid organisations led to stage two which involved the recognition and conceptualisation of more complex sectors, that include the first-level theory. These authentic sectors, still composed of formal organisations, include hybrid organisations (see Figure 24.2) which, with their conflicting principles, can blur the identification of accountable owners. As presented in the case studies, the lack of clarity about decision-making ownership contributes to human problems locally, nationally and internationally. The achievement of transparent accountability can be addressed by utilising the concepts of principal owners and prime sector adherence.

These conclusions discuss the impact of the findings of the chapter on organisational theory. In the first place they reflect on the need for rethinking organisational theory, and in the second place, they embark on a consideration of the possible direction and impact of the New Organisational Reality approach.

The Gap in Organisational Theory

My main criticism of current organisational theory is that it largely fails to take a sufficiently broad perspective of the definition of organisations. One major example is the failure to recognise hybrid organisations as a significant part of its theoretical territory. To ignore their impact, and the vast number and types of hybrids that exist, fails take to into account their scope and impact. Examples of hybrid organisations that come to mind include: family businesses,[8] political parties, the UK's Royal Family, the British Broadcasting Corporation (BBC), universities, the NHS, most large charities, non-governmental organisations (NGOs), a few banks, charity shops, social enterprises, housing associations, trade unions, parts of the legal system, some multinational companies, several governmental agencies, and numerous outstanding UK cultural organisations such as the National Theatre and the British Museum. All of these contain mix principles from one or more other sectors. Some hybrids are outstandingly successful, others are less so, and others have been outstanding disasters. A broader perspective would also require considering organisations and hybridity beyond formal organisations.

True, academic contributions to the study of hybrid organisations have increased dramatically and some theoretical approaches have attempted to absorb hybrid organisations within their own existing theories of formal organisations. More precisely, they do not offer an encompassing theory of hybrid organisations, but discuss parts or aspects of hybrid organisations. Of these approaches, institutional theory is widely regarded as one of the most significant and has been described by Andrew Pettigrew (quoted in the cover blurb for the second edition of the *SAGE Handbook of Organizational Institutionalism*;

Greenwood et al., 2018) as the 'default theory in management and organisation studies'. In view of the limitations of space I shall concentrate only on this approach.

Readers of the literature in this area, including myself, cannot fail to be impressed by the range of organisational issues that are now encompassed, and the eminent scholars who operate within its broad tent. Nonetheless, it is a struggle to understand its core definitions and boundaries. The comments from some of those within the tent is not reassuring on this account. The discomfort is evident in the blistering critique from Havaman and David (2008) in their contributions to the first edition of the *SAGE Handbook of Organizational Institutionalism*. The strength of the institutional perspective they say:

> is its sweeping reach . . . But the strength provided by this broad reach also generates a critical weakness. If institution and institutionalization mean everything and explain everything – change and stability; routines, values, and norms; intra-organisational, organisational, and inter-organisational structures and behaviours; cognitive, regulative, and a normative processes – then they mean nothing and explain nothing. (ibid., pp. 582–583)

What is called by the authors of that *Handbook* 'a contrary view' (ibid., p. 4), set out by Czarniawska (2008) and designed to be more supportive of institutional theory, is revealed to be hardly more reassuring, describing many contributions to the new institutionalism as 'confused' (Havaman and David, 2008, p. 779).

The critical constructive approach of Greenwood and his colleagues is closer to the approach of this chapter. Also writing from within the institutional tent, they claim 'that the most important institution in modern society is the organisation', and that institutional scholarship is 'missing an attempt to gain a coherent, holistic account of how organisations are structured and managed' (Greenwood et al., 2014, p. 1206). But there is an even more fundamental issue that will need to be addressed, and that is the steady change in the nature of organisations themselves, with the rise and impact of hybrid organisations and the entry into the New Organisational Reality that is discussed in the following subsection.

Reflections on the Potential Impact of a New Organisational Reality

The previous sections of this chapter presented a theory of ideal model sectors that was then superseded by the theory of authentic sectors which included individual formal hybrid organisations. Then, hybridity theory demonstrated its value in responding to the major problem of individual hybrid organisations: confused accountable decision-making ownership. At present, the body of existing theory offers a strong basis for understanding and responding to the possible existential problem of hybrid organisations. As discussed earlier, the ideal model sectors provided the major organisational responses to human needs and seem to be the logical starting point for the development of organisational theory. But we are now living in an era in which the focus on individual hybrid organisations has segued into an underwritten model that enables large-scale reproduction of hybrid structures.

My proposition is that there is already a strong case that, with apologies to Andrew Pettigrew, the default reality of many groups of organisations is already hybridity. Organisational practice has steadily accepted hybrid organisations as essential forms of formal organisation. At this juncture the role of governments and their agencies are important to this process. They have a long tradition of involvement in hybrid organisations (see, for example, Chapter 11 of this *Handbook*)). They also have the power, if not necessarily the resources, to establish large numbers of similar hybrid organisations. They can devise policies that require the creation of more or less similar types of organisation in particular areas of social problems. And hybrid organisations involved with the private or third sectors can appear to be an attractive way to cut costs and improve services.

The practical implementation of hybridity and the advance of NOR is demonstrated in research on housing associations. A relevant study is that of Nguyen et al. (2012), who trace the evolution of US housing policy towards greater hybridity. Utilising hybridity theory they note that, since the Housing Act of 1937, the delivery of public housing in the USA has evolved from a purely public model to a model of entrenched hybridity. They suggest that one benefit of the shift towards hybridity is that it 'has encouraged Local Housing Authorities' to harness the power of markets and employ business techniques, while also enlisting the services of nonprofits, volunteers and faith-based organisations to provide high-quality affordable rental housing tenant services (ibid., p. 470). Although the authors utilise just two case studies, the background to this work is the 3300 public housing agencies in the USA. This appears to be a large-scale slide into the NOR.

UK governments have taken a more transparent slide in their support for social enterprises, now widely regarded by scholars, if not by government, as hybrid organisations (Doherty et al., 2014). Social enterprises have proved difficult to define, and government, keen to establish their number, has undertaken research to solve the problem. The researchers immediately faced the dilemma of defining social enterprises and, in their attempt to solve the issues, decided to identify some 'core criteria' (UK Government, 2017, p. 7). Their main conclusions, supported by a panel of practitioners, were that: at least 50 per cent of income must come from trading or commercial activities; surplus profits must be used primarily to further social or environmental goals; these goals should be of greater or equal concern compared to financial goals; and social enterprises should have charitable status and legal form. Although their approach should be treated with some caution, they decided that there were 471 000 social enterprises in the UK.

It is certainly a reasonable set of criteria, but publicly accepting most social enterprises as hybrid organisations and utilising an organisational accountable decision-making approach would be a more profitable utilisation of public resources. Its concepts would not only better suit the counting exercise, but they would also make it possible to categorise the different types of hybrid enterprises, in addition to helping resolve problems emanating from the clash of sector principles.

These two examples are the tip of the NOR iceberg. The fact is that, globally, governments have widely implemented the key part of the NOR approach. Thus recent research by Bruton et al. (2015), drawing on 36 case studies from four industries in 23 countries, concluded that many state-owned enterprises were hybrid organisations although they were typically viewed dichotomously as either completely state or private (ibid., p. 121). State-owned enterprises represented approximately 10 per cent of global gross domestic product (GDP) and the authors make a powerful plea, referring to these hybrid organisations, that 'if management research endeavors to be more globally and broadly relevant, we argue that scholars should devote additional time attention to this important, adaptive, and enduring organisational form' (ibid., p. 29).

So far I have discussed the impact of the formal organisation element of the NOR and its link with public policy. In conclusion I look briefly forward to the additional development of the NOR in Chapters 27 and 29 of this *Handbook*. The first of these chapters analyses the often underestimated, sometimes almost hidden yet critical, role of volunteers in organisations. In Chapter 29 the theory of hybrid organisations takes a large step forward in response to my own plea for a broader boundary for organisational research. The practical problem has been one that I have wrestled with for a long while, as I and many other researchers had encountered the difficulties of attempting to understand the overlapping territory between formal organisations and the non-formal organisational forms of the personal world. More recent research has enabled me to identify a unique form of personal world organisation, the 'personal-organisation' (PO), and the hybrid relationships of these with formal organisations. This closes the theoretical gap between formal and non-formal organisations; increases awareness of the interdependence between different forms of organisation; improves knowledge and sensitivity to the advantages and disadvantages of those organisations; and introduces a new way of understanding and thinking about organisations.

NOTES

1. The names and aims of the sectors often vary from country to country, particularly that of the third sector which has been called nonprofit, voluntary or non-governmental as well as civil society, charity, and other terms.
2. Brunel University, Programme of Research and Training into Voluntary Action, Workshop for Voluntary Sector Staff, February 1979. This was the first workshop of the Programme of Research and Training into Voluntary Action (PORTVAC) that I founded a year earlier.
3. Based on confidential discussions with parents of handicapped children in the care of a large voluntary organisation.
4. The material in this paragraph is a summary taken from Billis (2010, Chapter 3).
5. Conservatorship is a draconian step. 'As conservator FHFA has the powers of the management, boards and shareholders of Fannie Mae and Freddie Mac. [Both] continue to operate as business corporations' (https://www.fhfa.gov/Conservatorship).
6. https://www.royalmarsden.nhs.uk/about-royal-marsden/who-we-are/foundation-trust-status.
7. http://www.paulharrisplasticsurgeon.co.uk/new-appointment-as-medical-director-of-private-care-at-the-royal-marsden-hospital/.
8. Family businesses as hybrids are discussed in Chapter 29 of this *Handbook*.

REFERENCES

Armour, S. and J. Healey (2008) 'Taxpayers take on trillions in risk in Fannie, Freddie takeover', *USA Today*, 7 September.
Baker, D. (2018) 'The future of Fannie and Freddie', *American Affairs*, Spring Vol. 1. https://americanaffairsjournal.org/2018/02/future-fannie-freddie/.
Berger, P. and T. Luckman (1971) *The Social Construction of Reality*, Harmondsworth: Penguin Books.
Beveridge, W. (1948) *Voluntary Action: A Report on Methods of Social Advance*, London: George Allen & Unwin.
Billis, D. (1984) *Welfare Bureaucracies: Their Design and Change in Response to Social Problems*, London: Heinemann.
Billis, D. (1991) 'The roots of voluntary agencies: a question of choice', *Nonprofit and Voluntary Sector Quarterly*, 20(1), 57–69.
Billis, D. (ed.) (2010) *Hybrid Organizations and the Third Sector*, London: Palgrave Macmillan.
Billis, D. (ed.) (2013) *The Symbiotic Relationship Between Social Enterprise and Hybridity*, Liege: EMES.
Billis, D. and R. Rowbottom (1977) 'The stratification of work and organisational design', *Human Relations*, 30(1), 53–76.

BMA (2018) 'Focus on taking on new partners – guidance for GPs', British Medical Association, updated 23 April. https://www.bma.org.uk/advice/employment/gp-practices/gps-and-staff/focus-on-taking-on-new-partners.

Bozeman, B. (1987) *All Organizations are Public: Bridging Public and Private Organizational Theories*, San Francisco, CA: Jossey-Bass.

Bruton, G., D. Ahistrom, S. Ciprian, M. Peng and Kehan Ku (2015) 'State-owned enterprises around the world as hybrid organizations', *Academy of Management Perspectives*, 29(1), 92–114.

Czarniawska, B. (2008) 'How to misuse institutions and get away with it: some reflections on institutional theory/ies', in R. Greenwood, C. Oliver, K. Sahlin and R. Suddaby (eds), *SAGE Handbook of Organizational Institutionalism*, 1st edition, Thousand Oaks, CA: SAGE, pp. 769–811.

Dean, H. (2010) *Understanding Human Need: Social Issues, Policy and Practice*, Bristol: Policy Press.

Department of Health (2003) 'Short Guide to NHS Foundation Trusts', updated 23 May 2018. https://www.wwl.nhs.uk/Library/Foundation_Trust/Foundation_Trust_Guide.pdf.

Doherty, B., H. Haugh and F. Lyon (2014) 'Social enterprises as hybrid organizations: a review and research agenda', *International Journal of Management Reviews*, 16(4), 417–436.

The Economist (2008) 'Fannie Mae and Freddie Mac: end of illusions', 17 July 17.

Fama, E. and M. Jenson (1983) 'Separation of ownership and control', *Journal of Law and Economics*, 26(2), 301–325.

Forrester, T. (2010) 'Is it time to start worrying about Fannie Mae and Freddie Mac again?' www.washingtonpost.com, accessed 28 October 2016.

Greenwood, R., C.R. Hinings and D. Whetten (2014) 'Rethinking institutions and organizations', *Journal of Management Studies*, 51(7), 1206–1220.

Greenwood, R., C. Oliver, T. Lawrence and R. Meyer (eds) (2018), *SAGE Handbook of Organizational Institutionalism*, 2nd edition, Thousand Oaks, CA: SAGE.

Grossman, S. and O. Hart (1986) 'The costs and benefits of ownership: a theory of vertical and lateral integration' *Journal of Political Economy*, 94(4), 691–719.

Havaman, H. and R. David (2008) 'Ecologists and institutionalists: friends or foes?', in R. Greenwood, C. Oliver, K. Sahlin and R. Suddaby (eds), *SAGE Handbook of Organizational Institutionalism*, 1st edition, Thousand Oaks, CA: SAGE, pp. 574–593.

Howard, J. and M. Taylor (2010) 'Hybridity in partnership working: managing tensions and opportunities', in D. Billis (ed.), *Hybrid Organizations and the Third Sector*, London: Palgrave Macmillan, pp. 175–196.

Jaques, Elliott (1976) *A General Theory of Bureaucracy*, London: Heinemann Educational Books.

Jaques, Elliott (2002) *The Life and Behavior of Living Organisms: A General Theory*, Santa Barbara, CA: Praeger.

Koppell, J.G.S. (2003) *The Politics of Quasi-Government: Hybrid Organizations and the Dynamics of Bureaucratic Control*, Cambridge: Cambridge University Press.

Lawler, J. (2018) 'Steven Mnuchin: legislation on Fannie, Freddie won't happen this year', *Washington Examiner*, 30 April.

Milgrom, P.R. and J. Roberts (1992) *Economics, Organization, and Management*, Englewood Cliffs, NJ: Prentice-Hall.

Nguyen, M.T., W. Rohe and S.M. Cowan (2012) 'Entrenched hybridity in public housing agencies in the USA', *Housing Studies*, 27(4), 457–475.

NHS Foundation Trust Directory (2018) 'What are Foundation Trusts?' https://www.gov.uk/government/organisations/department-of-health-and-social-care.

Nielsen, B. (2018) 'The US Congress is largely to blame', https://www.investopedia.com/.

Perry, J.L. and H.G. Rainey (1988) 'The public–private distinction in organization theory: a critique and research strategy', *Academy of Management Review*, 13(2), 182–201.

Popper, K.R. (1972) *Objective Knowledge: An Evolutionary Approach*, Oxford: Clarendon Press.

Popper, K.R. (1974) *Conjectures and Refutations: The Growth of Scientific Knowledge*, 5th edition, London: Routledge & Kegan Paul.

Popper, K.R. (1992) *Unended Quest*, London: Routledge Classics.

Royal Marsden Cancer Charity (2018), Annual Report, 2018.

Seidman, H. (1988) 'The quasi world of the federal government', *Brookings Review*, 6(3), 23–27.

Teasdale, S., H. Buckingham and J. Rees (2013) 'Is the third sector being overwhelmed by the state and the market?', Third Sector Futures Dialogues, Big Picture, Paper 4 Birmingham, Third Sector Research Centre, University of Birmingham.

Udy, S. (1959) '"Bureaucracy" and "rationality" in Weber's organisation theory: an empirical study', *American Sociological Association*, 24(6), 791–795.

UK Government (2017) 'Social enterprise: market trends', September, Department of Media, Digital and Sport.

Wamsley, G.L. and M.N. Zald (1976) *The Political Economy of Public Organizations*, Bloomington, IN: Indiana University Press.

25. Hybrid organisations in sub-Saharan Africa
David Littlewood and Diane Holt

INTRODUCTION

The Khayelitsha Cookie Company (KCC) is a hybrid organisation in South Africa that provides affirming employment for women from disadvantaged township communities, who are paid a fair wage and have equity in the venture. Cookswell Jikos is a hybrid organisation in Kenya that produces and sells energy-efficient cook stoves to achieve its environmental mission of household-level sustainable seed-to-ash cooking in Africa. In Zambia, the hybrid organisation the Mumwa Crafts Association connects low-income craft producers from remote rural areas with domestic and international markets, providing them with a much-needed stable source of income. These are just three examples of hybrid organisations in sub-Saharan Africa, the area of the African continent that lies south of the Sahara Desert. Hybrid organisations, which exist at the interface of the public, private and third sectors, and which span boundaries between them, can now be found across sub-Saharan Africa.

In recent times, we have seen a proliferation of hybrid organising, and a growth in the number of hybrid organisations globally (Haigh et al., 2015). It is increasingly suggested that such organisations have an important role to play in tackling 'wicked' global sustainable development challenges. Accompanying these developments there has been a surge in academic interest in hybrid organisations and organising (see, e.g., Billis, 2010; Jay, 2013; Doherty et al., 2014; Haigh et al., 2015; Powell et al., 2018). Nevertheless, there remains much about hybrid organisations that we do not know, particularly about hybrids in developing economies. More specifically there remains a relative paucity of work on hybrid organisations and organising in sub-Saharan Africa (Holt and Littlewood, 2015). This reflects wider limited business and management scholarship on sub-Saharan Africa (see Zoogah and Nkomo, 2013; Walsh, 2015). This chapter contributes towards addressing these gaps. Accordingly, the chapter has three main objectives:

- to examine the state of the research field on hybrid organisations and hybrid organising in sub-Saharan Africa;
- to explore the types of hybrid organisations found in sub-Saharan Africa and their characteristics, deploying a contextualised framework of Billis's (2010) theory of hybrid organisations;
- to identify challenges faced by different types of hybrid organisations in sub-Saharan Africa, and possible strategies for overcoming them.

The chapter is structured to address these objectives as follows. It begins with a review of extant literature on hybrid organisations in sub-Saharan Africa. This is followed by a discussion of Billis's (2010) theory of hybrid organisations which we contextualise for use in sub-Saharan Africa. This theory is then applied as a framework to explore the different types of hybrid organisations found in sub-Saharan Africa, and their characteristics, illustrated with examples. The challenges different hybrid organisations in sub-Saharan African contexts face are then discussed, along with strategies for overcoming such challenges. Finally, the chapter concludes with a summary discussion of its contributions to knowledge and theory, as well as identifying areas for future research and implications for policy and practice.

HYBRID ORGANISATIONS IN SUB-SAHARAN AFRICA: WHAT DO WE KNOW?

The term 'hybrid organisations', and notions of hybrid organising, have come to prominence relatively recently in the business and management field (Pache and Santos, 2010; Haigh and Hoffman, 2012). Indeed, in recent years we have witnessed a rapid growth in hybrid organisation scholarship (see, e.g., Battilana and Dorado, 2010; Battilana et al., 2012; Doherty et al., 2014; Bruton et al., 2015; Haigh et al., 2015; Mair et al., 2015; Kannothra et al., 2018; Powell et al., 2018). However, underpinning this recent interest and literature are earlier works. Firstly, work informed by new institutional theories focusing on how organisations cope with competing institutional demands and logics (Scott and Meyer, 1991; Scott, 2001; Hoffman, 1999). Secondly, extant studies in the public administration field (Lan and Rainey, 1992; Denis et al., 2015), and indeed across the wider social sciences, addressing issues of the blurring of boundaries between the public, private and third sectors (O'Neill, 1989; Billis, 1991, 2010).

As part of this growth in hybrid organisation scholarship in business and management a stream of research has developed examining hybrid organisations in sub-Saharan Africa (e.g., Rivera-Santos et al., 2015; Holt and Littlewood, 2015). There also exists a relevant wider cross-disciplinary literature on non-governmental organisations (NGOs) and the third sector in sub-Saharan Africa, and on how the blurring of boundaries between public, private and third sectors plays out in sub-Saharan African contexts.

In this chapter hybrid organisations are understood broadly as organisations that possess the structural features and characteristics of more than one sector (public, private and third). This understanding is founded on the notion that organisations in different sectors manifest generic features and characteristics that are in some way 'pure' and distinct (see Billis, 2010). According to Pache and Santos (2013), hybrid organisations span sector boundaries, incorporating elements from different institutional logics. After Doherty et al. (2014), social enterprises can be seen as a classic example of a hybrid organisation in that they combine properties and logics associated with private, public and third sector organisations. Another example of a hybrid organisation might be state-owned enterprises (see Bruton et al., 2015), which combine logics from the public and private sectors. Hockerts (2015), meanwhile, identifies some fair trade organisations as hybrids; these are organisations that aim to manipulate trading relationships to create income for poor, marginalised producers by charging a premium to conscientious consumers. Some organisations engaging in base of the pyramid (BoP) initiatives are also regarded as hybrids; these provide essential products and services (for example, health, transportation, finance) at an affordable price to poor customers who would otherwise not have access to such products, or only at a prohibitive cost. In these latter instances these organisations combine private sector logics with those of the third and/ or the public sector.

In business and management studies there is an emerging body of literature on hybrid organisations in sub-Saharan Africa. A significant proportion of this work focuses on social enterprises, as a specific type of hybrid organisation. In one early study, Thompson and Doherty (2006) consider the hybrid organisation Play Pumps as part of a review of global social enterprise cases, whilst Kerlin (2009) examines social enterprise cases in Zambia and Zimbabwe in her global comparative work. In 2011, a major research project was conducted on social enterprises in South Africa funded by the International Labour Organization and the Belgian government which examined 24 cases focusing on best-practice learning. This work looked at the backgrounds and histories, business models and target markets of the case study organisations and developed a range of tools, guides and training materials as well as reports addressing themes such as impact measurement (Fonteneau, 2011) and appropriate policy responses (Steinman, 2010; Steinman and van Rooij, 2012).

Social enterprises and social entrepreneurship in South Africa are now relatively well studied (see Urban, 2008; Karanda and Toledano, 2012; Kodzi, 2015; Littlewood and Holt, 2015b, 2018a; Claeyé, 2017), particularly compared to other countries on the African continent. However, increasingly research is also being conducted on social enterprises elsewhere in sub-Saharan Africa. For example, Cieslik (2016) examines a social enterprise community-based green energy project in rural Burundi, Holt and Littlewood (2017) research the bricolage activities of social entrepreneurs in Kenya, and Ciambotti and Pedrini (2019) explore the hybrid harvesting strategies of social enterprises in Kenya.

Cross-country comparative work is also being undertaken. The Trickle Out Africa research project examines social and environmental enterprises throughout East and Southern Africa (www.trickleout.net). Meanwhile, Rivera-Santos et al. (2015) present the findings of quantitative research examining social enterprises across 19 sub-Saharan African countries. They explore the significance of environmental characteristics on social entrepreneurship, focusing specifically on four African contextual dimensions (informality, acute poverty, colonial history and ethnic group identity), and find that these may influence how social entrepreneurs in sub-Saharan Africa perceive themselves and their ventures, as well as their choice of activity. Further recent cross-country studies include work by Littlewood and Holt (2015a) on the landscape of social and environmental entrepreneurship in Africa, whilst in another study Holt and Littlewood (2015) explore the identification, mapping and monitoring of impact in hybrid organisations, introducing their Hy-Map impact framework, and illustrating their discussions and its use with reference to case examples from Kenya, Zambia, Mozambique and South Africa. Finally, Littlewood and Holt (2018b) examine social enterprise resilience with reference to cases from multiple sub-Saharan African countries, Mirvis and Googins (2018) assess partnerships between international actors and African social enterprises, and Steinfield and Holt (2019) develop a theory of the reproduction of social innovation in subsistence markets drawing upon examples from across sub-Saharan Africa.

Bitzer et al. (2015) provide a wider focus for our review by presenting a collection of works on social and environmental innovation in Africa, encompassing case examples not only of social enterprise hybrids, but also of BoP-type hybrids and hybrid cross-sector partnerships. In its early incarnations BoP literature focused particularly on multinational corporations (MNCs) as the principal agents for BoP initiatives. It was suggested that there was a fortune available for those multinationals that could tailor their products and services to low-income consumers and markets, and that this would simultaneously benefit those consumers by providing them with needed goods and services (see Prahalad, 2004; Hammond and Prahalad, 2004). However, since these early writings, and as Kolk et al. (2014) discuss, approaches to BoP have evolved quite dramatically, exemplified in discussion of 'BoP 2.0' (Simanis and Hart, 2008) and most recently 'BoP 3.0' (Hart and Casado Caneque, 2015). Here, rather than searching for a fortune in the BoP it is suggested that firms can make a fortune with the BoP through processes of co-creation (London, 2009). BoP literature and practice is also now less MNC-focused; indeed Kolk et al. (2014) suggest that most initiators of BoP programmes are not the large MNCs originally envisaged in early work, but are often small local firms, not-for-profit charities or social enterprises, and in some instances even the state. Some of this literature focuses on BoP initiatives in sub-Saharan Africa contexts. Arnould and Mohr (2005), for example, examine the BoP innovations of local companies in Zinder in Niger, whilst McFalls (2007) looks at HP's i-Community in South Africa and the limits of 'inclusive capitalism' (see also Anderson and Kupp, 2008; Dolan and Scott, 2009; Simanis et al., 2008). Nevertheless, Kolk et al. (2014) identify a need for a broadening of the empirical base in BoP research, particularly in relation to Africa.

Research has also been conducted into other types of hybrid organisation in sub-Saharan Africa, both within the business and management field and across the wider social sciences. For example, there is a significant body of work on fair trade hybrid organisations in sub-Saharan Africa, addressing a range of issues including their international relationships, governance and their impact on producers, all explored with reference to varied fair trade products (see Becchetti and Costantino, 2008; Raynolds and Ngcwangu, 2010; Bassett, 2010). The tourism industry across sub-Saharan Africa is also populated by diverse organisational forms, many of which possess the structural features and characteristics of more than one sector and might be considered hybrids. Researchers have examined tourism hybrid social enterprises in sub-Saharan Africa specifically (see Von der Weppen and Chochrane, 2012; Van Wijk et al., 2015), but also organisations undertaking pro-poor, community-based and sustainable tourism, with each of these notions having its own body of literature. State-owned enterprises are furthermore prevalent in the tourism industry in sub-Saharan Africa, as will be discussed in this chapter, and can be considered a form of hybrid organisation (see Bruton et al., 2015). There is also a wider body of work on state-owned enterprises in Africa (Ariyo and Afeikhena, 1999), although there remains significant scope for further work in this area.

This section has reviewed the state of the field in research on hybrid organisations in sub-Saharan Africa, exploring what we do and do not know. In the following section we explore the theory of hybrid organisations proposed by Billis (2010) and which we contextualise for application in sub-Saharan Africa.

A THEORY OF HYBRID ORGANISATIONS IN SUB-SAHARAN AFRICA

In constructing his theory of hybrid organisations, Billis (2010) begins by reviewing extant literature, and through this identifying three major approaches to understanding hybrids.

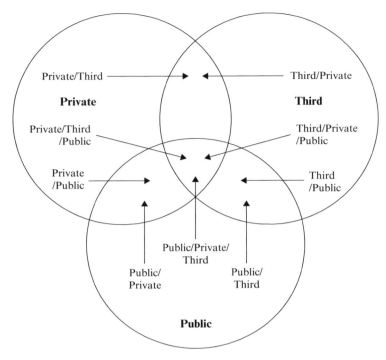

Source: Billis (2010, p. 56).

Figure 25.1 *Three sectors and their hybrid zones*

He argues that these are: the conceptualisation of hybrids as occupying points on a continuum between sectors; studies that emphasise a single sector (public or private), and explore organisations and their boundaries from the perspective of that sector; and studies that throw out the sector metaphor and view hybridisation as ubiquitous. However, Billis takes a different view, introducing his prime sector approach, arguing that hybrid organisations have their roots in and primarily adhere to the principles of one sector: public, private or third. Each sector then has three forms or zones of hybridity which it is possible for organisations to move or slide into, or indeed to be born into. Billis (2010) describes this latter scenario as 'enacted' hybridity and the former as 'organic' hybridity. He also distinguishes between 'shallow' hybridity, that is, a modest form of hybridity, and 'entrenched' hybridity where hybridity is embedded in governance and/or operations. Figure 25.1 is taken from Billis (2010, p. 56) and illustrates the three sectors and their hybrid zones.

Billis's model and theory of hybrid organisations are based on the idea that organisations in different sectors – public, private and third – present certain generic features and characteristics that are 'pure' and distinct, and that each sector has its own mechanisms for accountability linked to particular ownership types. In this chapter Billis's model is used as a framework for discussing different types of hybrids found in sub-Saharan Africa. However, in sub-Saharan African contexts the key building blocks of Billis's (2010) model

– namely, the public, private and third sectors – are different, at least in some respects, to those found in developed countries. There are additional complexities associated with sub-Saharan African contexts, with the public, private and third sectors manifesting and interacting in particular ways. This in turn has implications for the types of hybrids that emerge and can be found in sub-Saharan Africa. A more contextualised theory of hybrid organisations in sub-Saharan Africa is therefore needed. We will now explore the nature of these three sectors – private, public and third – in sub-Saharan Africa.

The Private Sector in Sub-Saharan Africa

Whilst recognising significant differences across sub-Saharan African countries – such as differences between South Africa and Mali – and also intra-country variability, the private sector in sub-Saharan African countries is generally quite different to that found in developed economies. This manifests in the presence of a large informal economy in many sub-Saharan African countries. For example, in 2006 informal economy employment in Kenya was estimated at 6 million in contrast to the estimated 2 million people working in the formal economy (Kapila, 2006). Across sub-Saharan Africa more widely it has been suggested that the informal economy contributes 75 per cent of non-agricultural employment, 61 per cent of urban employment and up to 92 per cent of new jobs (Commission for Africa, 2005; see also Holt and Littlewood, 2014). This significance of the informal economy clearly has implications for hybrids in sub-Saharan Africa. Such organisations may choose to locate themselves in the informal economy. They may also move in and out of the informal economy as circumstances change, straddling the boundary between the formal and informal economies. Hybrid organisations in sub-Saharan Africa may also deal with informal economy suppliers or distributers, they may work with informal economy enterprises who can for instance be the beneficiaries of their training and support, and they may also sell their products in the informal economy or in wider BoP subsistence markets. Such subsistence marketplaces are often characterised by institutional 'voids' (Mair et al., 2012; Parmigiani and Rivera-Santos, 2015) where market failures or inefficiencies may result from institutions that are absent or non-functioning. Although these voids can also provide opportunity spaces for hybrid organisations.

At the other end of the private sector spectrum, many large firms in sub-Saharan African economies are multinational enterprises, or their subsidiaries. Indeed, this may be the case to a larger extent than in most developed countries, although we do also recognise that there are a growing number of large African companies active in varied sectors including finance, telecommunications and consumer goods, and often serving BoP markets. Finally, full or partial state-owned enterprises are prevalent across sub-Saharan Africa, for example in the extractive industries, but also in the provision of public services such as railways, power, water, and managing tourism and wildlife resources.

The Public Sector in Sub-Saharan Africa

Whilst again there is significant variation across and within countries, the public sector in sub-Saharan Africa, particularly when compared to that in more developed economies, is characterised by limited resources and capacity, regulatory voids, and also challenges of corruption, excessive bureaucracy and limits to accountability. Sub-Saharan African contexts are also characterised by significant legal (Meinzen-Dick and Pradhan, 2001) and wider institutional (Lund, 2006) pluralism. Indeed, scholarship has identified a situation of 'dual' national and ethnic institutional structures in many African states where you have on the one hand national-level institutions, policies and bureaucrats, and on the other hand, powerful ethnic norms, institutions and traditional leaders (see Michalopoulos and Papaioannou, 2015). These dual national and ethnic institutions coexist, and at some times and places are in harmony, and at others in conflict (Herbst, 2000). Finally, within some sub-Saharan African countries, conflict, political instability and limits to government resources have resulted in other actors taking on the traditional role and responsibilities of the state, with varied consequences; for example, oil companies in the Niger Delta, or NGOs and donors in Malawi who at one time provided an estimated 40 per cent of the country's budget (*Guardian*, 2014). Taken together, this means there are significant complexities in what constitutes the public sector in sub-Saharan African contexts, which again has implications for the types of hybrid organisations found in such settings.

The Third Sector in Sub-Saharan Africa

Historically the third sector in sub-Saharan Africa has been heavily influenced by international dynamics and actors. International NGOs operate directly in sub-Saharan African countries and also act through local partner organisations to which they provide funds and support. Assistance for local and international NGOs in Africa is also provided by developed-country governments; international philanthropic foundations, for example, the Ford Foundation and the Bill and Melinda Gates Foundation; and international institutions such as the Commonwealth and the United Nations. This contrasts with the third sector in most developed countries where domestic funding sources, including government service contracts, and domestic organisations generally prevail. Another difference is the perhaps greater preponderance of community organisations that are unregistered and which operate informally in sub-Saharan Africa. The third sector, in at least some sub-Saharan African countries, may also be less able to hold government accountable compared to that found in developed countries; this may be particularly the case in conflict-affected or post-conflict countries, or those experiencing authoritarian rule.

In this section we have considered the application of Billis's (2010) theory of hybrid organisations in the context of hybrids in sub-Saharan Africa. This application is complicated by contextual factors in the sub-Saharan African environment, such as the prevalence and significance of the informal economy, the existence of dual institutions, as well as international influences on the third sector. These contextual factors in turn influence the types of hybrid organisations emerging in sub-Saharan Africa, but also how they emerge, that is, whether they are 'organic' or 'enacted', and the degree to which they are 'shallow' or 'entrenched'. In the following section we apply this contextualised theory as a framework to explore the types of hybrid organisations found in sub-Saharan Africa.

TYPES AND EXAMPLES OF HYBRID ORGANISATIONS IN SUB-SAHARAN AFRICA

As illustrated in Figure 25.1, Billis (2010) suggests that each sector – public, private and third – has three forms or zones of hybridity, representing nine hybrid zones in total. In this section we use this model and his prime sector approach as a framework to explore the types of hybrid organisations found in sub-Saharan Africa and their characteristics, illustrated with examples.

Types and Examples of Third Sector Hybrids

Third–private

These kinds of hybrid are common across sub-Saharan Africa. They are hybrids with the dominant logics and characteristics of third sector organisations that are engaging in some form of income-generating or business-like activities, albeit at quite a limited or superficial level. In recent times, in response to declining international donor funding, more and more third sector organisations in the developing world have started to move into social enterprise spaces. Billis (2010) might describe this process as one of organic emergence; whilst after Munoz (2010), such organisations may be considered 'proto social enterprises', or proto hybrids. One example of such a hybrid is the Africa Craft Trust, which implements craft development and training programmes across the Southern Africa region. The Bicycling Empowerment Network (BEN) of South Africa might be another example. It is legally registered as a public benefit organisation and addresses issues of poverty and mobility through the promotion of bicycles. BEN South Africa furthermore provides an illustration of the complex international networks and relationships within which many hybrids in sub-Saharan are frequently embedded. It is one of a number of social enterprises across sub-Saharan Africa that receive bicycles from the United Kingdom (UK) charity Re-Cycle (Bikes to Africa), which in turn describes itself as both a charity and company, thus demonstrating its own hybridity. Re-Cycle works with multiple organisations across a number of African countries, with these organisations undertaking various bicycle-related interventions. These organisations have varied legal forms, with some registered locally and others registered in the UK, and they have quite different operating models.

Third–public

These types of hybrids are also widely found in sub-Saharan Africa. Historically, public sector limitations and the inability of the state in many sub-Saharan African countries to meet basic needs has necessitated third sector organisations having to fill the gaps. They may be local third sector organisations receiving international funding, local subsidiaries of international third sector organisations, or community-based and informal member groups and associations. To varying extents across sub-Saharan African countries you also find some subcontracting of public services to local third sector organisations. For example, the not-for-profit social enterprise Learn to Earn (LtE) in South Africa undertakes training on behalf of the local municipality.

Third–public–private

Hybrids that primarily adhere to the principles and characteristics of the third sector but which engage with and have traits associated with both the private and public sectors can also be found in sub-Saharan Africa. One example of this is the social enterprise The Book Bus. The Book Bus Foundation is a UK-registered charity that undertakes literacy-related development interventions in Zambia, Malawi and Ecuador. Alongside delivering tens of thousands of books to rural schools in impoverished communities, volunteer tourists – who pay to travel with The Book Bus – also work in and with local schools to encourage reading and improve literacy. The Book Bus is also engaging with local education providers to ensure that its interventions add value and build capacity. Furthermore, it provides a mobile library service and is involved in library-building. The Book Bus began life as a third sector organisation, but through organic processes has moved into hybrid spaces, with its hybridity becoming more entrenched over time.

Types and Examples of Private Sector Hybrids

Private–third

These kinds of hybrid are also prevalent across sub-Saharan Africa, with significant variations in the types of private–third sector hybrid found there. A characteristic of many firms in sub-Saharan Africa is that they are highly embedded in their communities and that through generating employment, selling products and providing services, or through philanthropic giving, they can have a significant local, regional and national impact on development. In sub-Saharan African contexts therefore the boundary between traditional private sector firms and private–third sector hybrids can be particularly blurred.

One example of such a private–third sector hybrid is the Kenyan environmental enterprise Cookswell Jikos. This private–third sector hybrid sells energy-efficient charcoal- and wood-fuelled cooking stoves and charcoal ovens, as well as small packets of tree seeds, focusing particularly on BoP customers. Cookswell Jikos is a for-profit venture that aims to create a sustainable 'seed-to-ash' cycle of cooking in Africa. Its products are designed to reduce charcoal use in cooking, saving customers money, whilst also helping to reduce tree-cutting and preserve Kenya's forests. Another example of a private–third sector hybrid is the Khayelitsha Cookie Company (KCC), a social enterprise in Cape Town with the twin aims of producing the best cookies in South Africa, whilst empowering and improving the lives of previously unemployed and disadvantaged women from Khayelitsha, a deprived township community with a high unemployment rate. KCC is also strongly committed to training its staff, who have equity in the venture through a trust fund. Both Cookswell Jikos and KCC were born or enacted as hybrids, with hybridity entrenched from their outset.

Fair trade organisations which sell Fairtrade certified products or adopt wider 'fair trade' practices can also be considered private–third sector hybrids. Examples include the fair trade organisation Kuapa Kokoo, a farmers' co-operative in Ghana at the heart of the highly successful global Divine Chocolate venture; but also the social enterprise Alive and Kicking with production facilities in Kenya, Zambia and Ghana that operates using 'fair' employment practices, with profits used for community health-related outreach activities. Kuapa Kokoo is also a co-operative, a type of private–third sector hybrid that can be found in rural and urban areas across sub-Saharan Africa.

Other types of private–third sector hybrid include those found in tourism across sub-Saharan Africa, including eco, community and sustainable tourism ventures. For example, in Zambia the KaingU Lodge is an eco-tourism lodge which seeks to minimise its environmental footprint and maximise its positive social impact on nearby communities, including through the establishment and funding of the KaingU Community Trust. In Kenya, meanwhile, Gamewatchers Safaris and Porini Safari Camps seek to similarly minimise their environmental impact, support wildlife conservation, and contribute to community development through payments to local conservancies and their members.

Many microfinance providers may also be found within the private–third sector hybrid zone, although it is important to recognise the significant variation that exists in microfinance business models. At one end of the continuum, for example, are microfinance providers operating as traditional businesses whose primary goal is profit generation; while at the other are third sector organisations providing microfinance (ostensibly) motivated by a desire to alleviate poverty and which might be better considered third sector–private hybrids. However, also within this space one might find microfinance providers in the informal economy who may have different kinds of motivation, as well as community savings and credit groups whose origins and goals may vary, and which can play a variety of different roles in their communities.

Finally, the private–third sector hybrid grouping might also include semi-autonomous foundations established by MNCs. In the extractives industry in Namibia, for instance, a number of firms have established such foundations (see Littlewood, 2015). And it might also include some BoP initiatives; see London et al. (2010) for a description of multiple BoP initiatives in sub-Saharan Africa, including those run by MNCs and local companies but also international NGOs, development agencies, and through partnerships between multiple actors. In these latter cases it may be that they are better categorised as a different type of hybrid organisation.

Private–public

As in the developed world, private–public hybrids can also be found in sub-Saharan Africa. At a shallow level this manifests itself in private sector organisations both large and small fulfilling public service contracts. However, other types of private–public hybrids include joint ventures where the state is a minority shareholder. In 2008, for example, the Epangelo Mining Company (Pty) Ltd was established as a vehicle by Namibia's government to undertake joint venture investments in the mining industry (Littlewood, 2015). Hybridity is entrenched in such ventures, which can emerge organically – for instance, over time state actors take progressively greater equity in private sector ventures – or be enacted as a hybrid from the start. Other quite specific examples of private–public hybrids might include instances where extractive companies may create purpose-built communities to house their employees with their own local government structures, health and education facilities (Littlewood, 2014). Research undertaken on the extractive industry in Nigeria has also identified these forms of hybrids with oil companies assuming a 'quasi-governmental' role in response to state failures, with quite varied implications for communities and the reputations of the companies themselves (Frynas, 2005).

Private–third–public
These complex hybrids with the dominant logics of the private sector, but which also embody characteristics associated with the third and public sectors and engage with these sectors, can also be found in sub-Saharan Africa. An example is the South African National Lottery. The Lottery is now run by ITHUBA, a privately owned company in which the state has a shareholding but so do a number of third sector organisations including the Disabled People of South Africa organisation, the SANCO Development Institute which is the investment arm of the South African National Civic Organisation (SANCO), and Lottery Investments which is the investment vehicle for the National Education, Health and Allied Workers Unions. Proceeds from the South African National Lottery are also used to support the country's third sector.

Types and Examples of Public Sector Hybrids

Public–third
These types of hybrids can also be found in sub-Saharan Africa. At quite a shallow level they may occur in local government initiatives supported by a third sector organisation, whilst a more entrenched manifestation would be partnerships between public and third sector organisations. Reflecting the institutional pluralism prevalent in sub-Saharan Africa, public–third sector hybrids may also involve traditional authorities and institutions working with third sector organisations. Public universities and semi-autonomous public sector training institutions provide an example of public–third sector hybrids: there are now more than 500 public universities in sub-Saharan Africa (Brookings, 2018).

Public–private
Parastatals or state-owned enterprises are widespread throughout sub-Saharan Africa. Such organisations may be considered hybrids (after Bruton et al., 2015), as they possess the dominant logics of the public sector but also some characteristics of private sector organisations. Examples of such organisations abound across various sectors and are of different sizes, for instance the Basotho Enterprise Development Corporation founded in 1980 is a subsidiary of the Lesotho National Development Corporation and a parastatal of the Lesotho Government that establishes and promotes Basotho-owned businesses. In nearby Swaziland, the National Maize Corporation is a state-owned enterprise which aims to enhance food security whilst also creating wealth through effective grain procurement, storage and distribution. In Kenya the Geothermal Development Company (GDC) is a state-owned company which aims to fast-track geothermal resource development in the country. State-owned enterprises can also be found in the tourism sector, for instance Namibia Wildlife Resorts which runs tourism facilities in the country's protected areas. State-owned enterprises are often enacted hybrids, with their hybridity entrenched. However, illustrating the dynamic nature of hybrid organising and dynamism in Billis's (2010) model, state-owned enterprises may also be privatised, whereby they move into the private sector sphere of the model, and may even lose their hybrid status entirely. One example of such movement is the Kenya Tea Development Agency Holdings Ltd which was privatised in 2000.

Public–private–third

This is the final type of hybrid and is again prevalent in sub-Saharan Africa. Examples of this type of hybrid include national broadcasters like the South African Broadcasting Corporation (SABC) or the Ghana Broadcasting Corporation. Zimbabwe's CAMPFIRE Association might also be considered this kind of hybrid. The Community Areas Management Programme for Indigenous Resources (CAMPFIRE) is a community-based natural resources management (CBNRM) programme developed by Zimbabwe's government which is designed to promote the sustainable utilisation of natural resources and conservation through generating income for rural communities. At a local level CAMPFIRE is driven through rural district councils, which are the lowest level of government in communal lands. Through CAMPFIRE, community members receive direct payments from tourism activities in their areas, whilst several schools, clinics and income-generating projects have been established out of CAMPFIRE funds. CAMPFIRE also has benefits for the protection of wildlife areas and populations.

Summary

In summary, in this section we have explored the landscape of hybrid organisations in sub-Saharan Africa, identifying different types of such organisations with discussions informed by and structured around Billis's prime sector framework approach, which is contextualised for use in sub-Saharan Africa. Using a range of examples we have showcased the diversity of hybrid organisational forms that may be found in Africa. It should be noted that our discussions are by no means exhaustive, and are limited by the need for generalisation; within a group such as fair trade organisations or microfinance providers, for example, there is significant scope for further segmentation. In the following section we examine some of the key challenges faced by hybrid organisations in sub-Saharan Africa, addressing each of the three sectors (third, private and public), before discussing strategies through which these challenges may be overcome.

CHALLENGES AND STRATEGIES FOR HYBRID ORGANISATIONS IN SUB-SAHARAN AFRICA

To date, only limited consideration has been given by scholars to the challenges faced by hybrid organisations in sub-Saharan Africa, and to strategies for overcoming them. Where such analysis has occurred it has often focused on a particular type of hybrid, for example social enterprises or state-owned enterprises. Discussions in this section therefore address what remains a broadly underexplored topic, and in a way that attempts to integrate the similar and even shared challenges faced by different kinds of hybrid organisations in sub-Saharan African contexts.

Challenges and Strategies for Third Sector Hybrids

Hybridity amongst third sector organisations in sub-Saharan Africa can be a response to key external environmental challenges that such organisations face: namely, reductions in international donor funding, and increasing expectations from donors that individual programmes and the organisations running them should be more self-sufficient and sustainable. Third sector hybrids in sub-Saharan Africa also frequently operate in environments characterised by resource scarcity, and wider complexity and even chaotic conditions (after Alexander, 2014), with significant potential for environmental shocks or 'jolts' (Meyer, 1982) such as natural disasters, political instability or conflict, or economic turbulence. In the context of such external environmental challenges and turbulence, resilience is a key trait for third sector hybrids. Research suggests that the ability to face down reality and to see things as they really are is a key trait of resilient individuals and organisations, whilst values and beliefs that are strongly shared are also likely to help organisations and their internal and external stakeholders make sense of challenges and setbacks (Coutu, 2002). Furthermore, the ability to experiment and improvise, and a refusal to be constrained by environmental limitations (Holt and Littlewood, 2017), a condition prevalent in sub-Saharan Africa, have also been linked to organisational resilience. These capabilities and traits are therefore of key importance for third sector hybrids in sub-Saharan Africa to cultivate (Littlewood and Holt, 2018b).

A quite different challenge faced by third sector hybrids in sub-Saharan Africa is that of succession. Whilst this can be a challenge for third sector hybrids – and indeed wider organisations – everywhere, there seem to be particular dynamics associated with this issue in developing-country contexts, and these are especially acute in sub-Saharan Africa. Many third sector hybrids in sub-Saharan Africa are initiated and managed by individuals from outside of the beneficiary communities. That is, they are expatriates or highly educated and skilled local people. As a result, when these individuals move on, their organisations frequently decline and in some instances cease to exist.

An example of the social enterprise, the Mumwa Crafts Association (MCA), illustrates this point but may perhaps also indicate one way to mitigate it. The MCA is a craft producer association in Western Zambia with 3000-plus members who are spread across rural areas of the province. The members are organised into craft producer centres and their products are purchased and then sold by the MCA, which performs a market linkage role. The MCA has existed for more than 20 years and was founded in the context of numerous failed, often well-funded, craft projects in Western Province, where the projects ended after their predominantly expatriate leaders and managers moved on. In contrast to such projects, the MCA was developed bottom-up and led by local people, it is strongly embedded in the communities it serves, whilst local producer members also feel a strong sense of ownership. Communication with and accountability to the members is also strong.

Scaling is another challenge faced by third sector hybrids in sub-Saharan Africa. One way in which a third sector hybrid, Learn to Earn (LtE), in South Africa is attempting to overcome this challenge is through a franchising approach. LtE is a social enterprise in the Western Cape working in the field of skills development and job creation. It has created the Learn to Earn Association as a vehicle for the LtE model to be replicated in other parts of South Africa and internationally. Rather than establishing LtE branches, LtE assists other organisations with capacity-building to develop their own skills development and job creation processes. This approach is founded on recognition that all communities are different, they have their own particular dynamics and development challenges, and unique solutions to such challenges. Overall, this approach also facilitates local embeddedness and stakeholder ownership, which can have benefits in terms of sustainability and impact.

Third sector hybrids in sub-Saharan Africa like those elsewhere also face challenges in understanding and reporting impact. Such work can be time- and resource-intensive, whilst there may also be tensions between the kinds of metrics and reporting required for different stakeholders; for example, that conducted for international donors, that needed to ensure local accountability to beneficiaries, and that needed to help hybrids reflect on and improve their activities. Existing impact assessment frameworks, and wider performance management tools, even those tailored for third sector hybrids, may also be unsuitable or require significant modification for use in sub-Saharan African contexts. A recent framework for identifying, mapping and monitoring the impact of hybrids, which was developed by drawing upon research with hybrids in sub-Saharan Africa, may provide some guidance on this (see Holt and Littlewood, 2015).

Finally, mission drift can present a challenge for third sector hybrids in sub-Saharan Africa, as can maintaining the organisation's primary focus on its social and/or environmental mission in the face of imperatives for economic value creation and the need to ensure survival. This is particularly the case where third sector hybrids, which may be poorly resourced, engage with powerful state and private sector actors with their own particular goals and agendas for collaboration. In such scenarios a reflexive and critical perspective is essential for managers in third sector hybrids to assess the opportunities and threats stemming from such relationships.

Challenges and Strategies for Private Sector Hybrids

There are overlaps between the challenges faced by third sector hybrids and by private sector hybrids. For example, the business environment in sub-Saharan Africa is also challenging for private sector hybrids, which similarly face the prospect of environmental shocks or 'jolts' (Meyer, 1982), and operate in conditions of constrained resources, uncertainty and institutional voids (Mair et al., 2012) leading to market failures and inefficiencies where institutions are absent or non-functioning. Parmigiani and Rivera-Santos (2015) identify five types of institutional voids, particularly in subsistence markets – product market, labour market, capital market, contracting and regulatory – all of which present challenges of different kinds for private sector hybrids, and indeed other types of hybrids. These external environmental challenges are starkly illustrated in the World Bank's Doing Business ranking, with a preponderance of African countries positioned towards the bottom of the ranking (World Bank, 2019). As with third sector hybrids these environmental challenges require individual and organisational resilience and associated capabilities.

In the previous section the notion of embeddedness was discussed as a significant factor in the ownership of organisations by communities, and related to organisational sustainability. Embeddedness was also identified as having implications for social impact. Private sector hybrids that purchase from, employ or sell to the poor also require a strong understanding of the dynamics of subsistence markets if their interventions and activities are to be successful. Insufficient understanding of subsistence markets, and the needs and preferences of low-income consumers, has been linked to the failure of many early BoP interventions. The importance of local knowledge and of 'co-creation' of BoP interventions with the poor, who are recognised as more than just consumers, is acknowledged in more recent BoP 2.0 and 3.0 approaches (Hart et al., 2015). These may also be led by third sector hybrids, which are often perceived as having greater local knowledge and embeddedness, or through partnerships between such organisations and MNCs. Nevertheless, BoP interventions have also often been financially unsuccessful. Karnani (2007), for example, argues that there is no fortune at the base of the pyramid and suggests that BoP markets are quite small and costly to serve, whilst the poor are culturally heterogeneous and geographically dispersed. Thus whilst notions of 'win–win' and 'shared-value' creation are rhetorically appealing they can be difficult for firms to realise in practice. It is also argued by Crane et al. (2014) that in such initiatives trade-offs between economic, social and environmental value creation remain necessary.

A further challenge for private sector hybrids in sub-Saharan Africa comes when competing against more traditional private sector firms that may be able to offer lower prices, if for example they do not offer employees such favourable terms and conditions. For instance, it may be that employment creation is a key part of a for-profit social enterprise's mission, which might then restrict its ability to mechanise and automate production as this could threaten staff numbers. Private sector hybrids therefore need to be careful in their approach to the market and selective about the markets in which they compete. A strong understanding of their target market is important as is a clear sense of on what basis they compete.

The risk of imitation is another challenge for hybrids in sub-Saharan Africa where the enforcement of intellectual property – especially in subsistence markets – can be limited. Hybrids may develop innovative low-cost contextually appropriate products and services but quickly find these duplicated by both large (domestic and international) competitors as well as those in the informal economy. For example, the private sector hybrid Cookswell Jikos in Kenya now faces significant competition, not only from cheap imitation cook stoves made in the informal economy but also from imports. It has endeavoured to differentiate and emphasise the quality of its products, in terms of both robustness and design, but also in reducing fuel wood consumption and having wider positive environmental impacts. On the other hand, it also constantly innovates to improve efficiency and reduce costs in production and distribution.

A final challenge private sector hybrids may face is that well-intentioned NGOs and donor interventions may flood their markets; for example, an influx of donated energy-efficient cook stoves into a community or region. As before, a differentiation strategy may offer some protection against this risk.

Challenges and Strategies for Public Sector Hybrids

Finally, public sector hybrids in sub-Saharan Africa face some similar challenges to those discussed previously for third sector and private sector hybrids, such as resource constraints, operating in poorly functioning markets, and the challenge of assessing impact. Public sector hybrids may also be implicated in institutional failures and the creation of the wider complex and chaotic environmental conditions (Alexander et al., 2014) that third and private sector hybrids in sub-Saharan Africa are then required to navigate. For example, in Transparency International's Corruption Perceptions Index, where countries are scored and ranked based on perceived levels of public sector corruption, sub-Saharan Africa is the worst-performing region globally (Transparency International, 2017). This suggests that corruption is a major challenge for African public sector hybrids.

Hybrid state-owned enterprises in sub-Saharan Africa also face challenges, and have been criticised for high levels of bureaucracy, inefficiency, nepotism and a lack of accountability. In some instances they are even suggested as being instruments of national kleptocracy. Examples abound of failing parastatals and state-owned enterprises in sub-Saharan Africa; for instance, the repeated bailouts required by Namibia Wildlife Resorts and Air Namibia, the challenges faced by Eskom and SABC in South Africa, the historical losses at the National Bank of Kenya (now largely privatised), whilst Nigeria's President recently dissolved the boards of all the country's federal parastatals. At the same time, hybrid state-owned enterprises and parastatals have the potential to provide needed goods and services and be an important source of government revenue, if managed effectively, and with adequate autonomy and accountability to citizens.

In this section we have discussed the challenges faced by different types of hybrid organisations in sub-Saharan Africa, some of which are common across different hybrid organisational forms. We have also reflected upon possible strategies for overcoming some of these challenges, illustrated with examples of such strategies in action. In the following section we conclude our chapter by identifying our contributions to knowledge and theory, potential areas for future research, and the implications of our discussions for policy and practice

CONCLUSION

In this chapter we have explored scholarship about and the landscape of hybrid organisations in sub-Saharan Africa. This chapter provides various insights for research, policy and practice.

Insights for Research

The chapter contributes to the still limited knowledge about hybrid organisations in sub-Saharan Africa. As discussed in the literature review section, whilst there is an emerging body of work on such organisations there remains significant scope for further enquiry. Existing work also remains relatively fragmented, often focusing on particular types of hybrids, with few attempts to date to examine multiple hybrid organisation forms together, as occurs in this chapter. At a wider level, business and management scholarship on sub-Saharan Africa remains underdeveloped, with this chapter also aiming to showcase Africa as a rich, complex and institutionally diverse setting for further study. We encourage further business and management research on hybrids, and indeed wider organisations, in sub-Saharan Africa contexts.

A further contribution of this chapter relates to its contextualisation of Billis's (2010) theory of hybrid organisations. We have elaborated on this theory for use in sub-Saharan Africa, identifying additional complexities in how the three sectors manifest in such settings. This provides insights for future scholarship on hybrid organisations in sub-Saharan Africa, as well as for work examining hybrids in other developing-world or emerging-economy contexts with their own complexities.

A number of areas for future research are raised by discussions in this chapter. Firstly, we have explored hybrid organisations at the macro level of sub-Saharan Africa as a whole. There are, however, limitations to this macro perspective, notably that we are not able to capture the very significant differences between countries in sub-Saharan Africa and also within countries. How hybrid organisations manifest themselves in particular African countries linked to national, regional and local institutions, and the interactions between them, and with transnational actors, is therefore an area in need of further study. In-depth comparison of hybrid organisation ecosystems in two or more sub-Saharan African countries is also needed, as is more fine-grained analysis focusing on particular sectors, for example: private sector hybrids or public sector hybrids; subgroups within these sectors, for instance public–private hybrids; or types within these subgroups, for example state-owned enterprises and parastatals or fair trade hybrids. These hybrids could be looked at through the lens of particular sectors, for example tourism or energy; or with a focus on particular challenges, for example scaling. Finally, hybrid scholars might apply other theories of hybrid organisations than that proposed by Billis to the study of such organisations in sub-Saharan Africa, or indeed develop new theories based on African data and organisations.

Insights for Policy

Discussions in this chapter offer insights and have implications for policy. Firstly, it showcases the range of hybrid organisational forms that exist in sub-Saharan Africa. In so doing it illustrates the variety of options available to decision-makers during policy development, as well as examples they might look to. Secondly, the chapter considers the challenges different kinds of hybrids in sub-Saharan Africa face, some of which are specific to particular hybrid forms whilst others are more general, and also potential strategies for overcoming these challenges. This may provide insights for decision-makers designing policies and initiatives to support hybrids in overcoming such challenges, or that are seeking to tackle the causes of these challenges. Implications for policy are also apparent in the discussion of the need for public sector hybrids to be more accountable, autonomous and innovative. Finally, discussions in the chapter may encourage decision-makers to be reflexive about and avoid interventions and policies that can negatively affect the functioning of hybrids.

Insights for Practice

Finally, discussions in the chapter offer insights and implications for practice. These relate particularly to the challenges faced by different kinds of hybrid organisations and the strategies such organisations might adopt to overcome them. They might include measures through which hybrids might map and measure impact; how they might develop capabilities for resilience; the ways in which they can successfully scale, for example through franchising; and how hybrids might better compete with for-profit businesses. In conclusion, whilst there remains much that we do not know about hybrid organisations in sub-Saharan Africa, this chapter aims to provide a starting point for addressing some of the gaps in our understanding, whilst also offering insights for research, policy and practice, and guidance for future scholarship.

REFERENCES

Alexander, A., H. Walker and M. Naim (2014), 'Decision theory in sustainable supply chain management: a literature review', *Supply Chain Management: An International Journal*, 19(5/6), pp. 504–522.

Anderson, J. and M. Kupp (2008), 'Celtel Nigeria: serving the rural poor', Tilburg: TiasNimbas Case Study.

Ariyo, A. and J. Afeikhena (1999), 'Privatization in Africa: an appraisal', *World Development*, 27(1), pp. 201–213.

Arnould, E.J. and J.J. Mohr (2005), 'Dynamic transformations for base-of-the-pyramid market clusters', *Journal of the Academy of Marketing Science*, 33, pp. 254–274.

Bassett, T.J. (2010), 'Slim pickings: fairtrade cotton in West Africa', *Geoforum*, 41(1), pp. 44–55.

Battilana, J. and S. Dorado (2010), 'Building sustainable hybrid organisations: the case of commercial microfinance organisations', *Academy of Management Journal*, 53(6), pp. 1419–1440.

Battilana, J., M. Lee., J. Walker and C. Dorsey (2012), 'In search of the hybrid ideal', *Stanford Social Innovation Review*, Summer, pp. 51–55.

Becchetti, L. and M. Costantino (2008), 'The effects of fair trade on affiliated producers: an impact analysis on Kenyan farmers', *World Development*, 36(5), pp. 823–842.

Billis, D. (1991), 'The roots of voluntary agencies: a question of choice', *Nonprofit and Voluntary Sector Quarterly*, 20(1), pp. 57–70.

Billis, D. (2010), *Hybrid Organisations and the Third Sector*, Basingstoke: Palgrave Macmillan.

Bitzer, V., R. Hamann, M. Hall and E.L. Wosu Griffin (2015), *The Business of Social and Environmental Innovation: New Frontiers in Africa*, Cham: Springer International Publishing.

Brookings (2018), 'Higher education enrolment grows in sub-Saharan Africa along with disparities in enrolment by income', accessed 6 June 2018 at https://www.brookings.edu/blog/africa-in-focus/2018/01/10/figures-of-the-week-higher-education-enrollment-grows-in-sub-saharan-africa-along-with-disparities-in-enrollment-by-income/.

Bruton, G.D., M.W. Peng., D. Ahlstrom., C. Stan and K. Xu (2015), 'State owned enterprises around the world as hybrid organisations', *Academy of Management Perspectives*, 29(1), pp. 92–114.

Cieslik, K. (2016), 'Moral economy meets social enterprise community-based green energy project in rural Burundi', *World Development*, 8, pp. 12–26.

Ciambotti, G. and M. Pedrini (2019), 'Hybrid harvesting strategies to overcome resource constraints: evidence from social enterprises in Kenya', *Journal of Business Ethics*, DOI https://doi.org/10.1007/s10551-019-04256-y.

Claeyé, F. (2017), 'A typology of social entrepreneuring models in South Africa', *Social Enterprise Journal*, 13(4), pp. 427–442.

Commission for Africa (2005), *Our Common Interest*, Report of the Commission for Africa, accessed 6 June 2018 at http://www.commissionforafrica.info/wp-content/uploads/2005-report/11-03-05_cr_report.pdf.

Coutu, D. (2002), 'How resilience works', *Harvard Business Review*, 80(5), pp. 46–56.

Crane, A., G. Palazzo, L.J. Spence and D. Matten (2014), 'Contesting the value of the shared value concept', *California Management Review*, 56(2), pp. 130–153.

Denis, J.L., E. Ferlie and N. Van Gestel (2015), 'Understanding hybridity in public organisations', *Public Administration*, 93(2), pp. 273–289.

Doherty, B., H. Haugh and F. Lyon (2014), 'Social enterprises as hybrid organisations: a review and research agenda', *International Journal of Management Reviews*, 16, pp. 417–436.

Dolan, C. and L. Scott (2009), 'Lipstick evangelism: Avon trading circles and gender empowerment in South Africa', *Gender and Development*, 17(2), pp. 203–218.

Fonteneau, B. (2011), 'Overview of appropriate mechanisms for guaranteeing the social purpose and measuring the social impact of social enterprises in South Africa', Pretoria, South Africa: International Labour Office.

Frynas, J. (2005), 'The false developmental promise of corporate social responsibility: evidence from multinational oil companies', *International Affairs*, 81(3), pp. 581–598.

Guardian (2014), 'Malawi tightens budget strings to placate foreign aid donors', accessed 6 June 2018 at http://www.theguardian.com/global-development/2014/sep/10/malawi-budget-foreign-aid-donors-mutharika.

Haigh, N. and A.J. Hoffman (2012), 'Hybrid organisations: the next chapter of sustainable business', *Organisational Dynamics*, 41, pp. 126–134.

Haigh, N., J. Walker, S. Bacq and J. Kickul (2015), 'Hybrid organisations: origins, strategies, impacts and implications', *California Management Review*, 57(3), pp. 5–12.

Hammond, A.L. and C.K. Prahalad (2004), 'Selling to the poor', *Foreign Policy*, 142, pp. 30–37.

Hart, S. and F. Casado Caneque (2015), *Base of the Pyramid 3.0 Sustainable Development through Innovation and Entrepreneurship*, Sheffield: Greenleaf.

Herbst, J. (2000), *States and Power in Africa*, Princeton, NJ: Princeton University Press.

Hockerts, K. (2015), 'How hybrid organisations turn antagonistic assets into complementarities', *California Management Review*, 57(3), pp. 83–106.

Hoffman, A.J. (1999), 'Institutional evolution and change: environmentalism and the US chemical industry', *Academy of Management Journal*, 42(4), pp. 351–371.

Holt, D. and D. Littlewood (2014), 'The informal economy as a route to market in sub-Saharan Africa – observations amongst Kenyan informal economy entrepreneurs', in Sonny Nwankwo and Kevin Ibeh, *The Routledge Companion to Business in Africa*, London: Routledge, pp. 198–217.

Holt, D. and D. Littlewood (2015), 'Identifying, mapping and monitoring the impact of hybrid firms', *California Management Review*, 57(3), pp. 107–125.

Holt, D. and D. Littlewood (2017), 'Waste livelihoods amongst the poor – through the lens of bricolage', *Business Strategy and the Environment*, 26, pp. 253–264.

Jay, J. (2013), 'Navigating paradox as a mechanism of change and innovation in hybrid organisations', *Academy of Management Journal*, 56, pp. 137–159.

Kannothra, C.G., S. Manning and N. Haigh (2018), 'How hybrids manage growth and social–business tensions in global supply chains: the case of impact sourcing', *Journal of Business Ethics*, 148(2), pp. 271–290.

Kapila, S. (2006), 'Unleashing the entrepreneurial potential of micro and small enterprises in Kenya: some experiences and directions', Paper prepared for the Commission on Legal Empowerment of the Poor, presented at UNHAITAT, Nairobi, Kenya, 26 November.

Karanda, C. and N. Toledano (2012), 'Social entrepreneurship in South Africa: a different narrative for a different context', *Social Enterprise Journal*, 8, pp. 201–215.

Karnani, A. (2007), 'The mirage of marketing to the bottom of the pyramid: how the private sector can alleviate poverty', *California Management Review*, 49(4), pp. 90–111.

Kerlin, J.A. (2009), *Social Enterprise: A Global Comparison*, Lebanon, NH: University Press of New England.

Kodzi, Jr E. (2015), 'The clash of missions: juxtaposing competing pressures in South Africa's social enterprises', *Journal of Social Entrepreneurship*, 6(3), pp. 278–298.

Kolk, A., M. Rivera-Santos and C. Rufin (2014), 'Reviewing a decade of research on the base/bottom of the pyramid (BOP) concept', *Business and Society*, 53(3), pp. 338–377.

Lan, Z. and H.G. Rainey (1992), 'Goals, rules, and effectiveness in public, private, and hybrid organisations: more evidence on frequent assertions about differences', *Journal of Public Administration Research and Theory*, 2(1), pp. 5–28.

Littlewood, D. (2014), '"Cursed" communities? Corporate social responsibility (CSR), company towns and the mining industry in Namibia', *Journal of Business Ethics*, 120(1), pp. 39–63.

Littlewood, D. (2015), 'Corporate social responsibility (CSR), mining and sustainable development in Namibia: critical reflections through a relational lens', *Development Southern Africa*, 32(2), pp. 240–257.

Littlewood, D. and D. Holt (2015a), 'Social and environmental enterprises in Africa: context, convergence and characteristics', in Verena Bitzer, Ralf Hamann, Martin Hall and Eliada Wosu Griffin (eds), *The Business of Social and Environmental Innovation: New Frontiers in Africa*, Cham: Springer International Publishing, pp. 27–48.

Littlewood, D. and D. Holt (2015b), 'Social enterprise in South Africa', ICSEM Working Paper, No. 2015-02, Liege: International Comparative Social Enterprise Models (ICSEM) Project.

Littlewood, D. and D. Holt (2018a), 'Social entrepreneurship in South Africa: exploring the influence of environment', *Business and Society*, 57(3), pp. 525–561.

Littlewood, D. and D. Holt (2018b), 'Social enterprise resilience in sub-Saharan Africa', *Business Strategy and Development*, 1(1), pp. 53–63.

London, T. (2009), 'Making better investments at the base of the pyramid', *Harvard Business Review*, 87(5), pp. 106–113.

London, T., R. Anupindi and S. Sheth (2010), 'Creating mutual value: lessons learned from ventures serving base of the pyramid producers', *Journal of Business Research*, 63, pp. 582–594.

Lund, C. (2006), 'Twilight institutions: public authority and local politics in Africa', *Development and Change*, 37(4), pp. 685–705.

Mair J., I. Martí and M. Ventresca (2012), 'Building inclusive markets in rural Bangladesh: how intermediaries work institutional voids', *Academy of Management Journal*, 55(4), pp. 819–850.

Mair, J., J. Mayer and E. Lutz (2015), 'Navigating institutional plurality: organisational governance in hybrid organisations', *Organisation Studies*, 36(6), pp. 713–739.

McFalls, R. (2007), 'Testing the limits of "inclusive capitalism": a case study of the South Africa HP i-Community', *Journal of Corporate Citizenship*, 28, pp. 85–98.

Meinzen-Dick, R.S. and R. Pradhan (2001), 'Implications of legal pluralism for natural resource management', *IDS Bulletin*, 32, pp. 10–17.

Meyer, A.D. (1982), 'Adapting to environmental jolts', *Administrative Science Quarterly*, 27, pp. 515–537.

Michalopoulos, S. and E. Papaioannou (2015), 'On the ethnic origins of African development: chiefs and precolonial centralisation', *Academy of Management Perspectives*, 29(1), pp. 32–71.

Mirvis, P. and B. Googins (2018), 'Catalyzing social entrepreneurship in Africa: roles for western universities, NGOs and corporations', *Africa Journal of Management*, 4(1), pp. 57–83.

Munoz, S.A. (2010), 'Towards a geographical research agenda for social enterprise', *Area*, 42, pp. 302–312.

O'Neill, M. (1989), *The Third America: The Emergence of the Non-Profit Sector in the United States*, San Francisco, CA: Jossey-Bass.

Pache, A.C. and F. Santos (2010), 'Inside the hybrid organisation: an organisational level view of responses to conflicting institutional demands', ESSEC Working Paper, Document de Recherche ESSEC / Centre de recherche de l'ESSEC.

Pache, A.C. and F. Santos (2013), 'Inside the hybrid organisation: selective coupling as a response to competing institutional logics', *Academy of Management Journal*, 56(4), pp. 972–1001.

Parmigiani, A.E. and M. Rivera-Santos (2015), 'Sourcing for the base of the pyramid: constructing supply chains to address voids in subsistence markets', *Journal of Operations Management*, 33/34, pp. 60–70.

Powell, M., A. Gillet and B. Doherty (2018), 'Sustainability in social enterprise: hybrid organizing in public services', *Public Management Review*, 21(2), pp. 159–186.

Prahalad, C.K. (2004), *The Fortune at the Bottom of the Pyramid*, Upper Saddle River, NJ: Wharton School Publishing.

Raynolds, L.T. and S.U. Ngcwangu (2010), 'Fair trade Rooibos tea: connecting South African producers and American consumer markets', *Geoforum*, 41(1), pp. 74–83.

Rivera-Santos, M., D. Holt, D. Littlewood and A. Kolk (2015), 'Social entrepreneurship in sub-Saharan Africa', *Academy of Management Perspectives*, 29(1), pp. 72–91.

Scott, W.R (2001), *Institutions and Organisations* (2nd edn), Thousand Oaks, CA: SAGE Publications.

Scott, W.R. and J.W. Meyer (1991), 'The organisation of societal sectors: propositions and early evidence', in W.W. Powell and P.J. Di Maggio (eds), *The New Institutionalism in Organisational Analysis*, Chicago, IL: University of Chicago Press, pp. 108–142.

Simanis, E. and S.L. Hart (2008), 'The base of the pyramid protocol: toward next generation BoP strategy (Version 2.0)', Ithaca, NY: Cornell University.

Simanis, E., S. Hart and D. Duke (2008), 'The base of the pyramid protocol: beyond "basic needs" business strategies', *Innovations*, 3(1), pp. 57–84.

Steinfield, L. and D. Holt (2019), 'Towards a theory on the reproduction of social innovations in subsistence marketplaces', *Journal of Product Innovation Management*, 36(6), pp. 764–799.

Steinman, S. (2010), 'An exploratory study into factors influencing an enabling environment for social enterprises in South Africa', Geneva: International Labour Organization.

Steinman, S. and J. van Rooij (2012), 'Developing public policies for the social and solidarity economy in South Africa: the need for a state–civil society dialogue', *Universitas Forum*, 3, pp. 1–19.

Thompson, J. and B. Doherty (2006), 'The diverse world of social enterprise: a collection of social enterprise stories', *International Journal Social Economics*, 33, pp. 361–375.

Transparency International (2017), *Corruption Perceptions Index 2017*, accessed 6 June 2018 at https://www.transparency.org/news/feature/corruption_perceptions_index_2017.

Urban, B. (2008), 'Social entrepreneurship in South Africa: delineating the construct with associated skills', *International Journal of Entrepreneurial Behavior and Research*, 14, pp. 346–364.

Van Wijk, J., R. Van der Duim, M. Lamers and D. Sumba (2015), 'The emergence of institutional innovations in tourism: the evolution of the African Wildlife Foundation's tourism conservation enterprises', *Journal of Sustainable Tourism*, 23(1), pp. 104–125.

Von der Weppen, J. and J. Cochrane (2012), 'Social enterprises in tourism: an exploratory study of operational models and success factors', *Journal of Sustainable Tourism*, 20(3), pp. 497–511.

Walsh, J. (2015), 'Organisation and management scholarship in and for Africa . . . and the world', *Academy of Management Perspectives*, 29(1), pp. 1–6.

World Bank (2019), *Doing Business Ranking*, accessed 6 June 2018 at http://www.doingbusiness.org/rankings.

Zoogah, D.B. and S. Nkomo (2013), 'Management research in Africa: past, present and future possibilities', in Terri R. Lituchy, Betty J. Punnett and Bill B. Puplampu (eds), *Management in Africa: Macro and Micro Perspectives*, New York: Routledge, pp. 9–31.

26. The church, faith-based organisations and the three sectors
Johan Gärde

INTRODUCTION

The organisational life of faith communities and religious congregations is changing in post-secular environments with new interactions, opportunities for collaboration and social contracts between the public and private sectors and civil society organisations (secular and religious). Religious communities with shrinking congregations and faith-based organisations (FBOs) in a post-secular environment are developing strategies for networking and collaboration with the public and private sectors. They are utilising a new discourse of solidarity and inclusion, which also attracts a larger public that goes beyond the shrinking constituencies of their own members.

Collaboration has been accompanied by the growth of hybridity and hybrid organisations. Billis (2010) suggests that this occurs when an organisation from one sector, for example the civil society/third sector, adopts the different approaches and principles of the public and/or the private sector. As this chapter will show, hybrid organisational forms can bring with them the prospect of answers to difficult problems of communities and welfare. But they can also present their own inherent problems when the different principles become uncomfortable partners. I shall shortly illustrate this in a personal example.

The purpose of this chapter, and the research problem it addresses, is to understand better this complex territory of the hybrid arrangements that have arisen from the interaction between church, faith-based organisations and the three sectors. In order to achieve this, its more specific objectives are to:

- explore some of the drivers both for, and against, the growth of hybridity in the post-secular environment; and
- develop a rough draft of some of the new hybrid relationships between faith-based organisations and the other sectors.

I have drawn on my own research and other relevant approaches in addressing these objectives. Two points of explanation are required before the content of the chapter is outlined. Firstly, there are a variety of alternative names for the third sector, including nonprofits, voluntary, non-governmental organisations and civil society organisations. These will be used interchangeably. Secondly, much of the research relates to 'hybrid faith-based social service providers'. However, it does not distort my argument to include them more simply within the general category of hybrid FBOs.

The path to these objectives begins with a section on 'Internal Relationships' where the balance of attention is mainly inward-looking, in the sense that the focus is on religion, the church and faith-based organisations. Accordingly, it first describes a turbulent meeting at the Vatican resulting from the tensions between the principles of the mission-driven church and the very different business-driven principles of external consultants. This tension between different fundamental principles goes to the heart of the debate about hybridity. The next subsection provides an essential background to the chapter by examining the boundary discussions and interrelationships between religion, church and faith-based organisations. This sets up the following discussion which addresses the first objective by discussing how the driving force for and against hybridity in FBOs is principally related to their mission and vision.

The next section on 'External Relationships' is essentially 'outward-looking' since it focuses on relationships with European states, then on the more problematic 'failing states'. It responds to the second objective by utilising case studies in order to begin the process of mapping FBOs within the wider framework of civil society/third sector organisations. The chapter ends with a summary and conclusions.

INTERNAL RELATIONSHIPS

The Secular and the Sacred: Analysing the 'Culture Shock'

In the 1990s, I had the privilege of attending one of the first sessions when the world's biggest faith-based organisation, Caritas Internationalis, decided to launch a major organisational review. For the first time, it was decided not only to use in-house experts on mainly experience-based methodologies from the vast Catholic network, but also to employ external strategic planning consultants. The task was immense: to engage almost 200 countries and member organisations throughout the world, utilising a method mainly developed for the corporate sector and now slowly being tested among secular non-governmental organisations. Suspicion was widespread and many church leaders challenged this decision.

The session at the Executive Committee of Caritas Internationalis finally started in the main hall of Palazzo San Calisto in the Vatican. The two strategic planning consultants began to present the terms of reference of their task. After a couple of minutes, they were interrupted by a Monsignore from Eastern Europe who, without asking for the permission to talk, yelled:

> It seems that you don't know where you are! You are visiting the Holy Roman-Catholic Church with a 2000 year history and you haven't learned that we don't do anything without prayer and a chant to Virgin Mary. So dear brothers and sisters in Christ, let's sing *Salve Regina* together . . .

The assembled participants stood up, started to sing with one voice the hymn *Salve Regina* in Latin, which then became a protest song against secular-rational strategic planning in the shape and form presented by the external consultants. The cultural shock was obvious, the momentum for change lost, and the consultants had to resign. The story illustrates how contrasting concepts of organisational culture between a secular corporate-inspired approach and the sacred can cause tension and be a hurdle even in a situation when a major FBO was shifting from what Weber (1905) would label 'traditional' to what he called 'rational-legal' authority.

This phenomenon of 'culture shock' or severe tension at times of important change has been researched from an organisational perspective in the civil society/third sector by Billis (2010). He argues more broadly that such tensions sometimes reflect fundamental differences of principles and response to human need by three different sectors or 'worlds': the public, private and third. Thus, whereas private sector organisations are based on principles of shareholding, market forces and profit; third sector/civil society organisations are mission-driven and based on associations of members. And, where the different principles of the governance and operations of one sector begin to invade the principles of another sector, this has been conceptualised as 'hybridity' and the possible emergence of 'hybrid organisations'.

From the perspective of this theory, the consultants' approach in the Vatican story appeared largely drawn from their experience of the principles of private sector organisations. They lacked sensitivity to, and knowledge of, the mission-driven history, values and traditions of the Catholic church. I shall discuss below the question of whether the institutions of a particular religion are essential building blocks of civil society and the third sector. If so, according to the same theory, my earlier story could be interpreted as reflecting deep concern that the mission-driven (civil society/third sector) principles of the church would be damaged by hybridisation, in this case the intrusion of alien business-driven strategic planning.

In general, these new strategies of collaboration and the associated potential influx of public and private funding and different principles of organisation have increased the possibility that FBOs might move into hybrid territory. An increase in hybridity may bring with it not only benefits, but also potential tensions from clashing principles, as in the Vatican example. Moving beyond the Vatican story I go on to discuss in the following subsection the main institutions and forces that are influencing the growth of hybridity.

The Main Actors: Religion, Church and Faith-Based Organisations

This subsection focuses on the definitions and boundaries of the central components that drive or hinder the development of hybrid forms of faith-based organisation: religion, church and faith-based organisations themselves. But, in addition to these components, there are a huge number and variety of environmental factors that must be added to the equation. These will be discussed later, wherever possible in their own distinct environmental situations.

In order to prepare for the examination of boundaries and the discussion of hybrid faith-based organisations, I begin by providing a definition of religion. In this chapter I shall analyse and describe religion as a social phenomenon which is defined in mainly functionalist terms, in the sense of relating to issues such as life's ultimate questions and purpose surrounding, for example, the notions of ethics and values and religious belief systems (Durkheim, 1912 [1965]; Yinger, 1979; Parsons, 1937 [1961]).

This is complex territory. For example, the intricacy and dynamics of contributing factors for strengthening or weakening religious values in society has been demonstrated by sociologists of religion (Inglehart and Welzel, 2005; Pettersson, 2006). Other scholars have argued that the study of religion and religiosity in society is more multidimensional than the traditional discourse of secularism, pointing to phenomena such as 'desecularization, resacralization, de-Christianization and the emergence of a post-secular society'

(Nynäs et al., 2012, p. 115). Even substantive and metaphysical dimensions play a central role when religion is defined in essentialist terms with its transcendental claims, nature and the external configurations of symbols, rituals and other expressions of religious culture.

Even these few examples show that it is not surprising that there will be alternative views of the nature of religious organisations. Of these, two are particularly relevant for their impact on the perceived role of faith-based organisations. One perspective is put forward by Rochester and Torry (2010), who argue that 'religious organisations' have the fundamental purpose of worship. Their argument runs as follows: 'If a church no longer gathers for worship, then it is no longer a church, it is no longer a congregation and it is no longer a religious organisation' (ibid., p. 115). A religious organisation cannot hybridise.

They also suggest that faith-based organisations have a main purpose, which is not strictly religious but nevertheless has a structural connection to a religious organisation. They argue that there are three organisational arrangements for the provision of social welfare that are made between religious congregations and separate entities, which could be labelled 'faith-based organisations': (1) informal and less organised social care within the congregation; (2) more social action-oriented programmes, such as youth programmes; and (3) separate social associations and charities established by the congregations. And they link these arrangements to hybridity, which is seen to take place mainly in the third model.

From a sociology of religion perspective, the argument presented by Rochester and Torry, worship can also be understood from a more functionalist view of religious organisations, where the worshipping element is just one faith dimension but not the only one, since core faith aspects also include behaviour, experience and knowledge (Glock and Stark, 1965). These include, for example, those religious organisations in Islam and Buddhism that were set up primarily for reasons relating to the 'experience dimensions', such as Zen Buddhism and Sufi orders.

In addition to this mainly local congregational focus above, I suggest that there are additional dimensions relating to different faith traditions and levels of analysis. For instance, returning to a question I raised earlier: are the church and Islam part of civil society? In searching for an answer to this 'high-level' question, I will also briefly also utilise sociological and organisational ideas.

But, first, the church needs to be understood and explained, before trying to analyse it within the framework of civil society (Casanova, 2001, pp. 1041–1080). Church (and congregation) can be understood from different scientific disciplines, mainly where theologians from the subdiscipline of ecclesiology have elaborated their own definitions, types and categories in the three main Christian faith traditions of Catholicism, Orthodoxy and Protestantism. 'Church' or 'congregation' could in that theological and ecclesiological perspective be defined differently, with consequences for different views on authority. Some church leaders would also put forward the argument of the church as *sui generis*, something unique which cannot be categorised and cannot, for instance, be labelled as a non-governmental organisation (NGO) or third sector organisation (TSO).

From a sociological point of view, church, congregation, parish and/or Islam, depending on the levels of analysis, could all be part of civil society and also be defined as NGOs, civil society organisations (CSOs), TSOs or FBOs. From an organisational perspective Billis (2010, pp. 56–58) identifies nine types of overlapping hybrid zones between the three sectors. For the purposes of this chapter the three relevant hybrid zones are those that have their primary roots and adherence to the principles of the third sector. These are:

1.   third–public;
2.   third–public–private;
3.   third–private.

Within this framework FBOs would be part of the third sector or located within the global definitions and categorisation of civil society (Salamon et al., 1999; Keane, 2003). In that perspective the 'faith sector' is part of civil society and not a separate entity (Torry, 2012).

However, Islam is not an institution, but one of the world's biggest and most important religions and faith traditions, with different concepts of civil society (Hanafi, 2002). Although religion has been given more importance lately in the social and public spheres of society (Herbert, 2016), a religion in itself cannot be part of civil society. In contrast, the institutions of a given religion are, from a sociological point of view, essential building blocks of civil society, such as faith-based organisations from Christianity or Islam (Ebaugh et al., 2003; Herbert, 2016; Berger, 2005; Lunn, 2009). These institutional building blocks are what An'Naim calls 'normative components' of civil society, since 'religion is a necessary form of associational life for most people around the world' (An'Naim, 2005, p. 38, in Juergenmeyer, 2005).

This subsection has examined the boundary discussions, and interrelationships between religion, church and faith-based organisations. I began by offering a definition of religion and presented alternative views of the nature of religious organisations. The argument differentiated between the institutions and organisations of the civil society/ third sector on the one hand and religion which relates to life's ultimate questions and purpose on the other.

Having discussed some of the boundary issues confronting this exploration I now move on to the core of this chapter, which begins with a discussion of the critical role of mission and vision in relation to hybridity, and is followed by two subsections devoted to the critical external relationship of FBOs with the state.

The Internal Driving Forces for FBOs: Mission, Vision and Hybridisation

This subsection returns to that opening theme of the growth of hybridisation, building on the previous discussion of the boundaries between the key actors. It argues that one of the main driving forces for or against hybridity in faith-based organisations is mainly related to their mission and vision. Thus, in a study in Sweden which represents a Nordic welfare context, the organisational and institutional set-up of FBOs and their willingness to address major social issues and problems from a collaborative approach was seen to be linked to their vision and mission and capability to reach out to other congregations (Gärde, 2015). These could arise from:

1.   similar faith traditions and their institutions (ecumenical collaboration);
2.   other religious faith traditions (inter-religious collaboration); and
3.   other cultural and/or ethnic communities (inter-cultural collaboration).

In addition, there emerged a fourth pattern of collaboration with state agencies and/or private entities which could lead to different types of third sector hybrid organisations. Examples of the way in which different types of third sector/civil society organisations can enter hybrid territory when their welfare activities become overdependent on resources from the state/government sector and/or the private sector are presented elsewhere in this *Handbook*.

Based on this research, I suggest that at the core of every FBO stands the mission, as perceived by its concerned leadership and its constituencies. I describe the 'vision' as the overall view on faith, its ideological foundation and the religious ambition a person or organisation embraces. This can be compared with the concept of 'mission', which is how the overall view on faith, its ideological foundation and the religious ambition should be accomplished (Clarke, 2006; Milligan and Conradson, 2006; Torry, 2012).

The mission is not necessarily shared at all levels of a religious institution (Van der Ven, 1994). The same religious entity can have different agendas and sets of priorities, even more so if we are talking about congregations that are heterogeneous from a social, economic and ethnic point of view. Universal religious institutions such as Catholicism and Islam and, importantly for this chapter, their respective FBOs are challenged by different cultural and political contexts and have elaborate (internal) legal codes and procedures to handle internal and external affairs. Canon law and Sharia law are examples of legal systems that historically have influenced modern jurisprudence, and in modern times are sometimes in conflict with current civil and criminal laws (see De Cordier, 2009). For homogenous congregations, often Protestant or Orthodox national churches, religious faith is often part of the national heritage and shared by one ethnicity.

In order to further our understanding of the nature of hybridity within FBOs I now bring into the discussion an additional factor. This concerns the relationship between vision and mission or the distinctions between the progressive and conservative (vision) and the modern and traditional (mission) (Gärde 1999). Social scientists often tend to categorise religious congregations according to their social and political approaches, that is, whether they could be considered progressive (liberal) or conservative. Figure 26.1 may serve as a helpful analytical tool to help us understand the dynamics of hybridity within faith-based organisations and how they relate to their visions and missions.

One example that illustrates the application of the matrix in Figure 26.1 is that of the social movements of the Catholic church in Latin America, whose ecclesiastical base communities were progressive in their vision but often rather traditional in their mission. Their ways of spreading social messages were rudimentary and basic, low-tech and people-centred, and could thus be classified as Progressive-Traditional (PT) in that schema. During the 1980s many of these social movements were challenged by the traditional and centralised institutions of the Vatican which could initially be labelled Conservative-Traditional (CT) organisations. Traditional lay movements such as Opus Dei and Communione e Liberazione were renewed by the development of very

Vision ↓	TRADITIONAL	MODERN	*Mission* ←
PROGRESSIVE	PT	PM	
CONSERVATIVE	CT	CM	

Figure 26.1   Matrix on vision and mission of faith-based organisations

modern ways of spreading their mission, embracing information technology (IT) and advanced technological state-of-the-art tools and channels, often inspired by Protestant Charismatic North American congregations and becoming Conservative-Modern (CM) organisations. Other examples of the CM approach can be found outside the Christian spheres of influence, notably Islamic State which has been very successful in utilising internet and social media in spreading its version of Islam from the times of the Prophet Mohammad. Other religious sects and movements that see the external world as a threat seek to restrict their ways of transmitting their message through traditional means and have a zero-tolerant approach to collaboration and networking, and can be seen as variants of the CT model.

In order to extend the range of this analysis for the study of hybrid faith-based organisations I have drawn on the three-sector theory of hybridity (Billis, 2010). This enables me to make suggestions as to how the four types of the faith-based civil society/third sector organisations identified in Figure 26.1 overlap with the state/public and private sectors. We need, however, to add an additional proposition of this theory: that, because of the inherent contradictory principles of the different sectors, organisations will have roots and primary adherence and 'prime ownership' to the principles of one of the three sectors (Billis, 2010, pp. 56–57), which become important when very difficult organisational problems arise in hybrid forms.

The four types of FBOs in Figure 26.1 might consequently be analysed as follows:

- PT: religious and social movements mainly collaborating and/or networking with left-wing political parties and governments in the public sphere, and anti-commercial and critical of the private sector. These would have roots and prime adherence to the mission-driven principles of the civil society/third sector in a relationship of 'shallow' hybridity with the governmental sector. Their vision and mission is likely to act as a protection against hybridity with the private sector.
- PM: progressive religious and social movements actively working with civil society organisations and working in partnership with public entities. Often critical of private sector initiatives but with a pragmatic approach as long as it serves their vision. Although rooted in the civil society/third sector they are already likely to be in entrenched hybridity with the public sector, and susceptible to entering hybrid relationships with the private sector.
- CM: religious entities mainly concerned with their own mission and with developing their internal constituencies and membership, but open to collaboration mainly with the private sector and the public sector for charitable and philanthropic purposes. These appear unlikely to become hybrid organisations unless their collaboration with the private sector leads to conditions likely to influence their mission.
- CT: entities with conservative and traditional leadership which would aim at any cost to defend the core values of both vision and mission in a changing world. This category would also include religious sects that are intolerant of collaboration with other aspects of society that they view with suspicion and as a possible threat. These organisations appear unlikely to deviate from their pure 'non-hybrid' status.

This subsection has demonstrated the way in which, based on their mission and vision, religious entities can be usefully analysed in terms of four different types (PT, PM, CM, CT). These differences in mission and vision lead to variations in their degree of openness towards the surrounding society and are an important factor in the potential susceptibility to hybridisation of faith-based organisations. The discussion on mission and vision also inevitably touched on their external relationship with the state and its organisations and, to lesser degree, the private sector. The following section discusses these relationships in more detail and begins by exploring the relationship between faith-based organisations and their hybrids and European states.

EXTERNAL RELATIONSHIPS

Faith-Based Organisations, Hybridity and the Relationship with European States

This and the following subsection move the main focus of the chapter into what might be described as the external dimension of this exploration. This division is approximate, but it is nevertheless helpful in getting to grips with the complexity of the interactions between FBOs and hybridity. Again, in response to that complexity, this subsection mainly discusses the relationship between FBOs and European states. In so doing I draw upon the results of a major European research programme in addition to the research findings and theoretical approaches noted previously.

In this research programme 12 countries were analysed with a focus on the role of FBOs and their participation in social welfare provision, which has been a rich field for the global study of hybridity (Bäckström and Pettersson, 2016). Eight welfare types (social democratic, liberal, conservative, corporatist, social/capitalist, Southern European, liberal and post-communist), based on Esping-Andersen's (2013) typology, were tested empirically through national case studies in Northern, continental and Eastern Europe (Pettersson and Sjöborg, 2012). Several of these case studies are utilised, together with material from the previous section, in order to develop a modest typology of the relationship between the church and its faith-based organisations and the state and its governmental organisations.

In Germany, the welfare model has been marked by a 'privileged relation' between the government and the Roman Catholic and Evangelical Lutheran Protestant churches in what is called *Verbändeprivileg*, or 'relative priority' (Biendarra and Leis-Peters, 2012, p. 18) since the time of Bismarck at the end of the 19th century. This framework of collaboration has clear corporative elements and in many aspects can be seen as a hybrid where religious entities are not only state churches but also part of the public governmental structures for designing, funding and implementing welfare services.

The welfare set-up in the Nordic countries was different. While the state Lutheran churches had a central role in addressing charity and alleviating poverty until the mid-1850s, after that the local municipality was divided into civil and religious parts, with the former having the authority, responsibility and rights for implementing welfare activities. In a sense, these measures marginalised the church which, since then, has become a complementary partner to the state rather than replacing it, as was the case in Germany. In turn the state was challenged and reformed by the emergence of social movements, often progressive and advocating for change, and issues such as gender equality became high on the agenda in that northern context.

These social movements together with third sector organisations often collaborated with state agencies and were funded with public money; in some instances they were completely dependent on governmental funding. This raised questions regarding their integrity and independence. There were, for example, some Protestant FBOs with substantive funding from the Swedish government, sometimes for more than 90 per cent of their expenditure. In view of this extensive state funding there was little or no incentive for them to raise funds from their own members or from the wider public. As a result, the agendas, policies and the discourse between public sector and civil society or third sector organisations were almost the same as CSOs – including FBOs – as they were bound by the constraints of public spending and strict contractual requirements.

Drawing on the findings of the European research project, and other research discussed in the previous section of this chapter, it becomes possible to propose that there are four different types of interaction between the state and faith-based organisations:

1. Symbiotic hybridity between government rulers and faith-based organisations: the nationalist political movements of post-communist countries such as Russia are having an impact on civil society in general and the major Orthodox churches and other faith-based organisations in particular. This has led to a kind of symbiosis between governmental agencies and faith-based organisations, which are co-opted as a means of strengthening national identity. FBOs might thus be considered entrenched civic society (or third sector)–state hybrid organisations. On the other hand if, rather than being in a symbiotic relationship, the state controlled the mission of the organisation, then an FBO would be analysed more accurately as a state–third sector organisation.
2. Monopoly hybrid faith-based organisations such as Caritas and Diakonie in Germany are state-funded welfare entities, linked to the Roman Catholic and the Evangelical churches as well as to the German state. They have been part of a social contract established at the time of Bismarck and are located in a conservative social context.
3. Universal church faith-based organisations and hybridity for the common good: the new leadership of the Catholic church under Pope Francis is challenging the current church leaders and parish structures to become more involved in social matters and to elaborate new strategies on the 'preferential options for the poor'. This creates a new space for strengthened collaboration with secular NGOs, governmental agencies and 'all peoples of good will' (John XXIII, 1963, pp. 70,72). In this example the challenge of hybridity would be the extent to which strengthened collaboration might lead to mission drift.
4. Fusion hybridity can be seen in a non-European example where there is shared responsibility for the management of both religious property and assets (*waqfs*) and a shared obligation to fulfil the Islamic duties towards the poor (*zakat*). This welfare model has many variations, but is very often rooted in a solid fusion of the state and FBOs where religious assets are part of the apparatus of state ownership and control. While this model can be seen as related to the corporative welfare type described by Esping-Andersen but it is rooted in the different legal tradition of Sharia law, with a

plurality of Islamic jurisprudence. In view of the many variations of the model, and the absence of research in this area, it would be premature to attempt a sector analysis.

Verhagen makes a broader case about the relationship between governments and faith-based organisations when he argues that 'European FBOs are forced to modify their language of faith to bring into line with the dominant development discourse' (Verhagen, 2001, quoted in James, 2009, p. 11). In the last 20 years, the shift in international aid and development and the role of TSOs has led an increased number of Western-sponsored local organisations to become engaged in campaigning, advocacy and lobbying rather than to focus on welfare delivery or social and health-oriented aid. This shift of focus has led to ethical dilemmas and increased levels of hybridity between the public sector and civil society/third sector spheres. The following subsection enters the more problematic areas of situations in which the state might, to all intents and purposes, not exist, or be controlled by dictators, or be failing.

Hybridity and the Failing State

In stark contrast to the kinds of relationship between state and FBOs discussed above, there are examples of very different approaches. Some religious leaders have reacted against oppressive and dictatorial state regimes and some, like Archbishop Oscar Romero in El Salvador, who supported the creation of thousands of local-based communities uniting different parts of the country which promised a new kind of civil society, have paid for their opposition with their lives. Chile during the Pinochet regime was another example, where the Catholic church created a platform for social activism against the regime, and trade unions, youth groups, political parties, parish associations and popular education groups joined forces with it (Mercer, 2002).

In other countries marked by dictatorship, abuse of human rights and repression, the path of faith-based organisations in relation to the rulers took different directions. For example, some religious entities were convinced that the strong leader was a saviour and a guarantor for the threatened state, and became part of the repressive apparatus. That was, for instance, the case in Syria where the Baath Party and its leadership was supported by religious minorities, such as the Alawites and several Christian communities. In this context, governmental-organised non-governmental organisations (GONGOs) played a central role as a perverted form of hybrid organisations, servicing the needs of the ruling regime and its elites. Or, in attempts to please more liberal and moderate layers of society, new more modern 'NGOs' were created by relatives of prominent politicians using what looked like modern-style management to address the needs of society through charity and development projects (see, e.g., Frolic, 1997).

The failing state may also be accompanied by extreme poverty, humanitarian crises and lack of human security which are not only possible drivers for higher levels of religiosity, but are also highly likely to influence the configuration of civil society organisations (Pettersson, 2006) and the potential increase of hybrid organisational relationships. In these situations, the different agendas of foreign aid agencies often provide important external influences which will also contribute to this new and different landscape of NGOs and FBOs, as well as to their patterns of potential collaboration or conflict. In countries such as Somalia, Iraq and Afghanistan, billions of dollars of resources are pumped in from foreign donor agencies, completely changing the landscape of NGOs and the organisational structure of civil society – at least as long as the money is coming in.

These changes were apparent in Iraq after 2003 when the United States (US) toppled the Iraqi regime. Before then the Baath Party had a monopoly on social life and restricted the creation and functioning of a free civil society. The few FBOs that were tolerated could, in the main, only work with their own members, on a voluntary basis and under the strict control of the regime and its security apparatus. There were only a handful of registered NGOs and the few that were tolerated existed primarily to make propaganda for the regime. In such a situation it was difficult to talk meaningfully of a civil society/third sector. As part of a campaign by the American occupying forces to win the hearts and minds of the Iraqi population, however, efforts were made to transform and enhance civil society. The considerable volume of funding for this initiative was accompanied by the arrival of foreign private consultants and think tanks, often with close links to US politicians and decision-makers in Washington, which created a new organisational hybrid of 'Iraqi NGO'. Their governance and management structures were set up by the donors, and the local employees had to comply with conditions such as learning English and adopting the culture and behaviour of 'NGO workers'. In essence, this was a structure that was not built bottom-up from the Iraqi perspective and needs. Analytically, the prime ownership and roots of these Iraqi NGOs emanated from, and could be tracked back to, the US political elite.

This development of the Iraqi NGO provides an example of a growing phenomenon, resulting from a combination of geopolitics and foreign partners, which created new hybrid CSOs which became accepted as viable partners for foreign donors and were seen as 'moderate' and open-minded religious entities. This new hybrid is in many ways artificial but it can be seen as providing a useful organisational contribution to the implementation of life-saving operations under severe humanitarian conditions. The hybrid nature of the arrangements can be further complicated by the entry of the military with its own organisational structures, orders and mandate from the civilian authorities. This has led to a new review of what kind of organisation can be involved with humanitarian conditions, and the ethical dilemmas relating to this kind of civil–military and sometimes religious collaboration schemes. The review has put forward recommended minimum and common standards when it comes to quality assurance in the delivery of humanitarian assistance through a common framework of indicators (Sphere Standards, n.d.; Walker and Purdin, 2004).

By contrast we can identify an interesting example of the 'organic' emergence of local CSOs – often mainly FBOs – that are working in developing countries with the poorest and most marginalised populations and far from the attention of Western media and donors. Health and social services are delivered through religious orders, congregations, parishes and diocesan structures in sub-Saharan Africa where they frequently replace an absent state and corrupt governments. This has created strong local community-oriented organisations with well-developed networks and contacts with local leaders who are part of the civic fabric and have a strong sense of local needs. These hybrid FBOs mix local and foreign concepts of organisational configurations, management structures and governance, in a constant dialogue with potential foreign and local partners. Conceptually, they can be regarded as third sector-rooted organisations, probably with both governmental and private sector aspects of hybridity.

This discussion of what might be called the failing state has illustrated how, outside Europe, FBOs have also entered into hybrid-type relationships and the development of hybrid organisations in response to severe international social welfare problems. The following subsection attempts to take a further step forward by attempting to utilise the three-sector approach to tentatively explore the emerging landscape of hybrid faith-based organisations.

Hybrid Faith-Based Organisations and Sector Relationships

The story of events at the Vatican meeting illustrated the tensions between the mission and vision-driven associational principles of the church and the market-driven principles of the visiting consultants. The significant adoption of principles associated with the private sector by third sector organisations, including faith-based organisations, has led to the growth of hybridity and hybrid organisations. Similarly, the adoption of principles associated with the public sector has been illustrated throughout the chapter, and particularly in the with the discussion on symbiotic hybridity, monopoly hybrid faith-based organisations, universal church faith-based organisations, and fusion hybridity.

While the relationship between state and the public sector has received attention in this chapter, the relationship between faith-based organisations and the private sector has played a less prominent role. In part this may be due to the fact that the chapter has been significantly concerned with the provision of social services in which governments often have a major role. But it also reflects the long history of involvement and interdependence between state and religion where what we today call hybridity has a very long history.

The following brief case studies represent a modest attempt to conceptualise the emerging permutations of hybrid relationships between third sector faith-based organisations and the public and private sectors. As an entry point, and also as a potential basis for further research, I have attempted to analyse the case studies by utilising the three-sector theory (Billis, 2010). The first word of each category signifies the prime sector accountability, as described earlier. Accordingly, since my concern is with third sector organisations there are three possible combinations of hybrid organisation in which the third sector is dominant.

Third–private–public sector hybridity

The first case study is set in the multicultural suburb of Fisksätra in Sweden, where integration is the main problem. The suburb has high levels of immigrants from the Middle East and Africa, unemployment, family problems, criminality and drug abuse. These social problems cannot be handled by one sector alone. The social services department from the municipality did not have the capacity to reach out to certain target groups with potential high-risk factors for child abuse and/or domestic violence. In response to these problems a team of social workers and psychologists from both the public and third sectors was created where locally based NGOs could reach out to Arabic-speaking women with their peers – engaged communities and volunteers – who explained and designed the group intervention with relevant topics raised by the participating women.

The local housing company, the major private landowner in the area, had problems with development and the lack of a sense of community in the whole environment. The company hired professionals with a social commitment who also supported the projects that were implemented jointly with local NGOs. The commitment was long-term and not ad hoc and this finally yielded good results for all those concerned.

Importantly, religious extremism was also prevented through Muslim–Catholic– Protestant collaboration through religious dialogue and praxis, the so-called Diapraxis programme, supported by locally raised funds and public support from the European Social Fund. More widely, urban area studies show that faith initiatives in this sector often are successful as catalysts for social change (Beaumont, 2008; Dierckx et al., 2009).

Third–public sector hybridity

In Afghanistan, the humanitarian crisis and the need to reach out to vulnerable populations in times of turmoil led a group of Afghani and Swedish social activists to create an NGO in the 1980s during the Soviet occupation, with public funding from the Swedish government and other foreign donors. The uniqueness of this collaboration is that is localised and driven by participation by the main local stakeholders in the areas of content and decision-making.

The need for financial and human resources and a long-term joint approach was obvious, but difficult to build up during times of civil war, conflict and high levels of threats, with militias and religious extremist groups threatening the operation. Through the local network of tribal leaders with authority in different regions, it was possible to deliver aid in remote areas and to the most vulnerable groups. This group remains one of the main providers of humanitarian assistance in Afghanistan, and 30 years later there exist thousands of collaborators, activists, employees and volunteers.

Other examples are recent partnerships in international development aid where Islamic FBOs now enter into third–public hybridity in the West, such as Muslim Aid's partnership with United Methodist Committee on Relief; Christian Aid and Muslim Aid and the Catholic Agency for Overseas Development (Cafod) and Islamic Relief (James, 2009, p. 19). These networks are now tapping into public funding for common projects. One challenge for the Christian and Muslim FBOs is to adapt their 'faith language' into the 'dominant development discourse' (ibid., p. 11).

In Islamic countries, the hybridity is between the public sector and the FBOs, where the authority is either directly appointed by the government or influenced in different ways. A Sunni welfare organisation such as Makassed in Lebanon would have a substantial part of its payroll directly covered by the state and influenced by both Sunni politicians and religious leaders (Terc, 2006). That is part of the welfare mix and the Lebanese confessionalism with limited or no clear boundaries between the public and civil society spheres.

Third–private sector hybridity

The private sector comes into the picture where philanthropy and corporate social responsibility (CSR) are creating new innovative initiatives in key areas of concern (Van Marrewijk, 2003). Microfinance loans have been a success in several developing countries in Africa and Asia, where the banking sector has been transformed and now also cater for the needs of people and communities who previously had no access to credit. Civil society organisations needed to advocate for this to happen, and in several instances created microfinance institutions (MFIs) where the third sector and the private sector jointly were committed to provide microfinance loans, and later provided other needed financial and insurance services.

In each of these three categories, religious institutions with their faith-based organisations are playing a variety of central roles in order to gather together the communities and vulnerable people in remote areas.

SUMMARY AND CONCLUSIONS

Summary

This chapter had two interdependent objectives. The first of these was to explore some of the drivers both for, and against, the growth of hybridity in the changing environment. The second objective was to develop a cautious map of some of the new hybrid relationships between faith-based organisations and the other sectors. The various subsections provided the stepping-stones towards achieving those objectives.

Following the introduction, in the next section the scene was set with a brief personal story which illustrates the dramatic impact of the clash of the mission-driven values and principles of the church and the market-driven principles of the external advisers. We can also note here – the first of many occasions in the chapter – the way in which severe problems can instigate change. This is particularly the case in the later discussion about 'failing states'.

The following two subsections provided the foundation for addressing the first objective of better understanding the drivers of change towards, and away from, hybrid relationships. In order to do this the main 'internal' participants in these relationships (religion, church and faith-based organisations) were identified and analysed. The next subsection responded to the first objective and contended that vision and mission drive the forces for or against hybridity. Drawing on a number of different research sources, this concluded the inward looking section of the chapter with the development of a matrix (Figure 26.1) of four different types of faith-based organisations. The case was made that differences in their vision and mission are reflected in the openness of FBOs towards the surrounding society, and are consequently an important factor in the development, or otherwise, of hybridisation.

The next section of the chapter was mainly outward-looking. It began by drawing on a major European research programme in 12 European states in order to explore the relationship between faith-based organisations, hybridity and the European states. Based on these findings it became possible to propose four different types of relationships. This subsection concluded with the development of four types of interaction: symbiotic hybridity, monopoly hybrid faith-based organisations, universal church faith-based organisations and hybridity for the common good, and from outside Europe the example of fusion hybridity. The positive contribution of the welfare role of FBOs was noted, but so also were the questions being raised about their integrity and independence in the light of their dependence on government funding.

The mood changed in the following subsection in which attention was focused on hybridity and what was called the 'failing state', characterised by oppression and dictatorship, often accompanied by severe humanitarian conditions. Various types of hybrid interactions were illustrated and the impact of foreign consultants and donors in the development of 'top-down' hybrid NGOs was discussed. The subsection concluded by comparing these NGOs with the emergence of local, often mainly FBOs, with strong local community interaction and their awareness of local needs. This responded to the second objective of this chapter, which was to develop a draft or a modest map of the relationships between faith-based hybrid organisations and the three sectors.

Conclusions: Hybrid Faith-Based Organisations – Challenges and Responses

This chapter has discussed the diversity of the missions of faith-based organisations. It is important to remember that the mission for many FBOs goes beyond terrestrial problems and worries and enters other spheres of lives, with a focus on the metaphysical and spiritual dimensions of the human conditions of people. In contrast, other FBOs are more directly committed and focused on what is going on in the here and now, where faith plays a central role for engagement and social activism.

Nevertheless, despite this diversity, the general background is that the position of faith communities is changing: in a post-secular environment they are facing diminishing congregations. In response, these communities have developed a variety of ways of interacting and collaborating with public, private and other civil society organisations. Many of these interactions have led to hybrid types of organisation. This hybrid interaction with the public and private sectors, with their fundamentally different approaches and principles, has highlighted not only the tensions that can arise from the differences between those principles, but also potential benefits for faith communities.

Again, despite their diversity, there is ample evidence that FBOs from different faith traditions, together with public and private sector organisations and institutions, are finding the necessary space and opportunities for collaboration, cooperation and engagement, and the development of hybrid interactions. In part, reaching out by the church and its faith-based organisation, and the growth of opportunities for hybridity, is a result of internal factors such as diminishing congregations. But the subsection on the failing state has demonstrated the ways in which external pressures and severe problems have produced fertile conditions for the growth of hybridisation and hybrid organisations.

The picture that emerges is of a 'tug-of-war' between faith communities and their organisations which are striving not only to resolve the challenge of declining membership but also to respond to the challenge of wider humanitarian tragedy. The dilemma is to handle the *ad-intra/ad-extra* dimensions, such as the eroding membership base – that is, to survive as faith communities – but at the same time to allocate human and financial resources for external use. Tensions can occur within hybrid organisations as they struggle to cope with the changes that flow from collaborative schemes, such as the risk of being co-opted and/or controlled by public authorities that have different agendas (Williams et al., 2012). In Fisksätra it was not enough to work on religious and theological dialogue; real and substantive issues of common concern relating to the social problems in the area became both a starting point and a driver. And the work could involve challenges to the internal authority and leadership of FBOs. In the case of Fisksätra the local Imam and the Catholic parish priest were challenged by some members of their congregations who did not agree on the approach they were taking.

Further afield, in the aid industry, traditionally bilateral, multilateral and third-sector development and humanitarian assistance are three separate sectors with their own internal dynamics and challenges. The lessons learnt from interventions of previous years in Afghanistan and the Middle East and North Africa (MENA) region demonstrate the dangers in this high-risk environment, where higher degrees of collaboration between the sectors have become a necessity. Responses are being developed to meet the challenges. Thus, the response in the high-risk environment in Afghanistan and the MENA region has led to the need to find new levels of participation by the target groups and concerned stakeholders, not only in the implementation, but also in the design and decision-making.

Probably the main message of this chapter emerges from the three case studies, in which a high level of pragmatism was a common factor, with a common approach and a shared belief that reaching out to other stakeholders might contribute to the common good. What emerged from these cases and from other examples discussed in the chapter is the prevalence of the search for pragmatic solutions. Yet pragmatism, while essential, is not enough.

The environment is changing, as hybrid TSOs are certain to increase. Examples are the new Sustainable Development Goals (SDGs) and Agenda 2030; the 17 goals decided by 200 countries at the General Assembly of the United Nations in September 2015 provide a common framework for intervention by the public, private and third sectors. New schemes of collaboration across the sectors will be needed, and the old way of implementing development projects with three distinct sectors and limited collaboration between them is not regarded as viable any longer. In Sweden, for example, FBOs such as the City Mission and the Salvation Army are already shaping hybrid sector business organisations with the development of shops in commercial shopping malls.

Above all, the increasing part played by hybrid FBOs will require increased reflection and action. For example, a new strategic approach within FBOs will be required – as reflected in the opening example of Caritas Internationalis – taking into consideration the guiding core values and organisational culture, and how the vision and mission should be situated in a changing post-secular environment. And it is not just FBOs that will need to deepen their understanding of new and developing situations. In a world in which relationships between organisations from all three sectors are becoming even more complex, the need for research is essential. This is true in all parts of the world, but nowhere is the potential benefit greater than in the failing state. To better understand the relationship between hybrid organisations and the resolution of problems in such states possibly represents one of the most rewarding and yet most challenging areas of research facing academics. Hopefully, this chapter's exploration_of the relationships between hybrid faith-based organisations and sectors will make some contribution towards responding to those challenges.

REFERENCES

An'Naim (2005) The politics of religion and the morality of globalization. In Juergensmeyer, M. (ed.), *Religion in Global Civil Society*. New York: Oxford University Press, pp. 23–48.

Bäckström, A. and Pettersson, P. (2016) *Welfare and Religion in 21st Century Europe: Volume 1: Configuring the Connections*. London: Routledge.

Beaumont, J. (2008) Faith action on urban social issues. *Urban Studies*, 45(10), pp. 2019–2034.

Berger, P. (2005) Religion and global civil society. In Juergensmeyer, M. (ed.). *Religion in Global Civil Society*. New York: Oxford University Press, pp. 11–22.

Biendarra, I. and Leis-Peters, A. (2012) Germany, overview of the national situation. In Bäckström, A. (ed.), *Welfare and Values in Europe. Transitions related to Religion, Minorities and Gender, Volume 2, National*

Overviews and Case Study Report: Continental Europe: Germany, France, Italy, Greece. Uppsala University, Acta universitatis upsaliensis, Studies in Religion and Society 5. Sweden: Uppsala, pp. 13–54.

Billis, D. (ed.) (2010) *Hybrid Organizations and the Third Sector: Challenges for Practice, Theory and Policy*. Basingstoke: Palgrave Macmillan.

Casanova, J. (2001) Civil society and religion: retrospective reflections on Catholicism and prospective reflections on Islam. *Social Research*, 68(4), pp. 1041–1080.

Clarke, G. (2006) Faith matters: faith-based organisations, civil society and international development. *Journal of International Development*, 18(6), pp. 835–848.

De Cordier, B. (2009) Faith-based aid, globalisation and the humanitarian frontline: an analysis of Western-based Muslim aid organisations. *Disasters*, 33(4), pp. 608–628.

Dierckx, D., Vranken, J. and Kerstens, W. (2009) *Faith-Based Organisations and Social Exclusion in European Cities*. Leuven: Acco.

Durkheim, E. (1912 [1965]) *The Elementary Forms of the Religious Life*. New York: Free Press.

Ebaugh, H.R., Pipes, P.F., Chafetz, J.S. and Daniels, M. (2003) Where's the religion? Distinguishing faith-based from secular social service agencies. *Journal for the Scientific Study of Religion*, 42(3), pp. 411–426.

Esping-Andersen, G. (2013) *The Three Worlds of Welfare Capitalism*. Hoboken, NJ: John Wiley & Sons.

Frolic, B. (1997) State-led civil society. In Brook, T. and Frolic, B.M. (eds), *Civil Society in China*. New York: Routledge, pp. 46–67.

Gärde, J. (1999) Från invandrarkyrka till mångkulturellt samfund: En kyrkosociologisk analys av katolska kyrkan i Sverige. Dissertation, Uppsala University.

Gärde, J. (2015) Shrinking religious communities and thriving interreligious social work in postsecular Sweden. *Journal of Religion and Spirituality in Social Work: Social Thought*, 34(1), pp. 1–23.

Glock, C.Y. and Stark, R. (1965) *Religion and Society in Tension*. Chicago, IL: Rand McNally.

Hanafi, H. (2002) Alternative conceptions of civil society: a reflective Islamic approach. In Chambers, S. and Kymlicka, W. (eds). *Alternative Conceptions of Civil Society*. Princeton, NJ: Princeton University Press, pp. 171–189.

Herbert, D. (2016) *Religion and Civil Society: Rethinking Public Religion in the Contemporary World*. New York: Routledge.

Inglehart, R. and Welzel, C. (2005) *Modernization, Cultural Change, and Democracy: The Human Development Sequence*. New York: Cambridge University Press.

James, R. (2009) What is distinctive about FBOs? Praxis Paper, 22. Oxford: Intrac.

John XXIII (1963) Encyclical letter, *Pacem in Terris*. http://w2.vatican.va/content/john-xxiii/en/encyclicals/documents/hf_j-xxiii_enc_11041963_pacem.html (accessed 8 October 2019).

Juergensmeyer, M. (ed.) (2005) *Religion in Global Civil Society*. New York: Oxford University Press.

Keane, J. (2003) *Global Civil Society?* Cambridge: Cambridge University Press.

Lunn, J. (2009) The role of religion, spirituality and faith in development: a critical theory approach. *Third World Quarterly*, 30(5), pp. 937–951.

Mercer, C. (2002) NGOs, civil society and democratization: a critical review of the literature. *Progress in Development Studies*, 2(1), pp. 5–22.

Milligan, C. and Conradson, D. (2006) *Landscapes of Voluntarism: New Spaces of Health, Welfare and Governance*. Bristol: Policy Press.

Nynäs, P., Lassander, M. and Utriainen, T. (eds) (2012) *Post-Secular Society*. New Brunswick, NJ: Transaction Publishers.

Parsons, T. (1937 [1961]) *The Structure of Social Action*. New York: Free Press.

Pettersson, P. and Sjöborg, A. (eds) (2012) *Welfare and Values in Europe: Transitions related to Religion, Minorities and Gender, Volume 3*, Studies in Religion and Society 6. Uppsala: Acta Universitatis Upsaliensis.

Pettersson, T. (2006) Religion in contemporary society: eroded by human well-being, supported by cultural diversity. *Comparative Sociology*, 5(2/3), pp. 231–257.

Rochester, C. and Torry, M. (2010) Faith-based organizations and hybridity: a special case? In Billis, D. (ed.), *Hybrid Organizations and the Third Sector: Challenges for Practice, Theory and Policy*. Basingstoke: Palgrave Macmillan, pp. 114–133.

Salamon, L., Sokolowski, S. and List, R. (1999) *Global Civil Society*. Baltimore, MD: Johns Hopkins Center for Civil Society Studies.

Sphere Standards (n.d.) Sphere Standards, humanitarian charter and minimum standards 2019. https://www.spherestandards.org/ (accessed 9 October 2019).

Terc, M. (2006) A modern, integral, and open understanding: Sunni Islam and Lebanese identity in the Makassed Association. *Comparative Education Review*, 50(3), pp. 431–445.

Torry, M. (2012) Is there a faith sector? *Voluntary Sector Review*, 3(1), pp. 111–117.

Van der Ven, J.A. (1994) The communicative identity of the local church. In Provost, J.H. and Walf, K. (eds), *Catholic Identity*. Canterbury: SCM Press, pp. 26–37.

Van Marrewijk, M. (2003) Concepts and definitions of CSR and corporate sustainability: between agency and communion. *Journal of Business Ethics*, *44*(2/3), pp. 95–105.

Verhagen, K. (2001) The potential and pitfalls confronting Catholic NGOs in the world of microfinance (microcredit). University of St Thomas. http://www.stthomas.edu/cathstudies/cst/mgmt/le/papersnp/verhagen.htm (accessed 22 November 2004).

Walker, P. and Purdin, S. (2004) Birthing sphere. *Disasters*, *28*(2), pp. 100–111.

Weber, M. (1905) *The Protestant Ethic and the Spirit of Capitalism*. London: Allen & Unwin.

Williams, A., Cloke, P. and Thomas, S. (2012) Co-constituting neoliberalism: faith-based organisations, co-option, and resistance in the UK. *Environment and Planning A*, *44*(6), pp. 1479–1501.

Yinger, M. (1979) *The Scientific Study of Religion*. New York: Macmillan.

27. Volunteers and hybrid organisations
Colin Rochester, Angela Ellis Paine and Matt Hill

INTRODUCTION

Volunteers are playing a growing and increasingly important role in organisations across all three sectors: public and private as well as third. Their contribution to third sector organisations is (on one level at least) fairly straightforward – the theoretical framework developed by David Billis (2010) identifies volunteers as the sector's distinctive human resources – but the position with regard to the organisations in the other two sectors is more problematic. For Billis the private sector's distinctive human resources are 'paid employees' while the public sector is staffed by 'paid public servants' (ibid., p. 55). Within Billis's framework the presence of volunteers in these two sectors is in a sense anomalous and may indicate that an organisation in which they are involved contains elements of hybridity. In this chapter we discuss the role and status of volunteers in different kinds of organisation and review the ways in which their activities are organised. We have carried out this review in order to assess the extent to which the involvement of volunteers can be seen as a way of defining organisations as hybrid. Our discussion is largely centred on the experience of volunteering in England, although we will also take account of some relevant literature from elsewhere.

Direct evidence of the changing nature or experience of volunteering in hybrid organisations is hard to find. Some commentators have discussed the implications of hybridity for volunteers within the third sector (see Hustinx, 2014; Ellis Paine et al., 2010) but there is less discussion of volunteering within other hybrid settings. Indeed, even within the field of third sector studies, as Warburton and McDonald (2009, p. 825) argue, 'little is known about how these organisational changes impact upon the capacity and commitment of volunteers, and particularly those volunteers accustomed to working in a traditional institutional order'.

There is, however, a growing body of material which can help to throw some light on the role and status of volunteers in different kinds of organisation. There is a long history of volunteer involvement in parts of the public sector and there has been renewed interest recently in the role of voluntary action in parts of the United Kingdom's National Health Service (NHS) (Brindle, 2017; Lay, 2017; Galea et al., 2013; Hotchkiss et al., 2014; Mundle et al., 2012; Naylor et al., 2013), social care (Hussein, 2011; Volunteer Development Scotland, 2013), schools (Body et al., 2017), the criminal justice system (Hamilton, 2017; Britton and Calendar, 2016; Barnard and Britton, 2016), and volunteering is also common across the fields of leisure, heritage and cultural services (Nichols, 2017; Birchall and Simmons, 2004). Volunteer involvement is less common in the private sector but we have identified some useful literature including studies of the differences between all three sectors in the fields of tourism (Andersson and Getz, 2009) and social care (Hill, 2016).

The chapter is set out in six subsequent sections. In the first of these we try to identify the various kinds of organisation in which volunteers are involved. We approach this by revisiting David Billis's map of the 'authentic sector model' (set out in Chapter 24 of this *Handbook*) which brings together the ideal models of the three sectors – private, public and third – together with the hybrid forms associated with each of them. In the next section of the chapter we look more closely at the 'ideal type' of the third sector organisation – the association – which is owned and governed by its volunteer members who are also responsible for defining and carrying out its operational work. This, we suggest, provides a kind of template against which we can assess the extent to which these third sector principles are present in hybrid organisations. We then look at the role of volunteers in third sector hybrids and the changing relationship between them and paid employees. The next two sections look at the status and roles of volunteers in the other two sectors: the public sector and the private sector, respectively. The final section summarises our findings across the sectors and seeks to identify the part played by volunteers in each sector and the extent to which they can be seen as contributing to the hybrid nature of public, private and third sector organisations.

MAPPING HYBRID ORGANISATIONS

The geography of David Billis's 'authentic sector model' is based on an amalgamation of two types of organisation. The first of these is the 'ideal type' that represents the unambiguous exemplar of each of the three sectors – public, private and third or voluntary – which represents the 'fundamental and different ways of responding to human problems' that cannot be addressed by 'families, friends and . . . non-organisational social interactions' (Billis, Chapter 24 in this *Handbook*). The second type of organisation that completes the membership of the authentic sector model is the hybrid: an organisation which does not conform to any one of the ideal types but combines the organisational principles of more than one of them.

Each non-hybrid organisation can be defined by the ways in which they are owned and governed; the operational priorities by which they are driven; and the distinctive human and other resources they command. In the case of the private or for-profit sector the 'ideal type' is the managerially controlled 'firm', owned by shareholders and governed by the size of share ownership; with its operational priorities based on market forces and individual choice; staffed by paid employees and funded by sales and fees. In contrast, the public sector is organised through the legally backed 'bureau', owned by citizens and governed by public elections; with operational priorities based on public service and collective choice; staffed by paid public servants; and funded from taxes. And the ideal model of the third – or voluntary or not-for-profit – sector is the 'association' that is owned by its members, governed by private elections; with operational priorities that are based on members' commitment to their mission; relies on volunteers for its operational work; and is funded from subscriptions and donations (Billis, 2010, pp. 54–55).

While hybrid organisations may exhibit different and even contradictory organisational principles drawn from more than one of the sectors discussed above, Billis (2010, p. 56) argues that 'organizations will have "roots" and have primary adherence to the principles of one sector'. Hybrids based on the private sector are those which combine their private sector roots with public sector principles, or with third sector principles, or with principles drawn from both. Hybrids based on the public sector are those which combine their public sector roots with third sector principles, or with private sector principles, or with principles from both. And hybrids based on the voluntary or third sector are those which combine their third sector roots with public sector principles, or with private sector principles, or with principles drawn from both.

Billis also distinguishes between different categories of hybridity. In the first place he identifies the difference between 'shallow' and 'entrenched' forms. Shallow forms involve a comparatively modest degree of involvement with principles introduced from sectors other than the prime sector affiliation of any hybrid. Any tensions resulting from these changes can be easily accommodated without any significant challenge to the organisation's founding mission or organising principles. By contrast, the entrenchment of hybridity arrives when new elements are introduced to such an extent that they challenge the underlying mission and values of the organisation. His second distinction is between 'organic' hybrids that have changed over time 'from the steady accumulation of external resources' and those that have been 'enacted', or created as hybrids 'from day one' (Billis, 2010, p. 61).

This brief overview of the organisational geography of Billis's 'authentic sector model' enables us to identify the kinds of organisation in which we can expect to locate the involvement of volunteers. Clearly the non-hybrid form of the third sector association provides the starting point for a discussion of the role and status of volunteers in organisations. Equally clearly, volunteers have no place among the organisational principles of Billis's private and public sector ideal-typical organisations. Among the variety of hybrid organisations mapped by Billis we can expect to find volunteers involved in: (1) organisations with their roots in the third sector but which have been influenced by the organisational principles of the private and/or public sectors; (2) organisations with their roots in the public sector but which have been influenced by the organisational principles of the third sector; and (3) organisations with their roots in the private sector but which have been influenced by the organisational principles of the third sector. In this chapter we will discuss in turn each of these organisational forms, but only after we have looked more carefully at the third sector association and the ways in which volunteers have been involved in this kind of organisation.

THE 'PURE' THIRD SECTOR ORGANISATION: THE ASSOCIATION

The association is a unique kind of formal organisation in that it is entirely owned, managed and operated by its – volunteer – members. Its key organisational principles have been identified by Billis (2010, pp. 54–55):

- Its ownership rests entirely with the association's members who alone have the authority to make the key decisions that determine the future of the organisation.
- The governance of the association is in the hands of those members who have been elected by the membership to serve as the officers and committee of the association.
- The operational priorities of the organisation's work are 'driven neither by the need to make a profit nor by public policies but primarily by the association's own agenda' (ibid., p. 53).

- The human resources deployed by the association are the voluntary activities of their members and other volunteers. Other distinctive resources are provided by voluntary contributions in the form of subscriptions and donations.

These key principles define the association as an organisational form that is very different from the public sector bureau and the private sector firm. These are organised as bureaucracies with clear hierarchies of authority and accountability whose staff have clearly defined roles and responsibilities. By contrast, associations have been described as spaces for 'un-coerced participation' (Lohmann, 1992) where members/volunteers exercise a considerable degree of autonomy over their activities. Associational volunteers have been described as 'unmanaged' (Scott, 2010) and 'not biddable' (Kearney, 2001 [2007]): they can choose not only whether or not to volunteer but also on what terms they will participate. And, in the absence of the kind of command-and-control structure provided by a bureaucracy, associations are guided by the shared goals of their members and an agreed set of informal 'rules' governing what is accepted by them as appropriate behaviour (Smith, 2000).

VOLUNTEERS AND THIRD SECTOR HYBRIDS

Volunteers and Paid Staff in the Third Sector

By far the most common form of third sector organisation is the purely voluntary association. A study in the North of England, for example, found that only 31 per cent of general charities employed paid staff and the great majority of them relied solely on volunteers (Kane et al., 2010). And many of the third sector organisations that employ staff also rely heavily on volunteers: all charities have volunteer trustees, while many voluntary organisations also involve volunteers in operational roles. Furthermore the majority of those who volunteer in organisations are involved in those with third sector roots (Low et al., 2007). The extent and nature of volunteer involvement has changed and is changing, and varies considerably among third sector organisations not least according to the degree to which they have been influenced by the growing impact of the employment of paid staff and the need to access external revenue to meet their costs. There has been a marked increase over recent years in the number of paid staff employed in the third sector. According to the United Kingdom (UK) Labour Force Survey the total number of people employed in the sector rose by 24 per cent between 1997 and 2006, and the number of full-time-equivalent staff increased by 75000 between 2001 and 2006 (Kane et al., 2010). Over a similar period the proportion of the population that volunteers has remained static, although there is evidence that this phenomenon is not uniform across all organisations (Ellis Paine et al., 2010). It also seems that paid staff have replaced volunteers in some – but by no means all – third sector organisations, and that the impact of an increase in the numbers of paid staff on the role and status of volunteers varies from organisation to organisation (ibid.).

One way of addressing these differences is captured by the distinction between 'shallow' and 'entrenched' hybrids made by Billis (2010) and applied to third sector hybrids by Ellis Paine et al. (2010). 'Shallow' hybrids have 'moved into hybridity in a rather gentle fashion, causing minor disturbances, but not necessarily calling into question their basic third sector identity' (Billis, 2010, pp. 58–59). In the case of 'entrenched' hybrids, by contrast, the impact of public and/or private sector principles can have an effect on the basic values and mission of an organisation's original foundation.

Shallow Hybrids

A critical step in a process of change for shallow third sector hybrids is often the introduction of one or more paid employees to take on some of the operational work of the organisation that had originally been undertaken by volunteers. This has an impact on the role and status of the volunteers. They retain a major stake in the organisation but can no longer be regarded as its sole owners: as Ellis Paine et al. (2010, p. 106) argue, 'they have a role in decision-making and their views are generally taken seriously but they are not the ultimate power holders'. Increasingly, 'paid staff begin to take on greater significance and have more central and strategic roles in the organization'. At the same time, the operational roles played by volunteers continue to be shaped by the interests of individual volunteers as well as by the needs of the organisation, and their activities are 'organized informally, developmentally and inclusively' (ibid.).

Entrenched Hybrids

The entrenchment of hybridity in third sector organisations is to a significant degree the product of major changes in public and social policy which have had a significant impact on the sector and the position of many volunteers within it. Increasingly third sector organisations have been aligned with the interest of the state and seen as partners in the delivery of social welfare as well as participants in a competitive market place for the provision of public services (Harris, 2010). Third sector organisations have adapted their missions to meet the requirements of the state; increased the size of their income; employed considerably more staff; developed their capacity to compete for contracts; developed a more hierarchical and bureaucratic staff structure; and concentrated power in their chief executive officers and other senior paid managers.

Paid Staff and Volunteers: Changing Roles and Relationships

The growing numbers of paid staff employed in third sector organisations has been associated with significant changes in the part played by volunteers. There has been an increased focus on the need for personnel with professional competence and technical skills, rather than experiential learning which tends to favour paid staff over volunteers (Bondi, 2004; Weeks et al., 1996; Aiken and Thomson, 2013). In some organisations volunteers have been replaced – in part or in full – by paid staff who were considered to be more reliable and better equipped to meet demands for the efficient and reliable provision of public services (Buckingham, 2010; Eikenberry and Kulver, 2004; Cloke et al., 2007; Elstub, 2006). And in an increasing number of hybrids there has been a change in the characteristics of volunteers: Eikenberry and Kulver (2004), for example, highlight the replacement of community representatives on boards of trustees with entrepreneurial business representatives with specific skill sets. Other organisations have continued to involve considerable numbers of volunteers, and in some cases have expanded their volunteer numbers in response to the expansion of their provision of services. At the same time, however, they may increasingly rely on paid staff to take on strategic roles, with volunteers restricted to engagement in specific programmes or roles that are less skilled, less time-intensive, and more marginal to the organisation's core delivery and decision-making activities (Ellis Paine et al., 2010; Geoghagen and Powell, 2006).

Associated with these changing roles for volunteers and paid staff is a fundamental change in their relationship. As Carmel and Harlock (2008) suggest, the relationship between paid staff and volunteers within entrenched third sector hybrids is one of employer and employee, rather than the co-owners or co-workers who participate in associations or shallow third sector hybrids. There is evidence of tension between volunteers and paid staff (Weeks et al., 1996; Leonard et al., 2004), particularly for those within organisations where the roles of both volunteers and paid staff have changed over time through processes associated with organic, increasingly entrenched hybridisation.

Changing Approaches to Volunteer Management

The way in which volunteering is coordinated and managed is also changing, and is likely to be different in associations and third sector hybrids. While volunteer 'management' within associations is likely to be implicit, informal and based on mutual support, within hybrid third sector organisations it is more likely to be top-down, formal, rule- and work-based. The growing influence of private sector and public sector practices contribute to an increasing concern for standardised delivery and work practice, risk management and impact assessment, which drive formalisation processes across the third sector, including within volunteer management. Following Zimmeck (2001), management is 'home-grown' within associations and 'modern' within third sector hybrids; or, using Meijs and Hoogstad (2001) terms, 'membership management' is likely to be more common in associations and 'programme management' in third sector hybrids. Application forms, recruitment/assessment processes, role descriptions, induction, training, and ongoing supervision and management have become standard practices for volunteering within larger (hybrid) third sector organisations (see, e.g., Machin and Ellis Paine, 2008).

The introduction of increasingly formal volunteer management practices affects the volunteering experience. While on the one hand evidence suggests that volunteers think the organisation of their work has improved, on the other hand for some it has become too formal and bureaucratic (see Low et al., 2007), more about work than about conviviality (Rochester, 2013), for example. While volunteers often want their work to be well organised, and indeed have been instrumental in driving the formalisation of volunteer management practices, they rarely want it to become too work-like; as Gaskin (2003) found, they want a 'choice blend', well-organised volunteer roles and support, delivered in an informal flexible manner. Overly formal volunteer management processes can contribute to volunteers feeling disgruntled, sometimes to the point of leaving an organisation, and can put others off from joining (Low et al., 2007).

Volunteers, Hybridity and Third Sector Organisations

Together, we suggest, changes to the role, relationships, organisation and management of volunteers that have been associated with hybridity in third sector organisations are fundamentally affecting their position and identity, and ultimately shaping both the experience and outcomes of volunteering. Within associations and – to a considerable extent – in shallow third sector hybrids, volunteers exercise considerable autonomy over their own actions and play a significant part, as owners or members, in determining the direction of the organisation as a whole, while the organisation of their work is informal and based on mutual support. As the organisational principles of the public sector and/ or the private sector become established in the entrenched kind of third sector hybrid together with professionalisation, formalisation and bureaucratisation, the roles and activities of volunteers in these organisations are markedly different. They are reposi-tioned within them as (unpaid) staff (instead of owners or members) whose role is to carry out operational tasks specified for them under the supervision of paid managers (Ellis Paine et al., 2010, pp. 107–108).

These changes in the role and status of volunteers in increasingly entrenched third sector hybrids are neither universal or inevitable. 'Why is it, for example,' Ellis Paine et al. (2010, p. 110) ask, 'that some organizations have resisted the overwhelming drive towards professionalization and formalization and kept the spirit of volunteering alive and central to their organizational ethos, and some have not?' We have not answered this question in this chapter any more than Ellis Paine and her colleagues did in theirs, but we can suggest that one partial explanation may be found in the difference between organisations that are deeply rooted in the third sector and have become hybridised by a process of organic change, and those that have been created as a hybrid by a conscious decision on the part of those managing it. This distinction has been made by Billis (2010, pp. 61–62). Volunteering may have been deeply embedded in an organic hybrid, we sug-gest, whereas volunteering in enacted hybrids may not have been a fundamental part of its organisational culture. As Netting et al. (2004, p. 82) argue, 'an organisational culture pre-disposed to using volunteers is very different to one in which the incorporation of volunteers is an "add on" to an already busy schedule'.

The Impact of Hybridisation on the Volunteer Experience

The entrenchment of hybridity in third sector organisations has contributed to a pro-found change in the role and experience of volunteers. The future of the 'traditional' or 'collective' volunteer with a commitment to a specific cause (defined, among others, by Hustinx, 2001 [2007]) may be largely restricted to its contribution to associations and shallow hybrids. Volunteers in entrenched hybrids are more likely to find their place in Hustinx's 'new' 'reflexive' volunteering in which volunteers are involved in a series of shorter-term relationships with a variety of organisations, based on an exchange between the volunteer and the organisation. Rather than shaping the mission and strategic opera-tion of the organisation, volunteers are restricted to performing specific and operational roles. Instead of exercising a considerable degree of autonomy over the ways in which they carry out their roles they are increasingly subject to the supervision of managers and undergo human resource management procedures that are more appropriately designed for paid staff. For 'new' volunteers with their limited and conditional commitment to the organisation this regime may be perfectly acceptable (although some may find the degree of bureaucracy involved irksome), but the experience of volunteering it provides is very different to that expected or encountered by the 'traditional' volunteer.

VOLUNTEERS IN THE PUBLIC SECTOR

Introduction

There is no place for volunteers in the model of the non-hybrid form of public sector organisation characterised by Billis (2010) – the bureau – but there are and always have been, in fact, large numbers of volunteers involved in the public sector and there have been calls for the involvement of many more. Arguably, then, the involvement of volunteers in public sector organisations could be seen as an indication of their hybrid nature: rooted in the public sector but also involving some organisational principles drawn from the third sector. On the other hand the existence of volunteers who are essentially unpaid equivalents of paid employees, or whose contribution to the organisation is otherwise marginal, might be thought to lack sufficient weight to make a meaningful contribution to hybridisation.

In this section of the chapter we will review what is known about the involvement of volunteers in public sector organisations and discuss the extent to which their roles and activities can be seen as indicative of third sector organisational principles and thus form part of some kind of public sector hybrid. We will begin by assessing the overall scale of volunteer involvement in the public sector and then sketch out the history of that involvement. Following those introductory subsections we will look at the involvement of volunteers in four areas of public policy: schools, the police service, libraries and hospitals. The final subsection will provide some concluding remarks about these four areas and offer three models of volunteer involvement in the sector.

The Scale of Volunteer Involvement

Accurate empirical evidence of the scale of volunteer involvement in the public sector is hard to come by but what evidence there is suggests that it can be extensive. The most recent survey (by Low et al., 2007) found that nearly a quarter of volunteers in England identified the public sector as providing the main organisation with which they were involved. The authors expressed some doubt about the accuracy of respondents' identification of public sector organisations, but the survey does give an indication of the likely scale of volunteer involvement in the sector. We calculate that this percentage would amount to some 5.5 million adults whose involvement was equivalent to more than 374 000 full-time workers each year. A similar study of volunteering in the United States of America in 1999 reported a similar level of involvement: 27 per cent of volunteers had volunteered for a government agency (Brudney, 1999).

There is also evidence of significant levels of activity in specific areas of volunteer involvement in the public sector. According to the National Governance Association there are more than 250 000 school governors and trustees in England, 'one of the largest volunteer groups in the UK' (NGA, 2018), and this figure is likely to be matched – at least – by the numbers of those who volunteer in a variety of other capacities in schools (Body et al., 2017). Volunteers were also extensively involved across the criminal justice system, including 30 000 lay magistrates (Active Communities Unit, 2000, cited in Birchall and Simmons, 2004), 20 000 Special Constables (Police Specials, 2014), 10 000 Police Support Volunteers and the same number of Police Cadets (Barnard and Britton, 2016);

while the Police Federation of England and Wales claimed that there were more than 38 000 volunteers involved in 200 different roles across police services in 2017 (Hamilton, 2017; Suffolk Constabulary, 2017). Volunteer involvement is also common across leisure, heritage and cultural services, with one report from 2000 finding that 100 000 volunteers were involved in supporting heritage activities such as museums (Active Communities Unit, 2000, cited in Birchall and Simmons, 2004). And there are a significant variety and number of volunteers involved in the health service: one study identified almost 50 different 'things that volunteers do within the NHS' (Hawkins and Restall, 2006), while the total numbers involved in acute hospital trusts alone was estimated at 78 000 (Galea et al., 2013).

These figures have to be seen as tentative. There has to be some doubt about whether they are all public sector organisations; Low et al. (2007) suggested that some of the respondents to their survey had misidentified the sector within which their main volunteering activity had taken place. Furthermore, many volunteers are recruited and 'managed' by third sector organisations such as parent–teacher associations and hospital leagues of friends, rather than being directly coordinated by public sector organisations themselves, and it is not always possible to establish whether such volunteers have been included in the figures. The overall figures also fail to reveal just how uneven the distribution of volunteers is even within the individual fields. Galea et al. (2013, p. 1), for example, found a considerable variation in the numbers of volunteers involved in NHS acute hospital trusts – from 35 to 1300 – with differences not easily explained by the size of trusts. Similarly, Body et al. (2017, p. 9) reported that the scale of the contribution of voluntary action to the work of the primary schools they studied varied significantly: from 3 to 227 hours of volunteer time a week. On the other hand, they do provide a useful measure of the overall levels of volunteer involvement in the public sector.

The History of Involvement in the Sector

Volunteer involvement in public sector organisations is not new: it has a long and significant history. Some of the roles still played by volunteers, such as lay magistrates, Special Constables and school governors, are of long standing. Volunteer involvement in the health service did not disappear with the introduction of the National Health Service and, from the 1960s on, was promoted by the then Ministry of Health which provided guidance for the recruitment of volunteers and encouraged the employment of voluntary service managers in the NHS (Davis Smith, 1996). In 1969 the influential Aves Committee published its report on *The Voluntary Worker in the Social Services* which focused on 'the place of volunteers in the expanding role of social services' and their relationship with professional social workers (Aves, 1969, p. 195). One of the recommendations of the report led to the establishment of the Volunteer Centre UK to provide a continuing focus for volunteers in the public sector (Rochester, 2013).

This long history of volunteer involvement in the public sector has taken a recent turn since the general election of 2010 which led to the formation of the Coalition Government with its commitment to austerity and its rhetoric of the 'Big Society' (Alcock, 2010). These policy changes have produced severe cuts in public expenditure, together with attempts to improve the quality of public service delivery by involving service users and citizens in its design and implementation, and emphasising an enhanced role for the individual, the family and the community rather than the state in meeting social needs (Pestoff, Chapter 18 in this *Handbook*). These shifts represent important drivers for expanding the breadth and depth of volunteering in public sector organisations. Most recently they have led to major national campaigns to boost volunteer numbers in hospitals (Brindle, 2017; Lay, 2017) and in the police service (Hamilton, 2017; Suffolk Constabulary, 2017).

Volunteers in Schools

A recent important and pioneering study of volunteers in primary schools in the county of Kent (Body et al., 2017) has provided a detailed picture of the variety of the roles they play and the importance of their contribution to the work of the schools. Broadly speaking they fall into three main categories: those who serve as school governors, those involved in fundraising and those involved in the operational work of the school. Body and her colleagues found that in 67 per cent of the schools they surveyed volunteers regularly supported the school with management and leadership activities; in 71 per cent of them with fundraising activities (many of them involved with the annual school fair and other 'internal' activities, but comparatively few raising funds from 'external' sources); while as many as 96 per cent of volunteers regularly supported 'work in the classroom'. The great majority of the head teachers and other senior leaders of the schools surveyed by Body and her colleagues – 93 per cent – said that volunteers formed 'an important part of the school community' (ibid., p. 8) and nearly three-quarters of them would like to involve more volunteers in their school.

They identified three main ways in which the involvement of volunteers benefited the schools. First among these was that it provided increased support for the children and enhanced their experiences. Volunteers could, for example, deliver one-to-one support for children to meet individual needs as well as supporting whole school activities such as school trips. They were seen as possessing 'an array of different professional skills and expertise' which could be used 'to supplement and support teaching' (Body et al., 2017, p. 15). And volunteers could also be seen as providing adult role models and emotional support for some children. The second benefit of involving volunteers, according to some schools, was to provide 'strong links to the local community' (ibid., p. 15) and, as one head expressed it, they helped 'to develop a sense of community beyond the school gates' (ibid., p. 8). The third way in which voluntary action was of benefit to schools was that it responded to the pressures of depleted budgets both by providing increased capacity at minimum cost and by helping to raise additional funding.

This positive account of the contribution made by volunteers to schools needs to be set against the very uneven levels of volunteering reported by Body and her colleagues. They calculated that there was a discrepancy between 'approximately 72 minutes of volunteer time per pupil [per week] at one school, versus less than a minute of voluntary support for several others' (Body et al., 2017, p. 9), while 58 per cent of the schools surveyed 'struggled to attract the amount of volunteer support they would ideally like' (ibid., p. 8). Evidence from Body et al.'s study, nonetheless, suggests that the range and depth of volunteer involvement that could be found in all three aspect of the work of schools – governance, operational activities and fundraising – means that at least some of them should be considered to have a hybrid element.

Volunteers in the Police Service

By contrast, the rationale for involving volunteers in the police service appears to be more limited: they are valued for their ability to provide much-needed human resources in a time of restricted budgets. The large-scale and long-established involvement of volunteer Special Constables has always been seen as a means of supplementing policy manpower and has provided an avenue of recruitment for those seeking to enter the police as a career (Pepper, 2014; Mirrlees-Black and Byron, 1994). The comparatively recent proliferation of volunteer roles – and the demand for more volunteer involvement – appears to have been driven by similar demands. According to a report in *The Times* of 10 October 2017:

> Chief constables have spent £600 000 on a campaign to fill thousands of policing vacancies with volunteers. Unpaid members of the public are being asked to carry out jobs that were traditionally done by officers, from holding speed radar guns and monitoring closed-circuit television cameras to supporting elderly crime victims. (Hamilton, 2017)

The work of volunteers is organised along similar lines to that of paid staff – with formal, hierarchical management structures – and there is a lack of specialist management and support for them (Callender et al., 2018). Further research might provide us with evidence of the extent to which volunteers in the police service are subject to the same terms of service as the paid staff; if they are significantly different, and if they are accompanied by the expansion of the breadth and depth of volunteer involvement, this would suggest that hybridisation has taken place. Without that evidence, and unlike the involvement of volunteers in schools, there is no evidence at this stage to suggest that volunteers bring the organisational principles of the third sector to bear on the policy force.

Volunteers in Libraries and Leisure Centres

The replacement of some paid staff by volunteers in the police service – job substitution – has been even more marked in some of the areas most affected by funding cuts: public libraries and leisure services. Between 2010 and 2014, for example, the number of full-time staff employed in UK libraries fell by 22 per cent, from 24 746 to 19 308, while the number of volunteers doubled from 17 550 to 35 818 (CIPFA, 2014, quoted by Cooke, 2015). The impact on library services and leisure centres has varied markedly between local authorities. In some cases branch libraries and leisure services such as swimming pools, museums and parks have been closed, or have survived only because volunteers have stepped in to play a variety of roles to maintain the services. In other cases volunteers have taken over the work of frontline staff while a cadre of qualified professionals (such as qualified librarians) has been retained.

We do not yet have a comprehensive map of volunteering in these changing circumstances but we can identify some at least of the major landmarks. There appear to be two models of volunteer involvement in a library service: the 'community library' on the one hand, and the library run by experienced, trained information professionals and supported by volunteers on the other. The 'community library' appears to take on some of the principles of the third sector association, with their volunteers seeing themselves as owners of the library and central to the service: 'They open the building each day, stack the shelves, order stock and staff reception. They also do the cleaning' (Cooke, 2015). The local authority owns the books and the building while its staff may be seen as providing support. The alternative model places professional trained librarians at the centre of the library and as the main means of delivering its services. Volunteers play a valuable role, but essentially as subordinate to the professional staff and a means of 'delivering specific activities (storytimes, job clubs, reading schemes, etc) rather than taking on the day-to-day logistics of running a library' (Baber, 2018).

Nichols et al. (2015) have identified a more complex model of volunteer involvement across a wider spectrum of types of leisure services: museums and swimming pools as well as libraries. They focus on the transfer of ownership of public assets such as a library or a swimming pool to 'the community' in the form of a trust led by volunteers, and review the role of volunteers and/or paid staff in both governance and operational roles (ibid., p. 75). The transfer of assets of this kind would appear to establish ownership of the trusts established for the purpose, and bring about the transfer of the library or swimming pool from the public to the third sector. The outcome of this transfer could thus be seen as an enacted third sector hybrid.

Volunteers in NHS Hospitals

Volunteers are involved in dozens of different roles within NHS hospitals. A number of them are involved in an expanding array of governance roles, with varying degrees of decision-making powers ranging from a variety of patient representatives to board members in Foundation Trusts (Naylor et al., 2013; Mundle et al., 2012; Paylor, 2011). The complexity of the current NHS landscape and its governance structures makes it very difficult to assess the extent of the contribution made by volunteers to these arrangements. We believe that a careful examination of the roles played by volunteers in the governance of the NHS could well provide evidence of a significant contribution to growing hybridisation in its hospitals.

Volunteers are also involved in a great number of operational roles which carry out a variety of functions in hospital wards, clinics, departments and other facilities (Hawkins and Restall, 2006). The increasing proliferation of different volunteer roles in response to growing demand for NHS services at a time of growing budgetary constraints has led to a shift in how the health service views volunteers. While it continues to involve them as a low-cost means of carrying out low-skilled basic tasks (such as 'running the hospital shop or pushing a trolley around the wards'; Brindle, 2017) it has increasingly regarded volunteers as a way of improving quality and making a distinctive contribution to the NHS. The emphasis has – rhetorically at least – shifted away from the need to reduce costs and towards a concern to enrich services and improve the quality of care. Volunteers are seen as the means of adding 'a personal human touch' (Mundle et al., 2012, p. 16) and involving the community (Galea et al., 2013) in order to 'contribute to a better patient experience rather than to reduce costs (ibid., p. 13). And these aspirations are echoed in the recent calls for the mobilisation of a new 'army of volunteers to help on hospital wards', a scheme which its promoters claim 'will not be used as a cost-cutting alternative to paid staff' but will enable volunteers to 'do things that hard-pressed doctors and nurses do not have time for, such as comforting frightened dementia patients and ensuring that people will not die alone' (Smyth, 2018).

This shift in the role and status of volunteers in the NHS appears to be based on two assumptions. The first of these is that services will be enhanced if they are based on the principle of co-production: that they will be improved if service users and members of the community are involved in their design and delivery as well as paid staff. And the second principle is that the role of volunteers should be seen as extending and supplementing the work of paid staff rather than substituting for them (Naylor et al., 2013). But these findings should be treated with caution: as Mundle et al. (2012, p. 14) conclude, 'there are inconsistent definitions and uses of the term "complement" and "substitute" across the literature and no clear consensus on whether the work of volunteers is mainly a substitute or a complement for paid labour'.

If the ambitious plans for doubling the number of volunteers in NHS hospitals are realised (Brindle, 2017; Lay, 2017; Smyth, 2018), the need to address that lack of consensus will be given new importance. At the same time the NHS will need to improve the level of strategic direction for the involvement of its volunteers (see, e.g., Galea et al., 2013); tackle its failure to embed volunteering and volunteer support across organisations; and address 'inadequate and inconsistent structural support in the form of volunteer co-ordinators, of staff with the responsibility for volunteering' (VDS, 2013, p. 26).

But it will also need to clarify the ways in which volunteers extend and complement the work of paid staff – making a distinctive contribution – and thus can be seen as providing an element of hybridity in NHS hospitals alongside what appears to be a growing involvement in their governance.

Three Models of Volunteer Involvement in the Public Sector

In schools, hospitals and leisure services volunteers are taking on more varied roles and greater responsibilities for governance in public services. We know very little about the ways in which this trend is developing and the impact of these changes. We have rather more to discuss when we look at the ways in which volunteers are playing operational roles in public services. On the basis of the data we have at our disposal we can outline three broad models for the ways in which volunteering is perceived and acted upon in the public sector. And we can discuss these against the backdrop of the growing numbers and the more varied roles and tasks that have developed in public services.

In the first place there are areas of the public sector where volunteers continue to be seen essentially as auxiliaries, whose subordinate role is clearly differentiated from those of the paid staff and who provide either a source of cheap labour for the organisation or carry out specific tasks that are not seen as key functions of the staff. Our brief review of volunteers in public services identified this model as active in some parts of the health service, in some libraries and in some of the roles played in schools.

Unlike this model the other two have responded to the growing diversity and importance of volunteer involvement. In the first case, exemplified by the development of the police service and also seen in some libraries, volunteers have been seen as additions or substitutes for paid staff and have been treated in very much the same way as those they work alongside or have replaced. The police force has minimised the hybrid nature of the organisation by appearing to ignore any thoughts that the role of volunteers might be different or distinctive from its other human resources. In some libraries hybridity has rapidly become entrenched as volunteers have taken over the running of services.

The third model can, to a greater or lesser extent, be seen in organisations that have embraced the idea that volunteers bring something distinctive to the organisation, and is found in a number of schools, some aspects of the health service, and some libraries and leisure services. It contributes to organisational hybridity and raises some important issues. One key issue is the need to achieve some degree of clarity and consensus about the boundary between substitution and complementary activity on the part of volunteers highlighted by Mundle et al. (2012). The coexistence of two different kinds of human resources – paid staff and volunteers – can lead to tensions between them unless the distinction between their roles and those of the paid staff can be maintained. And this is made more problematic as the activities of volunteers are extended into a wider range of less distinct roles, and volunteers are involved beyond 'the fringes' (Naylor et al., 2013). What is clear, moreover, is that the extent to which volunteers are viewed as a distinctive form of human resources governs the need for the organisations in which they are involved to provide them with an appropriate and distinctive approach to their supervision and support.

VOLUNTEERS IN THE PRIVATE SECTOR

Introduction

The characterisation of the ideal-typical private sector organisation by Billis (2010) as the managerially controlled firm, staffed by paid employees and driven by market forces, suggests at first glance that volunteers are unlikely to be found in the for-profit sector. But, although they are less numerous than those we found in the third or public sectors, their numbers are not inconsiderable: a survey by Low et al. (2007) found that 11 per cent of their respondents identified the private sector as their primary site for volunteering, which suggests that there may be as many as 2.5 million volunteers involved in that sector. This figure may, however, be an overestimate because, as we have previously noted, the authors of the survey felt that some respondents were unclear about the identity of the sector in which they volunteered, and we have no means of verifying the numbers. The figure does suggest, nonetheless, that there is a surprising body of volunteers involved with the private sector.

While we know comparatively little about the involvement of volunteers in the private sector, we are aware that they can be found in two areas. In the first of these they are involved in private sector organisations that deliver public services – usually contracted by the state – such as care homes, some educational establishments, prisons and the probation service. And the second area in which volunteers are engaged covers a wide range of sports, arts and cultural organisations that are often run for profit (Hill, 2016). In the absence of wider evidence we will focus our attention on what is known about volunteers in private sector care homes on the one hand, and those who contribute to the work of privately run festivals on the other.

Volunteering in Private Sector Care Homes

Overall, volunteers do not play a major part in the activities of care homes. Hussein's (2011) analysis of the National Minimum Data Set in Social Care in England found that a large proportion (89 per cent) of the organisations providing social care to adults or older people – which included domiciliary as well as residential care – reported that their workforce included no volunteers at all. Amongst those that did, volunteer-involving organisations were 'almost equally prevalent within the voluntary and private sector (49% and 45% respectively)', while 'only 5% of local authorities' reported volunteer involvement in their social care workforce (ibid., p. 10). But those figures obscure the differences between the number of volunteers involved in each sector: while the average (mean) number of volunteers involved in voluntary sector programmes was 15.2, the average (mean) number engaged in the private sector was only 2 (ibid., pp. 10–11). Volunteers were thus involved in very small numbers in a minority of social care programmes in the private sector.

Our knowledge about why and how volunteers were involved in private sector care homes is based on an in-depth study of care organisations across all three sectors by one of the authors of this chapter (Hill, 2016) which offers some unique insights into the field. While some of the managers of the care homes saw them introduction of volunteers as a means of developing a drive towards improving the quality of care and helping to build better links with the community, all of the managers of care homes – regardless of sector – viewed volunteers essentially as a form of human resource. In the case of the private sector homes the involvement of volunteers was universally seen as an inexpensive extension to the work of their paid staff. Some of them also saw volunteering as a kind of recruitment mechanism through which they could trial potential employees; an approach shared by some of the volunteers, who saw volunteering as a route to employment. This approach to involving volunteers was only seen in private sector homes and was not explicitly found in any of the public or voluntary sector providers studied by Hill.

The view that volunteers provided cheap resources and, in some cases, a useful training ground did not translate into the involvement of volunteers in anything but auxiliary roles in the private sector care homes studied by Hill. As one manager said: 'I don't think we should be relying on volunteering to give that quality of care. I think therefore it still has to be . . . a cherry on top.' Hill canvassed a number of possible explanations for the limited role played by volunteers as well as their modest numbers in private homes. These included: the view from private sector employers that they were of lesser worth than the staff they employed; an unwillingness on the part of volunteers to engage in private sector organisations; resistance by staff and management within private sector organisations to the involvement of volunteers; reluctance on the part of volunteer brokers to place volunteers within private sector organisations; and wider societal aversion to involving volunteers in for-profit settings. Whatever the explanation – and Hill felt it would be a combination of those he identified – the evidence suggests that volunteers were likely to be seen as peripheral to the delivery of services rather than viewed as part of its core work.

Volunteers were often positioned on the periphery of private care home organisations, to the extent that they were sometimes viewed less as (superfluous) unpaid staff than as 'visitors' in a similar role to family members or friends. This, together with their limited scope for involvement, meant that volunteers were largely unsupervised and unmanaged. One volunteer reported by Hill summed up the nature of their involvement with the home: 'I take myself along there, I sign in the book and I go up and see my lady . . . sometimes there aren't any staff around and sometimes they don't say hello . . . I just go up and see my lady and I come down and sign out and then I go.' The lack of supervision involved meant that volunteers were able to make their contribution to the care of residents in ways they felt appropriate, but it also demonstrated a lack of investment by the owners in the work. The very unstructured and unsupported nature of volunteering in these homes, moreover, suggests that they may have developed into a very different form of hybridity which combined elements of the 'personal world' (see Chapter 29 in this *Handbook*) with a formal organisation.

Some private care homes had chosen not to involve volunteers in their work because of the cost of investing in them. According to another of Hill's respondents: 'because it is a private home they said "we love it, we are in for it but if we need to commit any finances – no"'. Those that did see the value of volunteers adopted more rigorous approaches to recruiting them than providers from other sectors, and placed a clear emphasis on recruiting volunteers who would need little ongoing support. Private sector providers were clearly more selective than those in other sectors, but their approach was not so much the wish to select the best possible people for the job as the need to be sure that they did not accept anyone to whom they would need to offer support.

Volunteers in Privately Run Festivals

A study by Andersson and Getz (2009) of the role of volunteers in running festivals in all three sectors provides supplementary information to what we have learned about their engagement in the private sector provision of care homes. The involvement of volunteers in festivals run by the private sector was on a smaller scale and for shorter periods than for those who were involved in either the public or the voluntary sector. Significantly, private sector involvement was limited to the period of the festival itself and did not extend to playing an active part in any long-term planning activities, as happened in public sector and, in particular, third sector-led festivals. At the same time, the underlying rationale for volunteer involvement in private sector festivals was different from that found in festivals run by the other sectors. It was narrowly instrumental and based on one or both of two considerations: it was likely to be part of a strategy aimed at creating a 'community feel' for the event – possibly to emulate the way in which the third sector organisations approached festival organisation – or, more simply, a means of accessing free or cheap labour.

Summary: The Role of Volunteers in Private Sector Organisations

While the evidence we have been able to deploy about volunteering in private sector organisations is very limited it seems clear that the presence of volunteers does not demonstrate that there is any significant degree of hybridity involved in them:

- In the first place, the rationale adopted by private sector organisations is largely instrumental and in line with their market-driven orientation. Volunteers are seen as human resources but of less value than paid staff.
- On the other hand, these private sector organisations do not make a great deal of use of these resources. Volunteers are largely treated as peripheral players: they are not seen as making a distinctive contribution to the organisation, but as auxiliaries.
- As a result, volunteers have not supplanted paid staff, which remain the dominant form of human resources in the firm.

- The organisations do not invest in their volunteers or provide them with more than a minimum of management. Many of them recruit volunteers who are 'ready-made' and do not need significant training or support. As a result, volunteers of this kind may be treated as potential employees.
- And, finally, the introduction of volunteers does not seem to have led to any significant changes in the behaviour of the organisation; their minimal involvement has avoided any tension arising between its paid staff and the volunteers; and volunteers have not disrupted any of the defining organisational features of the private sector firm.

SUMMARY AND CONCLUSIONS

This chapter set out to review the role and status of volunteers in different kinds of organisations across all three sectors with a view to assessing the extent to which their involvement can characterise the organisations concerned as hybrids. Starting from the map of the authentic sectors developed by Billis (Chapter 24 in this *Handbook*) we look in turn at the ideal type of the third sector association; at shallow and entrenched hybrids with third sector roots; at the involvement of volunteers in several kinds of public sector organisation which are potentially hybrid; and at some examples of private sector organisations which involve volunteers.

The existence of volunteers in public and private sector organisations might indicate that they have moved into the area of hybridity by drawing to some extent on one of the organisational principles of the third sector. But we tend to think of the involvement of volunteers in itself as a necessary but not sufficient key to identifying organisations with public or private sector roots as hybrid. We suggest that a significant level of hybridity will depend on the extent to which the role and status of volunteers in any organisation contribute to the implementation of one or more of the operational priorities of the third sector.

The most important of these principles is ownership. By the very nature of the sector concept, it is only third sector organisations that can be seen as being owned by their volunteer members and, as we have seen, many of them have come to share their ownership – or have even lost it – as a result of the development of hybrid forms. Public sector organisations are owned by citizens at large rather than by the members of these organisations, although we did find a very small number of cases – community libraries, for example – where volunteers could be seen as some of the owners of the organisation. And the ownership of private sector organisations is restricted to shareholders. The next level of importance in the hierarchy of organisational principles described by Billis (Chapter 24 in this *Handbook*) is governance. We can argue that volunteers play governance roles in schools and some public sector health services, although the numbers involved and the extent of their power and influence is questionable. We have found no examples of volunteers playing governance roles in the private sector.

As a result we suggest that the search for hybridity should focus on the breadth and depth of roles played by volunteers, and the extent to which they might have some influence on the ways in which hybrid organisations shape and pursue their ends; and especially the extent to which operational priorities are governed by a sense of mission rather than by market forces or public service.

Our review of third sector hybrids highlights the way in which the operational role of volunteers has changed from their experience in associations and shallow hybrids. Rather than playing a significant part in the overall direction of the organisation, or exercising any individual initiative in the work they undertake, they are increasingly treated as unpaid employees allocated specific operational tasks and subject to close supervision by paid managers. This approach has been developed as the result of the establishment in these hybrids of the organisational principles of the public sector and/or private sector, and the introduction of advanced levels of professionalisation and bureaucratisation. The extent to which third sector organisations have followed this path varies, but for some the continued existence of some of the key organisational principles of the sector is in some doubt.

The experience of volunteers in some public sector organisations may resemble those found in these entrenched third sector hybrids, but the overall picture of the public sector and its volunteers is rather more varied and nuanced. We identified three main models of the involvement of volunteers.

The first of these – which we found in some parts of the health service and in some libraries – restricts the involvement of volunteers to acting as auxiliaries, whose roles are clearly distinguished from and subordinate to those carried out by paid staff. They are seen either as a source of cheap labour or as a means of carrying out tasks that are not seen as part of the role of the staff.

In the second model, exemplified by the experience of the police service, organisations have responded to the need for greater diversity and increased value in volunteer roles. They have responded to this need by recruiting volunteers as substitutes for paid staff and treating them in very much the same way as their replacements. Volunteers are often recruited on the basis of a person specification and provided with a formal job description; they are trained to perform the role they are to play; their work is supervised by managers; and the performance of their duties is monitored and assessed.

Unlike the other two, our third model could be seen as a hybrid form. Found in some schools, some hospitals and some libraries, it is based in the idea that volunteers either play a significant part in or make a distinctive or complementary contribution to the organisation; and may do both. In this model volunteers are not auxiliaries or substitutes but, like their counterparts in associations and shallow third sector hybrids, can exercise their initiative and 'make a difference' to the work of the organisation.

Finally, our review of volunteers in private sector organisations suggests that their presence does not indicate that any significant degree of hybridity is involved. The involvement of volunteers is very much in line with market forces: they are seen as cheap labour and are provided with limited, if any, training or support. Their role is seen as quite peripheral.

Overall, the extent to which the involvement of volunteers in all three sectors is influenced by the principles of the third sector can be seen as limited although, within those limitations, it can be significant for at least some of the organisations concerned. Volunteers do not exercise ownership and the governance roles they play outside of the non-hybrid association can be extensive, but rarely command significant levels of power and responsibility. They do provide a distinctive form of human resources, although the degree to which they can express this distinctive character varies from organisation to organisation. And they can make a significant contribution to the ways in which the aims and activities of the organisations in which they are involved are developed. In this respect we would argue that volunteers help to define hybridity in some at least of the organisations found in the public and the third sectors.

These conclusions need to be treated with caution: the quantity and quality of the data we have been able to access provide some support for our argument, but there is a clear need for further and better-focused research to help identify the nature of the distinctive contribution made by volunteers to the organisations in which they are involved. This would not only provide better evidence of the ways in which volunteers help to define organisations as hybrid, but also help those responsible for the involvement of volunteers to provide the most appropriate forms of support and supervision for their activities.

REFERENCES

Active Communities Unit (2000) 'Volunteering and community activity today', Material assembled for the Active Community Cross-Cutting Review, Active Communities Unit: London.

Aiken, A. and G. Thomson (2013) 'Professionalisation of a breastfeeding peer support service: issues and experiences of peer supporters', *Midwifery*, 29, pp. 145–151.

Alcock, P. (2010) 'Building the Big Society: a new policy environment for the third sector in England', *Voluntary Sector Review*, 1 (3), pp. 379–389.

Andersson, T. and D. Getz (2009) 'Tourism as a mixed industry: differences between private, public and not-for-profit festivals', *Tourism Management*, 30 (2009), pp. 847–856.

Aves, G.M. (1969) *The Voluntary Worker in the Social Services: Report of a Committee jointly set up by the National Council of Social Services and the National Institute for Social Work Training under the Chairmanship of Dame Geraldine M. Aves*, Bedford Square Press of the NCSS and George Allen & Unwin: London.

Baber, G. (2018) 'The positive and negative impact of using volunteers in public libraries', University College London.

Barnard, E. and I. Britton (2016) 'Citizens in policing – a new paradigm of direct citizen involvement', *ECAN Bulletin*, 29, pp. 19–28.

Billis, D. (2010) *Hybrid Organizations and the Third Sector: Challenges for Practice, Theory and Policy*, Palgrave Macmillan: Basingstoke.

Birchall, J. and R. Simmons (2004) *User Power: The Participation of Users in Public Services*, National Consumer Council: London.

Body, A., K. Holman and E. Hogg (2017) 'To bridge the gap? Voluntary action in primary schools', *Voluntary Action Review*, 8 (3), pp. 251–271.

Bondi, L. (2004) '"A double edged sword"? The professionalisation of counselling in the UK', *Health and Place*, 10, pp. 319–328.

Brindle, D. (2017) 'New recruits in the fight for the NHS', *Guardian*, 6 December.

Britton, I. and M. Calendar (2016) 'Citizen involvement in policing: a critical but under-researched aspect of policing', paper presented at the Social Policy Association Conference, 4–6 July.

Brudney, J. (1999) 'The effective use of volunteers: best practices for the public sector', *Law and Contemporary Problems*, 62 (4), pp. 219–255.

Buckingham, H. (2010) 'Capturing diversity: a typology of TSOs responses to contracting based on empirical evidence from homelessness services', TSRC Working Paper 41, Third Sector Research Centre: Birmingham.

Callender, M., K. Cahalin, S. Cole, L. Hubbard and I. Britton (2018) 'Understanding the motivations, morale, and retention of Special Constables: findings from a national survey', *Policing: A Journal of Policy and Practice*, https://doi.org/10.1093/police/pay058.

Carmel, E. and J. Harlock (2008) 'Instituting the third sector as a governable terrain: partnerships, procurement and performance in the UK', *Policy and Politics*, 36 (2), pp. 155–171.

CIPFA (Chartered Institute of Public Finance and Accountancy) (2014) *CIPFA Library Profile 2014*, CIPFA.

Cloke, P., S. Johnsen and J. May (2007) 'Ethical citizenship? Volunteers and the ethics of providing services for homeless people', *Geoforum*, 38 (6), pp. 1089–1101.

Cooke, J. (2015) 'The volunteers that are keeping local libraries alive', BBC, https://www.bbc.co.uk/news/entertainment-arts-33475594.

Davis Smith, J. (1996) 'Should volunteers be managed?', in D. Billis and M. Harris (eds), *Voluntary Agencies: Challenges of Organisation and Management*, Macmillan: Basingstoke.

Eikenberry, A. and J. Kulver (2004) 'The marketization of the nonprofit sector: civil society at risk?', *Public Administration Review*, 64 (2), pp. 132–140.

Ellis Paine, A., N. Ockenden and J. Stuart (2010) 'Volunteers in hybrid organizations: a marginalised majority?', in D. Billis (ed.), *Hybrid Organizations and the Third Sector: Challenges for Practice, Theory and Policy*, Palgrave Macmillan: Basingstoke.

Elstub, S. (2006) 'Towards an inclusive social policy for the UK: the need for democratic deliberation in voluntary and community associations', *Voluntas*, 17 (1), pp. 17–39.

Galea, A., C. Naylor, D. Buck and L. Weaks (2013) *Volunteering in Acute Trusts in England: Understanding the Scale and Impact*, Kings Fund: London.

Gaskin, K. (2003) *A Choice Blend: What Volunteers Want from Organisation and Management*, Institute for Volunteering Research: London.

Geoghegan, M. and F. Powell (2006) 'Community development, partnership governance and dilemmas of professionalization: profiling and assessing the case of Ireland', *British Journal of Social Work*, 36, pp. 845–861.

Hamilton, F. (2017) 'Volunteer crimefighters to fill police vacancies', *The Times*, 10 October.

Harris, M. (2010) 'The contradictory policy environment', in D. Billis (ed.), *Hybrid Organizations and the Third Sector: Challenges for Practice, Theory and Policy*, Palgrave Macmillan: Basingstoke.

Hawkins, S. and M. Restall (2006) *Volunteers across the NHS*, Volunteering England: London.

Hill, M. (2016) 'Care home volunteering: exploring how sectoral status and the strategic positioning of volunteering affects the volunteer experience and the impact on residents', Paper presented to the NCVO/VSSN Annual Research Conference, Nottingham Trent University.

Hotchkiss, R., L. Unruh and M. Fottler (2014) 'The role, measurement and impact of volunteerism in hospitals', *Nonprofit and Voluntary Sector Management*, 43 (6), pp. 1111–1128.

Hussein, S. (2011) 'Volunteers in the formal long-term care workforce in England', *Social Care Workforce Periodical*, 13, pp. 1–36.

Hustinx, L. (2001 [2007]) 'Individualisation and new styles of youth volunteering: an empirical exploration' *Voluntary Action*, 3 (2), pp. 57–76; reprinted in J. Davis Smith and M. Locke (eds), *Volunteering and the Test of Time: Essays for Policy, Organisation and Research*, Institute for Volunteering Research: London.

Hustinx, L. (2014) 'Volunteering in a hybrid institutional and organizational environment: an emerging research agenda', in M. Freise and T. Hallmann (eds), *Modernizing Democracy: Associations and Associating in the 21st Century*, Springer: New York.

Kane, D., J. Mohan and F. Geyne Rajme (2010) 'Paid work and volunteering in the third sector in the north east of England', Northern Rock Foundation Third Sector Trends study report, http://www.nr-foundation.org.uk/downloads/North-East-workforce.pdf.

Kearney, J. (2001 [2007]) 'The values and basic principles of volunteering: complacency or caution?', *Voluntary Action*, 3 (3), pp. 63–86; reprinted in J. Davis Smith and M. Locke (eds), *Volunteering and the Test of Time: Essays for Policy, Organisation and Research*, Institute for Volunteering Research: London.

Lay, K. (2017) 'Army of volunteers to help on hospital wards', *The Times*, 7 December.

Leonard, R., J. Onyx and H. Hayward-Brown (2004) 'Volunteer and coordinator perspectives on managing women volunteers', *Non-profit Management and Leadership*, 15 (2), pp. 205–219.

Lohmann, R. (1992) *The Commons: New Perspectives on Nonprofit Organizations and Voluntary Action*, Jossey Bass: San Francisco, CA.

Low, N., S. Butt, A. Ellis Paine and J. Davis Smith (2007) *Helping Out: A National Survey of Volunteering and Charitable Giving*, Cabinet Office: London.

Machin, J. and A. Ellis Paine (2008) *Management Matters: A National Survey of Volunteer Management Capacity*, Institute for Volunteering Research: London.

Meijs, L. and E. Hoogstad (2001) 'New ways of managing volunteers: combining membership management and programme management', *Voluntary Action*, 3, pp. 41–61.

Mirrlees-Black, C. and C. Byron (1994) 'Special considerations: issues for the management and organisation of the volunteer police', Research and Planning Unit Paper 88, Home Office: London.

Mundle, C., C. Naylor and D. Buck (2012) 'Volunteering in health and care in England', Kings Fund: London.

National Governors Association (NGA) (2018) 'About the NGA', https://www.nga.org.uk/About-Us.aspx (accessed 19 February 2018).

Naylor, C., C. Mundle, L. Weaks and D. Buck (2013) 'Volunteering in health and care: securing a sustainable future', Kings Fund: London.

Netting, E., W. Nelson, K. Borders and H. Ruth (2004) 'Volunteer and paid staff relationships', *Administration in Social Work*, 28 (3/4), pp. 69–89.

Nichols, G. (2017) 'Volunteering in community sports associations: a literature review', *Voluntaristics Review*, 2 (1), pp. 1–75.

Nichols, G., D. Forbes, D.L. Findlay-King and G. Macfadyen (2015) 'Is the asset transfer of public leisure facilities in England an example of associative democracy?', *Administrative Sciences*, 5, pp. 71–87, https://www.mdpi.com/2076-3387/5/2/71.

Paylor, J. (2011) 'Volunteering and health: evidence of impact and implications for policy and practice', Institute for Volunteering Research: London.

Pepper, I. (2014) 'Do part-time volunteer police officers aspire to be regular police officers?', *Police Journal*, 87 (2), pp. 105–113.

Police Specials (2014) 'Welcome to PoliceSpecials.com', www.policespecials.com (accessed 14 November 2014).

Rochester, C. (2013) *Rediscovering Voluntary Action: The Beat of a Different Drum*, Palgrave Macmillan: Basingstoke.

Scott, D. (2010) 'Some preliminary remarks', presented to the conference on Volunteering Counts, Manchester, March.

Smith, D.H. (2000) *Grassroots Associations*, SAGE: Thousand Oaks, CA.

Smyth, C. (2018) 'Health chiefs ask millions to work as NHS volunteers', *The Times*, 27 November.

Suffolk Constabulary (2017) 'Nationwide campaign launched to recruit more volunteers to support local policing', https://www.suffolk.police.uk/news/latest-news/06-10-2017/nationwide-campaign-launched-recruit-more-volunteers-support-local (accessed 25 February 2018).

Volunteer Development Scotland (VDS) (2013) 'Volunteers and Older People's Care in Tayside', Volunteer Development Scotland.

Warburton, J. and C. Macdonald (2009) 'The challenges of the new institutional environment: an Australian case study of older volunteers in the contemporary non-profit sector', *Ageing and Society*, 29 (5), pp. 823–840.

Weeks, J., P. Aggleton, C. McKevitt, K. Parkinson and A. Taylor-Laybourn (1996) 'Community and contracts: tension and dilemmas in the voluntary sector response to HIV and AIDS', *Policy Studies*, 17 (2), pp. 107–123.

Zimmeck, M. (2001) 'The right stuff: new ways of thinking about managing volunteers', Institute for Volunteering Research: London.

28. Family businesses as hybrid organisations
Börje Boers and Mattias Nordqvist

INTRODUCTION

The objective of this chapter is to deepen our understanding of the nature of family businesses by analysing them as hybrid organisations. We define family businesses as businesses where one or several families own the controlling majority of the shares and are actively involved in the business (Chrisman et al., 2005; Chua et al., 1999). The focus of the chapter is on the theoretical notion of family businesses as hybrid organisations, and it draws on case research based on two publicly listed family firms. Publicly listed family firms are common around the world (La Porta et al., 1999) and they illustrate explicitly the hybrid character of family businesses by combining the logic of family ownership with the expectation of delivering shareholder value (Boers and Nordqvist, 2012). We argue that hybridity is especially apparent in publicly listed family businesses, where it arises from different underlying institutional logics related to the family and the market and the private and the public. The hybrid nature of this kind of business has an impact on their decision-making, their control and/or their governance more generally.

To analyse the two cases, we draw on literature on hybrid organisations, governance and family firms. The study of hybrid organisations has gained momentum in recent years (see, e.g., Battilana and Dorado, 2010; Battilana and Lee, 2014; Billis, 2010; Pache and Santos, 2013; and also this *Handbook*). The current focus seems to be on social enterprises as typical examples of hybrid organisations (Battilana and Lee, 2014; Doherty et al., 2014). Yet this phenomenon is not exclusive to social enterprises or the third sector: it is equally relevant for some public sector and for-profit organisations. The most common type of business is the family business (Dyer, 2003), which also represents a hybrid organisation, with the two domains of family and business constituting the source of hybridity. Family businesses have been portrayed as hybrid organisations in previous literature (e.g., Arregle et al., 2007; Boers and Nordqvist, 2012; Ljungkvist and Boers, 2017), but the concept of hybridity has not gained as much research attention as it deserves. The purpose of this chapter is to address this limitation.

In this chapter we argue that family businesses are especially interesting examples of hybrid organisations. Family business can be seen as the combination of two institutions – the family and business – into one organisation (Boers and Nordqvist, 2012; Leaptrott, 2005; Melin and Nordqvist, 2007; Nordqvist and Melin, 2002; Parada et al., 2010). The institutions of family and business can be connected to specific institutional logics: the logic of family ownership and the logic of the market. These logics, as we shall see, encompass different characteristics. The chapter then discusses earlier research on family business that is relevant to hybrid organisations. Subsequently it reviews literature with regard to the hybrid character of family business and institutional logics. We then go on to illustrate the hybrid character of family businesses from an institutional logics perspective empirically, drawing on two case studies, before discussing our findings and drawing some conclusions.

THE NATURE OF FAMILY BUSINESSES

Family businesses are the most common type of organised business activities across the world (see, e.g., Anderson and Reeb, 2003; Faccio and Lang, 2002; La Porta et al., 1999; Shanker and Astrachan, 1996). There is no single, widely accepted definition of what a family business is (Handler, 1989; Westhead and Cowling, 1998; Winter et al., 1998) but there seems to be agreement that the peculiarity of family businesses is rooted in the combination of the ways in which two subsystems of family and business influence their behaviour (Leaptrott, 2005; Pieper and Klein, 2007; Sharma, 2004; Tagiuri and Davis, 1996). A family's involvement as owners and managers in the business is seen as the factor that distinguishes them from non-family businesses (Astrachan et al., 2002; Chua et al., 1999; Shanker and Astrachan, 1996). And there is a continuing debate as to whether the family and the business can be seen as complementary or competing (Reay et al., 2015).

A useful approach to understanding the difference between family and non-family firms, as well as capturing the unique characteristics of family businesses, is to focus on the logic of family ownership (Brundin et al., 2014). Brundin et al. (2014) suggest that family businesses are driven by a specific ownership logic that is different from the financial market logic that often guides non-family businesses, such as publicly listed companies with diffused ownership. The logic of family ownership guides decision-making and behaviours in family businesses and emphasises, for instance, their distance from capital markets; their long-term orientation; their multiple financial and non-financial goals; their flexible governance structures; their short decision-making processes; the emotional attachment of their owners to the business; and the strong identification of the owners with their business. The logic of non-family ownership would instead focus on short-term orientation; emotional distance from the business by managers; a transactional relationship by the owners and the business; longer decision-making processes; and simpler kinds of orientation towards financial goals such as shareholder value and short-term profits (Brundin et al., 2014).

Several researchers argue that the logic of family ownership also defines some unique characteristics of family businesses that are useful as a point of departure in understanding the nature of family business from different perspectives. Even if family involvement and transgenerational intentions call for priorities in family businesses that are different to those experienced in non-family businesses, nonetheless family businesses also have to be profitable and financially successful if they are to be competitive and survive (Zellweger et al., 2012). For instance, Zachary (2011) and Goel et al. (2012) argue that the socio-psychological dimensions of a family business influence all other dimensions within that business. Similarly, Tagiuri and Davis (1996) argue that family businesses can have ambivalent attributes that are a result of the family's role in the business. Therefore, tensions may arise where the systems overlap.

More specifically, the tensions that arise in many family businesses that, we argue, constitute the essence of the hybridity of this type of organisation find their source in the overlap between the family business and the business system. This overlap has been conceptualised as a role overlap where people have to balance demands from different systems, depending on which role they play in a particular situation; that is, a family role or a business role (Gersick et al., 1997; Nordqvist and Melin, 2002). When an individual such as an owner, a manager or an employee, or a group of individuals such as the owner-family, the top management team or the board of directors perceive different, or even conflicting demands from the different systems, tensions will arise which may have an impact on decision-making and behaviour. One example is the existence of multiple goals in family businesses. There may be tensions between family-oriented non-financial goals such as harmony and family employment on the one hand, and business-oriented financial goals such as profit and lucrative compensation packages for top managers on the other. The next section of the chapter will focus more closely on the hybrid nature of family businesses.

THE FAMILY BUSINESS AS A HYBRID ORGANISATION

Peredo (2003) argues that the overlap between the logic of family and kinship (close relations between family members) and the logic of the market as introduced in the previous section, leads to a struggle within the family firm which defines its hybrid character of the firm. Borys and Jemison (1989, p. 235) define hybrids as 'organisational arrangements that use resources and/or governance structures from more than one existing organisation'. While these authors had in mind joint ventures and similar arrangements, the insights introduced in the previous section on family firms suggest that the family and the firm can be viewed in the same way as different organisations or as institutions that are held separate within the dominant logics of economics.

Family businesses have been mentioned as examples of hybrid identity organisations because they combine elements which would normally not be expected to be found together: a normative identity represented by the family and a utilitarian identity represented by business (Albert et al., 1999; Albert and Whetten, 1985; Whetten, 2006), which are seen as incompatible (Albert and Whetten, 1985). Research on dual and multiple identities (Foreman and Whetten, 2002; Pratt and Foreman, 2000) indicates that the combination of normative and utilitarian identities leads to tensions and conflict. Foreman and Whetten (2002) found that competing claims based on normative and utilitarian identities lead to conflicts for organisational members as to which they should embrace, while the assumption of dual identities implies increased complexity for the construction of an organisational identity. Golden-Biddle and Rao (1997) found that a hybrid identity could lead to conflict and required effort and care. Organisational members may feel torn between competing identity claims, while the members of family businesses may find that they make decision-making more complicated. Early research on family businesses depicted family and business as opposites and implied that one needed to take priority over the other: either family first or business first (Ward, 1987). It is now clear that this is a stark simplification that does not account for the complexity of the phenomenon that is 'family business'.

Another scholar to study hybrid organisational identity in a family business (Tompkins, 2010) takes a social actor lens and views organisational identity as institutionalised through identity claims. 'The presumed competing sets of priorities – normative and utilitarian – represented by family and business systems, respectively, present these organisational entities with dilemmas of leadership choice and style, strategic planning and purpose, and values and norms not addressed within mainstream organisational theory'

(Tompkins, 2010, p. 8). From this definition it becomes clear that identity incongruence is a result of competing logics derived from the two subsystems, that is, the family system and the business system.

Family businesses might be an archetype of hybrid organisations (Arregle et al., 2007). Drawing on Battilana and Lee (2014) we argue that (family business) research benefits from an institutional logics perspective which we elaborate in the following. 'Institutional logic' has become a buzzword and is very popular in recent research (Thornton and Ocasio, 2008). Institutional logics provide classifications and categorisations which shape individual cognition (ibid.). However, these categories and classifications are social constructions (Berger and Luckmann, 1966) existing at different levels. A common definition by Thornton and Ocasio (1999, p. 804) is: 'the socially constructed, historical patterns of material practices, assumptions, values, beliefs, and rules by which individuals produce and reproduce their material subsistence, organise time and space, and provide meaning to their social reality'.

Following this definition, research shows that different institutional logics have consequences for organisations (Besharov and Smith, 2014). Identity can be seen as linking institutional logics with individual and organisational behaviour (Lok, 2010; Thornton and Ocasio, 2008). In other words, the logics will be shaped by what organisational members perceive to be central, enduring and distinctive about their organisation (Albert and Whetten, 1985).

Family business research has so far not paid much attention to the consequences of multiple institutional logics. Recently, some studies have used the idea of institutional logic to study family businesses (Jaskiewicz et al., 2016; Zellweger et al., 2016), but these studies do not frame family businesses as hybrid organisations. Jaskiewicz et al. (2016) use the notion to study succession and argue that conflicts between family and commercial logics lead to different succession processes. Zellweger et al. (2016) use the idea to study pricing of businesses in intergenerational successions. And Miller et al. (2011) argue that family businesses are often more oriented towards a familial logic rather than a market or capitalist logic.

Thus, family businesses can be the setting for the combination of several institutional logics. Miller et al. (2011) argue that ownership can be seen as providing a social context that influences strategy and performance. Based on a study of family and lone founder ownership they argue that there are specific logics associated with family ownership and lone founder ownership, respectively. These logics are influenced by their social context: that is, for family owners the family, and for lone founders a broader range of stakeholders. This leads lone founders to be oriented more towards market and growth strategies, whereas family owners blend market and family orientation (Miller et al., 2011). Miller et al. (2011) studied publicly listed companies. In another recent study, not based on publicly listed firms, Brundin et al. (2014) go further and argue that family businesses can be characterised by a family ownership logic which includes seven core characteristics.

Besharov and Smith (2014) suggest that multiple institutional logics can have different consequences for organisations, and have developed a classification based on this perception which identifies four different possible outcomes depending on the compatibility and centrality of the logics involved, and which can be seen as four types of hybrid. Besharov and Smith's framework for assessing multiple logics in terms of their centrality and compatibility appears to be a useful way of analysing hybrid organisations (Battilana and Dorado, 2010) and also addresses the heterogeneity resulting from multiple logics. The issue of heterogeneity has also been raised in other research on family businesses (e.g., Melin and Nordqvist, 2007).

THE CASE STUDIES

We draw on two companies which are family-owned and have been listed on the stock exchange. We give some background information on them before discussing each company in more depth. Then we summarise some key issues.

As a background to our research we conducted in-depth studies of family ownership on the Swedish stock exchange. The study involved approximately 30 interviews with owners, managers, board members and other stakeholders in a large number of publicly listed family firms, and the data from our interviews were complemented by the use of archival data. In this chapter we focus on comparing two publicly listed, family-owned businesses. We selected these firms because they were very clear in their communication to stakeholders and minority shareholders that they were family businesses. They have therefore made their hybrid character explicit. Case company A eventually decided to leave the stock exchange, whereas company B is still publicly listed. In both companies the owning families hold a controlling majority. Table 28.1 shows how the case study companies are owned and the nature of the families' influence on the companies. The case companies are different with regards to ownership structure and family involvement and therefore illustrate the heterogeneity of the population of family businesses (Melin and Nordqvist, 2007).

Company A is a private bakery with 900 employees and total sales of SEK 3.3 billion. It is a family company, founded in 1897, and the fourth generation of Dansons are still active in the bakery with, among others, Fredrik Danson as chief executive officer (CEO) and his brother Ulf Danson as vice-CEO. Company B is a listed private equity company. The firm's business concept is to generate, over time, the highest possible return through the professional, active and responsible exercise of its ownership role in a number of selected companies and investment situations. Added value is created in connection with acquisition, development and divestment of companies. The main owner is the Lindskog family who control the firm through ownership held by private individuals and two major foundations. The Lindskog family are today a fairly large family with several branches.

Table 28.1   Family control in case companies

Company	Family ownership	Family involvement	External involvement
A	100% through family foundation	Family CEO and 5 family and 6 non-family members on the board of directors	External chairperson of the board
B	73.5% voting rights directly and indirectly controlled by family and through foundations	2 family and 5 non-family members on the board of directors	External CEO and chairperson of the board

The Bakery

Company A was listed on the stock market but did not find it easy for the owning family to handle the resulting demands. The value of the shares was very low and there was not much interest in trading them. Making a new offering of shares was not an attractive idea for the family because they felt they would be 'selling the family jewels' for much too low a price. They also felt that there were high costs associated with being publicly listed which did not bring commensurate benefits from them. One owner reflected:

> You're more independent outside the stock exchange. We can meet all our employees, for instance, and tell them exactly what's going on, about our results. They can ask me any questions, and I can answer and I don't have to say some information is confidential because it would affect the market. I couldn't be open like this before. (Family owner and chairperson of the board)

The differences between the bakery and its state-owned main competitor Toast became very evident to many consumers: 'We were media's baby during many years', one of the main owners said, and added, 'They wrote so much more about us than our size actually motivated. It was free advertising. A reaction nobody really had counted with.' The two brothers were also very welcoming to journalists and reporters. Some investors were disappointed when they realised that the family would never sell their stake in the firm. This was a key reason why there was decreased interest from a broader group in investing the firm:

> We were very open about the role and intentions of the family. We said that we would never let this firm be taken over by someone else. We were very honest, but nobody believed us. They thought as long as someone appears who is willing to pay enough. But for us this company doesn't have a price. It's still not for sale, no matter if someone offers us several billions for it. We've shown we're serious in keeping the firm by creating a trust for our ownership. (Family owner)

There were thus some negative sides of being a publicly listed company. Reasoning about why the family decided to delist their company, one family member said: 'We're not capitalists, we're industrialists, we're bakers. This is the greatest difference with family businesses. And sure, here the industrial is in conflict with the capitalist who invests on the stock exchange. The controlling owner has different values than other actors who invest in his or her company' (Family owner). Another family member added:

> It's important with a face behind a company. As we're growing older we realize that it's important with some new faces associated with this company and not just me and my brother. We don't want the firm to die with us. We want to show that this is a family business made of flesh and blood. All since the 1890s, our company, or brand is very much associated with our family and we think this is very good. (Family owner)

The same family member explained that it was important that an owner felt an attachment to the company they owned. He did not believe in neutral ownership:

> It's even better if we both own and manage the firm, even if no one in the next generation will become the CEO. The key is that there is a long-term orientation in how the firm is governed.

There are several members of the next generation already working in the firm. Many already have their own children, and I believe in even further generations down the road owning this company. The likelihood increases that there is a new entrepreneur in the family. I don't think the future is a big problem. We're open for the children's participation, at the same time as we don't force them to take part. We've been relaxed in relation to the expectations on our children. They do what they want. That's how we were treated by our father.

There were a number of incidents while the company was listed on the stock exchange that led to tensions with minority shareholders. The family owners were careful not to accept other substantial owners besides themselves, mainly because they did not want to lose control of the firm. Moreover, they did not want anyone outside the family to get involved and tell them what to do. This was the reason why they wanted to keep control of the shares (A-shares) with high voting power. This allowed them to get hold of capital but not to share voting control.[1] One of the largest minority owners asked at early stage to have a representative on the board. The family owners, however, did not want this to happen. They wanted to decide the board formation themselves:

I told them they couldn't have their own board member. We have the majority of the votes and we decide the team. No, they told us, we want a board member. This almost became a conflict between us and them. Perhaps it was a bit too rude from our side, but eventually they accepted it. After some time we suggested a person to them whom we had met some times. He seemed to be a good person. We said if you choose him it's okay. They accepted. This person is still in the board, more than 20 years later. (Family owner and chairperson of the board)

A private shareholder who controlled a notable minority stake also tried to enter the board. When he realised that the brothers would not allow this, he suggested other people who could represent him, but the two main owners did not accept this either:

We had to pay for this . . . He wanted a corner in the company, which we we're not interested in. We acted consistently. We said firmly no . . . The purpose of the individual shareholder to enter the board was different. It wasn't to benefit the company, but himself. He often came with suggestions on how we could sell the company and make good money. He just bought the shares, because he wanted the whole company to be sold. (Family owner and Chairperson of the board)

As a public firm they often encountered people who had strong opinions on how they should run the firm:

On the Stock Exchange there are many people who want to be the coach, the one that forms the team and decides the tactics and the strategy. Everybody thinks they know how to market your products. It happened often that especially one minority owner called and told me about possible customers, and what restaurants he had been to that did not sell our products, and why they didn't sell them. He said we need to do it this way instead. He called my brother during weekends and in the evening. I told him very early that we're the most capable of running this company. I think this was true, because no one of our competitors performed better during this period. We had the trust and confidence from the other shareholders to run this. He was the only one who tried to get involved and take over the management. (Family owner)

Beyond the general publicity that the bakery received about the firm and its products when it was publicly listed, the owners expressed some disappointment with the quality of the articles written by business journalists from a more market-oriented, investor's perspective. They described them as mostly opinions not based on facts, and sometimes comments based on false information and assumptions, or lack of depth in the analyses. 'I don't think the large, public companies were exposed to this. I found it very hard to experience, especially because what is written is seen as the truth,' one of the main owners said. He enjoys not being exposed to this type of treatment today and he is also glad that the company is not as exposed to pressures to follow specific fashions and trends.

The Equity Company

During the first years as a listed company, the demands on the equity company from the market and the minority owners were much lower than they are today. 'Now being a listed company causes a lot of problems for the top management team. They must write reports, and comply with codes that are absurd' (Family owner, board member). In general, this respondent had not perceived many problems with being a listed family controlled company, as long as information is direct, straight and honest and the firm performs well. In his view: 'Those who don't like us can sell their shares, that is why the stock exchange exists. Sometimes we forget that it's actually possible to sell shares'.

An external board member commented on the status of the firm:

> B is both a family business and a non-family business. To just say it's a family business is misleading. We're very careful to follow all the rules and codes at the stock exchange, we act as a public company and the board is not dominated by the family. It's a mix, because without a doubt there is a family that has significant influence and that can decide in difficult situations.

This respondent discussed the different demands on the company. While the company had to certain requirements as a result of publicly listed the family ownership was still strong and this made other demands on the company. He continued:

> Their [the family's] influence is exercised carefully today, but everybody in the board understands that they need to listen if for instance Per-Olof [owner, family board members] says something. At the same time, the board is competent and the members are not afraid of saying what they think. It's a very lively debate in the board. The family has decided to work through a strong Chairperson and board. The family is wise, they're not afraid of listening to others.

A former non-family CEO described in a newspaper interview how he perceived the multiple logics:

> B is not a company designed to maintain power. B has only one single purpose and it is the same for all shareholders. B only exists to give return to all the shareholders' investments . . . We don't belong to a sphere. I think this is important. We have no other considerations than to live up to our core values; return on investment, competence and shareholder friendliness. I feel no restrictions [from the family].

It needs to be noted, however, that the multiple logics within company B were not always aligned. An episode from their history illustrates this. In the late 1990s the company faced some difficult times. Some tensions and divergence in the view on how B should be directed led to changing the CEO and the chairman. The non-family CEO left in particular after some actions the family chairman took that were not liked by some family members, board members and minority owners. 'Sven [family owner and prior chairman of board of directors] was right in his analysis, but the way he acted was not acceptable', one interviewee says.[2]

Some interviewees argued that the reason why problems emerged between the family chairman and the non-family CEO had to do with more than personal tensions. Rather, the root of the problem was related to the circumstances for doing business through a listed investment company. In Sweden, market actors had for 50–60 years talked about investment company discounts. This basically means that the value of the shares within the investment company's portfolio is lower than these shares individually in the market. This is thus a problem for companies that invest completely, or partly, in other listed companies that individuals can invest directly in. At the same time, the beneficial tax situation for investment companies created opportunities. The CEO suggested a solution to the problem which was positive for minor shareholders, but perhaps less so for the majority family owners who wanted the firm to stay under the family's control. Some board members felt that the confidence in the firm and in Lindskog as an owner family was about to be lost:

> Nothing happened, and something really needed to happen. There was no shared vision from the family on how to deal with the situation. They weren't able to say; we've had family council, the board has met and we've talked with the foundation and we all agree, this is how we shall do. It finally worked out, but was unclear for a long time. (External board member)

A family member argued that the former CEO and chairperson saved the company through his actions. If he had not acted, the company would have disappeared and been lost for the family. The strategy implemented by Jansson meant that, if the firm did not manage to reach a certain performance level, its shares would be distributed to all shareholders. The family was not interested in this. They wanted to keep the control of the company. The problem was that the information about what he did was not appropriately distributed. 'In terms of the core of the issue, he was right', a family member said, and added:

> Because of earlier disagreements within the family and the fact that the board did not work as professionally as it does today, there was an unequal power balance in the firm. The CEO had managed to secure too much power and he outmanoeuvred people who didn't agree with him. Eventually my father thought that enough was enough, but perhaps he acted too fast and without considering all the consequences of his actions. I think this is the event that changed the firm from being a smaller, old family governed business to a very professionally governed business where the family still controls. (Family owner)

The changes at the CEO and board levels were deemed necessary to restore trust and confidence among investors and analysts. It was also seen as necessary to be able to recruit a new CEO. The former CEO and chairperson stayed as a regular board member for some years after the incident. An executive in an association for shareholders says:

> The firm is a good example of a listed company where the family played a very important for many years. In particular, the former CEO and chairman was dominant. There was a kind of revolution when [the CEO] came in and changed a lot of things. Sven seemed to agree with the

changes to begin with, but then he tried to stop it. I can actually understand that he wanted to stop it. (Executive of shareholders association)

When, in May 1998, a new chairperson was appointed to replace the previous chair he demanded that the family in the future should deal with differences in opinions in their private sphere. He thought it was essential that the family could show externally that they were united. Otherwise the confidence in the family as a main owner on the stock exchange would continue to decrease. 'It's very important. People knew this existed, and when family conflicts are evident the family ownership is weakened,' one interviewee said. 'In this sense, the family resigned from the operations but stayed as largest, interested and active owners,' said one interviewee, and added that the family became more 'capitalists' than before.

Summary of Key Issues

- Both companies were family-controlled and family members were actively involved in the company (see Table 28.1).
- Being listed put certain demands on the companies – for example, reporting and compliance with governance codes – which were considered a burden by the owning families.
- Being listed gave certain publicity but also raised public expectations that went beyond formal requirements.
- The public viewed family ownership critically, as there seemed to be a risk of expropriating minority shareholders. Likewise, minority shareholders speculated that the owning families might sell their shares if a high enough offer was made.
- Both companies had a central conflict during their time on the stock exchange: the bakery had issues with a minority shareholder who wanted a position on the board of directors; and the equity firm had problems with a stock options plan which resulted in the retreat of the family chairperson and the CEO.
- Both companies drew different conclusions from being listed: whereas the bakery delisted, the equity company remained on the stock exchange. The equity company became a more professional family business with a non-family CEO and chairman of the board.

DISCUSSION

In this section, we extend current research on hybrid organisations by taking an institutional logics perspective and analysing the key issues of the case studies with regard to the compatibility and centrality of their logics. We draw on Besharov and Smith's (2014) concept of logic multiplicity and its classification into four different types of hybrid depending on the degree of logic compatibility and logic centrality they exhibit. The four types are characterised by Besharov and Smith as the following:

- Contested organisations. These are organisations combining multiple logics with low compatibility and high centrality. The potential for conflict in these organisations is high due to competing logics that are central to these organisations.

- Estranged organisations. In these organisations, centrality and compatibility are both low. The multiple logics provide contrary implications for actions. However, due to low centrality, one logic is dominant and others are peripheral and this leads to lower ambiguity than in contested organisations.
- Aligned organisations. In these organisations the degrees of centrality and compatibility are high. Conflict between multiple logics, however, is minimal because the logics are represented among the different members and are reflected in the mission, strategy and identity of am organisation. This may give rise to conflicts but, as the multiple logics are compatible, multiple goals derived from these are consistent.
- Dominant organisations. In these organisations compatibility between multiple logics is high whereas their centrality is low. One logic in these organisations is dominant and prevails over the others. The risk of conflict between multiple logics is limited or non-existent.

Both of our case study companies are exposed to multiple logics, and the owning families are involved in both of them but to different degrees. Both companies can be characterised as contested organisation*s* (Besharov and Smith, 2014) while they are listed on the stock exchange. In this type of organisation, the potential of extensive conflicts due to multiple logics is high. Multiple logics are central for both organisations: they are businesses with strong, visible and operational involvement from the families as well as strong demands from the minority shareholders and others representing the market and shareholder value logic (Boers and Nordqvist, 2012; Boers et al., 2017). According to the logic of family ownership, owning families have a long-term and industrial focus, as well as a wish for autonomy towards the capital market (Brundin et al., 2014). In the case of company B the visibility of family owners also became an issue. Hence, both companies were family-controlled, publicly listed companies with contested multiple logics.

Companies A and B solved the conflicts differently. Whereas the owning family in company A decided to take back control of the company by delisting it and transferring its ownership into a foundation which is controlled by the family, company B stayed listed but the family withdrew from the operational management of the company and installed a non-family CEO and a non-family chairperson of the board. In terms of multiple logics and the framework developed by Besharov and Smith, the companies went different ways, as Figure 28.1 demonstrates.

As Figure 28.1 shows, company A can be characterised in the terms used by Besharov and Smith as an estranged organisation. This means that one logic – the family ownership

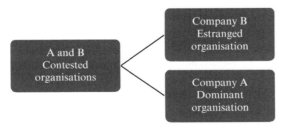

Figure 28.1   Development of multiple logics in companies A and B

logic – has become central to the organisation and other logics are much less significant. Even though the multiplicity of logics creates ambiguity, one logic is so dominant that conflicts are resolved in line with it. In case of company A, the owning family were always quite explicit that it was they who controlled the business and they who were in charge. This was made visible not only through the family's involvement in managing the company but also through the fact that the company carried the family name (Danson's Bakery). Delisting from the stock exchange eliminated the competing logic of shareholder value but did not entirely remove the business logic of the company, which still had to earn money (Brundin et al., 2014; Miller et al., 2011). And the bakery remained – despite no longer being listed – a professionally managed firm with an external non-family chairman of the board.

While company B was, like company A, a contested organisation it resolved the conflicts resulting from competing logics differently. It could be seen in Besharov and Smith's classification as a dominant organisation where one logic was central and other multiple logics were compatible. Company B could be described as a hybrid professional family firm because it was professionally managed by a CEO and a chairperson of the board who were not members of the family, but retained significant family influence (Stewart and Hitt, 2012). The shareholder value and market logic can be seen as the dominant logic. Even though the company is still family-controlled, the family's retreat from operational management has decreased the potential for conflict. Family members involved in the business have found their roles and used their influence as members of the board of directors.

The experience of our case study organisations shows that multiple logics can be handled in different ways, and that Besharov and Smith's framework provides a suitable way of explaining how they play out. It is important to note that the ways in which multiple logics are combined is not settled for all time. Instead, as Besharov and Smith emphasise, the relationship changes over time as circumstances change. Analysing organisations at multiple points in time allows us to observe changes in the treatment of multiple logics.

CONCLUSION

The arguments put forward in this chapter illustrate the hybrid nature of the family businesses. We chose to focus on publicly listed family businesses as a case of particularly explicit hybridity, as the result of the combination of family and business, private and public, and long-term versus short-term. The logics of family ownership and the market logic pose different demands on the companies and led to one company leaving the stock market. The exit from the stock exchange did not eliminate the hybrid character of the family business. Instead it led to the logic of family ownership becoming dominant, and changing the nature of the hybrid organisation from one in which logics were contested to one with a dominant logic. The kind of hybridity has changed with the circumstances but the organisation remains hybrid.

The main contribution to this study is the understanding of the logic of family owner-ship and its perspective on hybridity. Our study deviates from the ideal type of the social enterprise as hybrid organisation (Battilana and Lee, 2014) to show how family businesses are exposed to different logics. This enables us to extend the developing research on institutional logics by developing the conceptualisation of the family business as a hybrid organisation.

NOTES

1. On the Swedish stock exchange, vote differentiation is common: that is, majority shareholder control voting (A-shares) rights and float capital rights (B-shares).
2. The non-family CEO introduced a redemption programme which resulted in the dilution of the majority shareholder stake if the stock price had stayed under a certain level. The former family chairman bought shares in the company which raised the share price and the family stayed in control.

REFERENCES

Albert, S., and Whetten, D.A. (1985). Organisational Identity. In L.L. Cummings and B.M. Staw (eds), *Research in Organisational Behavior* (Vol. 8, pp. 263–295). Greenwich, CT: JAI Press.

Albert, S., Godfrey, P.C., and Whetten, D.A. (1999). *Hybrid Identity Organisations*. Provo, UT: Brigham Young University Marriott School of Management.

Anderson, R.C., and Reeb, D.M. (2003). Founding-Family Ownership and Firm Performance: Evidence from the S&P 500. *Journal of Finance*, 58(3), 1301–1328.

Arregle, J.-L., Hitt, M.A., Sirmon, D.G., and Very, P. (2007). The Development of Organisational Social Capital: Attributes of Family Firms. *Journal of Management Studies*, 44(1), 73–95.

Astrachan, J.H., Klein, S.B., and Smyrnios, K.X. (2002). The F-PEC scale of Family Influence: A Proposal for Solving the Family Business Definition Problem. *Family Business Review*, 15(1), 45–58.

Battilana, J., and Dorado, S. (2010). Building Sustainable Hybrid Organisations: The Case of Commercial Microfinance Organisations. *Academy of Management Journal*, 53(6), 1419–1440.

Battilana, J., and Lee, M. (2014). Advancing Research on Hybrid Organizing: Insights from the Study of Social Enterprises. *Academy of Management Annals*, 8(1), 397–441.

Berger, P., and Luckmann, T. (1966). *The Social Construction of Reality*. New York: Doubleday.

Besharov, M.L., and Smith, W.K. (2014). Multiple Institutional Logics in Organisations: Explaining Their Varied Nature and Implications. *Academy of Management Review*, 39(3), 364–381.

Billis, D. (ed.) (2010). *Hybrid Organisations and the Third Sector: Challenges for Practice, Theory and Policy*. Basingstoke: Palgrave Macmillan.

Boers, B., and Nordqvist, M. (2012). Understanding Hybrid-Identity Organisations: The Case of Publicly Listed Family Businesses. In A. Carsrud and M. Brännback (eds), *Understanding Family Businesses* (Vol. 15, pp. 251–269). New York: Springer

Boers, B., Ljungkvist, T., Brunninge, O., and Nordqvist, M. (2017). Going Private: A Socioemotional Wealth Perspective on Why Family Controlled Companies Decide to Leave the Stock-Exchange. *Journal of Family Business Strategy*, 8(2), 74–86.

Borys, B., and Jemison, D.B. (1989). Hybrid Arrangements as Strategic Alliances: Theoretical Issues in Organisational Combinations. *Academy of Management Review*, 14(2), 234–249.

Brundin, E., Samuelsson, E.F., and Melin, L. (2014). Family Ownership Logic: Framing the Core Characteristics of Family Businesses. *Journal of Management and Organisation*, 20(1), 6–37.

Chrisman, J.J., Chua, J.H., and Sharma, P. (2005). Trends and Directions in the Development of a Strategic Management Theory of the Family Firm. *Entrepreneurship Theory and Practice*, September, 555–575.

Chua, J.H., Chrisman, J.J., and Sharma, P. (1999). Defining the Family Business by Behavior. *Entrepreneurship Theory and Practice*, Summer, 19–39.

Doherty, B., Haugh, H., and Lyon, F. (2014). Social Enterprises as Hybrid Organisations: A Review and Research Agenda. *International Journal of Management Reviews*, 16(4), 417–436.

Dyer, W.G. (2003). The Family: The Missing Variable in Organisational Research. *Entrepreneurship Theory and Practice*, 27(4), 401–416.

Faccio, M., and Lang, L.H. (2002). The Ultimate Ownership of Western European Corporations. *Journal of Financial Economics*, 65(3), 365–395.

Foreman, P., and Whetten, D.A. (2002). Members' Identification with Multiple-Identity Organisations. *Organisation Science*, 13(6), 618–635.

Gersick, K.E., Davis, J.A., Hampton, M.M., and Lansberg, I. (1997). *Generation to Generation: Life Cycles of the Family Business*. Boston, MA: Harvard Business School Press.

Goel, S., Mazzola, P., Phan, P.H., Pieper, T.M., and Zachary, R.K. (2012). Strategy, Ownership, Governance, and Socio-Psychological Perspectives on Family Businesses from Around the World. *Journal of Family Business Strategy*, 3(2), 54–65.

Golden-Biddle, K., and Rao, H. (1997). Breaches in the Boardroom: Organisational Identity and Conflicts of Commitment in a Nonprofit Organisation. *Organisation Science*, 8(6), 593–611.

Handler, W.C. (1989). Methodological Issues and Considerations in Studying Family Businesses. *Family Business Review*, 2(3), 257–276.

Jaskiewicz, P., Heinrichs, K., Rau, S.B., and Reay, T. (2016). To Be or Not to Be: How Family Firms Manage Family and Commercial Logics in Succession. *Entrepreneurship Theory and Practice*, 40(4), 781–813.

La Porta, R., Lopez-De-Silanes, F., and Shleifer, A. (1999). Corporate Ownership around the World. *Journal of Finance*, 54(2), 471–517.

Leaptrott, J. (2005). An Institutional Theory View of the Family Business. *Family Business Review*, 18(3), 215–228.

Ljungkvist, T., and Boers, B. (2017). Another Hybrid? Family Businesses as Venture Capitalists. *Journal of Family Business Management*, 7(3), 329–350.

Lok, J. (2010). Institutional Logics as Identity Projects. *Academy of Management Journal*, 53(6), 1305–1335.

Melin, L., and Nordqvist, M. (2007). The Reflexive Dynamics of Institutionalization: The Case of the Family Business. *Strategic Organisation*, 5(3), 321–333.

Miller, D., Le Breton-Miller, I., and Lester, R.H. (2011). Family and Lone Founder Ownership and Strategic Behaviour: Social Context, Identity, and Institutional Logics. *Journal of Management Studies*, 48(1), 1–25.

Nordqvist, M., and Melin, L. (2002). The Dynamics of Family Firms: An Institutional Perspective on Corporate Governance and Strategic Change. In D.E. Fletcher (ed.), *Understanding the Small Family Business* (pp. 94–110). London: Routledge.

Pache, A.-C., and Santos, F. (2013). Inside the Hybrid Organisation: Selective Coupling as a Response to Competing Institutional Logics. *Academy of Management Journal*, 56(4), 972–1001.

Parada, M.J., Nordqvist, M., and Gimeno, A. (2010). Institutionalizing the Family Business: The Role of Professional Associations in Fostering a Change of Values. *Family Business Review*, 23(4), 355–372.

Peredo, A.M. (2003). Nothing Thicker than Blood? Commentary on 'Help One Another, Use One Another: Toward an Anthropology of Family Business', *Entrepreneurship Theory and Practice*, 27(4), 397–400.

Pieper, T.M., and Klein, S.B. (2007). The Bulleye: A Systems Approach to Modeling Family Firms. *Family Business Review*, 20(4), 301–319.

Pratt, M.G., and Foreman, P.O. (2000). Classifying Managerial Responses to Multiple Organisational Identities. *Academy of Management Review*, 25(1), 18–42.

Reay, T., Jaskiewicz, P., and Hinings, C.B. (2015). How Family, Business, and Community Logics Shape Family Firm Behavior and 'Rules of the Game' in an Organisational Field. *Family Business Review*, 28(4), 292–311.

Shanker, M.C., and Astrachan, J.H. (1996). Myths and Realities: Family Businesses' Contribution to the US Economy: A Framework for Assessing Family Business Statistics. *Family Business Review*, 9(2), 107–123.

Sharma, P. (2004). An Overview of the Field of Family Business Studies: Current Status and Directions for the Future. *Family Business Review*, 17(1), 1–36.

Stewart, A., and Hitt, M.A. (2012). Why Can't a Family Business be More Like a Nonfamily Business? Modes of Professionalization in Family Firms. *Family Business Review*, 25(1), 58–86.

Tagiuri, R., and Davis, J. (1996). Bivalent Attributes of the Family Firm. *Family Business Review*, 9(2), 199–208.

Thornton, P.H., and Ocasio, W. (1999). Institutional Logics and the Historical Contingency of Power in Organisations: Executive Succession in the Higher Education Publishing Industry, 1958–1990. *American Journal of Sociology*, 105(3), 801–843.

Thornton, P.H., and Ocasio, W. (2008). Institutional Logics. In R. Greenwood, C. Oliver, R. Suddaby and K. Sahlin-Andersson (eds), *The SAGE Handbook of Organisational Institutionalism* (pp. 99–129). London: SAGE Publications.

Tompkins, R. (2010). The Organisational Identity of a Family Business: The Role of Hybrid Identity in Organisational Events. Doctoral dissertation, George Washington University, Washington, DC.

Ward, J. (1987). *Keeping the Family Business Healthy: How to Plan for Continuing Growth, Profitability, And Family Leadership*. San Francisco, CA: Jossey-Bass.

Westhead, P., and Cowling, M. (1998). Family Firm Research: The Need for a Methodological Rethink. *Entrepreneurship Theory and Practice*, 23(1), 31–55.

Whetten, D.A. (2006). Albert and Whetten Revisited: Strengthening the Concept of Organisational Identity. *Journal of Management Inquiry*, 15(3), 219–234.

Winter, M., Fitzgerald, M.A., Heck, R.K.Z., Haynes, G.W., and Danes, S.M. (1998). Revisiting the Study of Family Businesses: Methodological Challenges, Dilemmas, and Alternative Approaches. *Family Business Review*, 11(3), 239–252.

Zachary, R.K. (2011). The Importance of the Family System in Family Business. *Journal of Family Business Management*, 1(1), 26–36.

Zellweger, T., Ganter, M., Sieger, P., and Patel, P.C. (2016). How Much am I Expected to Pay for My Parents' Firm? An Institutional Logics Perspective on Family Discounts. *Entrepreneurship Theory and Practice*, 40(5), 1041–1069.

Zellweger, T.M., Nason, R.S., and Nordqvist, M. (2012). From Longevity of Firms to Transgenerational Entrepreneurship of Families: Introducing Family Entrepreneurial Orientation. *Family Business Review*, 25(2), 136–155.

29. Hybrid organisations in the overlapping territory with the personal world
David Billis

INTRODUCTION

Organisational Foundations

The foundations of this chapter build on the theory presented in Chapter 24. There, the public, private and third sectors were presented as the three fundamental organised ways of responding to human problems. Each sector comprises an aggregation of formal organisations, those that have a public persona, an accountable structure and the resources to respond systematically to problems.

Formal organisations in all three sectors have the same core five elements of their structure. They are: owners, who all have a role in decision-making (with principal owners making the critical decisions); governance, the way owners are appointed (such as share-holding, public elections and private elections); operational priorities, the concepts utilised by owners and their agents to achieve their purposes; and other elements – distinctive human resources and other resources. It is accountability which is the overarching and the linking concept between the elements and principles of formal organisations. In this chapter I shall refer to this linking concept as the major principle.

Organisations in each sector have their own distinctive and competing set of principles for each of the five elements. Considering private, public and third sectors in this order, the driving forces and distinctive features of their principles according to the sectors are as follows:

- ownership: by shareholders, citizens, and members;
- governance: by size of share ownership, public elections and private elections;
- priorities: by market forces, public service and collective choice, and mission;
- human resources: paid employees in the firm, paid public servants in the bureau, members and volunteers in the association;
- other resources: sales and fees; taxes; membership fees, donations and legacies.

The distinctive principles of each sector produces Weberian-type ideal models. Although the majority of individual organisations adhere to these, an individual sector which consist of an aggregation of organisations is more realistically defined as a normal model.

It is normal because all sectors also contain hybrid organisations: those that have absorbed or been established with principles from other sectors. Hybrid organisations can cause confusion over ownership and accountability but also offer potential advantages such as benefiting from the best features of other sectors. The main objective of Chapter 24 was to develop a map of the three organisational worlds and their hybrids that would present the essence of a usable theory for better understanding organisational practice and theory. In so doing, the chapter reached the conclusion that we were now living in the New Organisational Reality (NOR) in which hybrid organisations were seen as far more extensive than was generally recognised, and that this had important implications for organisational theory.

The Purpose of this Chapter

What was noted, but not discussed, was that the three formal-organisational worlds operate within an all-encompassing 'personal world' of individuals, families, friends and neighbours. In addition the personal world also contains countless groupings that may be defined as the personal world arrangements for doing things. Unlike formal organisations they are not bound by publicly accountable principles but are essentially groups which are held together by friendship and conviviality and which do not seek or need a public persona. Despite the major contribution of families, friends, neighbours and groupings in response to human problems, they are the least well researched from an organisational perspective. Consequently, Chapter 24 left a large agenda of unfinished business that might be summed up in one question: where, if anywhere, does the personal world fit into the theory of hybrid organisations? This will be discussed in the following paragraph.

As the dominant actors in responding systematically to human problems, it is not surprising that most organisational research is preoccupied with formal organisations and, more recently, their hybrid organisations. In contrast, the personal world of individuals and their innumerable personal world groupings – arrangements for doing things – have received less attention from organisational theorists. The end result is a theoretical gap in the overlapping territory between the three sectors of formal organisations and personal world groupings. My aim is to increase the understanding of this territory by extending the theory and the map of hybridity to include the personal world. I intend to begin this process by moving beyond the limitations of the boundary-less categorisation of grouping and identifying what I will call a 'personal-organisation' (PO). This is not a formal organisation but will need to possess comparable characteristics if the theory of hybridity is to be extended to the personal world.

This introduction finishes with a summary of the chapter's main sections on the path to its conclusions. The first section provides a background to the overlapping territory by noting the work of several authors who have researched in this area and confronted the problems of hybrid relationships and tension. It confirms the value of exploring this territory and the potential value of developing useful organisational theory.

The next section, based on qualitative research with 15 book clubs, demonstrates how formal organisations and POs can be compared. It sets the foundation for the identification of different types of hybrid organisations in the overlapping territory. It concludes with a model of personal-organisations (Table 29.1) which differentiates its principles from those of formal organisations.

The chapter then responds to the main research objective by extending the three-sector map to include personal organisations. It begins by demonstrating the large potential scope of POs and distinguishes between inward-looking and outward-looking POs. It continues by discussing the case of the family and argues, after defining the family, that part of it can be regarded as a distinctive type of PO: the 'family personal-organisation' (FPO).

Table 29.1   Personal-organisations and sectors

Core elements	Third sector principles	Private sector principles	Public sector principles	Personal-organisations
1. Ownership (key decisions)	Formal membership	Shareholders	Citizens	Personally responsible leaders
2. Governance	Private elections	Share ownership size	Public elections	Trust-based
3. Operational priorities	Commitment to implement distinctive mission	Market forces and individual choice	Public service and collective choice	Consensus about purpose and regular meetings
4. Distinctive human resources	Members and volunteers in association	Paid staff in managerially controlled firm	Paid public servants in legally backed bureau	Responsible friendly members in available space
5. Distinctive other resources	Dues, donations, legacies	Sales, fees	Taxes	Few
Major principle	Accountability	Accountability	Accountability	Responsibility

The last main section speculates on the different ways in which hybrid organisations could arise from the personal world, and how principles of the personal world can be adopted by formal organisations. The chapter then closes with a summary and conclusions.

RESEARCH IN THE OVERLAPPING TERRITORY

This section presents the preliminary steps towards meeting the objectives of this chapter: to increase the understanding of the overlapping territory and consider its possible extension. It examines some of the literature that might provide insights into the experience of other researchers who have encountered the overlapping territory. In general, it is hoped that it will provide insights into the study of the overlapping territory and, more specifically, that it will explore whether the territory exhibits tension between formal organisations and groupings: an indication that hybridity might perhaps be present. As noted in the introduction, groupings were simply described as personal world arrangements for doing things. This section will also argue that there are organisations in the overlapping territory that already appear to be hybrid organisations. The foremost and most important of these are family businesses, whose title aptly describes their inherent hybridity between the personal world and formal organisations, and which will be discussed later in the chapter.

The first authors cited support the proposition that the territory exhibits tension between formal organisations and groupings. Although focused on interpersonal relationships rather than organisational structures, the seminal work by Eisenstadt and Roniger (1984) is a good starting point since a recurring theme in their analysis is the ambivalence, tension and conflict between the typical relationships in the personal world and 'the formalised organised structure' (ibid., p. 2). From this it is a small leap to assume that relationships between personal world groupings and formal organisations would also be ambivalent and tense. A not dissimilar approach is taken by Allan Silver, who elegantly compares 'friendship' which is 'quintessentially private' and is 'so contrary' with the associations that dominate the public domain, and their 'explicit contract, rational exchange, formal division of labor and impersonal institutions' (Silver, 1989, pp. 74–97).

Other work moves closer to the domain of organisations and hybridity and supports the proposition that hybrid organisations exist in the overlapping territory. For example, the major study by Bensman and Lilienfeld (1979, p. 179) describes 'informal social groups and networks . . . that have some characteristics of the private and some of the public'. They call these a 'quasi-public' area of life. In their use of the word 'quasi' they appear to be searching for a way to conceptualise a hybrid area of activity which has characteristics of both the personal and 'informal' types of organisation.

Coming from a different social policy and administration background, the ambivalence of the 'quasi-public' was evident in the period of the United Kingdom (UK) governmental creation of 'good neighbour schemes'. These attempted 'to mobilise local residents to increase the amount or range of help they give to one another' (Abrams et al., 1981, p. 9). However, those who left the scheme indicated that they disliked the need for formality in what was seen as a very different (non-organisational) world. The authors suggest that the schemes can 'act as a half-way house between the two worlds of informal care given by relations, neighbours and friends, and of formal care given by the statutory authorities' (ibid., p. 17). In what seems to be a description of the overlapping territory they hope that some form of their halfway house will emerge which could resolve the tension between the private and the public.

Other investigators of the overlapping territory have also been compelled to use a variety of names to describe groups that occupy that territory. Thus, even the influential economist Mancur Olson, who provided a detailed economic analysis of groups, abandoned his attempt at a definition of small groups. These, and also religious philanthropic organisations, did not have a 'significant economic interest' (Olson 1965 [1977], p. 6). Of significance is the seemingly incidental introduction of a term that encapsulates the dilemmas we are discussing: Olson refers to the 'unorganised group' (ibid., p. 8). Unfortunately no definition is offered.

In one of his studies, David Horton Smith, a distinguished researcher of the third sector, also seeking to understand the overlapping territory, distinguished between 'informal groups' and formal organisations. He introduces another name to describe the territory: he suggests that the 'semiformal organisation is a group that is almost but not quite a formal organisation, lacking clear boundaries and sometimes a clear leadership structure' (Smith, 1992, p. 252). Another researcher with deep interest in the third sector is Thomasina Borkman (2008), whose work on self-help groups succinctly expressed the paradox and dilemmas of her research. She argued that: 'as voluntary associations, self-help groups are quasi-public in that peers who are strangers meet in associations; because they are often small and do not advertise their existence, they are also quasi-private' (ibid., p. 213).

This quasi-public–quasi-private tension emerged as a key characteristic of the research programme on 'below the radar' (BTR) groups being undertaken by the Third Sector Research Centre. It seems that BTR 'has become a short-hand used to describe small voluntary organisations, community groups and more informal or semi-formal activities in the third sector' (Phillimore et al., 2010, p. 1). This body of research contains much useful material for an understanding of the interaction between the formal and the personal, and the presence of hybridity tension between the personal world and formal organisations. Phillimore et al. bring us back to an important theme of this chapter – the nature of accountability – and their finding that 'formal constituted structures did not necessarily evidence accountability as leaders often put friends or family on the board' (Phillimore et al., 2010, p. 16).

This section of the chapter has utilised relevant literature to confirm: (1) the presence of tension between formal organisations and groupings in the overlapping territory; and (2) the existence of hybrid organisations in the overlapping territory. It has provided reassurance that this might be a fertile area for additional research and the possible uncovering of a PO. But the review of the literature has also provided an important additional benefit. For example, the work of Eisenstadt and Roniger, Silver, and others in this field has demonstrated the existence of a different language in the personal world. It suggests that the PO would also have its own preferred use of organisational language that distinguishes it from formal organisations, and a few words did emerge as potential PO principles. These will be noted as they become relevant in the case study in the following section.

However, before moving to the heart of the chapter – the case study and the construction of a model of the personal-organisation – one further piece of research deserves attention. Unfortunately, although there is a now a rich body of publications discussing book clubs, reading groups and other names, few appear interested in their internal organisation. One exception is that by Long (2003), an impressively broad study, which does contain some organisational issues. The most relevant of these was the concluding analysis, which echoed a familiar problem, this time shared with reading and book clubs: 'the difficulty of classifying reading groups as either wholly public or private' (ibid., p. 221).

DEVELOPING THE MODEL OF THE PERSONAL-ORGANISATION

This section of the chapter presents the findings of the research on book clubs and the development of the model of the personal-organisation. But first, I answer the questions: why were book clubs chosen, and what methodology was adopted to analyse them?

In Search of the Personal-Organisation: Why Book Clubs?

This subsection responds to the above two questions and begins by discussing the parameters of the PO in order to consider whether book clubs would be suitable examples. Since the purpose of the chapter is to extend, if possible, the theory and map of hybridity, the main parameter for any new addition to the map will be the presence of a comparable organisational language. A map written in two different languages would confuse rather than enlighten the user. Given that the language of the only map of the three sectors and their hybrids is that of elements and principles, new additions to the map would need to abide by the same language and parameters. The elements can be regarded as the headline description of the five fundamental structural parts of the formal organisation: (1) ownership: person(s) accountable for 'life-and-death' decision-making; (2) governance:

accountability for the way owners are appointed, and guardianship of the organisational mission; (3) operational priorities; (4) the distinctive human resources; and (5) the distinctive other resources.

However, the elements are only useful if each of these headline descriptions is accompanied by the organisation's distinctive ways – or principles – of implementing them. Thus, in the theory of hybrid organisations the distinctive ways have been analysed at the level of the sector and the results summarised in Table 29.1. One important example is that the element of life-and-death decision-making is, in the private sector, implemented according to the distinctive principle of the size of shareholding. The comparison with the third sector is that the same element is undertaken by its own distinctive principle of voting by the formal membership.

The search for what eventually evolved in this chapter as the PO was the result of two separate strands of research. It began with a period of work on the theme of the organisational forms in the personal world and its overlapping with the third sector. This work culminated in 2012 with a paper that was the precursor of Figure 29.1 in this chapter (Billis, 2011). In essence, it focused on conviviality groups that were unambiguously part of the personal world, and identified: (1) those that move organically into hybridity with the third sector; and (2) those that include both friends and strangers, have explicit goals, and are often established immediately as hybrids. I also briefly noted that some of these might never become formal associations.

At this point I had become influenced by some early results from the second research strand: the work with book clubs. I had begun to analyse their key organisational characteristics and to appreciate their longevity, independence, and obvious determination and ability to maintain their 'non-bureaucratic' arrangements. Some of this material was

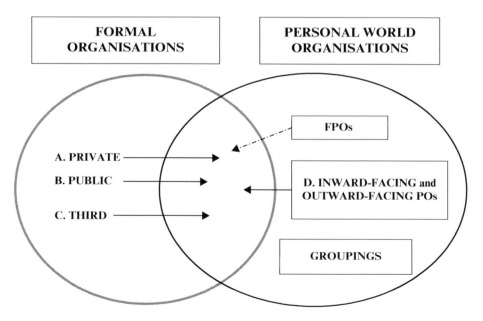

Figure 29.1   Formal organisations, hybrids and the personal world

utilised in one paragraph in the 2012 paper, although its significance in the search for the PO was not appreciated until a few years later when the work on this chapter began.

The research with book clubs was unplanned. It was the result of a serendipitous conversation with friends about these clubs. Two of them were members of book clubs and I was swiftly disabused of my naive assumption that these were primarily a place for conviviality. I still did not have any idea that there might be a PO, and it was the hidden nature of the book club that presented an irresistible opportunity for exploration.

A few weeks later I found myself enthusiastically undertaking initial pilot interviews with the two members. I was armed with a list of preliminary questions that were intended to provide broad topics, rather than any 'tick box' exercise. They were to be utilised according to the flow of the discussion in order to understand the key features of the club. The questions included: why and when was it established? Who established it? Who invited you, were you friends, or what? Why did you join? What were the dynamics of the club? For example, is there an informal leader, what is the role of the founder, do some members dominate, and why? What was the balance of activity between books and social? Has it changed over time? Do many members leave, why, and how do you get rid of them if necessary?

The preliminary list of questions resulted in lively discussions which augured well for a future project. Both interviews indicated that the clubs played an important role in the life of the – predominantly female – members. As the project continued, this initial opinion was reinforced and the valuable role of book clubs in the response to human problems became clearer.

One major dilemma still remained to be solved: how to gain access to additional organisations that were quintessentially private – a necessary requirement for their inclusion in the research? Looking online, searching for information in the local libraries or other sources were unhelpful, since their public persona immediately ruled them out. I would be unable to utilise my preferred problem-driven research methodology since, even if there were problems, they were unlikely to be made public.

Without a ready-to-hand alternative methodology I had drifted into an approach. Beginning with my pilot interviewees I was then recommended to an unknown third interviewee. I had begun my snowballing experience, and was following the broad footsteps of others confronted by a similar dilemma.

Methodology and Scope

Despite having heard about 'snowballing', I knew little about the methodology, and had never previously worked with 'invisible' groups. It just seemed a natural extension of my previous interview-based qualitative research which might now meet the organisational characteristics of book clubs. I needed to gain information about 'sufficient' clubs to provide useful tentative theory about the existence of personal-organisations. I decided that interviewing members from 18–20 clubs would provide sufficient different data for initial model-building. The downside was that setting up the interviews in this type of organisation took rather more time. For example, it is only practical to identify an interviewee after the previous interview has been completed and provided with the name and address of the next participant. And even then, the person would have to give their agreement and a convenient time would then need to be separately negotiated.

But how reliable is my version of snowballing? There does not appear to be research specifically concerned with utilising snowballing as a research methodology to uncover the organisation of invisible self-organised book clubs. It was certainly an unlikely possibility, even though there is a large body of research about book clubs. However Atkinson and Flint (2001), in a brief but important paper, discuss the pros and cons of utilising snowballing as a research methodology to uncover hidden populations. Summarising, they suggest that what is often called 'snowball sampling' is most frequently used in qualitative research primarily through interviews.

They point to a number of advantages – in addition to those noted earlier – that are claimed for snowballing; none of these seem to be particularly relevant for book clubs. On the other hand, their more detailed material on three 'deficiencies' seemed more pertinent. The first group of deficiencies concerned the lack of randomness in selection, overemphasising cohesiveness in social networks, and not being representative of the wider population. But 'representation' is essentially a political concept and not a consideration for a small private group. The second group of deficiencies included the difficulty of finding respondents and initiating 'chain referrals' which included people in authority providing their (prejudiced) route into the required population. Again, 'authority' is also not an issue in a small invisible group, although differences of influence are usually present in any informal grouping. The brief third group of deficiencies were concerned with maintaining confidentiality, a central feature of my approach, so this too was unproblematic.

Case Studies: Introduction

Altogether, a 'snowballed' member from each of 17 clubs was interviewed. It emerged that one of them was not an independent club and it was excluded. Another was not really a book club and was also excluded. The remaining 15 similar groups were analysed to see whether they might provide a tentative ideal model of a 'sector' including hybrid organisations that would serve as a bridge with formal organisations. Those requirements relate to the five elements of formal organisations, and the objective was to seek to match the findings from the remaining 15 clubs against those five elements. To reiterate, the five elements were ownership, governance, priorities, human resources and other resources.

Leadership and Personal Commitment

I begin by noting that several participants objected to the use of the word 'club', which they regarded as too 'formal'. They exhibited a strong sense of the organisational difference between the formal and the personal. In order to do justice to the organised nature of the groups whilst emphasising their personal world roots, the title 'personal-organisation' was chosen purely for the purposes of this chapter.

Book clubs can have very deep roots, with some claiming to have continuous records that go back to the 18th century (Hartley, 2002). More realistically, but still impressively, the clubs in the case study had an average age of about 15 years; eight clubs were up to ten years old, five clubs were in the range 11–30, and two were more than 30 years old.

In several cases lengthy membership had resulted in a reluctance to recruit new members; as one person put it, 'we have become a clique'. In another group, the interviewee pointed out that she had been 'trying for some time' to persuade the others to deal with the problem of recruiting new members. A third contributor, discussing the same issue, rather more colourfully suggested that, 'what we want are clones'. This issue of organisational sustainability can be summarised as 'managing the boundaries'. How are new members recruited and how, if necessary, is it possible to expel members who 'do not fit in'?

The interviews clarified the manner in which these small groups, all with a membership of 8–12, resolved these difficult questions, and how the clubs existed as a stable organisational form. They returned to the unanswered question of how the 'boundary questions' in the clubs were dealt with and, by implication, what the role of ownership was in these critical issues. Participants were asked who 'owned' the club. I explained that I was defining ownership in the sense that it involved an individual or individuals who were the most influential in decision-making. Although it was possible to use this definition, their preferred word to describe the influential person was 'leader'. And, since I had been searching for a distinctive language for the personal world, it seemed absurd to carry on using the alien and contentious concept of ownership. The participants were easily able to identify those who had more influence in decision-making than other members. Of the 15 clubs, 11 had generally accepted leaders of varying degrees of influence, of whom six were founders. The remaining four clubs had developed rules and procedures to organise themselves with some minimal coordinative leadership.

It appears that, even in these small groups, in order to ensure focus and sustainability, most of them required some form of appropriate leadership. To understand why this was required, I returned to consider what owners could do in reality. Put bluntly, the most stressful task was how to get rid of members. What sort of leadership exists in book clubs when faced with this most stressful decision? In one unique case, confronted with the difficulty of getting rid of an awkward person and her friends who threatened the stability of the club, the owner quietly brought a small group of confidantes together, the club was closed, and then restarted six months later. The more usual way of dealing with awkward members is more transparent and in keeping with the general ethos of the group. They were 'counselled' out, or diplomatically told that they did not fit in.

There was another challenge for leaders. When asked to estimate what was the approximate balance of time spent between books and social activities, the overall average was about 50 per cent on each. But this obscured the fact that there were two or three clubs at either end of the spectrum: some emphasising their prime focus on books and spending up to 70 per cent of their time on them; whilst several were more 'relaxed' and, for them, the 'social' aspect was the most important. It was essential to get the appropriate balance for the needs of the members. The challenge for leaders – the influential voices in the club – now appeared more multifaceted. They had to handle its boundaries but were also required to take the lead in getting rid of people, and to keep an eye on the balance between time spent on books and time spent on friendly social discussion.

The discussions concerning leadership made it clear that accountability, as the overarching element which holds the formal organisation together and holds people to account for their actions, was inappropriate. Nevertheless, a distinctive personal world concept was used instead of accountability. Sometimes, when participants were asked why they did certain things for the group, the phrase 'personal responsibility' was used.

Activities could range from taking on some administrative tasks, to volunteering to help with 'counselling-out' unwanted members. Personal responsibility was an implicit principle of becoming a member. A member could not be 'held to account' as in the formal sector. Nonetheless, the expectation was that the 'ways of doing things' of the group would be adhered to.

The first important conclusion was that it was personal responsibility that held the group together. It acted as an overarching major principle comparable to accountability. It is now also possible to respond to the question as to whether these personal-organisations have the equivalent of owners in formal organisations, those who make the key decisions. It is the personally responsible leaders or leaders, as seen in the case study, who comprise the equivalent of the owners in formal organisations.

Founders may naturally feel they have a special responsibility for leadership in 'their' organisation and they may act as the first amongst equals. But, over time, as seen in the case studies, the situation will change and the configuration of leadership will also change. Nonetheless, what was evident was the need of the clubs to have a leader or leadership even if, for some of the most stable and embedded clubs, very little was required of them.

Trust and Governance

In formal organisations the concept of governance was used to describe the way in which those who have a role in decision-making are appointed, such as elections or shareholding. Most of these words would be greeted with horror by book club members. Yet, decisions are made, and what will be looked for in this section is the principle which makes it possible to take decisions.

The interviewees naturally, without any prompting, provided substantial support. The most telling example was that 'trust between members was very important since it laid the foundation for a degree of criticism in the discussions'. Given that the discussions were the focal activity of the group, trust was a precondition for success. This was also the word that appeared in the literature of personal world language, but was not included in the discussion on the overlapping territory in the previous section of this chapter. Particularly impressive is the study by Seligman (1997 [2000]), who provides a persuasive argument for the important differentiation between 'trust' and 'confidence'. Seligman expresses enthusiasm for the views of Niklas Luhmann in providing the 'crucial distinction between trust in persons and confidence in institutions' (ibid., p. 18). He accepts Luhmann's argument that trust remains vital in interpersonal relationships, but not in functional systems.

In another important, but very different example, trust was linked with criticism. Without trust, several members expressed their unease about preparing tea and cakes when their turn came to host the monthly meeting. When asked whether they had friends in the group, when the answer was 'No', the criterion for friendship was usually whether they invited the person home for a meal. Being prepared to bake a cake was not a signal of crossing the boundary and becoming what was called 'real friends', but it was usefully described as 'friendliness': there was sufficient trust between members to be relaxed about any minor criticism.

Trust, as with responsibility, pervaded the entire group. It began when a new candidate was proposed for membership, usually sponsored by one of the group. It was an important criterion for acceptance. Can we trust them to fit in with the way we do things and the accepted style of interaction, the type of books we choose, the manner in which we discuss them, to read the chosen books, to make a reasonable presentation, and to play an active part in the discussions? Trust and personal responsibility were intertwined. A member was trusted because other members know that she possessed the necessary personal responsibility to do what was required. The following subsection presents the third, and final core principle.

Operational Priorities and Consensus

Priorities may be regarded as the distinctive principles which drive what work the organisation actually does. For example, in the private sector the distinctive principles are market forces and individual choice. The work of book clubs might be described as to read and discuss books in a systematic fashion which satisfies its members and also to provide a friendly social environment. The way of achieving this was a short-term programme deciding when and where the group would meet.

The diverse views of group members regarding the choice of literature and allied issues meant that setting priorities was not always straightforward. In a few cases the 'rules' of doing things were discussed at the time of the club's foundation, whereas others took a more leisurely path. But in all cases there could be a lengthy period of experimentation until they found 'what works'. Collaboration was essential if the unity and friendly character of the group was to be maintained, and in order to produce a satisfying discussion the process had to be based on the principle of consensus. Occasionally a vote might be taken, but a trust-based consensus was the natural principle that complemented personal responsibility and trust. The three most important principles – personal responsibility, trust and consensus – are in place, and the remaining principles of human and other resources will be briefly discussed as part of the model.

Resources

The resources of the book club were in essence the totality of the work of the members. They were not based on sales, fees, taxes, dues, donations or legacies but on individual personal responsibility, trust and consensual agreement. There were some modest tangible contributions which were spread amongst the group, for example taking turns to host the meetings and provide some food.

The Importance of Personal-Organisations

The case study suggests that POs may be important even if not formal organisations. They have objectives which they meet in a systematic fashion, an organisational boundary, longevity, reasonable stability of members, and they are self-sustaining. Furthermore, they respond informally to numerous individual problems faced by their members. These range from those faced by new mothers to the challenges of work, retirement and growing older. And all this is achieved within a coherent and distinctive set of often implicit organisational principles. These reasons justified describing book clubs, and other groups with similar basic principles, as personal-organisations. The evidence so far now makes it possible to present, in Table 29.1, personal-organisations, contrasting them with the three formal sectors that are defined in the introduction. In the table the principles of personal-organisations are compared with those of the three sectors of formal organisations.

The following section of the chapter explores the possibility that POs, with their distinctive personal world principles, may be widespread, going well beyond book clubs, in what has earlier been described as the 'primordial organisational soup' (Billis, 1993): the myriad of individuals, their interrelationships and groupings.

THE PERSONAL WORLD AND HYBRID ORGANISATIONS: EXTENDING THE MAP

This section of the chapter explores whether the scope and importance of personal-organisations (POs) are far greater than is immediately apparent. If this is so, it would be possible to extend the map and close the gap in the overlapping territory. This section will present an addition to an organisational map that in Chapter 24 already contains formal organisations and their hybrids. It first begins to identify types of POs that go beyond the case study, and differentiates the inward-looking and often hidden type from the outward-looking type.

Beyond the Case Study

Notwithstanding the work in this area, some of which was noted earlier, there remains much to learn regarding organisational forms in the personal world. With respect to personal-organisations this subsection discusses the possibility that they may potentially be a major feature of an enlarged map. To begin with, book clubs are only one type of inward-looking and hidden personal-organisations. They are not easy to uncover and a brief search suggests that many such groups will be found within broader titles such as sewing clubs, babysitting groups, singing groups and sports groups.

The second type of POs are important for the study of hybrid organisations. They adhere to the same basic principles described in Table 29.1 but, unlike book clubs, their activities may involve the production of an external product such as a performance for an audience: they are outward-facing. They may face additional challenges such as the need for resources beyond those of their members. Providing these activities does not make a significant impact on the fundamental principles in Table 29.1; they also will be defined as POs.

An example of research that indicates the potential scope of personal-organisations is related to findings from the case studies which emphasised the importance of the time devoted to socialising, and the deeper significance of baking a cake and the link with trust and friendliness. These findings are echoed in the far-ranging studies by Colin Rochester (2013). In the section on 'voluntary action as conviviality and expressive behaviour' (ibid., pp. 30–35) he points out that food and drink and 'the desire for conviviality is, in practice, closely allied to recreational activities and the constructive use of leisure time' (ibid., pp. 32). Rochester provides numerous examples of types of activities and specific organisations that fall under his heading of 'conviviality'. I surmise that a significant number will be personal-organisations.

Another area in which POs are highly likely to be present is that of self-help groups. Thomasina Borkman, a leading researcher in this area, points out that they go to great lengths to avoid anything (membership lists, donations) 'which would necessitate a public paper trail'. One example cited is the 'twelve-step anonymous group[1] [which] has an egalitarian and democratic structure with decision-making by consensus and a rotating and elected leadership; they are largely autonomous local groups who own no property, have no staff, and operate with almost no money' (Borkman, 2008, p. 213). Admittedly there is some ambiguity in the reference to 'largely' autonomous local groups, but it is difficult to escape the conclusion that these, and potentially many other self-help groups, are inward-looking personal-organisations.

Borkman's work also reminds us that there may also be many POs beyond self-help groups for which conviviality, whilst important, is not their prime purpose. There are also outward-looking groupings that wish to 'change things', as indeed self-help groups often wish to do. These groups may desire better political systems, changes in government policy, improved working conditions, greater gender equality, less pollution and, in democratic countries, numerous other continually changing concerns. Small local groupings are likely to choose the personal-organisation model as the natural way forward.

This discussion has provided support for the case that, in addition to clubs, there is a large range of POs, both inward- and outward-looking. Perhaps the most exciting of the remaining possible candidates for POs is the family, or at least a defined part of the family. The following speculations consider why the family is so important for the study of hybrid organisations and the overlapping territory.

The Family and the Family Firm

This subsection is limited to an exploration of whether the family, or part of it, can be regarded as a personal-organisation with its own principles, comparable to those in Table 29.1. If this is the case, it would lay the foundation for future analysis of hybridity in family firms based on the fundamental organisational principles of the family, rather than on its wide-ranging individual characteristics which result from its historic position as the global social institution. It is the family, which is an entity without meaningful business connections, rather than the family firm, that is the main topic of discussion, but I begin with some brief comments about the firm.

Family firms are a major presence in the economy of most societies. The statistics are emphatic. In 2014 there were an estimated 4.6 million family businesses in the UK, representing 87 per cent of all private sector firms (Oxford Economics, 2016), and other countries have even higher percentages. Although the family is not generally regarded as an organisation, the family firm is now widely accepted as a hybrid organisation. For example, there is considerable support from students of family businesses and others that, as Cater and Schwab (2008, p. 33) note: 'family firms represent hybrid organizations that embed business relationships in family relationships and try to serve both family and business needs' (see also Whetten et al., 2013). There is also agreement that the hybridity of the family firm brings with it distinct problems and can lead to 'warring family members' (Baron and Lachenauer, 2016).

The recognition of the significance of the hybrid family firms raises important questions about the nature of this hybridity. On one side of the relationship is the 'firm', an organisational form about which there is no shortage of information. On the other side is the 'family', with its own huge large body of literature which does not address it as an organisation – and therein lies the problem. In an aptly titled article, 'The Family: The Missing Variable in Organizational Research', Dyer (2003) clearly identified the problem with the existing body of family literature. The lack of organisational research, however, has improved since then, with several authors treating the family as an organisation (Scabini and Manzi, 2011; Scabini et al., 2006).

Although the missing variable is more visible, specific organisational research on the family only infrequently treats it as an organisation. It lacks a set of organisational principles comparable to that of the firm. Without such a theory of the built-in fundamental hybridity in family firms, the role of the family as an organisation remains undervalued and the understanding of hybridity in the family firm remains incomplete. To understand more it is helpful to return to the most important questions, which are: (1) What are the boundaries of the family organisation? and (2) What might be its set of organisational principles?

The logical starting point for an answer to the question of boundaries is to address the most contentious aspect of family analysis: providing a usable definition. My cautious working definition is of the inclusive family as a group of people who self-define themselves to be members of the family, and are accepted as such by the existing members. True, most members are likely to be related by blood or marriage, but I suggest this definition still holds.

My hypothesis is that within the inclusive family there are three tiers (not to be confused with the 'levels' in Table 29.1) that reflect their participation in the inclusive family. The first, largest, tier consists of those members who only occasionally, if at all, have contact with other members of the family. The second tier are the 'active' family members who, for example, maintain regular contact, participate and host gatherings, remember birthdays, and provide occasional support. The third, most important, tier is the nuclear family who, together with the active members, comprise what will be called the 'family personal-organisation' (FPO) that will be discussed next. In the search for a boundary to the FPO, the following subsection provides more detail about the three tiers, answers the questions about the boundaries, and considers whether the principles of the personal-organisation in Table 29.1 can be utilised in the FPO.

The Family Personal-Organisation (FPO)

First, some words of explanation. The three tiers serve as broad categories primarily to provide a definition of, and boundary for, the inclusive family. They also serve to highlight the active members and leaders as the central actors in the family organisation. These tiers should be distinguished from the larger number of different levels of organisational responsibility-based principles in Table 29.1. Thus, as will be seen, active members may find themselves at different times fulfilling different levels on the ladder of responsibility in Table 29.1. These comments are offered as a first attempt to lay the foundation for the hypothesis that part of the family can be conceptualised as a family personal-organisation. Any future research will doubtless need to reflect further on the concepts and the language.

I begin with the founders of the nuclear family that most likely consists of a pair of adults and their socially recognised children. In UK law, parents have legal rights and responsibilities (accountabilities): most importantly to provide a home, and protect and maintain the children. Amongst other important legal accountabilities are: maintaining discipline, choosing and providing education, agreeing to medical treatment, naming and agreeing to any change of the child's name. These legal obligations are only part of the reality of their full personal responsibilities, which might be summarised as providing a sustainable systematic response to the problems of the family. Depending on numerous factors including their ability and resources they will need to plan for the maintenance and continuation of the family, and much more.

The totality of expected activities and associated responsibilities required in order to maintain the family begin to make a case for considering the family as an organisation, and the parents as the personally responsible leaders. But the consideration of the family as an organisation goes further. The burden of the expected work in the family is such that leaders will wish to seek advice from trusted others. Typically, significant personal responsibility will be taken by a small number of people who might include grandparents, siblings and others who are trusted to contribute their experience, time and resources. On the ladder of decision-making in Table 29.1 these contributors, mainly from the pool of active members, act as a trust-based 'governance' group who advise and support the leaders.

It has been argued that trust arising from common ancestry and shared family identity (Corbetta and Salvato, 2004, in Sundaramurty, 2008, p. 89) have given the family businesses a 'comparative advantage' (Carney, 2005, p. 249). This abundance of trust present in families – recognising that this is not always the case – make it questionable whether the next level in the ladder of decision-making, deciding operational priorities, requires conceptualisation. The combination of trust and proximity may mean that it will naturally be absorbed by the governance group. But this is going beyond my main hypothesis, and in the absence of qualitative research there is a danger that this argument, dare it be said, could be seen as 'bureaucratic'. As with members of book clubs, family members might be unhappy at some of the language utilised so far. For example, the governance group may, depending on the problem, be an unplanned meeting with one or a few people. It is this totality of trusted confidants who may require a more appropriate name, but 'governance group' will suffice at this early stage of conceptualisation.

But I return now to the highly relevant contribution of grandparents, and not only for their governance-supporting responsibilities. The complexity, importance and changing nature of their participation is helpfully summarised by Gay Ochiltree (2006, pp. 1–3) in a paper which helps to illustrate their role in relation to several FPO principles. Ochiltree notes that: 'grandparents, mostly grandmothers, are the major providers of child care for preschool children . . . when both the parents are in the workforce'. In this example grandparents provide a valuable distinctive human resource and act as the responsible friendly members. It can be necessary for them to take on the role of personally responsible leaders since they may have to bring up grandchildren because their parents are unable to do so; often, for example, because of drug or alcohol abuse.

Ochiltree (2006, p. 2) also cites another author, Kornhaber (1996), who suggests that grandparents do not wish to be critical and intrusive and that they consequently adopt an approach of 'respectful cooperation' which enables them to have some say. This is an interesting phrase which reflects the difference of responsibilities between responsible leaders, yet emphasises the need for cooperation in personal-organisations. In using the word 'respectful' it also hints at the greater need for understanding and clarifying the difference in responsibilities in the family when compared with other personal-organisations.

Earlier in the chapter the need for appropriate language when discussing personal world organisations was emphasised. At this point it is important to stress that the family has a far greater range of activities and purposes than those covered by the FPO. These non-organisational activities, also undertaken by grandparents, are less tangible and, summarising from a number of authors cited in Ochiltree (2006), include helping with the children's emotional development, passing on to the grandchildren cultural knowledge as well as family traditions, and offering opportunities for emotional integration.

In conclusion, I hope that the material provided is sufficient to achieve the purpose of this subsection, which was to justify the foundation for the hypothesis that parts of the family are undertaking activities that cover the principles of a personal-organisation laid out in Table 29.1. In order to recognise the role of the family as the foremost societal institution, it has been conceptualised as a family personal-organisation consisting of the personally responsible leaders and some 'active' members of the family. The recognition of the FPO makes it possible to consider both the family firm and the family organisation as providing bridges between these two different forms of organisation, and the extension of the map of the overlapping territory.

The Extended Map: Explanations and Usage

This section presents and explains the key features of Figure 29.1. The circle on the left-hand side depicts the three sectors, with the arrowheads indicating that each of these sectors has its own hybrid organisations with the personal world, as illustrated in the overlapping territory of the two circles. A similar exercise is demonstrated in the personal world circle.

There is no significance in the positioning of the arrowheads in each circle. Thus, the principles of all three formal sectors could in theory influence the principles of the personal-organisations, both inward- and outward-facing types. Both inward-facing and outward-facing POs appear in the map in recognition of the proposition that there will be different – not inevitable – trajectories into a state of being influenced by the principles of formal organisations. Groupings have been included in order to indicate that some of these may be POs.

The larger area of the circle is occupied by the three formal organisations of each sector with their unique, unambiguous set of principles and their accountable structures. Hybridity between formal organisations is noted in the introduction to this chapter, and to avoid undue complexity is not included in the map.

The smaller (overlapping) area is occupied by two forms of hybrid organisation: formal organisations that have absorbed some principles from the personal-organisations; and personal-organisations that have absorbed distinctive principles from one or more of the three formal sectors. These will be discussed in the next section of the chapter.

Summary

The extended map now provides us with a number of possible new organisational inhabit-ants in addition to the three 'old-timers', the (non-hybrid) formal organisations of the three sectors. The newcomers are:

- the personal-organisation (PO and FPO);
- three new hybrids, rooted in the POs of the personal world that have absorbed the principles of one or more of the three formal sectors;
- three new hybrids resulting from the absorption of PO principles by each formal sector.

In total there are potentially seven new types of organisations: the new personal-organisation and six hybrid organisations in the overlapping territory. The next section of the chapter considers how some of the six hybrids might arise from POs and others arise from formal organisations.

BECOMING HYBRID ORGANISATIONS IN THE OVERLAPPING TERRITORY

Introduction

This section of the chapter first discusses the way in which hybrid organisations could arise from the personal world, and then how principles of the personal world can develop in the opposite direction and be adopted by formal organisations. Based on varying degrees of research, it focuses on some of the processes which have already led to, or might lead to, hybrid organisations in the overlapping territory.

Personal-Organisations and Hybridity with Formal Organisations

The inward-looking personal-organisation
This is a brief summary of a research project undertaken in collaboration with a group founded by several families with problem children. It was inward-looking, concentrating on supporting its own semi-permanent group of families. Support was provided on a voluntary basis by the members of the group. Without a formal structure it was led by a parent on the basis of consensus. For the first 18 months the small group managed without a public persona, and would fit into the definition of a personal-organisation.

A little later, the situation changed when several members of the group concluded that the unique support they were providing was needed not just by their own group, but also by the wider community. Support was secured from both government and private sources. Slowly, staff began to be employed. In the coming years, they moved organically into hybridity with the third sector. Eventually, they were meeting the needs of the locality and became 'entrenched' with a formal organisational structure, delineation of roles, a management committee and committee meetings, paid employees, formal systems of staff appointment and a significant budget.

The outward-looking personal-organisation
In contrast, the 'scenario' – possible events in the future – outlined below speculates on the possible organic move into hybridity of an outward-looking personal-organisation. It consisted of friends who had formed a small theatre group and had been performing in local venues primarily for their own pleasure. They just covered their costs. Their

principles were those of the personal-organisation, and their leader was quintessentially the first amongst equals.

As time goes by, they built a wider reputation and they were now making a surplus. There was tension between those who were attracted to the prospect of making serious money and those who wanted to keep to the 'good old days' of friends enjoying themselves. They needed to decide whether they wished to step on the bottom rung (external resources) of the ladder of hybridity (Table 29.1, Element 5) and enter shallow hybridity by adopting a typical source of income of the private sector.

From this point it can be speculated that there were a number of possibilities. For example, the tension of hybridity might be considered too high a price to pay, so they returned to their founding principles and remained a personal-organisation. Or, they might have sought ways to move to shallow hybridity by consensual agreement which still allowed them to retain their distinctive principles of leadership, governance and operational priorities. The next stage of hybridity (entrenched) in formal organisations occurs when the principles of one or both neighbouring sectors begin to significantly influence the group's operational priorities. In outward-looking POs the path to entrenched hybridity might occur by allowing profit to determine the performance priorities, by appointing accountable paid staff, and perhaps finally moving from a leader to an accountable manager. The possibility of reconstituting themselves by establishing a formal accountability-based organisation might prove to be an irresistible alternative.

The alternative approach to organic hybridity is enactment and is worth a brief mention. In this case a similar group of people, with the same PO principles, might decide – perhaps with the assistance of a hands-off benefactor – to immediately establish a hybrid theatre group. This seems rather less likely than the organic approach.

Formal Organisations and Hybridity with Personal-Organisations

Here I suggest that, in order for hybridity to occur, PO principles will be absorbed within the boundaries of formal organisations. The process of hybridity, based on the substantial organisational differences between formal organisations and the PO, is likely to be considerably different to the way in which the other side of the relationship discussed in the previous section develops. Based on the available research it has not proved possible to develop scenarios, and what are presented here are some early thoughts on the development of hybridity from the perspective of formal organisations. The first subsection below discusses the way in which PO principles are introduced into formal organisations. The second speculates on the organic absorption of principles, and the final subsection serves as a lead-in to the summary and conclusions of the chapter.

Introduction of PO principles

For managers in formal organisations, the language of personal world interactions can appear attractive: the perceived harsh language of managerial accountability might be replaced with, or exist alongside, more comfortable words. Hence, it is not unusual to find responsibility being used together with accountability; for leadership to be employed alongside managerial accountability; and for consensus to be used in conjunction with accountable decision-making.

However, my limited research in situations in which personal world language has been proposed for private sector usage indicate that it can be problematic and that it would be prudent to ensure that several preconditions are met: that each principle to be used from the PO has a clear workable definition and that the principles of the particular sector organisation, particularly the accountable organisational structure, be clearly understood and respected.

My main research in this area was accidental and only illustrates what can happen when the above preconditions are not met. I was invited by the regional director (RD) of a very large company who was unhappy with the working of his management team to analyse the cause of the problem and to provide an alternative organisational model. Individual confidential interviews with the RD and the team were undertaken and a report prepared which, with the agreement of each individual participant, was presented to all participants. What emerged was that the RD had previously delegated part of his work to his management team, who were instructed to work on the basis of consensus in the expectation of improved decision-making. Instead the reverse had happened and the situation had deteriorated. The team were squabbling about the allocation of work, decisions could not be made, or took far too much time, and personal relationships had worsened. Awkward questions were being put to the RD from peers outside the region, with the disconcerting possibility that the chief executive of the company might get involved.

The project took place well before my current research, but the evidence was sufficiently strong to demonstrate that consensus had failed. Today, a more sophisticated explanation could be offered. With the benefit of hindsight it is now evident that the RD, with the best of intentions, failed to take account of the preconditions noted above. He did not have a clear definition of what he was planning, and he did not appreciate the power of the contradictions between the principles of his organisation and the introduction of consensus. Possibly as a consequence he also could not see fit to secure the support of his peers and senior management team. My supposition is that, with greater understanding and appreciation of the PO principles and those of the formal organisation, where thought desirable, absorption of the principles will be possible and productive.

Organic absorption of principles
So far, the discussion has ignored those formal organisations that may have already absorbed, or been established with, PO principles. They deserve inclusion in the hypothesis but can only fleetingly be discussed in this chapter. My only comment is that when considering entrenched hybrid organisations, consensual decision-making may be essential in large organisations such as universities when they attempt to balance the principles of working in the market, fulfilling associational missions of research and teaching, and ensuring government support. What can now be added is the essential collaboration and working together on numerous committees and meetings which enable the university to function and, in many universities, are based on PO principles of consensus, personal responsibility and personally responsible leaders. Stefan Collini in his perceptive book discussing the purpose of universities (Collini, 2012, p. 134) makes a similar case in his criticism of the bureaucratic system that: 'two of the most important sources of efficiency in intellectual activity are voluntary cooperation and individual autonomy'. He follows this by suggesting that in contrast to the talk of 'accountability and productivity', 'cooperation and a sense of shared commitment to the enterprise is infinitely more fruitful'.

Organic absorption is different in smaller formal organisations, mainly those of the third sector. In these cases PO principles are easier to embrace, as a result of their close links to the personal world and their empathy with many of their organisational principles. In fact, it is well documented that small organisations represent the vast majority of the third sector (NCVO, 2018). It is a plausible assumption that many of them are third sector–PO hybrids.

Broader assimilation of PO principles

The broader assimilation of personal world principles by businesses, particularly those of the family, is confirmed and explained by Whetten et al. (2013, p. 488). They argue that: 'the reason why utilitarian organizations, such as businesses, suffer from a poor reputation is that they are perceived as being "too utilitarian" – the ends too often justify the means'. Ideally, they should be guided by a higher set of normative values and principles, where the 'requirements of being a family are coincidentally the ideals of being a business'. The authors wonder whether 'this is perhaps why so many companies engage in social practices and evoke values and principles reminiscent of family norms' (ibid.).

The large-scale assimilation of personal world principles is not confined to the private sector. A recent multimedia recruitment campaign by the British Army included an animation in which a voice says: 'Once you're in, you realise no one is a machine. The Army is a family' (Nagesh, 2018). But, as the *Harvard Business Review* reminds its readers, 'using the term family makes it easy for misunderstandings to arise' (Hoffman et al., 2014); 'In a real family, parents can't fire their children.' The authors suggest that this is precisely what occurs when the company is described as a family and then workers are laid off. The reality is that employees 'will feel hurt and betrayed – with real justification' (ibid.).

And yet, it would be unwarranted to suggest that the association with the family is necessarily for the purpose of securing competitive advantage, as is implied by Whetten et al. For example, in the armed forces and other organisations that are engage in life-threatening work, there may be an intrinsic duty of care above and beyond that of most formal organisations. The chapter now closes with a summary and conclusions.

SUMMARY AND CONCLUSIONS

Summary

The objective of this chapter was to test the hypothesis that the theory of hybridity could be extended to include the personal world with its 'groupings', and consequently bridge the gap (the overlapping territory) with formal organisations. The search began with a trawl through relevant literature which, combined with the experience of those who had already encountered the conceptual difficulties, enabled the first building blocks of a possible model of a personal-organisation (PO) to be put in place. Having done so, the chapter utilised a case study of book clubs in order to complete a model of POs which was set out in Table 29.1. This made it possible to differentiate between their principles and those of formal organisations. The hybrid territory between could now be explored using a common organisational language.

The chapter then responded to the main research objective by extending and explaining the new map to include personal-organisations (Figure 29.1), intended to demonstrate the considerable potential scope of the new POs. At this point the analysis began to consider the nature of hybrid organisations in the overlapping hybrid territory. Because of its importance the discussion started with the family firm and its link with the family. Could the internal, family organisation in itself be considered as some form of organisation? Families were therefore included in Figure 29.1, and the extended map and the overlapping territory which now contained six possible types of hybrid organisation were explained.

Finally, the concepts presented in the chapter were utilised to speculate on the ways in which: (1) hybrid organisations could arise from POs; and (2) how PO principles could be assimilated by formal organisations. This section concluded with some brief reflections on the broader assimilation of personal world principles based on the family.

Conclusions: Theory, Practice and Research in the New Organisational Reality

At the heart of this chapter is the identification of a typical organisational form – the personal-organisation – that, with its own hybrid characteristics, stands comparison with the formal organisation and enables the map of hybrid organisations to be expanded. It brings organisations into the personal world and represents the latest stage of development of a theory of hybrid organisations. These conclusions discuss the potential contribution of the POs with respect to its implications for organisational theory, practice and research.

Organisational theory

The inclusion of the PO with its distinct principles and its hybrid organisations with formal organisations, returns the discussion to the introduction and the section 'The Purpose of this Chapter'. Those paragraphs questioned the preoccupation of organisational studies with formal organisations and the paucity of research into the 'groupings' of the personal world.

This preoccupation was noted by Tsoukas who suggests that: 'ever since Weber, OT [organisation theory] has largely been concerned with the study of formal organisations' (Tsoukas, 2007, p. 608). The identification of the PO and its hybrid interrelationships challenges the preoccupation with formal organisations and makes it possible to develop a more encompassing and interrelated theory of organisations, as outlined in Figure 29.1.

This more encompassing theory draws its strength from a number of sources. In its early formulations, the strength of the sector theory was based on the four great responders to human problems: the three sectors of formal organisations, and the personal world. On reflection, the theory was substantially, but not entirely, organisational since it included what was assumed to be the non-organisational personal world.

That assumption has now been challenged by the uncovering of the PO. It brings greater coherence to the theory which becomes entirely organisational. It closes the gap between formal organisations and the personal world. And it brings into the theory organisations whose scope, size and impact may prove to be significant. It suggests that there is serious organisational life beyond hierarchy and power-based accountability.

There is a also a theoretical impact on the chronic problem of defining a robust boundary definition of the third sector. This has been partly resolved with the identification of

its distinctive principles, as illustrated in Table 29.1. It brings within the legitimate definition of the third sector those organisations that are rooted in the sector, but have also
absorbed principles drawn from POs. In contrast, POs are an integral part of, and rooted
in the personal world, although they may have absorbed principles from the three formal
sectors. Overall, the inclusion of POs and their roots in the personal world principles
means that there are now four great responders to human problems which – notwithstanding the substantial research still required – have their place in an encompassing and
interdependent general theory of hybrid organisations.

Practice

The intention was not only to contribute to organisation theory, but also to indicate how
this extended model might also have practical implications at the level of the individual
organisation. One strength of the theory may be its ability to avoid what Starbuck claims
is the fate of organisational theory since 1960 when it arrived. Since then, 'expansion
and affluence have brought pressures . . . to become self absorbed and irrelevant to its
environment' (Starbuck, 2003, p. 174). This is a worrying criticism since irrelevance must
surely spell the death toll of any usable theory.

The roots of hybridity theory in real organisations and human problems, and its
bottom-up development of concepts such as sectors, hybridity and most recently the
personal-organisation, are intended to be usable and respond to theoretical and practical
problems of the real world and its environment. Thus, the identification of the personal-
organisation and its hybrids represents an important contribution in the clarification of
the theoretical and practical problems of the overlapping territory discussed earlier in this
chapter. There, it emerged that a variety of different descriptions were used by researchers
working in the overlapping territory. The extended map (Figure 29.1) and explanations
now offer definitions of the types of organisations and their hybrids that inhabit the
overlapping territory. Each organisation can be analysed with the concepts described in
Chapter 24.

Finally, the practical value of the theory is highlighted in situations where individual
hybrid organisations are struggling with the competing principles of formal organisations and POs. This can be seen in Wuthnow's (1996) pioneering work which contains
numerous examples of the tensions between the 'private, largely invisible ways' of small
groups, and their management by the 'well-organised' structure of the national leadership
which 'commands huge resources' (ibid., p. 4). Many of the examples were manifestly the
consequence of the competing principles of formal organisations, in this case the third
sector, and those of the POs.

POs, the New Organisational Reality, and research

In Chapter 24 of this *Handbook* I argued that we are entering a period of the
New Organisational Reality (NOR), in which the growing recognition of hybrid
organisations will result in: (1) their being increasingly accepted as important and
normal types of formal organisation; (2) greater awareness of sectoral interdependence
between many formal organisations; and (3) increased sensitivity to the advantages
and disadvantages of hybrid organisation. These changes in acceptance, awareness
and sensitivity imply a change of approach and the possible entry into a different
organisational zeitgeist.

The ambition of this chapter was to increase the understanding of the overlapping organisational territory between formal organisation and the innumerable personal world groupings: arrangements for doing things. It was an ambition that is met by the findings that there are indeed personal world organisations, or personal-organisations, based on organisational principles comparable to those of the ubiquitous formal organisation. The consequence of this finding is that by using the expanded theory of hybrid organisations to include the personal-organisations we can now span the theoretical gap with formal organisations.

The current organisational zeitgeist began to be challenged by the increasing understanding of hybrid formal organisations. In future years it may be that a major contribution to the NOR will be the expansion of the boundary of current organisational approaches by including the organisational forms of the personal world. This second stage of the NOR could follow the same process noted earlier. It will also increasingly: (1) recognise the existence and importance of these forms of hybrid organisations with POs; (2) become aware of the interdependence of formal organisations and POs; and (3) develop sensitivity to the issues arising from the competing principles of the hybrids in the overlapping territory. But these are all possible areas for research in the future.

Nonetheless, until then, the new analysis in this chapter opens up a substantial potential area of exploration. Much of this is listed in the concluding summary of the section on 'The personal world and hybrid organisations: extending the map' which includes the seven new types of organisation. Three of these are hybrid organisations rooted in the personal world that have absorbed some principles from the three formal sectors, and three hybrids result from the absorption of PO principles by principles from one or more of the formal sectors. A few of these were briefly discussed in the following section, but each type opens up areas of research in itself. The seventh new type was that of the personal-organisation, which certainly deserves extensive research. And the development of a robust theory of families as organisations, and their hybridity overlapping with family firms, still remains as a suitably challenging and exciting area to close this list of potential research.

NOTE

1. The 'twelve steps' were developed by Alcoholics Anonymous to establish guidelines for the best way to overcome an addiction to alcohol. An anonymous group is one that does not have a public persona.

REFERENCES

Abrams, Philip, Sheila Abrams, Robin Humphrey and Ray Snaith (1981), *Action for Care: A Review of Good Neighbour Schemes in England*, Berkhamsted: Volunteer Centre.
Atkinson, Roland and John Flint (2001), *Accessing Hidden and Hard-To-Reach Populations: Snowball Researched Strategies*, Social Research Update, Summer 2001, University of Surrey.
Baron, Josh and Rob Lachenauer (2016), 'Surviving in the Family Business When You're Not Part of the Family', *Harvard Business Review*, 15 January.
Bensman, Joseph and Robert Lilienfeld (1979), *Between Private and Public: The Lost Boundaries of the Self*, New York: Free Press.
Billis, David (1993), *Organising Public and Voluntary Agencies*, London: Routledge.

Billis, David (2011), 'The Other Boundary of the Third Sector', ARNOVA, Annual Conference, Toronto.

Borkman, Thomasina (2008), 'Self-Help Groups as Participatory Action', in Ram A. Cnaan and Carl Milofsky (eds), *Handbook of Community Movements and Local Organisations*, New York: Springer, pp. 211–226.

Carney, Michael (2005), 'Corporate Governance and Competitive Advantage in Family-Controlled Firms', *Entrepreneurship Theory and Practice*, 29(3), pp. 249–265. SSRN: https://ssrn.com/abstract= 1507602.

Cater, John and Andreas Schwab (2008), 'Turnaround Strategies in Established Small Family Firms', *Family Business Review*, 21(31), p. 33.

Collini, Stefan (2012), *What Are Universities For?*, London: Penguin Books.

Corbetta, G. and C.A. Salvato (2004), 'The Board of Directors in Family Firms: One Side Fits All?', *Family Business Review*, 17, pp. 119–134.

Dyer, W. Gibb, Jr (2003), 'The Family: The Missing Variable in Organizational Research', *Entrepreneurship Theory and Practice*, 27(4), pp. 401–416.

Eisenstadt, S.N. and L. Roniger (1984), *Patrons, Clients and Friends: Interpersonal Relations and the Structure of Trust in Society*, Cambridge: Cambridge University Press.

Hartley, Jenny (2002), *The Reading Groups Book*, Oxford: Oxford University Press.

Hoffman, Raid, Ben Casnocha and Chris Yey (2014), 'Your Company Is Not a Family', *Harvard Business Review*, 17 June.

Kornhaber, Arthur (1996), *Contemporary Grandparenting*, Thousand Oaks, CA: SAGE.

Long, Elizabeth (2003), *Book Clubs: Women and the Uses of Reading in Everyday Life*, Chicago, IL: University of Chicago Press.

Nagesh, Ashitha (2018), 'New Recruitment Ads Released to make Army Look More Inclusive', *Metro*, 10 January.

NCVO (National Council for Voluntary Organisations) (2018), 'UK Civil Society Almanac', May.

Ochiltree, Gay (2006), 'The Changing Role of Grandparents', Melbourne: Australian Institute of Family Studies.

Olson, Mancur (1965 [1977]), *The Logic of Collective Action, Public Goods and the Theory of Groups*, 7th printing 1977, Harvard Economics Studies, Cambridge, MA: Harvard University Press.

Oxford Economics (2016), 'The UK Family Business Sector', www.oxfordeconomics/com/publication/open/263822.

Phillimore, Jenny, Angus McCabe, Andri Soteri Proctor and Rebecca Taylor (2010), 'Understanding the Distinctiveness of Small-Scale, Third Sector Activity: The Role of Local Knowledge and Networks in Shaping below the Radar Actions', Third Sector Research Centre, Working Paper 33.

Rochester, Colin (2013), *Rediscovering Voluntary Action: The Beat of a Different Drum*, Basingstoke: Palgrave Macmillan.

Scabini, Eugenia and Claudia Manzi (2011), 'Family Processes and Identity', in S.J. Schwartz, K. Luyckx and V. Vignoles (eds), *Handbook of Identity Theory and Research*, New York: Springer, pp. 565–584.

Scabini, Eugenia, Elena Marta and Margherita Lancz (2006), *The Transition to Adulthood and Family Relations: An Intergenerational Approach*, Hove: Psychology Press.

Seligman, Adam B. (1997 [2000]), *The Problem of Trust*, paperback edn 2000, Princeton, NJ: Princeton University Press.

Silver, Allan (1989), 'Friendship and Trust as Moral Ideals: An Historical Approach', *European Journal of Sociology*, 30(2), pp. 274–297.

Smith, David Horton (1992), 'A Neglected Type of Voluntary Non-Profit Organisation: Exploration of the Semiformal, Fluid-Membership Organization', *Nonprofit and Voluntary Sector Quarterly*, 21(3), pp. 251–269.

Starbuck, William (2003), *The Origins of Organisation Theory*, ResearchGate, https://www.researchgate.net/256043102.

Sundaramurthy, Chamu (2008), 'Sustaining Trust within Family Businesses', *Family Business Review*, 21(1), pp. 89–102.

Tsoukas, Haridimos (2007), 'New Times, Fresh Challenges; Reflections on the Past and the Future of Organizational Theory', in Tsoukas Haridimos (ed.), *The Handbook of Organization Theory: Metaphorical Perspectives*, Oxford: Oxford Handbooks. Oxford: Oxford University Press, pp. 607–623.

Whetten, David, Peter Foreman and W. Gibb Dyer (2013), 'Organizational Identity and Family Business', in Leif Melin, Mattias Norquist and Pramoda Sharma (eds), *The SAGE Handbook of Family Business*, Thousand Oaks, CA: SAGE, pp. 480–497.

Wuthnow, Robert (1996), *Sharing the Journey: Support Groups and America's New Quest for Community*, paperback edn, New York: Free Press.

Index